AMERICA IN
THE WORLD
1962–1987

CSIS

★★★★ 25th ★★★★
Anniversary

Center for Strategic
and International Studies

EDITED BY

WALTER LAQUEUR &

BRAD ROBERTS

AMERICA IN THE WORLD 1962–1987

A Strategic and Political Reader

ST. MARTIN'S PRESS

NEW YORK

© 1987 CSIS

All rights reserved. For information, write:
Scholarly & Reference Division,
St. Martin's Press, Inc., 175 Fifth Avenue, New York, NY 10010

First published in the United States of America in 1987

Printed in the United States of America

Library of Congress Cataloging-in-Publication Data

America in the world, 1962–1987.
  Includes index.
  1. United States—Foreign relations—1945–
2. United States —National security. 3. United
States—Military policy. I. Laqueur, Walter. ⊬ 1921 –
II. Roberts, Brad.
E840.A618   1987   327.73   87-23389
ISBN 0-312-01318-3

Contents

Acknowledgments

The following publishers and authors have generously given their permission to use extended quotations from copyrighted works. The chapter in which the excerpt appears is noted in brackets after the author's name.

From *National Security: Political, Military, and Economic Strategies in the Decade Ahead,* edited by David M. Abshire and Richard V. Allen. Copyright © 1963 by the Board of Trustees of the Leland Stanford Junior University. Reprinted by permission of Praeger Publishers and the Hoover Institution on War, Revolution, and Peace. Pages xi–xiv, "Introduction," by Arleigh Burke (appears in chapter 1 as "National Strategy"); pages 413–417, "Address to the Conference on January 23, 1963," by Senator Henry M. Jackson (in chapter 1 as "National Security"); and pages 687–705, "Strategic Leverage from Aid and Trade" by James R. Schlesinger [in chapter 7].

From *NATO in Quest of Cohesion,* edited by Karl H. Cerny and Henry W. Briefs. Copyright © 1965 by the Board of Trustees of the Leland Stanford Junior University. Reprinted by permission of Praeger Publishers and the Hoover Institution on War, Revolution, and Peace. Pages 11–19, "U.S. Policy Toward NATO," by the Honorable George W. Ball (in chapter 2) and pages 125–134, "The Crisis of the Alliance," by Hans J. Morgenthau (in chapter 2).

From *U.S. Interests in Africa,* by Helen Kitchen. Washington Paper 98. Copyright © 1983 by Praeger Publishers and The Center for Strategic and International Studies. Reprinted by permission of Praeger Publishers and The Center for Strategic and International Studies. Pages 75–104, "Is a Coherent Africa Policy Possible?" (in chapter 5).

From *NATO: The Next Generation,* edited by Robert E. Hunter. Copyright © 1984 by Westview Press and The Center for Strategic and International Studies. Reprinted by permission of Westview Press and The Center for Strategic and International Studies. Pages 28–36, "Leadership in the Alliance," by Helmut Schmidt (in chapter 2) and pages 37–51, "An American Perspective," by James Schlesinger (in chapter 2 as "An American Perspective on NATO Leadership").

From *After Brezhnev: Sources of Soviet Conduct in the 1980s,* edited by Robert F. Byrnes. Copyright © 1983 by The Center for Strategic and International Studies and Indiana University Press. Reprinted by permission of Indiana University Press and The Center for Strategic and International Studies. Pages 423–440, "Critical Choices in the 1980s," by Robert F. Byrnes (in chapter 3).

From *Preventing Nuclear War: A Realistic Approach,* edited by Barry M. Blechman. Copyright © 1985 by The Center for Strategic and International

Studies and Indiana University Press. Reprinted by permission of Indiana University Press and The Center for Strategic and International Studies. Pages 1–6, "A Practical Approach to Containing Nuclear Dangers," by Senator Sam Nunn and Senator John Warner (in chapter 4).

From *The Washington Quarterly,* copyright © 1978 through 1987 by The Center for Strategic and International Studies and Transaction or MIT Press/Journals. Reprinted by permission of MIT Press and The Center for Strategic and International Studies. Pages 91–103, vol. 2, no. 1 (Winter 1979) "Nationalism, Nations, and Western Policies," by Hugh Seton-Watson (in chapter 5); pages 8–22, vol. 2, no. 3 (Summer 1979) "From American Imperialism to Soviet Hegemonism," by Raymond Aron (in chapter 5); pages 3–17, vol. 3, no. 4 (Autumn 1979) "The Future of NATO," by Henry A. Kissinger (in chapter 2); pages 18–31, vol. 2, no. 4 (Autumn 1979) "Social Change and the Defense of the West," by Michael Howard (in chapter 2); pages 58–66, vol. 3, no. 1 (Winter 1980) "Negotiating with the Soviets," by Edward L. Rowny (in chapter 3); pages 118–129, vol. 3, no. 3 (Summer 1980) "Intelligence for Policymaking," by Richard K. Betts (in chapter 6); pages 3–12, vol. 4, no. 1 (Winter 1981) "Foreign Policy and the English Language," by Walter Laqueur (in chapter 6); pages 83–105, vol. 5, no. 1 (Winter 1982) "Twenty Years in the Strategic Labyrinth," by David M. Abshire (in chapter 1); pages 17–24, vol. 5, no. 4 (Autumn 1982) "On the Meaning of Victory," by Edward N. Luttwak (in chapter 2); pages 71–82, vol. 6, no. 2 (Spring 1983) "Anatomy of Policymaking," by Adam B. Ulam (in chapter 3 as "Anatomy of Soviet Policymaking"); pages 115–119, vol. 6, no. 2 (Spring 1983) "Reducing Japanese-U.S. Friction," by Saburo Okita (in chapter 5); pages 16–21, vol. 6, no. 3 (Summer 1983) "Congress and Intelligence Oversight," by Barry Goldwater (in chapter 6); pages 73–103, vol. 7, no. 4 (Fall 1984) "Extended Deterrence," by Walter Slocombe (in chapter 4); pages 14–19, *White Paper 1984* "The Three Requirements for a Bipartisan Foreign Policy," by Zbigniew Brzezinski (in chapter 6); pages 3–8, vol. 8, no. 2 (Spring 1985) "Foreign Policy Agenda," by Richard G. Lugar (in chapter 5); pages 9–13, vol. 8, no. 2 (Spring 1985) "Foreign Policy Agenda," by Jack F. Kemp (in chapter 5); pages 45–58, vol. 9, no. 3 (Summer 1986) "The Owls' Agenda for Avoiding Nuclear War," by Graham Allison, Albert Carnesale, and Joseph S. Nye, Jr. (in chapter 4 as "The Owls' Agenda"); pages 15–24, vol. 10, no. 3 (Summer 1987) "A National Strategy for the 1990s," by Amos A. Jordan (in chapter 1).

From *The Washington Quarterly,* vol. 2, no. 4 (Autumn 1979). Copyright © 1979 by The Center for Strategic and International Studies and Transaction. Pages 54–63, "The Pleasures of Self-Deception," by Roberta Wohlstetter (in chapter 6). Copyright © 1979 by Roberta Wohlstetter and reprinted with her kind permission.

From *The Washington Quarterly,* vol. 10, no. 2 (Spring 1987). Copyright © 1987 by The Center for Strategic and International Studies and MIT Press/Journals. Pages 21–33, "Technological Challenges to National Economic Policies of the West," by Harald B. Malmgren (in chapter 7 as "Technology and Western Economic Policy"). Copyrighted elsewhere by Harald B. Malmgren and reprinted with his kind permission.

From *The Need to Reshape Military Strategy, The First David M. Abshire Lecture, March 18, 1983,* by Senator Sam Nunn. Significant Issues Series, vol. 5, no. 4. Copyright © 1983 by The Center for Strategic and International Studies. Reprinted with permission. Pages 1–13 (in chapter 1).

From *International Communications Policy; Preparing for the Future, The Third David M. Abshire Endowed Lecture, October 8, 1985,* by Dante B. Fascell. Significant Issues Series, vol. 8, no. 4. Copyright © 1985 by The Center for Strategic and International Studies. Reprinted with permission. Pages 1–13 (in chapter 5 as "International Communications Policy: A Strategy").

From *Detente and East-West Relations" An Address by Sen. Hubert Humphrey to the Quadrangular Conference III.* Copyright © 1976 by The Center for Strategic and International Studies. Reprinted with permission. (In chapter 5.)

From *The Gulf: Implications of British Withdrawal,* by Bernard Lewis et al. Special Report Series No. 8, February 1969. Copyright © 1969 by The Center for Strategic and International Studies. Reprinted with permission. Pages 7–13 (in chapter 5).

From *U.S. National Security and the Third World: Toward an Integrated Approach, Scowcroft Panel Report,* edited by William Perry. Copyright © 1983 by The Center for Strategic and International Studies. (In chapter 5 as "U.S. National Security and the Third World").

From *Managing National Security: The Reagan/Mondale Challenge,* by Robert E. Hunter. Significant Issues Series, vol. 6, no. 13. Copyright © 1984 by The Center for Strategic and International Studies. Reprinted by permission. (In chapter 6 as "Managing National Security".)

From "An Address by Robert S. Strauss on U.S. Trade and International Economic Policy—A Strategy." An address to the International Economic Forum, The Center for Strategic and International Studies, November 17, 1986. Copyright © 1986 by Robert S. Strauss and reprinted with his kind permission. (In chapter 7 as "A Bipartisan Trade Strategy".)

About the Contributors

Arleigh Burke is a decorated naval officer who served as founding director of CSIS.

David Abshire was cofounder of CSIS, which he now serves as chancellor. This essay was written during his service as the U.S. Permanent Representative to NATO from 1983 to 1987.

Amos A. Jordan is the President of CSIS, having been appointed in 1983.

Henry Jackson was Senator from Washington (Democrat) from 1953 until his death in 1983.

Sam Nunn is Senator from Georgia (Democrat), currently serving as chairman of the Armed Services Committee.

George Ball was undersecretary of state from 1961 to 1966.

Hans Morgenthau was director of the Center for the Study of American Foreign Policy at the University of Chicago from 1950 to 1968 and counselor to the Departments of State and Defense.

Henry Kissinger was secretary of state from 1973 to 1977 and now serves as counselor to CSIS.

Helmut Schmidt was chancellor of the Federal Republic of Germany from 1974 to 1982.

James Schlesinger was secretary of energy (1977–1979), secretary of defense (1973–1975), and director of Central Intelligence (1973), and now serves as counselor to CSIS.

Michael Howard is professor of the history of war at All Soul's College, Oxford University.

Edward Luttwak is senior fellow at CSIS.

Robert Brynes is professor of history at Indiana University and directed the CSIS project on the Soviet Union in the 1980s.

Ed Rowny is special adviser to the president and the secretary of state for arms control matters. This essay was written during his service as representative of the Joint Chiefs of Staff to the U.S. SALT negotiating team.

Adam Ulam is director of the Russian Research Center at Harvard University.

Graham Allison, Albert Carnesale, and Joseph S. Nye, Jr., are professors at Harvard University's John F. Kennedy School of Government.

Sam Nunn is Senator from Georgia (Democrat) and **John Warner** is Senator from Virginia (Republican). They served as cochairmen of the CSIS working group on nuclear risk reduction.

Walter Slocombe was deputy undersecretary of defense for policy planning from 1979 to 1981.

Raymond Aron was a distinguished French author and educator who passed away in 1983.

Dante Fascell is a member of the House of Representatives (Democrat-Florida) and serves as chairman of the Foreign Affairs Committee.

Hubert Humphrey was vice president of the United States from 1965 to 1969.

Jack Kemp is a member of the House of Representatives (Republican-New York).

Helen Kitchen is director of the CSIS African Studies program.

Bernard Lewis is an historian of the Near and Middle East at Princeton University.

Richard Lugar is Senator from Indiana (Republican). This essay was authored during his service as chairman of the Senate Committee on Foreign Relations from 1985 to 1986.

Saburo Okita was foreign minister of Japan from 1979 to 1980.

Brent Scowcroft was assistant to the president for national security affairs from 1975 to 1977.

Hugh Seton-Watson was professor of Russian history at the University of London until his death in 1986.

Zbigniew Brzezinski was assistant to the president for national security affairs from 1977 to 1981 and currently serves as counselor to CSIS.

Robert Hunter served on the staff of the National Security Council from 1977 to 1981 and is currently a senior fellow at CSIS.

Roberta Wohlstetter is affiliated with Pan Heuristics, Inc. and is a member of the CSIS International Research Council.

Richard Betts is a research fellow at the Brookings Institution.

Barry Goldwater was a Senator from Arizona (Republican) from 1953 to 1986. This essay was written during his service as chairman of the Select Committee on Intelligence.

Walter Laqueur is chairman of the International Research Council at CSIS.

James Schlesinger (as noted above).

Robert Strauss was special representative for trade negotiations from 1977 to 1979.

Harald Malmgren was deputy U.S. trade representative from 1972 to 1975.

PREFACE

CSIS: 25 Years of Shaping the Future   *Amos A. Jordan*

The Center for Strategic and International Studies is a public policy research institute specializing in international affairs. To be relevant and to play a role in shaping the future it must step out ahead of the pace of events, identify policy challenges dimly perceived on the horizon, apply scholarship and experience to their study, and be ready with well-thought-out policy alternatives when the decision maker needs them.

The history of CSIS over its first quarter century reflects that anticipatory vocation. It is the story of a continuous learning curve, of exciting insight, of broadening perspectives, of gradual acceptance by the policy-making community, and of quiet satisfaction when ideas born in CSIS are translated into viable public policy. That it is also a history of steady growth, never a conscious CSIS objective *per se*, suggests only that the Center's approach and methods have thus far stood well the test of time. For the future it guarantees little. Just as its agenda must probe ahead of events, the Center's institutional approach and techniques must adapt to shifting opportunities and needs. The human race is on the move on this planet as never before. Change and complexities in international relationships beat upon us. As always, the CSIS task lies ahead.

Genesis

CSIS was born as the Center for Strategic Studies in a modest Georgetown townhouse in September 1962. It was organized as a self-funding arm of Georgetown University, an institution whose School of Foreign Service had already established a reputation for excellence in the field of international studies. The idea for the new Center had been conceived by Dr. David Abshire, West Point graduate and Korean War veteran who took his Ph.D. in history at Georgetown. His experience on Capitol Hill with the House minority leader's staff and later as a scholar with the American Enterprise Association (now the American Enterprise Institute) had instilled in him a conviction that the lengthy and theoretical studies being generated by most of the existing U.S. think tanks were of little practical use to the nation's policymakers. He saw a need for more concise, issue-oriented research that would serve up to the policymaker a balanced set of well-studied options. His chosen field for this approach was foreign affairs.

Abshire's concept was strongly endorsed by his AEA colleagues, including William Baroody, Sr., and Glen Campbell. It was Baroody's suggestion that the new Center move beyond its Georgetown University affiliation to serve as a conduit between the wider academic community and the national centers of decision. Baroody also deployed his considerable influence to secure initial foundation funding for CSS. The Georgetown University leadership, especially Father James Horrigan, S.J., dean of the Graduate School, was equally supportive.

The first step in the organizational phase was to find a president or director of sufficient prestige and experience to give the proposed institution instant credibility. In that quest, Chicago attorney and internationalist Morris Leibman (today a member of the CSIS Board of Trustees) played a decisive role. He helped to persuade the recently retired chief of naval operations, Admiral Arleigh Burke, to take on the task.

Thus when CSS opened its doors in 1962 it was armed with an innovative concept of service to the nation, strong leadership, a modest funding base, and affiliation with a strong university.

The Early Years

CSIS began with a 1963 budget of $150,000 and five employees. Its first full-time scholar was Richard Allen, later to become Ronald Reagan's national security adviser. Its first conference, in January 1963, was entitled National Security: The Demands of Strategy and Economics in the Decade Ahead. That theme, stressing the linkage between economics and security, has remained central to the CSIS agenda over the past quarter century. Two of the more articulate participants in that conference, Henry Kissinger and James Schlesinger, are now CSIS counselors after subsequent careers in the national leadership. In a letter to Abshire, Kissinger described that first conference as the most successful he had ever attended. The final report of the conference, published under the title *National Security: Political, Military, and Economic Strategies in the Decade Ahead,* became a standard reference for both practitioners and students of strategy throughout the 1960s and helped establish the Center's scholarly reputation.

Close on the heels of this promising maiden effort came research-based seminars on Soviet nuclear strategy and problems of the NATO alliance. In the mid- and latter 1960s, a new group of Center scholars, including Eleanor Lansing Dulles, Alvin Cottrell, and Norman Bailey, produced studies and panel reports on such ongoing issues as East-West detente, arms control, revolution in the Dominican Republic, and divestiture of the Panama Canal. In 1966, Representative Clement J. Zablocki, a Wisconsin Democrat and charter member of the Center's Advisory Board, launched the tradition of direct congressional involvement in CSS research by participating in (and editing the result of) a study on the incipient Sino-Soviet rivalry. Two years later, another panel report coordinated by Alvin Cottrell, soon to become the Center's director of research, foresaw the danger of political instability in the Persian Gulf states, specifically in Iran, following Britain's planned withdrawal from the Gulf area.

The Flowering

1968, a year of global political turmoil and change, proved to be a pivotal year for CSS as well. Dr. Philip Mosely, former director of studies at the Council on Foreign Relations and a renowned institution-builder in foreign studies, joined the Center's Executive Board in 1967 and was a prime mover in advancing CSS from a mere catalyst or compiler of research to a creator of original works. It was at his urging, too, that the word "international" was added to the Center's name in January of that year—in recognition both of the increasing number of foreign scholars engaged in the Center's work and of the emerging importance of the Third World to U.S. national security. In November, Mosely became chairman of the newly inaugurated CSIS International Research Council (today headed by Walter Laqueur) and enlisted some of the world's top foreign affairs scholars to help shape the CSIS agenda, broaden its horizons, and monitor the quality of its output.

This period also marked an expanded commitment to public affairs and publications efforts. New York Times columnist Arthur Krock, who became a member of the Executive Board in 1966, argued that the Center needed a journalist on its staff "to make our scholars understandable." Krock's protégé, Jon Vondracek of Time magazine, joined the Center a short time later and served for 20 years as the driving force behind the Center's communications activities.

In May 1971, CSIS moved to its present quarters at 1800 K Street with substantially greater space and access to the excellent conference and dining facilities of the International Club of Washington. The move was supervised by a new CSIS chairman, former Director General of the Foreign Service Ambassador John M. Steeves, who ably ran CSIS for three years during Abshire's stint as assistant secretary of state for congressional relations.

In the 1970s, too, CSIS gradually expanded its regional study capabilities, inviting scholars from some of the key regional powers to participate in its panels and conferences. The Latin American Program, which had begun in 1966, was enlarged under James Theberge, later to become ambassador to Nicaragua. An African Program was launched in the mid-1970s under the direction of Michael Samuels, soon to be succeeded by Chester A. Crocker (until his appointment as assistant secretary of state for African affairs in 1981). An important new dimension was added to the Center's work on the Middle East with the addition of retired Ambassador Robert Neumann to the staff, who also served ably at a later time as vice chairman of the Center. Also during the mid-1970s, Ray Cline joined the Center and began a series of well-received world power studies. All these new programs led to a series of multidisciplinary study projects on such issues as Soviet influence in the Caribbean and the security of the Western Mediterranean.

The 1970s also witnessed the introduction of many of the research and conferencing techniques that have become a CSIS hallmark. Panels of distinguished legislators, business leaders, and scholars from the United States and abroad were formed to examine emerging foreign affairs issues and produce published reports. Early panels addressed *Russia in the Caribbean, U.S. Military Research and Development Management, The Canadian Condominium,* and *U.S.–Philippines Economic Relations,* among other topics. Conferences were conducted at home and overseas on both security and economic issues. Seminars were held for legislators, congressional staffers, corporate representatives, and media leaders featuring such speakers as President Richard Nixon and Walter Rostow.

It was Steeves who inaugurated, in 1972, the *Washington Papers* series that remains today a primary CSIS vehicle for the rapid conveyance of important Center and external research findings in concise form to policymakers and the public. The *Papers* were immediately greeted with wide acclaim in the Washington community. Former President Gerald Ford, a charter member of the Center's Advisory Board, identified the source of their appeal. Ford, then Minority Leader of the House of Representatives, buttonholed Assistant Secretary of

State Abshire during a Capitol Hill reception. "You know what's so great about your *Washington Papers,* Dave?" queried the Minority Leader. "You can throw two of them in your briefcase, read one on the plane home and another on the ride back!"

When Abshire resumed the chairmanship in January 1973, his first priority was to strengthen the already considerable relationship between CSIS and Capitol Hill. First, the Advisory Board was broadened to include more Members of Congress. Such distinguished legislators as Senators Hubert Humphrey, William Roth, and Sam Nunn and Representatives Richard Bolling, Al Ullman, and John Rhodes became familiar faces at CSIS events. At one CSIS dinner discussion on East Asia, fourteen senators were present, all deeply engaged, between mouthfuls, in discussing the fine points of Japanese–U.S. relations.

As a part of the concerted effort to involve important congressional figures in major CSIS events, CSIS hosted its first Quadrangular Conference in June of 1973, cochaired by Senators Hubert Humphrey and William Brock. The Quad conference drew leaders from Europe, Japan, Canada, and the United States to examine the impact of trade, monetary, energy, and security developments on quadrangular relations. That first Quad Forum was rated by old CSIS hands as the best conference by the Center since the kickoff National Security Conference a decade earlier. The Quadrangular Forum has grown in prestige and influence since its first meeting and today constitutes a major, systematic process through which private sector experience and viewpoints can be injected into the annual Economic Summits engaging the same group of nations.

The following spring, in March 1974, Abshire began yet another congressionally oriented annual forum that continues to flourish. The Williamsburg Conference series was jointly conceived by Abshire and *Reader's Digest* Managing Editor Ken Gilmore as a means of bringing legislators and officials together with business and academic leaders in a relaxed setting to discuss a single issue of contemporary significance. In 1974, the issue was "The Great Power Balance and the Energy Problem"; in 1987, it was competitiveness and international trade.

Energy was understandably a major national concern in the 1970s, and CSIS soon became deeply engaged, both in policy research on the many issues involved and in a remarkably effective program of public education aimed largely at energy conservation. Energy expert Jack Bridges was brought in as CSIS director of energy programs. Bridges, an adviser to the Joint Atomic Energy Committee, had been among the first in the early 1960s to forecast a global oil shortage. He was widely regarded as far ahead of his time, particularly in the application of computers to the analysis of the energy supply problem. Bridges produced a comprehensive, computer-based assessment of energy vulnerability that was widely briefed to Congressional and corporate leaders. Determined to make his findings broadly available, Bridges contracted with Hanna Barbera Productions for an animated Flintstones cartoon to dramatize the precariousness of the oil supply situation and the essentiality of conservation. The cartoon was shown to an estimated TV audience of 100 million Americans and earned a Cine Award for animated film.

This pioneer success in the energy field led to a related and even more ambitious research and consensus building undertaking—the National Coal Policy Project. Directed by Frank Murray and launched in late 1976, this five-year program helped forge a consensus among coal producers, users, and environmentalists on more responsible coal production and utilization methods. It also inspired far-reaching legislation on the subject and provided a model process for conflict resolution efforts in a variety of fields. Amos (Joe) Jordan, who joined the Center in January 1977 from the Ford administration, where he had most recently served as deputy under secretary of state, supervised that project, as one of his first CSIS assignments as executive director.

The expanding focus and reputation of the Center in the 1970s, taken together with its increasing integration into the Washington policy-making process, encouraged several senior strategists to join its ranks. Henry Kissinger came to the Center in 1977 as a resident counselor and established his CSIS International Councillors group, bringing together some of the world's most respected bankers and captains of industry. In 1979, James Schlesinger also came aboard as a counselor after his remarkable career in three cabinet posts under both Republican and Democratic presidents. Similarly, Zbigniew Brzezinski, President Carter's national security advisor, arrived in the spring of 1981. In 1986, Robert McFarlane joined in the same capacity. These "statesman-scholars" continue as CSIS counselors, contributing a dimension of strategic insight unparalleled in the think tank community. CSIS was now in a better position than ever to challenge stereotypical foreign affairs concepts and to assume greater leadership in addressing the accelerating tempo of global change.

Others who joined the Center during this dynamic period of building included Admiral Thomas Moorer, retired chairman of the Joint Chiefs of Staff, the distinguished defense intellectual Edward Luttwak, former chief scientist of the Arms Control and Disarmament Agency Robert H. Kupperman, and energy expert Charles Ebinger. Each added a significant new dimension to the Center's overall capabilities.

As the hub of widening networks of scholars dealing with foreign policy studies, the Center needed a new medium for bringing to public and scholarly attention the best in strategic thought that these networks were generating. In 1978, to meet this need, *The Washington Quarterly* was launched under the editorial leadership of Walter Laqueur. The quality of its contribution to the national foreign policy debate can be judged from the selections in this volume.

The strong growth of CSIS in the 1970s could not have been achieved without the generous and continuing financial support of several hundred foundation, corporate, and individual donors. In 1971, the budget of about $600,000 supported barely a dozen scholars and staff; by 1981, the full-time staff had risen to more than 100 men and women and the budget to over $5 million. Most of the Center's success in generating that level of funding can be attributed to the drive and skill of David Abshire and the chief financial officer, Christa D. Konrad Dantzler, now the CSIS vice president for administration. Among their achievements just after the turn of the decade was a series of successful drives that raised over $5 million to endow five research chairs (the Center's only endowment as of mid-1987).

Maturity

The 1981 inauguration of Ronald Reagan propelled CSIS into the public eye. CSIS Advisory Board chairman Anne Armstrong was the President's selection as cochairman for the transition team. CSIS President David Abshire was asked to direct the national security transition. CSIS Vice Chairman Robert Neumann, now director of the Center's Middle East Studies Program, headed the State Department transition team. A number of individuals prominent in CSIS programs were given senior administration assignments, leading to unwarranted media descriptions of CSIS as "Reagan's foreign policy think tank." Such descriptions are far from accurate—the bipartisan tone and nonpartisan content of the Center's work are perhaps most convincingly demonstrated by the fact that when control of the Senate shifted from the Republicans to the Democrats in 1986, the chairmanship of the five committees most central to the work of CSIS passed from the hands of five Republican members of the CSIS Advisory Board to five Democratic board members.

But the Reagan presidency, the issues that have faced it, and the administration's responses to those issues have inevitably influenced the CSIS research agenda in the 1980s. His ambitious military force improvement program, his strategic defense initiative, his alliance and Third World strategies, his approach to the East-West confrontation and arms control, and his policies on international trade and technology transfers have all been assessed in CSIS studies.

The Center has continued since 1980 to build its in-house research capabilities. Programmatic depth was added to regional programs on Europe, the Soviet Union, Japan, Latin America, and the Middle East. CSIS reorganized its work on functional issues into five programs: Arms Control and Crisis Management, Energy and National Security, International Business and Economics, International Communications, and Political-Military Studies. Important new talent was brought into the Center with the appointment of a mix of younger analysts and more experienced practitioners, including James Woolsey, former secretary of the navy, Robert Hunter, former director of West European and Middle Eastern affairs for the National Security Council, world-renowned Africanist Helen Kitchen, energy expert Henry Schuler, political-military expert Barry Blechman, retired Army General Ernest Graves, whose manifold substantive and managerial talents earned him subsequent appointment as a senior adviser, maritime policy specialist Harlan Ullman, and William Taylor, appointed first as director of political-military affairs and later as executive vice president and chief operating officer.

This continued but slower evolution and growth in the early eighties had boosted the Center's permanent staff roster to about 140 and the budget to about $8.5 million by mid-decade. Current CSIS thinking is that these levels put the Center at about the right "fighting weight" for the foreseeable future. Indeed, in the period 1984–1987, there was no further expansion—in fact, a slight leaning down as programs were rationalized and productivity improved with the increased use of computers and word processors.

Of course the volume and quality of research output is a function of research methodology as well as staff size and quality. One of CSIS' strengths has long been its ability to pull together from all relevant disciplines and from all corners of the globe teams of the best available minds to address each study undertaking. Typically these have included both theoreticians and practitioners. Almost invariably they engage public and private sector policymakers who have a direct professional interest in the results and who have used them to good effect in their subsequent decisions. This kind of networking simultaneously brings both authority and impact to the Center's products.

Some of the most fruitful networking has involved the Congress. As a non-profit, non-partisan institution based in Washington, CSIS has had from its inception a fraternal relationship with the Congress, on both sides of the aisle. Four legislators, including Gerald Ford, were charter members of the Center's Advisory Board, and all four participated actively in CSIS programs. In the larger board of 1987, there are 23. But, in addition to these "members of the family," fully half of the Senate and about a quarter of the House were involved in various Center programs in 1986.

In 1980 CSIS inaugurated a new and, in the event, a highly successful vehicle for cooperation with the Congress. The first CSIS Congressional Study Group (CSG) in that year was co-chaired by Senator Sam Nunn (D-Ga.) and Representative Richard Cheney (R-Wyo.). Its task was to examine options for U.S. strategy in the 1980s. Other early CSGs studied the links between foreign policy and defense capabilities, the role of international communications, and the prospects for economic cooperation in the Pacific Basin. The CSG concept is a flexible one, permitting groups to be formed on an ad hoc basis as new issues arise and others are resolved, sometimes through legislation conceived in the CSG. In 1987 there are nine such groups examining a variety of regional and functional issues.

A key constituency and partner over the whole life of CSIS has been the academic world; the Center's affiliation with Georgetown University has never been a confining one. CSIS scholars, interns, and academic collaborators have been drawn from nearly 100 of the nation's and the world's best universities. The CSIS Soviet Studies Program, for example, serves as the focal point of a computer network launched in 1985 that links Kremlinologists from some 150 U.S. and foreign institutions.

In 1983 Joe Jordan, who had long served as David Abshire's deputy, became the Center's president and CEO. (Abshire, in turn, became U.S. permanent representative to the North Atlantic Council and, subsequently and briefly, special counselor to the President.) Jordan placed great emphasis on strengthening the scholarship of the Center, bringing in such outstanding analysts as Richard Bissell, Thane Gustafson, and Susan Pharr. Under his leadership, too, were begun a monograph series (the Significant Issues Series) and the bimonthly CSIS newsletter. Additionally, Jordan vigorously expanded the use of congressionally led consensus-building panels. As noted elsewhere, he also inaugurated the National Leadership Forum and the International Leadership Forum.

As observed earlier, the Center's outreach has not stopped at the nation's border. CSIS has provided a base for overseas visiting scholars and forums for foreign statesmen and study groups since its early years—CSIS' International Councillors first convened in 1977, and its International Leadership Forum in 1985. The ILF brings together each year both established and younger leaders from all corners of the world to wrestle with and propose answers to some of the most pressing problems emerging on the international agenda.

CSIS has traditionally sought to provide an objective meeting ground for business and government in the formulation of foreign policy. The business stake in sound policy is fundamental. Moreover, business insights on international issues are based on decades of hands-on experience and cannot be prudently ignored. John Yochelson, vice president for corporate affairs and director of the international business and economics program, built an extraordinarily effective series of research projects and meetings (with the assistance of Penny Thunberg and Paul Craig Roberts, holders of the Scholl and Simon Chairs, respectively) focused on international economic issues. The Quadrangular Forums, already described, have been a key element of this overall program throughout the early and mid-1980s.

Clearly, the significance of fast-rising change in world trade and technological patterns cannot be understood and sensibly addressed without the participation of those most directly involved. To the substantial array of activities already employed by the Center to facilitate bridging between governmental policy makers and business, Joe Jordan added the National Leadership Forum in 1984. The NLF brings together these two constituencies each fall, along with academic and other opinion leaders, to discuss major foreign affairs issues. CSIS also continues roundtables in a number of cities that permit local business leaders to engage in direct discussion with top Washington policymakers.

All these networks and cooperative relations have helped to make the 1980s the most productive and influential period in the Center's 25-year history. At any given time, CSIS is engaged in upwards of 50 distinct study projects involving hundreds of scholars and practitioners. Not all will effect needed policy change. Perhaps not all should. But the Center's work, in the aggregate, focuses a selected cross-section of talent on most of the crucial foreign affairs issues facing U.S. policy today and in the years ahead. In so doing it contributes authoritatively and constructively to the national foreign policy debate. That, in essence, is the function of a think tank.

The quality and impact of the Center's work is perhaps best demonstrated by an illustrative sampling of some of the major projects of recent years:

Soviet Studies: In order to understand better the domestic determinants of Soviet international behavior in the 1980s, CSIS brought together a network of nearly forty experts from the U.S. and abroad, whose study, *After Brezhnev*, continues to be in very high demand. Building on this beginning, CSIS formalized and expanded this Soviet network with the computerized SOVSET' system that has revolutionized the way Soviet scholars go about their work and has facilitated exceedingly effective cooperation on subsequent studies of Soviet party-military relations.

Nuclear Risk Reduction: A CSIS study group co-chaired by Senators Nunn and Warner generated the original concept of nuclear risk reduction centers, an idea endorsed at the 1985 Geneva summit by Reagan and Gorbachev. A subsequent CSIS study group defined concrete elements of such centers and its recommendations for specific consultative mechanisms were the subject of subsequent U.S.–Soviet negotiation and agreement.

The U.S. and the World Economy: The annual meetings under CSIS auspices of private sector leaders and economists from Europe, Japan, Canada, and the United States has generated two widely discussed studies of changes in the international economy and U.S. leadership. The common perspectives developed at these annual meetings have been a highly valued input to the economic summits.

Defense Reorganization: In the year before the defense reorganization issue burst onto the Congressional and media agenda, CSIS had organized an expert study group on this subject and issued a consensus report. Many of the recommendations of the group found their way into subsequent legislation.

Strategy and Arms Control: An integrated set of research and seminar activities focusing on the role of arms control in overall national strategy has resulted in a series of panel reports and other publications, such as *Reducing the Risk of Nuclear War* and *Negotiating from Strength,* that have been widely praised for looking beyond the rhetoric of public debate to grapple with the core issues.

Conventional Force Structure: A widely circulated study sought to gauge the impact of static defense resources for the strength of U.S. conventional forces. Conducted before defense spending tapered off, the study highlights largely unanticipated and quite severe cuts in conventional forces in the years ahead.

Crisis Management: CSIS has conducted a remarkably prophetic series of regional crisis simulations that have revealed weaknesses in the decision-making process and the limits of U.S. power in coping with Third World conflict.

Executive-Legislative Relations: A panel on executive-legislative relations suggested procedural changes in both branches that have gained wide support.

International Communications: CSIS is currently exploring, in collaboration with top legislative, administration, and business leaders, the far-reaching political, social, economic, and strategic impact of the information-communications "revolution" now in progress.

Independence

The formal affiliation between CSIS and Georgetown University was terminated on July 1, 1987. A 1986 panel chaired by Andrew Goodpaster had concluded, after an exhaustive analysis of the Center's operations and goals and its relations with the University, that a separation of the two institutions would be beneficial to both. CSIS welcomed this "invitation to independence." Less formal ties will continue. Georgetown President Timothy S. Healy, S.J., serves on the new CSIS Board of Trustees. A number of CSIS scholars remain on the University's faculty, and the Center welcomes, as it always has, large numbers of Georgetown students in its internship programs. Since the Center, from its inception, has been self-funding, there are no significant fiscal implications in the separation. CSIS has matured, is solvent, has an established reputation for excellence among its peers and in the community at large, and looks forward to its independent future with confidence, even exhilaration.

Throughout its existence, CSIS has benefited greatly from the committed leadership of a host of talented, creative individuals who have served as members of its Executive and Advisory Boards. As a fully independent organization, the role played by this external leadership has grown more important. The Center's chief policymaking body since its inception—the Executive Board—has performed its work quite effectively under the able leadership of Philip Mosely, Arleigh Burke, John Steeves, Nathaniel Samuels, Leo Cherne, and, mostly recently, Leonard Marks. This board has been supplanted by a new and distinguished 22-person Board of Trustees chaired by Ambassador Anne Armstrong. The 72-person Advisory Board has been led over the years by Karl Bendetsen, Fred Fay, Fred Seitz, and Anne Armstrong, and the board will continue to play an important role in the years ahead.

The Center's governing bodies, in-house leadership, and expert staff are in agreement that CSIS should adhere to the precepts that have guided its first quarter century as it moves into its second quarter. CSIS will remain nonpartisan, anticipatory, interdisciplinary, and relevant. It will continue to serve the public and the policy community with the best scholarship and judgment the world affords.

Introduction *Walter Laqueur*

In the prologue to Goethe's *Faust* the director of the theater states his philosophy in a few well-chosen words.

"Wer vieles bringt, wird manchem etwas bringen"

Which has been translated freely and not altogether accurately: "Give much, please many." Our assignment in preparing this reader has been unfortunately more difficult. We could not give remotely as much as we intended: Our initial selection was about three times as long as the present reader, and even this initial selection did not include some landmark articles that have been widely discussed and quoted over the years. We could not include, for instance, for want of space, articles on energy, even though the energy program was for years one of the main pillars of CSIS. Nor was the "please many" part of our brief. Our intention was to give a representative selection of articles, speeches, and reports published by CSIS since its foundation. Such a selection became by necessity a running commentary on U.S. foreign policy during this period. Sometimes these articles have made a certain contribution to defining the national agenda. Sometimes they have anticipated major issues before their real importance was generally recognized. Whatever the shortcomings of our publications over the years, we never claimed a monopoly of wisdom and foresight; there was always the awareness that in many situations there is room for legitimate discussion and dissent. We have been proud (and sometimes sad) that our contributions have so often been right, and we have provided a stage for them even if these views—as frequently happened—were not at all popular. But we have also practiced *glasnost* long before Mr. Gorbachev introduced this term into our political dictionary.

CSIS was founded in 1962; while I was not present at the creation my recollections do go back to the very early days when our headquarters (a pretentious term at that time) was in a small office on top of a grocery store at the corner of 18th and "I" Street opposite USIA (which has since moved), the Roger Hotel (which has been pulled down), and Washington's best political-economic-military bookshop (which is still going strong). The Center of Strategic Studies became the Center for Strategic and International Studies, while the number of those connected with it rose more than tenfold. So have its activities, and as these lines are written it has attained organizational independence. It is now, for better or worse, an integral part of the Washington political scene. Some surveys of this scene tend to attribute to

CSIS somewhat exaggerated influence, others claim to have detected a "party line" that does not exist—but no survey will fail to mention it.

This Reader spans a quarter of a century, and it is striking in retrospect how many of the basic problems facing U.S. policy makers and the American people have but little changed over this period—less, in any case, than during other comparable periods in recent history. The quarter of a century that passed between 1917 and 1942 witnessed enormous changes both on the domestic scene and in foreign affairs: twice in a lifetime America became involved in a world war; the Russian revolution and its repercussions profoundly changed the world scene; so did the rise of Hitler and of Japan as aggressive world powers; the world economic depression—to mention but a few of the major developments that took place. The world of 1942, in brief, was very different from the state of affairs that had prevailed under President Wilson.

Few comparable changes have taken place during the last 25 years. Deterrence and arms control are still among the major issues preoccupying the strategists. The state of NATO has remained a subject of frequent and sometimes heated discussions. There have been some local wars, including Vietnam, but in retrospect their impact has not been even remotely comparable to the outcome of the two world wars. Relations between the Soviet Union and China are still not cordial, and while currently there is promise for some change in Moscow, Soviet policy both domestic and foreign has changed remarkably little since Khrushchev's days. The problems facing the Third World, Latin America for example, are more or less the same. Churchill, de Gaulle, Adenauer, and some other leading West European leaders were still alive in 1962, but how little basic change has taken place in the domestic and foreign policy of countries such as Britain, France, Italy, and West Germany. (Spain, admittedly, is a welcome exception.) The Berlin Wall was erected in 1961—it still stands, and while relations between the two Germanies are now somewhat more relaxed than at that time, little has changed in Eastern Europe. Terrorism has figured prominently in the media in recent decades, but again, seen in historical perspective, how little difference has it made over the years.

There have been, as always, some exceptions: the overthrow of the Shah and the revival of an aggressive fundamentalistic Islamic movement, for example. Yet with all the apocalyptic rhetoric surrounding these events, most of that aggression has so far turned inward, and it is by no means certain how lasting the phenomenon is likely to be. For truly important changes one ought perhaps to look to the world economy rather than to world politics: the emergence of Japan and other Far Eastern countries as leading industrial powers;

the growing debt of the Third World—and of the United States; the economic stagnation of the Soviet bloc and its long-term social and political repercussions; the growing importance of high technology in every field.

But the fact that so many "old" problems persist does not mean that we are any nearer to satisfactory solutions: the present Reader is a good illustration of continued debate.

Some of our friends and collaborators who contributed to this volume have since died: Senator Henry Jackson (1912–1983), Senator Hubert Humphrey (1911–1978), Hugh Seton Watson (1916–1984), Hans Morgenthau (1904–1980), and Raymond Aron (1905–1983). These eminent men, whom we were happy to count among our friends, are so widely known and whose work is so well remembered to this day that further words of appreciation would only repeat what others have said about them. Phillip Mosely, my predecessor as chairman of the International Research Council, was not only one of the pioneers in the field of Russian and Slavic studies in this country, but he also greatly helped to put CSIS on the map, and provided wise judgment and firm leadership at the beginning of our steps.

Toward the end of his life, Raymond Aron said in an interview: "A love of truth and a horror of falsehood—this, I believe, lies at the very heart of my way of being and thinking. And in order to be able to express the truth, one must be free." We could not have thought of a better envoy for this Reader.

1

NATIONAL STRATEGY

National Strategy

Arleigh Burke

The United States is the most powerful nation on earth. Strategy involves the use of that power in its full array, economic, military, political, cultural, social, moral, spiritual and psychological, to accomplish national objectives in the world. A strategy that neglects any element of national power, or declines to consider any reasonable opinion concerning it, is no strategy at all. It is, at best, a tactical exercise and, at worst, a patchwork of expediency which will quickly unravel under pressure. Nor is a strategy without objectives a real strategy. It is at best a holding action.

Thus, national power and national objectives are the irreducible elements of strategy. To understand and wisely marshal the one, and arrive at consensus on the other, is the purpose of strategic discussions. Having the power, we have the grave responsibility to pursue that purpose. We could not, if we wished, ignore the responsibility. Our position has imposed it upon us. We can fail the responsibility, of course. We cannot avoid it. This does not mean a call for some sort of American empire. It does mean a clear call for American leadership.

The people of the United States have demonstrated, more than any other nation in history, that we do not wish to impose control on any other peoples of the world. After World War II, the United States poured money, materials, ideas, and equipment into countries which had been devastated by war—countries which had been our enemies as well as countries which had been our allies. Europe and free Asia, the countries of the Middle East, Latin America, and Africa have more freedom, more prosperity, better health, because of the generosity of the United States. Even the USSR, whose avowed goal has been our destruction, has been benefitted greatly by the United States.

But no matter how generous the impulses of a nation, there is a limit on how much a nation can give of its substance, as the United States is learning now with its rapidly growing national debt, with its imbalance of payments, and with the ever growing competition facing our exports. Strategy demands a realistic view of these factors as part of the overall consideration. They cannot be put into a compartment labelled "economics" and isolated from the larger discussion. The welfare of the goose, in short, is of strategic concern to the man whose golden eggs are sustaining the neighborhood. It should be of as great concern to the neighbors, as a matter of fact.

In addition to its responsibility to assist other nations, the United States has the responsibility to protect its own freedom, and the freedom of other peoples, from the efforts of the Communists to destroy all freedom. Southeast Asia, Latin America, the Middle East are areas where now there is continuous danger of more people, more nations, being forced to submit to absolute Communist dictatorship as in Cuba.

There are differences of opinion among the various Communists in the world, but they do have a common overriding objective: to destroy all that we stand for. The USSR and Red China may be at each other's throats, but the grand strategic objective of each remains the same.

Change is the essence of history. But the trend of future events will not change in the direction we desire unless we do something about it. Time alone will not bring about a change in the methods and goals of international communism. We have within our power the capability of eroding communism, but it will not erode of itself. We must carefully avoid the assumption that trends we desire will take place without our influencing those trends. Communism has not yet reached a high water mark, and it will take more than one or two reverses for the Communists to renounce their stated goals and become non-Communists. At the present moment the Communists—both Soviet and Chinese—exude confidence in the historically inevitable triumph of their system and the downfall of ours. *Their* objectives are clear.

What, then, can be done? What are the objectives which the Free World, and the United States in particular, should try to achieve?

Most essential is a fundamental re-evaluation of our desired goals. It appears that there are three basic policy choices open to us:

First, we could retreat before Communist blackmail, making avoidance of confrontation our objective and leaving the Communists to rule the world. That alternative is unworthy of consideration.

A second choice is to attempt to "co-exist" with the Communists, declaring that our basic goal is to live in harmony with our fellow man. Although this is a laudable and worthy goal, it has a serious flaw: the Communists use the doctrine of "peaceful co-existence" as an offensive weapon to be utilized in the destruction of the West. "Peaceful co-existence" is to the Communists a strategem which has already begun to pay dividends.

A third policy choice is this: to take initiative toward the elimination of Communists from positions of power, thus causing the erosion of the Communist system. This would involve recognition that the existence of the Communist Party precludes the attainment of real peace, and recognition that, until the means of power have been taken out of the hands of the Communist Party, there will be no chance for a just and lasting peace.

It is well to be reminded that the third alternative does not call for the physical annihilation of the opponent; rather, it seeks to undermine, erode, and deteriorate his position of power—his whole system. It aims at having in power in Russia and China governments with legitimate, limited aims.

The strategy which the United States follows may be the most important element in determining the events of the future. In developing strategy, all aspects of the problems which confront a nation must be thoroughly examined. This requires that the best advocates of the various possible courses of action be heard. It is not enough to select one of just several theoretical courses of action. And, of course, the strategy cannot be formed at all until the objectives are decided.

A thorough understanding of the relationships among people is needed for any strategy to be implemented effectively. Relationships among nations must be clear, simple, and uncomplicated. People in our own nation and those in other nations must have an unblurred understanding of what the United States stands for and what the United States wants to happen.

By our actions they will know us. A nation does not gain the confidence of another nation on demand. Nor does one nation have faith in the competence of another because the other loudly proclaims it.

A strong and cohesive Free World alliance depends on the demonstrated brainpower, manpower, machine power, and spiritual power of its individual signatories, and upon their willingness to commit those resources to the goals of the alliance.

The United States must take the lead in forming a strategic objective. From that point, the choices which will confront this nation also are enormous. Decisions which will affect all mankind and the future existence of the world will be made in our Capital. Wise choices involve the collation of the opinions of the best minds of the nation. It was to participate in that process that the Center for Strategic Studies held the Conference contained in this volume.

Twenty Years in the Strategic Labyrinth   *David M. Abshire*

There is a sobering truth at the heart of the contemporary debate on global strategy, a deeply painful awareness that the United States has not achieved a minimum of strategic competence for a long time and that its errors of strategy have proved more costly than once was thought possible. Over the past 20 years I have led a center of strategic studies and I think that some reflection on civilian and military strategists alike is in order.

The facts are undeniable. Basic miscalculations of strategy in Indochina led to the commitment of half a million men to an indecisive war in Asia that eventually took a tragic toll in American lives and morale, leaving us with a depleted military establishment. Concurrently, a fundamental misunderstanding of Soviet intentions led to the notion that Moscow would accept a nuclear truce based on mutual assured destruction (MAD) and thus would be content with parity instead of moving toward strategic superiority and nuclear blackmail. That misunderstanding has created one of this nation's foremost dilemmas for the next decade.

Nor has our record in the conduct of actual military operations been encouraging. During the past two decades, American success came early during the Cuban missile crisis, but that success must be measured against the episodic failures of the Bay of Pigs, Vietnam, and the aborted Iranian hostage rescue attempt. Today, there are serious Western military analysts who question whether the North Atlantic Treaty Organization (NATO) could fight a European war effectively or whether the Rapid Deployment Force (RDF) could function in its mission.

What went wrong with American strategic thinking? Could the analysis have been more accurate in predicting the rapidly shifting military and political developments of the two decades just ended? Within the armed forces, theorists have an especially complex mandate because by its nature the military is a traditional institution, and questioning strategic assumptions is difficult for military leaders. Thus, a basic irony of the last 20 years has been the degree to which strategic planning has shifted from uniformed to civilian leadership within the Department of Defense and strategic thinking has become the purview of civilian analysts outside the government itself.

What, then, can be said of the research centers—the "think tanks"—that have staked out policymaking spheres of influence for themselves during the past decades? Could they have done more? Did they fail to furnish ideas adequate to the challenges that faced the nation even while they staffed the executive branch and Congress with many of their leading civilian strategists? In short, should the research centers be assigned part of the blame for U.S. strategic failure in our time, and, if so, has the experience provided useful lessons for the decades ahead?

The Civilian Strategists

The creation of strategic research centers during the late 1950s owed much to a fundamental argument about the strategic premises at the time. As the Eisenhower era came to a reasonably successful conclusion, the advocates of the "new look" and "flexible response" philosophies—the extraordinary army intellectuals, Maxwell Taylor and James Gavin, who dissented from prevailing "massive retaliation" doctrines—helped trigger the first major reassessment of America's military conceptions since the Korean War. Having identified massive retaliation for what it was—not the viable long-haul strategy portrayed by administration advocates but merely a gigantic one-shot spasm—a number of academics and writers sought new institutional channels from which to influence and shape the policies ahead.

Of course, even during the Eisenhower years, there existed voices of military reform and reevaluation, although they were often in a state of academic isolation. The air force was the chief proponent of massive retaliation. It was also the military service leading strategic research at the time, if only because of the service's urgent need to evaluate weapons systems of unique complexity. Air force funding sponsored the expansion of the RAND Corporation, which had been founded in 1948. As early as 1954, Bernard Brodie, veteran strategist and by then a RAND Corporation member, called into question the wisdom of massive retaliatory doctrine as a deterrent to limited war. Brodie soon found allies in Albert Wohlstetter and others. In the lead chapter, "The Requirements of Deterrence" in his important edited collection, *Military Policy and National Security,* William Kaufmann also challenged John Foster Dulles's emphasis on massive retaliation. At the same time, Kaufmann conceded that his own proposal to confine the strategy to last-resort contingencies left a large vacuum in deterrence planning.

Others in academia and in the foundation world germinated ideas that would influence strongly the strategic directions of the next decade. Supported by Frank Barnett and the Richardson Foundation, Robert Strausz-Hupé founded the Foreign Policy Research Institute (FPRI) at the University of Pennsylvania, which had something of an "army" orientation (in contrast with RAND's "air force" emphasis) if only because active-duty Colonel William Kintner was in residence. The brilliant book on protracted conflict by Strausz-Hupé and his colleagues reinforced this emphasis on "hands-on" warfare. The book countered a popular tendency among military analysts of the 1950s to identify a single year of "maximum vulnerability"—some short-term crisis period—as the basis for strategic discussion.

Meanwhile, at Princeton's Center for International Studies, Klaus Knorr probed NATO's problems, following in the footsteps of the late Edward Mead Earle, the pioneer of military studies at Princeton during World War II. The growing sophistication of work in the field influenced—and was influenced by—Alistair Buchan's founding (largely with Ford Foundation money) of the Institute for Strategic Studies in London, whose initial output was limited mainly to an annual military balance survey.

Clustered at Harvard were former State Department Counselor Robert Bowie, games theorist Thomas Schelling, and Rockefeller colleague Henry Kissinger. Kissinger was also based in New York at the Council on Foreign Relations, which sponsored his landmark analysis, *Nuclear Weapons and Foreign Policy,* a best-seller at the time. Kissinger argued in the book that deterrence as contained in the strategy of massive retaliation eliminated a variety of more attractive diplomatic and strategic initiatives. In the Midwest, at the University of Chicago's Center for the Study of American Foreign Policy, Robert Osgood produced *Limited War: The Challenge to American Strategy,* which included a historical survey of limited wars and argued for the need to impose limits upon future international conflicts by limiting national war aims. Add to the above the existing research centers—including Princeton's Center for International Studies, Johns Hopkins School for Advanced International Studies (SAIS), and the Hoover Institution on War, Revolution and Peace at Stanford—with key spokesmen such as Arnold Wolfers, Paul Nitze, and Stefan Possony. All these individuals and institutions, each in a distinctive manner, could be identified as belonging to the new breed of strategic theorists and research centers crowding the national stage at the onset of the 1960s.

Regardless of partisan preference, the new breed welcomed with much enthusiasm John F. Kennedy's 1961 inaugural address, especially its commitment to defend freedom everywhere and by whatever means—a clear repudiation of the obsession with massive retaliation as a solitary shield for the United States. Nikita Khrushchev had already delivered his own major oration disavowing nuclear war and endorsing "wars of national liberation." The challenge was obvious: hopes ran high for new strategic uses of flexible response, for the possibilities of counterinsurgency doctrine, and for plans to expand foreign aid.

The optimism seemed well founded and the great emphasis on technique seemed most appropriate. Colonialism—at least its Western variant—was fading rapidly, and new nations, many of them politically and economically unstable, proliferated throughout the old colonial spheres of Africa and Asia. Massachusetts Institute of Technology's

(MIT's) Walt Rostow joined the the Kennedy administration and promoted his "take off" concept of development through aid. Economists associated with the American Enterprise Institute (AEI) and the Hoover Institution questioned the belief that the models appropriate to Western national development and economic growth could be applied with few difficulties to the developing countries—given an adequate level of assistance. The majority of the theorists in the country, many identified with bipartisan Eastern Establishment foreign policy, shared in the optimism and endorsed many of the new ideas.

Theory and Practice

The tests were not long in coming. The Bay of Pigs fiasco not only ended the hope for a simple, Guatemala-style (that is, CIA-sponsored) "counter-revolution" against Castro but also forced an abrupt halt to the blustery rhetoric much in evidence about a "surgical" American military intervention in Laos to block a Communist takeover. Although Kennedy wisely accepted blame for the Bay of Pigs, the president's inner circle successfully persuaded sympathetic journalists that somehow "they" had not been at fault. Rather, they argued the holdover Eisenhower appointees—especially at CIA and within the Joint Chiefs—had misled the young chief executive.

The actual lesson of the Bay of Pigs for strategic planning lay at a deeper level, however, far removed from the recriminations of the day and far more of a portent for the failures that came later during the 1960s and 1970s. The Bay of Pigs failed not because of any plot by hangers-on against the new president but for readily observable reasons: erroneous intelligence estimates, incrementalism, overcentralized control, and indecision by the president himself in the climatic moments. This was Vietnam in microcosm—well in advance.

Adding to the confusion in the Kennedy years was the disastrous Kennedy-Khrushchev meeting in Vienna, at which even the president deeply feared that Khrushchev could miscalculate Kennedy's determination to defend Berlin. Only the Berlin crisis and the dramatic Cuban missile confrontation managed to revive the standing, credibility, and charisma of the new president.

The Cuban missile crisis, though of historic importance, was so not only because of the reasons advanced by White House historian and Kennedy aide Arthur Schlesinger, Jr. For one thing, the missile crisis provided the decisive impulse for the Soviet naval buildup and its new blue water strategy. For another, the missile crisis taught the Kennedy administration and a good part of the civilian research institute and intellectual community a troubling lesson: the importance of increasing centralized civilian control of military decisions, even to the tactical level. Secretary of Defense Robert McNamara's Situation Room confrontation with Chief of Naval Operations George Anderson over the deployment of a picket ship used during the blockade would be replayed many times by President Lyndon Johnson over U.S. patrols in Vietnam. Kennedy had given all his advisers copies of Barbara Tuchman's *The Guns of August* as a warning against allowing events to drift out of control. In his mind, the dangers of the nuclear era demanded careful political control of every policy step from the top as well as the avoidance of initiatives at lower levels, especially by the military.

At the Department of Defense, meanwhile, Secretary of Defense McNamara was implementing the techniques of "systems analysis" and management approaches he had learned while running the Ford Motor Company. He made heavy use of his civilian "whiz kids," many brought in from the RAND Corporation and business schools, to direct day-to-day planning. Military establishments, if anything, tend to be overly traditional and opposed to innovation; yet the complications and complexity of rapidly changing modern weapons systems increasingly demanded cost effectiveness analysis. The obsession with management methods and the indifference to the human factors of conflict, however, made the dangers of the McNamara reforms at times outweigh the benefits. McNamara also abolished the Joint Strategic Survey Committee, which had been the long range planning dimension of the Joint Chiefs of Staff. The systems analysts were not just on tap; they were on top.

Admiral George Anderson, who was not reappointed as chief of naval operations, warned in a Press Club speech before he left to become U.S. ambassador to Portugal that the armed forces were in danger of too much management and too little leadership. He argued that "overcentralized structures are conducive to the abuse of power and compounding of mistakes. . . . The operations analysts—properly concerned with cost effectiveness—seem to be working at the wrong echelon—above the professional military level rather than in an advisory capacity to the military who should thoroughly appreciate their assistance."

It is ironic that as civilian strategists imposed their concepts of deterrence on the American defense community, in the Soviet Union the military apparently continued to set strategy as well as tactics. In Washington it was assumed that the Soviets would eventually accept the soundness of mutual assured destruction. Deluded by mirror-imaging, analysts ignored the ample evidence suggesting otherwise.

Marshal Sokolovskii's 1962 book, *Military Strategy,* reflected the

Soviet military's concern with the operational problems of warfare in the nuclear age—a concern that dominates their strategy and tactics to this day.

Military Strategy is a collective work by a group of 15 leading Soviet officers headed by Marshal V.D. Sokolovskii, former chief of the General Staff. Sokolovskii's book reflected the beginnings of a major shift in Soviet emphasis from land warfare in Europe to the global problems of strategic war. The book is Clausewitzian yet Marxist in outlook, in the sense that strategy and military doctrine are not treated as independent entities but vehicles designed to foster the overriding political goals of the Soviet state.

Unlike game theory, model building, and systems analysis approaches to strategy that were emerging in this country, the Soviet military authors strongly emphasized operational and war fighting factors, specifically troop morale and operational readiness. Although many U.S. civilian specialists argued that the art of war had been changed irrevocably by the advent of nuclear weapons, the Soviet military theorists continued their reading and updating of Clausewitz. The Sokolovskii book is striking in its unwillingness to address the issue of flexible response, then so critical in U.S. debate. The book called for continued pursuit of Soviet quantitative and qualitative superiority and even asserted that in a future war—presumably a nuclear one—the Soviet Union would be victorious because of "the real relationship between the political, economic and military forces of the two systems."

The Georgetown Center

Developments at this juncture in the strategic debate require that I inject a personal note. In 1962 I was the executive secretary of the newly founded Georgetown University Center for Strategic Studies. Under the leadership of our director, recently retired Chief of Naval Operations Arleigh Burke, Center staff carefully studied the new Soviet book. Burke, seasoned by his combat experience during World War II and by his negotiating experience with the communists during the Korean War, believed in the primacy of human elements in strategic calculations. From its beginnings, then, the Center pursued assessments that stressed not only conceptual innovations but studies of operational reality going beyond military aspects of strategy. Burke was determined not to make the new Center beholden to government largesse. He also urged that the Center seek diverse approaches to key problems and issues, and be policy oriented and free from "entangling alliances" with the personnel and presumptions of any administration in office, whatever the party.

It might be well to relate the history of this Center to the ongoing collective concerns of other research centers and institutes over the past generation. One should begin by noting the obvious: For 40 years the Council on Foreign Relations dominated foreign policy thought in the United States. Its influential leaders came from the Eastern establishment. Later, they were to be categorized ironically in a book criticizing their policy role in America's most tragic modern experience, the Vietnam War, as "the best and the brightest."

At its beginning the Center was outside this establishment, clearly determined to make its deliberations national and balanced, but equally determined to draw on the better known figures in strategic discussion including theorists at places such as the Hoover Institution and economists from the American Enterprise Institute. The study of strategy and economics was to be as important as that of diplomacy. If the Center was an idea that I developed, the idea became a reality only through the essential support of William Baroody Sr., head of the American Enterprise Institute.[1]

In January 1963 the Center's first conference in the Hall of Nations at the Georgetown University School of Foreign Service brought together the full range of America's strategic and economic thinkers. (Richard Ware of the Relm Foundation, which funded the conference, had always hoped to see some of the market-oriented economists better confront the problems of strategy.) Our first research associate, Richard V. Allen, and I had brought together persons already well known at that time—and some much better known now: Henry Kissinger, James Schlesinger, Robert Strausz-Hupé, Herman Kahn, Murray Weidenbaum, Otto Eckstein, Thomas Schelling, and Arnold Wolfers were among the 30 participants. Characteristic of the scope of CSIS strategic discussion since then, half the conference was devoted to political-military issues and the remainder to economic issues—first, the role of economic strategy, with Oscar Morgenstein, James Schlesinger, Karl Brandt, and Vergil Salera, and second, the role of the market economy in supporting defense requirements, with Otto Eckstein, Murray Weidenbaum, Edward Mason, Norman Ture, Irving Seigel, and Glenn Campbell debating tax and fiscal policies, the costs of alternative military strategies, and domestic U.S. defense costs.

What was unusual about that 1962 conference, and indeed distinctive about the Center, was that the experts who attended came not only from traditional Eastern universities and groups but reflected a national mixture cutting across the political spectrum. Moreover, rigorous economic analysis of the defense budget emerged as a major theme, possibly for the first time at a gathering of this sort. Economists, many from Western universities, who would become prominent in later administrations including the present one, joined in a lively debate over the issue of financing higher defense spending while dealing with both inflation and deficits—an issue that today has become critical.

The degree of prescient "futurology" displayed by the main speakers at the 1962 conference belies the now-fashionable perception among journalists and even some theorists that the United States "stumbled" into strategic disaster or "drifted" into "quagmires." Herman Kahn, for example, who had left RAND to form the Hudson Institute and had just published his controversial book, *Thinking About The Unthinkable,* delivered a paper constructing a 37-step "escalation ladder" to allow what Kahn called ". . . a methodological device which provides a convenient list of many options facing the strategist in a two-sided confrontation." He called the typical situation "a competition in risk taking." Thomas Schelling of Harvard stressed the problems of enemy intentions and the necessity of persuasion. He noted appropriately that the lesson of the so-called missile gap, a major 1960 campaign issue, was the primacy of perception in determining policy: One reacts to what he thinks he sees, not necessarily to what is actually there—a valuable insight for managing the arms race.

The degree to which the conferees anticipated the strategic problems of the 1960s and 1970s varied widely. Kissinger warned of the consequences of not assisting our allies with their own nuclear forces and ignoring the European elements of the alliance. Remedies were still within our control, he concluded, and the West was less imperiled by outside pressures than by a tendency to waste its own resources. In this he proved essentially correct: Despite all of NATO's problems between 1962 and 1982, the Atlantic partnership has muddled through—and the deterrent has worked.

In the Pacific and Southeast Asia, however, a very different picture emerged. There, the Vietnam War proved to be the major event of the 1960s and 1970s. The United States invested its energies and resources in an Asian land war with no clear preconceived plan. Gradual escalation did not result in our opponent backing down; his risk was minimized by the rules of the game that we set ourselves.

Some of the speakers at the 1963 conference did anticipate the problems. For example, Frank Trager argued that the Indochina war would be costly if fought on the communists' terms: "To defend Saigon, it will . . . be necessary to penetrate, undermine, threaten, and if necessary, attack Hanoi." Later in the decade the Johnson administration would rule out precisely this approach. Recalling Chinese intervention in Korea and the 1964 election campaign in which Johnson had described Goldwater as a zealot who would take the offensive recklessly in Vietnam and elsewhere, the Johnson administration committed itself instead to a process of graduated escalation until 1968 when it halted the bombing—after half a million Americans had been already committed to the war.

The possible economic cost of a lengthy military involvement in Vietnam was forecast at our 1963 meeting by Murray Weidenbaum, who spun out several scenarios examining the costs of alternative military strategies—hypothetical cases of an $18 to $20 billion a year "limited" war. (A later Weidenbaum study warned of the danger of not reporting frankly the actual costs of Vietnam and cautioned that the failure of federal fiscal policy to take them into account would produce an inflationary spiral.) If Weidenbaum's limited war scenario was a harbinger of the next five years, the debates of economists and strategists were harbingers for the debates of today. Participants grappled with economic strategies for U.S. allies, a key subject for the next 20 years, strategies now in utter disarray as the West German approval of the Yamal gas pipeline project demonstrated. Another panel argued over the role of the market economy in supporting defense requirements, an issue that today has come to be a seminal concern in the national debate over U.S. priorities. Despite the new emphasis on "supply-side economics," the issue has not really changed in two decades.

The military side was more mixed. Kahn's metaphor of an escalation ladder, the neat strategy—so gradual, so controlled, and so rational, which appeared to work so well in the short run during the Cuban missile crisis—proved to be a mammoth and tragic failure in Vietnam. The reason is easy to find. In the Cuban missile crisis, Kennedy threatened Khrushchev with unlimited action under certain circumstances. In Vietnam, Johnson took pains never to threaten Hanoi with ultimate destruction. The carefully rationalized and limited Vietnam escalation—and, later, de-escalation—assumed, like the escalation ladder itself, a rational cooperative opponent, who also would act incrementally and for limited objectives. But whereas the United States pursued limited objectives emphasizing limited means, North Vietnam was a nation totally committed to an unlimited objective, the total conquest of the South, with an overall military strategy using all its means and aimed at producing a final political result. That result was a decision by the U.S. commander in chief and Congress to withdraw from the war just as Prime Minister Mendes-France and the French National Assembly had done in 1954.

As the Tet offensive reached its stunning climax, American officials might well have remembered Sun Tzu's maxim that "The supreme excellence is not to win a hundred victories in a hundred battles. The supreme excellence is to defeat the armies of your enemies without ever having to defeat them." For we now know that for the communists Tet was a tactical defeat, but a television and political victory.

The gradual application of U.S. power in Vietnam led ultimately to the open-ended Asian land war against which General Douglas MacArthur and other military leaders had warned. Throughout the escalation, Secretary McNamara's kill ratios were faithfully presented to President Johnson to show that there was finally "light at the end of the tunnel." Unfortunately, what Clausewitz termed the "friction" of war—what distinguishes war in reality from war in theory—intervened.

Thus did Kennedy's and Johnson's best and brightest depart Washington, leaving in their wake a destabilized country torn apart by domestic dissent.

The Decline of Strategic Thought

The late 1960s were lean years for strategic studies centers. If the search for alternatives to massive retaliation had attracted those whom Theodore White labeled "action intellectuals" to strategic studies during the 1950s, years of disenchantment with the stalemated war in Vietnam led many to seek less exposed policy pursuits. The Students for a Democratic Society (SDS) and other student radical insurgent groups went on the rampage for a time. At Harvard, the Center for International Studies was ransacked, and certain scholars such as Thomas Schelling moved into new fields. Defense centers with a hard science orientation, such as MITs Draper Laboratories, were forced to disassociate themselves from the university.

The disclosure of CIA support for some strategic and international studies centers reinforced the suspicion of such centers in the academic world. Interest in and foundation funding for Soviet studies declined catastrophically, as did funds for critical foreign language training. Nor did the U.S. military escape unscathed, finding itself all-too-often barred from studying the Soviet adversary. As Robert Bathhurst has pointed out, the 1976 U.S. Army tactical handbook, *The Threat,* dropped the captions to pictures identifying Soviets and charts of Soviet tactics and equipment. At the Naval War College, no less, the 1972 curriculum included no lectures on Soviet intentions.

The research centers responded to this climate in different ways. The Foreign Policy Research Institute broke away from the University of Pennsylvania. At Georgetown, the SDS drove the ROTC off campus and attacked the Center as a CIA-funded front, only to learn that no CIA money or even government money had ever been accepted. McGeorge Bundy, by then head of the Ford Foundation, redirected his institution away from international studies primarily and toward urban problems. Even the RAND Corporation diversified and initiated urban and social welfare studies. Virtually the entire foundation community followed suit, except for the Scaife and Relm foundations. Interestingly, the Scaife foundation vastly expanded its funding for international security studies and fledgling centers at a time when the strategic studies community was at its lowest ebb.

There were new beginnings to be sure, but little noted at the time. Even before many intellectuals fled the strategic field, our Center had broadened its base and its name to reflect the broader environment within which purely strategic issues must be placed. It became the Center for Strategic and International Studies (CSIS). For us, Columbia's Professor Philip Mosely conceived and chaired a research council of international scholars. Using his CSIS affiliation, Chairman Mosely also tried to offset the decline in Soviet studies by leading a transatlantic panel of Sovietologists in an analysis of new trends in Kremlin policy. "The 1970s may well mark a new turning point in many crucial aspects of Soviet policy," he wrote.

Elsewhere several leading Eastern centers began major arms control and disarmament projects in response to the challenges posed by new technologies, such as the multiple independently targetable reentry vehicle (MIRV), and by the Nixon administration's interest in controlling certain aspects of the arms competition. At Brookings, a new wave of young thinkers on political-military affairs began to emerge, including Jeffrey Record, Roger Kaplan, and Barry Blechman. Meanwhile at RAND, despite an added domestic focus, James Schlesinger assumed responsibility for its strategic studies area, specializing in economics and resources rather than model building and systems analysis.

The systems analysts of the 1960s had turned out to be wrong not only in their definition of an appropriate strategy for Vietnam but also in their assessment of the Soviet Union. The rapid acceleration of strategic systems during the Kennedy-McNamara years led in time to reliance on the concepts of parity and mutual assured destruction. In other words, the United States returned to the nonstrategic conception of massive retaliation, in the somewhat altered form of the belief that, with both sides enjoying destructive overkill, the use of strategic nuclear weapons would be seen as totally irrational. The Soviets surely would level off their defense spending, the advocates of MAD argued. Unfortunately, as Secretary of Defense Harold Brown, a McNamara protege, ruefully conceded ten years later, something quite different happened: "We build, they build. We don't build, they build." For an extended period the CIA persistently underestimated the Soviet Union's annual expenditures on defense in what must be seen retroactively as a significant intelligence failure.

Scholars in Government

In the past 20 years, the national security policymaking process has been dominated by the strategic studies community. Henry Kissinger of Harvard, James Schlesinger of RAND, and Zbigniew Brzezinski of Columbia, unlike the earlier systems analysts of the McNamara era, took leadership positions at the very top of the government. Bringing a strong conceptual background to public office, these civilian strategists have had a unique opportunity rarely seen in Western democracies to transform their ideas into government policies. It is significant, however, that their policies have met with limited success, weakened by persistent domestic criticism and the failure of both allies and adversaries to play their "prescribed" roles in the international system.

Because of their stated commitment to the withdrawal of U.S. troops from Vietnam, Nixon and Kissinger sought freedom of action in dealing with the problems of the war they inherited. Meanwhile, the Sino-Soviet split had deepened and both countries held different perspectives on the situation in Indochina. In an effort to maximize their freedom of action, Nixon and Kissinger not only forced the opening to China but, simultaneously, developed an economic and arms control package with the Soviet Union, in retrospect signaling the zenith of detente.

As far as the private research centers were concerned, though, perhaps the period's most significant event was the ascendancy of the quintessential professor-strategist of the decade, Henry Kissinger, within the Nixon administration. Kissinger translated his conceptual analysis of the international system into a series of formidable "state of the world" reports unparalleled in the history of the presidency. Written in a scholarly style, they provided a detailed outline of the administration's strategy to establish a "structure of peace." In a sense, these reports stole the show from the outside think tanks.

At the same time, James Schlesinger moved from the RAND Corporation to the Office of Management and Budget, bringing with him a sure sense of strategic resource management. Catapulted from one important position to another, including chairman of the Atomic Energy Commission and director of Central Intelligence, it was as secretary of defense that Schlesinger made a valuable strategic contribution.

While Kissinger gave new impetus and ambition to U.S. foreign policy, Schlesinger, beginning in 1973, pushed for a reassessment of U.S. strategic doctrine. Officials in the Nixon administration had been disturbed by the excessive rigidity of U.S. strike plans if deterrence were to fail. These plans entailed the indiscriminate dumping of thousands of nuclear weapons on Soviet urban-industrial centers with little concern for limited contingencies below the MAD threshold. As the 1970 presidential foreign policy report pointed out: "Should a President be left with the single option of ordering the mass destruction of enemy civilians in the face of the certainty that it would be followed by the mass slaughter of Americans?"

In early 1974, the administration introduced greater flexibility into U.S. strategic doctrine. Rather than options emphasizing a massive reaction, Schlesinger stated the doctrine in the 1975 Annual Defense Department Report, "We now want to provide the President with a wider set of much more selective targeting options." Henceforth, U.S. officials facing a confrontation with the Soviet Union would have the capability of responding with precision and discrimination to Soviet attacks without necessarily triggering a full-scale exchange of nuclear weapons.

Schlesinger was also instrumental in reappraising NATO's theatre nuclear force posture and initiating the modernization of its tactical nuclear arsenal. With the end of the Vietnam War, the defense of Europe once again became the priority of the U.S. military. There was mounting concern about the continuing absence of a strategy for the 7,000 nuclear weapons stored in Europe, their vulnerability to Soviet preemption or terrorist attacks, and their low utility in actual conflict. Although Schlesinger's effort to give greater precision to NATO's flexible response doctrine was considerably hampered by European sensitivities to discussions of nuclear battlefield scenarios, he was successful in laying the groundwork for upgrading NATO's battlefield weapons and improving the peacetime security of the weapons.

In the diplomatic arena, the policy of detente began to fall apart by the mid-1970s, though dissenting voices had been heard earlier from both ends of the political spectrum. One of the critics, Zbigniew Brzezinski, became executive director of the newly-formed Trilateral Commission of Americans, Japanese, and Europeans. Brzezinski shared the group's intellectual leadership with several others, including Robert Bowie of Harvard and Henry Owen at Brookings. After beginning his career studying Soviet matters at Columbia's Russian Institute, Brzezinski had turned his attention increasingly from his concern for the balance of U.S.-Soviet power to a search for global order. The Trilateralists were not to study national or international security, but political and economic relations among industrial democracies, and were to establish new methods of private communication. Initially many Trilateralists reacted, in part against the priority Kissinger assigned to the U.S.-Soviet relationship as well as to the new economic policies of Secretary of the Treasury John Connally.

In the military field, Albert Wohlstetter's 1976 analysis of Soviet military spending was a devastating refutation of the official predictions of McNamara. Wohlstetter found that, since the early 1960s, the United States had systematically underestimated Soviet increases in their offensive forces. He challenged the traditional notions of the existence of an arms race and argued that the overestimates that had led to the missile gap myth during the 1950s had produced a "confessional literature" during the 1960s. Also, according to Wohlstetter, "dissonant sounds of reality were hardly audible in Establishment study groups meeting in Washington, Cambridge, and New York," an allegation I found overdrawn in relationship to the one center I knew best. But Wohlstetter was on target in his assertion that the facts proved "the United States has not been running a quantitative strategic race."

At about the same time Wohlstetter's article appeared, Richard Pipes led a study of Soviet strategy in Europe sponsored by the Stanford Research Institute. Pipes was highly critical of detente as a one-sided phenomenon, noting that it dovetailed with the Soviet strategy of trying to detach Western Europe from the United States. In a similar vein, Ray Cline at CSIS wrote a *World Power Assessment,* stressing the factor of "will" as the key to the strategic equation and attacking detente for its role in eroding Western will. Also under the same auspices, John Collins of the Congressional Research Service published his *American and Soviet Military Trends,* demonstrating a distinct advantage for Moscow in most areas of military capability.

It should also be noted that as early as 1972, Edward Luttwak warned in a CSIS *Washington Paper (The Strategic Balance 1972)* that an asymmetry in U.S.-Soviet strategic doctrine could well undermine U.S. arms control efforts. By then, partly for holding similar views, James Schlesinger had resigned as secretary of defense after differing with the president over the defense budget. Out of government, Schlesinger emerged as a critic of detente and U.S. preparedness levels, becoming a fellow both at CSIS and at Johns Hopkins's SAIS.

By the 1976 primary campaign, even the word "detente" had become a political liability, and President Ford announced that he had struck it from his vocabulary. Just as strikingly, the Trilateral Commission, which at its formation had agreed not to address international security issues, undertook such a study of the Soviet Union directed principally by Richard Lowenthal of West Germany. The Trilateral Report assumed greater significance when the new Carter administration tapped some 19 Trilateralists for leadership positions.

By then, private research centers were experiencing a notable revival, attracting not only former government policymakers such as Schlesinger but—in the case of CSIS—a former secretary of state and the most recent national security adviser. Both Henry Kissinger and, later, Zbigniew Brzezinski chose to join the Georgetown Center, thereby remaining closely attuned to the Washington policy world. In Kissinger's last two years as secretary of state, he had displayed a strong measure of interest in Soviet geopolitical strategy as it impinged, for example, upon such troublespots as Angola. After leaving office, his attention returned to the Soviet strategic threat, as he spent more time with colleagues in research centers and with analysts such as SAIS's Paul Nitze and John Lehman who were members of the newly formed Committee on the Present Danger.

Even more dramatic than Kissinger's turn to the problems of strategic reassessment was Brzezinski's return from his concentration on world order assessments to his first discipline, the problem of Soviet power. After the first year of the Carter administration, Brzezinski urged that the president recognize the destabilizing dangers of Soviet ambitions. Only after the Soviet invasion of Afghanistan did the entire administration belatedly agree, though some apparently only because of strong public and presidential pressures.

With distinguished and experienced foreign policy practitioners in residence, research centers like CSIS became in the late 1970s the focal points for national and international debate of key issues. Another case study can be drawn from this Center's experience. In September 1979, CSIS, under Kissinger's leadership, cosponsored a meeting on the future of NATO in Brussels. Future scholars may acknowledge this meeting as a critical moment in the history of the NATO alliance. Kissinger startled Europe with a blunt, grim assessment of NATO's urgent problems. While conceding that the alliance had been a remarkable success, he argued that the profound crisis confronting the West made it imperative for NATO to develop policies and force structures capable of meeting the current and impending Soviet challenge. In an age of strategic parity, he warned that U.S. allies could no longer demand strategic reassurances that "we cannot possibly mean or if we do mean, we should not want to execute because if we execute, we risk the destruction of civilization." Not only did the alliance require development of a strategic counterforce capability, Kissinger argued, but NATO should also build up conventional and theatre nuclear forces in Europe and—perhaps most important of all—design a credible political and military strategy for their use. Kissinger added that, although detente remained essential to further dialogue with the Soviets (thereby indicating that he had not repudiated his entire legacy), it could not on its own guarantee the West's security in the turbulent decade ahead. Defense must precede detente, Kissinger told his shaken European audience, confessing that he too had contributed in the past to an erroneous view of the relationship between East and West.

Kissinger's dramatic speech made headlines across Europe, and it triggered often vehement debate at the three-day conference. Professor Michael Howard of Oxford went so far as to state that he could no longer assign Kissinger's books in his classes because the latter's altered views—though not new at all—were at variance with his written work. Some Americans present, including recently retired NATO commander General Alexander Haig, might have stressed the deterrent effect of U.S. ground forces in Europe a good deal more, something minimized in Kissinger's talk. Klaus Mehnert and other Europeans argued in the same vein that even the most minimal deterrent would deter, and within weeks, at an International Institute for Strategic Studies (IISS) conference in Switzerland, McGeorge Bundy tried to rebut Kissinger's arguments with a similar assessment—that a minimal deterrent, properly managed, would do the job adequately.

For many Europeans, Kissinger's bold speech was considered downright indelicate, however accurate its evaluation. One much-disturbed European NATO official rushed up to me to complain that Kissinger should not have spoken as he did. Had he spoken the truth, I asked. He had, the official responded, but he should not have done so. I responded then, as I would today, that if the Vietnamese experience has taught Americans anything, it is that lack of public candor can end up with lack of public support in a crisis.

"Truthful indelicacy" remains a perennial problem for public officals. How can the real issues of European defense be discussed candidly, for example, without encouraging neutralism or Gaullism in Europe and possibly in this country as well? Officials in all the NATO countries have become increasingly circumspect in their public statements as the reactions to recent statements by President Reagan on limited nuclear war and Secretary Haig on nuclear weapons demonstrate. Increasingly the job of reassessment and strategy reconstruction is being left to the policy annals and private strategic studies centers on both sides of the Atlantic, "safe houses" where honest debate and controversial proposals on the alliance can still occur.

Never before in recent history have the nongovernmental research centers and the policy journals become potentially so important in filling a policy void. Thus, CSIS's Walter Laqueur could write in 1981 that if the Europeans did not move forward on theatre nuclear modernization, they should adopt a strategy of conventional force parity, something the United States should negotiate as an absolute condition of its continued support for the alliance. Such a hard-headed option could not have been made publicly, possibly not even privately, by any U.S. public official despite NATO's continued deterioration—or, possibly, because of it.

Other Dimensions of Strategy

These reflections have focused so far on the role of the study centers and their strategists in grouping our strategy in NATO and Vietnam. This discussion would not be complete, however, if I did not examine four other dimensions of strategy that can be decisive in determining a conflict either actual or potential. If we are to meet the challenges of the 1980s, it is essential that our strategy include technological, logistical, cultural, and resource vectors. The study centers may well have to assay the leading role in such an integration.

Technological considerations were not sufficient to excite Clausewitz's attention, and it took naval strategists and tacticians to generate breakthroughs. The situation on land began to change in the nineteenth century with the needle gun, and then in the next century with the machine gun and the tank. Technology trade-offs became part of the preparation for war. William James wrote in 1911, "Every up-to-date dictionary should say that 'peace' and 'war' mean the same thing, now *in posse,* now *in actu.* It may even reasonably be said that the intensely sharp competitive *preparation* for war by the nation *is the real war,* permanent, increasing; and that battles are only a sort of public verification of mastery gained during the 'peace' intervals."

As the century wore on and World War I became stalemated, Colonel J.F.C. Fuller wrote in an official paper: "Tools, or weapons, if only the right ones can be discovered, form 99 percent of victory. . . . In war, especially in modern wars, wars in which weapons change rapidly, one thing is certain; no army of 50 years before any date selected would stand 'a dog's chance' against the army existing at that date . . ."

Sputnik and subsequent allegations of a missile gap sensitized the American public in the early 1960s to the dangers of a loss in the technological race. Today, as Chairman Brezhnev has reminded us, "The center of gravity in the competition between the two [the U.S. and the U.S.S.R.] systems is now to be found precisely in [the fields of science and technology]. . . ." Obviously, a major strategic or diplomatic victory can be achieved without firing a shot. Advances in lasers and particle beams could be decisive in the future. In antisubmarine warfare, no one can minimize the impact on our triad of a major Soviet breakthrough. Historically, there has been a frequent failure to anticipate the impact of decisive technological development on the ever-shifting offensive-defensive balance.

These are issues that study centers addressed rather well from the very beginning. Organizations such as the Center for Naval Analysis and the RAND Corporation did much classified work, of course, but other work was done for public consumption. In 1969 at CSIS Dr. John Warner, former president of Carnegie-Mellon, chaired a panel study on research and development, one now being updated under the leadership of Dr. Frederick Seitz. That same year the Hudson Institute did a major study justifying the ABM system, which was widely used in Congress in gaining legislative support for Safeguard.

Technology has also been an area where Dr. Stephen Possony and Dr. Edward Teller at the Hoover Institution, former director of the Defense Intelligence Agency General Daniel Graham, and retired General George Keegan have contributed through the American Security Council and other organizations such as the National Strategy Information Center.

What has been especially lacking, however, is an assessment of the degree to which technology does and should determine strategy, as well as when oversophistication destroys effective use. In this context, the Harvard Center for Science and International Affairs was established in 1978 with a $4 million Ford Foundation grant as part of the Kennedy School of Government. The Center has focused on nuclear doctrine and arms control, energy and nuclear nonproliferation, arms transfers, and the military impact of new technologies. The Center's staff includes scientists and strategists such as Paul Doty, Albert Carnesale, Richard Garwin, and Michael Nacht. In addition, one of the Center's key activities has been the publication of *International Security,* which has rapidly become a leading journal in the field of strategic studies. Also associated with Harvard is the Program on Information Resources Policy, which is studying such critical issues as command, control, communications, and intelligence.

Despite the alarming erosion of engineering education in the

United States, technology is still the great American strength, and at a time of resource scarcity, it must become a vital part of our strategic reconstruction where we have comparative advantage. Strategy must drive technology in a direction that creates better protection for us and incentives for the Soviets to join in real arms reduction agreements.

Resources and Logistics

In the next 20 years, the weakest link in U.S. strategy could be the failure to maintain secure access to global energy, minerals, and other natural resources. This loss of access would restrict the flow of raw materials for civilian economies and of vital supplies required by military logistics. The problem of resources has been an enduring factor in the calculation of strategists. The Second Reich built the Berlin-to-Baghdad railway to increase access to petroleum. Japan went to war in 1941 largely because the Allies had denied it supplies of oil, tin, and rubber from Southeast Asia. Today, however, all nations face conflicts over resources—a dilemma that has serious implications for the Western alliance in its current state of disarray.

For the United States, access to resources was not a major problem during the Cold War era. For more than three decades, our military and civilian economies grew prosperous on cheap and readily-available energy. Strategically, Great Britain and its allies managed to secure the Persian Gulf area until the late-1970s by backing both Iran and Saudi Arabia, despite the intra-regional rivalry between those countries. But the 1973 Yom Kippur War and the ensuing Arab oil embargo changed the situation overnight. The West learned that not only could oil prices skyrocket but also that an interruption of Arab oil supplies could force NATO members to change their policies toward Israel and the Arab states. An alliance organized to defend Western Europe was unprepared to deal with the diplomatic and economic consequences of an oil supply interruption. To paraphrase Liddell Hart, the Organization of Petroleum Exporting Countries (OPEC) discovered how best to use the strategy of the indirect approach against the West.

In the years that followed, nothing seemed certain but increasing uncertainty. Although some Arab members of OPEC did not maintain their unified stand on oil prices and supply, they remained unified in their opposition to continuing U.S. support for Israel. With the exception of the Netherlands, our European allies shifted to a pro-Arab stance, which left the United States isolated in its Middle East policy, further straining the alliance.

As early as 1968 a few experts also became concerned over the potential for conflict in the Persian Gulf. A CSIS panel and study coordinated by Alvin Cottrell and myself cautioned that a withdrawal of British troops from east of Suez could destabilize the region. For an area that would witness the fall of the all-powerful shah and the bloody stalemate of an Iran-Iraq war, the conclusions of the panel, which included Bernard Lewis, Charles Issawi, Sir William Luce, and Michael Hourani proved to be prophetic.

In a very different study, *Toward Peace in the Middle East,* published in December of 1975, the Brookings Institution undertook to find a solution to the Palestinian problem. That study, which involved Zbigniew Brzezinski and William Quandt, was decisive in capping President Carter's Middle East policy.

Because geopolitics and diplomacy have come to affect energy supply and prices, soon after the Yom Kippur War national security analysts also began to focus on the interplay between U.S. strategy and energy problems. In 1974 President Nixon, with the aid of William Simon, established Project Independence. Its goals were to reduce U.S. vulnerability to oil cutoffs through increasing self-sufficiency in energy and diversification of oil imports. Above all, it sought a cost estimate of the security risks incurred by import dependence, one that could serve as a base for import tariffs and subsidies for alternative energy development.

Several research institutes followed suit with their own analysis and recommendations. The Ford Foundation sponsored two major studies, *A Time to Choose: America's Energy Future* (1974) and *Energy: The Next Twenty Years* (1979). The RAND Corporation issued several monographs including a 1974 study on preparing for oil import disruptions. The year 1979 marked the publication of other important energy studies: *Energy in Transition: 1985–2010* by The National Academy of Sciences, *Energy Future* by the Harvard Business School, and the report of the Workshop on Alternative Energy Strategies conducted at the Massachusetts Institute of Technology by Carroll Wilson. Throughout this decade, AEI pioneered in the field of deregulation.

CSIS first became deeply involved in the energy field in 1973 when Jack Bridges, a former adviser to the Joint Committee on Atomic Energy, joined the Center. Using all available forecast data and computer technology, Bridges developed a brilliant three-dimensional plastic energy display system showing how the energy problem affected future energy scenarios. Although some Washington policymakers had called Bridges an alarmist prior to the 1973 war, when the war began, he was asked to brief 80 senators and 250 congressmen with his display system. Overnight energy had become a major concern for U.S. strategic and foreign policy just as OPEC emerged as a critical factor in U.S. diplomatic and economic calculations.

CSIS also became involved in developing ways to expand the use of coal in the United States. The National Coal Policy Project sought to reconcile the differences among environmentalists, electric utilities, and industrial coal users. Its findings and recommendations published in 1979 brought national attention to the difficulties of using this most abundant U.S. energy resource. At MIT, Carroll Wilson also pursued the elusive solution to the coal problem, publishing *The World Coal Study* in 1980.

At the 1979 NATO Conference, fully two-thirds of the 120 delegates were assigned to topics such as energy economics and the Persian Gulf. Understandably but unfortunately, the debate over Henry Kissinger's speech overwhelmed CSIS's effort to launch a systematic European-U.S. dialogue on the problem of access to resources. To compensate in part for that initial failure, CSIS in the fall of 1979 undertook an independent project to integrate energy and national security issues under the direction of Charles Ebinger. That project report, *The Critical Link: Energy and National Security* due to be published early in 1982, synthesizes their findings on the continuing vulnerability of the West to oil import disruptions and the international implications of this vulnerability.

Conventional military thinking in this country adapted only slowly, however, to the full implications of this new strategic challenge. Although new maritime and logistic strategies were needed to overcome problems related to resource access in the Indian Ocean and Persian Gulf, Pentagon and think-tank research generally remained focused on the requirements for a possible NATO-Warsaw Pact war. To the traditional military analysts, weapons systems and other necessities required for a confrontation in Europe seemed more significant than those needed to keep the sea-lanes open elsewhere in the world. U.S. efforts in this respect in the early 1970s proved to be shortsighted. When the British withdrew from the Gulf, for example, the United States established facilities at Bahrain with two destroyers and a submarine tender, while the United States lacked even a single base in the Indian Ocean. Diego Garcia, fully 2,000 miles from the most probable site of naval action in the region, became a target for congressional opposition reminiscent of Congress's unwillingness to fortify Wake Island during the late 1930s. Admiral Thomas S. Moorer, while chairman of the Joint Chiefs of Staff and later at CSIS, continually warned of the coming dangers of such an oversight.

Only when the shah's regime collapsed and brought down the main pillar buttressing U.S. policy in Southwest Asia did the United States begin to take its first tentative steps toward providing a credible presence in the area. The seizure of American hostages in Iran and the tensions within the region that grew in subsequent months made a U.S. forces buildup in the Indian Ocean a necessity. Unfortunately, the buildup occurred largely by diverting ships and personnel from other parts of the world where U.S. forces were already less than adequate. Until recently, both the U.S. civilian and naval leadership have been slow to recognize the dramatic policy implications of the new energy-economics elements in national security, especially as these apply to the requirements of Persian Gulf defense, where the U.S. weakness was as much political as military.

Slowly, U.S. policy—first in the closing months of the Carter administration and now under President Reagan—has begun to confront the awesome problems involved in achieving a measure of stability in the region. Policies that might seem unrelated—reinforcing U.S. support for the Saudi regime, recommissioning old battleships and perhaps an aircraft carrier, developing new approaches to supply problems associated with maintaining a permanent force in the region through civilian manning and commercial long-term maritime charters—all reflected the slow and still uncertain U.S. effort to stave off a series of catastrophes for Western interests in the Gulf. John Norton Moore's Center for Oceans Law and Policy at the University of Virginia, along with CSIS, tried to confront these issues.

One critical dimension of the problem of resource access involves strategic minerals, first brought to national attention in 1980 not by a research center but by the World Affairs Council of Pittsburgh. The extraordinary report issued by the Council, led by its president, R. Daniel McMichael, in collaboration with MIT Professor Daniel Fine, helped to generate congressional hearings and to focus some executive branch attention on the most severe resource contingency for the decades ahead, especially in view of the large concentration of strategic minerals in central and southern Africa as well as in the Soviet Union.

The ability to assure adequate resource supply has not been a major problem for American strategists until recently. In a series of conflicts—from the Revolution through the Civil War and, most especially, World War II—American industry has displayed an ability, working in close conjunction with government's military and civilian leaders, to provide the requirements needed to maintain American armed forces. As a nation we have excelled at the logistical dimension of warfare, even to the extent that we were too prone to rely on strategies of attrition without maneuver and surprise.

Considering the national past, it seems strange yet appropriate to argue that the weakest link in American strategy over the next 20 years may well involve a massive failure in logistics. Such problems tend to be beyond the scope of the normal civilian research analyst, and only a few have addressed themselves to the problems, most notably Martin Van Creveld in *Supplying War*. The subject of potential logistical disaster emerged dramatically at CSIS's 1979 NATO conference when Admiral Isaac Kidd, recently retired as supreme allied commander, Atlantic, spoke about the disastrous deterioration of U.S. maritime capabilities. Although the strengthening of the American-flag fleet is crucial to NATO, it is absolutely essential for the projection of U.S. power in the Persian Gulf. Most of the civilian strategists had little interest in what he said. The aborted Iranian hostage rescue mission reminds us, in microcosm, of the broader strategic necessity of adequate logistical support. Without it, the Rapid Development Force will be largely a paper capability.

Cultural Dimension

The cultural component of U.S. strategy remains possibly its most neglected and misunderstood dimension. Some of the gravest miscalculations of the Vietnam War came from facile efforts to apply mechanically American concepts of democracy and self-determination to a distinctly different culture that already possessed a French veneer to its Asian essence. The only war in Southeast Asia fought in a way even partially appropriate to its culture was in Laos where about 200 civilian contract employees—not a wholesale military presence—worked with General Van Pao and his Meo tribesmen. The Meo's logistical system, by Saigon MAAG standards, was crude; yet it worked. The enemy was stalemated without the several hundred thousand U.S. troops then committed to an Americanized war in South Vietnam. Without pausing to review the specific elements in the cultural arrogance often displayed by Americans in their pursuit of victory in Vietnam, the question must be raised: How might we avoid repeating such mistakes—and avoid making equally disastrous newer ones—in Southwest Asia?

That the Muslim world, particularly in the Persian Gulf region, contains in embryo the ingredients for a Great Power confrontation remains an obvious point, reinforced each time Muslim fundamentalist culture confronts a modernizing, Western regime. Studies of cultural and religious affairs such as those at CSIS, including assessments that deal with the disparate collection of movements lumped together in the West as "Muslim fundamentalism," become, therefore, increasingly important to U.S. strategists. If we once again over-Americanize our strategy in a way that encourages too rapid modernization and inappropriate basing structures while ignoring the cultures of the region, we will have decreased the overall security.

Nor have we studied adequately the manner in which the United States communicates with other cultures throughout the world. The question of an effective public diplomacy can no longer be left to cultural affairs officers alone, but is vital to the strategic and diplomatic equation. My experiences as chairman of the Board for International Broadcasting and my involvement with Frank Stanton's panel on Public Diplomacy first taught me the importance of our much neglected international communications policy. If the tensions with the Soviet Union increase in the 1980s, the ability to communicate with the people of the USSR so that they will understand our peaceful intentions becomes absolutely critical. The same is true for Western Europe. No more striking example can be found than the neutron bomb issue, where reports about a tactical weapon with a limited destructive capability that could have compensated for Soviet tank superiority were so distorted that it became a monster weapon and its deployment was postponed.

In international communication there must be an understanding of the political and cultural environment. Knowledge of foreign languages and cultures are seriously lacking today in the United States. Unlike the Soviet Union, the United States has not devoted significant resources to studying its principal adversary. Although the 1950s and early 1960s were a flourishing period for Russian language studies and for research on the Soviet Union, the past 15 years have seen a decline both in funding and interest. Decreased government support and growing foundation inattention to existing research centers or university departments have led to a smaller pool of Sovietologists, fewer jobs for them, and, overall, less research on critical aspects of Soviet affairs. On national security grounds alone this situation must be reversed. Area studies on the Communist world must be revived.

There are recent encouraging signs that this trend is being reversed. The Sino Soviet Institute of George Washington University and CSIS completed a joint study that showed the cultural diversity in the Soviet Union, and James Billington has written perceptively on Russian intellectual history. Harvard's Derek Leebaert's edited collection, *Soviet Military Thinking,* clearly shows that the Soviet military has not subscribed to our strategic doctrine. Our own major undertaking at CSIS, directed by Professor Robert Byrnes of Indiana University, will analyze the Soviet Union's internal dynamics during the decade ahead. Some 25 scholars are divided into 7 working groups led by Robert Campbell (Soviet economy and energy), Maurice Friedberg (intellectual and cultural factors), Andrzej Korbonski (Eastern Europe), Gail Lapidus (demographic and social factors), Chip Blacker (military forces), Seweryn Bialer (political systems), and Adam Ulam (external factors).

A New Breed

By 1980 some extraordinary trends were evident. First of all, strategic study centers had begun to spring up around the world, with advance teams visiting the United States to find out how to establish them. In the 1970s, a CSIS was established in Indonesia, then an outstanding Center for Strategic Studies was formed by General Yariv in Tel Aviv, and the Al Ahram Institute was set up in Cairo under Dr. Boutros-Ghali. The Research Institute for Peace and Security under Dr. Inoki began an annual military balance study in Japan with the help of IISS in London. The University of Riyadh studied how to establish its own center, and other countries such as Spain, Portugal, and even Bangladesh expressed interest or had plans in progress.

With the emergence of a new generation of scholars, congressional staffers, and study centers, many of the older institutions underwent a revival. Under the leadership of former Kissinger staffer Winston Lord, the Council on Foreign Relations has moved toward the center of the strategic debate. It coauthored the 1981 panel report on Western security with leading European study centers: Karl Kaiser's German Policy Society, Thierry de Montbrial's French Institute of International Affairs, and David Watt's Royal Institute of International Affairs. Similarly, under the leadership of Henry Fowler, Kenneth Rush, and Francis Wilcox, the Atlantic Council of the United States initiated a series of highly relevant policy studies.

Significantly, the think tanks began to play an even more important role, if in a very different way from that of the 1950s. Undoubtedly in the United States this new role of the study groups originated partially in the breakdown of the foreign policy and defense consensus following Vietnam and Watergate, the frequent stalemates between the president and Congress, and the search for new ideas around which to build a new consensus.

Presidential candidates began to draw extensively on the think tanks for both ideas and advisers, Carter from Brookings and Carnegie and Reagan from the Hoover Institute, AEI, CSIS, and the Institute for Foreign Policy Analysis. Professor William Van Cleave of UCLA and Scott Thompson of the Fletcher School of Law and Diplomacy also produced a strategic options paper that influenced the thinking of Governor Reagan's campaign staff. Of special influence during the transition were the defense, foreign policy, and intelligence papers prepared by the Heritage Foundation under the direction of Ed Feulner. The papers were authored by innovative congressional committee staffers, many of whom subsequently joined the new administration. If Feulner tapped younger Hill talent, Presidents Carter and Reagan, on a more senior level, made numerous appointments from among the tested veterans of the Trilateral Commission and the Committee on the Present Danger. The latter contributed in many ways to the reversal in the decline of defense spending, while groups to the left, such as the Institute of Policy Studies and the Center for Defense Information, have raised strong dissenting voices about this policy.

In many respects, U.S. think tanks today are very different from their European counterparts. Never has a Tory or Labour government drawn upon the staffs of the highly respected British institutes, such as IISS and the historic Chatham House.

The Study Centers Challenged

Let us look ahead. Today's ultimate challenge is to devise a grand strategy that incorporates political, economic, logistical, technological, social, and cultural dimensions. My 20 years in the strategic labyrinth have led to the conclusion that a sense of certainty, most notably in evidence during the halcyon days of systems analysts in the 1960s, proved wrong in practice as well as dangerous both methodologically and morally. The American failure in Vietnam, the fall of the shah, and the Soviets' pursuit of military superiority have shown the degree to which our assessments must cope with uncertainty and unpredictability. The essence of effective strategy lies in its ability to accommodate the unexpected. If nothing else, strategy is a flexible art.

Any new effort to devise a grand strategy, therefore, must be tested constantly by such principles as freedom of action and economy of effort. Options must be devised to allow for change within our alliance system throughout the world, not only in Europe. U.S. defenses must not be tied to the weakest links in that system in the future, as has been the case in the past.

Frederick the Great observed that he who tries to be strong everywhere will be strong nowhere. The study centers must grapple with that classic strategic principle: economy of effort. This demands a sense of proportion and clearer objectives. Gone is the cheap energy that made possible high economic growth rates, and gone are many of the traditional markets for American goods. Gone, too, is the mammoth foreign aid and security assistance program, along with construction of U.S. bases around the world. Gone is the era when high percentages of gross national product could be allocated to defense spending with minimal political cost.

The public itself, after the shocks of Vietnam and Watergate, has little confidence in the existing national security process. The Atlantic alliance is in disarray, divided by the role of theatre nuclear weapons and their pending modernization, and by neutralist pressures, possibly historic in their sweep, throughout Western Europe. Meanwhile East Asia, especially Japan, has achieved major importance in the global economy despite its continuing military weakness. Southwest Asia, moreover, has become the energy heartland for the Atlantic alliance and Japan, just as Central and Southern Africa have for strategic minerals.

Within the United States, however, the legacy of the 1960s continues to haunt the process of adjustment. Thus, the complexity and expense of military technology and confusion in procurement policy have exacerbated micromanagement within the armed forces. This—combined with the newly-intrusive role of the Office of Management and Budget in weapons-system economics—has created an elephantine, strategic decision-making process. Management tends to override leadership in our fighting forces. The successful military campaigns of the last 20 years have been fought by countries like Israel, which has imaginative leadership, based on a decentralized command system that enjoys maximum flexibility for maneuver in the field. Never has an "agonizing reappraisal" been called for more desperately. Never before have the research centers had a greater opportunity to contribute to that reassessment.

A historical review is in order. Despite the efforts of a few scholars who have alternated historical research with policy analysis—such as Henry Kissinger, Bernard Brodie, Walter Laqueur, and Colin Gray—the historical dimension of strategic assessment largely disappeared during the 1950s. It fell victim to the tragic delusion that nuclear weapons systems required only systems analysis and game theory, dismissing as unnecessary the classical principles of military strategy.

This arrogant disregard for historical examples was compounded by elements basic to American character and culture. Historians D.W. Brogan and Russell Weigley have noted the American proclivity to rely heavily upon overwhelming superiority in personnel and equipment in a war rather than upon strategic initiative. Sometimes this costly combination works—as it did for Ulysses S. Grant. The South lost its rebellion for lack of manpower and supplies. General Grant's attrition warfare foreshadowed tactics used by World War I generals at Verdun and Paschendaele. Forgotten was the art of maneuver warfare as practiced by Lee and Jackson.

The U.S. mass production method of warfare during World War II was more acceptable to military leaders such as Eisenhower in Europe and Nimitz in Asia than to MacArthur, who lost fewer American troops in four years than fell during the Battle of the Bulge. Two decades later in Vietnam, Defense Secretary Robert McNamara's stress on "kill ratios," along with the Americanization of the war itself, fit appropriately into the traditional American style. Since World War II, we have pioneered, often foolishly, in the use of overwhelming weapons systems, nuclear and otherwise, leading often to a massive waste of energy and resources. The greatest attrition effort in human history, the strategic bombing campaigns, actually pushed the enemies into more total resistance. Impersonal management has replaced personal leadership as the key to waging war; massive fire power has substituted—badly for the most part—for skillful maneuver, battleground flexibility, and economy of force. We have somehow forgotten that the art of classical strategy has always been to upset the opponent and his equilibrium rather than to drive him to greater consolidation and resistance.

The American way of war finally has run its course. It failed us miserably in Vietnam. In the reinvention of American strategy, we must acknowledge those classical principles recognized by the great strategists of history—Alexander, Hannibal, Caesar, Frederick the Great, and Napoleon among them—who suffered from inferior physical resources, yet were capable of imposing their will on opponents by virtue of greater imagination. The psychology of command and rebuilding leadership to exercise such command remains critical. NATO, for example, continues to rest on a cumbersome defense, relying far too much upon uncritical acceptance of a war of attrition—the strategies of yesterday.

Even now, at a time when the democracies in our alliances enjoy at least twice the population and four times the gross national product of the Warsaw Pact countries, we are still unable to maximize economic resources so as to constrain the mounting Soviet military buildup. The technology and financial resources of the industrial democracies have become indispensable to the Soviets, enabling them to divert their available economic resources to military spending. All too apt is Lenin's wry observation that the capitalist countries would sell his fledgling Bolshevik dictatorship the rope with which capitalism would be hanged. Can we allow the situation to deteriorate further?

A Revival of Strategy

That this country and its allies require a strategic reformation, a basic rethinking of policies and doctrines, seems indisputable. Such reformations never originate solely through appropriate channels, however, whether in the military or in government. Imagination cannot be requisitioned.

Fortunately there have been signs that the country's leaders have begun to recognize the inadequacies of our present strategy. The war colleges have undergone an important revamping in departments such as the policy and strategy unit at the Naval War College. The Army War College began a remarkable reassessment with the study, *On Strategy: Vietnam in Context.* Looking to the future, Army Chief of Staff E.C. Myer has sought to introduce more flexibility into army doctrine. Chief of Naval Operations Admiral Thomas Hayward has created a long range planning panel to analyze the future roles of the navy. To his great credit, Marine Corps Commandant General Barrow has established a Center on Maneuver Warfare. Navy Secretary John Lehman, with his past association with FPRI and CSIS, has introduced new concepts in naval strategy that involve reacting at times and places of our own choosing. Former RAND Corporation economist Fred Iklé, as undersecretary of defense, has approached the logistical nightmare by examining the inadequate industrial base. President Reagan has reestablished the President's Foreign Intelligence Advisory Board—the board that under the Ford administration aided in establishing "Team B" to review CIA estimates and the entire intelligence process. Secretary Weinberger has called upon the Defense University to undertake a new role in strategic reappraisal through a new Strategic Concepts Center.

Some of these developments have been prodded in Congress by a bipartisan caucus of both conservative and liberal military reformers like Gary Hart (D-Colo.), Newt Gingrich (R-Ga.), Sam Nunn (D-Ga.), and William Whitehurst (R-Va.). Making a strong contribution to the vigorous new ideas emerging from the Congress have been members of congressional staffs, those at the research centers—figures such as Jeffrey Record, William Lind, and Edward Luttwak—and the work being done by mavericks within the Department of Defense such as John Boyd and Frank Spinney. A range of new concepts and proposals has begun to appear, although no consensus has been reached. In this regard a more integrated effort is being undertaken by a study group led by Senator Sam Nunn and Representative Richard Cheney (R-Wyo.) on grand strategy and Senator John Glenn (D-Ohio) on force structure and foreign policy, with participants drawn from a variety of study centers. In contrast to McNamara's whiz kids, who stressed operational and systems analysis, the new reformers emphasize the human elements, historical experience, and the primacy of strategy over technology.

What lessons can be drawn from the past 20 years of strategic studies? Too often, the centers assumed that American power was inexhaustible and could be projected successfully to any point in the globe in any degree desired. Too readily, we substituted counting for thinking. The systems and operations analysts served their purpose, but found their notions carried to a dangerous extreme. Our adversaries did not behave according to our prescribed, rational model. Strategic miscalculations were exacerbated by the traditional American faith in mechanization and quantification, expressed in massive wars of attrition. The economic effects of warfare were neglected, as were the cultural and psychological impacts, which affect fighting capability as much as weapons readiness.

Strategic studies centers now confront the result of their previous neglect of the human factor. Any new grand strategy that emerges must be based on the study of history and of classic principles that teach economy of effort and that seek to maximize freedom of action and flexibility. Can such a strategy fit intelligently into a new approach to arms control, Atlantic alliance policy, and new strategic imperatives elsewhere in the world?

This leads to a vast major oversight by the study centers, and by the executive branch, over the past 20 years: the failure to study closely the relationship between strategy and diplomacy. Their coordination is imperative. Strategy is the art of utilizing resources to influence the will and behavior of an opponent. Diplomacy is the art of negotiating toward mutually satisfactory goals. Our problems with SALT I and SALT II arose from a negotiating diplomacy that lacked an effective strategy. The geopolitical scale of recent energy crises likewise reflects a diplomacy devoid of a basic strategy. During World War II, we had an effective European theater strategy but lacked a diplomacy to cope with a growing Soviet interest in controlling Eastern Europe and Berlin. Strategy and diplomacy should never be separate entities. Each must inform and discipline the other. With the American way of war now an unaffordable anachronism, the synthesis of these two disciplines is essential. This issue is not being seriously examined either in government, the war colleges, the Foreign Service Institute, or in private study centers.

Toward a Public Strategy

In addition, our nation's grand strategy must be accepted and endorsed not only by a single administration but by successive administrations, by the leaders of both major political parties, by Congress, and by a majority of the public if we are to meet the cardinal requirement: unity of national effort.

Just as Walter Lippman urged creation of a "public philosophy," so Americans today need a public strategy that can be understood, argued, and defended by our countrymen. A public strategy provides the final dimension of strategic assessment: the social dimension. No effective grand strategy can exist in this democratic republic without a basic consensus and a firm political foundation. This became clear to me during the early 1970s, while serving as assistant secretary of state, when I became aware of the degree to which this country's major international miscalculations stemmed not from a misreading of international realities but from an inability to mobilize congressional and public support behind a specific policy objective.

Today, the issue of nuclear deterrence—its legitimacy—is increasingly under question. The alliance failed to unite over Poland. The nation is also divided over the issues and the strategy for providing security in the Middle East. In our own backyard, the Caribbean, there is the challenge of low level conflict, and the options for the United States in areas that have never known social justice or a strong middle class are difficult ones.

No effective strategy is possible, however, without unified support at home and a sense of legitimacy, which have been fitful or, at times, entirely absent since the Vietnam War. Whether Congress or the executive branch can achieve such unity without strong support from private sector groups—especially the research centers and the media—remains doubtful. The outside catalysts, the study centers, are essential to the formulation and public acceptance of a new strategy for America.

NOTE

1. In addition to Mr. Baroody and myself, others on the first executive board of the Center were Admiral Arleigh Burke; James B. Horigan, S.J., dean, Graduate School, Georgetown University; Professor Howard Penniman, chairman, Department of Government, Georgetown University; and Dr. W. Glenn Campbell, director, Hoover Institution, Stanford University. Chicago attorney Morris I. Leibman helped persuade Admiral Burke to take on this kind of public service and subsequently became a key board member. The University's president, Edward Bunn, S.J., and Byron Collins, S.J., were particularly supportive.

A National Strategy for the 1990s   *Amos A. Jordan*

It is a truism that Americans are not comfortable with the ideas of realpolitik. Instead, they are problem solvers who look to the clear identification of already pressing difficulties, the prompt and orderly marshalling of resources to confront those problems, and their rapid solution. The "can-do" mentality has served us well, and we should be proud of our accomplishments. But in today's rapidly changing, dangerous world, it must be supplemented by a propensity to look to the future, to view the world in coherent terms, and to put in place policies that support one another over the long term.

Of late, there has been a resurgence of interest in the U.S. Congress about national strategy. This interest can be traced to the view of current congressional leadership that the nation has been ill-served by the typical debates about foreign and defense policy that focuses on narrow issues and micromanagement. That leadership also reflects, to a certain degree, the growing sentiment in the American polity that the role of the United States in the world needs continual reexamination.

The purpose of this essay is to contribute to the process of (re-)articulating a national strategy for the years of challenge ahead. It delineates components of a strategic perspective by defining the concept of strategy and analyzing the ways in which the international environment shapes contemporary choices, advances six strategic propositions for the 1990s, and discusses the problems of resources and the process of making national strategy. It concludes with some observations about future strategic challenges.

Definitions

Strategy means many things to different people. A simple definition is a useful starting point: strategy is how a nation develops and applies all its resources to accomplish its objectives. National security strategy should be distinguished from military strategy. The former is a much broader concept than the latter, encompassing the full range of foreign and defense policy objectives and all the instruments of national power available for pursuing those objectives. This essay focuses largely on the subject of national security strategy, largely because the

United States has given too little attention to nurturing and using non-military instruments in advancing its interests. Moreover, there has not been a sufficiently widespread appreciation of the relationships among the various instruments. Nor has there been a firm grasp of the impor-tance of building structures and processes within the government to capitalize upon those relationships.

Strategy must proceed from national interests and objectives. These tend to be stable and are largely familiar to informed citizens. I note here only that they pertain to physical survival with values and institutions intact, a healthy domestic and international economy, vig-orous alliances, etc. The major objectives that support those interests are also reasonably clear, though somewhat more dynamic, for situa-tions change and new opportunities and challenges arise. Strategy itself is about choices of ways to pursue those interests, choices which are, in turn, based on priorities—whether explicit or implicit. Choices invari-ably entail risks. For a nation with global interests leading a worldwide coalition, such choices cannot be directed to a single immutable end or even set of ends. Our problem is not to draw a road map of how to get from (a) to (b) or (c). Rather, we are faced with the problem of con-tinual choice as the terrain around us changes. The challenge is to develop a template of preferences and priorities, of options and re-strictions, which we can choose as our situation changes. Only with such a template can we ask the tough questions of realistic strategy.

Environmental Imperatives

Strategy must deal with the world as it is, not as we wish it were. Four features of today's international climate critically condition our strategic choices.

The first such feature is the unreadiness of the American public to shoulder the responsibilities carried in the past. Whether from sheer weariness, continuing fallout from the Vietnam War, attrition of the so-called foreign policy establishment, or whatever, Americans are in-creasingly skeptical and unpredictable about external commitments. The vast majority of Americans take no interest in foreign affairs. Only a bare, eroding majority believes the United States should even play an active part in world affairs. The assumptions, convictions, and consensus which once underwrote confident, reliable American be-havior in the world have eroded and become progressively less per-suasive to our friends, our adversaries, and ourselves.

The political implications of this unhappy fact are self-evident: a constituency for responsible international engagement must be built in the public and the government if we are to have a coherent, credible, and consistent national security strategy. Congress has an especially important role to play in building this constituency.

The second prominent environmental feature is continuing global instability. Often violent and unpredictable, such instability results from the breakdown of empires and the concurrent fragmentation of traditional societies, from widening economic disparities aggravated by rising expectations and the communications explosion, and from a plethora of ethnic, racial, religious, and ideological rivalries. Of course, not all instability requires a U.S. response. Some is relatively benign and ought to be tolerated or even encouraged; some is essentially irrelevant to U.S. interests. But much of the instability is intrinsically damaging or could lead to wider dangers, and thus requires some kind of U.S. response.

The third feature is the growing diffusion of power throughout the international system. Our era has witnessed unprecedented changes in the nature and distribution of the military and economic instruments of influence.

In the military arena, power has shifted centrifugally to both ends of the conflict spectrum. At one end of the spectrum, nuclear weapons have revolutionized strategy. The fact that the USSR can dump the equivalent of 6 billion tons of TNT on the United States in a brief period, killing perhaps 150 million Americans, means, as James Schlesinger has observed, that "The old rules do not work . . . in the relationship between the nuclear superpowers." There are at least four or five other nuclear powers now, and perhaps that many more will join the club in the next decade.

At the other end of the spectrum—low-intensity conflict—the diffusion of power has been most pronounced. Dozens of weak nations and even weaker nonstate actors have regular recourse to terrorism, armed subversion, raids, and other forms of limited violence. The combination of interdependence and fragile infrastructures, particularly in developed states, makes this traditional form of warfare by the weak especially dangerous in our era and difficult to combat. Here, too, traditional strategic maxims need rethinking.

The diffusion of economic power has been less dramatic, but no less important, in affecting the national security of the United States. The growth of economies competitive with our own in the years since World War II has coincided with the growth of interdependence, energy shortages, and structural shifts away from primary production and heavy industry. These changes have vastly complicated our nation's harmonization of its defense and economic policies. We have paid far too little attention to the opportunities and challenges presented by this dimension of power diffusion.

Finally, any assessment of strategy must focus on the fact that a militarily powerful Soviet Union will contest American values, interests, and policies around the globe for a very long time to come. Zbigniew Brzezinski has forcefully articulated this enduring fact: "The American-Soviet rivalry is a long-term contest . . . a classic historical conflict between two major powers and is not susceptible to a broad and quick resolution, either through a victory by one side or through a grand act of reconciliation." An immediate strategic conclusion leaps from that assessment: we must prepare ourselves and gear our policies and programs for the long haul. As Chairman of the Joint Chiefs Admiral William Crowe recently expressed it, "We must prepare for a full-fledged marathon, not a wind sprint."

Despite the hopes of many, the well-advertised internal problems of the Soviet Union cannot be expected to paralyze it in external affairs. At most, they may somewhat slow the growth of its challenge. Communist ideology, Russian history, and the Soviet view of the world combine to ensure a vigorous, dangerous contest that we cannot shirk. On the other hand, we must guard against propagating a self-fulfilling prophecy of unremitting hostility leading to war. It is essential to leave the way open to a more cooperative relationship across the board, if the Soviets genuinely so desire. Indeed, we must actively encourage such a relationship on the basis of full but careful reciprocity.

Strategic Propositions

These imperatives and our national purposes cited earlier suggest the following six propositions as central components of a forward looking, yet realistic national strategy for the United States.

First, preserving the strategic nuclear balance between the United States and the Soviet Union is an essential foundation of all other components of the national strategy. Because of the centrality of nuclear stability, minimal risk here should be the rule. Thus a viable strategic triad of land-based intercontinental ballistic missiles, sea-based systems, and bombers should be maintained, along with a survivable system of strategic command, control, and communications—whatever the expense. Modernization of existing systems is required periodically, but simultaneous modernization of all elements of the triad ought not to be essential.

Second, a vigorous research and development (R&D) program aimed at developing strategic defenses for our offensive forces should be pursued. Such a program is justified by the need to test the feasibility of the concepts involved, to guard against Soviet anti-ballistic missile defense breakout, and to enable U.S. policy makers to judge the effectiveness, stability, and costs of various mixes of offensive and defensive systems. This R&D can and should be accomplished within the restrictive interpretation of the Anti-Ballistic Missile (ABM) Treaty and without pressure to rush to early deployment decisions.

Third, deep reductions in offensive nuclear arms (and conventional and chemical arms as well) should be vigorously pursued. Particular priority ought be given to reducing large intercontinental ballistic missiles (ICBMs) with multiple warheads because of the threat they pose to stability in time of crisis. Since nuclear weapons cannot be uninvented and cheating at the margin in nuclear matters could prove profoundly destabilizing, reductions should not aim at total elimination. And other stabilizing arms control measures should be pursued as well. These should include the more determined use of the Standing Consultative Commission to challenge confidence-eroding Soviet tactics (for instance, in telemetry encryption). The creation of nuclear risk reduction centers as envisaged at the Geneva summit would also be desirable, as would be the adoption of various other confidence-building measures as set forth at the Helsinki and Stockholm conferences. In all these initiatives, arms control should not be treated as a substitute for defense measures, but as an intrinsic element of national security strategy. In particular, arms control should not be sought in one isolated realm—nuclear, for example—in ways that will destabilize other realms—such as the conventional one.

Fourth, the United States must continue to deny the Soviet Union domination of the rimlands of Eurasia. Of particular importance are the three central strategic fronts in Western Europe, Southwest Asia (including the Persian Gulf), and Northeast Asia. To abandon this longstanding, key goal is to risk isolationism and a beleaguered fortress America.

This requires a coalition-based strategy. Insofar as feasible, the United States and its allies should preposition forces and matériel under a scheme of flexible basing. Such a strategy need not entail the presence of large U.S. ground forces, except in Western Europe. In Western Europe, marginal reductions in the number of U.S. troops could and should be made, and some of the heavy U.S. units should be converted to light ones. However, a force reduction of the order of one-third, which is sometimes suggested, cannot be achieved without sacrificing the forward defense of the Federal Republic of Germany, which is politically essential at this time. Moreover, substantial U.S. withdrawals could undermine the political cohesion and consensus that are essential for deterrence in Europe.

The retention of a small number—perhaps 100—theater nuclear

weapons in Europe is important to continuation of the flexible response strategy, which has kept the peace there for a quarter of a century and remains valid. Though theoretically possible, it is totally impractical in the foreseeable future for the West to build a sufficient conventional force to provide assured theater deterrence in the absence of a credible threat of nuclear escalation.

Some slenderizing of forward-deployed U.S. forces is also possible in Northeast Asia, given improvements in the force balance on the Korean peninsula, increased Japanese defense commitments, and the continuation of Soviet-Chinese rivalry. But there, too, balances are delicate and political sensitivies high, so that only marginal changes can be made without a wholesale revision of the required force projection capability.

In Southwest Asia, the denial of Soviet hegemony also requires visible, effective U.S. commitments, though in the first instance the instruments of this policy should be weighted heavily toward diplomacy and economic and military assistance. Militarily, we must strengthen the reserves earmarked for contingencies in the region and improve airlift and sealift to get them there.

Fifth, greater emphasis should be placed in U.S. strategy on long-term attrition of the base from which the Soviet Union builds and projects its military power. The first four propositions were aimed at containing Soviet power; this one is directed at eroding that power. In the first instance, it calls for a reinvigorated information program aimed at the Soviet Union, primarily at its non-Russian peoples. Such a program must convey to those peoples the truth about what is going on inside the Soviet Union and also about Soviet relations with the rest of the world. Voice of America and Radio Liberty are the primary but not the only instruments of such a strategy and should be provided with the modest increment in resources required to do a more effective job.

Such information programs also have important value in areas outside the territory of the Soviet Union but within its orbit, particularly Eastern Europe. Radio Free Europe and Voice of America should receive the modest resources needed as an urgent priority. Economic and political initiatives, applied with selectivity toward Eastern European countries, should accompany these renewed information and public diplomacy programs in order to loosen Soviet bonds over their satellites.

Priority should also be given to funding vigorous people-to-people, cultural and scientific exchange programs, as long as these are on the basis of reciprocity. Those subject to the rule of Moscow should know the truth about both East and West. We have nothing to fear from encouraging Americans and our free world friends to get to know the Soviet Union and its empire first hand.

The various economic instruments of the United States are of little use in directly pursuing a strategy of eroding the base from which the Soviet Union threatens the rest of us. Economic warfare against the USSR should be rejected as both nonproductive and unnecessarily provocative. But we should take care that our economic policies do not unwittingly strengthen the roots of Soviet power. Thus, although Soviet economic intercourse with the West could in the long term lead to the amelioration of East-West tensions, and therefore needs to be encouraged, we should ensure that trade between the Soviet Union and the West is exclusively in nonstrategic items and that it is not subsidized in any fashion.

Sixth, the United States ought to assist friendly regimes in the Third World wherever they have the support of their own people. The Nixon Doctrine retains its utility as a way for coping with insurgencies against such regimes, especially if augmented by a more constructive use of our economic strength. Overwhelmingly, in most less developed countries the need is primarily for economic aid, investment, and trade opportunities. To meet local conflict, the Nixon or Guam Doctrine called for self-help, primary responsibility for regional stability to be shared by neighbors, and "residual U.S. responsibility," meaning U.S. provision of military assistance as needed.

In coping with unfriendly, destabilizing Third World regimes, the United States should seek to provide limited help for their neighbors and domestic insurgents, if those insurgents have a genuine domestic base. The direct intervention of U.S. troops should be rejected in such circumstances, unless a vital American interest is in jeopardy. Except in special cases, too, it is wasteful and counterproductive to make other kinds of direct U.S. military responses such as blockades, nearby troop exercises, or naval shows of force. Gunboat diplomacy and other similar kinds of hollow threats are the favored approach of many to Third World problems, but will not work if the targeted people refuse to be cowed—which is increasingly the case.

The economic instruments of national strategy hold a greater promise of long-term success in the developing world than reliance on gunboat diplomacy or military force more generally. It is worth noting that foreign assistance takes only about 2 percent of the annual federal budget of the United States; we have probably received more foreign policy benefit per dollar from such assistance over the years than from any other international or defense program. Yet foreign assistance accounts are consistently starved by the Congress, and we are currently in a period of particularly harsh cuts. Of course, aid mistakes have been made, some of them at the insistence of the Congress, such as selling rather than granting assistance to nations which desperately needed it but could not afford to pay for it on commercial terms. Three years ago the Carlucci Commission set forth a number of reforms and policy initiatives to strengthen our foreign assistance programs, which remain valid today.

In the wake of the Iranian arms sales fiasco there is, of course, temptation to legislate further constraints on the provision of foreign assistance. But based on what we know so far, there is no need for fresh amendments to the Arms Control Export Act. The commander-in-chief needs more, not less, flexibility in the use of foreign assistance. It is a defense instrument that should be readily available to pursue national security strategy.

Trade and investment policies are often of equal or greater import than aid as tools of national strategy. As the world's largest market and, quite incredibly, also the world's largest debtor, the United States has tremendous economic and political leverage throughout the world. If the United States closes off a part of its market to a Third World country or pinches its investments there, the consequences for that nation's economic and political health are likely to be far greater than could be offset by any amount of foreign assistance or help through other American instruments. Yet, the economic policies of the United States are often considered without regard for these kinds of national security consequences. The Departments of Treasury and Commerce are not part of the National Security Council system—with the consequence that there is often an inadequate assessment made of the role that economic instruments can play and how they can reinforce or even substitute in some cases for the military instrument.

Resources

A vigorous strategy of global engagement cannot be had on the cheap. However, it is entirely affordable. The record of the last thirty years shows that that level of spending is politically sustainable—if our leadership will work at it. A wisely spent 6 to 6.5 percent of gross national product (GNP) is probably adequate and is certainly affordable. But because of past sins by both the administration and Congress, the United States now confronts a budget mess from which even somewhat larger amounts could not rescue us immediately. Indeed, it will take a few years to work out of the problem. With the large bow wave of procurement now sweeping over the defense budget, outlays will rise, even as budget authority is squeezed severely. The old temptation to preserve forces and modernization at the expense of readiness will be strong. But for both deterrence and defense reasons it must be resisted.

National thinking must be geared to long-haul continuity. The administration, the Congress, and the public must perceive the value of building a stable strategy and stable funding in order to meet the long-term challenges that confront the nation. Facing an invigorated Soviet Union, the United States can ill afford the on-again, off-again defense approaches that have marked the last two decades.

But the strategy-resources gap can never be closed. Nor do we have an option to substantially cut our commitments—at least at this juncture—since this increases rather than lowers risks. Some have argued that the strategy-resources gap can be straddled by U.S. prestige or that political capital can be spent to accomplish things not possible financially or militarily. But prestige can evaporate rapidly, particularly as a nation scales back its commitments. The prudent allocation of 6 to 6.5 percent of GNP would not increase the risks already inherent in U.S. strategy; appropriately spent, it could even reduce some of them. But even if some minor additional risk must be run temporarily while the country works out of the budget mess, that is preferable to unravelling national objectives and commitments.

Strategy and Process

The making of long-term national security strategy is hardly the rational and linear process we might hope. Military programs, security assistance allocations, trade policies, or the deployment of forces, for example, by and large are not logically derived from analyses of interests, objectives, threats, strategies, etc.

The chairman of the Armed Services Committee of the U.S. House of Representatives, Les Aspin, made a series of speeches on the floor of the House in March 1987 that address the subject of formulating national security policies. He pointed out that national security objectives and the means to achieve them become divorced in the U.S. decision-making process, so that mismatches of strategy and forces are inevitable. He proposed a series of reforms to the policy-making process such as the formal integration of expertise at the start of the process and the creation of a feedback loop, as well as access to detailed quantitative analyses of force balances, mixes, and costs—all in an iterative process in which the president would be involved from the start.

These are laudable suggestions which should be pursued, but they miss one central point, namely, that in a large complex democracy such as our own, with a separation of governmental powers, policy-making is not and cannot be a purely rational process. Deductive logic, from ends to means, is inevitably overwhelmed at many places along the route by politics. Induction and synthesis in these cases are as important as deduction and analysis.

Zbigniew Brzezinski has made a different suggestion to strengthen the process of defining and refining national strategy. He has proposed a formal planning staff affiliated with the National Security Council (NSC). This approach should be endorsed, but to be effective, such a staff must be fenced off from the day-to-day work of the rest of the NSC staff; otherwise, it risks being swept up in the flow of daily business as have comparable efforts in the Departments of State and Defense.

But such reforms (including bringing Treasury and Commerce into the NSC system as implied earlier) do not contain much hope for a long-term improvement in the national security policy-making process. Long-term improvement lies in the direction of building a better informed public and policy-making community, generating a broader consensus on national interests and objectives and the associated threats and risks, developing better trained and experienced experts who will be involved more intimately in the process, and stimulating a broader, deeper, and more widely shared dialogue among all the participants in the process.

The Congress has taken a first step in this direction with the requirement that the president submit an annual *National Security Strategy Report*. It is appropriate that the administration periodically rethink its national security goals, strategies, and resources, and present its conclusions to the Congress and the public. The first iteration in the process was released in January 1987, and provides a useful point of departure. It provides a comprehensive but largely unexceptional listing of U.S. interests and objectives, threats thereto, and the instruments of U.S. policy. It reflects both the strengths and weaknesses of conventional wisdom on the subject. It is strong on its analysis of the Soviet threat and of military instruments. But it seems to undervalue national interests outside of Europe, such as those in the Persian Gulf. Moreover, it reflects little appreciation of other threats to the United States beyond the Soviet one, such as the threat of nuclear proliferation, a major international economic downturn, or chaos in the Third World. Indeed, over the next decade many of the challenges to U.S. interests—many of them serious ones—will not be of Soviet origin. The *Report*'s discussion of the elements of national power gives only brief attention to political and informational elements, a particularly egregious oversight in view of the strong comparative advantage enjoyed by the United States and the West in this domain.

The concept of an unclassified but official national strategy statement must strike almost anybody other than an American as unwise. Since strategy must rest upon a realistic appreciation of the international environment and its threats and opportunities, and because resource constraints require that there be priorities among objectives, the publication of such a document could be of incalculable value to an adversary. Of course, the document can deal in such a level of generality that the adversary will not be informed by it, but then neither will the public nor the Congress. Inevitably, the president's first strategy report reflects this dilemma—it is so general that it does not add much. It is a useful document in bringing together familiar statements of U.S. foreign and defense policies, a credible first step in the process of informing the public and building consensus.

Conclusion

The importance of a strategic perspective to U.S. policy is growing. In the 1940s and 1950s, the United States could depend upon its preponderant military, economic, and political power to get by in the world. It was an era well-suited to the "everything is possible" American psyche. In the 1960s, this congenial situation began to give way as the nation discovered the limits of its power and resources. The 1970s witnessed a growing appreciation of the complexities of the world and stirred up the time-honored isolationist tendencies of the American body politic.

Looking to the 1990s and beyond, this need for a strategic approach to our problems can only grow. Four factors make this a near certainty.

First, the United States has shown little propensity to solve the resources problem outlined above. Indeed, the country is now moving toward a situation where continuation of past practices can produce disaster. If spending on the kind of strategy outlined above drops below the 6 to 6.5 percent level, the instruments of national strategy will suffer major cuts. The cumulative impact of such cuts will be to deprive the United States of the key factor needed to cope with the strategy-resources mismatch—flexibility. In an era when we cannot do everything at once or anticipate all challenges, the United States must maintain flexible instruments to apply as the situation warrants. Static or declining resources will have important implications for military instruments as well as other components of national strategy, such as the foreign assistance.

Second, the challenges of the coming decade look no easier than those of the last decade. Whatever one may think of Soviet Secretary

General Mikhail Gorbachev's public diplomacy or domestic policy, or even of his arms control intentions, it is clear that the United States will face a vigorous, innovative leader able to marshal continually growing Soviet military power. The capacity of the United States to deal with the Soviet Union continues to be impaired by inadequate understanding of the hows and whys of Soviet policy, and a major priority for the coming years should be enhanced understanding of Soviet strategy. Moreover, looking ahead, Soviet military power is far from being the only significant challenge.

Third, and more optimistically, a strategic perspective can enable the United States to prepare for opportunities in the 1990s that we have not enjoyed in the 1980s. We can anticipate opportunities in the developing world, for instance, that we have not enjoyed since the first wave of postwar independence, as the Western model recovers its vitality as a tool of international prosperity and peace. Similarly, we can anticipate opportunities to work with the Soviets to reduce the chances for war and, in a more general sense, to ameliorate rather than exacerbate our enduring competition.

Finally, we should anticipate that the 1990s will see a major national debate about how much Americans want to do internationally. The United States has always always been of two minds about its role in the world, compelled by a need to make it better or safer but also eschewing its entangling commitments. In recent years, the earlier apparent consensus on playing a major role in the world has waned. The decade ahead will see the final transition from the immediate post–World War II environment and a fresh need for choice. Americans are not well disposed to either the long haul or complexity, both of which are needed in international affairs. Nor are we well disposed toward complexity. But we do not live in the kind of world we might choose, nor can we afford to withdraw from it. Strategy must be the essence of managing these dilemmas.

Amos A. Jordan is president of the Center for Strategic and International Studies. This article is based on testimony delivered to the Senate Armed Services Committee in April 1987.

National Security

Senator Henry M. Jackson

We are all aware of the fact that the United States has come a long way since the end of World War II. Then we were wondering whether we could afford 14 billion dollars for a defense program. Today we are supporting a defense program that involves a 50-billion-dollar-plus budget.

Only a few years ago our problem was to create strength out of weakness. As we look to the decade ahead, we find that our essential problem is to use our strength wisely. It is well for us to keep in mind at all times that it is much easier to build strength than to use it wisely.

Now recently we have had an example (at least as far as we have gone) in the wise use of strength and military power. I refer, of course, to Cuba. Those of us who are involved in the practical side of this problem every day can certainly point with pride to the enormous impact that has come from that decision—to manage military power to achieve sensible foreign policy objectives. The impact is not applicable just to Cuba, but it has been world-wide. It is one of the rare times that we have been able to make the Soviets back down, I believe, since 1946, when President Truman in his usual understandable language indicated to Mr. Stalin that either they get out of Iran (Persia) or big things would happen. The Soviets understood, and started moving.

The effect of Cuba—as far as we have gone, and I emphasize that because we still have a problem of dismantling sooner or later what I think is the real missile, Castro—has been enormous on our allies, our friends, and the soft neutrals around the world. As a matter of fact, it is much like the experience that those who have run for office have gone through—that is, nothing succeeds like success. If you are running for office and losing, you don't have many friends, and the going is pretty rough. Yet as you make progress, and it looks like you're going to win, supporters start coming over to your side. A day or two before election they are all coming over on your side, and if they are not there a day or two before election, you can be sure they will be there a day after to explain how they have been for you from the beginning. Some of our allies and good friends have gone through that particular experience as a result of Cuba. It is a form, I suppose, of retroactive righteousness. But if it helps, so much the better.

The second point I would like to make is that there has been a splitting in the monolithic structure that the Communist world has been endeavoring to build. This at least complicates their situation, but it also leaves them with problems. I think we have to keep in mind that the mere fact there is a schism does not mean that we can relax. I spent eight days out in the field in Vietnam in December. I found that whatever ideological split there may be between the Moscow Communists and the Chinese, there is a meeting of the minds on the value of supporting "wars of national liberation" that Mr. Khrushchev referred to in his speech at the 22nd Party Congress last year. But, nevertheless, the schism can be considered a plus on our side.

The third development, of course, is India. In planning and looking ahead, we have to include at all times the obvious mistakes that the enemy will make. Who would have thought that China would help us do a job that we have been most unsuccessful in putting over, especially with India and other so-called non-aligned nations? That is, the necessity of their becoming (if they are neutrals) at least "hard" neutrals. We failed, but certainly the recent Chinese pressure has worked to our advantage in this regard. This has not been an easy task for the United States because we have had significant policy differences with India. If the United States had followed Mr. Nehru's policy and philosophy, we would not have had the arms to give him when he came so hurriedly to us for help. I am sure Mr. Nehru does not relish this on-the-job training program, but it may save others from a similar schooling.

At the same time this does not mean that we should ignore India, because the preservation of the territorial integrity of India—with 400 million people—is essential to the national security of the United States of America. It is in our own national interest to help preserve the integrity of that country.

Now these are some of the pulses, and there are many others. But I would like to look ahead a decade or so and pose some of the problems that come to mind, and that we need as a society to be thinking about.

First of all, the United States has military alliances with more than forty countries and provides military aid to more than sixty countries. But we were brought up on George Washington's Farewell Address, and we have had little experience in the management of alliances in periods short of open warfare.

It is clear, I think, that the next decade will see some heavy strains on our system of alliances. But if it is true, and I believe it is, that we must remain united in the Free World if the Communists are not to have success with a strategy of "divide and conquer," we must overcome these strains. This may be very difficult for us—and for our allies.

Possible questions for this group might be: how can we preserve and strengthen our alliances in a period when other states are gaining economic and military strength and are increasingly tempted to act independently? What means of influence are available to us? How best can they be used? Is there need for new political, economic, and military structures in the West?

Secondly, it would be well to consider the fact that we are providing economic assistance in a variety of forms to many countries. There is much dissatisfaction in this country with the results of economic aid. Yet it seems increasingly likely that the outcome of the world struggle will be decided by what happens within societies in the rest of the world, provided, of course, that we and our major allies remain militarily strong. The United States will probably have to continue many types of non-military programs and perhaps (and I hesitate to say this because it's not good news) increase certain types in the years ahead.

Therefore, questions that merit serious study are how can we make economic aid a more effective tool of foreign policy? What are the proper goals of economic aid? What are reasonable tests of success or failure? How can we develop a public opinion that will support the wise use of our economic strength as a tool of foreign policy, bearing in mind that this is a tool in which the United States has an enormous advantage.

A third observation. In every major country but our own, legislative bodies have been losing influence in relation to executive power in recent years. When you think about it, the reason is clear enough. The need to concentrate power of command in one man varies with the powers of others to inflict sudden damage. As questions of foreign policy become more complex and more delicate, the need for a strong executive obviously increases. This has been the universal experience in time of war, and we are living, indeed, in a Cold War, when the pressures for executive leadership—or for what Hamilton called "an energetic executive"—are very great, though less intense than in a hot war.

Therefore, questions of fundamental interest and concern to me are what adjustments will enable us to preserve a strong, effective Congress as a necessary check on the Executive? What changes in the way Congress handles its job can contribute to the development of clear, purposeful, national policy adequate to the challenges of our time?

And fourth. Wise national policies require both good organizations and good people. The people are indeed the critical factor in all of this, as Admiral Burke pointed out. And I might add you can have a very fine organization with inadequate people in it and the organization is not going to mean very much. But good people can even survive a poor organization.

More often than not, poor policy decisions are, in fact, traceable to inadequate people, to their inexperience, to their bad judgment, to their failure to comprehend the significance of information crossing their desks. Our Government does have, in fact, many first-rate people in it, but the number of critical jobs is far larger than the number of able and experienced people available to fill them.

The heart of the problem of national security is this: how are we going to use to the fullest the good people now in government? And how are we going to recruit our best people for key foreign policy and defense posts in the future?

I know that many things will be accomplished by this Conference. I do hope that one of the primary accomplishments will be to help bring better people into the area of national security. And secondly, if I may be so presumptuous as to observe, I hope your proceedings will be such as to be useful and meaningful to those people who will, in fact, make the decisions in the national security area of your Federal Government.

You have to ask yourselves: what are you here for? Well, you add to the great dialogue that is very important in the national security area. You make information available to your colleagues, and this gets printed and gets to the scholars. But in the last analysis, you really *do* have to ask the question: what can you do here to (a) get better people into the national security posts and (b) when they are there, what can you do to help them do a better job? This is really the heart of the problem and, I would trust, one of your top objectives.

Let me conclude by merely making this observation. As we look ahead ten years, or a decade, I think it is well for us to remember that the future that we are talking about is in fact the history that we are making day by day. And the page that we are working on, my friends, is bright with promise.

The Need to Reshape Military Strategy
Senator Sam Nunn

The Perspective

In the aftermath of World War II, the United States clearly possessed the most potent military and economic capability on the globe. In the 1950s and 1960s, the United States enjoyed a nuclear advantage, and the threat of escalation to nuclear weapons remained credible. During this period, our nation attempted to field conventional forces capable of coping simultaneously with major conflicts in Europe and Asia while holding sufficient military forces in reserve to handle a smaller contingency elsewhere. This was often labeled the two and a half war strategy.

In the wake of the Vietnam War, the Sino-Soviet split, and the emerging relationship between the United States and the People's Republic of China, our military strategy was adjusted to one of being prepared to fight one war in Europe or Asia, while also being able to fight a small war elsewhere. This was sometimes oversimplified by calling it a one and a half war strategy.

During the 1970s, America was confronted with significant changes: the advent of nuclear parity, greater American dependence on foreign resources and foreign trade, and vastly improved Soviet conventional military forces.

Since 1979, the announced purposes of U.S. military strategy have been substantially inflated, reversing the trend in the post-Vietnam era. Starting with President Carter's commitment to protect U.S. interests in the Persian Gulf, we have asked our military forces to take on new and demanding tasks in addition to traditional U.S. military obligations in Europe and the Far East.

Secretary of Defense Caspar Weinberger has testified that this administration's "long-term goal is to be able to meet the demands of worldwide war, including concurrent reinforcement of Europe, deployment to Southwest Asia and the Pacific, and support for other areas . . ." Some would say that this amounts to a three and a half war strategy.

Despite these expanding obligations, U.S. force levels have remained essentially static. The inevitable result has been a widening gap between forces on hand and forces needed to achieve our military strategy. The Joint Chiefs of Staff in 1982 recommended force levels that could cost up to $750 billion more than the $1.6 trillion requested in the administration's Five-Year Defense Plan.

In short, our military strategy far exceeds our present capability and projected resources. General David Jones, former chairman of the Joint Chiefs, recently stated, "The mismatch between strategy and the forces to carry it out . . . is greater now than it was before because we are trying to do everything." As Army Chief of Staff General Edward C. Meyer has commented, "We are accepting tremendous risks with the size of the forces that we have, to do what we have pledged to do."

A huge increase in force levels would be needed to provide any reasonable assurance that the United States could carry out the military strategy now in the posture statement. But these additional forces would cost many billions more than we can expect to allocate to defense spending. We will be fortunate in the current economic circumstances to maintain real growth in defense spending of between 5 and 7 percent per year. This obviously poses a serious dilemma.

A sound military strategy must be predicated on a calculated relationship between ends and means. Based on this definition, there would appear to be three alternatives: (1) alter our global national security objectives, (2) increase the resources for defense, or (3) change our military strategy.

Are we prepared as a nation to redefine our vital interests and, therefore, our military objectives? Do we write off Europe, or the Persian Gulf, or Northeast Asia?

If we are not so inclined—and I submit that we are not—are the Congress and the American people prepared to increase greatly the military budget over the current Reagan plan? The answer to this is obvious.

If we cannot afford to give up our national security objectives and we are not willing to spend huge additional funds for defense, then we are left with the third alternative: change our military strategy.

In determining a realistic and sound military strategy and in allocating our finite resources, we must begin with certain realities.

First, any new strategy must be comprehensible and convincing to the American people and their elected representatives. It must be understandable and clearly related to what this nation wants to protect and to the means available to do so.

Second, the threat of nuclear responses to non-nuclear aggression is becoming less credible. There is a growing aversion to nuclear weapons in the Western world that is beginning to be reflected in the various peace and freeze movements.

Certainly, there are some unilateral disarmers in the freeze movement, but there are also many sincere people who are searching for a defense and arms control policy entailing less nuclear risk. To them, I say frankly—we must place the conventional horse before the nuclear cart. Nuclear parity means that we can neither tolerate serious deficiencies in our nuclear deterrent nor continue to tolerate longstanding deficiencies in our conventional forces.

The bottom line is that even with the modernization of our nuclear forces, the nuclear "crutch" on which we have leaned for so long is no longer sufficient to compensate for conventional weaknesses. The conventional leg of NATO's defenses must come out of its cast. We must prepare our conventional forces to deter and defeat conventional aggression.

Third, any new U.S. strategy must be based on a partnership with our allies. Indeed, no discussion of U.S. military strategy can ignore America's historic and continuing dependence on powerful allies as a means of fulfilling our own national security objectives. Today, the United States enjoys in Europe and Asia a network of allies whose combined economic power and potential military power exceeds our own, although none devotes as much of its national wealth to defense as the United States. As NATO specialist Tom Callaghan has stated, "The Alliance must pool its enormous industrial and technological resources, eliminate all unnecessary duplication of defense efforts, and share the financial burdens and economic benefits."

Fourth, hard choices are unavoidable. We lack the budgetary and manpower resources to do everything we now wish to do simultaneously. Two years ago the Reagan administration announced a program to modernize most of our strategic nuclear forces, increase and modernize our conventional force structure, building a 600-ship Navy, and improve readiness, sustainability, and military pay across the board. It is now obvious that the Reagan program cannot be fully implemented.

The Strategy

Needed—A Viable Conventional Strategy

With these dilemmas, questions, and realities in mind, I believe that our principal military challenge is the development of a military strategy and military forces that deny the Soviet Union any prospect of achieving its objectives through conventional aggression. While maintaining a nuclear deterrent, such a strategy would

- provide a much broader firebreak between conventional and nuclear war;
- confront the Soviets, rather than ourselves, with the grim choice of being denied the fruits of military success or assuming the terrible risk of crossing the nuclear threshold;
- counter attempted Soviet conventional aggression in a manner that would leave the Soviet empire and the Soviet military establishment in a far weaker position at the end of hostilities;
- refuse a NATO occupation of the Soviet Union. As the late Field Marshal Bernard Montgomery remarked, "There are only two ageless principles of war—don't invade Russia and don't invade China."

In developing a viable conventional strategy, we must focus on Soviet weaknesses and Western strengths.

Exploiting Soviet Weaknesses

In wartime, Soviet force planners would confront a number of inherent weaknesses, including the tenuous land lines of communication connecting European Russia with Soviet forces in the Far East, the unreliability of their Warsaw Pact allies, and the lack of easy Soviet naval access to the high seas. We should establish a set of new military goals that would exploit these weaknesses.

First and foremost, I suggest a broad military goal that I would label "Keeping Russian Forces In Russia." We have looked at the huge Soviet land mass as an asset to the Russians. It can also be converted into a serious liability for them. Across this huge land area, the Soviets have tenuous lines of communication and limited access to the sea. They have potential adversaries on most of their borders.

We should let the Soviets know that if they invade Europe or the Persian Gulf, we would seek to tie down their forces in the Far East and in other areas of the Soviet Union. We would not seek to accomplish this through direct assault on these forces but rather through destruction of their lines of communication. I am under no illusions that this will be an easy task, but every step we take to add to our own capability for this mission greatly increases deterrence, both militarily and psychologically.

While I do not believe the West should count on the Chinese opening a second front if the Soviets invade Western Europe, I do believe the Soviets would think long and hard if they believe that their Far East forces could be isolated.

Our military capabilities also should send an unmistakable message that Eastern Europe will not be a sanctuary if the Soviets invade Western Europe. Eastern Europe is a potential Achilles' heel for them.

It should be made clear to the Soviets that, in the event of European war, violence will not be confined to Western Europe—that their forces in or passing through Eastern Europe will be subjected to attacks ranging from deep aerial strikes to commando and partisan raids.

To wage war against NATO, the Soviets must move massive forces and supplies from western Russia across Eastern Europe including Poland and Czechoslovakia, countries whose peoples have long resented—and occasionally resisted—membership in the Soviet empire. In a war we should not permit Moscow to count upon their continued, even if enforced, loyalty. In the 1950s, we trained and fielded special stay-behind forces dedicated to disrupting Soviet military activity in occupied territory and to promoting indigenous popular resistance. This concept should be revived; the very recreation of such forces would strengthen deterrence by putting the Soviet Union on notice that it could not expect a free ride in Eastern Europe in the event of an invasion of Western Europe.

Another element of keeping the Russians in Russia would depend on our navy. In peacetime, the navy plays a vital role in the nuclear deterrent and operations in support of American interests overseas. In wartime, the primary goal of our naval forces should be to deny Russian use of the sea.

This has been described as "gaining sea control" or "defending the sea lines of communication." I would put it more directly and simply as "sinking the Soviet fleet and bottling up the remnants." I would include the Russian merchant marine and fishing fleet which operate in concert with the Soviet navy.

By sinking and blocking their fleet we would gain sea control, protect the lines of communication, and also, at war's end, leave no viable opposing navy to threaten us, whatever the outcome on land. This task is no longer a matter of battle force against battle force in a World War II manner, but primarily our submarines and aircraft operating against enemy submarines, land-based air, and surface ships.

As part of this task, our naval forces, assisted by land-based air, should have the mission of controlling the choke points that limit Russian access to the sea. The best way to keep the Soviet navy in its proper place is to keep it bottled up in the Norwegian, Baltic, and Black Seas, and the Sea of Japan.

Even if we have to repaint some air force planes navy blue and gold, we must insist that our naval strategy be based on full utilization of land-based air. I do not believe that we should take on Soviet naval power through massive employment of our carrier-based air power directly against heavily defended ports and naval installations in the Soviet homeland.

Enhancing Western Strengths

We must also design our strategy to take advantage of our military strengths. The United States and its allies possess marked advantages over the Soviet Union in ocean access, tactical airpower, antisubmarine warfare capabilities, the training of our military manpower, and advanced technologies such as precision-guided munitions, microelectronics, and cruise missiles.

If properly exploited, our technological advantages can in no small measure offset the Soviet Union's longstanding superiority in numbers. By properly exploited, I mean utilizing our technological know-how not just to improve weapon performance but also to enhance cost-effectiveness, operability, maintainability, and reliability.

One area in which our technological prowess can be brought to bear is our tactical air power. U.S. tactical air power has long enjoyed advantages both in quality and in pilot skills. We should dedicate ourselves to the goal of achieving tactical air superiority in any theater of operations deemed vital to the United States within a few days after the outbreak of hostilities.

By providing improved conventional munitions for delivery from standoff ranges as a top procurement priority, we can apply our technological genius to multiplying dramatically the military effectiveness of our existing aircraft. We must also maintain our advantages in tactical intelligence and command and control.

This stepped up tactical air capability should be accomplished primarily through the Guard and Reserve forces. The Guard and Reserves in all four services have demonstrated repeatedly that it is possible to maintain a degree of readiness and combat skills equivalent to or even superior to that of their active duty counterparts.

If we truly want to increase U.S. defense capabilities within reasonable budget resources, we should also plan to increase the role of our reserve forces in many other areas. Countries as disparate as Israel, Sweden, and the Netherlands have shown what is possible to do with properly trained and properly equipped reserve forces.

Integrated active and reserve forces could yield the United States a less costly, yet more combat-effective, force structure characterized by later, readier reserves. The time has come to stop parroting the virtues of the total force concept and make it a reality. Truly ready reserve forces are perhaps the best defense bargain available.

Tasking Our Allies

I have outlined a number of changed military tasks for U.S. forces. When implemented, these new capabilities would greatly enhance NATO's ability to carry out its longstanding doctrine of forward defense.

The imperative question must now be posed. If U.S. forces are to undertake these new tasks and continue to provide an effective nuclear deterrent, what should be the role of our allies?

Before discussing Europe, I must add that the Japanese clearly must be consulted with respect to their announced goal of defending the air lanes and the sea lanes within 1,000 miles of their homeland. Clearly, that is something we should expect from our Japanese allies, and that is something their own prime ministers have announced as their goal.

We clearly must rethink NATO's present doctrine of forward defense. The political desirability of conceding as little European territory as possible to an invader is not at issue. What is at issue is whether that objective is properly served by the current organization, disposition, and operational doctrine of NATO forces dedicated to Europe's forward defense. I do not believe that it is.

A large gap exists in NATO's ability to implement the sacred principle of forward defense. NATO is thus confronted with a choice: either to drop the concept of forward defense as part of NATO's doctrine, or to convert forward defense from a theory into a reality by reallocating the NATO defense burden.

U.S. ground forces are and must remain a vital part of the defense of Europe. To implement properly the new Army-Air Force doctrine of Airland Battle, our forces must emphasize maneuverability and flexibility, lighter reinforcements, special operations forces, communications, and second echelon attack.

The allies, however, must increasingly provide the basic ingredients for Europe's initial forward defense, including heavy ground forces, more effective utilization of their vast pool of trained reserves, and the possible employment of barrier defenses. In short, if U.S. forces in Europe are to assume the primary responsibility for disrupting and destroying Soviet second echelon forces, European units must assume the primary responsibility for holding the first echelon in check. In my judgment, the United States should take steps over time, in close consultation with our allies, to make these shifts. If the Europeans do not adjust, military gaps which presently exist will quickly become even more pronounced. If it is politically essential that forward defense remain a key part of NATO's strategy, it is no less politically essential that our European allies explain to their citizens why they are not providing the forces to implement the forward defense of their territory.

The Persian Gulf

Each of the changes I have proposed would provide U.S. forces more flexibility to meet contingencies outside Europe including the Persian Gulf while still contributing to the defense of Europe.

We should, however, take a closer look at the Rapid Deployment Force: its purpose, its size, its composition, and its command arrangements. When this is done, I believe we will find that the RDF should be built mainly around the navy, marine, and light army forces that already have long experience and training for just such purposes.

We should not plan to slug it out tank for tank with Soviet forces in areas along the Soviet periphery. We must structure our forces for tasks that are achievable. This means emphasizing light, strategically mobile reaction forces designed to beat the Russians to the vital ground and thereby confront them with the choice of backing off or firing the first shot in a war between two nuclear-armed states. We should also strongly emphasize tactical air and other military capabilities designed to isolate Soviet field forces by severing their lines of communication.

Arms Control

Arms control must be an inseparable component of any military strategy in the last quarter of the twentieth century. Our arms control efforts must, like our military strategy, reflect certain realities.

We must recognize that a coalition military strategy demands a coalition arms control strategy. Our arms control efforts must enjoy the confidence of our allies as well as our own citizens. We must develop a bipartisan approach to arms control that has some hope of continuity beyond one administration.

I have suggested a number of proposals in the last several years toward these goals. They include creation of a bipartisan commission to oversee our arms control efforts, improving hot line communications between the United States and the USSR; regular visits and exchanges between U.S. and Soviet defense and military leaders; establishment of a U.S. and Soviet manned crisis control center to help prevent an accidental nuclear war; the Cohen-Nunn guaranteed build-down proposal in which both sides would eliminate two warheads for each new one added; and a proposal to reduce significantly battlefield nuclear systems in NATO. In regard to battlefield nuclear weapons, the increasing obsolescence of many of them and the continuing absence of any persuasive doctrine for their use make certain battlefield systems prime candidates for a unilateral reduction. Such a reduction would signal our good faith bargaining position and present to the Soviets a challenge to reciprocate—or to explain to the European public why they refuse.

A Reshaped Strategy Needed Now

The U.S. political, economic, and military margin for error has diminished significantly since World War II. Our principal adversary is stronger but so are our allies. We now face the need to reshape our military strategy. In so doing, we need to engage our minds as well as our pocketbooks. More money for defense is a necessity, but spending more money without a clear sense of ultimate purpose or priority will not result in sound strategy or adequate security.

I recommend a military strategy that places a premium on out-thinking the potential aggressor, a strategy that

- seeks to apply our strengths against his weaknesses, not our weaknesses against his strengths;
- requires a greater contribution by the allies, and substantially greater cooperation among us all;
- includes fully exploiting our technological advantages including tactical air and improved munitions;
- makes better use of our Reserve and National Guard;
- in particular seeks to avoid depending on nuclear weapons to deter conventional attack.

In an era of nuclear parity, defense and deterrence are inseparable. The ability, actual or perceived, to wage war successfully is the best means of avoiding the necessity to wage it at all. This should be the driving force behind our objectives, our goals, and our strategy. As General George C. Marshall observed: "If man does find the solution for world peace it will be the most revolutionary reversal of his record we have ever known."

In a nuclear age our task is clear but awesome—we must reverse the record of history.

2

THE FUTURE OF WESTERN SECURITY

U.S. Policy Toward NATO

The Honorable George W. Ball

Alliances have rarely had a good reputation. As an institution they need the services of a dilligent press agent. Napoleon's rude remarks on the weakness of alliances are a part of his legend. Bismarck's comments were less quotable but equally scornful.

But contempt for alliances was not invented in the Nineteenth Century. Pericles said it all—and said it better—long before, when, according to Thucydides, he observed that within the classical alliance

> the great wish of some is to avenge themselves on some particular enemy, the great wish of others to save their own pocket. Slow in assembling, they devote a very small fraction of the time to the consideration of any public object, most of it to the prosecution of their own objects. Meanwhile each fancies that no harm will come of his neglect, and that it is the business of somebody else to look after this or that for him; and so, by the same notion being entertained by all separately, the common cause imperceptibly decays.

Pericles' prediction as to the inevitability of decay of the classical alliance is not applicable to NATO, since NATO is not—or, at least, not merely—a classical alliance. We should never forget that it is something more—something quite different.

And so I should like to recall some elemental facts about this Atlantic institution—an institution with a name that, in Prime Minister Pearson's words, sounds like a new breakfast food, but an institution that has nevertheless served us well as the central structural framework for the defense of the free world.

NATO was born in a time of crisis. It developed its present shape and form during a sustained period of tension. Today the fact—or at least the appearance—of relaxation between East and West is subjecting it to a new strain and test.

In today's relaxed environment there is danger that NATO may gradually lose some of its vitality through apathy and a kind of international wishful thinking. The present generally good state of economic health on both sides of the ocean has produced a pervasive sense of well-being, almost of euphoria. The Atlantic world feels increasingly strong and confident of the future. There is danger that, if this happy state persists for long, some may be tempted to regard the obligations of a massive enterprise such as NATO as unnecessarily heavy and some of our European friends—out of a sense of new-found confidence—may be led to consider NATO as too much an American show. There is already an apparent trend that way.

No human institution is ever perfect, and over time we should continue to improve further the present NATO alliance. But at the same time we must be extremely wary of any suggestion that the alliance is, of course, a good thing but that the NATO structure is a bad idea. Such a suggestion, if seriously regarded, could do great harm. For it might reduce NATO to the status of a classical alliance—an alliance inactive in peace and impotent in war.

An Unprecedented Alliance

Let me recall certain obvious facts about the character and meaning of NATO—facts that we sometimes overlook but which we can never afford to take for granted.

The first relates to the nature of NATO as we now know it. If NATO is not just a classical alliance, what is it?

I suppose it can be accurately described as a full-fledged collective defense arrangement of an unprecedented kind. Obviously, the foundation stone of NATO is the common commitment of the member states that an armed attack against one shall be considered an armed attack against all. But NATO rests on far more than that basic assurance.

NATO expresses the indivisible nature of Western defense. Within its structure the member states have created a unified force of great power and dimensions operating under a unified command. This command, in turn, is subject to a Council of Permanent Representatives that serves as a conduit for political guidance from the member states.

This is NATO today, but we sometimes forget that it was not born full-armed. As first established in 1949, it was little more than the Council and a collection of committees. In fact, there was a saying in those days that "before we established NATO the Russians could march to the Pyrenees in a fortnight. It will take them much longer now; they will have to walk through all those committees."

Stalin was the author of NATO's present structure. It was only after the Korean invasion, when the West first fully comprehended the magnitude of the Communist danger, that the member nations created a Supreme High Command under General Eisenhower and revamped NATO to make it an effective instrument for collective defense.

The road by which the Western world arrived at this point was long and bloody.

Any illusions as to the virtues of an old-fashioned alliance will be dispelled if one recalls the early years of the first World War. We must never forget the events of 1914 to 1918—nor will be permitted to do so if one can judge by the spate of books presently being written about that period.

The story of those years is a tragic chronicle of unnecessary slaughter. In 1914, 1915, 1916, and even 1917 the two principal allies— France and Great Britain—worked largely at cross purposes. There was little joint preparation and management. Planning was only haphazardly coordinated. Strategies, more often than not, were divergent and self-defeating. In fact, it was not until April of 1918—and then only through the efforts of a great French statesman, Georges Clemenceau—that the Entente powers finally pooled their resources under the strategic command of General Foch, as Commander-in-Chief of the Allied Armies in France. Soon thereafter—out of disarray—came unity and victory.

Thanks to Sir John Slessor, I need not point out that in the second World War the same Allies once again went into battle without adequate coordination. In his stimulating essay he describes quite vividly the lack of contact between the British and French staff that prevailed up to six months before the outbreak of the war. Again there was no common policy and no combined strategic planning.

But we have profited—and with good sense we can continue to profit—from all that. Today we have achieved what has never before been possible in peacetime—an effective unified command. This we must cherish and preserve. It is an invaluable resource of the free world. Let us not assess it too cheaply. For if the lack of a unified command proved tragic in 1914, it would be even more catastrophic today. This nuclear age would permit no war of attrition but only of destruction, and we would not have four years—or even four days—to organize a unified command.

It is not enough, however, merely to safeguard what we have. Like any living organism, NATO must grow and change in order to survive. Several of the essays considered by this group emphasize two major pieces of unfinished business:

First, we must develop ways and means for managing the nuclear deterrent power of the West in a manner that will take account of the aspirations for participation by member states not now possessing atomic weapons. At the same time we must avoid the manifest dangers of proliferation.

Second, we must continue to perfect NATO as an instrument by which the member nations can concert policies with respect to problems that arise not merely within the NATO area but elsewhere in the world.

Each of these pieces of unfinished business is, in my view, complicated by the same central difficulty—that most of the nation states which form the membership of NATO are not large enough by themselves to play roles commensurate with the requirements of the present age.

Managing the Nuclear Deterrent

Clearly this is true with regard to atomic weapons. The defense of the West requires not merely that an individual nation have the ability to mobilize vast resources of men, money, material, industrial plant, and technology, but also that there be unity of control of the life or death decision of nuclear destruction.

I am sure that no one here favors nuclear proliferation as an objective of policy. Its dangers are manifest. For first one country, then another, to develop a national nuclear system could not help but heighten feelings of distrust within the Western alliance, while at the same time increasing tensions between the free world and the Communist bloc. The multiplication of national deterrents would increase the danger that a nuclear holocaust might be triggered through accident or miscalculation. At the same time it would multiply the chance that—at some point—nuclear weapons might fall under the control of an irresponsible individual or government. And finally, it would render progressively more difficult the achievement of an ultimate agreement to control or limit nuclear armament.

But the road toward proliferation has no logical ending—and as we start down that road there are no logical stopping points other than the limits which nations impose on themselves or the limits imposed by the availability of resources or technology.

The renunciation of proliferation as a general principle is clearly not good enough. Such a solemn pronouncement is unlikely to influence the decisions of individual governments. Unless we can produce workable alternatives, proliferation will almost certainly occur whether we like it or not.

Here is where the political organization of Europe becomes relevant. If Europe were sufficiently far advanced toward political unity that it could by itself manage and control an atomic deterrent, we could hopefully look forward to an effective and integrated Atlantic defense founded on a true nuclear partnership. But this is not the case today nor is it likely to be for some time. Effective nuclear control means the delegation to a central executive of the power of life or death involved in the use of atomic weapons. Obviously this presupposes a very high degree of political unity—a degree that far transcends anything immediately in contemplation.

Meanwhile, time will not stand still. Whatever the situation today—and the evidence on the point is confusing—we would delude ourselves if we assumed that the gifted and vigorous people in several of the countries of Western Europe would not sooner or later insist on playing an effective role in their own nuclear defense. If we provide no opportunity for even partial fulfillment of this quite natural desire, the consequences are easily foreseeable. Political pressures for the multiplication of national nuclear deterrents will accumulate—and governments will yield to them. The process moreover will feed on itself; the decision of one country to build a nuclear deterrent will almost certainly increase pressures for similar decisions in others.

The dilemma we face cannot, therefore, be safely brushed aside. If we regard the proliferation of national deterrent systems as undesirable and if we consider that the present exclusion of a large part of the members of the Western alliance from nuclear management is not likely to last, what other options do we have?

It is our attempt to answer this question that led us in 1960 to propose the creation of a multilateral nuclear force. I recognize that this force has become a subject of some controversy not merely among you *cognoscenti* in this dialogue but in similar discussions elsewhere. Yet, as I see it, those who challenge the wisdom or effectiveness of such a force are yet to suggest an adequate alternative.

The multilateral force we are proposing would be organized within the framework of the Western alliance. To constitute a truly international force, we have felt that it should meet four conditions:

First, it should be assigned to NATO by all countries participating in the force. To meet this condition, we propose that it be collectively owned by the participants and that all participating nations share in the costs of creating, maintaining, and operating it.

Second, it should not be predominantly based on the soil of any one nation. To meet this condition, we are proposing a sea-based force consisting of Polaris-type missiles mounted on surface warships. This force, deployed on the high seas, would operate outside the national limits of any state.

Third, it should be managed and operated by nationals of all participating countries under such conditions that it could not be withdrawn from the alliance to serve the national uses of any participating government. To meet this requirement, we propose that the ships themselves be manned by mixed crews of nationals of the participating nations.

The United States Joint Chiefs of Staff and the Secretary of Defense have concluded that an efficient first-class force can be created in this fashion. SACEUR has stated he would welcome the force as a significant addition to NATO's deterrent forces.

Fourth, the decision to fire the Polaris weapons should be a collective decision of the participating nations. One proposal is that political control be exercised through an executive body representing the participating nations. Obviously this control question is the heart of the matter. We are confident it can be solved.

In an ideal world we could no doubt devise less elaborate means for managing nuclear weapons. But we must work within the limitations of existing political arrangements. Those limitations arise from the fact that Western political institutions have not evolved in pace with the march of our technology. Until the West has achieved a far greater political unity than it possesses today, we believe that the development of a multilateral force is the best available course to pursue.

Not only does it offer the most effective means of dealing with the nuclear problem in the present political framework, it can also make possible a gradual and constructive evolution within that framework. The multilateral force would provide a new opportunity for working toward a greater unity in Europe and a closer partnership between the two sides of the Atlantic.

For the striking progress that has been achieved toward these goals in the past decade and a half has, to a considerable extent, come about from necessity—from the fact that governments have been compelled to cope with specific and immediate problems in Europe and the Atlantic area. And, as we seek to cope with the problem of nuclear management, I have no doubt that we shall—of necessity—make further strides toward a greater political unity in the years ahead.

Over the long pull, it will not be abstract principle but importunate necessity—the urgent need to get hard things done in order that we may survive and flourish—that will move us toward the attainment of the ultimate objective of unity and partnership.

Toward Effective Political Consultation

If the lack of political unity in Europe complicates the management of nuclear weapons systems within the NATO alliance, it also limits the development of NATO as an instrument for effective political consultation.

This question of consultation has been a favorite subject for discussions in dialogues such as you have been having here at The Center for Strategic Studies. A strong case can be made—and is frequently made—for greater consultation among NATO members—particularly with regard to world problems that lie outside the scope of the alliance.

The logic of this is clear enough. The member nations of NATO represent 90 percent of the industrial strength of the free world. They are, in Dean Acheson's words, "the central power which will support—if it is to be supported at all—a non-Communist world system."

I do not mean to suggest that, in the modern decentralized world, it would make sense to reserve the management of world affairs to an exclusive board of directors drawn solely from the NATO nations. Such a proposal would be an affront to friendly nations the world over that are playing responsible roles in their own areas. The United States, for example, has military alliances with twenty-eight countries in addition to its NATO partners.

At the same time it is clear that unity of policy among the members of NATO is an essential component of free-world power. To quote Mr. Acheson again: "If the center is not solid, relations with the periphery will not provide strength."

Unity of policy should presumably be hammered out through consultation. But consultation—essential though it be—can be fruitful only if all powers concerned are determined to make it so. It can produce little, for example, in the face of rigid philosophical differences such as those we have encountered in attempting to develop a common economic policy toward Cuba. It will also produce little when the consulting parties hold widely differing concepts of responsibility for world problems.

It is this latter point that imposes the most severe limit on the efficacy of consultation today.

Until the second World War the metropolitan nations of Europe spread their dominance over vast areas of the world through colonial arrangements. But, with the crumbling of the great colonial systems and the emergence in their stead of half a hundred new states during the turbulent years since the war, world power relationships have had to be vastly revised.

During this period the world interests of European states have greatly altered; at the same time America has had to devise new concepts of world responsibility.

I mention this dichotomy between interests and responsibility for it is, I think, fundamental to the question of consultation. We Americans have few national interests—in the narrow sense—outside our own territory, but we have assumed vast world responsibility.

The result is an unequal allocation among the Atlantic nations, both of responsibility and of the burden of decision that goes with it. This imbalance derives from the imperatives of history—not from deliberate American choice. We are aware that policy and responsibility must not be divorced. We recognize that no nation can be expected to share one without the other.

The United States today is quite prepared to share both with its NATO partners.

So far, however, such sharing has been severely limited by differences of attitude within the NATO alliance. The willingness to accept world responsibility—as distinct from the preservation of national interests—is, in our observation and experience, not universal among the NATO membership.

Hopefully this is a passing phenomenon. For the past decade and a half most European nations have been preoccupied with pressing postwar business—the liquidation of colonial arrangements and the building of strong domestic economies. Now this business is largely finished.

Yet this alone will not solve the problem. The problem will never be fully solved until Europe gets on further with the achievement of its own unity—until it organizes itself on a scale commensurate with the requirements of the age.

There are quite obvious reasons for this. The undertaking of world responsibility requires a world view. The discharge of such responsibility under post-colonial conditions must be based on the command of vast resources for defense and foreign aid—and on the will to use them. Western Europe collectively has more than enough resources, but a fragmented Europe cannot efficiently mobilize them in support of a common effort and a common view.

The existing structure of Europe, therefore, sets limits to the effective sharing both of responsibility and decision. But this does not mean that—within the limits thus imposed—we should not continue to improve the present imperfect allocation.

In fact, the United States is quite ready to go forward in sharing its responsibilities around the world wherever there is a will on the part of its European partners to share—and this includes a willingness to provide resources to make that sharing effective.

It was this thought which underlay President Johnson's comment in a speech to the Associated Press in New York when he said, in speaking of our Atlantic relations:

We also welcome agreed new mechanisms for political consultation on mutual interests throughout the world with whatever changes in organization are necessary to make such consultation rapid and effective.

I approach the end of my observations with three general conclusions:

The *first* is that NATO as it exists today—an Atlantic alliance with a unified force in being under a unified command—is an extraordinary peacetime achievement—a platform of accomplishment on which we should continue to build. And we should be wary, indeed, of any actions that might reduce its full effectiveness.

The *second* is that we cannot safely ignore the problem of widening participation in the management of our atomic defense—complicated as it may be by the fragmented structure of Western Europe. And unless you gentlemen are able, out of the collected wisdom represented here, to come up with a better solution than the multilateral force, I strongly urge your support for that proposal.

Finally, if NATO is to fulfill its purpose as the central arrangement for the defense of the free world, it must gradually extend its concern to the larger questions of free-world policy. Here again the limitations that obtain are not hard to isolate. They do not derive from any fault in the institutional structure of NATO but rather from the limited sense of world responsibility—as distinct from national interests—felt by many of our NATO partners.

These then are some of the problems for which we must find solutions over the coming months and years. Effective solutions will not be achieved merely by tinkering with the NATO structure but rather by progress in achieving a greater cohesion in relations among the member nations. This, it seems to me, is already in process. It has already produced substantial results but there is much more to be done.

NATO, therefore, should not be regarded as an end in itself. It should be thought of as one of the pillars in a more comprehensive Atlantic relationship—an Atlantic relationship we must achieve in due course if we are to gain that ultimate goal of which Woodrow Wilson spoke with such prophetic passion—the "universal dominion of right, by such a concert of free peoples as shall bring peace and safety to all nations and make the world itself at last free."

The Crisis of the Alliance

Hans J. Morgenthau

The Western alliance has ceased to be an instrument for policies to be pursued in common by its members. A *tour d'horizon* of the world scene presents a shocking picture of disintegration. There is not a single of the outstanding issues of world politics on which all members of the alliance see eye to eye. The United States stands alone in its policies vis-à-vis China, South Vietnam, and Cuba. The United States stands also alone in its policies concerning trade with the Communist nations. Great Britain, on the one hand, and West Germany and France, on the other, have taken contradictory positions with regard to Berlin. As concerns the German question as a whole and the over-all relations between the West and the Soviet Union, irreconcilable divergencies of interest and policies have made abstention from initiative and a passive commitment to the status quo the order of the day. Greece and Turkey have been on the brink of war over Cyprus. In Africa, the allies go their separate ways; Portugal, in particular, stands virtually alone. The policies of the United States and France toward the United Nations are diametrically opposed. A similar cleavage separates France from the United States and Great Britain in the field of disarmament. As concerns military strategy and the policies implementing it, the United States is at loggerheads with its major European allies on two basic questions: the role of conventional forces and the disposition of nuclear weapons.

The members of the Western alliance have only one obvious interest in common: protection from Communist aggression and subversion. But such an interest is not a policy; it is an objective requiring common policies for its realization. It is both illuminating and disturbing to note that the allies come closest to pursuing common policies, of however dubious value in themselves, in the conventional military field which is least likely to require common action in the foreseeable future, and that it is almost completely lacking in common policies in the political and economic spheres, which the Soviet Union itself has declared to be the arena where the fate of the world will be decided.

The Problem of Risks

What accounts for this decline in the fortunes of an alliance which a decade ago still appeared as the indispensable foundation for the security of the West? The decisive factor in this decline has been the transformation of the American nuclear monopoly, one of the foundation stones of the Western alliance, into a bipolar nuclear threat. That new "balance of terror" has rendered the Western alliance, as presently constituted, obsolete.

In the pre-nuclear age, nations who had certain interests in common would try to defend and promote these interests by coordinating or pooling their diplomatic and military resources. Thus nation A would go to war on behalf of the interests of nation B, or vice versa, when it thought that the defense and promotion of the other nation's interests were in its own as well. By thus reasoning, a nation would take a double risk: it could be mistaken about the identity of the interests involved and be drawn into a war without its own interests being sufficiently engaged, or it could miscalculate the distribution of power on either side and allow itself to get involved in a war which it would lose. What a nation had to guard against in its relations with its allies was a diplomatic blunder or a military miscalculation. If it failed to do so, it would as a rule risk at worst defeat in war with the consequent loss of an army or of territory.

The availability of nuclear weapons has radically transformed these traditional relations among allies and the risks resulting from them. Nuclear nation A which enters into an alliance with nation B, nuclear or non-nuclear, runs a double risk different in kind from the risks a member of a traditional alliance must face. In honoring the alliance, it might have to fight a nuclear war against nuclear power C, thereby forfeiting its own existence. Or ally B may provoke a war with nuclear power C on behalf of interests other than those contemplated by the alliance and thereby force A's hand, involving it in a nuclear war on behalf of interests other than its own. That latter risk is magnified if B is also a nuclear power, of however small dimensions. If B were to threaten or attack C with nuclear weapons, C might, rightly or wrongly, consider B's military power as a mere extension of A's and anticipate and partly prevent the commitment of A through a first strike against A. Or A, anticipating C's reaction against itself or seeking to save B through nuclear deterrence, may commit its own nuclear arsenal against C. In either case, B, however weak as a nuclear power, has the ability to act as a trigger for a general nuclear war.

B, on the other hand, too, faces a double risk. It may forfeit its existence in a nuclear war fought by A on behalf of its interests. Or it may find itself abandoned by A, should A refuse to run the risk of its own destruction on behalf of the interests of B.

It is this radical difference in the risks taken by allies in the pre-nuclear and nuclear age which has led to a radical difference in the reliability of alliances. In the pre-nuclear age, ally A could be expected with a very high degree of certainty to come to the aid of ally *B* at the risk of its own destruction. Here we contemplate the reverse side of the mechanics of deterrence. The very same doubt that deters *C* disheartens *B*. *C* cannot be certain that *A* will not actually forfeit its existence by resorting to nuclear war and, hence, is deterred. *B*, on the other hand, cannot be certain that *A* is willing to forfeit its existence by resorting to nuclear war and, hence, is disaffected.

It is ironic that the event which foreshadowed the decline of the Western alliance virtually coincided with the establishment of that alliance: the first explosion of a nuclear device by the Soviet Union in September 1949. While the destructive effects this event was bound to have upon the Western alliance could be, and actually were, predicted, the policies of the Western allies for almost a decade took no account of these effects. Three new facts were required to open the eyes of Western statesmen to the ever more acute contrast between the official declarations of unity of purpose and the institutions intended to serve common military action, on the one hand, and the crumbling political and military foundations, on the other. These facts are the new foreign policy of the Soviet Union, the Suez Crisis of 1956, and de Gaulle's initiative of January 14, 1963.

Soviet Foreign Policy Since Stalin

The foreign policy of the Soviet Union has fundamentally changed since Stalin's death in 1953. The greatest asset upon which the foreign policies of the nations of Western Europe could bank was the foreign policy of Stalin. Whenever there was a slackening in the Western effort, whenever there appeared cracks in the fabric of the Western alliance, Stalin could be counted upon to make a drastic aggressive move demonstrating to the members of the Western alliance how necessary for their survival the alliance was.

Kremlin policy since Stalin is of a different nature. It is not, at least for the time being, a policy of direct military aggression or serious military threats. Soviet leadership has explicitly and emphatically ruled out nuclear war as an instrument of policy. Their policies are aimed not so much, as were Stalin's, at the conquest of territories contiguous to the Soviet empire by diplomatic pressure or military threats as at the subversion of the whole non-Communist world through the impact which Soviet power, derived primarily from its technological and economic accomplishments, makes upon that world.

That policy of "peaceful" or "competitive coexistence" has been widely misunderstood as indicating a radical change not only in the tactics but in the goals of Soviet foreign policy as well. We have tended to read into "coexistence" a measure of permanency, which, as Mr. Khrushchev reminded us emphatically many times, it cannot have in the philosophy of communism; it is intended to be an intermediate tactical stage in the inevitable decay of capitalism. Thus we took genuine "coexistence" to be an accomplished fact rather than a state of affairs to be striven for and to be achieved only if the West has become so strong that the Soviet Union has no choice but to "coexist" with it. In consequence of this misunderstanding, the association with the United States appears to some of our European allies less vital than it once was. Thus the absence of unmistakable pressure, primarily of a military nature, at the confines where the Western alliance and the Soviet empire meet, has contributed to loosening the ties of the Western alliance.

Suez and Its Aftermath

The intervention of the United States, in conjunction with the Soviet Union, against Great Britain and France during the Suez Crisis of 1956 provided what might be called "the moment of truth" as concerns the political vitality of the Western alliance. It made empirically obvious what before could only be deduced from general principles—that the United States was not willing to risk its own existence on behalf of interests which were peculiar to its allies. The Western alliance proved to be much less comprehensive, cohesive, and reliable than official ideology and the array of common institutions had indicated.

From the state of affairs thus revealed, de Gaulle drew two alternative conclusions. The Western alliance, in order to regain its vitality, required a worldwide coordination of the policies of its major members, and to that end he proposed in 1958 a political triumvirate of the United States, France, and Great Britain. Since that proposal remained stillborn (the United States did not even dignify it with and answer) de Gaulle turned to the other alternative: the national nuclear deterrent. President de Gaulle, in his press conference of January 14, 1963 and subsequent statements, has declared traditional alliances for all practical purposes to be obsolete and has proposed to replace them with national nuclear deterrents. He proposes to assimilate nuclear weapons to conventional ones in that at least their deterrent function be controlled by national governments on behalf of traditional national interests. France would use its nuclear weapons, as it has used its army, navy, and air force in the past, for the purpose of exerting pressure upon a prospective enemy.

How has the United States reacted to this crisis of the Western alliance? As long as the crisis was not acute, the United States proceeded as though the foundations upon which the Western alliance had been erected in 1949 were a kind of immutable datum of nature and as though the factors which would make the crisis sooner or later inevitable did not exist. The extraordinary complacency and sterility which characterized the alliance policy of the United States in the 1950's not only precluded changes in policy taking into account the objective changes that had already occurred, and anticipating those which were sure to occur in the future, but also caused American power to be abused or not to be used at all for the purposes of the alliance.

Our intervention in the Suez crisis in 1956 is but the most spectacular and disastrous example of the capricious and devious disregard of the interests of our allies which marked that period of American foreign policy. Yet it is but the other side of the same medal of complacency and sterility that the United States during this period failed to exert within the alliance that positive political leadership which was its due by dint of its predominance and which its allies expected of it. Now that the leadership of the Western alliance has slipped from its hands, it is a cause for melancholy regret to remember how anxious our allies were then for American leadership to assert itself, and how often, during the crisis of that period, publications such as the London *Economist* implored the United States to that effect—and did so in vain.

Some U.S. Policy Choices

Now that the crisis of the Western alliance has become acute, five possibilities offer themselves to American policy: restoration of the status quo, drift, isolation, "Atlantic Union," pragmatic cooperation with a united Europe. Of these possibilities, only the last two present feasible policies.

In order to do justice to these possibilities, it is necessary to remind oneself that the momentous event which has transformed the objective nature of international relations and undermined the foundations of the Western alliance is the availability of nuclear weapons to more than one nation. This transformation, while recognized in the abstract, has not been able to affect our traditional modes of thought and action. Hence the dilemma which the Western alliance faces. On the one hand, the unity of the West is as necessary in the face of Communist subversion as it was in the face of military threats, now temporarily shelved. On the other hand, for the reasons mentioned above, that unity of interest can no longer be translated into common policies through the instrumentality of a traditional alliance. Where, then, can a new foundation for Western unity be found?

The Proliferation of Nuclear Weapons

On rational grounds, there is much to be said in favor of a return to the *status quo ante* January 14, 1963, that is, nuclear bipolarity. The use of nuclear weapons as instruments of national policy by more than two nations greatly increases the risk of nuclear war, for erected into a general principle of statecraft to be followed by any number of nations, it would issue in the indiscriminate proliferation of nuclear weapons and thereby destroy the very mechanics of mutual deterrence. These mechanics repose upon the bipolarity of nuclear power. Detection systems, such as radar and sonar, are capable of identifying nuclear delivery systems in action, but they cannot identify their national identity, except in a limited way through the calculation of the projectory of land-based missiles. In consequence, retaliation requires that *a priori* determination of national identity, which bipolarity provides. Thus an anonymous explosion, caused by a seaborne delivery vehicle and destroying parts of the east coast of the United States, would automatically be attributed to the Soviet Union, calling forth nuclear retaliation. If a multiplicity of nations possessed such devices and the United States had tense relations with only two to them, such an anonymous explosion could with certainty be attributed to no one nation, however much suspicion might point to a particular one. And a new nuclear diplomacy would try its best to deflect suspicion and retaliation from the guilty to an innocent nation. In the face of such a contingency, a rational nuclear policy would become impossible.

Yet, however great the risks of nuclear proliferation are and however much nuclear bipolarity is to be preferred to nuclear proliferation, the latter could have been prevented only through nuclear disarmament or at least the enforceable prohibition of nuclear tests. In the absence of either, it is futile to oppose proliferation. What is necessary—and also difficult—is to create political conditions likely to minimize the risks of proliferation and in the end to deprive proliferation even within the Western alliance of its rational justification.

The Multilateral Force

Yet we have insisted upon trying to restore the status quo. As the instrument for that restoration, we have chosen the multilateral seaborne nuclear force (MLF), a fleet of surface vessels armed with nuclear missiles and manned by mixed crews recruited from different allied nations. This force is intended to serve three main purposes: the retention of the ultimate control over the use of nuclear weapons in American hands; the prevention of the proliferation of nuclear weapons by giving the allies a share in planning and operations; and the satisfaction of the alleged nuclear appetite of Germany without giving her actual control over nuclear weapons. This is not the place to enter into a discussion of the technical, military, and specific political shortcomings of this device and the improbability of its success. It is only necessary here to point to two of its qualities, which shed an illuminating light upon the deficiencies of our foreign policy: the commitment to a status quo which has been bypassed by history, and the attempt to meet a political problem with a military device.

It is easier, both intellectually and in the short run politically, not to face up to the impossibility of restoring the *status quo ante* January 14, 1963, to keep the legal facade of the Western alliance intact, and to leave the crucial problems unattended. This policy of drift into which a stymied policy of restoration is likely to degenerate is of all the possibilities before us the most dangerous, for it combines in an incompatible interconnection the legal commitments of a traditional alliance with nuclear proliferation. It gives those of our allies who possess nuclear weapons the power to reduce to a minimum our freedom of choice with regard to nuclear war. Both France and Great Britain see the main purpose of the national nuclear deterrent in their ability to use that deterrent as a trigger with which to activate the nuclear deterrent of the United States. As the British White Paper on defense put it on February 13, 1964: "If there were no power in Europe capable of inflicting unacceptable damage on a potential enemy," the enemy might be tempted "to attack in the mistaken belief that the United States would not act unless America herself were attacked."* Or as the London *Economist* said in commenting on this White Paper: "The bombers also give Britain the ability to involve the United States in a nuclear war for which the Americans have no stomach, the argument being that the Russians would be led to loose off an attack on the United States if any foreign nuclear bombs went off on their territory, since they would not have time to see the Union Jack painted on its warhead."† In other words, proliferation combined with traditional alliance commitments turns the obsolescence of the Western alliance, as presently constituted, against the survival of the United States. Allies of the United States armed with nuclear weapons could virtually decide whether the United States shall live or die.

* *The New York Times,* February 14, 1964, p. 1
† *The Economist,* February 15, 1964, p. 587.

Isolation or Atlantic Partnership

Faced with this unacceptable possibility, the United States has two alternative courses of action. It can try to escape the risks its present policies vis-à-vis Western Europe entail by severing the ties of the alliance and retreating into isolation. This alternative is likely to become more tempting as frustrations multiply and awareness of the risks sinks in. Intercontinental nuclear strategy, taken as the sole determinant, would indeed make this alternative feasible. The military security of the United States would not be appreciably affected by whatever course the nations of Western Europe, separated from the United States, would take.

Yet the worldwide conflict in which we are engaged is not primarily of a military nature. It concerns two different conceptions of man and society, and in that conflict the survival of our way of life is at stake. That way of life is an upshot of Western civilization, of which Western Europe is the fountainhead. It is an open question whether our civilization, still unsure of itself, could survive without being able to draw upon the example and the cultural resources of Western Europe. It is even more doubtful whether our civilization could survive in a world which, after the defection of Western Europe, would be either indifferent or hostile to it. It is for this ultimate reason that isolation, however tempting in the short run, is no longer an acceptable alternative for the United States.

The other alternative is presented by the grand design of Atlantic partnership which John F. Kennedy formulated on July 4, 1962 in his "Declaration of Interdependence." That design has remained in the realm of political rhetoric, but it contains a political concept which alone promises to combine Western unity with nuclear power. In order to understand its import, it is first necessary to remind ourselves again of the political character of the crisis of the Western alliance.

The Western alliance is in disarray not because the United States has monopolistic control over the nuclear deterrent, but because the members of the alliance pursue different and sometimes incompatible policies, on behalf of which they might want to use the nuclear deterrent. If the policies of the members of the alliance were in harmony, the issue of the locus of the nuclear decision would lose its present political sting and de Gaulle would have had no need to raise the issue of the national nuclear deterrent. For the nations of Western Europe, either severally or united, would then consider using nuclear weapons for the same purpose as the United States, and vice versa, and the issue of the locus of the decision would be of technical, but no longer of substantive importance. This is, then, the crucial question: how can the different policies of the members of the Western alliance be brought into harmony?

The Need for Statesmanship

Members of alliances have had to face this question since time immemorial, and insofar as they were successful, they have answered it by a supreme effort of statesmanship. For it is one of the great constructive tasks of the statesman to transform an inchoate and implicit community of interests into the actuality of operating policies. This is the task before us today. However, it must be doubted that we shall be able to perform it. Four facts support that doubt.

Statesmanship, that is, the ability to think and act in the specific terms appropriate to foreign policy, has been at all times and in all places an extremely rare commodity. For reasons which are imbedded in our historic experience and the political folklore stemming from it, it has always been in particularly short supply in Washington. It is unlikely, although it is not altogether impossible, that of the few among us who possess the intellectual qualities of statesmanship, one will rise to that eminence of political influence and power that would be necessary to equip the foreign policy of the United States for that creative task.

The chances for the achievement of that task are further diminished by the unprecedented complexity and diversity of the policies to be harmonized. This task cannot be achieved, as de Gaulle recognized in 1958, through the ordinary processes of diplomacy. It requires a virtual fusion of the foreign policies of the members of the Western alliance under centralized direction. In the heyday of NATO, we could at least hope for a political "Atlantic Union" to form a permanent political foundation for the military alliance. In the heyday of a revived nationalism, the leading members of the Western alliance, short of being faced with a direct military threat against them all, are not likely to bring forth simultaneously the political vision, determination, and skill necessary to achieve this rationally required goal.

Two further factors militate against this likelihood: the increase in the political and economic strength of the nations of Western Europe and the corresponding decline of that of the United States. The forging of a political "Atlantic Union" out of several independent political units requires, as de Gaulle has correctly seen, a paramount power which is willing and able to impose its will, if need be, upon a recalcitrant member. In other words, in such an "Atlantic Union" the United States would of necessity be predominant. Yet when in the

1950's the United States had the power, and when its allies urged it to play that predominant role, the United States did not have the will to do so. Now even if it had the will, it would not have the power to make its will prevail.

It is exactly because an "Atlantic Union" would be dominated by the United States that de Gaulle is opposed to it in no uncertain terms. The opposition of the other major European powers has remained implicit. But their desire for emancipation from the United States is obviously incompatible with the pursuit of a political "Atlantic Union."

Goals for the United States

The United States cannot afford to lose sight of political "Atlantic Union" as the ultimate goal; for nuclear proliferation, inevitable as it is likely to be, can be rendered tolerable only if its centrifugal and anarchic consequences are counterbalanced by the politically unified use of proliferated nuclear weapons. As long as political union is unobtainable and since traditional alliance commitments joined with nuclear proliferation, as pointed out above, are intolerable, the United States must strive for three goals: to mitigate the consequences of proliferation by limiting the number of independent nuclear deterrents, to bring its alliance commitments for the time being into harmony with the interests it has actually or potentially in common with its allies, and in the end to render proliferation innocuous through united political control.

The first goal requires of the United States active support for the political unification of Europe. For since proliferation appears to be inevitable and political "Atlantic Union" unattainable, a European nuclear deterrent controlled by a European political authority is the best attainable alternative. Such support implies a radical change in our present policies which, by trying to isolate France, render the political unification of Europe impossible and seek in vain to restore the Atlantic alliance on foundations which no longer exist.

The second goal requires similarly a radical change from the dogmatic insistence upon the restoration of an unrestorable status quo to the pragmatic adaptation to circumstances which for the time being are not subject to our control. We must narrow the gap between our comprehensive legal commitments and the limited sphere within which our interests and policies still coincide with those of our allies. Otherwise we shall run the risk, to which improvident great powers have succumbed in the past, *vide* Germany in 1914, of getting involved in a war not of our making and on behalf of interests not our own.

Finally, we must look beyond these short-term adaptations to the ultimate goal not only of our alliance policy but of our over-all foreign policies as well: the minimization of the risk of nuclear war. The substitution of a European nuclear deterrent for a multiplicity of national ones is a step in this direction. Political "Atlantic Union" would be another step, impossible to achieve at present but to be sought for a not too distant future.

In the end, we must look for a settlement or at least decontamination of the great political issues which at present divide the world and conjure up the risk of nuclear war. We shall thus deprive the nuclear powers of the incentive to use nuclear weapons as instruments of their national policies. And we shall deal with the present crisis of the Western alliance, seeking first to take into account the new circumstances of the crisis and, then, to overcome the crisis itself not only as isolated moves aimed at short-term goals but also as steps toward the ultimate goal of banishing nuclear war itself.

The Future of NATO

Henry A. Kissinger

It is somewhat strange phenomenon for me to talk to a NATO conference in Brussels in the presence of so many old friends, who will consider my words an unnecessary interruption in the thoughts they are getting ready to launch at the conference sessions. When I see my old colleague Ambassador de Staercke sitting here, it is almost like the old days; he functions as my conscience as he always has.

I think I speak for all of you when I thank the foreign minister for the extraordinary arrangements that have been made.

At the beginning of the conference, the most useful thing I can do is to outline the concerns that I have about the future of NATO, the problems that in my estimation require solution, if we are to retain our vitality and if we are to remain relevant to the challenges before us. Since the early 1960s, every new American administration that has come into office promises a new look at Europe, a reappraisal and a reassessment. Each of these efforts has found us more or less confirming what already existed and what had been created in the late 1940s and early 1950s, with just enough alliance adaptation to please the endlessly restless Americans who can never restrain themselves from new attempts at architecture.

Without going into which of these proposals were right, or if any of these specific proposals were necessary, I think the fact that in the late 1970s we are operating an alliance machinery and a force structure under a concept more or less unchanged from the 1950s should indicate that we have been depleting capital. Living off capital may be a pleasant prospect for a substantial period of time, but inevitably a point will be reached where reality dominates. And my proposition to this group is that NATO is reaching a point where the strategic assumptions on which it has been operating, the force structures that it has been generating, and the joint policies it has been developing, will be inadequate for the 1980s.

I have said in the United States, in my SALT testimony, that if present trends continue, the 1980s will be a period of massive crisis for all of us. We have reached this point not through the mistakes of any single administration. Just as the commitment to NATO is a bipartisan American effort, the dilemmas that I would like to put before this group—admittedly in a perhaps exaggerated form—have been growing up over an extended period, partly as the result of American perceptions, partly as a result of European perceptions.

Nor is this to deny that NATO, by all of the standards of traditional alliances, has been an enormous success. To maintain an alliance in peacetime without conflict for a generation is extremely rare in history. And it is inherent in a process in which an alliance has been successful, in which deterrence has worked, that no one will be able to prove why it has worked. Was it because we conducted the correct policy? Was it because the Soviet Union never had any intention to attack us in the first place? Was it because of the policies of strength of some countries, or the policies of accommodation of other countries? So, what I say should not be taken as a criticism either of any particular American administration (even granting that there was one period of eight years in the past in which no mistakes were made) nor of any specific policies of European nations, but rather as an assessment of where we are today.

The Global Environment

Let me first turn to the strategic situation. The dominant fact of the current military balance is that the NATO countries are falling behind in every significant military category, with the possible exception of naval forces where the gap in our favor is closing. Never in history has it happened that a nation achieved superiority in all significant weapons categories without seeking to translate it at some point into some foreign policy benefit. It is, therefore, almost irrelevant to debate whether there is some magic date at which Soviet armies will head in some direction or another. I am willing to grant that there is no particular master plan nor is there any specific deadline; I do not even consider that the present Soviet leaders are superadventurous. That is fundamentally irrelevant.

In a world of upheaval and rapid changes, enough opportunities will arise in which the relative capacity and the relative willingness of the two sides to understand their interests and to defend their interests will be the key element. I do not believe the Soviet Union planned Angola, or created the conditions for intervention in Ethiopia, or necessarily had a deadline for the revolution in Afghanistan. But all of these events happened to the detriment of general stability. I would consider it a rash Western policy that did not take into account that in the decade ahead we will face simultaneously an unfavorable balance of power, a world in turmoil, a potential economic crisis, and a massive energy problem. To conduct business as usual is to entrust one's destiny to the will of others and to the self-restraint of those whose ideology highlights the crucial role of the objective balance of forces.

This is my fundamental theme. And I would now like to discuss this in relation to specific issues.

The Shifting Strategic Balance

First, at the risk of repeating myself, let me state once again what I take to be the fundamental change in the strategic situation as far as the United States is concerned, and then examine the implications for NATO.

When the North Atlantic Treaty Organization was created, the United States possessed an overwhelming strategic nuclear superiority. That is to say, for a long period of time we were likely to prevail in a nuclear war, certainly if we struck first and for a decade perhaps even if we struck second; we were in a position to wipe out the Soviet strategic forces and to reduce any possible counterblow against us to an acceptable level. And that situation must have looked more ominous to the Soviet Union even than it looked favorable to us.

If we think back to the Cuban Missile Crisis of 1962, which all the policymakers of the time were viewing with a consciousness of an approaching Armageddon, one is almost seized with nostalgia for the ease of their decisions. At that time the Soviet Union had about 70 long-range missiles that took 10 hours to fuel, which was a longer period of time than it would take our airplanes to get to the Soviet

Union from forward bases. Even at the time of the Middle East crisis of 1973 (the alert), we had a superiority of about eight to one in missile warheads. If one compares this with the current and foreseeable situation, we are approaching a point where it is difficult to assign a clear military objective to American strategic forces in a strategic nuclear exchange.

In the 1950s and for much of the 1960s, NATO was protected by a preponderance in American strategic striking power which was capable of disarming the Soviet Union, and by a vast American superiority in theatre nuclear forces although, as I will discuss, we never had a comprehensive theory for using theatre nuclear forces. Since all intelligence services congenitally overestimate the rationality of the decision-making process which they are analyzing, it is probable that the Soviet Union made more sense out of our nuclear deployment in Europe than we were able to make ourselves. In any event, it was numerically superior. And it was in that strategic framework that the allied ground forces on the continent were deployed.

No one disputes any longer that in the 1980s—and perhaps even today, but surely in the 1980s—the United States will no longer be in a strategic position to reduce a Soviet counterblow against the United States to tolerable levels. Indeed, one can argue that the United States will not be in a position in which attacking the Soviet strategic forces makes any military sense, because it may represent a marginal expenditure of our own strategic striking force that does not help greatly to ensure the safety of our forces.

Since the middle 1960s the growth of the Soviet strategic force has been massive. It grew from 220 intercontinental ballistic missiles in 1965 to 1,600 around 1972-1973. Soviet submarine-launched missiles grew from negligible numbers to over 900 in the 1970s. And the amazing phenomenon which historians will ponder is that all of this has happened without the United States attempting to make a significant effort to rectify that state of affairs. One reason was that it was not easy to rectify. But another reason was the growth of a school of thought to which I myself contributed, and many around this conference table also contributed, which considered that strategic stability was a military asset, and in which the historically amazing theory developed that vulnerability contributed to peace and invulnerability contributed to risks of war.

Such a theory could develop and be widely accepted only in a country that had never addressed the problem of the balance of power as a historical phenomenon. And, if I may say so, only also on a continent that was looking for any excuse to avoid analysis of the perils it was facing and that was looking for an easy way out. When the administration with which I was connected sought to implement an anti-ballistic missile program inherited from our predecessors, it became the subject of the most violent attacks from those who held the theory that it was destabilizing, provocative, and an obstacle to arms control; initially the ABM could be sold only as a protection against the Chinese and not against the Soviet threat. In any case, the ABM was systematically reduced by the Congress in every succeeding session to the point where we wound up with a curious coalition of the Pentagon and the arms controllers, both finally opposed to it: the Pentagon because it no longer made any military sense to put resources into a program that was being systematically deprived of military utility, and the arms control community because they saw in the strategic vulnerability of the United States a positive asset. It cannot have occurred often in history that it was considered an advantageous military doctrine to make your own country deliberately vulnerable.

Now we have reached that situation so devoutly worked for by the arms control community: we are indeed vulnerable. Moreover our weapons had been deliberately designed, starting in the 1960s, so as to not threaten the weapons of the other side. Under the doctrine of "assured destruction," nuclear war became not a military problem but one of engineering; it depended on theoretical calculations of the amount of economic and industrial damage that one needed to inflict on the other side; it was therefore essentially independent of the forces the other side was creating.

This general theory suffered two drawbacks. One was that the Soviets did not believe it. And the other is that we have not yet bred a race of supermen that can implement it. While we are building "assured destruction" capabilities, the Soviet Union is building forces for for traditional military missions capable of destroying the military forces of the United States. So in the 1980s we will be in a position where (1) many of our own strategic forces, including all of our land-based ICBMs, will be vulnerable, and (2) such an insignificant percentage of Soviet strategic forces will be vulnerable as not to represent a meaningful strategic attack option for the United States. Whether that means that the Soviet Union intends to attack the United States or not is certainly not my point. I am making two points: First, that the change in the strategic situation that is produced by our limited vulnerability is more fundamental for the United States than even total vulnerability would be for the Soviet Union because our strategic doctrine has relied extraordinarily, perhaps exclusively, on our superior strategic power. The Soviet Union has never relied on its superior strategic power. It has always depended more on its local and regional superiority. Therefore, even an equivalence in destructive power, even "assured destruction" for both sides, is a revolution in the strategic balance as we have known it. It is a fact that must be faced.

I have recently urged that the United States build a counterforce capability of its own for two reasons. One, the answer of our NATO friends to the situation that I have described has invariably been to demand additional reassurances of an undiminished American military commitment. And I have sat around the NATO Council table in Brussels and elsewhere and have uttered the magic words which had a profoundly reassuring effect, and which permitted the ministers to return home with a rationale for not increasing defense expenditures. And my successors have uttered the same reassurances. And yet if my analysis is correct, these words cannot be true indefinitely; and if my analysis is correct we must face the fact that it is absurd in the 1980s to base the strategy of the West on the credibility of the threat of mutual suicide.

One cannot ask a nation to design forces that have no military significance, whose primary purpose is the extermination of civilians, and expect that these factors will not affect a nation's resoluteness in crisis. We live in the paradoxical world that it is precisely the liberal, human, progressive community that is advocating the most bloodthirsty strategies and insisting that there is nothing to worry about as long as the capacity exists to kill 100 million people. It is this approach that argues that we should not be concerned about the vulnerability of our missile forces, when, after all, we can always launch them on warning of an attack. Any military man at this conference will tell you that launching strategic forces on warning can be accomplished only by delegating the authority to the proverbially "insane colonel" about whom so many movies have been made. Nobody who knows anything about how our government operates will believe that it is possible for our presidents to get the secretary of state, secretary of defenses, chairman of the Joint Chiefs of Staff, and director of the CIA to a conference called in the 15 minutes that may be available to make a decision, much less issue an order that then travels down the line of command in the 15 minutes. So the only way you can implement that strategy is by delegating the authority down to some field commander who must be given discretion so that when he thinks a nuclear war has started, he can retaliate. Is that the world we want to live in? Is that where "assured destruction" will finally take us?

And therefore I would say—what I might not say in office—that our European allies should not keep asking us to multiply strategic assurances that we cannot possibly mean or if we do mean, we should not want to execute because if we execute, we risk the destruction of civilization. Our strategic dilemma is not solved by verbal reassurances; it requires redesigning our forces and doctrine. There is no point in complaining about declining American will, or criticizing this or that American administration, for we are facing an objective crisis and it must be remedied.

Theatre Nuclear Forces

The second part of this problem is the imbalance that has grown up in theatre nuclear forces. In the 1950s and 1960s we put several thousand nuclear weapons into Europe. To be sure, we had no very precise idea of what to do with them, but I am sure that Soviet intelligence figured out some purpose for these forces; and in any event it was a matter for this disquiet. Now one reason we did not have a rational analysis for the use of these factors was the very reason that led to the strategic theory of "assured destruction." Let us face it: the intellectually predominant position in the United States was that we had to retain full control of the conduct of nuclear war and we therefore had a vested interest in avoiding any "firebreak" between tactical nuclear weapons and strategic nuclear weapons. The very reasoning that operated against setting a rational purpose for strategic forces also operated against giving a military role to tactical nuclear forces. And this was compounded by the fact that—to be tactless—the secret dream of every European was, of course, to avoid a nuclear war but, secondly, if there had to be a nuclear war, to have it conducted over their heads by the strategic forces of the United States and the Soviet Union. Be that as it may, the fact is that the strategic imbalance that I have predicted for the 1980s will also be accompanied by a theatre imbalance in the 1980s. How is it possible to survive with these imbalances in the face of the already demonstrated inferiority in conventional forces?

If there is no theatre nuclear establishment on the continent of Europe, we are writing the script for selective blackmail in which our allies will be threatened, and in which we will be forced into a decision whereby we can respond only with a strategy that has no military purpose but only the aim of destruction of populations.

I ask any of you around this conference table: If you were secretary of state or security adviser, what would you recommend to the president of the United States to do in such circumstances? How would he improve his relative military position? Of course he could threaten a full-scale strategic response, but is it a realistic course? It is senseless to say that dilemma shows that Americans are weak and irresolute. This is not the problem of any particular administration, but it is a problem of the doctrine that has developed.

Therefore, I believe that it is urgently necessary either that the Soviets be deprived of their counterforce capability in strategic forces, or that a U.S. counterforce capability in strategic forces be rapidly built. It is also necessary that either the Soviet nuclear threat in theatre nuclear forces against Europe be eliminated (which I do not see is possible), or that an immediate effort be made to build up our theatre nuclear forces. Just as I believe it is necessary that we develop a military purpose for our strategic forces and move away from the senseless and demoralizing strategy of massive civilian extermination, so it is imperative that we finally try to develop some credible military purposes for the tactical and theatre nuclear forces that we are building.

The Role Of Ground Forces

And third, it is time that we decide what role exactly we want for our ground forces on the continent. These forces were deployed in the 1950s when American strategic superiority was so great that we could defend Europe by the threat of general nuclear war. And they were deployed in Europe, as I have often said, as a means of ensuring the automaticity of our response. Our forces were in Europe as hostages. Everybody had a vested interest in not making the forces too large. We wound up with the paradox that they were much too large for what was needed for a tripwire yet not large enough for a sustained conventional defense. I tried for the years that I was in office to get some assessment of just what was meant by the 90-day stockpile that we were supposed to have, and what the minimum critical categories were. I know that my friend whom I admire enormously, General Alexander Haig, has done enormous work in improving the situation; nevertheless I would be amazed if even he believed that we can now say that our ground forces by themselves can offer a sustained defense without massive, rapid improvements.

The Political Context

If the chairman will permit, I will move to a few political considerations.

Everything that I have said about the military situation would be difficult enough to remedy, but the situation is compounded by theories to which, again, I myself have no doubt contributed. In 1968, at Reykjavik, NATO developed the theory—which I believe is totally wrong—that the alliance is as much an instrument of detente as it is of defense. I think that that is simply not correct. NATO is not equipped to be an instrument of detente; for example, every time we attempted to designate the secretary general of NATO as a negotiating partner with the Warsaw Pact, it was rejected. But this is a minor problem, and detente is important. It is important because, as the United States learned during Vietnam, in a democracy you cannot sustain the risk of war unless your public is convinced that you are committed to peace. Detente is important because we cannot hold the alliance together unless our allies are convinced that we are not seeking confrontation for its own sake. Detente is important because I cannot accept the proposition that it is the democracies that must concede the peace issue to their opponents. And detente is important so that if a confrontation proves unavoidable, we will have elaborated the reasons in a manner that permits us to sustain a confrontation.

So I have always been restless with those who define the issue as "detente" or "no detente." All Western governments must demonstrate and must conduct a serious effort to relax tensions and to negotiate outstanding differences. But there is something deeper involved in the West. There is in the West a tendency to treat detente quite theatrically; that is to say, not as a balancing of national interests and negotiations on the basis of strategic realities but rather as an exercise in strenuous goodwill, in which one removes by understanding the suspiciousness of a nation that is assumed to have no other motive to attack. This tendency to treat detente as an exercise in psychotherapy, or as an attempt at good personal relations, or as an effort in which individual leaders try to gain domestic support by proving that they have a special way in Moscow—that is disastrous for the West. And it is the corollary to the "assured destruction" theory, in the sense that it always provides an alibi for not doing what must be done.

Against all evidence, we were told that the ABM would ruin the chances of arms control. The fact was that Premier Kosygin in 1967 told President Johnson at Glassboro, N.J. that the idea of not engaging in defense was one of the most ridiculous propositions that he had ever heard. By 1970, when we had an ABM program, however inadequate, it was the only subject the Soviet Union was willing to discuss with us in SALT. When we gave up the B-1 bomber, we asked the Soviets to make a reciprocal gesture. We have yet to see it. When we gave up the neutron weapon, we were told that this was in correlation with the deployment of the SS-20. (If so, the result was in inverse correlation with the SS-20.) And now we are told that of course we are all for theatre nuclear forces, but first let us have another effort at negotiation. I saw a report about a distinguished American senator returning from Moscow the other day who said: "It is virtually certain that cruise missiles will be deployed and that NATO will undertake a build-up of its own unless negotiations to a new treaty are begun soon." If this is our position, all the Soviets have to do is to begin a negotiation to keep us from doing what they are already doing, negotiation or no negotiation.

Such a version of detente leads to unilateral disarmament for the West. I favor negotiation on theatre nuclear forces, but the talks will accelerate the more rapidly as we build such theatre nuclear forces. Then we can consider some numerical balance or some deployment pattern, but we cannot defer the strategic decisions we must make for the sake of initiating a negotiation. We must have detente, but the detente must be on a broad front in the sense that all of the NATO nations must pursue comparable policies. The illusion that some countries can achieve a preferential position with the U.S.S.R. is theoretically correct, but it is the best means of dividing the alliance. The illusion that some subjects can be separated for individual treatment of detente, while conflict goes on in all other areas, turns detente into a safety valve for aggression.

My fundamental point is that we need a credible strategy; we need an agreed strategy and we need to build urgently the required forces. We cannot wait two or three more years. We cannot conduct a foreign policy, even though each of our political systems encourages such a policy, in which we ease the domestic positions of the individual countries by pretending that single forays to Moscow can solve our problems.

Unfortunately, the time frame of the evolution of programs that I have described is longer than the electoral period of most of our leaders. Therefore our leaders in all of our countries have an enormous temptation to celebrate the very successes that lead to a differential detente either as to subject or as to region. How is it possible that the states that have 70% of the world's gross national product will not conduct a common energy policy? This is not just because it has become a shibboleth that "we must not have confrontation;" when have nations been confronted by a massive decline of their economies without being willing to confront those who are contributing significantly to the decline? And after all, it takes two to make a confrontation.

How is it possible that in the Middle East, two totally conflicting theories on how to proceed are being carried out simultaneously? How can it be that both Egypt and the PLO must simultaneously be encouraged, sometimes I confess by our own government? But fundamentally the Europeans are playing one card and we are playing another, so that both the radical and the moderate elements are being strengthened simultaneously. One of us has got to be wrong, and it is just an evasion to pretend that we work one side of the street and the Europeans work another side of the street, because what is really involved in Europe is an attempt to gain special advantages. Yet it is a situation in which the market conditions do not permit special advantages, but where, on the contrary, once it is accepted that oil is a political weapon, even the moderates have no excuse for *not* using it as a political weapon.

I'm not trying to suggest what the correct answer is, but I am saying that the nations represented around this table ought to ask themselves whether the two years of special advantages that either of them might gain is worth the 10 years' disaster that could easily befall them.

I know we have many alibis. We have the alibi that none of the things I said is inevitable because there is China. And we have the alibi that, after all, the Soviets have never stayed anywhere and they're in deep trouble themselves. And we have the alibi that we can make such great progress in the Third World that all of this is irrelevant.

In my view the Chinese have survived for 3,000 years by being the most unsentimental practitioners of the balance of power, the most sophisticated, and the ones most free of illusion. China will be an alibi for us only if we do what is necessary. China will not be on the barricades that we refuse to man as the victim of the forces which we have unleashed. So it is certain that we can have cooperation with China only if we create a balance of power.

Now the theory that the Soviets can never stay where they have been is amazingly widely held and supported by exactly one example: Egypt. I don't count Somalia-Ethiopia because I consider their departure from Somalia as a voluntary Soviet switch from one client to a larger client. And in Egypt the fact of the matter is that the balance of power was in favor of those that we supported and those who learned in three wars (in two of which we approached a U.S.-Soviet confrontation) that they could not achieve their aims by Soviet arms. And only after that demonstration was there an Egyptian switch. So we are right back to our original problem.

And the final nostalgia—that of the "noble savage," the Third World, that we're going to sweep them over to our side: I have to confess I cannot give this an operational definition. As for the Third World nations now meeting in Cuba, when I was in office I never read their resolutions, I regret to tell you, which is just as well because I might have said something rather nasty. But I would think it is statistically impossible that over the years that these Third World nations have been meeting, the United States has never done anything right. Even by accident we're bound to do something right. I defy anybody to read through these documents to find one reference on even the most minor thing to something that the United States has ever done right. What are the prospects of progress in a world in which the Cubans can host the nonaligned conference?

It seems to me a nostalgia, not a policy, to appeal to radical elements in the Third World to change their operational politics. They cannot, because the radical element is required for their bargaining position, a position between us and the Soviets, and because its ideology is hostile to us. Therefore, paradoxically, the more we approach them the more they are likely to pull away from us.

I'm not saying we should not deal with the radical elements of the Third World or that we should not do the best we can in the Third World. All I'm saying is the Third World is not our alibi, it is not our escape route; we may not lose there but we are not likely to win there by repeating their slogans.

Conclusion

This is not intended to be a depressing account of difficulties. It is not to say that we have no favorable prospects. It is simply to point out that problems neglected are crises invited.

In the thirtieth year of NATO we have come far and have achieved our principal purpose. If we do not address ourselves immediately to at least some of the problems I have mentioned, we will face the potentiality of debacles. And the weird aspect of it is that there is absolutely no necessity for it. The weird aspect is that the nations assembled in this room have three times the gross national product of the Soviet Union and four times the population. The Soviet Union has leadership problems, social problems, minority problems; all they have in their favor is the ability to accumulate military power and perhaps that only for a transitory period.

So if one looks ahead for 10 years, and if we do what is necessary, all the odds are in our favor. The challenges I have put before this group do not indicate that we are bound to be in difficulties, but only that we can defeat ourselves. And by contrast, one can say we have an extraordinary opportunity to rally our people, to define new positive programs even for negotiations with the East if we do what is necessary.

Or to put it another way, our adversaries are really not in control of their own future. Their system and their conditions in many ways make them victims of their past. We around this table are in the extraordinary position that we can decide a positive future for ourselves if we are willing to make the effort. We are in the position to say that the kind of world in which we want to live is largely up to us.

Dr. Kissinger's Comments to the Press After the Brussels Conference on NATO, September 3, 1979

KISSINGER: Out of politeness to my friend the foreign minister, I will not read the 50-minute statement that I have prepared for this occasion since he has already hinted that I shouldn't do this. I think you should direct your questions either at the foreign minister or whoever else may be available.

Q: Dr. Kissinger, you said that one of the problems in your opening speech was your poverty of the English language, I believe. Do you regret now using words like mutual suicide, extermination of civilians, bloodthirsty and mad colonels? Is that why that speech was misunderstood?

KISSINGER: I haven't seen the text since it has been transcribed, so that the "mad general" is a particularly felicitous phrase that I don't remember. But leaving it aside, there are two points you have to remember: English was established as the official language of the United States at its founding, but there's no evidence that this injunction of the founding fathers was necessarily carried out.

To answer your question, I think it is imperative that we face the consequences of the theory of mutual assured destruction. That theory involves the mutual extermination of civilians and I do not regret having said this. It makes no sense to rely on threats which have the most catastrophic consequences. I want to reiterate that I believe that the defense of Europe and of the United States is indissoluble. I believe that the United States must guarantee the defense of Europe. But I believe that both Europe and the United States have a joint interest in developing a defense doctrine that our leaders can explain to our publics over an extended period of time, and I do not regret having used these phrases. I regret that the interpretation has been given to them that this meant that the United States is no longer prepared to defend

Europe, and I can see how my somewhat classic language might have led to this, but the analysis I stand by.

The conclusion, I believe, requires us to develop a strategy that we can defend before our publics and that our opponents will believe over an extended period of time. And the final thing to remember is that the situation that I have described will not arise for two to four years, so that with effort we can reduce the dangers that I have described. This was my purpose.

Q: Doesn't the contrary theory that you were advocating—that of counterforce—simply interpose a different level of combat between the beginning of the war and the destruction of civilization in any event? To ask the question, what percentage chance do you think there is of fighting a nuclear war with counterforce and having it not lead to the destruction of civilization?

KISSINGER: Let me first of all make—let me stress—the following point here. The United States throughout the postwar period has been more dependent on its strategic forces than the Soviet Union has been on its own. Therefore, the loss of war-fighting capability for the United States strategic forces changes the situation more radically than a similar change would change it for the Soviet Union. Nor do I say that the preferred United States strategy should be strategic nuclear war. I am simply asking everybody to look at the 1980s. If present trends continue, the United States will not be able to reduce significantly the military capacity of the Soviet Union for strategic nuclear war. The Soviet Union will have an advantage in theatre nuclear forces of 3 to 1 and in conventional forces of 4 to 1. In those circumstances some kind of political crisis, perhaps not even triggered by the Soviet Union, is inevitable.

I do not believe that nuclear war will automatically escalate to the extermination of civilians because the danger of that and the consequences of that for every political leadership are profound. I simply want to create a situation in which we can extend for a while longer the military protection that the United States extended to Europe through the 50s, 60s and early 70s. In time, the tendency of strategic forces, either through mobility or going to sea, will be towards invulnerability. At that point, I hope that the theatre nuclear forces and the conventional forces will be sufficiently strengthened to make up the gap. So we are talking here about five-year periods. And it is never going to be an easy decision, but it is at least a decision that is more plausible.

The next question that one has to keep in mind is not only what one does in a crisis, but the likelihood of a crisis. And the likelihood of a crisis, in my view, is reduced if the United States has a plausible war-fighting capability and is not forced to protect its vital interest and the vital interests of its allies by the exclusive threat of what I called on Saturday "mass extermination of civilians." It's a very serious problem which will affect the morale of our society and our willingness to conduct a serious foreign policy, not just in Europe but around the world, and I do not want to suggest that it has an easy answer or has a recent origin.

Q: (Inaudible) . . . try for some kind of strategic superiority again?

KISSINGER: The fact of the situation is that, contrary to all theories, and contrary to our own expectations, the Soviet Union has built a capacity to destroy the American land-based forces, even though the Soviet Union requires that less that we do, because they already have superiority in conventional forces. I am saying that we should acquire a capability to pose an equal threat to the Soviet land-based forces. That threat, of course, will not necessarily be exercised. It may make a crisis more risky but it may make a crisis also less likely. And our objective after all is to prevent crisis. It may also force the Soviets to give up some of their land-based forces and go to a less destructive system.

Q: Dr. Kissinger has been advocating a strengthening of the theatre nuclear forces so that the United States does not have to rely on their pathetic arsenal; but for the European countries it would make a big difference if the conflict on our soil is to be fought with tactical nuclear weapons or the so-called grey area weapons or strategic weapons?

KISSINGER: Now, I have indeed said that the strengthening of theatre nuclear forces—and I would like to point out that the current administration in Washington is also favoring the strengthening of theatre nuclear forces so this is not a point I've made in opposition to our administration. The argument for theatre nuclear forces is not to spare the United States the decision to go to strategic nuclear war. The argument is to prevent the Soviet Union from believing that they can blackmail Europe by threatening it separately with nuclear war and thereby creating a gap in the continuum of risks which they could face. And this is especially important in the face of the strategic balance that I described, which is either equivalence or effective equivalence. In these conditions I believe it is too dangerous. We are also inferior in theatre nuclear forces, but the intention is not for the United States to escape the decision to be involved. The intention is to raise the risk for the Soviet Union in initiating hostilities in Europe.

Q: Some estimates say the Soviet Union will need to begin importing oil by mid-1980. Do you foresee the possibility of a direct confrontation between the United States and the Soviet Union in the present Gulf area over energy resources?

KISSINGER: Let me just make a general comment about Soviet intentions. I don't think one should conduct a debate as if the Soviet Union had a fixed plan in which on a certain date they will move into one area and then into another area. But I believe history also shows that a country may not have a plan but the evolution of the balance of power can be such that it is tempted into actions that, when it began to build the forces, it may not even have envisaged.

Secondly, we face in the world today many crises that can arise without being caused by either of the two superpowers but which will involve the vital interests of the superpowers once they begin, and in which therefore the relative capacity to reinforce and to run risks will determine the outcome. Thirdly, there are parts of the world—and this gets to your question—in which economic interests may become so heavily involved that they will lead, at least indirectly, to a confrontation. I do not think that the Soviet Union necessarily has a plan to occupy the Middle East, but I do believe that if the Soviet Union should become an oil importer, its already strong interest in the political complexion of the Middle East is bound to increase. Therefore, the tensions that are inseparable from the process of development and from the process of political evolution could be magnified, so that in the 80s the Persian Gulf area is at least one area in which we must have a capacity to protect our friends and to give them a certain measure of security, whether or not they will be directly threatened.

Q: During three days we have listened to a discussion about the situation in several points of the world but we didn't hear much discussion about the situation in Eastern Europe. Don't you believe that the situation, the internal situation, the succession crisis in the Soviet Union, and the crisis situation in several Eastern European countries are also a factor of this European and world balance of forces? Military forces.

KISSINGER: Excuse me. I think that it is a mistake to assess the global situation in entirely military terms. Certainly, the succession problem in any communist country and particularly in the Soviet Union will raise questions. The comment was made in our conference this afternoon that, in the past, historical experience has shown that whenever there is a succession in the Soviet Union the military complex, precisely because it will play such a role in determining the outcome, is likely to have a claim on even larger resources, so that at the end of the process we are likely to find an even stronger Soviet Union which will attempt to negotiate whatever detente it then envisages from a position of even greater strength. This was a judgment that was put forth in our country, not by me, but it is one that I find very plausible.

There is no question that the Soviet system, economically and politically, faces grave difficulties and necessities of adjustment. It is also true that it has been relatively most efficient in the military field. Therefore, the question is, "What will they emphasize during and after the succession?" Nobody can be sure. I think the best way to encourage a hopeful resolution is, one, to be strong enough not to create temptation for military pressure; second, to be conciliatory enough to indicate a readiness for negotiation; and third, to steer the negotiations to specific rules of international conduct and not simply to create in a general atmosphere attempts to identify diplomacy with psychiatry. If we can meet those three conditions, I think we can get through the 80s.

Q: (Inaudible) . . . East European countries. For instance, in Poland today where the dissidence is so important, what is the stability of some (inaudible)?

KISSINGER: I think every communist country faces the phenomenon—almost every communist country in Eastern Europe faces the phenomenon—that after having been in power for a generation it is very dubious. I would say none of them could win a free election. And, therefore, especially in Poland where the church is so strong and where the visit of the pope has elicited a degree of enthusiasm that no Polish leader could generate, it shows certain anomalies in the situation that over a historical period are bound to have their effect.

Q: Dr. Kissinger, you've talked about the challenges facing the alliance and highlighted some of the possible ways in which these tensions could come to bear differentially on the United States and on Europe. Could you talk a little bit about any recent changes in the political climate in Europe and in the United States which will make it more difficult or easier for the alliance to respond to the challenges you've outlined?

KISSINGER: Well, first to take the situation of the United States. As compared to the period when I was in office, that is the early 70s, the Vietnam War, and then the Watergate period, it is forgotten today that every defense budget was confronted by a substantially hostile Congress. This had a dual effect because it caused the administration which I served to submit lower defense budgets to begin with in order to prevent the Congress from cutting them even further, and then on top of it the Congress cut them by some $34 billion in the first Nixon administration, so that there was a relatively lower readiness to engage in defense programs.

Secondly, I think the United States is beginning to come out of the trauma of the Vietnam War, and in our public there is a sort of inchoate feeling that the United States must not constantly be on the defensive in international affairs. So I believe that our administration would find considerable public support for the kind of policies that the majority of the Americans here at the conference have outlined. And, indeed, one would have to say the major opposition for this policy would come from the liberal wing of the Democratic party and would be supported by most of the Republican party and the middle-to-conservative spectrum of the Democratic party.

In Europe the divisions did not go so deep in the early 70s and therefore the change did not have to be so drastic. But in most European countries, and almost all the major European countries, I think there is a greater readiness to face the situation that some of us have attempted to describe here, and my impression of the conference was that there was a substantial consensus behind the analysis even if there were some differences as to remedies. But even the differences as to remedies were not really so much of principle. I'm not saying there was unanimity but I think that the political and psychological climate to do what is necessary is better both in Europe and the United States than it has been throughout the 70s.

Q: Is it possible for the United States to develop its strategic forces in a manner that you suggest to counter the Soviet strategic forces within the limitations of the SALT agreement now negotiated? And the second part to that question is do you foresee the SALT agreement being ratified?

KISSINGER: Well, I believe that it is possible to do this within the limitations of the SALT agreement and I have so testified. I do not like the protocol in the SALT agreement and I have strongly urged the Senate to make clear that it will terminate and that it cannot be resubmitted in its present form for extension. I believe that it would be inimical to the modernization of theatre nuclear forces if the protocol were continued or if even negotiations about its possible continuation were conducted.

I also urged on the conference today, that before we go into SALT III we have a serious consideration within the United States and after that with our allies as to what exactly it is that we are trying to accomplish, so that we avoid the decision of having either to turn down an already negotiated treaty with all the consequences for political creditability or accepting it with some of the doubts that have been expressed. But to answer your question specifically, I do believe we can do within the constraints of SALT II—if we do all of the things that we are permitted to do—that part that concerns the strategic forces. We cannot do what is needed with theatre nuclear forces. Therefore, the protocol must end in 1981.

Leadership in the Alliance

Helmut Schmidt

It is really not that difficult for a political leader to guide his or her country. All one has to do is to satisfy the farmers, plus the labor unions, plus industry and business, plus perhaps even the parliament, and nowadays (at least in Europe) of course the female constituency, the pacifist constituency, plus the bishops and the generals and a few others—and even maybe the allies in Europe and North America!

To be serious, there is a danger today that political leaders will abandon the tightrope-walking art of conducting political leadership, both internationally and domestically, and replace it by playing to the television-watcher's ears and eyes. This method is of a tempting simplicity. All one has to do is to learn from the ratings and public opinion polls how to be even more sympathetic and congenial with the TV audience next time. In both parts of the alliance, leadership is tending to become the art of courting not only the media but—much more important—the audience.

This creates a new kind of demagoguery that can very well mean the end of leadership. If the electronic media, in particular, have played up Lebanon, then audiences expect one to talk about Lebanon. If they have played up Qadhafi, one has to stand before his audience as though he were willing to launch World War III against Libya.

As a foreign minister, Henry Kissinger did not do this, at least he didn't fall for this kind of temptation to any greater extent than did any of his contemporaries in Europe. In my view, Henry's speech was really a fine example of conscientious leadership by reason rather than by show business tricks.

I will try to resist the temptation to argue with Henry's splendid analysis, perhaps with one or two minor exceptions. The first exception I will mention at once.

In the second part of his talk, Henry dealt with the control of intermediate-range ballistic missiles (IRBMs). This chapter was a masterful piece of hindsight rationalization of the U.S. nonconcept in this field from the end of 1976 through 1983—eight years altogether.

Let me explain. In the first phase, 20 years ago, President John F. Kennedy unilaterally withdrew U.S. IRBMs from European soil, seemingly at the time a *quid pro quo* in the framework of solving the Cuban missile crisis. Being a young man or—as Henry correctly told you—a rather junior participant in the international debate at that time, I did support the Multilateral Force (MLF) proposal in particular because I understood there to be a political danger to Europe from the fact that there existed no counterweight to the Soviet SS-4s, SS-5s, and other IRBMs, all of which were targeted against Western Europe.

The MLF was dropped by President Lyndon Johnson. Afterwards, the second phase of that story lasted for a great number of years. The problem was totally neglected because, in the meantime, the Limited Test Ban, the Nonproliferation Treaty, SALT I, and the ABM Treaty were achieved and the SALT II talks were under way, giving the impression of an ever-growing area of nuclear parity and equilibrium.

The third phase started in early 1977 when President Jimmy Carter abolished the groundwork for SALT II, which he had inherited from President Gerald Ford and Henry Kissinger, in order to try a totally new approach for SALT II and, at the same time, a totally new approach toward the Soviet Union in general.

We Europeans cautioned in vain against such an undertaking. We then asked the U.S. president to include Soviet IRBMs—SS-20s and Backfire bombers—in SALT because we (or at least I) considered them to be of a strategic nature. These weapons threatened my nation with political blackmail and with annihilation, thereby threatening to separate Europe from the United States. By my mentioning this 1977 story, one can see that by then we had already subscribed to the analysis of the political dangers inherent in the unequalled existence of the SS-20s—an analysis that Henry has now given us in January 1984.

But it so happened that in 1977 President Carter refused and Zbigniew Brzezinski boldly told us, or told me, that it was none of my business. Consequently, when Carter met Leonid Brezhnev in Vienna in May 1979, IRBMs, Backfires, and SS-20s were not even mentioned at the negotiation table. This was irritating because the fourth phase had already started, a little before May 1979, and had become manifest in NATO's "double track" decision at the end of that year—in my view still a very sensible decision, if a couple of years too late.

That was followed by a fifth phase or rather by an interlude. Carter asked us to try to help him with the U.S. Senate in order to get the SALT II agreement ratified. The Europeans did try to be helpful during 1980, only to hear from the next president that SALT II was no good at all, and only to understand a little later that, nevertheless, President Reagan had in fact observed SALT II despite his earlier rhetoric.

We then urged him to start negotiations on INF, but it took a long time to get them started. Then came 1982 and 1983. The last part of the story is, I think, still fresh. The actual deployment of U.S. missiles on European soil may not yet be the end of the story.

I have talked about the German side of the coin not in order to complain but in order to arrive at conclusions based on that sequence of contradictory behavior and requests made by the leading country. My general conclusion is that since 1976—not only in the INF but in many fields of dispute with the Soviet Union—there has not been a continuity of aims or plans vis-à-vis the Soviet Union. Nor has there been any consistency of military plans, of posture on arms control diplomacy, or of economic behavior vis-à-vis the Soviet Union.

An embargo on grain was imposed, then lifted 12 months later; then an embargo on pipeline equipment was imposed and lifted again three months later—all without any consultation with European allies. And Henry Kissinger made the true remark that, despite earlier rhetoric by President Reagan and his administration, they have now come around to the middle of the road. This was similar to what happened to President Carter after three years, having entered the international strategic scene from the ideological Left much as his successor later entered it from the ideological Right.

I do blame the Russians for many things, but I find it difficult to blame them when they say that they cannot really read the Americans clearly enough. A couple of days ago, my friend U.S. Secretary of State George Schultz spoke of the U.S. willingness for a thaw—the Stockholm Conference being in the offing. I assume that U.S. intentions are good and clear, but, I ask myself, can the people in the Kremlin see that? And will they believe it?

The NATO double-track philosophy of 1967, drawn up under the chairmanship of Pierre Harmel, was more or less adhered to by the Americans for nine years altogether, until the end of 1976. In contrast, we Europeans wanted to stick to it much longer. In fact, we have never given it up. Leo Tindeman's talk was just one additional example, as was Lord Carrington's speech at the IISS last year. In my view, Peter Carrington's speech was one of the best any of us gave last year. It is still worth reading, especially because he is going to become NATO's secretary general.

Whether under the leadership of Edward Heath, James Callaghan, or Margaret Thatcher, there is quite a bit of continuity in Britain's grand strategy vis-à-vis the Soviet Union. There is a quite striking continuity in Paris from Charles de Gaulle through Georges Pompidou and Valery Giscard d'Estaing to François Mitterrand. The same is true of most West European countries, including my own—at least over the last 17 years—in spite of all the changes in all our countries from conservative to labor and back, from Social Democrats back to Christian Democrats, and so on. The same was also true in Japan until the arrival of Yasuhiro Nakasone, who seems to be trying to increase the degree of Japanese international involvement.

The one great exception is the United States. I am strongly convinced of the necessity for U.S. leadership. I have said this often. I really do believe it. I have urged it time and again. But U.S. leadership in the alliance is possible only if the United States and its people can again fulfill two prerequisites: first, a basic strategic understanding among the political elite in the United States, plus the will to stand up publicly for it and, if necessary, to fight for it, and, second, the will to understand and to take into consideration and discussion the strategic interests and views of the other NATO partners in North America and in Europe, as well as those of Japan.

Otherwise, strategic leadership would be doomed to go under because of the day-to-day processes of muddling through and because of strategic melodies pitched to the public's changing moods. In addition, the leader will be tempted to replace or supplant political leadership with sheer military-like command—taking decisions unilaterally, asking his allies "to please follow suit and please do so within a couple of days." (I could give a number of examples on that.) But if such a thing happens, then afterwards some people will become perplexed and annoyed about the so-called lack of Japanese or European loyalty or about a lack of decisiveness, of courage, or of the will to sacrifice enough financially.

That kind of leadership cannot work. It will not work. It certainly will not lead to a commonly accepted grand strategy for the alliance vis-à-vis the Soviet Union.

This morning I personally accepted Henry Kissinger's reply to Ambassador André de Staerke's question about whether or not it was true that a grand strategy should only be decided in collaboration with and in cooperation among allies. Henry answered that national strategic goals had to be clear first. Only then should one combine and bridge gaps and articulate compromises. I think this is certainly true. For instance, in the case of Germany—a divided nation living on the potential central European battleground—we of course have our own strategic considerations.

In practical terms, both stages have to go hand in hand: to define your strategic interests nationally *and* to combine those and compromise with the strategic interests of one's allies. Any attempt to articulate one's friends and allies may prove to be dangerous.

Let me give just two examples. First, if the present administration in Washington had had the will to understand Europe, and especially European political psychology, it would have avoided letting the "Star Wars" speech give the impression of a desire to end or even to violate the ABM Treaty. It would have avoided infuriating the so-called peace movements in Europe in many speeches and would have avoided supplying them with cheap ammunition for their psycho-propaganda. A second example: If some German politicians had had a better understanding of U.S. psychology, they would have avoided giving the wrong impression of being willing to acquiesce to Soviet pressure.

During the Eisenhower and Kennedy years, and again during the Nixon and Ford years, we Europeans did not feel tempted to make statements like those that one hears from time to time nowadays: "You Americans are just ideologues, but we Europeans are the ones who understand the practical, pragmatic art of maintaining the balance of power and of maintaining peace." Also, during the earlier years we were not told by Washington that we Europeans were just immoral pragmatists and also that the Americans were the real humanists, the legitimate and only courageous fighters for freedom of the individual and human rights.

In those periods, neither side painted other people or states white or black, friend or foe. If containment was and—I am sure—is going to be an important part of the goals of our alliance, then obviously any strategy or any grand strategy must start with analyzing the adversary's posture and capabilities, his interests and goals, his past behavior, his history, and the probabilities of his future behavior or action.

Regarding history, by the way, in reading William Hyland's paper on the Soviet dimension—which is, indeed, a thought-provoking paper—I was struck by the fact that an analysis of Soviet strategy seemed possible without reference to Russian history or Russian national psychology. An attitude, which Hyland's paper ascribes to the Reagan administration, is even being presented that understands Soviet foreign policy, and I quote: "to be a product of the USSR's domestic structure."

In my view, Soviet foreign policy is much more a continuation of Russian history. The Kremlinologists of our days should devote ample time to studying Ivan I, to studying Ivan IV (the "Terrible"), to studying all the Czars who carried the title of "Gatherer of Russian Soil"— which, over the generations, meant first the conquering of other peoples' territories southward to the Caucasus and the Turkish borders, eastward toward Kamchatka, westward to the Baltic and the Vistula and, afterwards, the Russification of the inhabitants.

One should also study the hitherto unended expansionist trend—

Peter the Great and the Czars until 1914—in order to understand Russia's inherent strategic trends. Of course, they should also study Russia under Lenin, Stalin, and later on, and also, of course, Sino-Russian relations during the last 100 years and Russo-Japanese relations (not just after World War II).

In my view, today's Russian strategy is 75 percent Russian and only 25 percent communist. The attempt to spread communism all over the world seems to me much more an instrument of Russian strategy than an ultimate goal.

One also ought to study the history, for instance, of Russian-German relations. If in his paper Mr. Hyland mentions my country only in the context of the appalling vision of containment by neutralization of Germany, he should also have said that there is Russian anxiety over Germany. In fact, there are three main Russian anxieties: Germany, the United States of America, and China.

One has to study the Russians' perennial persecution complex—their obvious security concern, which, for instance, makes their Afghanistan border seem secure only if there are Russian soldiers on both sides of that border. One has to study their equality complex—and the list of the dangerous anxieties and complexes may not even be complete as yet. For instance, the zest for equality with the West can be detected in Peter the Great as much as in Khrushchev's talk at the United Nations only 20 years ago.

One should also read less of Marx and Lenin and more of Dostoyevsky, Pushkin, Leskov, Tolstoi, Solzhenitsyn, and so on in order to understand at least one basic fact: that the Russians have always been willing—and, in my view, will continue to be willing—to rally behind the czars or the Kremlin if they thought or were made to believe that Mother Russia was being endangered.

In defending Mother Russia, they have an unequaled capacity to suffer. Sometimes one even gets the impression that they have a passion for suffering. It is because of this latter fact that all those quixotic or exotic ideas of economic warfare against the Soviet Union, or of a full-scale arms race in order to strangle them economically, are, in my judgment, grossly invalid. In such cases, Russians would be told that the West is after them, that they must not permit the fight to be lost, that therefore they need to tighten their belts further—and they will do it. Most of them didn't like Stalin at all, but they fought on against Hitler despite the loss of the lives of 20 million Russians, because they were not only made to believe, but they knew as a fact, that Mother Russia was in deep danger.

In studying Russian psychology, one will also find that the people are afraid of war; they are a peace-loving people. They ought to be shown—by our modern electronic media—that we are a peace-loving people too. Or let us show them what one could gain by economic cooperation, as has been put before us in Richard Davy's excellent paper.

Despite my living only 30 minutes away by car from the Iron Curtain (for a Soviet tank it might be 45 minutes, not more) and despite the fact that I live just five minutes flight time away from the airfields of their fighter bombers, I have never felt any military inferiority complex vis-à-vis their enormous military power. Among other reasons, I am not afraid because I know how highly Marshals Ogarkov and Ustinov judge Germany's conventional forces, which in the case of mobilization would number more than 1.2 million soldiers within a couple of days—all of them fully trained, because we have maintained the draft and national service for almost 30 years.

By the way, he who complains about an alleged lack of will for sacrifice (in my country, for instance) should understand that the Germans accept that their homes are to be the main battleground in all NATO's plans. Imagine asking this from the people in Idaho or in the states of New York or California or Texas or in England or France. The Germans have also agreed to play host to five or six armies on their soil, all of which are under foreign command, all on territory roughly as big as that of the state of Oregon, but with 60 million inhabitants compared with the 2.5 million in Oregon. There also are 5,000 nuclear warheads. On top of that we have the draft.

I do share the view in Robert Komer's paper that an initial conventional defense should be able to hold for weeks rather than for days. I think he is right that such a capability would highly enhance deterrence. I also think that General Franz-Joseph Schulze's paper is correct when, at the end, it says:

Improved conventional capabilities could enable NATO nations to react in a crisis generated by the apparent threat of aggression in a manner that neither undermines the firmness of its own governments and peoples nor provokes a resort to war by others. Our present dependence on possible early use of nuclear weapons threatens to undermine the two purposes of our alliance: namely the credibility of the deterrence of the adversary and effective reassurance of our own people.

There already exists a tangible, voluminous, and potent conventional capability. In my view, our conventional capabilities are very underrated and underestimated. We clearly need more conventional ammunition; we clearly need more conventional close ground support from tactical aircraft. But much of that could be provided over time by shifting aircraft from dual capability to conventional tasks and by using money that is now spent on nuclear ammunition for conventional ammunition.

It is a mistaken idea that wars are won by making budgets and by spending money. Of course you need some money. But if you want to show a potential aggressor that you are able to defend yourself in actual warfare, the first thing you need to have is soldiers—men in uniform.

Second on my list of priorities is motivating one's soldiers—assuring that they know that they are fighting for the right cause and have a probability of being successful. Third is military skill and training, and fourth is the education of the military—from noncommissioned officers on up to the top commanding officers of divisions and army corps—to make decisions when they are on their own and not wait for commands from higher up. Only on the last line of my order of priorities does one come to budget—of course it takes money to buy aircraft and ammunition and tanks.

In my view, military posture and plans have to serve the same goals as arms control and diplomacy. They have to serve the same grand strategy as well.

I want to stress my conviction that today's economic mess is now a greater danger to the coherence and political stability of our alliance than is the Soviet threat. This may change again in the near future. But I am deeply worried about the fact that, right now, the American public seems to believe that the world is in for a general economic upswing. This is not true. This is an impression that Americans extrapolate from what they experience inside the United States. It is not true in any place in Europe. Instead, we have growing unemployment.

Let me add an economic commonplace: In the medium term, economic growth depends on investment in fixed capital. But as long as real interest rates are many times higher than real growth, then the latter cannot be stimulated and will not happen. Investment in fixed capital will be creeping and staggering and therefore—given the fact that all the European industrial countries are geared to produce investment goods—unemployment will grow.

Keynesianism in one country may seem to be a good thing, even or especially so if you call it "supply side economics." It shows that Keynes was a genius. If a country spends $200 billion more than it earns per year, this has to have some effect on its economy and employment figures.

The United States is not truly following Keynes, because he thought the money was to be printed. The United States does not print the money any longer—and I praise Paul Volcker for that—it simply imports it. The richest economy in the world has now become the greatest importer of capital.

Americans may live with that. But the reason behind it is a real interest rate that the world has not seen since the birth of Christ—especially not in the middle of a depression, which is what we have in South America, in great parts of Asia, and to some degree in a number of regions of Europe: Northern France, the Borinage, the Ruhr Valley, and Middle England, all old smokestack industrial areas. And it may spread. One has to find a remedy for the cause of these high U.S. interest rates, which is the deficit.

I would like to point out to American friends that the wise people who initiated the North Atlantic Treaty did foresee such a situation and stated in Article Two of that treaty that NATO members will try to abandon contradictions in their international economic policies and enhance cooperation among all members.

The present rather egoistic budgetary policies of by far the biggest economy in the alliance are certainly a danger to the future cohesion of the alliance; they are certainly an offense against the spirit of the North Atlantic Treaty.

In order not to be misunderstood, let me give one assurance: I speak as a great friend of the United States and as a man who knows that the security of Europe and others outside Europe—including Japan—hinges on the United States and depends on U.S. leadership. I speak as a man who is a great friend of the United States who admires the country for its vitality and generosity.

An American Perspective on NATO Leadership

James R. Schlesinger

For some 25 years, I have been a NATO buff. During the troubled 1970s I worked long and hard to sustain our involvement in NATO. I mention these credentials at the outset. Everybody ought to make clear his credentials—whether they be professedly pro-American, before a tirade, or pro-NATO, before a disquieting analysis.

The organizers of this conference have achieved some novelty, in that the conference has, indeed, turned out to be different. The difference comes in the breaking of the normal routine—in Chancellor Schmidt's oration of last evening. This is not the first time that the chancellor has uttered some of his views, but it was the first time to my knowledge that he has gathered all of them together in a single speech of one hour, appropriately titled, I believe, the *Summa Contra Americanos*.

Many of us would have agreed with much of the substance of his remarks. But the tone was plain wrong—especially for American ears and sensibilities. As a consequence, I feel that he significantly detracted from the effect of those substantive comments (for which, incidentally, he has had an enthusiastic American audience) by creating, even in some surprising quarters, sympathy for both President Carter and President Reagan. If the means employed to effect a change in American opinion and policy is simultaneously to alienate the supporters of Jimmy Carter and Ronald Reagan, one inevitably will have a shrinking audience.

Last night we were informed that *above all* Marshal Ogarkov and Marshal Ustinov were impressed by the 1.2 million men that West Germany could put in the field. I think indeed that they are impressed by this mobilization capability. They would, however, be far more impressed if those forces were effectively equipped. But however impressed they might be, I still doubt that they will regard West Germany's contingent as decisive. For the Soviets the critical element is and will remain the role of the United States, the other superpower.

So, lest we be too readily swept away, I think it is important to express a few home truths. No less than the intra-alliance trade in weapons, candor also should be a two-way street. Let me deal with these home truths in two areas—first on the issue of the budget and military capabilities, and then on the nature of U.S. foreign policy.

Military Spending and Capabilities

The numbers that I will present now are not symbolic numbers—as in "Soviet foreign policy is roughly 75 percent Russian, 25 percent Communist"; they are real numbers. U.S. defense spending now exceeds 7 percent of the U.S. gross national product (GNP). By contrast, laying aside subsidies to Berlin, support for the border guards, and the like, the share of the German GNP allocated to the Ministry of Defense has shrunk over the decades and is now some 2.5 percent. If the United States allocated to its Department of Defense the same share of GNP that the Federal Republic allocates to its Ministry of Defense, U.S. federal spending would shrink by an amount approaching $200 billion a year.

I mention that number with a certain low cunning. Some of you will have already discerned that, were we to follow the German example in regard to defense spending, it would virtually eliminate the federal deficit. A decline in U.S. deficits would no doubt bring down interest rates, both real and nominal. However, under this hypothetical situation of such a reduction in defense spending, I do not know whether the capital flow to the United States (which so rightly concerns Chancellor Schmidt) would diminish simply because interest rates had declined, or whether the capital flow would increase because of the more desperate search for a safe haven.

U.S. defense spending this year will exceed $240 billion. That is 12-fold the comparable spending by our larger European allies—a little less in the case of the United Kingdom, which rivals the United States with regard to the share of GNP going to the military establishment. Yet, it is almost 15 times German military spending, at the current rate of exchange.

Upon what is all this money being spent? I must now go into a subject once characterized by Helmut Schmidt as the alliance "division of labor." Thus I shall discuss certain burdens that the United States bears alone, or virtually alone, on behalf of the alliance. The United States bears virtually all of the intelligence and reconnaissance costs of this alliance, including space satellites. None of our allies is required to make these expenditures that alone, at the current exchange rate, would equal half of the German defense budget.

Whether or not one agrees with recent American comments regarding maritime strategy, the United States maintains what is known as a "blue water navy." That naval force bears a global responsibility in behalf of this alliance. Sometimes its role may be unwelcome to Europeans, as in the case of Grenada, but clearly it is welcome in establishing a deterrent in the Persian Gulf—from which Western Europe and Japan obtain the energy resources needed to sustain their economies. The United States does this not because it is dependent on the Persian Gulf, but because it alone in the alliance has the necessary mobile forces. Navies do not come cheap. The cost of the U.S. Navy alone is more than four times German defense spending. Since World War II Germany itself has not been required to maintain anything on the order of a blue water navy—only a coastal defense force.

The United States also bears the cost of 97 percent of the total nuclear capabilities of the alliance—the backbone, incidentally, of alliance strategy. In addition to these burdens, it continues its deployments to supplement regional military forces in Korea and in Western Europe, operating 7,000 miles and 3,000 miles respectively from the United States. That deployment, which the United States has sustained for almost 40 years, remains indispensable to the security of Western Europe, because, in this era, the European nations by themselves cannot deter the Warsaw Pact powers—without the stiffening presence of the only superpower available to the Western European democracies, the United States.

To sustain these distant deployments imposes upon the United States special problems of manpower rotation and also serious logistical problems. Both involve additional costs. The United States pre-positions both equipment and supplies. Indeed we are now going up to six division-sets pre-positioned in Europe. That implies redundancy and extra cost. The United States also must maintain the airlift and sealift capabilities to move its forces, which perforce must operate far from the U.S. shores. In sum, the United States is obliged to sustain a very complex and costly set of military responsibilities and requirements. By contrast, the Federal Republic of Germany has been asked to perform one simple task—to provide a stalwart conventional capability in the heart of Europe. That straightforward task lends itself to economy in resources. I trust that enough has been said to make clear that comparative effort cannot appropriately be measured by manpower contributions on the Central Front of NATO.

Last night there was a good deal of talk that featured manpower comparisons. So let me say this: When the portion of population under arms in the German armed forces reaches the level that the United States achieves under the all-volunteer force, criticism by German leaders of the lack of the draft will seem less captious and rhetorical.

To be sure, I have always been a supporter of the draft. Along with Colonel Alexander Haig, then with the NSC, I helped make in the spring of 1970 the last pitch to the administration not to go over to the all-volunteer force. We were told, firmly, by Richard Nixon, to desist. That battle was lost then. The draft was abolished in the Nixon administration and then subsequently the Selective Service System was unwisely abolished in the Ford administration. (I might say parenthetically that I do not recall any great applause from Bonn for Jimmy Carter when he attempted to restore the system of registration.) I continue, now as then, to support restoration of the draft. So, incidentally, does Richard Nixon. But the draft is a technical matter only tangentially related to the defense of Europe. It is not an appropriate basis for denigrating the American defense effort.

Regarding the distribution of effort within the alliance, we have regularly indulged in something of a fiction in dealing with Congress, perhaps most notably during the period of the Mansfield amendment— I myself have participated in that fiction. Some on the Hill might even call it a confidence game, but I call it putting the best face on things. We have had a regular refrain: "as SACEUR has pointed out, our NATO allies provide 40 percent of the ships, 50 percent of the aircraft, and 90 percent of the manpower of the alliance." That statement sounded good. It was *intended* to sound good—and deflect congressional criticism of the European effort. But there were severe problems with it.

First, the statement dealt only with those forces that were earmarked to the principal NATO commanders. It thus excluded the greater part of the U.S. military establishment not formally committed to NATO, but clearly related to the defense of Europe. Much of it has as a priority the reinforcement of NATO.

Second, the statement simply ignores critical differences in complexity and quality. A $3 billion carrier (if it were earmarked) is the equivalent of a World War II destroyer, one-fortieth its size. Perhaps this is most dramatically indicated with respect to tactical air capabilities. The U.S. Air Force now includes some 26 tactical air wings of high quality, most not formally committed to NATO, but slated for its reinforcement. Bear this in mind when you hear assertions about the Warsaw Pact having air superiority—for such "analyses" ignore quality and involve only the earmarked forces. Even for the earmarked forces alone, the quality of U.S. aircraft over Soviet aircraft is probably best indicated by the performance of U.S.-supplied F-15s and F-16s over Soviet-supplied MiGs—in the 1982 Mideast War—with 102 MiGs downed and zero Israeli losses. (That suggests one should remain skeptical regarding the numbers game sometimes played by NATO intelligence.)

Third, such arguments ignore what the relative defense efforts *should* be. For example, in relation to GNP, German defense spending has fallen since the days of Konrad Adenauer. The relatively light burden of the German defense effort is sometimes disguised—either by making attacks on the Americans for not having the draft or by pointing out that German defense spending has grown by higher percentages in recent years. Starting from so low a base means that percentage increases do not reveal the national effort involved.

Candor, as I have said, requires a two-way street. The GNP of the Federal Republic of Germany is half that of the Soviet Union. The Soviet Union has the full range of capabilities as does the United States—including a blue water navy, intelligence and reconnaissance, and a massive nuclear capability—even larger in volume and in cost than that of the United States—plus an air defense system. If one lays aside those components of military forces, a nation with a GNP 50 percent that of the Soviet Union should be doing more in providing that stalwart conventional capability in the heart of Europe that is the only military responsibility assigned to the Federal Republic.

If one recalls the narrow range of German capabilities and responsibilities, one is nevertheless surprised to discover that the German defense budget, remembering that its GNP is 50 percent of the Soviet level, is roughly 5 percent of the dollar estimate of Soviet defense spending—5 percent! German production of military equipment— even in that narrower range in which they compete with the Soviets— has been running roughly 8 percent of the Soviet level. There is no reason why German forces themselves, *including the reserves,* should not now be fully equipped.

Last night we heard about the 1.2 million men that the Germans can put in the field. Fine! They should be equipped. If they are not appropriately equipped, they become part of an equivalent of Mao's People's War. I do not think that People's War is the model that the Federal Republic wishes to follow.

These are, to be sure, not the things I said to the Congress when I was secretary of defense. I state them to you now, because I fear that European irritation with the United States may have led to a lost sense regarding what the respective roles have been and should be. I have singled out the German defense effort—not because it is less effective in producing military forces than other nations, but more effective. I single it out also because of Chancellor Schmidt's comments last night and during his years in office. While high in quality, the German defense remains, nonetheless, surprisingly limited. It is not properly the basis of invidious assertions about the American defense effort.

A European commentator should therefore be careful in talking about relative performance. Since World War II, the United States has willingly taken on responsibility for the protection of Europe because, in the immediate postwar period, there was no one else to do it, and the United States could do it easily, given its vast superiority in nuclear weapons. Now, however, the balance is much closer. There is much work for all to do. If the deterrent is to be made more effective in this era, it will require a much larger European effort. Sniping at the Americans will not solve the problem.

The American Style in Foreign Policy

Let me turn to the other aspect of the American nation that I wanted to discuss—its instincts in foreign policy. We heard last night that it is crucially important for Americans to read the history of Russia. (Though the voice may be that of the former chancellor, the words are those of Egon Bahr.) But if we are all to read the history of one superpower, we should all, I believe, also be prepared to read the history of the other superpower. It might be illuminating.

The American nation is quite different in its underlying assumptions about foreign policy from all the nations of Europe. In the first place, it has no dynastic past. It shed its dynastic past at the time of the American Revolution. Subsequently it was warned by the "Father of His Country" against "entangling alliances"—reflecting his concern (and experience) that America might be too readily caught in the caldron of ideological, national, and dynastic ambitions that was Europe. Indeed, as we have observed the two European civil wars of this century from our own distant shores, Washington's disdain for Europe's dynastic past and national tensions may not seem wholly without validity.

On the old Continent, reflecting Europe's dynastic past subsequently transformed into modern nationalism, a political calculus developed embracing such concepts as *Realpolitic* or *raison d'état*. This is foreign to the beliefs of the American people—although you will find a smattering of Washington officials, journalists, college professors, and the like, who can talk in terms of European *Realpolitik*. These last are frequently the most welcomed visitors to Europe.

The United States is largely a romantic country. It has encountered little opposition and does not think in terms of moves and countermoves in a never-ending game. It sees no reason that it can't accomplish its presumably formidable objectives. Its history is marked by a belief in Manifest Destiny—abetted by a Puritan past in which the American nation was foreordained to be a Beacon unto the World. In order, therefore, to understand American policy, one should not simply go through a careful calculation of the national interest. However important such a calculation may be to officials of the Department of State, it would acquire little visceral support among the American people.

As a result of that Puritan missionary zeal, political eruptions occur in the United States that are somewhat confusing in Europe. One such example was called Wilsonianism in which the United States stepped forward to make the World Safe for Democracy—a commitment that has not as yet been entirely lived up to. Carterism—especially in its emphasis on human rights—was a later version of Wilsonianism. Whether or not it reflected a grasp of *Realpolitik*, it was close to the fundamental spirit of the country. That can be confirmed by that master politician, Franklin Roosevelt, who very astutely manipulated these underlying beliefs of the American people to achieve what he regarded as the national interest.

The Puritan impulse helps to explain why, as Henry Kissinger mentioned yesterday, there is an American tendency to try to innovate every four years. The Puritan impulse—an atavism if you will—may not be enormously helpful in the formulation of policies designed to achieve the national interest. But no one should fail to understand the large role that it has played in the past and continues to play in the deployment of American forces in Europe. That deployment ultimately is driven more by a sense of mission than by a calculation of the national interest.

I shall give you a small anecdote along these lines. Some years ago, I devoted almost six months achieving what was regarded at the time as unachievable—defeating the Mansfield amendment on the floor of the U.S. Senate. That vote rather surprised the majority leader, who discovered that he had lost only after it was too late.

Some weeks later, as I basked in a new complacency, I got some intelligence from one of my liaison people that the chairman of the Senate Appropriations Committee, John McClellan, was on the warpath. It was reported that he intended to remove our forces from Europe, which the Appropriations Committee can do by the simple act of writing legislation that "no monies appropriated under this Act shall be used to sustain American forces in Europe." I immediately went up to see the old chairman—of whom I was immensely fond. He was then 81 or 82 years of age. He was not a figure likely to be understood by Europeans. He had grown up, a hard-shell Presbyterian, in a small town in Arkansas. Although I had frequently urged him to come over to NATO, he had never done so. He was one of those Americans that, as Chancellor Schmidt suggested last evening, did not have much experience in Europe. Nonetheless, he had steadily supported spending 2 or 3 percent of the U.S. GNP on the protection of Europe, though he himself had never been there.

McClellan quickly and bluntly got to the point. He indicated that he was tired of the Europeans. I asked him why. He had heard of this fellow De Gaulle who had thrown us out of Paris. I confessed that indeed had happened, though it had occurred some six years earlier. I pressed the case that, whatever the misbehavior of the French, whatever the tenets of De Gaulle's policy, the United States had an obligation to the other peoples of Europe—to Germany above all, simply because of our responsibilities that flowed initially from the occupation, and to the Dutch, to the Danes, to the Belgians, to the Norwegians, and to others. The old gentleman responded to that argument. He finally relented and agreed not to press his amendment. Then he said, "You told me you were going over to NATO tomorrow." I responded, "Yes, sir"—and once again I encouraged him to come. He said, "Tell them for me: they're just a bunch of damned ingrates."

I did not deliver that message at that time. I cite that experience today because McClellan's attitude is the quintessential American attitude: such things as sympathy or gratitude are more important than reasons of state. American support for Europe does not reflect any precise calculation of the national interest. Otherwise why would we spend 7 percent of GNP to help defend those whose own estimate of the value of their security apparently was only, say, 3 percent of their GNP? Americans support Europe out of a sense of moral obligation.

Europeans are, in the view of Americans, good people; thus, they are *deserving* of our protection. That protection does not arise out of a sense of *Realpolitik*. Michel Jobert, one of Jean François Poncet's predecessors, said some years ago, in private, that the Americans have so clear a national interest in remaining in Europe that they *must* stay here whatever Europeans do. You can abuse them, you can insult them, and, because of the compulsion of that national interest, they must remain.

We have had other examples of Jobert's belief, both antagonistic and benign, but it reflects a fundamental misconception regarding the forces that move the American democracy. In the American democracy, no expert opinion, no government bureaucracy, no East Coast establishment would be able to maintain forces in Europe—unless the American public believes that *it is right*.

As I suggested earlier, we may be a strange nation given to romanticism in foreign policy, but our missionary zeal has served Western Europe and other countries well since the close of World War II. Some of that zeal, no doubt, is based upon the simple desire to defang the Communists, but much of it is based upon the belief that America has that pressing international obligation.

In the long sweep of American history, if one observes the cycle of American international involvement, it swings suddenly from isolation to overcommitment and then back again. So, in simple terms of European *Realpolitik,* in terms of a true appreciation of the national interests in Europe, I think that a better understanding of its American protector is required. It is a vital interest for Europe to keep the Americans committed. That implies understanding American attitudes and motives, not just assuming they are (or should be) the same as those in Europe.

Problems in NATO

Let me turn now to some concrete issues facing the alliance. At this conference we have, as usual, talked about whether or not there is a crisis in NATO. That crisis cannot be primarily military for the military balance is not changing that rapidly. It is a real problem in NATO that, from time to time, we have the heralding of false crises. To be sure, we have had some real crises in the past—the Skybolt episode, the Suez crisis, and the expulsion of NATO from Paris—but we have also had false crises.

The death of nuclear deterrence, announced here in Brussels at a CSIS meeting in 1979, is announced with greater frequency than is the death of God. It is about as relevant. The root issue regarding nuclear deterrence is not whether Europeans can have 100 percent confidence that the Americans will exchange New York for Hamburg, or New York for Paris. If there is a 20 percent chance or a 30 percent probability or a 50 percent probability—something less than 100 percent— what calculations must go on in the minds of the leaders of the Kremlin? Clearly they are not going to move. Nuclear deterrence, though diminished, is alive and well.

Perhaps the crisis is one of too many announced crises. I can recall, from the early days of NATO, an air force colonel who kept on his desk a rubber stamp that said: "In this perilous moment in the history of the alliance. . . ." He used that stamp with great frequency. Although the kind of discontent currently within the alliance is not unique, I believe it to be different—qualitatively different. Today there is a degree of mutual disenchantment. There are a number of reasons for their mutual disenchantment. They have been well stated by the panel on public opinion. Both Elizabeth Noelle-Neumann and John Rielly have provided excellent papers, which go much more to the heart of the alliance problems than does the Pershing missile deployment.

There is the American discovery, a little belated, that for some reason or other—one difficult to discern in the eyes of Americans— Europeans take European security less seriously than Americans have taken European security. The Americans have been coming over here since the demise of massive retaliation arguing that, if we wish a high-confidence deterrent, it is essential to have a stalwart conventional capability. That has been stated repeatedly by various secretaries of defense. Yet not all that much has happened—even though the ideological resistance to strengthened conventional forces, in the name of preserving nuclear deterrence, has now happily disappeared.

Americans must come to understand that the modesty of the response is not due to Europeans failing to hear the message. Americans keep on proselytizing for strengthened forces—like the American visiting Paris who seems to believe that, if he repeats his message frequently enough in English to the French waiter, ultimately the fellow will understand. Something of that sort has gone on with regard to these issues of European defense. It is not that the Europeans have failed to understand; they have understood quite well both the message and its implications. They differ from the Americans, however, regarding the nature and gravity of the Soviet threat. (As a matter of fact, I myself believe that the Europeans are probably a bit more accurate in their assessment of the Soviet threat than are the Americans.) Perhaps more important, the Europeans are sufficiently satisfied with a low-confidence deterrent that they do not want to put up significantly more resources to raise the confidence level. Meanwhile, the Americans, misunderstanding the problem, go on preaching the gospel of a high-confidence deterrent.

Increasingly the question of who is bearing the burden is the source of disenchantment in the United States. The resentment applies even more strongly in the case of Japan. The present U.S. recovery is masking a political problem, perhaps most starkly revealed by the U.S. $100 billion trade deficit. That is scarcely an insignificant sum even by U.S. standards. Somewhere down the road it will, almost inevitably, bounce back on the Japanese. For the American public the simple question is: why should the United States encourage import flows at the expense of U.S. jobs from a nation that is putting up less than 1 percent of its own GNP for defense?

Increasing irritation with out allies occurs far less in the American elites than in the general public. On the political Right, this exasperation has led to global unilateralism—whatever in God's name that may mean. It has no logical underpinning; it simply reflects a frustration on the Right that U.S. policy must be circumscribed by the attitudes of its allies—a simple fact of life if we will only recognize it. On the political Left, this irritation has led to renewed doubts about the military budget—increasing doubts, which are reflected in the Rielly paper.

At the same time the Europeans have discovered that the great Sir Galahad of the West has weaknesses that were not discerned during those early days after World War II—weaknesses in a political system that was designed in the eighteenth century and has something called the "separation of powers," which means the dispersion of power. Europeans have discovered that the great protector indeed has feet of clay. This is clearly reflected in the opinion surveys with the decline of European admiration—to put it euphemistically—for the United States. Over the course of the last decade, any visitor from the United States has been amply, if painfully, reminded of that decline.

This new understanding of the defects of the U.S. political system is reinforced by the "outsider syndrome." Since the disenchantment with Washington that came with the Watergate affair, the American people have elected as president men whose principal virtue has been that they have never been contaminated by any experience in foreign policy. Europeans, quite understandably, have been irritated by what appeared to be the erratic weakness of Jimmy Carter, and they have been almost equally irritated by what appeared to be the erratic strength of President Reagan.

This erratic quality, which flows partly from the dispersion of power and partly from the outsider problem, has led to European doubts about U.S. political wisdom—doubts that regrettably have been thoroughly justified. Indeed, they have become increasingly justified as the power of the United States has fallen—for the Free World has become even more dependent upon the wisdom and judiciousness of U.S. policy. In this very period in which we need wiser and steadier policy, we have become more erratic.

What Is to Be Done

This is the background to the present discontent within the alliance. All these issues have been discussed in various panels. The question is: What should we now do? Let me say, picking up a few comments from the panels, that the old formulas won't do. The legitimacy of the postwar dispensation is under challenge. There is a ferment out there. That ferment reflects far more than the gender gap that we discussed this morning. The American people, who began to doubt whether it was necessary to destroy villages in Vietnam in order to save them, have now developed a few inhibitions about an all-out nuclear strategy—when the other fellow can respond. And we cannot, "Star Wars" or otherwise, take away that capability of the Soviets to respond. The Catholic bishops have now weighed in. There is a problem that the youth, particularly in Europe, do not share the old views—referred to rather disarmingly as the problem of the successor generation.

Thus, there is this ferment out there. There is the peace problem. We do not need old answers to new problems.

In addition, Soviet propaganda has become more subtle and effective. No longer is it the old, clumsy *apparatchiks* dropping in from time to time in their blundering way. The new breed is better groomed and more ingratiating. They arrive at the UN or in Western Europe (notably in Germany) and, in contrast to their predecessors, are utterly charming. Soviet propaganda has become more impressive. As we talked about Eastern Europe in one of the panels, somebody quite rightly observed that the West needs differentiation in its policies toward the East—rather than impose uniform punishment on those who have had the misfortune to be victims of Soviet rule.

For at the same time, the Soviet Union is engaged in a reassessment of its own Western policy *(Westpolitik)* and is differentiating among the Western nations with some care. Most significantly, it has focused a major effort on West Germany, which in Soviet eyes has now undergone a conversion from the West German revanchism of old to a state of potential reasonableness—unlike some others in the Western alliance.

From this follows a very simple conclusion. Given the greater subtlety of Soviet propaganda, preserving alliance cohesion has now become the predominant goal. It is even more important than the deployment of Pershing missiles or whether or not the Europeans really achieve the 3 percent real growth in defense spending to which they have committed themselves. Therefore, all of our public comments should be carefully gauged according to the realization that the fundamental defense of Western freedom lies in preserving the cohesion of the alliance. I am not one to underestimate the need for strong military forces. If, however, in the (possibly fruitless) quest for such forces, we break up the minimal consensus necessary in the alliance, we will have done ourselves more political damage than we will have achieved military benefit.

This points to something that the Reagan administration must accept—indeed all administrations must accept. From time to time Americans have been annoyed to discover that, for some reason or other, Europeans do not wish to see the Cold War resumed in the heart of Europe—just because the Russians dispatched military forces into a country (Afghanistan in 1979) that they had politically taken over a year earlier—or because of conflicts in the Caribbean, Central America, the Horn of Africa or wherever. A gratuitous spillover of Third World struggles into Europe is unacceptable to the Europeans—and Americans simply have to accept this reality.

Europeans, whatever the Americans tell them, are also not going to end their contacts with East Germany or Eastern Europe. Indeed, the ferment in Eastern Europe is one of the new realities we are obliged to take into account. If the United States continues to press Europe that détente must be either indivisible or invisible, the Europeans will shrug off these pressures—and conclude that the Americans are unwise and dangerous. We Americans will have to accept the fact of differential détente—because *nobody* in Europe is going to accept the premise that, because of what is going on in El Salvador or Nicaragua, the Cold War should be returned here in the heart of Europe.

Our ideologues won't like it. Sometimes our realists won't like it. But it is a fact of life within the alliance.

Let me turn back to the issues of arms control and alliance arms policy. Europeans generally believe in arms control more fervently than do most Americans. Nonetheless, to ridicule arms control—as in 1980-1981—whatever the intellectual merits may be, will surely undermine the cohesion of the alliance.

In an era in which the problem is conventional forces, this alliance will not flourish militarily unless the Europeans are prepared to take the lead—including the financial burden. If the Europeans are willing to settle for a low-confidence deterrent, no amount of hectoring from the United States will lead them to spend the vast sums needed to achieve a high-confidence deterrent. Hectoring will pay few dividends, but it will serve to weaken the alliance.

Europeans may be willing to settle for a lower-confidence deterrent than the Americans urge upon them, yet it is primarily the Europeans who would have to pay to raise the confidence level in the deterrent. And there is a good deal of vocal support for improving the conventional forces. Many now believe that they have seen the light—and the light is that nuclear warfare is no fun! (No more than did Horatio should we require a ghost come from the grave to tell us that, my Lord!) All have seen the light, and, therefore, there is a good deal of superficial babble about the need to get rid of nuclear deterrence. "No first use" is a rational though pernicious version of that desire.

In my judgment, we should have a full-fledged conventional deterrent. I myself have been making this plea for some 25 years. Yet, over the course of those years, I have lost confidence in the probable success of that plea. Moreover, the economic environment that must sustain such increased defense expenditures has deteriorated with the continuing recession in Europe. And even the political base has to some extent deteriorated. The belief that we are actually going to create a stalwart, all-out, full conventional capability is, I fear, akin to Samuel Johnson's definition of second marriage: the triumph of hope over experience.

Cross-Atlantic Sniping

These, for better or worse, are the realities. I must say that sniping back and forth across the Atlantic is unlikely to help very much. We have a changed situation. We have new challenges. We should seek to understand them. We should not spend so much time using each other's weaknesses as a justification for doing less. That is the easy and fatal way out—but more quickly fatal for Western Europe than for the United States.

Yet we have had a good deal of needless sniping. Last night I listened to Helmut Schmidt with some perplexity. For two years during the SALT II negotiations, I fought to keep out of the negotiations the so-called forward-based systems—the American nuclear deployments in Europe. I did it because it was the right policy—but also at the urging of most Europeans. For in that period, the Europeans would go wild at the notion that theater nuclear weapons should be lumped together with strategic weapons. Imagine my amazement last evening to discover the historical anomaly that Jimmy Carter was being chided for *not* including theater weapons in the SALT II discussions when he took over as president. In short, Jimmy Carter was damned for following the advice steadily offered by Europe for six years.

We have observed similar inconsistencies on economic issues. When one came to the Continent some years ago, German bankers were prominent in offering advice. Americans were told quite firmly that they *must* fight inflation. They must bring to an end this steady rise in the price level. "Think of our experiences of 1923—and beware! You're on a dangerous slope; you must do whatever you can." Yet, when interest rates were put up to fight inflation, we received entirely different advice, which came down to: "the results of fighting inflation are unacceptable to us."

Some years ago, U.S. Treasury Secretary Michael Blumenthal said: "Let the free market work; let the dollar find its own level." He was immediately accused of talking the dollar down, which I take to be an offense. Nonetheless, as the dollar has risen in recent years, we have had numerous examples of doing precisely what Blumenthal was then accused of doing: many attempts, though this time abroad, to talk the dollar down.

There is a problem here of "crying wolf" too often. I realize that the great power in an alliance inevitably will be criticized more than the lesser powers. Yet, this kind of sniping back and forth—and we've had some illustrations here of late—will not help with the long-term goal of sustaining freedom. Sustaining freedom is more important to all of us—including to those of us from Europe—than is the dubious pleasure of scoring points off the American democracy.

Today I have provided, not a summary of the panels, but, instead, an American perspective. With respect to Europe's defense we must follow Europe's lead. Above all, however, all of us—in Europe and North America—must work to avoid divisive issues and to maintain alliance cohesion. The preservation of this alliance of democracies, unique in the world's history, is the fundamental political goal for all of us—for those who value security and for those who value freedom.

Social Change and the Defense of the West   *Michael Howard*

I

In the nineteenth century, Western society entered one of the greatest transitions in the history of mankind. For a thousand years its economy had been predominantly agrarian. Now it became increasingly industrial; and with the change in the means of production, as Marx was not alone in observing, there came a fundamental shift in societal values. One of the questions which particularly interested social and political thinkers throughout the century was whether industrial societies would be any less prone to warfare than their feudally structured predecessors. Liberal sociologists such as Auguste Comte suggested that industrialization would bring about an end to war altogether. War, they maintained, had been an activity peculiar to feudal, agrarian civilizations and their nomadic predecessors. In the new industrial age it would serve no purpose. The new social structures and patterns of behavior would not accommodate themselves to it as an institution; so inevitably it would disappear. And what these liberal thinkers hoped, conservative leaders feared. Throughout Western Europe, the spread of bourgeois pacifism and materialism created, among military men, something like horror. War indeed was to be welcomed as an antidote to it. In Imperial Germany, the army did its best to confine recruitment to the reliable inhabitants of country districts, regarding the cities of the Rhineland and the Ruhr as hotbeds of pacifism and socialism. In Britain, Edwardian statesmen were appalled by the physical unfitness of recruits from the urban slums and wondered how "a street-bred people" could endure in the struggle for national survival which, in that era of Social Darwinism, seemed increasingly probable. Whether with pleasure or apprehension, the view was widely held that the products of industrial societies would be neither able nor willing to fight.

But able and willing they were, and fight they did. When war came in 1914, the city-bred peoples of Western Europe showed no lack of capacity to adjust to it. Units raised from urban areas—in Britain from the industrialized Midlands, in Germany from Silesia and the Ruhr—fought as courageously and perhaps rather more skillfully than did those from such traditional military areas as the West Country or the Mark Brandenburg. Furthermore, without the organizational and technical skill of the bourgeois entrepreneurial classes, once the military leadership could bring itself to make use of it, the war could never have been sustained at all. Finally, the morale of the "street-bred people" on both sides remained heroically staunch through five terrible years. It was in the backward, still largely agrarian Russian Empire that revolution came, not in the highly industrialized West. And the experience of the Second World War was to provide yet stronger evidence of the capacity of industrialized societies to endure the most terrible of hardships and ordeals and still provide loyal and efficient armed forces.

Why did Comte and his followers prove so wrong? Why did industrial societies prove quite as apt at warfare as their agrarian predecessors? Two schools of thought arose to give an explanation. The Marxists maintained that Comte and other bourgeois sociologists had quite simply failed to perceive that war was as inherent in the capitalist order of society as it was in the feudal. It was a continuation of industrial competition by other means; and so far from unfitting the population for war, industrial society, through the disciplines it imposed through factory modes of production, simply turned it into more docile and malleable cannon fodder. Capitalism and militarism were interdependent, indeed indistinguishable; so only the overthrow of capitalism would bring about the end of war.

There were, however, other sociologists who tried to salvage something of their predecessors' hopes. Schumpeter in Europe, Veblen in the United States, attributed the successful militarization of industrial society not to the inherent nature of capitalism as such, but to the atavistic survival of feudal attitudes, structures, and ideologies; not only in Imperial Germany and Japan but, to some extent also, Veblen pointed out, in the social structure of England. The effectiveness with which these most advanced of industrial societies adapted themselves to war was due, they considered, to the continuing habit of deference to, and emulation of, a military ruling class; one whose survival, so far from being necessary to the capitalist leaders of industrial society as the Marxists maintained, was positively harmful to them. Veblen indeed expressed the hope that the war would go on long enough for the English officer-class to kill itself off completely, so that a more equitable, efficient, and peace-loving society could grow over their graves.

Both schools of thought gave partial explanations of a highly complex phenomenon. Certainly, in both British and German society, continuing patterns of social deference, the acceptance of the leadership of a traditional and notionally landed ruling class, did much to preserve both military discipline and social cohesion.[1] But even before the

First World War ended, a new kind of militarism was emerging which owed nothing to preindustrial survivals and indeed reacted violently against them. This was based not on subordination and obedience to traditional authority but on demotic values: individual toughness, group cohesion on an egalitarian basis, personal rather than class leadership qualities, combined with an understanding and mastery of technology. This was the spirit of the American and Australian armed forces. It was that of the new air forces of all nations. It was that of the new storm troops who spearheaded the German attacks in 1918 and who were to transmit it through the *Freikorps* to a new generation of German soldiers. It was not, as good socialists would have wished, a proletarian spirit, but it was *classless,* and that gave it a far wider appeal.

This new militarism, entirely indigenous to advanced industrial societies, was to provide much of the appeal of fascism everywhere. It combined the glamour of new technology with the promise of escape from the drab confines of bourgeois morality into a colorful and heroic world in which violence was not only permissible but *legitimized.* It reached its apogee in Nazi Germany, but it was latent throughout Western civilization and to some extent still is. In the form of the comic strip, it was to penetrate and perhaps mold the consciousness of the very young. The fighter pilot, the Panzer leader, the resistance group, above all, the *para,* that international symbol of *machismo,* these were to become the military archetypes with which adventurous adolescents could identify themselves, and who provide so much more dramatic an image of war than do the patient, invisible navies, the bureaucratized mass-armies, and the disciplined destructiveness of the bomber fleets whose operations were actually decisive in the Second World War.

That such a military spirit still exists in the West will not come as much of a surprise to anyone who has to deal with adolescent or prepubescent males, or even to anyone passing a well-stocked toyshop; though obsession with the Second World War itself probably nowhere reaches the levels characteristic of the United Kingdom. In a more generalized fashion, this emphasis on ruggedness, masculinity, and physical endurance is far more typical of the younger generation in the West than is the soft hedonism which older generations invariably fear to be sapping the fiber of their national strength. There may have been, during the two decades immediately following the Second World War, an understandable emphasis on the restoration and improvement of material standards, which combined with an equally understandable search for social equity to dominate the values of the postwar generation. But such emphasis on material welfare usually breeds its own antidote. In the 1890s, the desire to escape from the intolerable stuffiness of bourgeois society led, among other things, to the spread of *volkisch* youth movements and sports clubs, which were ultimately to prove seedbeds of the new militarism described above. The same spirit has in our own day produced a revolt against "consumerism" that is widespread throughout Western society and that now, as then, sometimes takes bizarre and even violent forms.

There is thus on the face of it no more reason why the societies of Western Europe and North America should today be any less able to adapt themselves to military activity than they have been at any time during the past hundred years, even though changes in social *mores* may impose on that activity new forms to which traditionally minded military professionals may find it difficult to adjust. There would be major economic and political difficulties involved in any such adaptation, but there always were. The military profession as such is not popular, but outside the Kingdom of Prussia it never was. The increasing difficulty of recruitment, as the growing diversification of society created alternative and more lucrative occupations, was observed by Clausewitz in the early part of the last century. It is true that the military now require a far higher proportion of trained specialists whose skills are better regarded by other sectors of the economy, but this is a problem of resource allocation common to all advanced countries; and although the West does not have the social-control mechanisms available to its adversaries, it has, in this as in other respects, a proportionately greater abundance of such skills. National service in Continental countries is accepted without enthusiasm, but accepted it is, and there does not appear at present to be any great pressure to abolish it. Even in Britain, when national service was abandoned in 1958, this was done for economic reasons which owed nothing to social or political protests. In the United States, hostility to the draft became politically significant only as the result of compulsion to serve in a peculiarly unpopular and morally ambiguous war. Now, as in the past, military institutions are accepted by the great majority of the population as a disagreeable necessity, and it is left to governments to decide what their size and shape may be.

On these governments, there do, of course, come short-term economic and political pressures of varying intensity; and it is these, rather than any deeper social patterns, that limit the military effectiveness of the West. And it is here that the invalidity of the Marxian doctrine, of the inevitably militaristic nature of monopoly capitalism, becomes fully evident. In the first place, there is an inherent resistance on the part of the possessing classes to public expenditure in any form and a preference for money to be left to fructify in their own pockets; and here defense suffers from the same disabilities as any other activity of government. In the second, there is the economic diversification we have already noted, that creates so highly competitive a market both for labor and for investment. And, in the third place, the representative nature of the pluralist democracy, which is the normal political form of advanced capitalistic societies, gives an urgency to pressures which in command economies are mediatized through the bureaucratic process. There is no reason to suppose that in communist regimes there is any less demand for lower taxes, better schools, more easily accessible welfare systems, and greater investment both in heavy and consumer-oriented industries than there is in the West. What these regimes lack however are those institutions, above all a free press and openly elected responsible representative bodies, which prevent resources from being allocated entirely according to priorities determined by closed bureaucratic and political elites. And it is precisely the existence of these institutions, as I understand it, that we in the West are concerned to preserve. They present us with problems, but of a kind that very few other societies are privileged to enjoy.

II

The difficulties that we experience in creating a militarily effective defense posture in the West thus arise not from any moral deficiency in our societies but from precisely those characteristics in them that we wish to defend and that our adversaries would wish to eliminate. Nor can those difficulties be blamed on any deep political divisions within Western Europe; much less on any skillful subversion by our adversaries. Indeed, given the profound social and political cleavages that have divided the societies of Western Europe during the past hundred years, it is remarkable how much support the alliance has commanded across the whole political spectrum. It must be admitted that this is due less to any skillful political management by the statesmen of the West than to the brutality and blunders of the Soviet Union, which have effectively destroyed the very powerful appeal that it exercised in the 1930s, as an ideal alternative society. The Soviet brand of Marx-Leninism now commands the allegiance of only small and isolated minorities within Western communist parties, while the mainstream of the socialist movement has turned its back on it altogether. That does not mean that left-wing parties in the West are necessarily any less hostile to what they see as "monopoly capitalism" and the imperialist neocolonialism which they see as being so closely associated with it. The Marxist creed seems to them none the less valid because of the perversions inflicted on it by Stalin, and even by Lenin. But, in terms of political action, this does not lead them to regard the Soviet Union as an ally for whose protection they would wish to exchange that of the United States. The position of the communist parties of Eastern Europe can have a limited appeal for Señor Carillo, Signor Berlinguer, or even M. Georges Marchais. To talk of "Eurocommunism" is a totally misleading oversimplification, but all the effective communist parties in Western Europe are deeply rooted within national political systems which they show few signs of wishing to exchange for a Moscow-dominated hegemony. Some, like the PCF, are neutralist, embracing with enthusiasm the idea of *défense à tous azimuths* and staunchly supporting the *force de frappe*. Others, like the PCI, accord the alliance a grumbling acquiescence. All use it as a convenient whipping boy; but it remains remarkable how little trouble these parties have caused the alliance over the past 30 years.

Opposition to and doubts about the alliance extend of course far beyond the official communist parties. A liberal, pacifistic tradition is a continuing, ineluctable, and, to my mind, admirable element in the Western political system, and its influence, in Northern Europe and the Netherlands in particular, has probably caused more problems to North Atlantic Treaty Organization (NATO) leaders than any amount of communist activity. Those influenced by it range from saintly men of penetrating intelligence to mindless fanatics impervious to reasoned argument, but it would be morally disreputable as well as politically foolish to treat them simply as a nuisance, far less as enemies. More often than not, the questions they raise and the criticism they make about Western defense postures are entirely legitimate. They furnish our societies not only with a conscience but also with a critical intelligence. If sometimes they deal with society not as it is but as we would all wish it to be, at least they save us from the cynical *immobilisme* that is the besetting sin of bureaucrats and the academics who tend to associate with them. They are the "philosophers" whose freedom of expression Kant modestly claimed to be a condition of Perpetual Peace, and with whom a dialogue is the essential prerequisite of a free society.

So the alliance must continue to live with and take notice of its critics, as it must continue to accept the political legitimacy of left-wing, including communist, parties in Western Europe. Nothing would bring the alliance more quickly into disarray than if it could convincingly be depicted as the creature of the Right, a new Holy Alliance directed not at maintaining the political and territorial sovereignty of its members but at preserving a particular structure of society about whose merits there was deeply felt disagreement. It is a military alliance to defend its members against external aggression; not an instrument for the suppression of social change, either in Western Europe or anywhere else in the world. That NATO should be championed by the more right-wing elements in Western Europe, those groups who not only have the greatest stake in the existing order but are temperamentally most concerned about questions of national defense, is natural enough. But if it had not also been supported by those parties of organized labor which represent the true center of gravity in industrial societies, especially the Labour party in Britain and the SPD in Germany, it would have disintegrated long ago.

The support of organized labor is the more important in the light of a problem which is particularly severe in Britain but which might in the event of a prolonged economic recession become more widespread. Like so many of our difficulties, there is nothing very new about it. Long before 1914 it was baptized "anarcho-syndicalism"; now it is better known as the English disease. It consists of the *ungovernability* of key elements in society; the arbitrary determination of certain groups to pursue their own short-term economic interests without concern for the rest of the community. Lightning strikes by civilian workers for purely parochial causes—usually without any deeper political motivation—can create havoc in delicate defense systems, and they are impossible to deal with unless the government enjoys the support, or at least the acquiescence, of organized labor as a whole. More widespread *dirigiste* measures of a kind essential in a serious military emergency would also be inconceivable without full labor support; and labor support, in Europe, means the backing of full-blooded socialists and, in many cases, communists. Such support can be relied upon, as it could in 1914 and in 1939, only for the most basic and obvious of emergencies: the defense of one's own territory or that of one's neighbors against a threat to national survival. It is this minimalist definition of the alliance's goals that is likely to maintain the consensus behind it, whatever the temptations might be to extend its objectives whether ideologically or geographically. Any action, however strategically desirable, by which the alliance appeared to be extending its support to oppressive regimes elsewhere in the world, would have seriously divisive consequences within the Western European political community.

III

The problem is, of course, to convince the peoples of Western Europe that there is, or plausibly might be, a "threat to national survival." It is a concept that the generation which has had no experience of the Second World War and its immediate aftermath has some difficulty in assimilating. For the military, it may be enough to indicate the strength and dispositions of the armed forces of the Soviet Union, those alarming capabilities which might one day tempt the Soviet leadership into the disastrous course of applying military means to solve their political problems. But the military specialist does not have to concern himself with the reasons why another state may wish to attack his own. It is enough that it should have the capacity to do so, and it is his job to see that the costs of such an action would be so high as to clearly outweigh any possible benefits. But this can be done only by the allocation of resources which involve his own society in heavy and continuing costs; and to make such costs acceptable to a skeptical and now profoundly undeferential public opinion, it is necessary to demonstrate a strong possibility that the Soviet leadership intends, or one day might intend, to use their military strength to overrun Western Europe. Soviet military capability *as such* is no more evidence of aggressive intent than is that of the United States. Although it is no doubt true that it greatly exceeds what our own military leaders would consider adequate for the territorial defense of the Soviet Union, there are too many alternative explanations—atavistic Soviet suspicions of the outside world, the growing collusion of Soviet adversaries East and West, the primacy enjoyed by the military in Soviet bureaucratic processes, a determination to demonstrate superpower status in the only way open to her, above all an understandable determination that any future conflict will be fought out on the soil of her adversaries rather than her own—for this to be accepted as prima facie evidence of aggressive intentions. Indeed Western perceptions of Soviet strength bear a strong family resemblance to the fears expressed by the German General Staff about the growing might of the Russian Empire before 1914; yet, as we now know, the intentions of that empire, though certainly not purely defensive, were far from predatory. As Clausewitz indicated, military grammar does not necessarily dictate political logic.

This military imbalance is thus not in itself likely to be enough to persuade the peoples of Western Europe that a plausible threat exists to their national survival which can be countered only by the acceptance of considerable additional costs. The people of Mexico and Canada, after all, coexist quite happily with the military power of the

United States. It is necessary to show what lawyers would call *mens rea,* aggressive intentions. For a skeptical generation that would far rather spend its money on something else, the question has to be answered: Why should the Soviet Union wish to attack Western Europe? Or is it, like Hitler's Germany, the kind of militarized society that regards war and conquest not as an instrument of policy but as a way of life?

It is now necessary to say something about the nature of "the threat"; for if indeed the Russians have the same kind of predatory intentions towards us as Hitler had towards them, a determination to conquer our territories and remold our societies as servile dependencies, then there is indeed an overwhelming case for evoking the latent military elements in the West and, at whatever the economic and social costs, creating Nations in Arms to defend our independence; which would require not simply well-equipped professional armed forces to take the first shock of the Soviet attack but well-trained and highly motivated reservists, disciplined "stay-behind" guerrilla forces, and, above all, an elaborate and convincing system of civil defense against nuclear attack. That this can be done in the face of a clear and present danger even by the most bourgeois and pacific of societies was demonstrated by the United Kingdom in 1940. The fact that it has *not* been done, but that Western Europe remains free none the less, will be attributed by some to the benignity of Soviet intentions, by others to the effectiveness of nuclear deterrence. Obviously, over the past 30 years, the Soviet leadership has calculated that the costs of any attack on the West would outweigh any possible benefits; but the same could be said about Western intentions towards the Soviet Union. Did the Russians ever wish to attack us anyway, and do they now?

This is the question that must be convincingly answered, and comparative figures of military strengths are simply not enough. Between the two conflicting views of the Soviet Union, one as an implacable predator, the other as a society obsessed with internal problems, paranoid about the external world and driven reluctantly into an arms race by the competition of far wealthier and more sophisticated adversaries, there is room for a wide range of opinions. The first of these is more general, oddly enough, in the United States than it is in Western Europe; not because Europeans have any greater confidence than have their American allies in Soviet benevolence, but perhaps because they have a livelier appreciation of the weaknesses of the Soviet Union and see in much of her behavior a familiar if disagreeable pattern that has changed little since the days of Peter the Great.[2] Without taking sides in this classic debate, beyond suggesting that the two concepts are not mutually exclusive, it can be suggested that, barring further self-inflicted wounds such as the Soviet leaders delivered against their cause in the "Prague summer" of 1968, the image of the Russians as predators may be one that Western peoples find increasingly difficult to accept, at least so far as their own territories are concerned. Historians are beginning to scrutinize with some care the stock explanations of the origins of the Cold War, and to question the validity of those fears of Soviet aggressive intentions which were used to justify the creation of the alliance 30 years ago. The original extreme and iconoclastic form of this "revisionism" as set out in the works of such writers as Gar Alperovitz and Gabriel Kolko has now been substantially modified, but few students of the period would now accept the simplistic views of the Soviet threat which were current in the early 1950s. A doctrine rejected by the bulk of the academic community is not likely to remain tenable for very long by those school teachers and publicists who mold public opinion. Too many documents have been released and too many memoirs written for the simple and heroic certainties of a quarter of a century ago to be acceptable to a new and properly skeptical generation. And if we were wrong about "the threat" then, they will quite rightly ask: Are we any more likely to be right now?

IV

The danger is that, in rejecting the simple and exaggerated fears of the postwar era, the intellectual leaders of Western society will fail to appreciate the more solidly based anxieties that underlie them. Those who cried wolf in 1948-53 may have been the victims of their own fears, but they were quite right in perceiving that, whether they were really threatened by a Soviet attack or not, the international environment was such that a stable and prosperous society could be built in Western Europe only on the basis of military security convincing enough to reassure its own members and discourage those who wished, by whatever means and for whatever motives, to disrupt it.

For whether they had predatory intentions or not, the cold hostility of the Soviet leadership to the West was made unmistakably clear after the Second World War, and there is no sign that it has ever abated. Whether or not Stalin had any plans for military attack during the last six years of his life, there is no doubt that he would have liked to absorb the whole of Germany into the Soviet system, and weaken the remaining states of Western Europe by every means in his power. These means would have been political, at least initially. Even in Germany the role of the Red Army would have been to enable the spearhead of the proletariat, the KPD, to complete the revolution begun by Karl Liebknecht and Rosa Luxembourg without foreign-backed intervention. It is a basic principle of Marx-Leninism that the revolution cannot be carried abroad on the points of foreign bayonets, but, where the workers are defending their revolution against the forces of reaction, whether indigenous or foreign, Soviet armed forces could not be expected to fold their hands and sit idly by. And it was by no means clear to anyone that there was not a "revolutionary situation" in Western Europe in the chaotic aftermath of the Second World War, which would enable the communists to complete the work begun, and interrupted, after the First. The communist parties of Western Europe, furthermore, were loyal to Moscow. The links forged before 1939 had been strengthened by the admirable performance of the Soviet peoples during the war, which enabled the Soviet Union to project itself, with good reason, as the true rescuer of the peoples of Europe from the menace of fascism. It is not surprising that the Russians had many friends in high places as well as low.

It is seldom that empires grow as a matter of settled policy. More often they expand, as did the British in India, reluctantly and piecemeal, with repeated and sincere disclaimers of predatory intent. Every step of Soviet expansion westwards could be justified (as was the contemporaneous expansion of U.S. power to the farther shores of the Pacific) by impeccable considerations of national defense. Obviously the whole of Germany must be controlled. How else could the Soviet Union feel safe from the invasions which had devastated her in two world wars? But with Germany under control, Russian suzerainty over Scandinavia would need to be assured, and defense facilities could reasonably be demanded at Copenhagen and the North Cape. The rest of Western Europe might be left alone on the strict understanding that they afforded no kind of toehold to the military power of the United States, but they would have to give firm guarantees of good behavior and of course do nothing to impede the historic development of socialism within their borders. An inverse Monroe Doctrine, in short, would have been proclaimed for Europe, excluding all intervention by the powers, or rather the power, of the Western hemisphere.

This was the real danger that faced the statesmen of the West after the war. They had no reason to suppose that Stalin's Russia would not act exactly as all great powers (their own included) had always acted when they had the chance, and even less to suppose that they had abandoned the fundamental principles of Marx-Leninism, which made it impossible for them to see the pattern of world-politics as anything other than a Hobbesian state of war, or to view capitalist states as anything other than long-term enemies bent on their destruction. So even if the myth of an imminent Soviet attack on Western Europe, deterred only by an American commitment to her defense, does not stand up to scholarly analysis of the documents, it was, like all myths, a dramatic representation of an underlying truth.

V

Does it remain true after 30 years? All the above arguments may be convincing, but that was a full generation ago, and an enormous amount has now changed, in Soviet society as well as in our own. In the first place, alarming as many of the developments in Western society may seem, no serious Marxist thinker would maintain that they add up to a classic "revolutionary situation." Least of all is this evident in West Germany, the country of most immediate concern to the Soviet Union. Indeed, it has been the total absence of any signs of such a situation ever developing, thanks to the *embourgeoisement* of the proletariat and the revisionism of the official communist parties, that has driven the idealists of the New Left either to nihilistic terrorism or to abandoning orthodox politics altogether in favor of ecological and kindred protest movements. Further, if a revolutionary situation *were* to develop in the West out of an economic recession compounded by an energy crisis, leading to massive unemployment and a drastic fall in the standard of living, it is doubtful whether the leaders it would throw up would look to Moscow for leadership, or whether the Soviet government would see it as being in their best interests, economically and politically, to exploit such a situation. To embarrass and weaken the economy of Western Europe is one thing; to cause its total collapse, with all the implications that would have for the well-being of Eastern Europe, is quite another. In any case, the precedents of the 1930s suggest that, in mature capitalist economies, such catastrophes strengthen the parties of the extreme Right rather than the extreme Left. It is notable that the appeal of left-wing policies in Western Europe has steadily waned as the economic situation has grown worse.

Further, it is only fair to recognize that the present generation of Soviet leaders is quite unlike that of Stalin, Molotov, and Vishinsky. They are conspicuously disagreeable people, but they have not fought their way to power through the thickets and quagmires of revolutionary conspiracy. They have come up through the established hierarchies of political and economic management, and their successors are likely to do the same. They are likely, as "scientific" Marxists, to view Western Europe in terms of cold calculation. What would the costs be of conquering us, and where would be the benefits? There is no revolutionary situation to exploit. The proletariat of the West is now by Marx-Leninist standards hopelessly corrupt. The communist parties are divided between revisionists and adventurists, neither of whom would provide docile instruments of Soviet control. The advantages which the Soviet Union at present gains from East-West trade depend on a flourishing capitalist economy in the West, and it is doubtful whether anyone in the Soviet leadership is under any illusions about this. Why should the Soviet leaders wish to turn a prosperous, productive, and relatively friendly Western Europe into another group of fractious and hostile dependencies.

These are the questions being posed by intelligent and well-informed young skeptics, and we cannot deny their force. Whatever opportunities of expansion and control the Soviet leaders may see elsewhere in the world (and the skeptics have something to say about that as well), it is very doubtful whether they see any in Western Europe or are likely to in the foreseeable future. This Soviet attitude towards its Western neighbors is an essential panel in a diptych of which the other consists of the armed strength of the alliance. It would be quite unrealistic to assume that the Russians have been deterred from attacking us solely by their perception of the military costs involved. It is probably many years since Western Europe presented itself to them as an attractive, even if an attainable, prize. It is not only the strength of the locks on their doors that protects aging spinsters from rape.

VI

We may accept therefore that there is at present little in the nature of Soviet society[3] or Soviet political intentions to justify the ringing of alarm bells in the West, the evocation of the militaristic elements in our society, and the conversion of the nations of Western Europe into garrison states. Indeed, to do anything of the kind could easily make the situation more dangerous, rather than less. The Soviet leadership is no more prone than we are ourselves to accept that the military preparations of its neighbors are purely defensive, and to refrain from responding in kind. But we should be wary of drawing too much comfort from the best-case analysis presented above. It has to be pointed out that, in disorderly societies, aged spinsters *do* get raped. Further, the record tends to show that states, especially powerful states, have seldom calculated their self-interest as coolly and correctly as political scientists could do on their behalf. (On any calculation of self-interest, would the United States have gotten herself involved in Vietnam?) The Soviet leadership has not abandoned its doctrinaire hostility to the West; Soviet publicists are commendably frank in explaining that "peaceful coexistence" does not mean the end of an ideological struggle which they could not terminate even if they wanted to. Whatever short-term accommodations may be made and however long they last, they remain in a Hobbesian state of war with us, and there is nothing that can be done about it. And it requires very few dealings with Soviet officials to bring home to the most starry-eyed of Western intellectuals how glacial and impermeable remains the permafrost beneath the shallow topsoil of official "peaceful coexistence."

Most important of all, it has to be pointed out that wars in Europe have very rarely begun with a settled intention of conquest on the part of the aggressor. To say that the Soviet Union today is not like Hitler's Germany, or even Stalin's Russia, may be perfectly true, but it is of limited relevance to our problems. When Germany attacked France through Belgium in 1914, and again in 1940, it was with no plan of conquest and settlement. Even in 1940, Hitler had, at least initially, no plans for transforming the *societies* of Western Europe, only of neutralizing the military power of their states. *Social* transformation followed only insofar as it was necessary to ensure the continued subordination of the defeated adversary. Both in 1914 and in 1940, Germany would have been happy to see Britain and France continue to flourish as prosperous and pacific communities with complete domestic freedom of action, so long as they had neither the political will nor the military capacity to interfere with German intentions elsewhere. Her intention was to eliminate the threat which French and British power posed to her freedom of action, not to conquer either of them.

This seems to me to be the appropriate analogy with the intentions of the Soviet Union towards Western Europe today. We are not a prey to be devoured. We are a potential threat which might have to be neutralized, reluctantly and in extremis, in full consciousness of all the social, political, as well as military costs involved, and only if all else fails. The Soviet Union would undertake the invasion and occupation of Western Europe without enthusiasm, simply to destroy our military power and ensure our continued debilitation. But as other countries have found in other circumstances, it is a lot easier to put troops into a defeated country than to take them out, and the Russians would then find, in spite of their very best intentions, that they had another chunk of ungovernable empire on their hands. It is an embarrassment that we should do our very best to spare them.

It would be going far beyond the bounds of this paper to suggest in any detail the circumstances in which the Soviet leadership might feel tempted to launch such an attack. (Indeed, in military exercises, NATO leaders sometimes find it as difficult to sketch a convincing political scenario for a Russian invasion as to devise means of checking it if it were to come.) One might have to visualize a preemptive strike, on the analogy of the Schlieffen Plan, in an Armageddon triggered off by a crisis elsewhere in the world. Another and more plausible possibility would be a situation in Eastern Europe so explosive that the Russians felt unable to contain it unless the source of infection beyond the Iron Curtain could be eliminated; and the history of empires, both Roman and British, provides plenty of precedents for such defensively intended punitive strikes. In either case, the attack would be improbable unless the Soviet military could promise rapid success without nuclear escalation, and the alternative appeared to be the disintegration of the Soviet Empire. But it is in precisely these circumstances that wars usually begin.

It would be pointless to multiply scenarios. Few wars, if indeed any, have started in any way foretold in advance, and none have ever pursued the courses predicted for them. But whatever the circumstances, it will remain the task of Western military leaders to ensure that their Soviet opposite numbers are never in a position to give such advice to their political masters, and their own political masters must provide them with the means to do so.

VII

This is the situation that must be explained to the skeptical peoples of our societies. The danger they have to face is probably not one of invasion directed towards the conquest of our societies and the destruction of our liberties, but of a disarming attack with strictly limited military objectives; though how secure our societies and liberties would be if such an attack were to succeed is another matter. Such a threat presents problems for military planners that are beyond the scope of this paper to discuss, but it may be remarked in passing that the distinction between such limited and total intentions is one that has not always been made in the works of Western strategists. A defense posture which is designed to deter the Soviet Union from a *Niederwerfungskrieg,* a war of total conquest, could be disastrously inapplicable if the intention was simply to destroy the bulk of our forward conventional capabilities, occupy a stretch of territory, and then offer generous peace terms long before the decision had been taken to initiate nuclear escalation.

What concerns us here are the implications of all this for our societies. These are simple, but they are neither reassuring nor new. The first, admittedly, is not without comfort for us: we do not confront a threat of totalitarian conquest such as could be countered only by a militarization of our societies. The second is that our security, our political freedom of action, and our stability in the event of a crisis depend on the provision of effective armed forces capable of deterring any attack by their evident capacity to impose intolerable costs on the attackers. And if this is not done, there are only three options open to us. The first is to continue to deter attack by the threat to initiate the use of nuclear weapons; but today this means accepting the use of nuclear weapons against us on at least a comparable scale. The second would be to back up our regular forces with sufficient reserves and territorials to fight a long and destructive war of attrition. The third would be to make the best terms with the adversary that we could get; and we must not be surprised or outraged if the political leaders of Western Europe, faced with so appalling a choice, were to opt for the last.

This then is the price that our societies have to pay, not perhaps for "national survival," but to guarantee our continuing independence. It is a situation that has to be clearly and repeatedly expounded: only if adequate conventional forces are maintained will statesmen be spared the agonizing dilemma outlined above. The difficulties of maintaining these forces will be no less in the future than in the past. They will be all the greater if we allow ourselves to believe that, in an age of nuclear equivalence, nuclear deterrence still offers an easy way out, or that technology can somehow eliminate problems that can only be solved by trained, well-equipped fighting men. The military has the obligation to state their requirements with clarity and moderation. Like all demands for massive public expenditure, they will, very properly, be contested and scrutinized. Vociferous minorities will remain stubbornly unconvinced of their necessity. But there is nothing inherent in the structure of our societies or the nature of our political systems to prevent them from being met.

NOTES

1. But not in France; an exception which limits the validity of Veblen's analysis as well (in view of the agrarian structure of much of French society in 1914-1918) as that of the Marxists.

2. There is also a greater readiness to accept Russia as historically part of the European community, to regret her self-imposed alienation, and to welcome any indications that she wants to be reconciled. That this applies even more strongly to the captive nations of Eastern Europe goes without saying. It is perhaps significant that Europeans tend, however inaccurately, to speak of "the Russians" rather than "the Soviets," seeing them as a people rather than a regime.

3. To deal with social and cultural patterns within the Soviet Union would far exceed the bounds of this paper and the capacity of its author. But it would be generally agreed that while Soviet society remains docile to its leaders and has an old-fashioned respect for its armed forces, it shows little tendency toward the kind of irrational militarism which might distort its government's calculations of *Realpolitik*.

On the Meaning of Victory

Edward N. Luttwak

The West has become comfortably habituated to defeat. Victory is viewed with great suspicion, if not outright hostility. After all, if the right-thinking are to achieve their great aim of abolishing war they must first persuade us that victory is futile or, better still, actually harmful. To use Stalinist language, one might say that the struggle against war requires the prior destruction of the very idea of victory. Accordingly, we are being told insistently that it is very unfortunate for the British that they have won the Falklands war: now they will have to garrison the islands at great cost, and sooner or later they will have to fight again—unless they give up their re-conquest—thus making their victory futile.

Never mind that the British successfully defended their principles, and never mind the rather splendid performance of Her Majesty's forces. The right-thinking know better: principles are old men's abstractions that young men are asked to fight for, and war, they insist, is a dirty and squalid business that evokes only the worst in man and serves no purpose. It was a great pity, of course, that the cameras of our network news were not properly accommodated by the British, otherwise we would have been able to enjoy carefully edited footage showing seasick British soldiers en route to the island, and then the wounded crying out in pain and finally at Port Stanley a British child mutilated ("in bitter irony") by a British bomb. It was also most inconsiderate of the British not to allow a TV-star correspondent of ours to interrogate the Queen in proper style ("How do you feel about sending your son towards his probable death?").

But everything missing in the Falklands was abundantly provided in Lebanon. Never mind that the Palestine Liberation Organization's (PLO) pretensions to military power were swept away in a crushing defeat that finally forced Yasir Arafat's men to take refuge among the civilians of Beirut; never mind that the Syrians were soundly beaten both in the air and on the ground. Above all, let us have no cold-blooded Realpolitik. For otherwise we might recognize a rather substantial result of victory in the decline of the Soviet Union's influence in the region to its lowest point since the beginning of its great and costly enterprise in the Arab world, almost 30 years ago. Superpowers, like other institutions known to us, are in the protection business. When they cannot protect clients, they lose influence, not just locally but worldwide.

To ignore such things is easy when the right-thinking have as much to work with as they had in Lebanon: not one wounded child but a great many and, of course, all those picturesque ruins. Only the most documented experts in the Middle East's instant archaeology could have known that much of the footage showed ruins of the civil war—those so greatly photographed in Damour, in fact, dated back to the PLO's devastation of that formerly Christian city.

The casualty figures provided another reminder of antiquity: when we read in the *Historia Augusta* that the army of Claudius II killed 320,000 Goths and sunk 2,000 Gothic ships, should we believe those numbers? And what about the huge numbers in Herodotus? It was assumed that the historian's dilemma could not arise in our statistical age—until there came the reports of the *Washington Post* and the *New York Times* correspondents in Beirut. Their Herodotus was the suitably authoritative head of the Red Crescent ("the Palestinian Red Cross"), who happens to be Arafat's brother. Thus our newspapers wrote of thousands of children killed, tens of thousands of civilians wounded or dead, and hundreds of thousands made homeless by Israeli bombing. (Did the United States supply the several hundred heavy strategic bombers needed for the job? How did the Israelis hide them all these years?)

No ancient scribe fond of large numbers could have done better than our press. Armed with these most useful numbers, the right-thinking recovered the ground lost in the Falklands. But it was not enough to prove that war is hell; it was also necessary to demonstrate that victory had to be futile for the Israelis, and positively harmful to the United States. Greatly disappointed by the refusal of the Latin American governments to retaliate against the United States for siding with the British, the right-thinking were given a new and better opportunity for gloomy prognostications that would hold the principle that victory equals loss: the Arabs would be "radicalized"; i.e., they would turn to the Soviet Union for support; the Arabs would withdraw their funds from U.S. banks and the Treasury; the Arabs would impose an oil embargo. Such fears were apparently so credible that they were shared by sundry senators, and even by some senior officials in the executive branch. Considerable gloom was thus duly distributed to dampen the unfortunate reflex of public opinion, whereby many obtained some satisfaction from the Israeli victory over Soviet arms.

But the right-thinking had to do even more; they had to persuade the Israelis to derive no benefit from victory. In part the evidence was provided by the advocates themselves. Having first produced so much film and so many photographs as well as acres of newsprint on the sufferings of the Palestinians, they could now argue quite correctly that Israel's reputation would suffer greatly from its venture; and then, of course, it could be argued persuasively that the Palestinians would only be further embittered by their defeat. Above all, it was insistently claimed that the PLO would win (or had won) a "political victory," precisely because of its military defeat. Inadvertently perhaps, some truth was thus told, inasmuch as Palestinian national ambitions must receive greater consideration to the degree that Israel's survival is less and less in serious question, owing to her military strength.

On the basis of such arguments, it could be claimed that Israel's victory was merely tactical, and eventually would be counterproductive, given its cost in blood, political support, and money. In the same vein, it has been argued most persuasively that the Allied victory in 1918 was futile because it set the stage for another World War two decades later; and that even in 1945, victory was ultimately harmful for the victors, because the British lost their economic strength in fighting that war, while the United States and the Soviet Union merely created the circumstances in which they would be locked in permanent confrontation with war-created atomic weapons and eventually with thermonuclear weapons so dangerous that they endanger the very survival of both.

The right-thinking can thus uncover evidence for the futility of victory in virtually every case that comes to mind in any period of history. That great father-figure of the right-thinking, Arnold Toynbee, wrote much to prove that the Romans were in fact ruined by their victory over Carthage, and Toynbee was perfectly consistent in his other capacity, as a Foreign Office expert: he was a very energetic supporter of appeasement during the late 1930s and indeed until the bitter end. After all, he argued in print that 1918 was a futile victory, and would perform likewise in writing of every Western victory that took place in his lifetime.

The hopelessly old-fashioned British and the aggressive Israelis remain unpersuaded. Our own *vox populi* has never, in fact, accepted the contention that war can yield no good result regardless of motive or circumstances. But at least our own enlightened elite, especially the media elite, knows the truth. Thus in the United States the process whereby all war is made unacceptable no matter what its purpose ("debellicization") is nowadays well advanced. For nuclear war the work has been fully done. Any U.S. general who would dare to emulate his Soviet counterparts in asserting that nuclear weapons—if only tactical—might actually serve to win in some circumstance or other, would earn himself the classic assignment to that deskless office in the remotest corridor of the Pentagon. The right-thinking are very firm in insisting that any use of nuclear weapons must inevitably result in all-out nuclear war, in which no rational purposes can be achieved so that the very concept of victory can have no meaning. And that, of course, is the view relentlessly promoted in classrooms and lecture halls, in countless editorials, in the speeches of our worthies, in sermons from the pulpit, and in the pontifications of our superstar television announcers.

At the opposite end of the spectrum of conflict, the sheer impossibility of victory in fighting guerrillas has acquired the status of a certified truth in right-thinking circles. (Hence the further offense of the Israelis, in defeating guerrillas.) Already during the Indochina war the principle was established that victory was a nongoal. To speak of it was deemed conclusive evidence of protofascism by the media elite. More remarkably, any talk of victory was taken as a sure symptom of provincial naivete, by the very people who were directing the fighting (Messrs. McNamara, McGeorge Bundy et al.). Having established that costly and futile war as the canonical case, the right-thinking could then argue that any active U.S. role in an insurgency would unfailingly yield another Vietnam. The president's decision that no American may carry a rifle in San Salvador was a true measure of the progress of debellicization.

Given the widespread acceptance of the claim that the United States cannot hope for victory in either a guerrilla war or a nuclear war, it is now the urgent priority of the right-thinking to close the unfortunate gap in the middle whereby medium-sized conventional war retains the possibility of victory. Thus their loud insistence that the medium-sized conventional wars fought by the British and Israelis must yield certifiably futile victories.

There is no doubt, to be sure, that victory always has its price, and that it may be very high. Victory is often a terrible thing for the victors. Only defeat is worse still: while it may contain some well-hidden advantage, it usually brings not only material loss but also demoralization in its wake. The British and Israelis both won costly victories; the Argentines, the PLO and the Syrians suffered defeats whose evil consequences are not truly diminished by the frenetic attempts that others may make to denigrate victory and promote the virtues of defeat.

The prominence of so many influential American voices in such mystification suggests that our own society is threatened by a process of debellicization that would deny any opportunity for victory, and thus for any purposeful resistance to aggression. Unless that process is firmly opposed, unless we refute the counsel of impotence, the only possible policy choices left open will be appeasement or outright retreat.

On Learning from Wars

It is notoriously difficult to derive valid tactical operational strategy, or even technical lessons, from the wars that others have fought. Misinformation and the sheer lack of information are the least of our difficulties. Much more serious is the multiplicity of contexts and facets in warfare. When we contemplate the most intricate of human mass activities, we see not merely through a glass darkly but rather through the dazzling refractions of a diamond. We see one truth tactically and another technically, while an operational view may yield yet another result, and the higher levels of strategy several more.

Consider, for example, the technically superior, but tactically vulnerable, operationally useful but strategically dubious antitank missile. Is that a weapon that we should rely upon to contain Soviet armor in Europe? Or, in assessing a course of conduct, and its protagonist, what are we to say of Rommel, who was a tactical mediocrity, an operational genius, and the very worst of (theater) strategists? How then would we answer the question that national leaders will earnestly ask in war: is X a good general?

Far more than the usual abundance of contradictory evidence, it is the multiplicity and the divergence of the facets of war that denies any clear identification of its valid lessons. In the absence of any self-evident truths, military bureaucracies intent on suppressing unwelcome lessons can do so all too easily, and just as easily they can select out the lessons that usefully serve to confirm their established doctrines and equipment preferences.

The classic case is, of course, the Russo-Japanese War of 1904-1905. Had the European general staffs appraised correctly the lessons that now seem so clear in hindsight, the fighting of 1914-1916 would have been radically different; the armies of Europe would have gone to war without horses, lances, and swords receiving in exchange many more machine guns as well as heavy howitzers, trench mortars, great quantities of barbed wire, and an entrenching tool for each soldier.

But in fact the lessons of the fighting in Manchuria had scarcely made any impression at all on the armies that went to war in 1914. The ready explanation is, of course, the extreme remoteness of the Manchurian theater of war, and the somewhat exotic character of the antagonists. That is certainly a plausible explanation, but it happens to be utterly false. The events of the Russo-Japanese war were reported in the press in great detail and with much acute analysis. Beyond that, solid works of scholarly precision were soon published. Above all, several European armies (as well as our own) sent battlefield observers to the scene—an especially talented group of officers, as it happens—who wrote very detailed tactical and operational reports that may still be consulted with advantage. The evidence so clearly presented in all these sources should have been conclusive and it should promptly have induced great changes in the cognizant armies. Yet nothing happened.

The ready explanation is that the abundant information on the war was simply ignored by the general staffs, even the reports they specifically commissioned. That too may seem plausible, especially if one's estimate of the intellectual caliber of the pre-1914 general staff officers has been fashioned by Barbara Tuchman's well-known work, *The Guns of August.*

Again the plausible explanation is utterly false. The military journals of the period are full of closely reasoned debates about the lessons of the Manchurian fighting, and the evidence was also very carefully reviewed in a multitude of internal staff working papers. (To read those documents is to discover just how false is the legend that portrays those men as harebrained uniformed peacocks, wooden-headed martinets, and neurotic war-lovers.) Thus it was neither the lack of information nor a willful disregard for the evidence that obscured the true lessons of the Russo-Japanese war. A far more subtle process was at work. The truths of the fighting were neither unknown nor ignored but rather subverted, by ad hoc "Manchurian" theories:

- The failure of the cavalry on both sides proved nothing, because neither side had "real" cavalry; Russian horses were mere ponies; and Japanese horses were few.
- The war was fought between two essentially weak armies, hence their immobility, and the resort to entrenchment.

- The siege operations at Port Arthur were inept on the Japanese side and hopeless on the Russian, hence the slow pace of the fighting and the old-fashioned employment of heavy howitzers and mortars.
- The Russian infantry was undisciplined and Japanese infantry physically weak, hence the failure of foot soldiers on both sides to defeat the machine gun by dashing assaults.

Thus social predisposition (in favor of the cavalry), tactical dogmatism (against the machine gun and entrenchment), technological pride (which protected the light 75mm gun of the French and its Krupp counterpart against the claims of heavier howitzers and cheaper mortars)—all played their varied roles in making persuasive the appropriate Manchurian theories of negation. Imposed change is always uncomfortable, often disruptive, and sometimes just intolerable. When there is a powerful desire to believe the untrue, we can all become very inventive in our distortions and in 1904-1905 there was an exceptionally strong impulse to invent theories that would explain away what was happening in Manchuria. For that war was most unsatisfactory to all. It was not the war of great maneuvers, that being the only kind of war that the Germans could accept, because only great maneuvers would allow victory to the outnumbered. It was not the war of irresistible infantry offensives that the less-industrialized French needed to reconquer their lost province; and it was certainly not the war of small units, which was the only kind of war that the small British army could then fight. Hence the unconscious rejection of lessons that would have imposed the abandonment of cherished goals or else intolerable change. As we contemplate the record of recent wars, as we try to extract their valid lessons, we should simply assume that the established military bureaucracies will unconsciously invent all the Manchurian theories they might need to explain away unwelcome evidence.

At least for the cause of military analysis, it is fortunate that we now have two very different wars to examine. Their diverse evidence can help us to sort out valid lessons, while making it more difficult to give plausibility to "Manchurian" theories.

Thus, for example, on the most basic of issues: why did the British soldiers outmatch their enemies so greatly? Those of our bureaucrats in and out of uniform who support the perpetuation of the All-Volunteer Force, deem the answer obvious: the British troops were professionals, while their enemies were mere conscripts. But this typical attempt to select out desirable evidence is promptly undone by the other war: in Lebanon, Israeli conscripts and reservists did very nicely against professional long-service Syrian troops and full-time PLO fighters.

Of course there are some who will discount this counterevidence, on the grounds that the "Israelis fought only against Arabs," in the words of a senior U.S. general. That of course is the most comprehensive of all Manchurian theories, for it can be exploited to explain away not merely one part of the evidence but all the evidence of all the wars fought by the Israelis. That the Syrians at least are far better soldiers than the Argentinians is beyond all doubt, and it is also perfectly possible that they are better soldiers than the various enemies whom that nameless general had fought in Korea and Vietnam. If that is so, the question becomes more interesting and more directly relevant to our own concerns: why can both the British and the Israelis in their very different ways field units that are so cohesive and highly motivated, and how can they turn out so many junior officers of such quality in combat leadership?

What is it, then, that these two very different armies have in common as far as these all-important basics are concerned? As far as unit cohesion is concerned, the answer that clearly emerges is that in both armies the fighting units are not mere administrative entities through which soldiers and officers rotate in and out. They are, rather, very stable social groups, each with its own internal sense of loyalty, each with its own distinctive ethos. The soldiers who fought so well in the Falklands did not truly belong to the British army; they belonged to their regiments, in which they would serve their entire service lives in stable association with their fellow soldiers. Our newspapers described the Royal Marine Commandos as "elite" troops. But it would not be a safe procedure, in a pub conversation with one of their members, to question the elite status of the Scots Guards, or of any Guards for that matter, or of any of two dozen more regiments, not counting obvious elite troops, such as the paratroopers, SAS, Gurkas, the Argylls, and more.

From their regimental system, the British obtain a very high elite content in their small 176,000-man army. Now that the U.S. Army is also small—very small indeed at 776,000 men and women, considering our global responsibilities—we too should seriously consider that system. The regimental mystique is not to be obtained in our case by the issue of tourist-shop badges and insignia or by playing up unfelt traditions. Instead, it is by way of a functional specialization that a real group identity can begin to arise, i.e., Arctic regiments, mountain regiments, desert regiments, tank regiments, jungle regiments, commando regiments, and so on. Needless to say, such units are unlikely to see combat in their nominal specialty, but in the meantime their strong sense of identity will have generated cohesion. Regimentalization is, of course, a very inefficient way of assigning men but, if efficiency were decisive, then surely accountants and economists should head our armed forces.

Alternatively, we might emulate the Israeli model, particularly since it might serve to redeem our National Guard and reserve forces. Their reserve units can be fully ready for war in three days or so; ours, we are told, would need three months or more, even though U.S. reservists serve on duty roughly the same number of days as the Israelis do.

The Israeli model achieves the same stability as the British: soldiers are assigned to a specific brigade and battalion, and there they remain throughout their years on active duty, and beyond that during the annual reserve call-ups as well. An initiative has been launched by the present chief of staff of the U.S. Army, General E. C. Meyer, which begins to provide a modicum of stability for our units, but the computerized manpower-management crowd strongly opposes that sort of thing because it results in "inefficiency," as some units become undermanned and others overstaffed. That is perfectly true, of course, and yet we need more, much more, of the sort of inefficiency that we have so recently seen at work on the hills around Port Stanley and in Lebanon.

Much more disruptive still would it be to accept the evidence that would lead us to recast the training of our young officers. West Point is an institution already quasi-antique and greatly respected, and even the new Air Force Academy is already sacrosanct. It would be outright sacrilege to suggest that we should stop the present procedure whereby all cadets are educated to become future generals (and technically trained, bureaucratically skillful, politically sensitive generals at that) and to turn out instead junior fighting leaders.

It is precisely in our technological-managerial age that the technological-managerial education given to our young officers has become less and less useful, if not actually counterproductive. Why should four years of electrical engineering and economics prepare a young man to lead others in combat? Why not teach war and tactics instead, in a course lasting perhaps one or two years instead of the present four? And why should fighter pilots receive a full-scale university education, instead of being taught how to hunt and kill with their machines? In due course, those who remain in the military career can receive all the education they need, but only *after* they have done their junior duty in the realm of combat.

Once upon a time, when this nation was young and primitive, it made eminent sense to use West Point in order to provide skills that civil society so greatly lacked. And in a nation of pioneer farmers, urban craftsmen, and frontiersmen, it was right to believe that the status of the leader could best be assured by teaching him social graces, bourgeois manners, and book knowledge. But in our suburban society, where half the population receives some kind of higher education, it is the skills and aptitudes of war that are missing and it is those that the academics should provide.

What ensures the status of the junior officer in both the British and Israeli armies are three things of supreme importance to the soldiers he leads: his greater willingness to take personal risks in order to reduce the risks imposed on his men, his greater knowledge of the hardware and software of soldiering, and his personal store of combat tradecraft. Those, surely, are the things that junior officers should be taught, and not sociology and economics, electrical engineering, and management—especially when the figure of the long-service combat sergeant is rapidly disappearing from the scene.

Another example of a most uncongenial lesson, which classic Manchurian arguments try to obscure, is of a radically different character. The British, it will be recalled, employed North Sea car ferries, container ships, passenger liners, and transport aircraft to sustain the logistic demands of an operation of exceptional range. The U.S. Navy does, of course, deploy a great deal of specialized logistic and amphibious shipping and would not have to resort to improvisations in order to stage an intervention on the scale of the Falklands. Along with the air force it could sustain a much larger operation solely with service-issue ships and aircraft but although large, their capacity is not large enough: We have three marine divisions, but only enough amphibious shipping for one division and-a-bit; we have 13 large carriers, but in a serious conflict we may need 15 or 20; and even a limited-war commitment of the Rapid Deployment Force (RDF) could easily require more transport-aircraft capacity than the air force now has.

It would thus be most useful to plan ahead for the use of mobilized civilian equipment, in order to survey ships and aircraft, and then develop and build bolt-on weapon rigs, containerized radar sets, boxed communication centers, and other such things for ships, as well as loading gear and add-on electronics.

Unconsciously repeating all the objections that the Admiralty raised in 1915-1916 against Lloyd George's demand for a convoy system (when convoys were finally introduced the number of sinkings declined sharply and immediately), the navy holds that civilian ships are unusable, since their crews would be undisciplined and their skippers would be incapable of keeping stations, while the ships themselves would be virtually useless because of their inherent design. And yet in the recent fighting, we saw civilian-manned British ships operating successfully not merely in a war zone but actually under fire; and we saw too how additional Harriers were deployed aboard an ordinary container ship, converted within a few days to serve as an aircraft carrier of sorts. If the British can improvise even an aircraft carrier, can we not at least plan ahead to employ civilian transport ships that might be desperately needed?

Similarly, the air force now proclaims itself short of airlift capacity and its claim is valid. The additional airlift, however, would not be needed on a day-to-day basis, but only in rare military emergencies to deliver large intervention forces. So why not rely on the great mass of aircraft in our commercial fleets for some of that surge capability? There is already, to be sure, a program that is meant to do just that, but the total airlift capacity involved remains quite small, and the air force is reluctant to use its funds for the purpose. We do need a larger fleet of airlifters of the C-5 variety, as only they can carry the heaviest and largest weapons; but for the great bulk of our airlift needs, civilian aircraft would be eminently suitable. The refusal of the air force to exploit fully the vast potential of the largest commercial air fleet in the world reminds us that military bureaucracies will never greatly favor arrangements that do not provide more officer slots for our over-officered armed forces.

In the three detailed articles that follow, much of the most important evidence of the two wars is carefully reviewed. As we seek to extract the valid lessons, let Manchuria be remembered.

3

UNDERSTANDING
THE SOVIETS

Critical Choices in the 1980s

Robert F. Byrnes

A central theme of this book is that Soviet leaders face increasingly acute challenges to undertake changes in their system and in certain of its policies. These challenges have been generated by the regime's successes in modernizing a traditional society, in impelling vigorous and long-sustained economic growth, and in making a more powerful place for itself in the world of nations. Having successfully transformed the old society, the leaders must decide, probably during the decade of the 1980s, whether and how they can adapt and alter the political order in ways necessary to make the new society work effectively. The basic question is: can a narrowly constituted political elite, comfortable in the security of its achievements and power and reluctant to face the hazards of change, generate the will to move innovatively to meet potential threats of stagnation, instability, and decline? Can it choose wisely between the disagreeable and the intolerable?

The Converging Dilemmas in the 1980s

The Soviet leaders' central problem derives from the convergence in the 1980s of several basic dilemmas, all coming to a critical point at about the same time; all cumulative, complicated, and closely and irrevocably interrelated; and all demanding hard policy choices that will greatly affect the Soviet system and its role in world politics for years ahead. These years promise to be as crucial as the late 1920s, when the Soviet leaders debated the policies that they should adopt after they had consolidated Communist rule and completed reconstruction from war and revolution.

None of these quandaries is new. All are fundamental and reflect long-term developments. The Soviet leaders have long been aware of them and have been struggling to evade them or to resolve them in a piecemeal way. Above all, the problems have become crucial at a time when the Soviet Union must complete the transfer of its highly centralized authority from Brezhnev to Andropov and then to a new generation. These are delicate and even hazardous undertakings in a political structure in which contending interest groups can be ruthless.

Changing a Conservative System and Society

The Soviet Union is an authoritarian state ruled by a stable, aged oligarchy determined to preserve full party authority and deeply committed to the status quo within the Soviet Union. The Soviet population is generally patriotic and at least outwardly submissive to whatever policies the leadership adopts, although apathy and discontent are widespread, especially among non-Russians: some areas of social life remain outside effective government control; and the Soviet peoples have shown shrewd skills in circumventing official policies they do not approve. The government and the country have benefited from three decades of economic growth, rising standards of living, steadily increasing military strength and prestige, and success in world politics, but this period has recently come to an end. Like all countries at all times, the Soviet Union faces a number of serious issues. These threaten to become acute in the 1980s.

Introducing fundamental transformations into any complex modern society is difficult, but it is especially so for a system that has become immobile and even frozen and is tied to an outmoded and perhaps irrelevant philosophy, allegedly revolutionary and internationalist but actually conservative and nationalist.

Ironically, the Soviet Union faces a new set of demanding choices in part because of its successes. By moving peasants into the urban world and providing two or three generations of workers the opportunity to move up and to assist their children to reach even higher class status, the leaders have fostered the creation of skills and knowledge, aspirations and appetites that the system would find increasingly difficult to satisfy, even if its economy were booming and opportunities for higher education and advancement were not declining. Soviet emphasis upon science, education, status, and the rights of workers and peasants has made the issue of social mobility especially acute. Like Count Witte in the 1890s, and indeed all Russian rulers since Peter the Great, Soviet leaders from Lenin through Brezhnev have appreciated that education in unprogressive societies leads to revolution, but that ignorance produces defeat. Careful Soviet monitoring of education has prevented the accumulation of violent pressures for change, but the provision of training and education to millions has enlarged pressures for upward mobility and created skepticism in a society based on faith.

The growth of nationalisms in this multinational state, that of the Russians as well as those of the minorities, has intensified the issue of governance. This phenomenon is related to the growth of national consciousness and the establishment of national states elsewhere in the world, but it is also a consequence of Communist fostering of minority cultures within the Soviet Union.

Russian nationalism has a longer history than most of the other Soviet nationalisms. It has blossomed because of the prominent role Russians play throughout the Soviet system and because of their visible contribution to the rise of the Soviet Union as a world power. The burgeoning thrust of Russian nationalism inevitably collides with the interests of the other ethnic groups, who are increasingly self-assertive and who seek higher status, increased freedom from Russian rule, and greater access to the instruments of authority. These hostilities are sharpened by economic, social, and religious discontent, especially in the Baltic republics, Ukraine, and Central Asia, and by the visible flattening of Slavic population growth at a time when most of the increase in the Soviet population comes from Moslem non-Russians in Central Asia.

Regime efforts to base itself on Russian national tradition as a means of stimulating support among the Russians and other Slavs naturally alienate the non-Russian half of the Soviet population. The party's simultaneous efforts to emphasize Soviet patriotism and to suppress extreme Russian nationalism have turned some Russian nationalists, Communists as well as noncommunists, against the system. In short, the rise of competing nationalisms is creating a bundle of annoying, increasingly serious strains that may constitute a powder keg in another generation or two.

The many varieties of dissident movements that keep coming up like flowers through cracks in concrete are another assertion of values that differ from those of the state, particularly because these attitudes now appear among the professional elite, a crucial class in any authoritarian society. Dissidence is a reflection of stubborn human nature. It expresses individualism against authority, old traditions and religious beliefs against the official state creed, and the eternal problems any dictatorship faces as its seeks to enforce total discipline in a modernizing society at a time when its coercive, material, and normative methods of social control are slowly losing effectiveness.

Marxist-Leninist faith and revolutionary enthusiasm among the population died long ago and left a vacuum, and the heroic period of Soviet history has ended. Evidence from party programs to pulp literature reflects disillusionment, pessimism, decline of the work ethic, and evaporation of civic morale.

The general rejection of official values and a turning away from a sense of national purpose toward nostalgia and the cultivation of private interests have led to widespread corruption, the decline of self-discipline, absenteeism, the second or unofficial economy, consumerism, and cynicism. Alcoholism has become a serious social curse. This is not the kind of society Lenin had in mind in 1917.

Many of these problems are similar to those in Western societies, but they are especially corrosive to a Communist system that seeks full control and imposition of its values. The visible conflict between the leaders' determination to preserve the system and the inexorable flowering of social, national, and spiritual forces that demand change creates one of the most serious dilemmas the rulers face and one closely related to their other challenges.

The Changing World: Technology, Especially Communications

Preserving an established authoritarian system is becoming increasingly difficult because the Soviet Union cannot isolate itself from a world going through changes of every kind at an ever more rapid and increasingly universal pace. These transformations of values, customs, habits, dress, economies, means of communication, and every aspect of human life have spread to every part of the globe. Even "the winds of freedom" that helped destroy the old empires have invaded the Soviet Union.

Some Russian rulers, such as Peter the Great, and Soviet leaders—Stalin in the first Five-Year Plan and at an increasingly rapid pace Khrushchev and Brezhnev—in a gingerly way established relationships with the West. The expansion of economic and cultural ties with the most advanced countries has introduced forces for change, beginning with the elites, those most involved, and then seeping slowly down through society. Louis XIV declared that nations touch only at the top, but this century's revolutions of transportation and communications have destroyed that old truism, even in an age of censorship and jamming. Contact with other countries through acquisition of scientific ideas and technical products, cooperative economic programs, participation in international conferences, exchange of scholars and graduate students, increasing access to foreign technical literature and selected belles lettres weakens authority at home. The Soviet government seeks a fire that will not burn. It wishes to be in the world, but not of it. It is struggling, as the tsars did, with the eternal problem of Western influence, trying to borrow on the one hand and to keep infection away on the other, but its participation in the affairs of the world has increased at an ever greater rate in the last two decades and therefore the choice has become ever more painful.

Soviet participation in the world market under Brezhnev illustrates this change and the problems it raises. In the late 1960s and throughout the 1970s, Soviet and Eastern European leaders increased trade with the West and borrowed heavily to evade the hard decisions concerning decentralization of the economy and the reallocation of resources among the military, capital investment, and the consumer. The Communist leaders hoped these injections would modernize their economies, increase the supply of satisfactory consumer goods, and resolve basic economic problems. Far from eliminating the need for innovation, this approach created an enlarged set of problems, thus making the need more urgent. Economic involvement with the West introduced more external influences, including inflation and recession; increased consumer appetites; softened the popular view of Western Europe; helped bring about systemic crisis in Poland; and at the same time exhausted the Western cornucopia as a *deus ex machina*.

The dilemma that contact with the West raises is especially visible and acute because a new era, the age of information, is transforming the West even more rapidly than the steam and jet engines did. Knowledge is becoming the world's most important product, as agricultural research, atomic weapons and energy, medical science, and discoveries affecting every aspect of life demonstrate. The age of the university, miniature electronics, automatic machinery, computers, and satellites is inevitably a worldwide age. The production of information and the development and manufacture of the equipment which produces knowledge and distributes it quickly are transforming all societies.

The countries that recognize this transformation, join the world, and contribute are becoming stronger. They also develop closer relations with other states and peoples, export their political systems and values, open themselves up to ideas, and become increasingly interdependent. A country that restricts this flow, controls the number and use of Xerox machines, prevents automatic dial telephoning between its own cities, reduces telephonic and other communications with other states, and tries to isolate itself inevitably slips toward decline. It forces itself into an eternally unsuccessful effort at "catching up," hampered by restraints of its own creation.

The Soviet leaders must soon make a hard choice concerning this challenge by defining their relations with this new technology and changing world because the transformations in the outside world that technology creates will not wait. The options are all hazardous, particularly because Soviet leaders cannot isolate the choices in the field of information from decisions they must make about other problems. Withdrawal from contact with the world is virtually impossible and would be costly even in the short run. Maintaining a wall with carefully monitored turnstiles is difficult, ineffective, and in a perverse way increases fascination with the outside world. Moreover, tightening restrictions is more difficult than earlier and would weaken further the vitality of national life, make the Soviet Union technologically more backward, and reduce its effectiveness in the competition for influence abroad. On the other hand, reducing or eliminating barriers would be fatal to control, first in Eastern Europe and then in the Soviet Union itself.

Most observers agree that the most likely response to this series of options will be increased repression and cultural isolation, combined with a determined effort to obtain the fruits of Western advance without the infections, basically an impossible task and one that will make the dilemma ever more acute.

The Slowing Economy: "Swollen State, Spent Society"

The economy of the USSR, having grown consistently since 1890, except during the two world wars, is the second largest in the world. It benefits from abundant natural resources, a large population, a vast industrial base, and potential for continued growth. During the 1970s, it profited from a windfall in foreign trade: its exports of oil and gas at sharply rising world prices enabled it considerably to expand imports of Western science, technology, and food products. At the same time, the economy displays grave systemic weaknesses.

The most visible determinant of Soviet policy in the 1980s and the most complicated, far-reaching, and difficult policy decisions are the consequences of the slowing rate of economic growth and unprecedented conditions of resource stringency. Years of economic growth at a constantly diminishing rate, from seven percent in the 1950s to five percent in the sixties, to four and then three percent in the seventies, enabled the Soviet leaders simultaneously to increase investment, the size and quality of the armed forces, and the standard of living. However, they now face a period in which the annual rate of growth will at best average 2 or 2.5 percent and may decline to one percent and virtual stagnation. The declining rate of growth reduces funds available for investment just when aging plant demands new equipment and when new needs arise.

In addition, the growth of labor supply will decelerate in the years ahead, falling to about 0.4 percent per year in the 1980s. Most of the increase will be among non-Russians in Central Asia, a population far from the most advanced infrastructure and main sources of raw materials, less skilled than the Russians, and generally unwilling to leave their homes or their region. On the other hand, bringing industry to areas where population is increasing would have very high capital costs and would intensify problems among ethnic groups.

Labor productivity will continue to decline: it is now zero or even negative because of insufficient capital investment, poor organization, failure to innovate, restrictions on labor mobility, and the government's continued inability to provide sufficient consumer goods as material incentives for an apathetic working class that has large savings accounts but nothing to purchase.

Most embarrassingly, agriculture remains an expensive problem. In spite of massive investments over the last twenty years (about one-third of all Soviet investment), greatly increased attention from government, and an annual increase of two percent in agricultural production, Soviet agriculture proves less and less capable of meeting consumer demands for more and better food. Even in 1982, Soviet citizens ate only two-thirds as much meat as Poles did. The cost of imported grain in 1981 was about $16 billion in hard currencies. American specialists estimate that the Soviet Union will import 25 to 40 million tons of grain annually throughout the 1980s (it imported 44 million tons of grain in 1981-82), and that other agricultural imports, including meat, will remain at the high levels of 1975-82. These massive purchases have riddled the hope that the Soviet Union could become self-sufficient with regard to food and have weakened the myth that the Soviet Union was or could become a model for other developing countries to emulate. Above all, they make the Soviet Union to some degree dependent upon the United States and other grain growers and therefore affect the conduct of Soviet policy.

Government policies designed to keep food prices low for workers have created a structure in which the consumer's market price is about one-half the cost of the produce to the state. The food subsidy in 1980 was about $50 billion and about $70 billion in 1982, 8 or 9 percent of Soviet GNP. The annual per capita cost of food subsidies then was about 195 rubles, somewhat more than an industrial worker's monthly wages and fifty percent more than the combined per capita expenditures for health and education. However, the Soviet government remains unwilling to introduce reality into pricing.

Soviet agriculture suffers bouts of poor weather, but its problems lie deep in the system and its operating procedures. Collectivization and the dead hand of centralized control of planning and management share responsibility. Government by a city-based apparatus since 1917 has neglected and penalized the rural folk. The basic backwardness of rural life, from mud roads to dreadful housing, poor schools, and grossly inadequate consumer goods, the exodus of the young to the cities, and the aging of the agricultural labor force have led to low productivity of farm labor.

The basic trouble is that central control and direction of the economy are an essential part of the political system. Major changes in the economy, which many Soviet specialists recognize as necessary, would undermine the controls party leaders consider crucial. Making or tolerating major innovations therefore strikes at the system itself.

Within this central dilemma, other equally awkward perplexities persist. Thus, the declining rate of growth makes the choices on allocation of resources among the military forces, capital investment, and the consumer both decisive and painful. Reducing or even freezing the level of military spending to free resources for investment or the consumer would require a heroic effort by the rulers and create serious political strains. Most Soviet leaders would consider such a step strategically dangerous, especially if the reductions affected R and D and production of new weapons at a time when they believed the United States was leaping ahead with new technology. Indeed, only a solidly entrenched leadership convinced that the need for innovation is desperate would decide to limit military expenditures, a course that many outside observers consider vital.

Increasing investment to stimulate growth, unleash new energy resources, develop new territorial complexes, and replace aging machinery would force the leaders to reduce or freeze military spending or consumer goods production or both. Similarly, increased attention to the consumer sector would directly affect the resources available for the military and investment.

Changing allocations of resources is particularly difficult because the immediate interests of central institutions and elites and of millions of Soviet citizens are so visibly engaged and because this conundrum is so tightly related to others, to potential ideological quarrels among the leaders, and to the character of the system. Party and bureaucratic opposition to relaxing familiar controls is great. Many workers oppose innovations because change would threaten job security, create sharp wage differentials to increase incentives, and raise prices by ending subsidies. All those benefiting from the system fear, justifiably, that changes in the economy would lead to ever greater pressures for further innovations. In addition, significant changes within the Soviet economy would encourage pressures for innovation in Eastern Europe, which would threaten stability, especially in Poland.

Most Western observers and many Soviet economists recognize the need for specific changes in the management of industry, especially for relaxation of the connections between the planner and the manager and between the manager and the consumer, and for a turn toward market socialism. They also recognize the need for changes in agriculture, including decentralization of control from Moscow, encouragement of private plots, vast improvements in rural life, the phased end of food subsidies, and perhaps even a return to the New Economic Policy of the 1920s. They agree that increased production and improved quality of consumer goods are now a prerequisite for Soviet economic growth. They also recognize that reducing production of consumer goods and the standard of living would affect in a negative way every aspect of Soviet life, beginning with productivity. Most Soviet citizens, accustomed to steady improvement in living standards, have visibly higher expectations than earlier and are aware of the gap between their own levels and standards of living elsewhere, even in Eastern Europe; the Soviet standard of living is about one-third the American. Keeping the Russian worker reasonably satisfied may provide the regime its greatest challenge. In fact, the situation is so grave that skilled observers conclude that the system must somehow meet consumer demands for such basic elements as food, housing, and health care to assure continuing stability.

In short, great pressures for changes in the Soviet economic system exist, ideas are abundant, and the potential for dramatic change and improvement is high. On the other hand, the political hazards and bureaucratic inertia are equally strong. Prospects for change are therefore problematic. Most outside observers believe that military expenditures will remain at least at the same absolute level, even if the Soviet Union and the United States reach effective arms control and reduction agreements. In sum, reform or innovation is risky and disagreeable. On the other hand, stagnation is intolerable. Sooner or later, Soviet leaders must make hard choices. Most observers believe that the Soviet government will seek to stimulate recovery by tinkering with the economy, especially through "organizational" and "mobilizational" changes aimed at increasing production of consumer goods.

Eastern Europe

The Soviet Union dominates the regimes and the policies of Poland, East Germany, Czechoslovakia, Hungary, Bulgaria, and to some extent Romania. These countries greatly enhance the USSR's power position because of their geographical location, natural resources, population, and productive capabilities. Stalin saw Eastern Europe as a barrier against the West and as the first step beyond the Soviet frontiers toward universal Communism. His successors see it as a vital part of the Soviet empire, one which ensures that the Soviet Union is a great European power. A Communist Eastern Europe provides a point of pressure against Western Europe. The Warsaw Pact constitutes a useful military alliance and diplomatic instrument. Different East European countries serve in a variety of ways as Soviet proxies in foreign areas, as purveyors of arms and economic aid to revolutionary movements in various parts of the world, and as links to Communist parties and to international front movements. The Soviet presence maintains Communist rule in those countries, serves as a barrier against the West, and helps to legitimize the Soviet system in Soviet eyes. Above all, rule by Communists loyal to or subservient to Moscow strengthens faith among Communists everywhere and creates fear among others that a Soviet Eastern Europe represents a permanent step toward Communist world power. A reversal of this situation would lead to unraveling of this central doctrine in the Communist faith.

Eastern Europe as a whole remains visibly unstable, even though Communist rule seems solid, except in Poland. Much of this instability derives from a history that thirty or forty years cannot overcome, for these peoples have created instabilities for all their conquerors. Soviet rule has revived East European nationalisms, aimed now against the Soviet effort to transform their cultures. The peoples resent Communism because it violates their histories and traditions, because the Soviets imposed it, and because the usurped authority of their rulers rests on Soviet power.

The social and cultural tensions that have developed in the Soviet Union have bubbled in Eastern Europe, too, only with greater visibility and effect. East European economic rates of growth have slowed greatly; in Poland they have been negative since 1978, and in most countries, especially Czechoslovakia, they are stagnant or declining. Prospects for improvement in the 1980s, except for Hungary, are dismal. Each state also faces the delicate problem of transferring authority to another set of rulers at some point in the 1980s.

Soviet rule under Stalin in particular exploited these peoples mercilessly, but they have been an expensive dependency and growing economic drain since about 1970, tieing down vast numbers of Soviet manpower and enormous Soviet resources. The Soviet Union granted these countries subsidies of $20 billion in one form or another in 1980, and the dependency is likely to remain high, particularly in oil and gas.

Poland is the heart of the Soviet empire, as it was of the Russian empire a century ago. In the 1980s it plays the central role in Soviet relations with the West that it has often played before. The collapse of the Polish party and economy illuminates the serious instabilities that wrack this potentially explosive area and the way in which the major hard choices converge and affect each other. The situation in Poland places an additional heavy strain upon the Soviet economy, and those contemplating the introduction of innovations into the Soviet economy must consider the ultimate effects of such changes in Poland and elsewhere in Eastern Europe.

As the consequence of national history and of a crisis which has matured over two decades, the great bulk of the Polish nation has rejected not just particular leaders, policies, incompetence, and corruption but the Communist system itself in a genuine, unplanned, if abortive, revolution from below. As far as one can tell, all Polish youth have rejected the system. Only the sense of responsibility that Poles have learned in crises since 1956, deserved fear of Soviet military intervention, and the dependence of the Polish Central Committee, military leaders, and security apparatus on the Soviets have prevented civil war, Soviet invasion, and international crisis. Poland is a cancer that the Soviets may freeze into temporary remission but one for which even a miraculous economic recovery would provide no certain cure.

The choices in Poland are even more troubling than those the Soviet economy offers, and Soviet leaders possess few if any options. Tinkering or palliatives would at best slow economic decline and perhaps prevent violent outbreaks: the gap between policy and reality is too wide, and the Communists have squandered too many years. Salvation from now-cautious Western bankers is most unlikely, with or without default and bankruptcy.

If the Polish regime could bring itself to honor its 1980 agreements concerning trade union and other rights—and if it could win Soviet approval for such a stunning reversal—the Polish appetite for sweeping reforms would grow. A government attempt to regain direct but discreet control of restored popular forces, even if the church restrained them, while it maneuvered between the vigilant Soviet Union and a watchful West, would require political skill a weak and divided party could hardly sustain. Moreover, such innovations in Poland would signal pressures for comparable changes elsewhere in Eastern Europe and in the Soviet Union's western regions. The inevitable reaction of the great mass of conservatives in the Soviet government, especially in the armed forces, to proposals that threaten to weaken the Soviet grip on the main approach to Germany and Europe would clearly prevent such a policy.

Another Soviet option, the most likely one, is that of reasserting Soviet authority over its East European empire, particularly Poland. This choice would mean supporting the military junta, or an even more reactionary group if Jaruzelski is not successful; strengthening those instruments that retained Poland for the Communists (the party apparatus, the military forces, and the security police); tightening all controls; relying on the presence or proximity of Soviet forces to ensure submission; and intervening directly if that should prove necessary. This is not an inviting prospect, but one to which the failures of the last thirty-five years have brought them. Such a policy would involve paying great attention to the transfers of authority throughout Eastern Europe in the 1980s. The Soviets would also seek to strengthen and tighten the Warsaw Pact and to provide limited economic assistance in dire crises, just as they provided $8 billion to Poland in 1981-82. At the same time, they would press these regimes to reduce the Soviet subsidy by raising the price of energy supplies, organizing new bilateral and multilateral trading agreements under the Council for Mutual Economic Assistance (CMEA), and arranging that these states help build Soviet pipelines and other capital enterprises.

All this would only reiterate the unsuccessful policies of the past three decades. The effect would increase apathy in the Polish economy and resentment against the Soviet Union. Restricting access to the West to carefully monitored turnstiles would increase alienation of the intellectuals and the youth already disaffected and simultaneously heighten the West's attraction to the entire population. The impact upon Western Europe, the Middle East and the Mediterranean states, the United States, and indeed most of the world would constitute a serious blow to Soviet prospects and adversely affect Soviet options on the other converging dilemmas. Indeed, some Soviet leaders must worry about the high cost of maintaining empire, the way in which its unraveling might begin with any loss of control over Poland, and the high cost of intervention and open Soviet occupation of Poland. But they cannot now escape.

A century ago Russian leaders recognized that no solution existed for "the Polish problem." The situation in Poland was a millstone around all efforts to introduce political, economic, or social reform into the Russian Empire: "The Poles, like the poor, we will always have with us." The Polish issue also divided Russia from the West European states, as it does again. Holding on to Warsaw cost Russia Constantinople a hundred years ago, and Warsaw bears a heavy price a century later. Poland and its economy remain major touchstones of Soviet policy and reveal the complicated and difficult nature of the hard choices Soviet leaders face. The Polish situation is so grave and the instabilities of some of its neighbors of such concern to Soviet leaders that maintaining the vigilant grip on the territory and people and returning Poland to some kind of "normal" Communist rule will constitute a main determinant of Soviet policy throughout the 1980s.

Opportunities Abroad

Events beyond the Soviet empire's frontiers, including developments in which the Soviets play no direct role, affect Soviet conduct and also raise policy dilemmas. Such developments demonstrate that Soviet leaders must take into consideration the complexities of an ever-shrinking and more interdependent world in reaching decisions. Some occurrences raise concerns for Soviet security. Others promise bright opportunities for Soviet advantage through meddling or scavenging but at the same time create problems because Soviet actions would affect other complicated and interrelated problems. In the 1980s, these factors and the presumed revival of American strength and resolution will force Soviet leaders to choose between taking advantage of tempting lures of expansion elsewhere in the world and maintaining the positive kinds of relations with the West that will enable the USSR to face its domestic dilemmas and to achieve its main goals in Western Europe. Relations with the People's Republic of China complicate foreign policy choices greatly because the Soviets see the Chinese as rivals for influence among radical and revolutionary forces.

In sum, the Soviet Union has limited ability to maneuver in its foreign policy, as it does in its domestic problems, and it faces a series of hard choices. Ironically, these dilemmas reflect in part Soviet foreign policy achievements in the 1970s, when the Soviet Union construed detente as a one-way street requiring no Soviet restraint. These policies ended the SALT process and provoked a massive military effort in the United States, alienated much of the Third World, and produced a negative effect on Soviet economic relations with the West. Both the successes and the costs of these policies sharpen the dilemmas the political system faces in the 1980s.

The Soviet leaders' main concern is to help prevent a nuclear war by preparing for such a war and using fear of war outside the Soviet Union to weaken resolution in other societies.

The United States is the principal Soviet adversary, a powerful country with strong military forces, an enormously productive and inventive economy, and such vitality that both its high and its low culture have gained permanent influence in much of the world. In fact, comparison of the vigor of American culture and the moribundity of Soviet culture and of their relative impact everywhere in the world, even in Eastern Europe, illustrates the weakness of the Soviet Union in all fields of competition except military.

However, the United States suffers, as does most of the world, from a numbing recession that as yet has no end in sight. The apparent, perhaps temporary, decline of American confidence and resolution, the social and intellectual fissures that disturb its serenity, its economic problems, and the perpetual uncertainties of American foreign policy weaken its role in the West. Leading an alliance of countries, particularly democratic ones, over a prolonged period of time has always proved difficult. Even so, Soviet leaders must keep the United States and its policies in mind whenever they make decisions on modifying the Soviet political structure, entering the era of information, resolving domestic economic issues, choosing alternatives in Poland, and considering actions anywhere in the world.

Even though it is underdeveloped and weak, and will remain so for at least another generation, the People's Republic of China also exerts a visible influence on Soviet conduct. The Soviet leaders and people have a deep irrational fear of the Chinese. The Soviet leaders still see themselves as the high priests of the international Communist movement and regard China as a keen rival for that movement's tattered flag. Beyond these ideological ambitions and quarrels lie ancient and deep national hostilities and conflicts of national interest, represented in the 1980s by Chinese opposition to the Soviet role in Vietnam and to the Soviet invasion of Afghanistan. Soviet maintenance of massive military forces on the Chinese borders at the expense of longterm economic growth demonstrates the depth of the Soviet preoccupation with China. Soviet options with regard to China are limited by reluctance to abandon positions in Southeast Asia and Afghanistan or to revise relationships with India, by the visible clash of Soviet and Chinese national interests as neighboring states, and to a lesser degree by ideology. However, the major Soviet concern is not so much the China of 1982 or even of 1990, but that American and Japanese aid may help increase Chinese economic and military power so that China may one day become a serious and unrelenting threat. The greatest fear, of course, is that the United States, Japan, and China, and possibly a unified Western Europe, will one day encircle the Soviet Union.

The Soviet leaders see Western Europe as a crucial area in which Soviet influence and leverage can grow. In spite of its remarkable political and economic recovery since 1945, cooperative efforts unthinkable as recently as forty years ago, and construction of bases for increased cooperation and even unity among democratic states, Western Europe lacks confidence and self-assurance. The area is vulnerable to outside pressures and no longer feels certain of the American guarantee of security and peace. Skillful Soviet diplomatic and psychological use of their huge military forces; disagreements between the United States and its allies over Soviet power and policy, strategies, trade, and the division of responsibilities and costs; and the effects of the so-called peace campaign have enriched the culture of appease-ment and fueled neutralist and even pacifist movements that will be-devil Western policy makers throughout the decade. Those movements will probably reach one of their peaks in the controversy over theater nuclear weapons, and 1983 may therefore witness an impressive Soviet "peace" campaign, based on attractive Soviet arms proposals, just when the West Germans especially are reaching decisions about the installation of weapons to counter the long-established SS20s.

Western Europe represents no military threat to the Soviets. How-ever, its existence, its freedoms, and its prosperity exert a continuing powerful appeal throughout Eastern Europe and the Soviet Union. Western Europe is therefore both a source of infection and an area of opportunity, one in which Soviet leaders see an important role for pa-tient, opportunistic diplomacy, but one in which they must approach their limited options with immense skill and tact, using both the carrot and the stick and somehow conducting themselves at home and in Po-land in such a way as not to strengthen West European fears.

Areas further afield are less attractive than Western Europe but nevertheless influence Soviet conduct. The more than one hundred new Third World countries and some older ones vary greatly one from another, but many are fragile constructs and suffer from serious mal-adies: insecure new institutions; internal discord; dreadful poverty side by side with spectacular new wealth; generally rising popular expecta-tions; ethnic, religious, and social divisions; resentment of their former imperial rulers; and powerful anti-Americanism. Many have ambitious radical leaders who seek quickly to transform their countries and make them important in world politics. They invite Soviet interest and sup-port, and Soviet achievements and authoritarianism attract some lead-ers.

In many of these countries, previous performance, distance, So-viet inability to compete with the United States and Western Europe in providing economic assistance, and the sorry economic performance of all Communist states in recent years hamper Soviet prospects. The So-viets' need to take sides in sensitive conflicts (such as between Iran and Iraq) and Soviet policy on Afghanistan and on religion hampers them in many areas, especially in the Moslem world.

Even so, Soviet leaders must conclude that a number of oppor-tunities to advance Soviet interests in several different areas of a cha-otic and even anarchic world will appear in the 1980s. In some cases, they may be able without significant cost or hazard to increase anarchy and disorder in regional and world politics, undermine Western influ-ence, and create conditions from which they may benefit openly, merely by providing direct or indirect support through proxies, such as

Cuba, radical and revolutionary movements, terrorism, and disruptive countries, such as Libya.

In other cases, countries in several different parts of the world will on some occasion offer attractive opportunities for meddling or scavenging, as Angola, South Yemen, and Ethiopia did in the 1970s. Soviet choices in each case would presumably reflect careful calculation of benefits and costs and of the effect upon the other complicated and interrelated problems for which they seek solutions.

Latin America, especially Central America, offers an especially attractive area for a carefully calibrated Soviet policy, combining the skills of the sympathetic observer and the speculator, of the nationalist and the Communist. The Soviets can profit from the deep fissures within each state and the disagreements among them, the strength of anti-Americanism, and Cuba as an instrument. On the other hand, Soviet leaders appreciate the sensitive concern with which the American public and any American government would face any expansion of Cuban and/or Soviet influence in Central America.

Finally, the Soviet leaders' decisions and conduct in the Middle East will reflect their alert and keen interest in the enormous potential benefits a deeply divided Iran could provide. Their choices here would represent the other interrelated concerns, the kinds of openings or opportunities which arise, timing, and Soviet evaluation of American firmness in defending American national interests, and that of other countries, in that part of the world. When considering all these attractive opportunities, the Soviet leaders must recognize that their ability to act is sharply limited by the other hard choices they face.

Conclusion

The new leadership that will one day emerge into power after Andropov, like that associated with him, has been carefully selected, trained and monitored. As far as outsiders can tell, the members of the younger generation (those now in their fifties and sixties) apparently share the values of present leaders, embrace and benefit from the party-state system, and view the Soviet Union, Eastern Europe, and the world in much the same way as their elders do. They entered political life after Stalin's death, and they are probably eager to set aside those who have ruled for such a long time. They seem more aware of the grave character of Soviet problems and more eager to "get the country going" than their elders have been. The failures of the system, the convergence of a number of critical problems, and the centrality of these rites of passage suggest that internal affairs will attract the bulk of their interest. The speed and skill with which Andropov moves this new generation into some share of power will greatly affect Soviet policy over the next decade and long into the future.

Most outside observers consider that resolute and far-reaching internal changes within a decade are necessary to prevent the erosion of Soviet power, future instabilities of a serious character within the Soviet empire, and perhaps as a consequence aggressive diplomatic and other forceful actions outside the empire. At the same time, these observers generally agree that the immobile character of the system, the absence of a reform mechanism, the thorny nature of the problems, and the ways the issues are interrelated limit the likelihood of major changes. They also conclude that the Andropov generation and those close to it will originally at least emphasize more law and order, labor discipline, Soviet nationalism, and moderately tighter police measures and negative incentives to increase productivity. Such a series of policies would produce stagnation, or even some decline in the Soviet economy, but not an immediate decline in military power or collapse, because both the system and the Soviet people are stubborn and adaptable.

In short, most observers see muddling through or muddling down as one likely choice within the Soviet Union and in Eastern Europe and in Soviet policy in the world at large. Such an option, common among political leaders everywhere, would delay fundamental decisions until the 1990s.

Under Andropov, the debate over policy choices may sharpen. Candidates jostling for place and power may advocate changes primarily to advance the interest of their bureaucratic or territorial constituencies or simply to amass power. Policy disagreements may arise within the leadership, and some candidates may adopt demagogic postures for change merely to strengthen their positions in the leadership. However, the problems are such that intense concerns will almost surely break through the now dominant apparent unanimity and that some members of the elite will advocate fundamental changes. No one can forecast whether or when such debates or disagreements will become acute or how the leadership will resolve them.

Whether Andropov and his colleagues, or their successors, would have the authority, resolution, and skill to carry through such transformations is a great unknown, because the oppositions to innovation are strong and entrenched. However, the death of Brezhnev and other senior Politburo officials does raise the possibility that the new leaders will act upon the recognized need for changes.

I believe that some present and probable future leaders, as well as many members of the Soviet elite, recognize the need for structured changes in the system and for major policy changes after sixteen years of immobility. Andropov and his colleagues may therefore attempt and somehow carry out important changes, beginning with a peace campaign with genuine arms reduction proposals as the centerpiece. But resistance to change is powerful and determined.

Outside actors, including the United States, can have little or no direct influence on how the Soviet Union chooses to manage its internal affairs. The United States and its allies should at least recognize the character of the challenge the Soviet Union presents and should be prepared to use their considerable strengths at appropriate times to contain Soviet power. The West should appreciate that the contest will be a long one, that it is at heart a political struggle, not a military one, that managing or controlling the competition will remain crucial, and that no quick solutions or early answers are likely. The struggle is a test of two civilizations, two cultures, each with its own strengths and weaknesses. If the United States and its allies should succeed in improving the quality of life in their societies and establishing consistency and coordination in their foreign policies, they may be able to nudge the Soviet Union into policies that make the system more tolerable for its citizens and less threatening to the world. But if the world outside the Soviet empire descends further into economic and political disarray, the incentives for the Soviet leaders to reform their internal system and to moderate their ambitions abroad will correspondingly decline.

Negotiating with the Soviets

Edward L. Rowny

Our modern Western civilization springs from a heritage not shared by the Soviet Union. Greek rationalism has influenced us to seek ways of resolving disputes among nations by peaceful arbitration or, if resorting to war was necessary, by limitation of its destructive effects. The persisting influence of Roman law has caused us to think optimistically that such rational solutions can be made subject to regulation by law. Our Judeo-Christian ethic, as exemplified in the Book of Revelation, teaches us that war is the result of sinfulness. War, in the words of Saint Augustine, is a "sad necessity for combatting evil." Western thinkers—Erasmus, Thomas Aquinas, Voltaire, Kant, Rousseau, and Bentham, to mention only a few—have made powerfully compelling arguments for international government as a way of peaceably settling disputes between nations. Western intellectuals have expressed faith that solutions will prevail because of their intrinsic merits and have evidenced hope that such solutions can be furthered through the negotiating process.

In sum, we have been conditioned to believe that problems between nations are solvable, that they can be negotiated, and that the solutions will be just ones. These ideas, held by the "philosophes" of Europe at the time of the American Revolution, were absorbed by our own "philosophes"—epitomized by Benjamin Franklin. Faith in reason and a commitment to Jefferson's "illimitable freedom of the human mind" furthered in America the European concept of the perfectibility of man.[1] Thus, overriding cultural and historical influences on our basic approach to negotiations have inspired Western intellectuals with a faith in the power of logical reasoning to solve fundamental problems and to conquer evil. Since the end of World War II the United States has been the nation most determined to bring advanced weapons technology under effective international control.[2] The basic approach we have adopted and our drive toward arms control have resulted in our becoming both pragmatic and impatient in negotiating. We believe the solution to differences is "to split down the middle," as in collective bargaining, and to constantly "get on with it." The undertaking *itself* is held to be important.

Russia, to a great extent because it adopted Eastern Orthodoxy, was cut off from the Greco-Roman secular heritage and the Protestant Reformation and became culturally isolated from the West. Russia's history and tradition is rooted in absolutism, secrecy, and authoritarianism. Western concepts of liberty, egalitarianism, rights of the individual, and rule of law have been largely alien to the Russian tradition. The two centuries of Tartar rule, which isolated Russia from the West during the period of the late Middle Ages and early European Renaissance, had a profound influence on separating Russia culturally from the West and ushered in a belief in the merits of absolutism. This unquestioned authority of the state over its individual members has been the predominant historical feature of Russian society—both under the Russian tsars and under Soviet commissars. For centuries, individuals in Russian society have been bound in one form or another to service to the state; throughout Russian history, state interests have determined the social order—not the other way around.

Russia's attempts, beginning with Peter the Great, to increase contacts with the West were accompanied by efforts at restricting such contacts to a small, educated, noble minority, thus keeping the great masses of the Russian people ignorant of—and hostile to—foreign influences. This long history of authoritarian control and isolation from the West has persisted down to the present time.

In both Tsarist and Soviet diplomacy, negotiations have been used, according to contemporary experts on the Soviet Union, "as a device to manipulate the atmosphere of world politics."[3] Soviet disarmament proposals aim to create a "world public opinion" designed to have a greater effect on the decision-making process in Western democratic countries than in Communist countries.[4] Thus there has developed an ideological conviction that Russia occupies a special place in the world with a unique mission to perform. This conviction still provides the framework for the Soviets' basic approach to negotiations. They see a perpetual conflict between "right" and "wrong" and advance their ideas in the conviction that "right" socialism will win out over "wrong" capitalism. Soviet negotiators appear to believe that the solution to differences is to adhere to principles, to shun compromise, and to be patient.

The Process

With this background in mind, let us briefly examine the nature of the negotiating process itself. Past experience in negotiating with the Russians and now the Soviets reveals certain Western strengths, as well as weaknesses. Yet I am convinced, after over six years of continuous negotiations with the Soviets, that American negotiators both fail to maximize their strengths and permit the Soviets to exploit our weaknesses.

The notion that the process of negotiation should be looked upon as a means toward an end and not as an end in itself appears too obvious to deserve detailed treatment. The negotiating process should ideally be a neutral process of finding a just settlement between opposing claims and objectively supportable points of view. However, an examination of the record shows that the negotiating process involving the United States and the Soviet Union has not in the past been a neutral one.

The strengths the United States brings to the negotiating process stem from the strengths inherent in our democratic institutions. Our system of government, broadly based on popular support and safeguarded by checks and balances, should give us confidence that the intellectual and moral bases of our positions are sound. Furthermore, the bureaucratic process in the United States is rather flexible and less rigidly doctrinaire than that of the Soviet Union. And, importantly for the negotiating process, the United States draws strength from being more volatile and unpredictable. We Americans are tolerant and long-suffering up to a point; but once aroused, we can and do act swiftly and decisively.

Americans conduct negotiations as a problem-solving exercise; the Soviets look upon negotiations as a competition and consider them as just another aspect of an ongoing struggle.

One of the strengths of our systematic and democratic processes in the United States is that we tend to examine all aspects of a problem and to arrive at what we believe to be a fair and reasonable solution. We then expect the Soviets to accept our solution or match it with a comparably fair or reasonable one. The Soviets, on the other hand, feel uninhibited about adopting extreme positions. Although they eschew compromise, *they* constantly call upon *our* "sense of fair play" and "spirit of compromise."

To a much greater extent than the Soviets, we tend to "mirror image" our adversary. Rather than recognizing that we and the Soviets are different—historically and culturally—we tend to assume that they have the same goals and are like us. Soviet negotiators are trained to exploit this weakness. They go to great lengths to conceal differences and to pretend that they have similar goals.

We put great stock in our flexibility and disdain Soviet inflexibility. While at times this works to our advantage, more often the Soviets exploit our penchant for flexibility. By displaying a patient willingness to "wait us out," Soviet negotiators stick to positions laid down by their higher authorities and deviate from them only rarely. Dr. Kissinger, as a result of this negotiating experience, confirms this view that the outstanding quality of the Soviets is enormous persistence in whatever course they are pursuing. As he put it: "We lack patience in negotiations . . . if we haven't made a new proposal for three months, we start getting restless."[5]

In negotiating with the Soviets, American negotiators often signal to the Soviets the "bottom-line" or "fall-back" position. We seem to believe that by doing so we will make our position more "credible" and the Soviets will follow our example. To be sure, our negotiators, having adopted what they believe to be fair and reasonable positions, have the best of intentions of maintaining them. But the Soviets do not feel compelled to follow our example. Instead, they wait us out in the belief that our desire to display flexibility and to compromise will in the end cause us to agree to terms closer to theirs. Unfortunately, they are all too often correct.

Americans tend to believe that we must give rationally supportable arguments for our positions, and that once we have done so we need not repeat our rationale. The Soviets, in contrast, often state positions without giving the rationale upon which they are based. The Soviet "rationale" is often no more than an assertion like "The reason is clear" or "It is so for objective (or for obvious) reasons." The Free World press often judges such Soviet statements to be of equal value to ours simply because their statements emanate from official governmental sources. Furthermore, the Soviets seldom tire of repeating their positions, however illogical or unsupportable, whereas we quickly tire of repeating our positions and arguments.

The Soviets often resort to a technique variously referred to as "cherry picking" or "taking the raisins out of the cake." By showing inflexibility on issues (or by avoiding them altogether) the Soviets induce us to advance various alternative proposals in the hope that the Soviets may be attracted to one of them. After we have put forth several such proposals, usually in the form of "balanced packages," the Soviets pick out from them the parts they like and ignore the parts they do not like. Unfortunately, we often forget—or overlook—the conditions under which our "packages" were initially offered. The end result is that we often agree to what they find acceptable while they reject what they find unacceptable.

The cliché "What's mine is mine and what's yours is negotiable" is a well-known Soviet technique, which time and again they use to advantage. We fail to appreciate that the Soviets habitually pocket concessions we make but fail to agree explicitly to concessions on their side.

The Soviets, as a negotiating tactic, press for us to "agree in principle." They then exploit our unwillingness to "haggle over the price." The net result is that we fail to insist on removing ambiguities or to seek explicit agreement upon what at the time seem to be unimportant details. While we tend to assume that the Soviets will live up to the "spirit" of such agreements, the Soviets utilize every loophole and go to the full limit the language technically allows.

Soviet negotiators, like Alice in Wonderland characters, use words to mean what they want them to mean. Our attempts to reach agreements based on objective analyses and estimates are labeled by the Soviets as "subjective" because, as they sometimes put it, "figures lie and liars figure." On the other hand, they label as "objective" the statements made by high Soviet officials simply because their officials made them. Even when the Soviets express a willingness to argue a case on its merits, their arguments are often expressed in vague phrases such as "all factors having been duly considered" or "well-known factors bearing on the situation."

The Soviets are secretive and reveal little about the details, state of development, or deployment of their strategic offensive arms, holding that such details are "military secrets." We, on the other hand, publish such information in the *Congressional Record,* in official "Posture Statements," and in our open press. This not only results in a grossly one-sided advantage for the Soviets but gives them opportunities for quoting those in the United States who voice views contrary to established government policy. Soviet negotiators seldom need to search for arguments to use against ours; they find them ready-made in our media.

The Soviets are masters at using propaganda to help their negotiations. Of the many examples which could be drawn upon to demonstrate this point, one is the notable case, associated with SALT, that occurred in March 1977, when the United States put forth its "comprehensive" proposal. The Soviet leadership immediately—and incorrectly—branded the proposal as one-sided in favor of the United States. We did not aggressively or firmly counter these assertions and hence allowed the perception to grow that the Soviets were correct. While I am not arguing that we ought to emulate them, it should be clear that the Soviets benefit from such practices. Predictably, the Soviets after a time begin believing their own propaganda.

The examples given here represent only a portion of the differences in the established patterns of United States and Soviet negotiations. They have been presented to show that we need to recognize that the Soviets have a basic approach to negotiations that differs from ours, and that in many respects they conduct negotiations in a manner which shows that they are more unlike than like us.

Character and Style

Our historical and cultural background has led us inexorably into the current dysfunctional "era of negotiations" and has influenced in fundamental ways our basic approach to, and conduct of, these negotiations. United States negotiators are pragmatic, impatient persons who cannot say no to extreme Soviet proposals and are willing to "split down the middle." Soviet negotiators are patient and doctrinaire realists who draw enormous strength from their stubborn adherence to their own principles.

It has not been my main purpose here to add to the spate of

recent discussions concerning our crisis of spirit in the West, except to note that the Soviets place us at a disadvantage in the negotiating process. They display a conviction that they know and believe in their goals, in contrast to the self-doubts and questioning we have over our goals.[6]

Shortly before his death Alistair Buchan commented on the challenge facing America and the West:

The Soviet Union, now in most significant senses the equal of the United States in long-range strategic power, with an increasing ability to project its influence to distant areas, less dependent on the fortunes of overseas Communist parties, may appear to be becoming more assertive and more influential at a time when the United States and its allies are becoming introspective or uncertain of their interests.[7]

Further he felt that:

We do not (therefore) know whether our western societies possess the internal coherence, the fidelity to their own ideals, to confront those societies that are led from the top downwards in a prolonged test of wills.[8]

De Tocqueville, a century and a half ago, expressed great admiration for the United States and faith in its future. Yet he wondered if we could overcome our greatest handicap, that of conducting a successful foreign policy with our potential enemies.[9] It is more than a passing coincidence that another prescient Frenchman (who travelled to Russia at the same time de Tocqueville travelled to the United States) concluded his journal with the words, "I do not blame the Russians for being what they are, I blame them for pretending to be what we are."[10]

Although our history and our heritage have placed us in an "era of negotiations," we must recognize that the process of negotiating cannot correct the precarious situations brought about by nuclear parity—and possible future inferiority—in the field of strategic offensive arms. I do not share the widely held current view that the process of negotiation is more important than the goals we seek, or that such negotiation necessarily helps us attain our goals. At the same time, I believe that if we allow our negotiating strengths to be minimized and our weaknesses to be exploited, negotiations can only increase the dangers we face. Accordingly, it behooves us to improve our negotiating ability. The first step toward such improvements is the recognition that the Soviets have a basic approach to negotiations that differs from ours and that they utilize a different set of techniques in conducting such negotiations.

Practical Consequences

We negotiate with the Soviet Union on limiting strategic offensive arms because we believe that it is in our national interest to do so: first, because we believe it will increase stability and decrease the risk of the outbreak of nuclear war; second, because we doubt the wisdom of continuing to develop and deploy arms which, we hope, will never be used; third, because we believe that the outcome of such negotiations could result in enhanced security; and finally, because it might lead to savings in defense outlays. These encouraging beliefs reflect the predominant strain of thinking in the United States and, indeed, in the Western world. However, comparable beliefs do not appear to be shared by the top leadership of the Soviet Union. For this reason we should critically reexamine our convictions and the possible consequences of their pursuit through negotiations.

Let us take a brief but critical look at each of our beliefs on limiting strategic offensive arms. First, do negotiations on limiting strategic offensive arms increase stability and reduce the risk of nuclear war? Perhaps—and again, perhaps not; the answer depends on the specifics involved. If the process results in an even-handed agreement, the risk of outbreak of nuclear war can be diminished. If, on the other hand, an agreement emerges which confers a real or perceived advantage to one side, the chances of nuclear war in fact increase.

Second, many Americans nurture a deep-seated conviction that the very act of negotiation results in reduced tensions and thereby lessens the probability of outbreak of nuclear war. This conviction, so firmly rooted in democratic societies in the West, is not shared in Eastern societies. Indeed, our history is replete with instances of our having been lulled into a false sense of security because we believed that the risk of war had been minimized simply because negotiations were taking place. For example, Tsar Nicholas II's appeal in 1898 for disarmament proved subsequently to be self-serving, and, according to a leading historian, sprang from the Russians' realization that their artillery was inferior to that of the Austrians. It is all the more ironic that the Tsar's appeal should have been described in the Western press as "beautiful music," and the dawn of "a new epoch in civilization."[11] As another example, the outcome of the Washington Naval Agreement of 1922 demonstrated that our conviction that negotiations on disarmament would prevent war was misguided. While the naval disarmament program temporarily saved funds and reduced frictions, it contributed significantly to the weakness of the United States and Great Britain and played into the hands of Japanese adventurism. The net results were the early and nearly catastrophic defeats in World War II.[12] Five years later, in 1927, the Soviets at the World Disarmament Conference in Geneva called for the total abolition of all armed forces, the first in a series of Soviet propaganda efforts which have had wide appeal in the West because of their simplistic idealism. The continued pursuit of disarmament in the 1930s by the Western democracies and the simultaneous build-up of arms by the Axis powers created an unstable international climate and helped bring on World War II.[13]

Third, there is a widespread belief in the West that a nuclear war would be so devastating that it would be suicidal for any leader to allow a war to occur—much less initiate one. A variation of this belief is that nuclear war is "unthinkable," therefore unworthy of serious attention. While practically everyone agrees that nuclear war should be avoided, and although most agree that the probability is low that a nuclear war will in fact occur, it does not follow that one side is justified in failing to prepare for the eventuality. Indeed, failing to prepare for the "unthinkable" war undermines, rather than enhances, deterrence.

Fourth, we also need examine the claim that limiting strategic arms will enhance our security. Such a result might indeed come about (it is of course this belief that provides the primary impetus for our current negotiations with the Soviet Union), but we must examine critically the terms of any agreement. Whether our security interests have in fact been served is an *empirical* question, not a matter of faith. Not all strategic arms limitation treaties are good for us.

Mutual security in an age of nuclear parity is enhanced if both sides are equally deterred from initiating a nuclear war. It is further enhanced if both sides refrain from taking risks that could result in the outbreak of such a war. The results of negotiations on limiting strategic offensive arms must therefore satisfy two conditions: (1) they must provide for mutual deterrence; and (2) they must contribute to stability in crisis situations.

Satisfying these conditions is difficult in our current quest for a satisfactory agreement on limiting strategic offensive arms. The first condition is difficult to satisfy because of the differing views held by the United States and the Soviet Union on how deterrence is achieved. Our concept of nuclear deterrence is that either side could survive a preemptive strike and still inflict a crippling blow upon the other. The Soviet concept appears to be that deterrence is best achieved by the achievement of Soviet war-winning capability. In fact, official Soviet doctrine holds that "an early dispersal and evacuation (of the population of the Soviet Union) could reduce losses [to] between five and eight percent."[14] These percentages translate into from 12 to 20 million casualties, the losses the Soviet Union suffered in World War II, and therefore not necessarily considered by them to be "unacceptable." In other words, our beliefs are not necessarily determinate; the Soviets must also consider themselves deterred.

Another difficulty in assuring deterrence arises from the differing nature of the strategic arms possessed by the two sides. The Soviet Union has placed primary emphasis on its numerous and powerful land-based ICBMs (intercontinental ballistic missiles), whereas the United States has developed a more evenly balanced triad of ICBMs, SLBMs (submarine-launched ballistic missiles), and heavy bombers. The United States' concept of deterrence thus relies upon a combination of the three elements of its triad, while the Soviets base their concept primarily on ICBMs, the most destabilizing of the categories of strategic offensive arms. Soviet ICBMs have a combination of warhead size and accuracy sufficient to eliminate the major portion of the U.S. ICBM force. Furthermore, the current generation of American ICBMs is fixed and thus easily targetable. Thus the United States could be left after a preemptory strike with a severely reduced weapons inventory and our leaders faced with the difficult task of deciding what actions to take, especially since the Soviets would still retain more than enough weapons to hold our cities at risk. Accordingly, unless the Soviets drastically reduce their ICBM force or the United States immediately embarks upon a program designed to make its ICBMs less vulnerable, deterrence will be seriously eroded during the early to mid-1980s.

There is not much basis for believing that an emerging agreement will result in economies. The United States will need to deploy additional forces in order to assure that deterrence is maintained. While it is theoretically possible that an agreement on strategic offensive arms could result in savings for the United States, such an agreement could only be accomplished if the Soviets were significantly to reduce their strategic offensive arms—an unlikely event since they continue stubbornly to resist even modest reductions. Knowing the appeal that economic savings has in the United States, the Soviets press their arguments with Americans. They continue to attribute weaknesses to the capitalistic society and contrast them to the strengths of their own centrally controlled economy. Accordingly, our emphasis on cost reductions is exploited by Soviet allegations that our military-industrial complex needs to build arms to keep the United States' economy strong and unemployment down.

Conclusion

The failure of American negotiators and policymakers to accept the basic differences between us and the Russians has produced several dangerous consequences. We fail to exploit our own advantages in the negotiation process, and consequently pay heavily in the form of unbalanced agreements. Moreover, by permitting the Russians to impose their own style on these negotiations, we inadvertently adopt Soviet goals and make them our own. We therefore fail to evaluate the actual content of the negotiations as we should, and make the negotiation "process" an end in itself.

We need to set ourselves rational objectives and then bring all our national talents and energies to bear on the problem of achieving them. We have several advantages vis-à-vis the Soviet Union and should manage to exploit them. But the first step in this process is the recognition that our goals are not the same because our national values and basic beliefs are dissimilar.

If a more realistic approach to negotiation with the Soviets is adopted, we can look confidently to a future in which our own interests can be greatly enhanced by strategic arms limitations treaties. But if we continue in the same mold, such treaties will inevitably favor our opponents.

NOTES

1. Henry Steele Commager, *The Empire of Reason* (Garden City, N.Y.: Anchor Press/Doubleday, 1977), chap. I and II, passim.
2. James E. Dougherty, *How to Think About Arms Control and Disarmament* (New York: Crane, Russak and Company, 1973), p. 55.
3. Lincoln P. Bloomfield, Walter C. Clemens, Jr., and Franklyn Griffiths, *Khrushchev and the Arms Race* (Cambridge: M.I.T. Press, 1966), p. 5.
4. Dougherty, op. cit., p. 70.
5. "Is There a Crisis of Spirit in the West?: A Conversation with Dr. Henry A. Kissinger and Senator Daniel P. Moynihan," *Public Opinion,* vol. 1, no. 2, May/June 1978, pp. 7-8.
6. Ibid.
7. Alistair Buchan, *The End of the Postwar Era: A New Balance of World Power* (New York: E.P. Dutton, 1974), p. 7.
8. Ibid., p. 5.
9. Alexis de Tocqueville, *Democracy in America* (New York: Alfred A. Knopf, 1963), vol. I, pp. 232-236.
10. Marquis de Custine. *Journey for our Time: The Journals of the Marquis de Custine,* Edited and translated by Phyllis Penn Kohler (New York: Pellegrine and Cudahy, 1951), p. 90.
11. Barbara Tuchman, *The Proud Tower* (New York: Macmillan, 1962), pp. 229-230.
12. Henry W. Forbes, *The Strategy of Disarmament* (Washington: Public Affairs Press, 1952), pp. 28-29.

13. John Toland, *Adolf Hitler* (Garden City, N.Y.: Doubleday and Co., 1976), chap. 13, passim.
14. *The 1969 Soviet Civil Defense Handbook,* translated into English at Oak Ridge, Tennessee, p. 68.

Anatomy of Soviet Policymaking *Adam B. Ulam*

Contemplating the vast volume of Kremlinology produced in this country since World War II, a layman might well paraphrase Karl Marx's famous thesis on Feuerbach and complain that various experts have only interpreted the Soviet Union in different ways, while the urgent need is to find out how its policies can be changed. There have been many prescriptions as to how the United States, through its own policies, might influence the U.S.S.R. to alter a disquieting pattern of Soviet behavior on the world scene. But before trying to formulate such prescriptions, we must first of all try to understand the process of Soviet policy-making.

To repeat what this author wrote in another study, "The student of Soviet affairs has as his first task to be neither hopeful nor pessimistic, but simply to state the facts and tendencies of Russian politics. It is when he begins to see in certain political trends the inevitabilities of the future and when he superimposes upon them his own conclusions about the desirable policies of America towards the U.S.S.R. that he is courting trouble."[1] American policymaking ought to profit by a dispassionate analysis of the Soviets' motivations and actions but it cannot be a substitute for such analysis.

The fulcrum of the Soviet political system is the 20-odd full and alternate members of the Politburo and those Central Committee Secretaries who are outside it. Yet we still need to know more about how this group operates and its relationship to the wider Soviet political elite and to the Soviet people at large. For our purposes, it is especially important to establish some analytical guidelines about how the inner ruling group arrives at its decisions on foreign policy and to what extent it is susceptible to influences from the larger international environment.

Elitist and secretive as the process of Soviet decisionmaking is in general, it is especially so when it comes to foreign policy. One may find occasionally in the Soviet press and in the utterances of lower officials fairly far-reaching criticisms, particularly of the country's economic systems and performance. It is almost inconceivable for such public discussion to take place in connection with any major Soviet position on international affairs. This taboo is observed also when it comes to Moscow's past foreign policy.

Those who see the Soviet system moving toward pluralism or who hypothesize about the growing influence of the military in decision-making disregard the exclusive prerogative of decisionmaking to which the inner ruling group, especially in the Brezhnev era, has held with such tenacity. Even Nikita Khrushchev, who intermittently attempted to enlarge his political base by using the Central Committee to curb his fellow oligarchs, guarded jealously the party's monopoly of power. He could speak slightingly in the presence of foreigners about Andrei Gromyko, then "only" minister of foreign affairs, but not yet a member of the charmed circle; and he dismissed Zhukov largely because the marshal had helped him in his 1957 scrap with the Vyacheslav Molotov faction, and it was intolerable that a professional soldier should be allowed to interfere in settling future disputes on the Soviet Olympus.

In their turn, Leonid Brezhnev and his colleagues were especially insistent not only on preserving the party's role as the only source of political power, but also on recouping the narrower oligarchy's prerogative as final arbiter in policymaking. There is a Soviet equivalent of the U.S. National Security Council, but it is presided over ex officio by the general secretary, and nothing indicates that it is more than an advisory body to the Politburo. Since 1964 the Central Committee has been relegated again to being a forum where decisions of the top leadership are announced and perhaps explained in greater detail than they are to the public at large, but not debated. Emperor Paul I once told a foreign ambassador that the only important public figures in Russia were those to whom he talked, and even their influence disappeared once they were no longer in actual conversation with the sovereign. The only participants in the decision-making process in the U.S.S.R., outside the 20-odd members of the inner circle, are those whom it chooses to consult, and only while it does so. Unless he is simultaneously a member of the Politburo, the status of the head of an important branch of the government—the armed forces, security, foreign ministry, or economic planning—is similar to that of a high civil servant in the West rather than that of a minister and policymaker.

Because of its very rigidity, and in view of the average age of the ruling oligarchy, the pattern we just sketched is likely to become exposed in the future to increasing strains and might well break down, at least temporarily, during a succession struggle or a situation similar to that of 1956-1957 and the early 1960s. Then the inner group splits into hostile factions and, especially on the latter occasion, the leader found himself increasingly out of tune with his senior colleagues.

For the present and immediate future we must assume, however, that the U.S.S.R. will continue to be governed under a system where policy options and moves are freely discussed by and fully known only to some 25 people, and the ultimate decisions are made by an even smaller group—the 13 or 15 full members of the Politburo.

This being so, we have little reason to expect basic changes in the Soviet philosophy of foreign relations. The present leaders and their prospective successors have seen the Soviet Union develop from the backward, militarily and industrially weak state of the early 1920s to one of the two superpowers of the post-1945 world. They have been brought up in the belief that the Soviet Union's connection with the worldwide communist movement has been a source of strength to their country, and it is only recently that they have had occasion for doubt on that score. Their formative years witnessed the Soviet system surviving the ravages of terror and the tremendous human and material losses of World War II. As rising bureaucrats in the immediate postwar period, the people of the Politburo generation could observe how Soviet diplomacy managed to offset the Soviet Union's industrial and military inferiority vis-á-vis the principle capitalist state, and even when the country's resources had to be devoted mainly to the task of recovery from the war, the U.S.S.R. still managed to advance its power and influence in the world at large.

In brief, very little in their own experience or in the international picture, as it has evolved during the past 20 years or so, could have persuaded the Kremlin that its basic guidelines for dealing with the outside world needed revision. The external power and influence of the U.S.S.R. has been used in propaganda at home to demonstrate the viability and dynamism of the Soviet system and its historical legitimacy. Granted the essentially conservative approach of the present leadership of the Soviet Union toward international affairs, one could hardly imagine it responding to a specific internal emergency by contriving a dangerous international crisis. But the Kremlin still persists in seeking to impress upon its people the paradoxical dichotomy of world politics: the imperialist threat remains as great as ever, and yet the U.S.S.R. is steadily growing more powerful. Both beliefs are seen as essential to preserving the cohesion of Soviet society. The average Soviet citizen is never to be dissuaded from seeing the capitalist world as a source of potential danger to his country and its allies. By the same token, he must not lose faith in the ability of his government and its armed forces to repel this threat and to ensure even in this nuclear age the security and greatness of the U.S.S.R. and of the entire socialist camp. It would take an extraordinary combination of domestic political, social, and economic pressures to form a critical mass capable of impelling the regime to change its outlook on world politics.

It is virtually impossible to conceive of the Soviet system surviving in its present form were its rulers to abandon explicitly, or even implicitly, the main premises behind their foreign policy. Practically every feature of Russian authoritarianism is ultimately rationalized in terms of the alleged foreign danger inherent in the existence of the "two struggling camps," one headed by the U.S.S.R. and the other, the capitalist one, by the United States. Writing at the most hopeful period of detente, and painting a very rosy picture of the future of Soviet-American relations, Georgi Arbatov still had to add the caveat, "There can be no question as to whether the struggle between the two systems would or would not continue. That struggle is historically unavoidable."[2] If the struggle continues, the Soviet citizen must be made to believe that his side is steadily forging ahead on the world stage. Otherwise, what can compensate him psychologically for his perception—increasingly unsuppressible—that life is freer and materially more abundant in the West?

To be sure, this official rationale of Soviet foreign policy becomes vulnerable in cases where its ideological premises cannot be readily reconciled with the nationalist ones, and it is mainly on that count that one can foresee the possibility of popular reactions at home affecting the course of foreign policy. Tito's apostasy could be dismissed by the Kremlin as being in itself not of great significance. The burdens inherent in standing armed guard over Eastern Europe or in suppressing the Afghan insurgency have been explained in the official media by the necessity of warding off the class enemy and, less explicitly, in terms of Russia's historical mission and interests antedating the Revolution. All these developments could be interpreted as still not in conflict with the thesis that communism is a natural ally and an obedient servant of the Soviet national interest.

However, the Sino-Soviet conflict has struck at the very heart of the ideology/national interest *Weltanschauung* of Soviet foreign policy. In his *Letter to the Soviet Leaders,* Aleksandr Solzhenitsyn formulated very cogently the essential dilemma that has confronted the Kremlin in public since the eruption of the dispute, in fact since Mao's forces conquered the mainland. It is another communist state, and precisely because it is communist, writes Solzhenitsyn, it has posed the greatest threat to Russia's future. Thus, even when it comes to the outside world, he charges, one can readily see how this false ideology has had disastrous consequences for the true interests and security of the Russian people and threatens it eventually with having to fight for survival.

This is not the isolated opinion of a writer and dissident who abhors every aspect of communism. Fear of China because of its enormous size, vast industrial-military potential, and the nature of its regime and ruling philosophy is probably the most visceral reaction of the average Soviet, insofar as his outlook on world affairs is concerned. No other aspect of the regime's policy has had as wide approval among the Soviet population as its efforts to contain and isolate the other great communist state.

It is important to note that even this problem has not been allowed to affect the official rationale of Soviet foreign policy. This rationale is still couched in terms inherited from the era when the world communist movement was monolithic in its subservience to Moscow. When it first erupted in public, the Sino-Soviet dispute might well have prompted a foreign observer to prophesy that its implications were bound to change not only the Kremlin's actual policies, but its whole approach to international situations. The confrontation between ideology and reality inherent in the clash ought to have led to a thorough reevaluation of the former, not merely as a justification but also as an operating principle for foreign policies. The U.S.S.R. should have abandoned even the pretense that what it was doing in Africa, the Near East, and other areas was in the furtherance of socialism.

Yet, in fact, such secularization of Soviet foreign policy has not taken place. One might object that the U.S.S.R. has tried to cope with the Chinese problem without any ideological inhibitions. It has attempted to enlist the United States in a joint effort to stop or delay China's nuclear development. It has encouraged India to attack and fragment China's only major ally in Asia. The Kremlin viewed with equanimity the massacre of the pro-Beijing Indonesian Communist party, and it encouraged and helped Vietnam in its open defiance of its huge neighbor. Ideological kinship has not restrained the Soviet Union from hinting at times that it might have to resort to a preemptive strike against China.

Yet, for all such unsentimental measures and attitudes, the Soviet leadership has refused to draw what to an outsider would be the logical deductions of its predicament with China. The doctrine of the two camps is still being maintained as stoutly as when the two great communist powers were linked "by unshakeable friendship" and alliance against a potential capitalist aggressor. China's departure from the straight and narrow path of "proletarian internationalism" has been explained in the official Soviet rhetoric as a temporary lapse, while even at the most hopeful periods of peaceful coexistence, the conflict with the capitalist world has been presented as an unavoidable and permanent feature of world politics. There have been fairly serious armed clashes along the Sino-Soviet border, and a sizable proportion of the Soviet armed forces is deployed along the frontier. Those Russian military manuals, however, that are accessible to the public discuss at length the dangers and various scenarios of conventional and nuclear warfare between the U.S.S.R. and the capitalist powers, while not even alluding to the possibility of a war with another communist power.

This bizarre pattern of behavior cannot be ascribed solely to the Soviet leaders' cynicism and ability to divorce their actions entirely from their words. Nor can it be attributed to some lingering ideological scruples. Given a truth serum, a Soviet statesman would readily confess that barring something very unexpected, the danger of unprovoked capitalist aggression against the U.S.S.R. is virtually nil, while the possibility of China someday advancing territorial and other claims on his country is very real indeed. The immobilism of the Soviet foreign policy doctrine finds its roots in the nature of the political system as a whole. The 13 or so men at the apex of the Soviet power structure have to think of themselves not only as rulers of a national state, but also as high priests of a world cult, which in turn is the source of legitimacy for the system as a whole and for their own power in particular. Could that legitimacy (and with it, the present political structure of the Soviet Union) endure, were its rulers to renounce one of the most basic operating tenets of communist political philosophy?

To a Westerner it might appear that the regime could greatly strengthen itself by curtailing its expansionist policies abroad and by concentrating on raising the living standards of the Soviet people. It would gain in popularity, the argument would continue, by being more explicit about the real dimension of the problem the U.S.S.R. faces in relation to China and by putting the alleged threat from the West into proper perspective. But it is most unlikely that the present generation of leaders would, or feels it could, afford to heed such arguments. They remember how even Nikita Khrushchev's modest and clumsy attempts at domestic liberalization and at relieving the siege mentality of his countrymen had, in their view, most unsettling effects on the party and society. Without a continuing sense of danger from abroad, economic improvement at home, far from being an effective remedy for political dissent, is in fact likely to make it more widespread. For the die-hards within the elite, even some of the side effects of detente, such as increased contacts with and knowledge of the West, must have appeared potentially harmful, because they brought in their wake ideological pollution and threatened the stability and cohesion of Soviet society.

History has played an unkind trick on the masters of the U.S.S.R.

Probably no other ruling oligarchy in modern times has been as pragmatically minded and power-oriented as the current Soviet one. Compared to them, even Nikita Khrushchev, who joined the party in 1918 during the Civil War, showed some characteristics of a true believer. Ironically, it is precisely because of power considerations that the rulers cannot disregard ideological constraints on their policies.

A superficial view of Soviet politics would lead us to believe that a Soviet statesman enjoys much greater freedom of action, especially in foreign affairs, than his Western counterpart. He can order and direct rather than having to plead or campaign for his program. If he has to persuade others, it is a small group rather than an unruly electorate or a partisan legislature. The Politburo's decisions are not hammered out in the full glare of publicity or subjected to immediate public debate and criticisms. Whatever the fears, hesitations, and divisions among the rulers, they seldom become known outside the precincts of the Kremlin. Hence, how can a democracy avoid finding itself at a disadvantage when negotiating with the Kremlin? Neither budgetary constraints nor fear of public opinion can deflect Brezhnev and company from a weapons policy or an action abroad that they believe to be necessary for their purposes and for the prestige and power of the U.S.S.R.

This picture, while correct in several details, is greatly misleading overall. The structure of the decision-making process in the U.S.S.R. enables the Kremlin to be free from many of the constraints under which nonauthoritarian governments must operate. Yet, the nature of the Soviet political system creates its own imperatives, which the leaders must heed and which may make the leaders' choice among foreign policy options more difficult and cumbersome than is the case in a democracy. Superbly equipped as it is for moving rapidly and effectively on several fronts, the Soviet political mechanism has not shown equal capacity during the last 20 years for effectively braking the momentum of its policies once launched. Whether the Soviet political mechanism can develop such braking devices must be of special interest to any student or practitioner of international affairs.

The immediate background of Soviet policies in the 1980s lies in the series of agreements and understandings reached between the U.S.S.R. and the United States, as well as other states of the Western bloc, which set up the foundations of what has come to be known as detente. It would be a gross oversimplification on our part to view detente as simply an attempt by the Kremlin to deceive the West or, conversely, as a definitive change in Moscow's philosophy of international affairs. Soviet leaders sought a temporary accommodation with the West and a consequent lowering of international tension for reasons inherent in their interpretation of the world scene as of 1970.

Even if undertaken solely as a tactical maneuver, detente was not cost-free for the Soviets. Domestically it gave more resonance to the voices of dissent and placed the government under the obligation of relaxing restrictions on Jewish emigration, a concession that would have been unthinkable a few years earlier. Abroad, it was bound to raise doubts and suspicions in the minds of the Soviet Union's clients and friends. Only a few weeks after the Nixon-Brezhnev summit, Anwar Sadat ordered some 20,000 Soviet military personnel out of Egypt, a step very largely motivated by his conviction that his country's foreign policy now had to be more balanced between the two superpowers.

The Soviet policymakers' usual skill at having their cake and eating it too was thus put to a severe test. The 1972-1973 period offers a convincing example of the Soviet Union's sensitivity to its antagonists actual policies and of the importance it places on its perception of the overall condition of the noncommunist world. In 1972 the economy of the West as a whole was still flourishing and expanding. Political stability appeared to be returning in the United States. With his successes in the international field, Nixon was virtually assured a second term. This political and economic strength of the West, as well as several other international developments, added up to compelling reasons for the Soviets to pull in their horns.

How long this restraint would have prevailed in the councils of the Kremlin and whether there was any possibility of a more fundamental alteration in Soviet foreign policy remains unknown. Within a year and a half of the inauguration of detente, the premises on which the Soviets' restraints had been based began to crumble. By the end of 1974 Moscow was bound to conclude that the West was not nearly as stable and strong politically or economically as it had appeared to be in 1972.

Beginning in 1974, the U.S.S.R. became much less concerned about U.S. reactions to its policies abroad, even the ones that were openly directed at undermining the influence and interests of the United States and its friends. Unlike the case of the 1973 Middle Eastern conflict, Soviet actions in Angola, Ethiopia, and South Yemen betrayed little hesitation or fear that they might bring effective U.S. countermeasures or even seriously damage overall Soviet-U.S. relations, thus diminishing the benefits the U.S.S.R. was reaping from detente. To be sure, the Soviets have always been aware of how sensitive the United States is to what happens in the Middle East, and in comparison the average American knows little and cares less about Angola or South Yemen. However, what should have been cause for alarm to U.S. policymakers was not so much the targets but the character of

Soviet activities in Africa. It was not merely another example of the Soviet skill at scavenging amidst the debris of Western colonialism and wresting yet another country from its nonaligned or pro-Western position through ideological appeal or an alliance with the local dictator or oligarchy. Angola was the testing ground for a new technique of Soviet imperial expansion.

The experiment was allowed to succeed and thus became a precedent for further employment of this technique. Non-native, up to now Cuban, troops would be used to establish Soviet presence in the country and to maintain the pro-Soviet regime in power. Thus, wars of "national liberation" could be carried out and won by the pro-Soviet faction, because it was helped not only by Soviet arms and advisers, but also by massive infusion of communist bloc troops. Had the general international situation remained similar to that of 1972-1973, it is unlikely that the conservative-minded Brezhnev regime would have attempted such a daring innovation as projecting Soviet power into areas thousands of miles away from the U.S.S.R.

The reasons for the Kremlin's confidence that this innovative form of international mischief-making was not unduly risky were probably very similar to those that persuaded North Vietnam about the same time to launch a massive invasion and to occupy the south. A North Vietnamese general spelled out candidly the rationale of his government's actions and why it was certain the United States would not interfere. "The internal contradictions within the U.S. administration and among U.S. political parties had intensified. The Watergate scandal had seriously affected the entire United States . . . It faced economic recession, mounting inflation, serious unemployment and an oil crisis."[3]

This revealing statement illustrates well the hard-boiled pragmatism of the Soviets and their disciples and how free they can be of the dogmas of their own ideology in their socio-economic evaluations of a given situation. According to classical Marxist-Leninist doctrine, an internal crisis impels the capitalists to act more aggressively and to seek a remedy for economic troubles, as well as to distract the attention of the masses through imperialist adventures. Here we had quite a realistic analysis of the reasons for this country's acquiescence in North Vietnam's flagrant violation of the agreement it had signed only two years before, and of the debilitating effects of domestic crisis on a democratic country's foreign policies. The statement demonstrates once again how in their calculus of potential risks and gains in world politics, the Soviets tend to go beyond the arithmetic of nuclear missiles, tanks, and ships and pay even closer attention to the psycho-political ingredients of the given situation. It did require a degree of sensitivity to U.S. politics to perceive how seriously American foreign policy was harmed by reopening the wounds of Vietnam and by pitting Congress against the executive branch. The Watergate affair had crippled America's capacity to act effectively abroad, especially when it came to meeting the Soviet and/or communist challenge in the Third World.

It was less remarkable for the Kremlin to draw the proper lesson from the energy crisis that now grips the West's economy. If the world's leading industrial nations were incapable of synchronizing their policies to counteract or soften the blow from the Organization of Petroleum Exporting Countries, a blow more serious in its implications to the West than anything done by the Soviet Union since World War II, how could they be expected to mount concerted action to deal with the Soviets' expansion in Africa or outright invasion of a neighboring country?

The effect of the Soviets' redefinition of detente in light of the economic crisis in the West weakened American leadership, and the fissiparous tendencies within the Atlantic alliance could be observed at the 1979 Vienna Brezhnev-Carter summit. Anxious as the Russians were to seal SALT II and to prevent relations between the two countries from deteriorating, there was little at Vienna of that studied courting of the Americans that had characterized the 1972 Moscow conference. This time there were no grandiloquent declarations about both countries scrupulously respecting each other's broad policy interests throughout the world. Instead, Brezhnev chose to lecture Carter and his entourage in public on the impermissibility and uselessness of trying to link the fate of SALT II and detente to Soviet restraint in foreign policy. "Attempts also continue to portray social processes taking place in one or another country or the struggles of the peoples for liberation as 'Moscow's plots or intrigues.' Naturally, the Soviet people are in sympathy with the liberation struggle of various nations . . . We believe that every people has the right to determine its own destiny. Why then pin on the Soviet Union the responsibility for the objective course of history, or what is more, use this as a pretext for worsening our relations?"[4] With the worldwide configuration of forces now much more in their favor than it had been in 1972, it was probably genuinely incomprehensible to the Soviet leaders how anyone could expect them to abide by the same obligations and cautions they had pledged to observe on the earlier occasion.

Choices and Projections

Their actions in the recent past and present offer a suggestive guide to Soviet leaders' choices and decisions in the future. While it is of little use to try to divide the Kremlin decisionmakers into hawks and doves or to try to divine who might represent the hard or soft factions, there is within the Politburo and its affiliates a considerable division of opinion when it comes to foreign policy. These differences, however, are not found in any permanent groupings or factions, but in the fluctuation between two main tendencies present in the mind of the leadership as a whole.

One such approach might be likened to that of the rentier. This view holds that the U.S.S.R. can afford to be patient and circumspect in its foreign policies, eschew risky ventures abroad, and continue to collect the dividends of its past successes and the inherent and worsening afflictions of the capitalist world. The rentier's attitude is based not so much on the preachings and certitudes of Marxism as on the deductions from the historical experiences of the Soviet state, especially since World War II, when the United States has been its only real rival for worldwide power and influence. The Americans have been unable to oppose effectively the Soviets' advance, and they are unlikely to do so in the future. The cumbersome procedure of American foreign policymaking and the unruly democratic setting in which it operates will always place the United States at a disadvantage vis-á-vis the flexible and unconstrained apparatus of Soviet diplomacy. Hence, it is unwise to provoke the Americans and risk a confrontation, when the U.S. position is bound to grow weaker and that of the U.S.S.R. stronger in the natural course of events.

The rentier puts the "imperialist danger" in a pragmatic perspective. It does exist as a general tendency within the capitalist world, but with proper caution on Moscow's part, it will not assume the form of a concrete menace. The United States was not able to threaten the U.S.S.R. at the time of greatest American superiority. It is not likely to do so now, when there is general awareness in the West of what a nuclear war might mean. The Reagan administration's early rhetoric has already been blunted by the realization that the Soviet Union cannot be intimidated and that both the economic realities and the realities of European politics will not permit the United States to regain superiority in strategic weapons or to match quantitatively those of the U.S.S.R.

The rentier would urge the Soviets to moderate the pace of their nuclear arms buildup and to be prepared to offer timely concessions in the course of negotiations. The U.S.S.R. has already gained great political advantages from having surpassed the United States in several categories of these weapons and would compound the gains by making what the world at large (if not the Pentagon) would hail as a magnanimous gesture—say, stopping the production of the Backfire bomber. Piling up arms eventually becomes politically counterproductive. The goal is to disarm the West psychologically and prevent it from recouping the momentum toward political integration; and Soviet military intimidation, if kept up for too long, is bound to have the opposite effect.

The same reasoning would apply to the general guidelines of Soviet policies throughout the world. Having established bridgeheads in Africa and the Caribbean, the Soviet Union would be making an error by trying to expand them too blatantly. The problems facing the United States in those areas are essentially intractable, and it is much better for Moscow to wait upon events in the Third World than to attempt to give history a push, for example in South Africa. The U.S.S.R. must refrain from any action likely to touch on a raw nerve of American politics, such as identifying itself with the extreme Arab position on Israel or reaching too obviously for control of the oil routes. In most of these areas of contention, time is essentially working for the Soviet Union, and precipitate actions by the Soviets might tend to reverse the trend.

The rentier's case on this last point becomes most debatable when the Politburo discussions turn to Eastern Europe and China. But even there, the rentier instinct would plead for a conservative approach. Soviet bloc countries can always be handled, though preferably not by military means. In China, it is true, time does not seem to work in the Soviets' favor. But for the balance of the 1980s and probably considerably beyond that, China can be contained, provided that the West and Japan do not launch a massive effort to help Beijing modernize its economy and become a major industrial (and hence military) power. Therefore, the need to contain China makes it all the more important to exercise restraint and blend firmness with conciliatory gestures in their approach toward the West.

The other side of the Soviet leadership's split personality might be called that of the speculator. For him the imperialist danger is not merely a doctrinal or propaganda phrase. It is not that he believes any more than the rentier that the United States is about to attack the U.S.S.R. or engineer a revolution in East Germany or Poland. But only the constant growth in power by the Soviet Union and its avowed readiness to contemplate nuclear war have kept the West off balance and have prevented it from more explicit attempts to undermine the socialist camp. The U.S.S.R., therefore, must not desist from active and aggressive exploitation of the weaknesses and vulnerabilities of the world capitalist system, even where it involves a possibility of a major clash with the United States. Such brinksmanship becomes especially important for the immediate future, because any lessening in the Soviets' militancy would be read by Washington as a vindication of tough U.S. rhetoric, would encourage the United States to play to the hilt the China card, and could embolden the West Europeans to follow Washington's pleas to join in applying economic pressures upon the Soviet Union.

The speculator would not desist from trying to enhance and exploit whatever military advantages the U.S.S.R. has already secured over the United States. To give up any of those advantages would be a grave mistake politically, even more so than militarily. It is awe of Soviet military might that has kept the United States from interfering in the Czechoslovak and Polish crises, has made the Europeans fearful about offending Moscow by imposing effective economic sanctions, and in fact makes them ever more eager to propitiate the Soviet colossus with trade and credits. Any slackening in the arms buildup would be taken in the West as confirmation of the thesis that internal economic and other problems have made the U.S.S.R. more malleable on defense and international issues and that consequently one can pressure the Soviets to alter not only their military and foreign policies but also their domestic ones. One has to negotiate with the United States and NATO on tactical and strategic nuclear arms, but to offer any one-sided concessions, even if not substantive, would be most damaging for the U.S.S.R.'s image and bargaining position.

The speculator would stress the necessity of militancy, and not only from the angle of relations with the West. In the years ahead some Third World leaders might well be tempted to imitate Sadat's gambit and exploit the U.S.S.R. for their own purposes, only to switch to the other side once the Soviet connection had been fully exploited. In retrospect it may have been a mistake to make Egypt the fulcrum of Soviet policies in the Middle East and to pour so much money and effort into buttressing its regime without obtaining a firmer grasp on its internal politics. Future Soviet ventures in the Third World must not only lead to a temporary discomfiture for the West, but also result in firm Soviet ideological and military control over the new client.

Analysts in the West and even some figures within the Soviet establishment keep pointing to Afghanistan as an illustration of the dangers of overt and precipitate Russian aggression. In fact, Afghanistan, for all its troublesome aspects, has served as a salutary lesson to those of Moscow's proteges who might contemplate following Egypt's example and try to get the benefits of Soviet political and economic support

while maneuvering between the two camps. For all the initial indigna-
tion, the Afghanistan coup served to strengthen the Muslim world's
respect or fear of the U.S.S.R. When a mob tried to attack the Soviet
embassy in Teheran, it was protected (unlike the embassy of another
power) by the forces of that very fundamentalist Muslim regime. Direct Soviet military intervention is not something to be used too often,
but once in a long while it serves as a useful reminder that the
U.S.S.R. is not to be trifled with.

Similar considerations indicate that the Soviet Union cannot afford to be a passive observer or just assist occasionally and indirectly
in the erosion of U.S. influence in Latin America or that of the West in
general in Africa. In fact it is doubtful whether this process can continue to benefit the Soviet Union's interests, unless the latter promotes
it energetically with more than just rhetoric and military supplies. All
radical and liberation movements are inherently unstable and volatile
in their political allegiance. If rebuffed in their pleas for more active
Soviet help, they may turn to others or tend to disintegrate. It would
thus be a mistake for Moscow to stand aside if and when armed struggle erupts in South Africa or in the case of a violent confrontation
between the forces of Left and Right in a major Latin American country.

Our speculator tends to question, not explicitly of course, the thesis that "the objective course of history" must favor the Soviet cause.
Where would the U.S.S.R. be today if it had allowed "objective factors" to determine the fate of Eastern Europe? In Latin America, Africa, and Asia one ought not to confuse the emotional residue of
anticolonialism and local radicalism with a secular tendency toward
communism or with automatic gravitation of the new and developing
societies toward the Soviet model. Anticapitalism and perhaps anti-
Western sentiments may be the common denominator of most radical
and liberation movements in the non-Western world. But once in
power, if they feel they can afford it, such movements tend to seek
freedom from any foreign tutelage. Their leaders have grown sophisticated enough to understand the complexities of the international scene
and, if left to themselves, they would prefer to be genuinely non-
aligned and able to play one side against the other.

It is not by patiently waiting upon events but by bold coups that
Soviet power and influence have been projected into all areas of the
globe, and it is not the "inherent logic of economic and social development" but the greatly expanded naval and airlift capabilities that have
maintained and enlarged those enclaves of influence. And so for the
balance of the 1980s the objective course of history must continue to

be carved out by strenuous Soviet efforts including, when necessary, the use of military force.

Political and economic stability is a natural ally of the capitalist world. The U.S.S.R., therefore, can have no interest except in special cases in a general U.S.-Soviet understanding that would lessen the intensity of political ferment in the troubled areas of the world or reduce appreciably the present level of international tension. The speculator rejects the practicality or desirability of any long-term accommodation between the U.S.S.R. and the United States. Even if it pursues the most peaceful policies, the United States will always represent a standing danger to the Soviet system and the socialist camp, simply by virtue of what it is. Close relations with the democracies lead inevitably to ideological pollution at home and to the weakening of that political vigilance and social discipline that is sine qua non of a communist regime.

The rentier and the speculator would disagree most violently concerning the degree of urgency of the Chinese problem. The activist rejects emphatically the notion that the U.S.S.R. can afford to sit and watch while China's economy is being modernized and its stockpile of nuclear weapons keeps growing. Some efficacious solution to the problem must be found during the next few years. Perhaps the intrafaction struggle that has been going on in China since the Cultural Revolution might assume the proportions of a civil war. Barring that rather slim hope, the U.S.S.R. would have to take some measures beyond simply trying to contain China. Perhaps Beijing could still be enticed to paper over its dispute with the Soviets and be pushed again onto a collision course with the United States. Conversely, a moment might come when the Soviets will have sufficiently intimidated the West to compel it to leave them a free hand for even the most drastic resolution of their Chinese dilemma. Since the Sino-Soviet dispute heated up, and even when relations between Washington and Beijing were at their worst, it has in fact been America's nuclear power that has been a key factor in restraining the Soviets from trying to resolve the conflict by force.

Neither of the two impulses currently coexisting in the minds of the Politburo is likely to achieve complete mastery during the balance of the decade. Ascendancy of the rentier mentality would clearly make the Soviet Union much less of a destabilizing force in the world arena and in the long run could open up prospects of a major change in the Soviets' philosophy of international relations. The speculator motif, if dominant, would greatly increase the danger of an all-out war. For the immediate future the Soviet leaders can be expected to seek a middle course between the two approaches, the benefits and risks of either determined by their perceptions of the strengths and weaknesses of the noncommunist world.

NOTES

1. Henry L. Stimson and McGeorge Bundy, *On Active Service in War and Peace* (New York: Octagon, 1947), p. 644.
2. Georgi Arbatov, "Soviet-American Relations," in *The Communist* (Moscow: February, 1973), p. 110.
3. Fox Butterfield, "Hanoi General was Surprised at Speed of Saigon's Collapse," *New York Times,* April 26, 1976.
4. Quoted in *State Department Bulletin,* no. 2028 (Washington, D.C.: USGPO, July 1979), p. 51.

4

ARMS CONTROL AND CRISIS MANAGEMENT

The Owls' Agenda for Avoiding Nuclear War

Graham Allison, Albert Carnesale, and Joseph S. Nye, Jr.

Could the United States and the Soviet Union fight a nuclear war sometime before the end of this century? The answer to this question cannot be a categorical no.

If the United States and the Soviet Union engage in a general nuclear war in the foreseeable future, is it possible that the results of this war could advance the national interest of either? The answer to this question is certainly no. President Reagan's oft-repeated one-liner expresses a profound truth: "A nuclear war cannot be won and must therefore never be fought." The fact—a general nuclear war cannot be won—demands the imperative: it must never be fought. But between the fact and the imperative lies a large policy challenge.

If a nuclear war could not be chosen by rational leaders of either the United States or the Soviet Union as a way of advancing national interests, how then could such a war occur? In addition to the deliberate choices, the ingredients would include unintended consequences, unanticipated actions by third parties, accidents, misperceptions, and malfunctions of organizations, machines, and minds. Such factors are not unknown in the history of great power competitions.

Recall World War I. At the conclusion of the war in 1918, how would each of the principal actors in the sequence of events of 1914 that led to war have assessed the balance sheet? The Kaiser in Germany—gone. The Austro-Hungarian empire—destroyed. The Russian Czar—shot, his monarchy overthrown by a communist revolution he abhorred. England had sacrificed the flower of its youth and exhausted economic advantages built up over a previous century. Yet the war occurred—not by accident, but by a combination of purposive choices by governments that triggered chains of events that ran out of control to consequences no one would have chosen.

As we enjoy the 41st year of peace—or at least the absence of global war—since the conclusion of World War II, it is appropriate to be grateful for the achievement of the past four decades, but mindful that the nuclear era has repealed none of the laws of history. Indeed, in the crises of the recent past, for example the Cuban missile crisis of 1962 or the superpower crisis surrounding the Yom Kippur war in the Middle East in 1973, it is possible to identify significant numbers of close calls and to develop not-implausible scenarios leading from actions that occurred to a nuclear war.

The purpose of this essay is to assess the risks of nuclear war between the United States and the Soviet Union and to advocate greater urgency to an underattended agenda of actions for reducing those risks. In contrast to the usual treatises on defense issues, we focus less on the nuclear weapons themselves and more on factors that affect the probability of their use.

Formal arms control negotiations about numbers and types of weapons are not unimportant. For example, an agreement to cut current nuclear arsenals in half could have beneficial political effects. But it would not in itself significantly change the basic shape of the problem we face. Each superpower would retain the ability to destroy the other's society. A nuclear war still could not be won, and no sane leader would choose nuclear war as the solution to his problem. Structural arms control agreements (i.e., those affecting the structures of nuclear arsenals) can be useful, but even more can be accomplished by actions the United States can take independently and in concert with the Soviet Union aimed directly at the risks of nuclear war.

Over the past few years, the Project on Avoiding Nuclear War at Harvard University's John F. Kennedy School of Government has put this question to dozens of groups. In most groups of 50 or more, at least one respondent selected each answer—from "almost certain" to "almost no chance."

Specialists in national security are much more optimistic in their responses than the general public. Nearly half of the public says nuclear war is likely before the end of the century.[1] Specialists' answers cluster between 1 in 100 and 1 in 10,000.

Not much is proven by this finding. In this realm, there are specialists but not experts. Fortunately, since Hiroshima and Nagasaki, we have had no experience with nuclear war. Indeed, the sharp disjunction between the general public's views and those of the specialists reminds one of Lord Keynes' observation that when the views of the general public and the community of economists diverge, the general public is almost invariably the wiser.

In assessing risks of nuclear war, specialists focus primarily on deliberate choices of governments. Here the central truth of the past decade and of the decade to come is that no sane leader would choose a major nuclear war as the solution to his problem. Specialists in national security tend to discount the fears of the public, explaining their exaggerations as reactions to irresponsible scaremongering—of which there has been a great deal. But the general public's view also reflects two notions rooted in common sense. First, they observe that complex systems—at least all the complex systems they see—sometimes fail. Second, human beings—again at least all the human beings they see—make mistakes. For these reasons the public tends to be skeptical about a conclusion that an event is impossible just because it would not make sense.

Over the past two and one-half years, our project has attempted to examine systematically each of the principal paths to nuclear war, and to explore scenarios down each of these paths. This analysis leaves us closer in our overall assessment to the specialists than to the general public. Nonetheless, we agree strongly with the public's view about failures of complex systems and human errors. These factors are certainly more important than most strategists or policymakers have recognized.

Intentional War and Inadvertent War

A besetting sin of nuclear strategists is their tendency to think solely in terms of rational actors carefully calculating responses to each other's actions. The logic of nuclear strategy has been strongly affected by game theoretic formulations in which two players calculate their strategic choices in the light of their opponents' strategic choices. By building forces and taking decisions which close off any rational use of nuclear weapons by our opponent, we reduce the risks of nuclear war. War would start because an aggressor might perceive tempting opportunities. The prospects of war (and aggression without war) can be reduced by eliminating such opportunities.

This rational actor model, which we call Model I, captures important historical truths which the democracies discovered belatedly in the 1930s. And it helps to explain why nuclear deterrence has not broken down over the past four decades. The rational model is not wrong as much as it is insufficient. It is insufficient because the real world of nuclear deterrence does not consist solely of two players coolly calculating strategies for a competition played in a laboratory. Nuclear deterrence is played among small groups of (primarily) men with different backgrounds, and different historical memories embedded in large complex organizations, which are difficult to control centrally in peacetime, and which may perform in unexpected ways in a time of crisis. In short, events may get out of control, and war may break out or inadvertently escalate. These fears of inadvertent war through loss of control constitute a second model, Model II, of how a nuclear war might begin.

Some Model I theorists scoff at the notion of accidental war and belittle the significance of Model II. It is difficult to find any historical cases of accidental war, and there have been impressive technological improvements over the last two decades that have reduced the prospects of such an event. Redundancy of warning and time for human errors to be corrected have been built into strategic systems. The most important point about stories of false warnings and faulty computer chips is how far they have been from launching a nuclear war.

Model I strategists have a point. Purely accidental war is unlikely, but accidents are only one of the possible causes of inadvertent nuclear war. World War I was not accidental. The Austro-Hungarians started it deliberately and the German Kaiser gave them a diplomatic blank check. But they thought they were starting the Austro-Serbian war which would end quickly and result in a Russian diplomatic defeat (as had occurred in 1909). Events got out of control. Intricate alliance structures and offensive military action plans complicated last ditch efforts to manage the crisis. Psychological stress contributed to a sense of fatalism in the minds of key leaders. World War I was not accidental, but its size and scope certainly were not anticipated and its results were far from what any of the principal actors would have chosen.

The moral of the story is that both Model I and Model II factors are important. Few human events as complex as modern war are purely inadvertent, but few are purely intentional either. It is the interplay of Model II and Model I, particularly at a time of crisis, that is critical to planning the avoidance of nuclear war. And the consideration of Model II factors leads to different priorities in the policy agenda than does strategic thinking that stresses primarily rational calculations.

Replaying Past Crises

For perspective on the risks of nuclear war, it is useful to recall two important crises in the nuclear era: the Cuban missile crisis of 1962 and the Middle East crisis of 1973. In both cases, the risks of war dramatically increased.

In October 1962, the Kennedy administration discovered the Soviet Union in the process of an unprecedented attempt to install intermediate-range ballistic missiles outside Soviet borders, 90 miles from U.S. shores on the island of Cuba. After a week of secret deliberations at the highest level of the U.S. government, President Kennedy chose to confront the Soviet Union publicly, demanding withdrawal of the missiles and imposing a naval quarantine of Cuba to demonstrate U.S. resolve. There ensued a week of nuclear bargaining. U.S. strategic nuclear forces stood at their highest level of alert ever. Bombers of the Strategic Air Command, armed with nuclear weapons, dispersed to military and civilian airports across the country. Quick Reaction Aircraft, armed with nuclear weapons, were on alert in Europe. Before the week was over, a Soviet surface-to-air missile in Cuba had shot down a U.S. U-2 over Cuba (whether under orders from Moscow, or unauthorized, we still cannot determine); another U.S. U-2 had strayed over the Soviet Union in what could have appeared to the Soviets as a last-minute surveillance of their missile fields, raising a squadron of Soviet fighters.

About this incident, Soviet Chairman Khrushchev wrote to President Kennedy:

One of your reconnaissance planes intruded over Soviet borders in the Chukotka Peninsula area. . . . The question is, Mr. President: how should we regard this? One of your planes violates our frontier during this anxious time we are both experiencing, when everything has been put into combat readiness. Is it not a fact that an intruding American plane could be easily taken for a nuclear bomber, which might push us to a fateful step?[2]

U.S. electronic intelligence ships repeatedly violated Cuban territorial waters—risking capture by Cuba, as we came to appreciate more after North Korea captured the Pueblo some years later. In accordance with its standard operating procedures for a nuclear alert, the U.S. Navy identified, tracked, and forced to the surface Soviet submarines that entered the area from which they could have launched missiles against the United States. Fuses leading from events that occurred to an authorized or unauthorized use of nuclear weapons are not difficult to identify. Three sketches may suggest the range of possibilities.

First, suppose the Kennedy administration's management of the Cuban missile crisis had been no more effective than its management of the Bay of Pigs fiasco 18 months earlier. In 1961, a new president and his advisers, unfamiliar with each other and with their jobs, authorized a covert invasion of Cuba that in retrospect appeared certain of failure. A CIA-trained and -led force of some 1,400 Cuban exiles, insufficient to withstand the first wave of resistance, landed at the Bay of Pigs. Contingency plans called for them to fade back into the Escambray mountains, if necessary, though planners failed to note that when the landing site was changed, the invasion force was left separated from the mountains by 60 miles of impassable swamp.

The president and his key associates believed that they had authorized an operation recommended unanimously by the Central Intelligence Agency and the Joint Chiefs of Staff (JCS). In fact, the Chiefs had simply approved the project; they had not provided an estimate of the likelihood of success. And while the project had the full support of the covert action arm of the CIA, it was based on estimates of a likely uprising within Cuba that the intelligence arm of the CIA found incredible. U.S.-sponsored air support, too extensive to remain unacknowledged but too limited to be of much real help, was canceled after the first several sorties. After two days of denial, the operation had to be acknowledged by the U.S. government. In the end, an operation authorized as covert, low risk, and with a high probability of success became a major public failure for which the president had to assume personal responsibility.

One cannot help but be struck by the could have beens when replaying the hand in the Cuban missile crisis. Kennedy determined at the outset to seize the initiative, making the first public move in order to define the face of the issue. If he had been forced to pick among U.S. options in the first 48 hours, there is little question that he would have ordered an air strike. In fact, the president took a week to consider the options, to probe the estimates of consequences, and to choose among the alternatives.

Were such a crisis to arise today, the president and his advisers are not likely to have, or to believe that they would have, more than 48 hours to decide without reaching the point of a probable leak. Investigative reporters, officials who talk to the press, greatly intensified competition between print and electronic media (which has largely eliminated the possibility of the president convincing a publisher to hold a story, as Kennedy did with the publishers of the *New York Times* and the *Washington Post*), a vast increase in the numbers and sophistication of the Washington press, and the growth of Soviet intelligence—all make somewhat quaint the notion of a week of secret deliberation by the dozen key officials at the top of the U.S. government.

What if Kennedy had felt it necessary to act and authorized the air strike, which was his initial preference (and which some advisers, including Dean Acheson, advocated throughout the crisis and in retrospect)?[3] The air strike that would have occurred would not have been the surgical strike the president wanted, but the much more massive air strike the air force had planned. Targets included not only the missiles themselves, but the Soviets' surface-to-air missile sites, the Cuban airfields, and the guns opposite the U.S. base at Guantanamo. Though this issue was not discussed at the time in the Executive Committee of the National Security Council, in retrospect it is clear that such an air strike would have appeared to the Soviets as a precursor of invasion, which it would in fact have been in the minds of some in the U.S. government.

Here a major crossroads would have been reached. If the Soviets failed to respond to the air strike, many in the United States would have pressed for the invasion follow-on: why leave the job half done? Whether in response to the air strike alone, or the air strike followed by an invasion, the Soviets might well have responded by closing Berlin. If so, could governments strained by the management of one crisis have managed two crises simultaneously? Given the NATO commitment to Berlin, there can be little question that the Kennedy administration would have attempted to break the blockade of Berlin, with the likely result that U.S. and Soviet troops would come into direct conflict for the first time in the postwar era. Given the decisive Soviet conventional advantage, at what point, if any, would the United States have considered the use of nuclear weapons?

A second scenario begins with the penultimate step of the crisis. At the end of the week of public bargaining, Kennedy offered Khrushchev a public stick and a private carrot. The stick demanded withdrawal of the missiles and threatened to bomb them out by the beginning of the next week unless Khrushchev agreed to withdraw them. The carrot, communicated privately by U.S. Attorney General Robert Kennedy to Soviet Ambassador Anatoliy Dobrynin, promised withdrawal of U.S. Jupiter missiles in Turkey, as Kennedy had previously intended, if the Cuban missile crisis was successfully resolved.

What if Khrushchev had simply failed to respond to this offer? No one can say with certainty whether the president would have executed the threat, although the majority of his advisers believed at the time that the air strike would take place early the next week. If the air strike had begun, might not some of the Soviet missiles in Cuba have been fired against U.S. targets, including Miami or Atlanta? If one or more of these cities had been struck, whether authorized or unauthorized, how would the United States have responded?

A third scenario involves combinations of paths like those above and unanticipated consequences, accidents, and misperceptions. If on Saturday, October 27, when a U.S. U-2 was shot down over Cuba and a second U-2 strayed over the Soviet Union, there also had been an accidental sinking of a Soviet submarine, might Khrushchev have reacted irrationally? If, during the nuclear alert, either accidentally or in an unauthorized fashion, one of the Quick Reaction Aircraft armed with nuclear weapons in Europe had delivered a nuclear weapon against a Soviet target, what then? If, during some combination of events, there had been mechanical failure, or if we had mistakenly perceived the Soviets readying a launch from Cuba, or if a third party, such as Castro, had bombed Washington with conventional weapons, or a dozen of other possibilities, would historians of World War III have portrayed it as any less inevitable than World War I?

The 1973 crisis between the superpowers occurred at the end of the Yom Kippur war. The specter of a decision to use nuclear weapons remained much more distant than in 1962. But the complexities of managing crises that include uncontrollable allies remind one of another aspect of 1914, and may offer more striking parallels to the future.

On October 6, 1973, Egypt and Syria launched a surprise attack against Israel. After a week of losses, Israel moved to the offensive, regained lost ground, crossed the Suez Canal, and was surrounding the Egyptian Third Army. This triggered a superpower crisis of 48 tense and uncertain hours. Henry Kissinger, assistant to the president for national security affairs, flew to Moscow for a special meeting, on October 20, at which the superpowers agreed to call for a ceasefire in place between Israel and Egypt. On October 22, Kissinger went to Israel and extracted from the Israeli cabinet acceptance of the ceasefire. And yet, on October 24, the fighting resumed and soon the entire Egyptian Third Army was surrounded and in danger of being annihilated.

Having accepted Kissinger's assurance about the ceasefire, Moscow felt betrayed. The Soviets, determined to prevent the destruction of the Egyptian Third Army, prepared to introduce their own airborne troops to stop the Israelis. On the morning of October 24, Washington faced the fact that Israel was pressing forward, in spite of previous agreements and Washington's repeated demands; Moscow was loading airborne divisions in preparation for direct intervention; and U.S. intelligence reported that Soviet ships carrying nuclear weapons had passed through the Bosphorous and entered the area.

Under these circumstances, Washington ordered a nuclear alert, raising U.S. forces worldwide to Defense Condition III for the first time since the Cuban missile crisis. Washington's purpose was to signal to Moscow its determination to prevent Soviet intervention in the area. The fact that Kissinger, the primary actor in this drama for the United States, intended the alert to be secret, and thus failed to inform our European allies or to prepare the U.S. public, indicates the extent to which events were forcing the pace of decisions, and how little the participants foresaw the consequences of their choices. By morning, changes in the status of two and a half million men worldwide had aroused alarm in Europe, curiosity among the U.S. public, and had precipitated a crisis of public confidence in itself.

Fortunately the alert, plus pressure on Israel, led both the Soviet Union and Israel to pause. Whether the nuclear alert played a larger role in Moscow or in Tel Aviv remains uncertain. But by manipulating the nuclear risk, in the sense that the United States had set in motion a chain of events that could lead to nuclear war, the United States signaled the importance it attached to the stakes.

"What ifs" abound. If Israel had persisted, as it could have done, and Moscow intervened, as it probably would have done, how would the United States have responded? If Moscow had intervened, would the Israelis have attacked Soviet aircraft transporting troops to the area? If Moscow had retaliated against Israel, as it certainly would have done, how would the United States have reacted? If the nuclear weapons identified by U.S. intelligence were nuclear warheads for Scud missiles that the Soviets had emplaced in Egypt, short-range missiles capable of attacking Tel Aviv or Jerusalem, how would the Israelis have reacted, or the United States?

This case highlights the challenge of influencing the behavior of an adversary and an ally simultaneously in crises in which allies are taking actions that their patrons are unable to control. Indeed, in this crisis, if the United States and the Soviet Union had not had a relationship in which communication via the Kissinger link permitted each to interpret correctly the other's meaning, could the 48 hour period have been managed? If the interests of the two superpowers had been more competitive than in this case, where both wanted Israel to stop without encircling or destroying the Egyptian Third Army, could the crisis have been successfully resolved? If the decision makers in question had been less able than both Kissinger and Brezhnev proved to be in this instance, what might have happened? And if the actions and reactions in the actual case had been accelerated by accidents, like the Israeli bombing of the U.S. Liberty ship in 1967, or the provocative act of a fifth party like Libya's Qadhafi, what might have happened?

Hawks, Doves, and Owls

This examination of the Cuban missile crisis of 1962 and the Middle East crisis of 1973 indicates that the system of nuclear deterrence is far from perfect. Views differ on how to improve it. We have described elsewhere the differences that exist between Hawks and Doves over the requirements for effective deterrence in Model I terms.[4] The

Hawks' motto is "peace through strength" and their historical metaphor is Munich. Doves, on the other hand, believe that the risk of nuclear war is increased by overarming. Even though we might intend to deter the other side by adding more weapons, the real effect may be to increase fears of attack, and to provoke the other side into rash actions that could lead to war. Doves draw a lesson from 1941, when the United States cut off oil supplies to Japan in an effort to deter it from attacking Southeast Asia. Instead, this act helped to provoke the Japanese surprise attack on Pearl Harbor.

Hawks and Doves each have a point. If we want to reduce risks of nuclear war, we need policies that avoid both temptation and provocation. But the battle between Hawks and Doves misses an even more important point. If nuclear war ever breaks out, it may be less because of deliberate decisions than because of events getting out of control. To dramatize this set of concerns, we add a third bird to the nuclear aviary—the Owl. History is full of cases where rational decision makers were tripped up by nonrational factors with disastrous results. World War I is the Owl's historical metaphor.

Faced with the dangers of inadvertent nuclear war, what is to be done? We should not ignore the Hawks' and Doves' concerns about the right degree of threat according to Model I, but we should look more carefully at the additional and underattended agenda advocated by Owls. Three clusters of issues addressed by the Owls' agenda will be considered: reducing the impact of accidents, limiting misperceptions, and preventing and managing crises.

Reducing the Impact of Accidents

Faulty computer chips, fouled up communications in the midst of international crises, crazy orders issued by overly zealous military commanders: these are among the images comprising mankind's nuclear nightmares. Model I strategists maintain that unintended nuclear use is a remote possibility. Under normal conditions, they appear to be right. Unfortunately, we cannot count on conditions always being normal. Abnormal times, replete with uncertainty, ambiguity, insecurity, and tension, are bound to occur, with an attendant increase in the likelihood of nuclear error. In light of the potentially catastrophic consequences of accidental or unauthorized nuclear use, further reduction of this risk is eminently worthwhile.

Short-range theater nuclear weapons are especially dangerous. NATO deploys a large arsenal of these weapons, especially nuclear artillery shells, in Western Europe. Its purpose is to help deter Soviet aggression there, and there is little doubt that it serves that end. The mere existence of these "fuses to the doomsday machine" so near the inter-German border would have to be taken into account by any Soviet leader contemplating a military move westward. But is this contribution to deterrence (in terms of Model I) worth the increased risk of inadvertent nuclear war (in terms of Model II)?

The military functions currently assigned to short-range theater nuclear weapons, including the destruction of massed formations of tanks and other armored vehicles, could be accomplished by conventional weapons based on newly emerging technologies or, where necessary, by intermediate-range nuclear forces deployed well away from the battlefield. Most Western military commanders in the field believe that in the event of a large-scale invasion by Warsaw Pact forces, NATO's nuclear weapons near the inter-German border would be overrun before presidential release authority for their use was received. The granting of such release early in a crisis would decrease the danger of losing these weapons, but only at the cost of increasing the danger of premature or unwarranted use. While deterrence may be strengthened by Soviet fears of such use, those fears haunt the West as well. On balance, we judge the contribution to deterrence made by short-range theater nuclear weapons to be clearly outweighed by the dangers of inadvertent use. Accordingly, we would reduce reliance on them and to the extent politically feasible, withdraw them gradually from likely regions of conflict.

Battlefield nuclear weapons are not the only ones that might be detonated accidentally or without proper authorization. Land-based theater nuclear weapons, just as the warheads on U.S. land-based intercontinental ballistic missiles and long-range bombers, are equipped with permissive action links (PALs). These devices serve as sophisticated electronic combination locks designed to prevent arming of the weapon until a secret coded combination, provided at the time release authority is granted, has been entered. Unlike these land-based weapons, U.S. nuclear forces at sea are not equipped with PALs. Proponents of this exemption for the U.S. Navy argue that it is needed to compensate for the relative difficulty of communicating with forces at sea, especially in the wake of a Soviet attack on our land-based and airborne communications transmitters. The ability of our sea-based nuclear forces to retaliate in the absence of an express order from the president or an authorized successor, they maintain, diminishes the potential effectiveness (and therefore the likelihood) of a Soviet first strike. This argument has merit, but it does not justify a blanket exemption from PALs for all nuclear weapons on surface ships and submarines.

Communication with surface ships is almost as reliable as with land-based strategic forces, even after a Soviet attack, so installing PALs on surface-ship-based nuclear weapons would neither undermine deterrence nor encourage a Soviet limited attack on U.S. communications facilities. If a strong case can be made for having some nuclear weapons available for immediate use in the event of naval nuclear warfare initiated by the adversary, presidential authorization could be given to unlock the PALs on some suitable weapons beyond the range of Soviet territory.

Submarines present a more challenging communication problem and, therefore, it might not be desirable to have locked PALs on all of the submarine-based nuclear weapons within range of the Soviet Union. If the Soviets knew for certain that our second strike could only be launched on orders from Washington, they might have an increased incentive for a surprise decapitating strike on our capital. Fortunately, the choice is not limited to all or nothing. Even if PALs were installed on all submarine-based nuclear weapons, they need not all be locked all of the time. Some might be unlocked routinely, and most or all of them could be unlocked when ordered by appropriate authorities. If, for example, PALs were installed on all weapons and half of them were locked at any time, deterrence would hardly be diminished, yet the chance of accidental or unauthorized use could be reduced by half.

Most promising of the hardware fixes to the problem of inadvertent nuclear use are improvements in the command, control, communications, and intelligence (C^3I) system. This has been one of the items of highest priority in the Reagan administration's strategic modernization program, and rightly so. A vulnerable strategic C^3I network (i.e., one of the kind many specialists believe we now have) invites catastrophe by encouraging decapitation and undermining deterrence. It promotes the granting of release authority early in a crisis and perhaps even the adoption of a launch-on-warning strategy for land-based ICBMs for fear that the release and launch messages may not be communicated in a timely manner if and when actually needed. It fosters early use of large numbers of nuclear weapons in carefully coordinated intricate patterns of attack achievable only with a sophisticated (and surviving) C^3I system. And it diminishes our ability in the event of war to carry out the military operations essential to our security and the security of our allies. These considerations argue strongly for improving the survivability and endurance of our C^3I network.

Limiting Misperceptions

Prudent decision making requires facts. But facts alone are not enough. They are filtered through the minds of policymakers. History offers all too many examples of misperceptions of adversaries' capabilities and threats. A sound strategy for avoiding nuclear war must attend to perceptions, as well as to reality.

Regular discussions between U.S. and Soviet officials at the summit, cabinet, high military, and working levels can contribute greatly to mutual understanding of how each side sees its own interests, the other's interests, and risks. Summit mania may be unavoidable—certainly if summits are held but once every six years. The goal, however, should be to have meetings between the leaders and the United States and the Soviet Union at regular intervals, making them as routine as possible in order to reduce political pressures for announced results from each session. Perhaps it would be possible to have regular meetings, even at the highest level, at which there would be no agreements as a matter of policy, relying on special ad hoc meetings for negotiations and agreements.

Regular meetings of the secretaries and state and defense with their Soviet counterparts offer promise, again more for the clarification of perceptions and interests than in the search for agreement or tangible results. Regular meetings between the Chairman of the Joint Chiefs of Staff and the Chief of the Soviet General Staff, like the meeting that took place between JCS Chairman David Jones and Soviet Chief of Staff Ogarkov as part of the summit meeting in 1979, were judged by U.S. participants as enormously useful in providing a better sense of the adversary, of what we do that most concerns him, and of how issues of relatively little importance to us, but of great importance to him, could be resolved.

Mechanisms and procedures such as the crisis control center suggested by Senators Sam Nunn (D-Ga.) and John Warner (R-Va.) might not play a significant role at the height of a crisis. At such a time, leaders will try to centralize decision making. But they could do useful work in the period prior to crises by exchanging data, developing capabilities for technical transmissions, and establishing the meaning of particular terms. While any such center would offer temptations to both sides to exploit it for intelligence purposes, as both would undoubtedly do, the benefits are important for a more open society such as ours.

If one takes seriously the factor of Soviet perceptions of U.S. strategic forces and their own in the balance of deterrence, official U.S. statements about the nature, extent, and importance of perceived or possible future Soviet military advantages made for the purpose of mobilizing public and congressional support for defense programs can have unintended effects in weakening deterrence. More careful attention needs to be given, therefore, to the impact of such statements on Soviet perceptions, and the perceptions of allies, as well as on the U.S. Congress.

U.S. declaratory policy and procedures can importantly affect our own, and the Soviets', perceptions of nuclear weapons. Is the nuclear taboo to be reinforced or undermined? Political rhetoric and military training sometimes suggest that nuclear weapons are no different from other instruments of war fighting and should be used just as weapons have been used in the past. But if our strategy for reducing the risks of nuclear war means to draw a bright line between nuclear weapons and all others, we need to emphasize the fact that nuclear weapons are essentially weapons of terror. U.S. statements and deployments have affected the evolution of Soviet thinking and should be considered carefully in this light.

Finally, a strategy to limit misperceptions would not cut off communications between the United States and the Soviet Union as a sanction. To assuage domestic pressures for reactions against Soviet actions that violate agreements of our values, sanctions have a role to play. Invariably in such situations, U.S. leaders are tempted to reduce or even to cut off contacts with the Soviets. But this temptation should be resisted, for it is in times of worsened relations and heightened tension that the communication links provided by official and nongovernmental contact are most needed.

Preventing and Managing Crises

Owls place primary emphasis on preventing and managing crises because crises greatly increase the prospect of nuclear war. Crises are characterized by an increase in threat and stress and a compression of time. These factors constrain rational decision making and reduce the ability to respond to the effects of accidents.

Since World War II the United States and the Soviet Union have developed some de facto rules of prudence to prevent and contain crises. The superpowers have not engaged each other's forces in combat, they have not threatened each other's vital interests, and they have not used nuclear weapons against anyone. These rules represent a restraint of antagonism that should be recognized, enhanced, and extended. At the same time, it is clear that the U.S.-Soviet relationship is fundamentally competitive, even during crises. Both nations wish to reduce the chances of intended or unintended war, but each also wishes to manipulate the fear of that outcome in order to deter or coerce the other side. The task of crisis prevention and management is thus more complex than it first appears.

Discussions of crisis prevention and management with the Soviets serve several useful functions. Such talks could help to sensitize the leaders to the issues involved and to the perspectives of the other side, to clarify perceptions of relative interest in specific geographical areas, and to reinforce and extend specific negotiated agreements, like the U.S.-Soviet Incidents at Sea Agreement, or establish new devices, like a jointly staffed crisis-monitoring center.

Communication between the superpowers is clearly an essential component of any system for preventing crises. It is also essential to think in advance about how to communicate about the termination of crises that might spill over into war. War termination is a taboo topic, but it is too important to ignore. The existing hot line—which is really a slow teletype link first established between Moscow and Washington in 1963—could be quickly destroyed in a nuclear war. The two sides jointly should establish multiple mechanisms for reliable and rapid communication between them not only in peacetime, but also after armed conflict—even nuclear conflict—has begun. In addition, we should take the lead in encouraging the establishment of such hot lines among all five of the countries known to have nuclear weapons.

In addition to such bilateral and multilateral measures, there are a number of independent steps we can take to improve our own procedures for preventing and managing crises. The current situation is far from adequate. For instance, there is virtually no staff continuity in the National Security Council (NSC) between administrations. Most NSC files are removed as private presidential papers. As a result, there is no collective memory center in our system for quick reference at a time of crisis. For example, there is no complete set of transcripts of communications between the president and his Soviet counterpart. Former NSC officials we interviewed described difficulties in ascertaining what exactly was agreed between Kennedy and Khruschev in the Cuban crisis, or in gaining access to key documents at the height of the Middle East crisis of 1973. A core professional staff in charge of critical, national NSC files would make a significant difference.

The United States must also find better ways to prepare our own leaders to deal with nuclear crises. Many new political appointees with responsibilities related to nuclear weapons arrive at their jobs with little knowledge of or background in U.S.-Soviet relations, nuclear weapons issues, or crisis decision making. Their training for dealing with potential nuclear crises is generally inadequate. As one former official put it, "new leaders are given a one day briefing that is like force feeding from a fire hose." They cannot possibly absorb it before they are caught up again in business as usual. We need to find more efficient ways of giving them information on nuclear deployments and practices, the kinds of crisis situations that might arise, and the mechanisms available for dealing with such crises. Some compilation of lessons learned from the experience of former officials is also needed. Active participation in crisis simulations can also be a valuable experience.

We should also be taking a number of steps to reduce the dangers of chaos that might follow from a Soviet or terrorist nuclear attack on Washington. Given such dangers of decapitation, it is essential that at least one of 17 constitutionally designated successors (and an appropriate staff) be outside of Washington at a time of crisis. In a serious crisis, it would be more important to have the vice president located in an alternative command post than in Washington. Yet the latter is what is currently planned.

Finally, there are important steps to avoid if we are to prevent and manage nuclear crises. Two simple rules of thumb are "don't multiply crises" and "don't use nuclear alerts for political signaling." On Model I reasoning, both are clever means to enhance the credibility of our deterrent threat. But in Model II terms, both are potential paths to nuclear disaster. It has been suggested that if the Soviets initiate a crisis in a region (or of a type) in which they have an advantage, the United States should respond by initiating another crisis in which it has the advantage. For example, Soviet aggression against U.S. interests in the Persian Gulf region might be countered by U.S. action against Cuba. Such action is likely to be counterproductive because it would increase the likelihood of accidents. Similarly, nuclear alerts are a dangerous form of communication, especially during crises. When some form of alert appears necessary to ensure the survival of our forces in case of an attack, preference should be given to low-level or partial alerts.

Conclusion

In conclusion, the most worrisome risk of nuclear war between the United States and the Soviet Union in the 14 years remaining in this century has frequently been misidentified. This risk arises neither from the likelihood that the leaders of the United States or the Soviet Union will deliberately choose nuclear war, nor merely from the possibility of a technical accident. Instead, nuclear war could emerge from some combination of deliberate choices, accidents, and unforeseen consequences.

Identifying and addressing this source of risk of nuclear war generates an agenda of actions. Some of the actions can be taken independently by the United States. Some can be taken only in concert with the Soviet Union. The specific proposals discussed above for reducing the impact of accidents, limiting misperceptions, and preventing and managing crises are meant to be suggestive of a much larger agenda— an Owls' agenda—that has been underattended in our national debate.

Focusing on this agenda does not require one to demean the necessity for actions to make nuclear and conventional deterrence more credible. The national debate between Hawks and Doves, between those who emphasize temptation and those more concerned with provocation will continue, as it should. The Owls' agenda offers some common ground, on which individuals destined to disagree forever about Star Wars or the nuclear freeze can agree on actions to take now to reduce the risks of nuclear war.

NOTES

1. The Public Agenda Foundation, *Voter Options on Nuclear Arms Policy* (New York: The Public Agenda Foundation, 1984); *Time,* January 2, 1984, p. 51.
2. Graham Allison, *Essence of Decision: Explaining the Cuban Missile Crisis* (Boston: Little, Brown & Co., 1971), p. 141.
3. Dean Acheson, "Homage to Plain Dumb Luck," *Esquire,* February 1969.
4. Graham T. Allison, Albert Carnesale, and Joseph S. Nye, Jr., *Hawks, Doves, and Owls: An Agenda for Avoiding Nuclear War* (New York: W. W. Norton & Co., 1985), pp. 206–222.

A Practical Approach to Containing Nuclear Dangers

Senator Sam Nunn and

Senator John Warner

The fundamental and overriding reason for attempting to negotiate arms control arrangements is to reduce the danger of military conflict between the two great powers, particularly a conflict that involved an exchange of nuclear weapons. Although it might prove feasible in such an eventuality to limit damage to moderate levels, the danger that any use of nuclear weapons would escalate to an exchange of catastrophic proportions is substantial enough that efforts to reduce the likelihood of such a contingency deserve a high priority. The risk of war between the great powers appears to be low at present; even so, the stakes potentially at risk are sufficiently grave to merit substantial efforts to bring about even marginal reductions in whatever dangers exist.

With few exceptions, attention to arms control negotiations in recent years has tended to focus on ways to reduce the size or to alter the characteristics of U.S. and Soviet nuclear arsenals. Increasing stocks of nuclear weapons are presumed to increase the risk of nuclear war by introducing uncertainties and instabilities in the balance of power between the United States and the USSR. Similarly, weapons with certain characteristics—particularly those which could be used to destroy the strategic forces of the other side—are believed to increase the risk of nuclear attack because of their effect on the incentives each side would perceive to initiate an exchange in the event of a crisis. Thus, arms control negotiators have concentrated on attempting to bring about "deep cuts" in strategic arsenals, and also to eliminate preferentially those weapons believed to make the strategic balance less stable.

In short, nuclear arms control negotiations have been attempting primarily to reduce the risk of nuclear war indirectly. They have been concentrating on the "capabilities" of the two sides to wage nuclear war. These efforts obviously are important and should be continued. But there is also the matter of "intentions." In addition to having certain capabilities, a nation needs a reason to wage war—either a malevolent intention of its own or a perception that an opponent has such an intention and therefore it would be prudent to strike first.

Negotiations can do little about malevolent intentions. In these cases it is essential to maintain powerful military forces capable of making clear to a potential aggressor that the cost of initiating conflict would be far greater than any potential gain. Negotiations, however, can help to reduce the possibility of erroneous perceptions of the other side's intentions—to facilitate communications between the two nations in crises and to build confidence in both states that the other does not intend to initiate conflict. Even if one side does have malevolent intentions, negotiated measures of confidence-building and communications can strengthen deterrence by reducing the danger of war by accident or inadvertence. Nuclear confidence-building measures can serve the additional function, in the event of a war between the two great powers, of assuring each nation that the conflict could be maintained on the conventional level and not escalate to the use of nuclear weapons.

One of the benefits of this approach to nuclear arms control is that it typically involves relatively small and noncontroversial steps, often technical arrangements that can be put in place without being complicated by the sharp political and ideological differences between the United States and the USSR. Indeed, the two nations already have reached several agreements that can be considered part of this general approach to reducing the risk of nuclear war. But there are many other things that could be done—pragmatic, politically feasible means of reducing the danger of the use of nuclear weapons.

Since 1982, we have cochaired a working group established to develop, evaluate, and—when appropriate—promote specific, pragmatic, and politically feasible means of making the use of nuclear weapons less likely. In addition to ourselves, the working group included James Schlesinger, the former Secretary of Defense; Brent Scowcroft, President Ford's National Security Advisor; Richard Ellis, United States Commissioner on the U.S.-USSR Standing Consultative Commission; Bobby Inman, formerly Deputy Director of Central Intelligence; William Hyland, formerly Deputy National Security Advisor (who served as the group's secretary); William Perry, formerly Under Secretary of Defense for Research and Engineering; Don Rice, President of the RAND Corporation; and Barry Blechman, a senior fellow at the Center for Strategic and International Studies. The Nunn-Warner Working Group on Nuclear Risk Reduction was established to explore pragmatic means of making the use of nuclear weapons less likely—means of improving communications and understanding between the United States and the USSR and measures to help build confidence between the two great powers that neither intends to initiate a nuclear conflict.

The group has met periodically over the past two years to consider a variety of ideas and proposals. In November 1983, it issued an interim report recommending that the United States and the USSR consider establishing "Nuclear Risk Reduction Centers" in their respective capitals to carry out a variety of functions that would contribute to a reduced danger of nuclear conflict. These centers would maintain a twenty-four-hour watch on situations that could lead to nuclear confrontations. They would be linked by sophisticated, real-time communications channels and might also include liaison officers from the second nation among their staffs. In addition to their roles during and prior to crises, they could serve as the forum for a variety of negotiations and information exchanges during normal times—all intended to control nuclear risks.

A wide range of measures that might also be considered for U.S.-Soviet negotiations could help to reduce the risk of nuclear war.

For one, it would be possible to enhance the physical means of communicating between the two nations in the event of a nuclear crisis. The United States and the USSR agreed to install a dedicated communications link for the use of the two heads-of-state in the wake of the Cuban Missile Crisis. The "Hot Line" Agreement was completed in 1963 and improved in 1971 when a satellite communications system was added to the existing land lines. In 1984, the hot line was improved again when the United States and the USSR agreed to add a facsimile transmission link to the existing teletype system. Additional measures are possible. President Reagan, for example, has proposed that an additional communications channel be established between the U.S. Department of Defense and the Soviet Defense Ministry for the exchange of technical information in the event of a crisis. He also has proposed that the two sides agree to upgrade the communications links between their respective capitals and their embassies in Moscow and Washington. (The text of the Defense Department study that recommended these measures is included in Appendix C.)

Second, the United States and the Soviet Union could exchange much more information about their respective nuclear forces and doctrines, with a view toward clarifying ambiguities, reducing suspicions, and building confidence of nonhostile intent. The two sides, for example, could maintain a common data base describing their strategic forces. Such a data base was created for the SALT II Treaty; it would be a relatively easy matter to update it periodically and to expand it to include forces not now counted.

The two great powers might also agree to notify each other prior to tests of strategic missiles and aircraft. The SALT II Treaty includes a requirement that certain types of tests be announced in advance. The United States has proposed to expand these requirements in the START negotiations; the Soviet Union has made somewhat related proposals.

Thought might also be given to instituting periodic meetings between military representatives of the two great powers. As explained by Wade J. Williams in Chapter 9, such a dialogue could help to improve mutual understanding and reduce suspicions on the two sides. In these periodic meetings, or in other forums, it might be helpful if each side informed the other of the types of strategic operations, tests, or development programs that caused concern. Such talks need not lead to any sort of formal agreement (and probably would not), but they could lead each side to eliminate practices which the other found needlessly provocative. For example, the USSR sometimes launches several missiles at one time in military exercises. This causes some concern when detected by U.S. warning systems. Similarly, the Soviets have complained about certain U.S. exercises involving strategic bombers. A frank exchange of views on these subjects might lead to unilateral actions to avoid certain practices.

For that matter, it might be possible to negotiate formal, mutual restraints in certain strategic operations or tests of certain types of strategic weapons. Obviously, any such proposal would have to be examined carefully on its merits; there would be risks as well as benefits in virtually any such proposal. Still, the idea bears exploration. Alan J. Vick and James A. Thomson explore limits on strategic operations in Chapter 7. Sidney D. Drell and Theodore J. Ralston analyze the potential utility of limitations on certain weapon tests in Chapter 6.

Third, the United States and the USSR might agree on joint planning for certain contingencies involving nuclear threats by third parties. Despite their very real differences, the two great powers do have certain interests in common—controlling the risk of nuclear terrorism being one of them. In the years ahead, nuclear weapon capabilities will almost certainly spread to additional nations. The risk that a weapon might fall into the hands of a subnational group or rogue national leader may be small, but it will almost certainly rise over the years. It would be prudent for U.S. and Soviet representatives to discuss how the two nations might behave in various contingencies; to think through possible crises and map out potential forms of cooperation. For example, what if there were an unexplained nuclear explosion somewhere? How would the two sides react? Or say there was a threat from a terrorist group to detonate a weapon if certain demands were not met? Or what if a nuclear weapon or the fissile material for one or more weapons were discovered to be missing? Or what if an intelligence agency determined that a subnational organization was on the verge of acquiring a nuclear capability? Joint planning for these types of contingencies—simply talking through the types of actions which would and would not be helpful—could well facilitate effective cooperation should the threat ever become real. Barry M. Blechman discusses the possible use of Nuclear Risk Reduction Centers to control the danger of nuclear terrorism in Chapter 4.

Finally, the United States and the USSR could agree to certain physical measures to help reduce the risk of accidental or inadvertent nuclear war. Victor A. Utgoff describes one such idea in Chapter 8 of this volume. He analyzes the costs and benefits of an agreement by the United States and the USSR to install unmanned, tamper-proof radars at each other's missile fields. These radars would detect the launch of a missile with an extremely high probability and send an encrypted signal back to the other nation. Different, and also encrypted, signals would also be sent at other times to ensure that the system was working properly. The installation of such a system would complement each side's early warning satellites, helping to avoid unnecessary—and possibly provocative—reactions to false warnings of attack and building confidence that neither side would attempt a surprise attack. As Utgoff points out, these types of unmanned, remote-sensor systems might have other applications as well in helping to reduce the risk of nuclear war.

In short, there are many potential practical steps to reduce the dangers implied by the existence of nuclear weapons. Each such measure requires careful and objective evaluation; none are without some costs and risks. Still, these ideas are worth exploring. We commend them to the attention of citizens and officials.

Extended Deterrence

Walter B. Slocombe

Why "Extended" Deterrence?

It is occasionally a useful exercise to think why we use all those familiar adjectives in the jargon of strategy—what makes the strategy "countervailing?" To whom is the destruction "assured?" Why must the capability be not merely "hard-target" but also prompt? And, for present purposes, to whom, or where, or against what is the deterrence "extended?"

This is legitimately a three-fold question because the deterrence is extended in several senses. First, it is extended nationally, for it represents an effort by the United States to extend the credibility of its nuclear power to the protection of other nations—most relevantly, the European NATO allies of the United States. It is a tribute to the continuing power of the national idea that while there is considerable debate whether the United States would or should be permitted to use nuclear weapons in the defense of, for example, Germany, there is practically none about whether the other 49 states would use such weapons for the defense of Alaska.

Second, deterrence is extended geographically. The threats which are to be discouraged are, for the most part, directed at regions close to the Soviet Union and remote from the United States. The fact that we seek to extend deterrence over great distances has a significant political consequence; to the degree that forces based in the United States are regarded as unsuitable to carry out the threats implicit in geographically extended deterrence, where should the forces that will be relied on be based and how, if at all, are the host countries to participate in the decision to use the weapons?

Third, extended deterrence promises nuclear retaliation not just for the gravest challenges to the security and existence of the United States, but goes further to threaten such retaliation—or first use—in order to discourage attacks that, while serious, pose less of an ultimate threat to U.S. interests.

Indeed, the jargon betrays the problem. Reliance on the ultimate threat of nuclear weapons to deter attacks on the United States itself is deterrence *simpliciter;* denominating as only extended deterrence the making of threats to deter attacks on U.S. allies is to assert that there are significant differences in the gravity to the United States of the threat posed by such attacks. Basically, successful deterrence, like a successful alliance, depends on all concerned—front-line allies, their more remote partners, and potential attackers—being convinced that an attack on any part of the alliance is in fact a threat to the vital interests of the most powerful ally. In a fundamental sense, the debate over extended deterrence is a debate over collective security, over the degree to which it is literally true, and not merely a pious Cold War formula that an attack on one NATO ally is an attack on all.

The problem of extended deterrence is simply the international and political problem of the credibility of retaliation with potentially suicidal consequences against serious, but not inevitably fatal, threats. From this perspective the debate over the extension of U.S. nuclear deterrence to Europe finds its counterpart in the debate over U.S. capacity to deter less than all-out attacks on the United States itself. The whole debate about the "window of vulnerability" and the significance of the vulnerability of U.S. intercontinental ballistic missile (ICBM) silos simply recasts the question of extended deterrence in a nongeographical, nonnational context. Just as threats of mutual obliteration may be thought less than adequately credible to deter attacks on U.S. allies in Europe and elsewhere, so such threats may be thought less than adequate to deter limited attacks on military forces in the United States itself.

The Chronic Crisis of Extended Deterrence

A quick review of the history of the role of nuclear weapons in NATO's strategic and political situation gives a useful perspective on the current debate. There can be no doubt that extended deterrence now faces a crisis. There cannot, however, be much doubt that extended deterrence has always been in the throes of crisis.

The uneasy history of U.S. nuclear guarantees to its overseas allies has gone through several phases. Only in the immediate postwar era, before the first Soviet atom bomb test, have U.S. nuclear forces relative to those of the USSR matched the theoretical requirements of high confidence extended deterrence. For a brief period after World War II, the Soviet Union lacked, and was believed by military and political leaders on both sides of the Atlantic to lack, any serious capability to attack the United States with nuclear weapons. During that period, when fears of an imminent Soviet attack on Western Europe were greater than they have been at any time since, the U.S. threat to respond to such an attack with nuclear weapons—though in terms of capability it may well have fallen short because of the limitations of the number and power of the nuclear weapons the United States then possessed—did not lack for credibility.

That dominance was fleeting. By the early 1950s, following the Soviet acquisition of nuclear weapons, the U.S. government became acutely conscious of the strains inherent in relying on a threat to launch a general nuclear attack on the Soviet Union as a response to a Soviet attack on U.S. allies. The declaratory policy of massive retaliation then espoused should in no way obscure the fact that during the Eisenhower administrations senior U.S. leaders, including the president, had grave doubts about the prudence, effectiveness, and even morality of relying on attacks on Soviet cities and industry—about all the weapons were capable of at that time—as the primary means of preventing a Soviet assault on Western Europe. Indeed, whatever the public simplifications may have been, the doctrine of massive retaliation itself was not a threat to level Moscow at the first sign of Soviet obstreperousness, but rather a warning that future Soviet aggression along the lines of Korea would find the United States less ready than it had been in 1950 to let the Soviet Union and its proxies define the geographical scope of the contest and the character of weapons used.

The immediate reaction of the U.S. administration and of the NATO alliance as a whole to doubts about general nuclear war as a way of defending Europe was to focus on the use of nuclear weapons in a manner that would be more effective militarily and more credible politically. The concept of limited nuclear war, and in particular the use of smaller nuclear weapons for militarily decisive intervention in battlefield operations, was the response.

The turn to tactical nuclear weapons seems to have had two sources. The first was technological. In the few short years between 1945 and 1954, the United States had gone from an extreme shortfall of weapons relative to targets to a position of nuclear plenty. Large numbers of smaller and far more flexible nuclear weapons were now— or would soon be—available. The second impetus was economic. The alternative of relying on conventional defense was rejected as too costly for an administration committed to fiscal retrenchment, and too troubling politically for a Europe still less than a decade removed from the destruction of World War II.

In a sense, theater nuclear forces (TNF) have never recovered from the enthusiasm of their early days. Small, "clean" nuclear weapons deployed with units in the field, not at air bases far in the rear, would carry the burden of deterrence and, if necessary, defense. Just how they would be decisive, especially once the Soviets could reply in kind, was never fully explained. For a period, however, Western leaders publicly espoused the view (later attributed to rigid Soviet artillery marshals) that nuclear weapons were just big cannon. As Field Marshal Bernard Montgomery, then Deputy Supreme Allied Commander Europe, blithely put it to a meeting in London in 1954. "With us [at SHAPE] it is no longer: 'They may possibly be used.' It is very definitely: 'They will be used, if we are attacked.' In fact, we have reached the point of no return as regards the use of atomic and thermonuclear weapons in a hot war."

NATO has spent the last 30 years returning to the very question Montgomery was so sure was closed. The period of hearty confidence that the deployment of large numbers of flexible, tactical nuclear weapons would solve NATO's deterrence problems was remarkably short lived. It did not last even for the time necessary to deploy the new weapons. A series of events brought the doctrine into almost immediate disrepute. Probably the two most important events were leaked reports of the 1955 Carte Blanche exercise showing the massive German civilian casualties that would accompany use of battlefield nuclear weapons to defend Western Europe and the Soviet testing in 1957 of an intercontinental ballistic missile heralding an era of absolute U.S. vulnerability.

One suspects, however, that the real problem was that the U.S. government had hoped TNF would produce decisive battlefield results at tolerable cost, while Europeans hoped TNF would set off general escalation. Growing consciousness of what the attempt could do to both partners prompted some quick rethinking.

The response to this crisis diverged into two schools. One sought to find a way to make the use of nuclear weapons more credible by making it not merely a step to mutual oblivion but also a strategically meaningful act—largely a response to U.S. vulnerability if escalation went very far. The second sought a way to make the use of nuclear weapons unnecessary—an approach produced by the conviction that primarily, conventional defense was both necessary and possible.

Responses of the first school included the political effort to devise a nuclear capability that was not exclusively provided by the United States. This effort took a variety of forms ranging from implementation of dual key systems through proposals to develop and deploy uniquely European nuclear forces under the control of a new NATO structure. It is not entirely coincidental that this was also the era of determined deployment of British and French independent nuclear forces.

From the U.S. side, one important aspect of the response in nuclear doctrine to recognition of Soviet capability against the United States was the articulation of a policy of preparing relatively large-scale but still limited nuclear targeting options. This policy sought to find a set of targets that went beyond battlefield use, which had been recognized to be principally destructive in the very Western territory it was to defend, and yet stopped short of massive attacks on the Soviet homeland—now recognized as likely to bring down an equivalent Soviet response on the United States and therefore of limited credibility.

The second school of response to the emergence of Soviet intercontinental forces and recognition of the terrible cost of large-scale use of battlefield nuclear weapons in Europe was the increased belief, in the United States at any rate, of the possibility of a conventional defense of Europe. Reinforcing this concept was the view that NATO had previously exaggerated the degree of Soviet conventional advantage and the scale of NATO effort necessary to offset it.

None of these responses to the perceived difficulties of heavy reliance on theater nuclear weapons for NATO deterrence was outstandingly successful. Europeans greeted Secretary of Defense Robert McNamara's articulation in 1961 of a U.S. doctrine of controlled strategic nuclear response with dismay. They feared an American scheme to limit nuclear war to Europe. When it became clearer, as Soviet forces began to match Soviet boasts, that no U.S. counterforce attacks could destroy the Soviet ability to retaliate against U.S. cities and industry, U.S. enthusiasm for the idea declined as well.

The efforts to increase credibility by a larger European role in nuclear attack decisions took concrete form in the multilateral force (MLF) idea. The plan foundered on the inability to reach a workable scheme for European decision making. A continent that, for all its common heritage and shared interests, could not agree on a supranational policy on the price of wine, barley, and sheep meat (mutton), found it hard to agree on how to decide on nuclear war—and eventually Lyndon Johnson lost patience with the attempt.

The effort to build a much stronger conventional capability fared little better. However attractive the idea was to specialists (mostly within the United States), it petered out, despite the problems on the nuclear side, as the immediate threat receded with the easing of the Berlin crisis and as the United States found its military energies for conventional forces diverted to Southeast Asia.

The decade of the 1960s was not entirely unproductive in shaking NATO's faith in a nuclear deus ex machina. By 1967, NATO was prepared to adopt a new statement of its doctrine. The policy of "flexible response," embodied in MC-14/3, proposed to deter by having forces able to meet aggression at whatever level of violence—including nuclear weapons—was necessary, while seeking to contain the scope of the fighting. This was a clear step beyond its predecessor of a decade before that had pledged the alliance to virtually immediate use of nuclear weapons.

The policy of flexible response has many critics and it lacks intellectual elegance, but it does have some of the important advantages of verbal compromise in a situation where there are no easy ways to reconcile conflicts of interest and the difficulties of taking action. It preserves the commitment of U.S. nuclear weapons and creates uncertainty in Soviet calculations, while recognizing the inherent advantages of having a conventional defense adequate at least to delay the use of nuclear weapons until large-scale conventional defeat has made such attacks necessary.

But the compromise of 1967 by no means terminated the argument. With unquestioned Soviet achievement of parity, with U.S.-Soviet agreement on limited restriction of intercontinental strategic arms—but not on theater systems—and with a variety of new tensions in the European-U.S. relationship over economics, Vietnam, oil, and the Middle East, debate continued over the credibility and extent of the U.S. nuclear guarantee. The United States, by the Schlesinger doctrine and the countervailing strategy, sought to revive the concept of controlled strategic response originally articulated by Secretary McNamara in the early 1960s. Responding to European concerns about an arms control deal being made over their heads and to Soviet deployments indicating a continued interest in being able to make strategic nuclear threats to Western Europe, the alliance agreed on deployment of Pershing IIs and ground launched cruise missiles (GLCMs) while simultaneously pressing negotiations to limit such deployment on both sides. The alliance may not always avoid repeating its own history, but it does learn. The intermediate range nuclear forces (INF) debate proceeded in a substantially more realistic political context than the MLF debate.

Challenges to Flexible Response

None of the steps taken by the alliance has stilled the controversy. Distinguished U.S. spokesmen have joined in questioning the credibility of the U.S. making any nuclear response to a Soviet attack in Europe. In Europe even more than in the United States, concern has been aroused at whether reliance on nuclear threats is worth risking the cost that making good on such threats would entail.

Consequently the alliance is turning to a new phase in the seemingly endless debate about extended deterrence. The general directions of criticism of current policy may be summed up in three questions:

Isn't there a nuclear alternative to current concepts? Is there not a way to defeat or deter by imposing unacceptable but less than total costs, some new way either doctrinally or operationally to use nuclear weapons that will ease the problems of credibility, effectiveness and destructiveness that have undermined past reliance on nuclear weapons?

Isn't there a conventional alternative? Is there not some way to avoid relying on nuclear weapons by creating a situation in which there is no need for threats of nuclear escalation because NATO can defeat a Soviet assault by direct conventional defense?

Isn't there some political way out, a way to rely on European rather than U.S. nuclear weapons? So far the possibility of a European deterrent remains the least discussed of the three possibilities. In the long run the outcome of persisting doubts about relying on American nuclear weapons could well be not massive European rallying to alliance conventional defense but growth in European nuclear forces, with all the attendant political problems of such forces.

Nuclear Changes

Those who seek a different, but still a nuclear, way of solving the problem have advanced a variety of proposals for changing the weapons and nuclear doctrines on which NATO relies.

One approach urges the need, in place of heavy reliance on battlefield nuclear weapons, to use long-range nuclear weapons to disrupt, inhibit, and prevent the massing and echeloning of Soviet forces well behind the front, and to destroy the airbases, supply systems, and command and control on which the Soviet onslaught would depend. NATO has always maintained that it stands prepared to strike behind the front line, but now this school of thought argues that, with improved target acquisition capabilities, it becomes possible to do a great deal more in this area. Because this approach tends to focus on targets in Eastern Europe between the Elbe and the Vistula, it threatens to arouse all of the traditional European fears about counting on fighting a nuclear war in Europe only. Nor is it self evident that the Warsaw Pact is significantly more vulnerable to deep strike nuclear attacks than NATO, if only because of NATO's heavy reliance on airpower, and therefore on airfields. Massive U.S. reinforcement of NATO's conventional defense presents a variety of targets (airfields, seaports, and prepositioned equipment storage areas bases) for limited nuclear attack which are, in their way, every bit as tempting as the Soviet tank formations are supposed to be for NATO.

A second and related approach may be termed a policy of no early first use. Without renouncing nuclear escalation altogether, or hoping to find the long-sought Grail of a militarily decisive target set for nuclear weapons, it is argued that NATO should take a series of steps to ensure that such a decision can be postponed as long as possible and made by political, not military, decision makers. An important element in this approach would pull NATO's nuclear weapons back, both literally from the inner-German border and figuratively from immediate battlefield missions. The INF decision fits conceptually very well with this approach, for Pershing IIs and GLCMs are more survivable and are optimized for deep strikes.

Proponents of this view hold that, with deployment under way, NATO can and should substantially reduce its commitment to the use of nuclear weapons on the battlefield. To symbolize that change in policy and to reduce pressures for early use of nuclear weapons, NATO should, it is argued, retire many nuclear weapons of dubious utility for long-withheld strikes (air defense weapons and atomic demolition munitions [ADMs] are usually mentioned in this context.) Such reduced numbers of artillery shells and short-range missiles as are retained should be pulled well back from the frontier, while dual-use aircraft are transferred back to the conventional battle. The resulting NATO theater nuclear force would be smaller and more survivable, and would embody a doctrine under which nuclear attacks would be reserved as a means of escalation after conventional defenses failed, not as a means of forcing the result.

In general, the efforts to ease the present problems by changes in nuclear plans propose to shift the threat of nuclear attacks made by NATO away from the battlefront and toward the rear, away from West Germany and its borders with East Germany and back toward Soviet soil, and to seek relief from the pressures to use nuclear weapons early by survivability and disengagement of battlefield forces.

Conventional Changes

Often politically, if not conceptually, contrary to these proposals to restructure NATO's nuclear reliance are proposals to get far more serious about conventional defense.

Proposals for improving NATO conventional defense exemplify the familiar, but not for that reason necessarily false, arguments for such steps—that the conventional imbalance is greatly exaggerated, that technology or public support or the inherent advantages of the defense are on NATO's side, that NATO already spends very nearly enough both in money and manpower to mount a formidable conventional defense, and that for all these reasons conventional defense along conventional lines is feasible and desirable.

The most orthodox version of this view maintains that modestly greater efforts, modestly more cooperation, and modestly improved weapons can produce quite large enhancements of NATO's nonnuclear capability. This view—which may be called a "conventional conventional" approach—has been advanced with logic, rigor, and conviction by moderate experts in the United States for years. Today it is exemplified by General Bernard Rogers' call for NATO commitment to four percent increases in defense spending and Robert W. Komer's plea for a more coalitional approach to alliance defense.

A variety of observers have enlivened the conventional force improvement lobby by suggesting that fundamental new approaches to nonnuclear defense are feasible—and probably necessary. Symptomatic of this approach, Neil Kinnock, the new leader of the British Labor Party, stresses that while his party would abjure nuclear threats, even perhaps in retaliation, the alternative strategy on which it would rely, though certainly nonnuclear, would by no means be conventional.

Prominent in this category are those who argue that emerging technologies offer ways to use the West's scientific and technological skill to make up for the shortfalls in more standard conventional forces that have created the present imbalance, and that are likely to persist despite calls for orthodox enhancements. In a sense, the proponents of emerging technologies argue that technology can do for conventional defense what battlefield nuclear weapons were supposed to have done for nuclear defense when they were propounded in the 1950s, namely apply Western skill and inventions, not unattainable numbers, to render the Soviet armored juggernaut ineffective by high-efficiency, high-leverage attacks on the concentrations which that strategy requires.

Other conventional changes have been advanced that do not rely so much on new inventions as on new thinking and new political attitudes. One is the argument that NATO's effectiveness and its perceived seriousness in conventional defense could be enhanced by the creation of large-scale physical barriers along the inter-German border. Another, and by no means contradictory view, argues that the time has come finally to abandon any suggestion that forward defense must be a static defense and rely instead on tactics of maneuver and defense in depth. In its extreme form this emphasis on new tactics includes an argument that NATO should develop the capability to engage in counteroffensives into Eastern European territory. This, it is argued, would frustrate Soviet efforts to concentrate on areas of the front they select and even, by threatening Soviet dominance of the satellites, impose on the Soviets a potential political cost to a war of long duration. Other proponents of fundamental departures in the conventional field include those who call for a massively increased reliance on reserves and mobilization and on concepts of civilian defense.

It is at least possible that the growing controversy about nuclear weapons in Europe has altered the political landscape of the debate over increased conventional defense. In the past, European resistance to significantly increased emphasis on conventional defense was as much political as economic. Conventional defense was seen not merely as costing more money, but as, either explicitly or implicitly, allowing or inviting the United States to leave Europe. With increasing recognition of the potential costs and risks to Europe of excessive reliance on nuclear weapons, Europeans, particularly those of the moderate left, may be growing more willing to recognize that they, even more than the United States, have a self-interest in a more credible conventional defense.

Clearly these proposals for improving conventional defense offer considerable potential. Nonetheless, serious problems remain with a largely or exclusively conventional defense. Emerging technologies are still emerging; even if only modest increases are required in budgets, they are not necessarily going to be forthcoming. Tactical doctrines of both barriers and maneuver, whatever their military merits, present political difficulties for West Germany and its already strained politics of security.

Proposals for stronger, even exclusively, conventional defense fail in too many instances to confront how very great the conventional defense problem is. Better conventional defenses could discourage quick limited-scale attacks intended to obtain large gains cheaply—if indeed the Soviets think such attacks are feasible. They could buy time and add uncertainty. If, however, one establishes the goal as a conventional defense against a prolonged and determined Soviet assault, one has to cope with the fact that whether or not the Soviets would be good at a blitzkrieg, Russians have long been very good at attrition. Current official Soviet doctrine, in its quest for the daring offensive breakthrough, is not an exemplification but a repudiation of Russian history. Historically, Russia has won wars by the gradual massing of numbers and by a willingness to take terrible losses until those masses can grind down a possibly more sophisticated but less numerous or less determined foe. Official Soviet enthusiasm for quick victories may reflect a judgment that in the long run the costs of being a modern Kutuzov are too high, but NATO can hardly afford to count on that.

No First Use?

Accompanying some calls for greater conventional efforts are plans proposing that NATO would pledge not to use nuclear weapons first. Many advocates of such a no-first-use posture would delay its declaration and implementation until there had been substantial improvements in conventional forces, but there is an element in the no first use argument which suggests that the pledge should precede rather than follow such improvements. It is argued that first use would be militarily ineffective, that it is blatantly incredible, and that the threat to initiate the use of nuclear weapons in the defense of Europe has come to produce not solidarity but divisiveness in the alliance. In any case it is claimed that a threat to use nuclear weapons first perpetuates the myth that nuclear weapons are a panacea for NATO's problems and thereby encourages evasion of those conventional force improvements that are feasible and needed.

It is, however, extremely debatable whether a no-first-use pledge would help enhance either transatlantic unity or conventional defense. The commitment of nuclear weapons is an important manifestation of

American solidarity with Europe. Revoking that commitment pledge might or might not be believed by the Russians—or the European Left—but there is every reason to believe it would gravely trouble Europeans who take the alliance seriously. So far, there is no reason to believe that a U.S. no-first-use pledge would calm European concerns about nuclear war enough to foster a joint commitment (endorsed by the bulk of the nuclear opposition) to vastly enhanced conventional defense.

Discussion of this issue should also cope with the inherent arrogance of assuming that the question of first use is essentially a subject for Western debate. Soviet doctrine in this as in all things is obscure, but it is probable that the Soviet Union regards the prompt neutralizing of NATO's nuclear capability as a high priority in any attack on Western Europe. In order to carry out this mission, the Soviet Union could at a very early stage use nuclear weapons against NATO's nuclear capabilities.

Alliance politics and Soviet plans aside, the traditional arguments for including an ultimate nuclear threat in NATO's deterrence doctrine continue to have validity. Militarily, the possibility that the allies will use nuclear weapons against mass Soviet conventional forces must influence Soviet judgments as to the prudence of massing armor sufficiently for the conventional breakthrough their doctrine requires. In time perhaps those tank concentrations will be as vulnerable to conventional assault as to nuclear, but there is little reason to believe that time has come yet. It is hard to see how a no-first-use pledge could avoid reducing Soviet uncertainty as to the consequences of aggression, and thereby increasing their willingness to attack. The size of the effect may be debatable: the direction seems clear.

Moreover, the possibility of first use plays a unique role in whatever hope there may be of containing a war in Europe once it was started. The Soviet Union, in deciding whether to embark on a course of aggression that threatens the freedom and independence of the democracies of the alliance, could not mistake NATO's capacity to deny the USSR any fruits of victory by using NATO's nuclear arsenal. The USSR could only mistake our will to use that capacity. The objective of deterrence is to ensure that there is the least possible chance that the Soviet Union would make that mistake.

We must, however, force ourselves to consider the possibility that, under the pressure perhaps of some now unforeseeable internal or foreign crisis, the Soviet leaders would, having persuaded themselves of a good chance of initial conventional success, estimate as tolerably low the chances of successful NATO conventional defense and the risk of nuclear escalation, if that defense fails. So self-persuaded, they might then launch an attack.

Thereafter, the point could come when NATO's conventional defenses would begin to fail. Then the alliance would have the greatest need to convince the Soviet Union, even in so disastrous a situation, that it had mistaken NATO's resolve, that it should pull back and reassess the prospects.

If the alliance, having failed in efforts to defeat the attack directly, could not somehow force a Soviet recomputation of likely losses against attainable gains, it would be faced finally with only two awful choices. Those choices would be acquiescence to Soviet military conquest or unleashing the full power of the U.S. nuclear arsenal. Each of these choices seems self-evidently intolerable—until the full and true consequences of the other are taken into account.

The potential of limited nuclear attacks to force that recalculation is, arguably, the chief contribution to deterrence and the principal justification for maintaining the capacity for the first use of nuclear weapons. Such attacks—whatever their direct military effect, and that effect could be substantial, though far from decisive in a traditional military sense—would serve to show the Soviets in the most direct and concrete way that the West, and specifically the United States, was in fact prepared to use the means that it had to prevent an end it could not tolerate.

No one can responsibly be confident that such an effort to compel restraint and retreat would be successful. The confusion, even hysteria, that would follow, and precede, such an attack might well drive both sides further and further toward the abyss, not persuade them to draw back. But there is a chance—and some would rate it a high chance—that faced with absolute proof of NATO's will to use nuclear weapons on a limited scale, the Soviet Union would pull back and terminate the war on terms acceptable to the West.

That is a chance worth retaining, and if only for that reason, a no-first-use pledge is a bad idea.

A Four-Point Program

To say that NATO should not abandon the possibility of initiating the use of nuclear weapons and that the basic policy of flexible response remains an appropriate one, is not to say that there should be no changes in Western tactical and theater nuclear weapon deployments, plans, and doctrines. In addition to pressing for whatever can be done to increase conventional capability, the following measures should be implemented in consultation with all the NATO allies:

Significant numbers of the U.S. tactical nuclear weapons in Europe are for the obsolescent Nike-Hercules air defense missiles and for ADMs. These amount to almost 20 percent of the total. Neither system is politically workable or militarily effective. In particular, reliance on ADMs should be replaced by efforts to secure agreement to the construction of significant passive barriers along the inner-German border. Removal of these weapons, in addition to whatever symbolic value it would have, would free for more useful military tasks the personnel and facilities presently used for their storage and protection.

A role remains for battlefield nuclear forces, in the form of weapons for artillery and short-range missiles, but nuclear weapons should be pulled back significantly from the frontier. This would reduce pressures for unnecessarily early release or delegation of authority to use such weapons. Obviously, Soviet proposals to create a nuclear free zone embracing virtually the whole of the Federal Republic of Germany are unacceptable, but there is a serious political or military case for pulling the battlefield weapons back far enough to give reasonable confidence that their advanced presence would not become a complication rather than a help in the event of attack. Concomitantly, NATO should increase the survivability of the command and control structure necessary for decisions on and employment of theater nuclear weapons.

Except for the Pershing IIs and ground-launched cruise missiles now being deployed, most NATO theater nuclear weapons are of the 1960s vintage. Clearly, improvements and modernization will be required, although the inherent controversiality of any such measures has made Western European governments unusually skittish on the subject. The focus of modernization should be on survivable, dedicated, relatively long-range systems. They should be survivable, which includes reduced reliance on air bases, to facilitate a policy of ensuring that the decision to use nuclear weapons could be delayed until it was clear that such use was necessary to forestall conventional collapse, and not accelerated out of a fear of Soviet preemption. They should be dedicated, not dual capable, to avoid the political, arms control, and most important, military complications of forces being withheld or diverted for nuclear roles when they could make a crucial contribution to conventional defense. They should be relatively long-range so they could be used in strikes whose military objective, apart from demonstrating NATO resolve, would be to disrupt the Soviet rear, not affect the immediate battle, which would, by hypothesis, be taking place on the west side of the inner-German border.

Finally, within the policy of flexible response, NATO should move toward the formal articulation of a policy of enhancing its conventional capability and configuring its nuclear capability so as to make clear that the decision to use nuclear weapons would be able to be deferred for a significant time. While NATO should formally reserve all its options, including battlefield use, declaratory policy should explicitly embrace the concept that initial use might be directed well behind the battlefront, and even onto Soviet territory.

In an ultimate sense, the credibility of extended deterrence depends not on the details of forces or doctrine, but on the basic recognition that extending America's nuclear commitments to Europe does not, in fact, really involve the attempt to push nuclear deterrence beyond the limits of truly vital American interests. The United States is committed to the security and integrity of Western Europe not because the independence of Western Europe from Soviet domination serves European interests but because it is essential to the independence of the United States. Only as long as that proposition is both true and perceived to be true can extended deterrence work, and as long as it is so perceived, extended deterrence can continue to work.

5

POLICY CHALLENGES

From American Imperialism to Soviet Hegemonism

Raymond Aron

Thirty years ago, professors of international relations and men in the street would have characterized the world in more or less the same terms. The first, in their learned way, baptized the interstate system as "bipolar"; the second placed the rivalry between the United States and the Soviet Union at the center of the world scene, often underestimating the overall military, economic, and maritime superiority of the American republic. Twenty years ago (1958), when Nikita Khrushchev launched his quasi ultimatum over Berlin, and then again a few years later during the Cuban missile crisis, a terrified humanity held its breath.

Today, the professors and the men in the street might agree on some things, but no longer on a characterization of the world. Rather, they might agree that the world could no longer be characterized in a simple way. Must one replace the Moscow-Washington bipolarity with the Moscow-Beijing-Washington triangle? Which of the great duellists now possesses military supremacy? Does the East-West conflict still maintain the global importance which we ascribed to it at least until the 1960s?

To be sure, the United States and the U.S.S.R. continue to merit the special role which they arrogate to themselves and which the observers grant them: the only states that possess a complete panoply of weapons on the earth, on the seas, in the air, and in space, from handguns to megaton bombs; the only ones capable of projecting their military power in any corner of the globe; the only ones who participate in the conquest of space. Moreover, from now until the end of the century, they will conserve the essential elements of their dominance, whatever the development of the People's Republic of China may be in the next 20 years.

Why is there a shattered image of the world, instead of the excessively simple structure of the cold war? The basic reasons are these:

The confusion between the Soviet Union and Marxism-Leninism, which transformed a great power rivalry into an ideological war, by now belongs to the past: the so-called socialist camp has fallen to pieces. The P.R.C. condemns Soviet "hegemonism" as public enemy number one. The intelligentsia may dream of Belgrade or Havana as the true Marxist Mecca: Tito or Castro against Goliath, be it capitalist or Stalinist. Between the quasi Stalinism of North Vietnam and the quasi-genocidal terrorism of Kampuchea, how is one to choose? China supports Phnom Penh because Moscow supports Hanoi. Communist parties in power rekindle the historical quarrels of their nations.

Yet, it would be too simple to eliminate the ideological dimension and return to the chess game of the chancelleries. In Asia, the Russian and Chinese empires have elevated the same ideology to the status of a state truth, and accuse each other of betraying the truth; at the same time, they have stripped their maneuvers, alliances, and hostilities of any ideological garb: power politics pure and simple emerges from the language which camouflaged it.

Elsewhere, things go on similar paths. The triumph of a "progressist" or Marxist-Leninist party does not necessarily lead to the alignment of the country in the Soviet camp. To be sure, it often does; but, even in the absence of such an alignment, a regime which considers itself "socialist" conducts quite a different diplomacy from that of the moderate or pro-Western state which it overthrew. The entry of a communist party into the government in Rome or Paris would constitute an international event with unforeseeable consequences: an extreme interpretation—catastrophe or episode without a future—might please the soul, but it would falsify reality.

The Russo-American relationship has itself become ambiguous and equivocal. Is it getting nearer to a condominium or a fight to the death? Are the two superpowers exhausting their quarrel little by little, or are they only play acting? The agreements on strategic arms limitations, in the last analysis, rest on reciprocal distrust. Henry Kissinger hoped to conclude a series of partial agreements with Moscow which would restrict the revolutionary or ex-revolutionary strength.

Did Kissinger succeed or fail? Has Brezhnev's Russia (as George Kennan claims) become a conservative power from which the United States and its allies have nothing much to fear? Or, rather, as the dissidents argue, is it still the same—prudent, but ever ready to exploit any occasion to extend its sphere of influence or domination, more ambitious than during Stalin's time because it has greater means, more stable domestically because the gerontocrats who have survived so many seismic shocks have "routinized" their reign and their despotism?

Containment used to be the key word and the inspiration for

American bipartisan diplomacy. But bipartisan diplomacy no longer exists outside the Atlantic zone. On all subjects—the "China card," SALT (Soviet-American Strategic Arms Limitation Talks), Africa, the defense budget—the intellectuals of the East Coast, whether Republican or Democrat, who conceived and supported bipartisan foreign policy in the postwar period are now divided, often to the point where yesterday's friends no longer speak to each other.

The two superpowers have not lost their military superiority, but what have they done with it? Is strength which is never used a true strength? In 1950-1953 the United States failed to achieve victory against North Korea, half of a country saved by the intervention of Chinese "volunteers." The United States was defeated by North Vietnam, another half-country—defeated in the sense that North Vietnam achieved its goal without, however, having defeated the American expeditionary force. Did the Soviet Union need 40,000 tanks to repress the Hungarian revolution, or to establish control over the Marxist-Leninists in Prague who dreamed of socialism with a human face?

The diplomats, with less cynicism than Stalin—how many divisions does the Pope have?—never forgot in their negotiations the number of armed men represented by each ambassador. Today, the number of special advisers—cultural, scientific, commercial, information—symbolizes total diplomacy, illustrates the new dimensions of diplomacy.

From all this emerges a greater question: Where is the essential component of the relations between states? On the one hand are the accumulation of arms, the technical progress of nuclear or conventional weapons; on the other hand are the national economies linked to a world market. For the first time, as the historians have noted, a world market is no longer bounded by a world empire. European industry depends upon petroleum from the Persian Gulf. National and multinational businesses import indispensable elements for their own machines from countries with low costs and salaries. Our relations with our partners in the European Economic Community, with the OPEC (Organization of Petroleum Exporting Countries) countries, with the U.S.S.R. and Eastern Europe are concerned, above all else, with commercial exchanges and, secondarily, with cultural exchanges. The socialist countries do not belong fully to the empire of the merchants; but they are attached to it through recourse to the high priests of the private banks in order to finance their purchases in the West.

*   *   *

Aside from, or more significant than, the traditional strategic-diplomatic relations between states, it is the complex network of inter- and transnational relations which constitutes what might be termed a world society. Ideas and information cross borders and cover the entire planet in a few moments. Technical innovations and scientific discoveries spread with incredible speed. In this traditional society, the states no longer play the lead role.

In this way, one explains the enormous diversity of the images from which the professors of international relations hesitate to choose. Which conforms best to the actual reality? I do not propose to discuss the abstract merits of these various descriptions, which are more complementary than mutually exclusive. I take as my point of departure the distinction between an *interstate system,* dominated by the balance of power, and the *world society* over which no actor can exercise sovereign supremacy, and I ponder the roles of the United States and the Soviet Union in the one and the other. Has the relative decline of the United States signaled the passage from American imperialism to Soviet hegemonism?

Weapons and Diplomacy

The Russo-American rivalry has taken two distinct forms in Europe and in the rest of the world. In Europe, the line of demarcation was slowly formed between 1947 and 1955, leading to two coalitions, the Warsaw Pact and the North Atlantic Treaty Organization (NATO). The frontiers have not changed, and neither side has used force to modify them. In Asia and the Middle East, the two superpowers have acted in the wings, if not on stage, but their troops have not encountered each other on the battlefield.

Both of the two limited wars in which American expeditionary forces engaged have had an accidental quality. Stalin would probably not have given the green light to Kim Il-Sung if Washington had let it be clearly known that it would not tolerate the invasion of South Korea by the troops of the North. The hostilities would not have lasted for three years if Truman had listened to the Chinese warnings delivered by the Indian ambassador. Similarly, the United States, hostile to the French return to Indochina, changed its mind following the victory of Mao Zedong in China. Following the Geneva Conference, it no longer wished to perpetuate a Korean situation in Vietnam in extremely unfavorable conditions: the South Vietnamese army, unlike that of South Korea, did not balance the troops mobilized by the other half of the country.

Aside from these two campaigns, the interstate system changed, following decolonization, revolts within countries, and the transfer of allegiances from one camp to the other. The United States and the Soviet Union intervened in the internal politics of the countries between them, but under a frequently impeccable juridical camouflage. The United Nations Charter does not forbid a country to buy weapons abroad or to ask for the assistance of another country. The United States or the Soviet Union reply to this kind of demand as they withdraw their diplomats, advisers, and troops when the local government asks for it. President Sadat achieved the withdrawal of Soviet advisers. The revolutionary government of Ethiopia similarly obtained the withdrawal of extra American diplomats and military personnel.

Sometimes the legal cover does not stand up to close scrutiny. The Anglo-French expedition in response to the nationalization of the Suez canal failed for many reasons. It would only have succeeded if it had provoked the quick fall of Nasser and the immediate arrival of another ruler. Encouraged by the Soviet ambassador and the American position, Nasser held on; the British pound sterling did not stand up and the Anglo-French troops withdrew without glory. At the same moment, the Soviet troops crushed the Hungarian revolution, following an appeal from a peasant-worker government led by Janos Kadar. The juridical camouflage was worth no more than that of the Anglo-French forces occupying the canal zone to separate the Israeli and Egyptian belligerents. In 1968, the Russians improved the public explanation for the movement of their armies along with those of their allies of the Warsaw Pact. Aside from the crises of 1956 and 1968, the superpowers intervened in the internal affairs of other states without explicitly violating international law. Such intervention took place either openly, through the shipment of arms or advisers, or clandestinely, looking toward the destabilization of a regime through support for its enemies or for recalcitrant ethnic minorities. In this sense, it can be said that gunboat diplomacy has become outmoded.

In the Middle East, Israel and the Arab countries have fought four wars: 1948, 1956, 1967, and 1973 (omitting the "war of attrition" of 1970). All ended by a cease-fire, never by a peace treaty. In 1956, France and Great Britain participated in the operation; since then they have been excluded from negotiations in times of crisis. This exclusion was not because of their role in 1956, but rather because, when states wage war, only those other countries capable of projecting their power onto the battlefield count. In 1956, 1967, and 1973, Russo-American negotiations, behind the scenes at the Security Council, influenced the duration of the hostilities and the modalities of the cease-fires.

Russians and Americans abstained from combat—permitting the Israelis to achieve victories on the ground—but in 1973 they resupplied their allies. They then imposed a cease-fire to save the Egyptian army, surrounded in the desert.

In a crisis of this sort, when the Kremlin seemed to be on the verge of sending airborne divisions to the Middle East, what balance of power decided the test of wills? That of the forces available in the theatre (the American Sixth Fleet, the Soviet fleet in the Eastern Mediterranean, and the squadrons available in ground bases)? Or was it not the global American and Russian forces, nuclear and conventional alike, all over the globe? I think that no one, including Messrs. Kissinger and Nixon, can reply with certitude. The Kremlin was not eager to risk its troops against the Israelis, but could not tolerate a total Israeli victory over Egypt. For his part, Henry Kissinger wanted to spare Egypt a defeat which would have prevented Sadat from conducting a peace policy. Once a Syrian-Egyptian victory had been excluded, the Russians and Americans wanted essentially the same thing. On both sides, the balance of force—both local and global—was calculated, a confrontation was avoided, and the verdict of (foreign) armies was accepted.

Whether one is speaking of Ethiopia or South Yemen, Afghanistan, Mozambique or Angola, is there a relationship between Soviet successes and the number of nuclear warheads, missiles in silos and submarines at the disposal of the two sides? The number of tanks or air squadrons of the two sides along the demarcation line in Europe? Apparently the reply is self-evident. The liberation movement in Mozambique stems from Marxist or progressive ideas. But, it was not in Moscow, but rather in our European universities that the African liberators learned their ideology. In Angola, the "progressist" movement triumphed because the American Congress refused the necessary funds to support the nonprogressist liberation movement. The balance of strength within Ethiopia or Angola did not depend on the global balance between the U.S.S.R. and the United States, but on the capacity or the will of the West and the Kremlin to aid their party.

But the apparent separation between the local balance of force and the global relations of the two superpowers is never radical. The interventions of Cuban troops in Africa are based on the existence, in the Soviet camp, of air transport, a series of air bases, and even, perhaps, airborne divisions in case of need. In the Middle East, the Kremlin tolerated the Israeli victory of 1967 and hesitated to commit its airborne divisions in 1973 because of American power, rather than because of purely local circumstances. In the Cuban missile crisis of the autumn of 1962, all the advantages were on the American side:

locally, the Army, Navy, and Air Force of the United States enjoyed a crushing superiority; in addition, the Americans' strategic nuclear arsenal was three to four times as great as the Soviets'. How can one establish the role of strategic and conventional theatre forces in the outcome of the crisis?

It is best to draw prudent conclusions. The central balance, that which involves Europe and the strategic weapons of the superpowers, influences crises and diplomatic confrontations and their outcomes when the armies confront each other or when recourse to arms by the superpowers appears probable or at least possible. In contrast, when the Russo-American rivalry unfolds within states, the global balance of strength only influences the protagonists indirectly. Nothing succeeds like success: if the east wind appears to triumph over the west wind, the arguments for progressist movements suddenly become the more convincing. Then, the global balance between the United States and the Soviet Union changes year by year in favor of the latter.

Arms Control

The Soviet Union has always had a substantial armed force. It suffices, for example, to compare the number of tanks on the two sides—50,000 Soviet tanks as against only 10,000 American ones—to gain the impression that henceforth the Russians will dominate the Americans. One could easily multiply the statistics: the Soviet military budget grows every year by 3 to 5 percent. It represents some 13 or perhaps 15 percent of the GNP of the Soviet Union, triple that of the United States (5 percent). Even in the strategic nuclear field, it is the Soviets who have made the most progress, deploying two new submarine-launched missiles and three land-based missile systems. The Americans have only deployed a single new submarine-launched missile (Trident), MIRVed the Minutemen and Poseidons, and improved the precision of their nuclear warheads. During the past decade, the negotiations on strategic arms limitations (SALT I and SALT II) have accompanied and concealed the Soviet ascent.

The SALT agreements are inspired by the doctrine of "arms control," the central idea of which is to establish a balance of arms such that neither side will be tempted to use them. Arms control does not imply disarmament or the reduction of weapons to a minimum: if each of the superpowers possessed only 100 missiles, they would risk being disarmed by a first strike, and instability would immediately result.

The Americans have focused their attention on strategic weapons, those which can strike Soviet targets from American territory (or vice versa). SALT tends toward the creation of "stability," not between the overall military strength of the two sides, but between a category of nuclear weapons and intercontinental launchers. Now, to the extent that these agreements achieve their goal, they "neutralize" these arms: stability prevents their utilization at least for a direct attack against them or against national territory. What remains, then, of their deterrent force? The very principle of SALT cannot fail to pose with increasing urgency the question which Europeans have been asking for 20 years: Is European security guaranteed by the conventional forces of NATO or by the thermonuclear arsenal of the United States?

In the beginning of NATO, the presence of American troops in Europe symbolically eliminated the distance between the Old and New Worlds. *Ich bin ein Berliner.* A pact limited to strategic weapons digs a ditch between Western Europe and the United States. The long Russo-American controversy on the Backfire bomber suddenly illuminates the logic and the paradox of these negotiations: If these have for their object the equality or equivalence of an isolated sector—long-distance launchers—the Americans logically proscribe an intercontinental capacity for the Backfire; but, used in theatre operations, this bomber contributes substantially to the battlefield strength of the Soviets, even while it adds nothing to their arsenal of intercontinental launchers— logical in an agreement on certain weapons, illogical in an agreement including all weapons.

Between the moment of the elaboration of the doctrine of arms control and the conclusion of the discussions of SALT II, technical advance has overtaken diplomacy.

The famous book by Albert Wohlstetter, *The Delicate Balance of Terror,* has acquired a new significance. The number of nuclear warheads in each missile, and the precision of its guidance system, permits one of the two to destroy almost all the land-based missiles of the other in a first strike. This would leave the attacked side with only the option of responding with submarine-launched missiles, heavily damaging the industrial and urban centers of the enemy, but with the certitude of receiving the same response. After a first strike against the land-based missiles of the other, the attacker conserves his thousands of nuclear warheads for a third strike.

Given the hypothesis of equality (or equivalence) of the destructive capacity of the superpowers, only a counterforce action is plausible. It may be that one of the two (or both) possesses a first-strike capability against the other's land-based missiles. In this case, the one could back the other into a corner, forcing him to negotiate after having lost the majority of his terrestrial force, or responding by decimating the attacker's cities, risking an escalation to a suicidal orgy of violence. The multiplying objections that arise against SALT II demonstrate the impasse at which the negotiations limited to intercontinental launchers have arrived: the agreement does not "stabilize" the relationship between intercontinental weapons, even though it separates the European theatre from the nuclear weapons of the superpowers.

Even worse, the Americans discover that, due to an excess of faith in their resources and their technology, they have in some ways been reached or even passed. Masters of miniaturization, they endowed the Minutemen III with three nuclear warheads (of 170 kilotons). The Soviets, far less artful, worked on large missiles, whose ability to carry destructive packages is far greater than that of the American missiles. In the SS-18, the Russians insert eight nuclear warheads, with two megatons. From now to 1985, the 303 SS-18s—all MIRVed—will threaten the destruction of the American land-based missiles.

The experts believe that, in the space of a few years, with or without the ratification of SALT II, at the highest level of intercontinental missiles, the U.S.S.R. will achieve a certain superiority. But, quite apart from any polemics, it is clear that the practice of arms control has favored neither disarmament, nor the stability of the level of intercontinental missiles, nor the security of Europe. The failure is due in part to the doctrine itself (the isolation of one type of arms), in part to technical innovation (MIRV, increased accuracy of guidance). The technicians have thus made stability impossible, even while the diplomats obstinately search for it. Soviet inferiority in miniaturization turned into superiority, that of the superior delivery capability of their heavy missiles. The optimists rejoice in the doctrine of mutual assured destruction, unaware that, at the very same moment, the deterrent force of nuclear weapons becomes less and less plausible.

Numerous Europeans interpret the American doctrine as an attempt to preserve the territorial United States from the ravages of war. The neutralization of strategic forces is said to exclude Soviet and American territory from the eventual theatre of operations. I am not convinced by this explanation. By stationing 200,000 or 300,000 of their troops on European soil, the Americans have condemned themselves to an unprecedented disaster if they do not prevent, by all possible means, the invasion of Europe by Soviet armies. Two ideas govern the thought and action of the leaders and advisers in Washington:

1. Russo-American rivalry is written in the great book of history, but it can take more or less violent forms; it can be conducted on a greater or lesser level of intensity.

2. The common interest of the two powers and of all mankind is to avoid an *unthinkable* war.

These ideas are reasonable and worthy of support, but they leave a doubt behind: the path of diplomacy is affected by the available arms on each side. What effect would a SALT treaty have on future confrontations between the two superpowers? In the foreseeable conditions of 1982 or 1985, would a confrontation like the Cuban missile crisis or the Yom Kippur War have the same outcome?

China

Has the diplomatic activism of the heirs of Mao Zedong changed the structure of the interstate system? Even before the death of the great helmsman, the Sino-Soviet conflict had forced the Kremlin to place 44 divisions and one-quarter of the Soviet air force along the border. The resources necessary to maintain a vast army in the Far East reduce the available resources in the West. Whatever the relations between China and the United States or Western Europe, the Chinese perform a great service to the West by their hostility to the Soviet Union. In the language of Marxism-Leninism, one may speak of an objective alliance. Objectively, the enemy of my enemy is my friend.

In 1978, something changed: China opened to the external world and adopted the line of the four modernizations (agriculture, industry, army, and technology). Deng Xiaoping substituted efficacy for ideology (not, however, without citing an appropriate phrase from Mao which supports his current policies), and he has not hesitated to ask the West for machinery and for the dollars to pay for it. The objective alliance took on a new face on the day when the West decided to help Chinese modernization with credit and know-how, thus helping the economic and military reinforcement of China.

How great an interest does the West have in reinforcing China? There is no shortage of Europeans and Americans who speak about an eventual conflict between short-term and long-term interests. What will be the line of Marxist China tomorrow? The leader of the modernizing faction, Deng, is more than 70 years old. Would a modernized and potent China conduct a policy which suits the moral and material interests of the West? These objections could easily be multiplied, but the question for today is whether we should respond to Chinese advances. We sell entire factories to the Soviet Union and give the Russians the key. Should we not do the same for the Chinese? We do not sell either weapons or nuclear plants to the Russians, but what if the Chinese want these from us? The United States has said that it will not sell weapons to Beijing, but will not oppose the Europeans if they wish to do so.

The Russians watch the rapprochement between China and the West with a jaundiced eye. For our part, we must have no illusions about the military significance of this objective alliance. If the Soviet Union launched a limited operation at one or another of the hot spots along the Sino-Soviet border, the United States would have neither the desire nor the means to intervene. By the same token, if the Soviet Union launched an attack toward the Atlantic, the Chinese would not come to our aid. China is not the substitute ally for Western Europe that Russia was for France at the beginning of the century.

The Kremlin probably considers it a mortal danger when China achieves an alliance with Japan and modernizes with Western assistance. But the threat is only a medium- or long-term one. The Chinese army is 20 years behind the Russians in quality of equipment, and Japan spends only 1 percent of its GNP on defense. I doubt that the United States will obtain any concessions from the Russians by playing the "China card"; rather, the reverse seems more probable. The Vietnamese wanted to liquidate the Cambodian regime of Pol Pot, and the Russians, at the very least, were not vexed when that liquidation came about shortly after the recognition of the P.R.C. by Washington.

It is only reasonable that the Chinese should denounce Soviet hegemonism as the world enemy number one. From their point of view, there is every reason to do so: they do not have a common border with the United States, but they have one of 2,000 kilometers with the Soviet imperium in Asia. The same is true for a great part of the world. In Europe, the Soviet Union maintains a superiority in troops and materiel, without forgetting their nuclear superiority (SS-20s, MIRVed, and mobile). More than the United States, the U.S.S.R. is resolved to project its power everywhere when the occasion presents itself, and the Kremlin has the means available for expeditionary forces: a dozen airborne divisions of its own, plus those offered by allies like Cuba and East Germany.

The Soviet leaders probably do not agree with those American professors who see military force playing an increasingly minor role in international relations. In the interstate system, one counts divisions, missiles, and the will to use them. In this sense, Soviet hegemonism has replaced American imperialism.

The World Market

At the end of the war, the United States dominated the world market even more than the interstate system. The North Korean army, then the Chinese volunteers, held the American expeditionary forces and exposed the limits of the military force of the United States. The era of European colonization was over. Others besides the Japanese acquired the means and the organization necessary for the modern art of war. As for the American nuclear monopoly, it did not terrify either Moscow or Beijing: both moral and political motives dissuaded Washington from using it, even against the communist "aggressors."

Over the world market, however, the Americans reigned alone: As the financial, commercial, and industrial center of the Free World, they placed their surplus disposal capital in external investments; they held the first place in the world in a majority of advanced technologies; 6 percent of the population of the planet consumed 50 percent of the raw materials used by all mankind. An abnormal situation, it could not endure and favored the creation of international organizations like the IMF (International Monetary Fund), GATT (General Agreement on Tariffs and Trade), and the United Nations.

The Marshall Plan, the subsequent recovery of Europe and Japan, responded to the logic of an interstate system and, at the same time, to that of a world economy, just as the leaders in Washington conceived of it themselves. Thirty years after the Marshall Plan, what is left of American supremacy?

In terms of per capita production, the most advanced European countries have now passed the United States when the calculation is made in terms of the official exchange rate. And even if one assumes that the undervaluation of the dollar falsifies the figures, the per capita production of Switzerland, Sweden, and West Germany is either very close, or equal to that of the United States. There remains one superiority, decisive for the interstate system: the United States is the only country to combine high productivity with a large population and immense space. The Japanese population is half that of the United States, and is concentrated in a very small area. Western Europe is divided into states, the most populous of which do not exceed one-quarter that of the United States. Japan and Western Europe lack raw materials and energy, and they depend on their foreign trade far more than the Americans. Competitors of the United States within the world market, neither the Japanese nor the Europeans constitute rivals within the interstate system. They live as protected states, even when the American republic condemns the invasion of goods "made in Japan."

Until 1971, the Bretton Woods system was maintained, no matter what it was actually worth. The overvaluation of the dollar favored simultaneously the expansion of international commerce, the growth of European exports, and the investments of large American corporations abroad. Since 1971, and especially since 1973, the United States has imposed a floating exchange rate. It is always in Washington that the monetary regime of the world is decided, regardless of the negotiations which precede or camouflage the American decisions. Finally, in certain sectors—civil aviation, petroleum technology, information, the conquest of space—American technology continues to pave the way.

Does the monetary role of Washington derive from the role played by the United States in the interstate system? In the absence of gold, only the dollar can serve as a world currency. Neither the government of Bonn nor that of Tokyo wants the mark or the yen to become the world reserve currency (even though the two currencies are sometimes used as reserves). So, under present circumstances, the world's central banks must choose between two highly unattractive alternatives: let the dollar drop (which they fear for economic and commercial reasons), or defend the price of the dollar—which obliges them to buy billions of dollars. Until 1971, the Europeans forced themselves to maintain the fixed price between gold and the dollar and between the dollar and the principal currencies (not without several revaluations of the yen and the mark). Since then, the Japanese and the Germans have oscillated between support for the dollar and letting it slide. At the moment, the monetary authorities of Bonn and Washington seem agreed upon a method of defense of the price of the dollar.

The GIs are no longer in Berlin, but do the Europeans have the means and the will to challenge the economic monetary policies of Washington? The dollar becomes quite naturally the pound sterling of the twentieth century. Probably the gold standard requires a dominant currency; only the dollar can hold that place—and it holds it very badly. Only a European currency, in the fullest sense of the term, could lift the mantle of supremacy from the American dollar.

The fall of the dollar produced a challenge to American prestige, just as the victorious revolt of OPEC demythologized American supremacy. The abandonment of Vietnam and the quadrupling of the price of oil removed a number of American illusions and canceled the superstitious awe of Washington by the members of the world market. "They do not tolerate": the phrase passed from the vocabulary. "They" *will* tolerate, because military or economic responses would be ineffective.

The Two World Markets

The Marxist-Leninists speak of two world markets, one capitalist, the other socialist. In fact, the two markets cannot be compared. The second involves only Eastern Europe and Cuba, to which Vietnam was recently added—an adhesion imposed by the Soviet Union to consolidate the ties between Moscow and Hanoi and to perpetuate the opposition between Hanoi and Beijing. The countries of Eastern Europe have expanded their trade with the Western economies. Restricted to the Soviet zone of Europe, without convertible currency, the so-called socialist world market does not represent a substitute or a rival to a world market centered around the United States. In fact, it is marginal in relation to the international economy.

The U.S.S.R. participates feebly in aiding the developing countries, and in practice, even those nations that proclaim themselves Marxist or progressist do not leave the capitalist world market. It is to the advanced capitalist countries that the producers of petroleum sell their black gold; it is in the American banking reserve that they deposit their surplus dollars. Even those African governments that have taken power thanks to Soviet aid, reestablish relations with the West and do not leave the capitalist market.

Where the leaders profess socialism or sovietism, Moscow tries to obtain naval and air bases (Guinea, South Yemen, or Mozambique); they attempt to improve their position by means of influence acquired over the armed forces of the country.

In Africa, the intervention of Cuban troops (carried by Soviet airplanes) opened a new phase marked by the use of military forces far from the U.S.S.R. These fighting units are resupplied and held together by an airlift, thanks to the use of air bases granted by friends. The Soviet technique of expansion rests almost entirely on military force and on infiltration or political propaganda, almost never on economic relations. In Africa, the United States is considered the fulcrum of the world market, the Soviet Union one of the two great military powers in the world.

Does Soviet expansion in Africa and in the Middle East endanger the balance of power or the world market? Everything depends on the geopolitical location and resources of the country which passes from one allegiance to another.

An anti-Western regime in Iran or a revolution in Saudi Arabia would suddenly overturn the economic order and the politico-military equilibrium. Has the United States still the means and the will to fight against such events that belong to the internal affairs of other sovereign countries? Even in a nationalist regime dominated by the Shiite church, the leaders will probably not give up the riches of black gold; thus, they will sell their oil, but they will worry less about the world market or the interests of the consumer states. They will not maintain the security of the Persian Gulf on behalf of the Occident. A change in regime in Saudi Arabia would produce even graver consequences. Would the new masters conduct the same pricing policies, the same quantity of production? The cement of the de facto alliance between the Saudis and the Americans is the fear of revolution that haunts the royal family in Riad. Traditionalist and religious, the royal family— whose ancestors unified Saudi Arabia—supports with its petrodollars moderate, anti-Soviet and antipropagandist regimes. But the United States would no longer have any means of putting pressure on a radical Islamic regime.

The order of the world market would be at the mercy of leaders hostile to modern civilization, hostile above all to capitalism. In both cases, the functioning of the world economy would depend on men who were foreign to its logic. One can imagine revolutionaries in Teheran and in Riyadh, more nationalist than progressist, religiously anti-Soviet, slowly reentering the world market and accepting its contradictions after a time of troubles. But in such a case the shock to the United States, far more than the defeat in Vietnam, would have repercussions across five continents and force the leaders in Washington into an agonizing reappraisal.

The American military presence in Turkey or Saudi Arabia is dependent upon the good will of the leaders in Ankara or Riyadh. Certainly, it was the same for military facilities first provided, and then withdrawn by the Soviet Union upon request of Egypt and Somalia. But the Soviet failure in Egypt (in Somalia the failure was the price paid for success in Ethiopia) concerns the interstate system. In return, a rupture between Iran or Saudi Arabia and the United States would involve the world economy indispensable to American prosperity and, more still, to that of its European allies.

That rupture would symbolize the impotence of the United States in conserving the allegiance of those countries most indispensable to American interests. American power in the diplomatic game comes in large part from prestige. In Washington, the current leaders want to reign without gunboat diplomacy. In the last analysis, this aspiration is ill-founded: modernization by itself erodes traditional authority, uproots the masses, and multiplies the grievances against the men in power and their American protectors. The Shah, a modernizing despot, concentrated on himself all the resentments, from those of the students to those of true believers. The Americans helped their friends prepare against a military coup; but against a popular revolt, inflamed by religious chieftains, neither the Iranian army nor the American advisers had an effective strategy.

The enfeeblement of the United States in the world economy aggravates the original contradiction of the contemporary world: world market without world empire. The American supremacy created the illusion of an empire. Propaganda attacked the American empire, confusing under this label two very different phenomena. Beijing did not hesitate; it supported the shah against the rebels, be they religious or lay. From the moment that Deng Xiaoping imposed the line of the four modernizations, Beijing stood up against anything that would undermine or destabilize international exchanges. Besides, these threats to the world market also reinforce Soviet hegemonism: if the Soviet Union controls Middle East oil through the intermediary of progressist governments, it holds the European economy hostage and enlarges its military empire.

The Soviet attitude, viewed from the outside, appears ambiguous. Without belonging to the world market, the U.S.S.R. feels the effects of the crises which sweep through it. It does not desire chaos in a country on its frontiers, but it does not want to ignore the chance which is offered to it by a religious revolt. The West, in Iran, rested its hopes on a modernizing but despotic regime; the regime which will follow it, aside from the religious reaction, will move it farther away from Washington, even if it does not embark upon the road to Moscow.

American Decline and Soviet Power

The distinction between the international system and the world economy does not suffice to give a clear and simple picture of international relations at the end of the 1970s. But it clarifies the passage from American imperialism to Soviet hegemonism.

The American republic, in the eyes of observers, appears in decline for three basic reasons:

1. The SALT treaties, of American inspiration, leading to equality or equivalence of intercontinental nuclear forces, perhaps to Soviet superiority, which produces global superiority (since the Soviet Union has more divisions and more tanks than the United States).

2. The incapacity of the United States to prevent the social and religious upheavals that provoke a shift in loyalty in certain countries of vital importance in the world market.

3. The reduction in the margin of superiority of the American economy compared to its commercial competitors, and the permanent crisis of the dollar.

In moving toward the United States, China's behavior conforms to the eternal logic of power politics. The U.S.S.R. is closer to the vital territorial centers of China than the United States. In addition, American military power, assuming that it acts, tends not to reach out but to reinforce threatened countries. Aside from the conquest of the American continent achieved at the end of the last century, there is no American imperialism comparable to that of czarist or Soviet Russia. In Vietnam, American strategy remained defensive; its objective was to prevent the communism of Hanoi from swallowing up the South. The intervention in Vietnam does not resemble imperialism in the normal sense of the term, which refers to the conquest of territory or of peoples. As for the imperialism defined by multinational corporations and foreign investment, China does not fear it; it rather calls for it. China counts on the blind passion for profit characteristic of capitalism to obtain credits, science, and technology necessary for its modernization.

If the Chinese use a different word to describe and denounce Soviet action—a word the West translates as "hegemonism"—they are right, even if the word does not exactly correspond to reality. The U.S.S.R. exerts its domination in Eastern Europe by military power and fixes the limits of tolerable diversity among the regimes in the socialist community. China fears encirclement by the Soviet Union and its allies. Japan and the United States judge that the military reinforcement of China contributes to the stability of Asia in the interstate system. The opening of China to trade with the West enlarges the world market.

Could China's choice of American imperialism rather than Soviet hegemonism be repeated tomorrow on other continents? In Latin America, the U.S.S.R. is far away and the United States is close at hand. Aside from Cuba, there are few Russians and many Americans. By the same token, in Iran there were, and in Saudi Arabia there are, many Americans and few Soviets. The Egyptians received thousands of Soviets, military advisers and technicians: they sent them away. In other African countries, the Russians lost the sympathies of the people even where the regimes opted for socialism (Mali, Guinea). The Black students who return from the East denounce the racism to which they were subjected. The Cubans apparently do better in Africa than the Soviets.

There are three theatres where, directly or indirectly, the East-

West conflict is being pursued: Africa, the Middle East, and Europe. In Africa, the Russians have changed the rules of the game by sending Cuban troops and their own military advisers. The final destiny of those countries governed by liberation movements or parties which embrace socialism has not yet been determined. For economic reasons, they may return towards the West. But the Soviets strive to assure the permanence of their success by military means. Hegemonism against imperialism, the Chinese would say, weapons against merchandise. Today imperialism is the indispensable conjunction of capital and Western technology.

In the Middle East, there is no direct Moscow-Washington conflict, there is rather the revolt of the masses or of progressist minorities against the despots, modernizing or not, tied to the United States. These revolts sometimes symbolize the death of tradition, sometimes the suppression of liberty, sometimes the support of a throne fallen into disrepute. In this region, it is the world market that is challenged, not by Moscow but by the peoples, eventually for the greater glory of Moscow.

In Europe, the frontiers of 1945 have slowly been stabilized and crystallized. Bonn and Pankow have accepted each other. The two coalitions continue to face each other peacefully, even as they make preparation for a test in which the West does not believe. The lack of belief is not because the Europeans have confidence in NATO, in conventional forces, or in the American nuclear umbrella. They, rather, trust the prudence of the Bolsheviks, sensitive to the incalculable perils of massive attack against Western Europe, and to the importance of the economic aid they receive from the West.

The period into which we are entering appears anything but calm and tranquil. The American republic has not found a bipartisan policy, a vision of the crisis, or a definable will. The Iranian revolution illustrates the precariousness of the regimes on which, faute de mieux, American diplomacy is based. In Europe, the Soviet Union does not have the prestige of a liberating power, but instead that of the most powerful army on the planet.

Such a great accumulation of weapons, such a misunderstanding of the risks: Are we victims of our illusions, or can we at this point rely upon the wisdom of the Soviets?

International Communications Policy: Preparing for the Future   *Dante B. Fascell*

Today is a special honor for me, for this lecture series was established to honor David M. Abshire, a personal and professional friend of many years, a man for whom I have the highest respect, a man whose contributions have left a mark not only on the Center for Strategic and International Studies but on the public affairs of the United States and on the conduct of international relations.

When I was invited to give this lecture, I was given an opportunity to speak on any topic I selected. On the eve of a major summit meeting between the leaders of the United States and the Soviet Union it was tempting to continue the themes so crucial to the Atlantic alliance that were developed so lucidly by my two distinguished predecessors in this series, Senator Sam Nunn and the minister of foreign relations of Belgium, Leo C. Tindemans. I decided instead to speak on international communications policy because of its inherent, fundamental importance to the United States and because it has been an issue to which David Abshire has for many decades devoted a tremendous amount of his enormous energy and analytical and intellectual skills.

Almost 15 years ago, David Abshire and I began to seek a solution to a problem besetting the U.S. government. Radio Free Europe and Radio Liberty had already been on the air for nearly 20 years, a product of the intelligence community. Their control and operation by a covert agency, however, was inconsistent with increasing public demands for openness and accountability. Our task was considerable.

Foremost on our minds was to preserve an important voice for the United States; in this instance, to keep a channel of communication open. Eventually, the concept of a Board for International Broadcasting emerged from a careful review and subsequent legislative action. David Abshire became the first chairman of the new board. The mandate of the two radios was reaffirmed and strengthened, carrying to the peoples of Eastern Europe and the Soviet Union information they were being denied.

We were very specific about the kind of information, however. We recognized then, as I continue to believe today, that objectivity must be the underlying principle of the charter of the radios. The mechanism set in place, the Board for International Broadcasting, has one single overriding priority, to protect that principle. If we played with the content of information to suit our daily needs, we would be gambling with the purpose of the radios: to inform, to educate, and, in the final analysis, to undo a terrible injustice. If we strayed from the truth, we would merely be joining the countries of Eastern Europe in denying their people knowledge.

The motivation behind that effort was not simply meant to preserve an entity. Rather, it was intended to promote the unwavering principle of freedom of speech and to take advantage of an unending resource—information.

The success of Radio Free Europe/Radio Liberty in forging new channels of information has become increasingly clear over the long run. The Congress recognized its effectiveness and recently set up Radio Marti to bring to the people of Cuba a precious resource denied them by their government—the truth.

Lately, we have been engaged in a new effort to open another channel of communications and information, the National Endowment for Democracy. Although it is still in its infancy, we can already point to successes. I am confident that over time we will see emerge a new sort of communication network reaching out to the rest of the world.

Communication is more than just international broadcasting, exchange programs, or even satellite links. What has been termed the "explosive convergence of fast computers and modern telecommunication" has made communications a revolutionary force for change. Already the fusion of technologies is changing our politics, our economy, international relations, and the ways in which people think about concepts such as community and property.

Yet, as we look back over the last few decades, at ingenious creations from Intelsat to Worldnet, I am concerned that we have not recognized the relationship between the seemingly separate pieces of the larger information and communication puzzle. We lack a comprehensive approach that will enable us to develop a policy capable of interlocking the myriad of U.S. interests in this complex and dynamic field. To prepare for the future we must act boldly and decisively to create new ways to produce coherent policies that integrate into our foreign policy all the disparate interests involved in communications.

The Communications Revolution and the United States

Although the communications revolution has already brought about massive social changes and promises even greater changes in the future, it is of particular and immediate significance to the United

States, for the technologies of the new age of communication have increasingly become a principal engine of U.S. economic leadership and growth. These new technologies have fueled much of our current prosperity and may be the key to our continuing strength.

For generations the United States has been the leader in communications technology. Today we are showing the way in the development of information resources. Despite the gloomiest reports on Japanese and West European developments, the United States still maintains the largest and freest market. Unlike the former we are not hostage to foreign markets, and our market is not as fragmented as that of the European Economic Community.

Yet, complacency will lead us nowhere and will permit us only to relinquish our lead to more aggressive countries that have staked their future on this emerging industry. The importance to the United States of the advances in communications and information technology can be seen from the changes it has already brought.

Our own economy has already undergone a significant transformation. Here are some relevant facts:

- In 1984, IBM's revenues exceeded those of the entire U.S. steel industry by 50 percent.
- The manufacture of information technology today produces yearly revenues for U.S. companies of some $110 billion, an amount that almost equals the yearly activity of the entire automobile industry. It is estimated that by 1994, the dollar amount will triple and will represent approximately 6 percent of our gross national product (GNP).
- The worldwide number of jobs in the information industry has already increased sixfold from 10 million to 60 million.
- Information technology exports have risen from $4 billion in 1965 to $35 billion in 1980.
- In 1982 the export of information-based services represented half of $60 billion worth of service-related exports.

These are but a few dramatic examples of a trend that has already been under way for some time in an area of our economy that is recognized as a leader in terms of growth, employment generation, and innovation. These changes have already had an impact on many other sectors to varying degrees.

Many industries would find it difficult to survive without access to good communications. Let me cite a few examples. The first is the international financial community. Today, most fund transfers and other financial transactions are conducted via telecommunications connections: links between satellite and data processing networks, which permit long distance access to stored data. With the concomitant spread of U.S. banks overseas, the dependence of banking on telecommunications and information technologies has become absolute. Furthermore, the emergence of alternative satellite systems is certainly encouraged not only by international finance's reliance on telecommunications but on the increased future need of finance and other industries.

Another participant in the information age is the news media, which has the technology to broadcast worldwide over satellites. Even the U.S. government has been affected by this aspect of communications, as we have seen in the influence of television on crisis management with regard to Iran and Lebanon. Three years ago under the leadership of the United States Information Agency (USIA), the United States launched the Worldnet program, another piece of the puzzle. Although USIA is struggling with the implications of international television and TV reporters are relentlessly rolling back the limits of their medium, the *International Herald Tribune, Wall Street Journal,* and *USA Today* have already initiated international daily newspapers. The success of these news media operations, however, depends not only on the ability of journalists to communicate through telecommunications networks, but also on their unhindered freedom to discover and report news. Some nations impair media operations by requiring journalists to be licensed or accredited, by denying their visas, or by requiring prior consent for the publication or broadcast of information.

In the United States such hindrances are prohibited by the First Amendment, which expresses the values that must be the sine qua non of U.S. policy judgments in all areas of the information arena. From our point of view, not only do these values encourage the free flow of information, but the importance of these democratic values justifies diplomatic efforts to encourage other nations to adopt them.

A third participant in the information age is the education community, including both teaching and research institutions. The information age is partly an education age, for only with lifelong education and training will individuals be able to adapt and adjust to a rapidly changing society. The new age requires a new kind of literacy, in government as well as in the private sector, which includes an understanding of technology.

As dramatic as many of the changes wrought by advances in communication technology have already been, one can look forward to even more. Here are just a few indications of the scope of changes yet to come:

· It is estimated that the combination of computer and telecommunications services and equipment will reach $500 billion by 1990 for the U.S. economy alone.
· Currently there are 6 million computers in the United States. It is estimated that by the end of the decade more than half of the U.S. households will possess a computer.
· The demand for satellite telecommunication has increased to the extent that it is anticipated that new satellites will be launched at the rate of 200 for the next decade in the United States alone.
· The world use of the telephone should increase exponentially because only nine countries have three-fourths of all phones now in use.

Impact on International Organizations

The exceptional growth in communications technology means that policies governing the area of new communication satellites, cables and microwaves, and the entire electromagnetic spectrum have become increasingly crucial to virtually every sector of our economy. Thus constant attention is focused on policy-making at every level of government. This, in turn, has placed new strains on multilateral institutions that have maintained the technical oversight of global communications.

For a century the International Telecommunication Union (ITU) has been the focal point for the international regulation of communications. The ITU today is facing the same disruptions felt in other areas because of the blurring of traditional distinctions between telecommunications and computer technologies. As the users of data communications increase, the ITU's job of coordinating the allocation of frequencies in a finite electromagnetic spectrum will become increasingly difficult. As technology becomes more sophisticated and the interdependence of nations increases, tensions will mount unless ways are found through international agreement to balance interests and treat all nations fairly.

The growing strains are not limited to the ITU. In fact, the United States has been faced with challenges in such other organizations involved with one aspect or another of communications and information—the UN Educational, Scientific, and Cultural Organization (UNESCO) and Intelsat, as well as in the UN General Assembly. Discussions about the free flow of information in UNESCO—an organization from which the United States has withdrawn—concentrate on the philosophical struggles between those nations that do not generally wish to restrict information flow and those that view restrictions, such as prior consent, as fundamental. Such discussions may not have a direct bearing on the outcome of today's business and government activities in information technology. Yet the conclusion of such a debate will influence, in the long run, the kinds of principles a majority of nations will adopt. From such principles these same nations will extract future standards for business and government activity.

While the United States debated its membership in UNESCO, another storm gathered closer to home. Intelsat, headquartered in Washington, challenged a U.S. initiative to promote the entry of the private sector into the satellite communications business. This conflict itself is indicative of the changes communication technology is presenting. It provides a dilemma for policymakers who wish to preserve the remarkable achievement of Intelsat—a functioning organization providing a worldwide telecommunications network—while at the same time bringing the vigor of the private sector to bear in this important area. I believe that the United States cannot afford to allow the demise of the only global communications system both because we still believe in the objectives we established in creating Intelsat and because the proposed systems taken all together can not begin to duplicate the global system that now carries 70 percent of U.S. worldwide communications.

The possible introduction of new energies in the development of space communications may signal a transition, during which the share and responsibility of government will begin gradually to shift into the hands of the private sector. As we advance in this new direction, the U.S. government will have to take great care to resolve these apparent contradictions in a way that both protects Intelsat and permits the force of competition to inject new dynamism into the use of space.

Another area in which rapidly changing communications technology is confronting international policymakers and international organizations with new choices is that of international trade. Trade in information-processing products—computers, terminals, software, and related equipment—has increased faster than almost any other trade sector. This, in turn, has produced new questions about who has rights to what. These are new dimensions to old issues—patents and copyrights. When data is crossing borders at the speed of light, how does one determine licensing fees, duties, and myriad other issues? These problems will continue to be a major focus of attention under the General Agreement on Tariffs and Trade (GATT) and the World Intellectual Property Organization and are already the subject of numerous bilateral discussions between governments.

Communications is one area in which the role of international organizations has proved of great value and importance. It takes cooperation for the technologies to operate. The tendency for such organizations to be politicized by extraneous issues is a potential threat to fulfilling the promise of new technologies. This is an area in which we need a much more effective diplomatic effort.

The International Arena

The international implications of the communication and information revolution is by no means restricted to technical discussions. It has become a central part of the politics of international relations. A communications infrastructure is central to any nation's ability to conduct its internal or external affairs. If a nation has no communications infrastructure, how can its people take their goods to market or even find out where the markets are? How can they attract investment?

The communications and information revolution is perceived by many nations as exacerbating the development gap between the rich and poor nations of the world. The attempts of developing nations to redress the imbalance through support for a New World Communication Order is evidence of this perception. Information technology can help to solve many of the problems of the developing world, or it could increase the tensions between the industrialized and developing nations. Ways must be found through bilateral and multilateral organizations such as international development banks to achieve equitable solutions and encourage the developing nations' participation in the new age. The U.S. government has a key catalytic role to play in this regard.

The U.S. Response

Since World War II, the United States government has accomplished a great deal with respect to international communications: it has encouraged a free flow of ideas globally, nurtured abroad a receptivity to the opportunities offered by information technologies, and promoted international cooperation through such initiatives as Intelsat. Despite this record I remain concerned that the foreign policy community has not paid sufficient attention to these new technologies and their implications for our foreign policy.

Information and communications form the core of U.S. governmental relations with other nations. The information age, by changing both the character and content of U.S. international relationships, challenges our government to rethink our traditional approach to foreign policy.

Thus far our approach to these issues all too often has led us to deal with each problem in isolation from the other. Yet the salient characteristics of the information age are that all the component factors are interrelated and involve international considerations—from the computer and telecommunications sectors, to the financial and trade sectors, to the news media and education communities, and to the foreign policy and national security communities.

The problem is not that we don't understand the separate problems, but that until now we have failed to create a way that will permit overall coordination and control so that no one entity impairs the ability of the United States to formulate and pursue its national interest. In short, we lack a national strategy with respect to an entire area of human endeavor that is important to our security and our economy.

At a time when our competitors in the world economy increasingly present a unified national approach to global markets, which includes sophisticated cooperation between government, business, finance, and labor, the United States can no longer afford a fractured response. We must find new ways to link the strength that internal competition gives us to the necessity for external cooperation to meet keen competition.

For those of us active in the field of foreign affairs, communications is only one area in which we all note the increasing difficulty of distinguishing between foreign and domestic policies. Moreover, what once were seen as economic or business issues are now also seen as political issues. How to integrate all of these concerns into coherent policy is one of the central challenges confronting our government.

Where do we go from here? Planning and implementing a national strategy on anything is a virtually impossible task in a country as complex and diverse as the United States. Both economic and political power are diffused as a matter of policy and history. The task is made even more difficult with a concept as broad as communications. Communications is as intangible as a philosophy and as concrete as a ringing telephone. There is no easy way to segregate the concept from the technology, to divorce domestic concerns from foreign affairs, or to isolate political decisions from economic realities.

Nevertheless, an effort must be made to develop a national strategy. Communications is just too important to the future economic and political strength of our nation.

We need a mechanism for systematically and periodically reviewing all our options. We must be certain that we are taking the right steps both in the private sector and in the public sector, and taking them together. For that reason I believe that a permanent presidential council should be established to act as an advisory body on national strategy to the president, Congress, and the private sector.

To be effective, such a group should include all the principal actors involved in the two concerned branches of government and representative leaders from the private sector. Under the auspices of the CSIS Congressional Study Group on International Communications and Information, such a body has already effectively been created. I would recommend simply putting an executive branch stamp on this group, calling it the Presidential Council on International Communications and Information Policy.

The council I envision would not have any direct role. Its basic purpose would be to recommend a coherent framework within which the United States would

- maintain its lead in technology;
- assure that communications-related exports remain a driving force of our national economy;
- and use its foreign policy apparatus to promote U.S. interests, to safeguard and promote our cherished values, and to further the prosperity of our citizens.

The task of effectively coordinating policy within the executive branch would seem to be an easier matter than forging a common approach between government and the private sector. In practice, however, there are considerable shortcomings within the government, particularly in the area of foreign affairs. There are problems of both resources and coordination.

Federal agencies are doing many of the things we need to do. In the international political arena we are modernizing such important foreign policy tools as the Voice of America and Radio Free Europe/Radio Liberty. We have inaugurated Radio Marti. All these are important long-term instruments for promoting the free flow of ideas and commerce—concepts central to the growing importance of the whole range of communications technology referred to as the information revolution.

The White House, the Departments of State and Commerce, the Agency for International Development (AID), and other agencies have given higher priority to advancing U.S. trade opportunities in communications and other areas. The Department of State has established a new Bureau for International Telecommunications Policy. A senior interagency group meets to coordinate policy. All these help but they are still not enough.

We cannot expect our diplomats to do more in the complex areas of trade and communications, perform their traditional duties, and discharge other important new duties in areas like drugs and terrorism without any increase in resources. Yet, at a time when our involvement in global politics and the world economy has grown by geometric proportions, the diplomatic resources we have at our disposal have remained static in absolute terms and have shrunken greatly in relation to our needs for a more effective foreign policy. In 1960 when 10.3 percent of our GNP was trade related, we had 3,608 foreign service officers. Today the percentage of our GNP related to trade has grown to 20.5 percent while diplomatic personnel are virtually the same, 4,038, of whom only 208 belong to the Foreign Commercial Service. If we are to do a better job in the field of international communications and trade, then our resource commitment obviously needs to rise to meet our very real needs. But more resources will not be enough.

Across the whole field of foreign policy and especially in communications and information policy we need policy integration, not just policy coordination. We cannot afford to settle for the least common denominator of policy between competing agencies and interests. We must have policies that are the best we can produce and produce quickly in a rapidly changing international environment. Too often what passes for serious policy is a series of peace treaties between competing centers of power. Such a system is not good enough for our competitors or our adversaries; we will settle for such a system only at our peril.

Within the government, policy integration, rather than coordination, can only flow from presidential recognition of the need for a more carefully integrated approach to policy. Such a recognition should not lead to yet another bureaucratic actor. The National Security Council (NSC) provides an appropriate mechanism, but it needs to upgrade its attention to communications issues both by assigning these tasks to a new deputy assistant adviser to the president for national security affairs and by providing that official with appropriate staff support.

Upgrading the NSC's role in this area would be enhanced by a careful review of the management of such issues by the Office of Management and Budget in coordination with the Congress.

Early tasks for the NSC to review are the adequacy of U.S. assistance for communications infrastructure in developing countries through both AID and multilateral institutions and the improvement of the effectiveness of U.S. diplomacy at international organizations by assuring better coordination of all U.S. diplomatic and economic activities.

In pointing out new steps that should be taken I would be remiss if I left the impression that little has been done that is useful. I recognize and applaud steps that this administration and especially Secretary of State George P. Shultz have taken toward giving these issues the priority they deserve. I am particularly appreciative of the decision to incorporate the communications policy function in the Department of State within a new bureau. I laud this latest step. The bureau will serve to institutionalize attention to international communications technology in the policy-making process. And I believe that it is especially appropriate that the institution that is responsible for the conduct of U.S. foreign policy should have the responsibility for international policy in this area.

Yet at the State Department more remains to be done. Flesh must be put on the bones of the new bureau. A viable career for officers specializing in these issues must be assured; staff resources must be upgraded at embassies to deal with these issues; and policy functions within the department must be carefully integrated.

The Department of State has made great strides in improving its technological capabilities in data processing and communications, but until now it has not developed a plan for ensuring that members of the career Foreign Service understand the implications of the information age. The core of any effective foreign policy is information about the needs, desires, plans, and activities of other nations and international organizations. This information must be collected and analyzed by Foreign Service members trained for that purpose. Failure to recognize the challenges of the information age could impair the Foreign Service and, with it, the rational and effective foreign policy responses.

Finally, I want to say a word about the private sector. All of you are here today because you recognize the importance of this subject to our nation. We all appreciate the outstanding leadership Dave Abshire has provided in gaining priority for information and communication issues and for getting the prestigious Center for Strategic and International Studies to focus needed attention on them.

But all of you in the private sector need to do more on your own. Our democratic government does listen and does respond to the needs of our citizenry. The more citizens, corporations, unions, think tanks, and universities that focus attention on these issues, the more effectively and more promptly your government will act to assure that the promise of the revolution in communications and information technology will be fulfilled in a way that strengthens America's security, enhances America's prosperity, and advances the cause of freedom around the globe.

Detente and East-West Relations

Senator Hubert H. Humphrey

Any discussion of detente brings to mind the English adage, "The king is dead, long live the king." Now somebody is going to say, what do you mean by that? I simply mean that we've taken a much more realistic attitude about detente, that some of the great expectations that were the phenomena of the 1960s and 1970s are passing into history, and we're beginning to look at detente in a much more realistic fashion. But I think it should be said that the ice has been broken in U.S.-Soviet relations. Whatever your point of view may be about detente, it does at least symbolize that we are in a process of communication. The two superpowers are now focusing on specific issues in their relations, and devoid of theatrics and dramatics, the Soviet-American dialogue must henceforth be based on an ongoing political process as well as on solid accomplishments. I try to define detente not as an accomplishment as such, but rather the creation of a political environment in which it is possible to work toward solutions that may relieve some of the tensions which exist between our two great systems. If you look at it as a process rather than a fact of achievement, I think you're in a much better position.

It is the issues at the heart of the East-West relations that I would like to address. By focusing on concrete problems, we avoid the windy generalities about East-West relations which obscure rather than clarify reality. In focusing on these problems, we need to keep in mind two central facts, as I see them:

First, businesslike, well-organized Soviet-U.S. efforts to resolve problems of common concern must continue. I say "must continue" because the process of continuation of these relationships will reduce the risk of war. It will contribute to sensible reductions in the vast and costly arsenals which both nations now possess. It may help to promote stability at a time of growing international violence and anarchy, and it hopefully will cause both superpowers to recognize their obligations and responsibilities to the rest of humanity.

It also is important to realize that these efforts will not soon radically (and I emphasize the words "soon" and "radically") change the international situation. I think this becomes more clear if we note that the benefits which were supposed to flow so quickly from improved Soviet-American relations have not materialized.

Detente has not brought an end to Soviet support of "liberation movements" in the Third World, as we know, or the established Communist parties in the industrialized nations. I don't think we should have expected that to happen. It has not meant a bonanza for Americans or the American business community.

It has not caused a liberalization, to any substantial degree, of Soviet suppression of internal dissidence. (I would put in a caveat here that I do think that the Soviet Union is more concerned about world public opinion than it used to be. It has gained a stature of power and respect—or at least acceptance—in the world to the point where, in dealing with its own internal dissidence, it is somewhat more concerned about outside opinion.)

It has not produced a reduction of Soviet defense expenditures. And so-called detente has not meant that we cease to regard each other as strong competitors and political adversaries.

Failure to realize these expectations is at the heart of much of the current frustration and disenchantment with detente and Soviet-American relations in the United States and Europe. But quite frankly, the expected benefits from detente, like the expected benefits from the United Nations, were oversold. We like to do that here. Our journalism contributes to it. Our whole sense of media, of advertising and public relations, always oversells practically everything that's on the market, either in ideas or goods.

Taking these things together, the need for continuing U.S.-Soviet cooperation in problems of common concern and the unlikelihood that these efforts soon will produce radical change in the Soviet system should provide the basis for a more mature relationship with the Soviets.

It should be a relationship that will embrace both competition and cooperation as instruments of peaceful change; a relationship shed of any illusion that a conservative Communist nation is going to abandon completely its ideology, goals, and tactics because its main adversary expects it to do so.

To say this, however, is not to say that a constructive Soviet-American relationship means that we must be morally indifferent to the denial of human rights within the Soviet Union. Such an attitude was sadly evident when the President refused to see Mr. Solzhenitsyn.

I recognize the substantial limitations of fundamentally altering Soviet internal policies by our actions or our relationship. But that doesn't mean that we should not persist in our proper goals, the democratic ideals and relationships which we believe lend themselves to peaceful cooperation. In other words, this is no excuse for turning our backs on those who express outrage at Soviet policies of suppression and denial of human rights. I don't know whether we can really change them a great deal but I don't believe that we ought to hush up. I believe that we have a responsibility to our own set of values, and those values ought to be constantly placed before the world community.

To this end I believe it is imperative that we insist on scrupulous fulfillment of the Helsinki Agreement through careful monitoring of the manner in which the Soviets treat their dissidents and how the question of freedom of movement is administered. I am not so naive as to believe that we're really going to make them toe the mark. But I think they ought to be reminded. More people in this world want freedom of movement than to be locked up; and more people want free exchange of ideas than to be denied expression of creative thought. We ought to be on the side of freedom constantly—not necessarily belligerently—but firmly and intensely.

Normalizing relations with the Soviets should not mean that we acquiesce through our silence to Soviet internal policies or practices. We had a period of acquiescence in this world in the time of Hitler. People did acquiesce, in Germany and elsewhere, who knew that Hitler's policies were wrong. There was too much acquiescence in America both to Japanese imperialism and German Nazism with people saying it wasn't any of our business. The fact is that *freedom* is our business. The fact is that democratic ideals are our business. And whenever we sell them out by silence or by negotiation, we do it at our peril.

Now it's one thing to say that we cannot alter these policies and practices. It is another thing to say that Soviet-American relations—at any cost—should be an end in themselves to preserve the status quo. I am not one who underestimates the tremendous importance of Soviet-American relations. I think the peace of the world depends on it, at least in the foreseeable future. Nor have I ever been known as a Soviet baiter. To the contrary, I recognize the accomplishments of their society in material things. I recognize many of the great contributions that have been made by their science and technology and many other areas. In fact the Russian people, over the centuries, have made great contributions to the culture of the world.

But if we must abandon the long-term goal of peaceful change within and without the Communist system as the price of U.S.-Soviet relationships, I suggest to you it can never endure.

The inflated rhetoric of summit diplomacy should, therefore, now cease. I am not opposed to summit diplomacy: to the contrary, I think it is a part of the diplomatic scene and will continue to be so. But I think summit diplomacy has to be well organized. It has to be put in a proper framework. It ought to be something that we know is going to happen, and it should be prepared for without extravaganzas or spectaculars. The time has come for American politicians to speak far more realistically of what can and what cannot be gained in East-West relations—and that goes on both sides. We should stop frightening ourselves with horrendous tales of Soviet aggression and Soviet penetration on the one hand, and recognize on the other that we're in for competition. I don't mind the competition myself. As a matter of fact, I think it keeps us alive and on our toes.

Let me now move from the general to the particular. Let's talk about specific areas in the current scene of U.S.-Soviet dealings. There are three priority areas that I believe are at the core of a more realistic Soviet-American relationship. The first, obviously, is to continue the SALT talk process and obtain (hopefully) in the near future, a new, meaningful, and acceptable agreement. I understand the difficulties. I don't think we ought to expect miracles or quick solutions. I want to say explicitly that my remarks here are not meant in any way to prejudge the tentative proposals which Secretary Kissinger discussed in Moscow. I was one that urged the Secretary to continue the discussions in Moscow. I believe he ought to walk the extra mile no matter how difficult it is to obtain better understandings with people and, hopefully, agreements.

I have only read news reports of the Secretary's discussion with the Soviet leadership.

The reduction of the Vladivostok ceilings, as I have read them, is an encouraging sign of progress. I am less certain about the proposals on the cruise missile issue because of the lack of information in the press accounts. What I am about to say is my own personal view of the way we should handle some of the very difficult issues facing us in the upcoming and continuing negotiations.

I stress the word "meaningful" when discussing SALT. In the SALT negotiations, we are now past the point where we must sign a document with the Soviets just to demonstrate our fidelity to the concept of more normalized relations. We want a document that *means* something, that *does* something—but we don't need one just to encourage ourselves to continue the process. Because once you sign documents that lend themselves to violation, you do not serve the cause of peace, or the cause of reduction of misunderstanding, or of tensions.

The qualitative content of the agreement—not the agreement itself—is the real measure of progress in the field of arms limitation. What is the pivotal element in a new SALT II agreement that would cover strategic weaponry and cruise missiles? Unless testing and deployment of strategic or intercontinental-range cruise missiles can be avoided, and I underscore strategic and intercontinental, it will be difficult to secure a substantial arms control agreement. The strategic cruise missile is an arms control nightmare. Its verification problems would be immense because of its characteristics and the fact that there would likely be great numbers deployed. There is just no way that you can know how many cruise missiles a B-52 or a submarine can carry. The only way to avoid this problem, therefore, is to forbid its testing and deployment. A ban on testing of strategic or intercontinental cruise-range missiles might be verifiable. If further studies indicate this is the case, concluding an agreement on such a ban should be a high priority of negotiations. And while the negotiations are underway, we should not prejudice their outcome by proceeding with the development and testing of strategic-range cruise missiles ourselves.

Now I differentiate between the strategic and the limited distance missile. I am convinced that America is strong enough by any measure, militarily, economically, politically, and socially to forego the addition of a costly new system of air and sea-launched strategic cruise missiles to its nuclear arsenal. I recognize that if the other side does it, all bets are off. But I'm talking about whether we take the lead and clearly we have the lead, at least in the technology.

America's lead in cruise missile technology is, of course, only temporary. If the ceilings on strategic arms established in Vladivostok should be raised to include the strategic cruise missile, a new SALT agreement will be of limited value, since its provisions with respect to cruise missile deployment could not be adequately verified. I know of no one today that thinks that you could properly verify cruise missiles. I predict that if an agreement should be negotiated, which included the cruise missile, it would have a very difficult time getting through the Senate. If we take the arms control process seriously, and believe that it is in our national interest, we must strive to avoid the testing and deployment of those weapons systems that cannot be measured with certainty. The only way that we dare negotiate these agreements is if we can be reasonably secure in verification. Trust does not really exist. We have to have an alternative to trust, which is the technology of verification. I do not believe for a minute that Secretary Kissinger or President Ford can afford to jeopardize the SALT process by allowing the testing and deployment of strategic-range cruise missiles to occur.

SALT is at the top of our arms control agenda. There are, however, several other critical items which merit attention. First, the task of reducing tension and confrontation in Europe must continue with renewed vigor at the MBFR (Mutual Balanced Force Reduction) negotiations. The Soviets have shown very little inclination to come around to any understanding here.

Secondly, the cooperation that we have elicited from the Soviets and others in the field of nuclear nonproliferation should continue and we ought to press for it and expand it. I am happy to say the Soviets have been very cooperative in this area. The threshold of the Test Ban Treaty recently negotiated should be renegotiated at a lower, and meaningful level. The ultimate goal should be a comprehensive nuclear test ban.

Finally, we should initiate discussions with the Soviets on conventional arms limitations building on our expertise and cooperation in the nuclear field. I feel that there really is no advanced security in the arms race. It's a constant game of who gets ahead and who catches up. It's catch up, get up, spend more, lifting the threshold of danger. And I am sure that Soviet negotiators are not going to negotiate away what they think is their security, and I hope and I believe none of our negotiators are going to negotiate away what is our security. When we are talking arms control, we are talking life and death. We are also talking about whether or not we can keep away from going bankrupt, because defense expenditures are rising at a horrendous pace. There is pressure in this country to get them to rise even faster.

Now the second area for U.S.-Soviet negotiation is what appears on the face to be more simple—it's economic. I would like to discuss just one issue here, and that's food.

Though Soviet grain purchases are the single most important variable in the world wheat market, their unwillingness to accept and cooperate in the establishment of adequate food and fiber information, which reveals supply and future needs, is disruptive and injurious to our bilateral economic relationship and to world food security. We simply have to insist they join in.

The Soviets have literally smashed our markets time after time. They come in with these huge purchases which disrupt the commodity market, which are of little or no benefit to the farm producer, which throw the commodity futures into a turmoil, and we have let them get by with it for years. Why haven't we asked them to do as the Japanese or other grain customers do? The Japanese and others take food supplies on a regular, week-by-week basis, not putting pressure on our transport system, upon our shipping system, not putting pressure on our markets, and have a reasonable understanding as to what is going to transpire over a crop year.

Fortunately, the recent negotiations conducted by Mr. Bell of the Department of Agriculture and Mr. Robinson of State have lent themselves to a better situation. There is already, however, some concern that the recent U.S.-Soviet grain agreement leads the Soviets to believe they can ignore their responsibilities as a significant element in the international food system. In other words, "they're taken care of." International norms in many fields are there for the Soviets to see. Western trading partners must be more insistent in their demands that these norms be obeyed.

Consultations about an international system of grain reserves are taking place in the wake of the Rome Food Conference. Success in this endeavor, which is important, will be impeded if the Soviets do not join or cooperate. If they refuse to join in building up their reserves—and I say *acknowledged* reserves for I happen to think they have a secret strategic reserve, but I'm talking about reserves that are available for the world community and for themselves—if they refuse to join, and must therefore go into the world market every time their production falls below domestic need and demand, the world grain market will be subject to endemic instability. Instability in these markets is disaster for American agriculture, because we are the reserve producers. We have got our economic life at stake. The largest business in America is not General Motors, or U.S. Steel, or computers. They are like a peanut stand. The real business of America is agriculture. That's one thing Washington doesn't understand. It's incredible, but there isn't a single agency of this government except one, the Department of Agriculture, that is even interested in agriculture, except in an emergency. The Federal Reserve Board ignores it. The State Department ignores it, except when it gets to be critical in terms of some world crisis. The Commerce Department ignores it. The White House ignores it. It is as if it didn't exist. It is the number one thing we have. Everything else we have, we have competitors for. And many of them outcompete us. But when it comes to agriculture, we say, "Well, we've got those old farmers out there. They'll still do it."

I want to tell you if I had my way, the American farmers would make you say uncle a few times until they got some attention. I think it's important that we emphasize this, but I don't think my message gets through and I will be very frank with you. I have been to all these sophisticated seminars now for over 20 years in Washington. I have never yet heard a conference on agriculture that they didn't complain about the farmer. And he is our most reliable producer. He saved us most of the time before and he is still saving the nation. He is the only thing we really have going for us except the sale of weapons. He is the big exporter. And yet he is given little or no consideration in economic policymaking of America domestically or internationally, except when it suddenly appears there is a crisis.

If we can get agreement of like-minded countries to create a system of building up their food reserves, it should be made manifestly clear to the Soviet Union that non-participating countries will enjoy a lower priority than others with respect to exports and reserves of participating countries in time of global food shortage. They either cooperate, join in, or take a second class status on the availability of supplies. I think that has got to be clear. If the Soviet Union expects to reap the advantages of an interdependent, international economic system, it will have to accept the responsibilities that go with those benefits. And as a United States Senator, I am going to look after U.S. interests. U.S. interests are not being protected by the kind of willy-nilly, ad hoc, in-and-out relationships that the Soviet Union preserves today in the international field of food and fiber. So I want the message to them to be clear. I believe in selling the Russians anything they can't shoot back, if they can pay cash. Anything. I believe in trade. I don't believe in trying to be mean about it or antagonistic. I believe that they are a good customer. I want them as a good customer for years and years and years to come. And I want us to be a reliable exporter and reliable producer. But we have got to have ground rules. And if they are not going to abide by the rules, they are not going to get the benefit in times of crisis. That is the way we have got to play the game.

Now it's important that American policymakers should not underestimate the critical importance of food worldwide, and particularly in our international relations and in our relations with the Soviet Union. Shed of any illusions that grain exports will overnight produce political miracles, I have every reason to believe that the Soviet behavior could be moderated by their continued dependence on America for food commodities. There is no way that they can produce enough for themselves, unless God Almighty changes the climate, because 85 to 90 percent of all the productive land of the Soviet Union is north of the latitude of Minneapolis, Minnesota. And we know that north of that, corn, soy beans and wheat are always in difficulty. It would be like trying to produce enough food for all of the Soviet Union in Canada. It cannot be done.

Now they can make their estimates of 215 million metric tons: that estimate is sort of like the President's budget—a lot of guesses that don't add up to a single thing in fact.

Last year we got an estimate of $8 billion for offshore oil leases. We got one billion. Anybody that fails that much in school has flunked. But these estimates, all these Soviet estimates, don't mean a thing. What you need to do is take a look at the traditional pattern of production as related to the estimates. The minute you start to do that, you begin to understand the facts.

A third area that I wish to discuss is the formulation or formation of a more enduring political relationship where cooperation moderates competition. There are no easy ways, no secret formulas. Tough and businesslike negotiations are the best route to progress in East-West relations. This means, for example, trying to persuade the Soviet Union to join with the United States in exercising a moderating, rather than an inflammatory, influence in the Middle East. There may have been some reasonable success already. I have some reason to believe that one of the reasons the Soviets didn't blast the Sinai Agreement was because they needed food. But the very time that the Sinai Agreement was before the Congress, they were also in the market for American food and, as you know, there was some doubt as to whether there were going to be deliveries. We both have the same responsibility to moderate conditions in the Middle East. This kind of successful negotiation involving a specific threat to peace is much more important to improving relations than general declarations or political atmospherics.

These three specific areas—arms control, economic policy, and political negotiations—should be the focus of East-West relations in the period ahead. Success in each of them is important. But there doesn't need to be linkage. We need a limitation on armaments. We need a system of international grain reserves and world grain information—food information. We need progress, step by step, towards peace in the Middle East. It will be difficult enough to make progress in each of these areas individually. If we limit them and make progress in one dependent on progress in all, the task will be impossible. And if we make one-sided concessions in one of these areas, in an effort to persuade the Soviets to change their stance in another, we will only expose ourselves to being considered a novice at the whole thing—just unwilling to recognize the facts of life.

We should signal clearly to the Soviet leaders that they can achieve solid benefits by cooperation in each of these areas. A strategic arms race, an unstable world food market, tension and conflict in the Middle East and elsewhere—none of these are in their interest or ours. They can work with us to avoid these dangers. But we must also make it clear to them that progress can be achieved only if they, no less than we, are prepared to make concessions. Agreements must be based on a solid mutuality of interests.

In about a month, the 25th Party Congress will occur in Moscow. During this meeting important decisions will be made about the Soviet Union's economic policies and its foreign policy. Looking ahead it is clear that the Soviets are on the threshold of a generational turnover among the party leadership and hierarchy. I believe there are hardly any of the original revolutionaries left, if any. There is a whole new generation. By actions and statements which make clear to the Soviets the principles we believe should govern East-West relationship, we may have a unique opportunity now to influence the development of a Soviet foreign policy of restraint and responsibility and the emergence of a less repressive domestic society. This can be achieved not by being soft or making foolish concessions or compromising in any way our national interests.

Firmness, not belligerency, but firmness is in order. But we must couple this attitude with encouragement of the forces of moderation in the Soviet society against the ideologues, the supernationalists, and the military. To achieve this, the American political leaders should focus on the three areas that I have described, seeking concrete progress on the basis of the principles that I tried to outline. I believe that these will serve the interests of both countries.

All of this will be hard to do in an election year, unless both political parties approach this issue in a responsible and realistic manner. I want to see the Soviet-American relationship discussed and debated in the coming Presidential election. But I want the candidates to use restraint, and to recognize their responsibility to the world community as well as to our own electorate. If they do not, and if demagoguery is substituted for sensible discussion, great harm could be done to the cause of influencing the evolution of a less aggressive Soviet foreign policy. If inflammatory rhetoric or exaggerated promises become the coinage of a Presidential campaign in discussing Soviet-American relations, we only aid and abet those Soviets who want to return to the cold war for their own purposes. And let me tell you they have cold war warriors too. It isn't just here in the United States. I urge candidates in both parties to take the high road of reasoned statesmanship, speaking honestly, openly, to East-West issues that must now be tackled. In this way, progress in our relations with the Soviet Union can continue even while we go about the process of choosing America's new leadership.

If we seek world peace, there are no alternatives to a constructive Soviet-American relationship. That's what I started with, that's what I end with. If we wish to have America turn its attention and energies to urgent domestic problems and pressing world responsibilities, the process, the slow, tedious, and at times agonizing, process of normalizing relations with the Soviet Union must continue, expecting no miracles, but working for some advancement.

Foreign Policy Agenda

Jack F. Kemp

"Democracy," writes Jean-Francois Revel, "may, after all, turn out to have been a historical accident, a brief parenthesis that is closing before our eyes."[1]

Then again, democracy may be the greatest and most enduring creation of man. The key to democracy's future lies not in the stars, but in ourselves—and especially in the leadership of the United States.

Today, we as a nation are stronger: We are better able to defend ourselves and our allies than we were four years ago. NATO has exhibited strength and cohesion in the face of an all-out Soviet effort to block Pershing II and ground-launched cruise missile deployment. There are five active liberation movements opposing Communist rule: in Angola, Mozambique, Cambodia, Afghanistan, and Nicaragua. The democratically elected government of El Salvador is holding its own against insurgent attacks. We are consolidating our strategic relationship with Israel. Our strong national economic recovery is fueling economic prosperity throughout the world, and democratic capitalism is replacing socialist ideology as a model for developing countries.

But in many areas the record is far less encouraging. International terrorism has grown into a new form of warfare against the democracies, and we are uncertain in our response. Poland's struggles for liberalization have been brutally suppressed, even as we speak of expanding trade with the East. Technology leaks from West to East are costing us $20-$50 billion each year to offset Soviet expropriation of our own industry and ingenuity—an enormous problem that has yet to generate the necessary unity among Western allies.

Radical elements criss-crossing cultural and geographical bounds threaten stability in all regions of the world, from Moslem extremists in the Middle East to Vietnamese invasion forces in southeast Asia, from Cuban troops in southern Africa to PLO operatives in Central America.

The adequacy of our vital defense buildup has been exaggerated both by the critics of defense spending who want to cut back, and at times by the administration in recounting its accomplishments.[2] In particular, speaking as a strong supporter of the President's strategic force modernization efforts. I believe that we have failed to assign strategic forces the budgeting priority or urgency required.

Without pretending to address all the compelling national security issues that will command our attention over the next four years, I would like to raise three general questions that are likely to be central to our nation's future.

Will We Align Ourselves with the Forces of Freedom?

After repeated legislative battles, Congress has united behind support for El Salvador, but has found itself polarized over assistance to Nicaraguan freedom fighters. Why?

Many opponents of covert aid to Nicaragua argue that it is wrong for us to intervene in the internal affairs of another country.[3] But it seems to me that there is a logical inconsistency in approving aid to governments to defend themselves and their people against radical insurgents, while refusing to aid democratic forces threatened with extinction because totalitarians have already captured their government. As Charles Krauthammer writes, "The great moral dilemmas of American foreign policy arise when the pursuit of security and the pursuit of democracy clash. 'Contra' aid is not such a case."[4]

Managua is the geopolitical epicenter of our own hemisphere. If we cannot muster the national will to help those who would liberate that city, who beyond our shores can be confident of our support?

After the sham elections in Nicaragua last year, there are no responsible internal voices that view the Sandinista government as having any moral legitimacy. Perhaps the time has come for free nations to review the diplomatic recognition accorded the Sandinista regime, and explore the possibility of conferring formal recognition on more worthy representatives of the Nicaraguan people.

Finally, I applaud our government's decision to eschew the Sandinista-inspired judicial charade at the International Court of Justice. What a cruel hoax on the precepts of justice and international law that the World Court should be used to legitimize the "right" of the Sandinista regime to oppress the Nicaraguan people.

The Soviet Union and its surrogates like Cuba and Nicaragua have no tradition of law or respect for the sovereignty of other states— or the integrity of the individual. Yet by appealing to the best within us—the precious Judeo-Christian ethics embodied in our legal system—lawless states attempt to use our very honor as a weapon against us; and while we are held in check they can work unhindered to destroy the democratic forces that free people would champion. If our values are to survive, we must be prepared to defend them. I believe that our policy toward the freedom fighters in Nicaragua and elsewhere must be placed in this philosophical context.

Will We Devote the Resources Necessary to Provide for Our Own Defense?

After a decade of disinvestment in defense, the Reagan Administration has struggled over the last four years to rebuild our strength. Yet again this year—notwithstanding the landslide defeat the American people gave the Democratic anti-defense platform—voices are being raised in Congress and elsewhere to protest defense increases at a time of a growing federal deficit. This is questionable economic policy; it is even worse national security policy.

The simple fact of the matter is that we do not really control the level of spending needed for defense; our adversaries do. Either we provide the levels of funding necessary to protect our national security interests, or we must redefine those interests to exclude the protection of key allies, vital world resources, and the prospects of millions of the world's people for a free and independent future.

It cannot be repeated often enough that the single greatest Soviet strategic objective since World War II has been to isolate the United States by rupturing our alliance with Western Europe. When responsible spokesmen in the United States suggest that we should withdraw our forces from Europe as a means of economizing on defense spending, how can any European fail to question our commitment to NATO's defense? How can others criticize our NATO allies for falling short of 3 percent defense growth, while calling for a defense budget freeze here at home? The antidote to neutralist sentiment in Europe is Western confidence and strength—neither of which can be achieved if the United States' commitment to defense is seen as transitory and uncertain.

While general purpose forces command the lion's share of the defense budget (some 80 percent), strategic programs command the greatest attention. Chief among these in the immediate future will be the President's Strategic Defense Initiative (SDI)—an effort I strongly support. But thus far, the SDI is nothing more than a Carrollian "grin without a cat"; presently there is no plan or commitment to deploy strategic defenses. I know such a plan can materialize as soon as we decide that we are serious about strategic defense—and I believe that should be soon. In fact, the case for the MX missile would be greatly enhanced if its planned deployment were coupled with a commitment to a near-term active defense.

I have heard some lament the upcoming debate over the merits of strategic defense, when in their opinion that issue was settled with the ratification of the ABM treaty. But this does not take into account the fact that much has changed since then, or admit the simple possibility that we were wrong in abandoning active defenses—as our experience since signing the ABM treaty would suggest.

First, developing technologies long ago rendered mutual assured destruction an illusory doctrine (if indeed it ever made any sense). Second, Soviet efforts in strategic defenses—some in violation of the ABM treaty—bring the Soviet Union to the edge of an ABM breakout capability, while we have no comparable potential in the United States. And finally, as a practical matter, we signed the ABM treaty with the understanding that there would be a follow-up on agreement limiting offensive weapons—which we never obtained. Our SALT I delegation and the Congress both warned that such a failure in the arms control process could jeopardize "the supreme national interests of the United States." At a minimum, we should ask ourselves now whether that warning was right.

Even with our renewed commitment to defense, the Soviet Union continues to outspend the United States in military investment each year. In the 1975-1985 period, Soviet spending will exceed ours by $450 billion, of which a full $250 billion is in the area of strategic forces. And in this fiscal year, with all the attention given the SDI, Soviet spending on strategic defenses will be in excess of $6 billion, versus only a couple of hundred million for the United States. Given this disparity in effort, we simply do not have the luxury of repeating past mistakes where we put off paying bills and allowed our defenses to decline. Over the not-so-long run, such complacency only increases the cost of defending the United States and heightens the risk that we will find ourselves inadequately prepared to defend our interests and our country.

Will We Honestly Address the Merits of Arms Control?

Despite a decade of bitter experience with the limitations of arms control agreements with the Soviet Union, there is still a widespread tendency to view arms control as an intrinsic good, rather than as a component of our national security policy. Instead of looking to our defense requirements, members of Congress often evaluate weapons systems from the standpoint of whether they further the prospects for arms control.

As a case in point, consider the history of the MX missile system. That program has been subjected to a maze of arms control constraints, from MIRVing to launching restrictions to verification windows; and judging from recent Congressional debate, its greatest utility would seem to be the "bargaining chip mission." The question of its strategic utility has long been lost to arms control concerns.

Today there is scarcely a single major U.S. strategic program unhampered by arms control restrictions imposed not by agreement, but unilaterally by Congress. We identify a need for sea-launched cruise missiles (SLCMs); the Congress requires that the President submit a report on how a limit on SLCMs could be monitored. We are beginning to develop an antisatellite capability (while the Soviets already have an operational antisatellite system); the Congress requires a report on the prospects for an ASAT arms control ban, and unilaterally suspends U.S. testing until the report is submitted. The President reports that the Soviets are violating SALT II in multiple counts; the Congress passes a "sense of the Congress resolution" that we should continue our policy of adhering to SALT II ("interim restraint").

Isn't it time to stop and reexamine the wisdom of such Congressional second-guessing? Congress can do nothing to constrain the Soviets. We can do everything to constrain the President and ourselves. In this time of difficult negotiations with the Soviets over arms reductions. President Reagan needs Congressional support, not unilateral obstacles.

In my opinion, there is something fundamentally wrong with 535 members of Congress trying to act as arms control negotiators. Congressional initiatives are unilateral by their very nature. Congress is precluded by the Constitution from negotiating with the Soviet Union; and it seems to me that what Congress is forbidden to do directly, it should not do indirectly by means of unilateral constraints.

This is not to say that Congress should keep hands off arms control. On the contrary, Congress has a vital role to play as skeptic and critic. For example, I believe Congress should challenge the SALT II related decision not to deploy additional Minuteman IIIs, and should oppose any decision to dismantle Poseidon submarines that is driven by arms control rather than defense considerations. In particular, the role of Congress may prove of central importance in addressing the issue of Soviet noncompliance with existing arms control agreements.

It is beyond dispute that the Soviet Union materially has breached the terms of its international agreements. These violations are not minor technicalities. They go to the heart of agreements reached between this country and the Soviet Union that were intended to address the fundamental requirements of deterrence and peace. In many instances, the violations cited result from actions undertaken by the Soviet Union prior to signing the agreements, meaning that the Soviet leadership signed agreements with the United States never intending to honor their word.

The individual violations are serious enough in their implications for our defense requirements. But beyond this, it is now clear that throughout the years we have been negotiating arms control, the Soviet Union has engaged in a systematic pattern of violating arms control agreements, while directly benefiting from U.S. adherence to those agreements.

We have yet to come to terms with the implications of this record of Soviet noncompliance. What does this mean for U.S. security? What does this mean for our adherence to existing agreements? What does this mean for the future of arms control? And what does this tell us about our relations with the Soviet Union? These questions demand answers.

In his monumental work, *How Democracies Perish,* Jean-Francois Revel documents how the Soviets have perfected the use of peace as an instrument of war. Summits, negotiations, and trade have yielded ever greater Soviet military expansion. Soviet disinformation and other active measures have sowed dissension within the Free World. Defenseless Third World countries have been toppled, while the West has been loathe to intervene.

Revel does not condemn democratic peoples for a reluctance to confront totalitarian advances. Rather he reserves his contempt for those political leaders entrusted with preserving democracy, who betray that trust through willful ignorance, negligence and lack of courage.

There are many hopeful signs that the democratic impulse has taken hold on both sides of what Churchill called the "Iron Curtain," and in many corners of the world. I firmly believe that the progress of history runs against tyrannies and toward the direction of freedom. But history does not help those who refuse to help themselves.

We, as Americans, carry special responsibilities. There are certain fundamental concepts about human dignity and the rights of man which, if not defended by America, will not be successfully defended by anyone else. But with our perseverance, there is no stopping our great democratic revolution, so that one day, all people may know the treasures of freedom.

NOTES

1. Jean-François Revel, *How Democracies Perish* (New York: Doubleday & Co., 1983), p. 3.
2. See "Can America Catch Up?" Committee on the Present Danger, Washington, D.C., November 1984, #27.
3. Apparently most members of Congress do not oppose covert aid per se: Congress provided a reported $250 million this year to the mujahedeen in Afghanistan (a

move which I strongly support), while denying a request for less than one-tenth that amount for freedom fighters in our own hemisphere.
4. "Support the Contras," *The Washington Post*, January 11, 1985.

Is a Coherent Africa Policy Possible?   *Helen Kitchen*

A Nigerian novelist who recently returned to his homeland after spending more then 20 years in the United States has been sorting out his impressions of the American psyche. Referring "mainly to American institutions" rather than to Americans as individuals, T. Obinkaram Echewa writes:

Americans apprehend rather than comprehend ideas. They do not have the discipline or the endurance to wrap their minds around a thought. Instead they prefer to grab, snatch or make a stab at it. Their mental energies are usually exerted as pulses rather than as continuously flowing force. Americans tend to be direct and literal rather than allusive and figurative, stark rather than subtle. They are happier dealing with statistics than with nuances. . . .

If you give an American child a package, he will quickly tear off the wrappings. If he finds a toy inside, he will start to play with it immediately. He will play feverishly for a while and then discard the toy out of boredom. Later, he might take it apart to see what makes it go. By contrast, a traditionally reared African child is inclined to savor the mystery of what is inside the package for some while. When he eventually uncovers the toy, he will play with it only a little at a time, so as not to use it up.[1]

Mr. Echewa has struck close to home. The episodic pattern of U.S. policy toward Africa since World War II cannot be understood, much less corrected, unless it is viewed as part of a broader American inclination to approach problems in the foreign policy realm as elsewhere with a task force mentality. Thus, the major U.S. commitments of senior-level attention in Africa to date—to Zaire in the 1960s, to Angola and Rhodesia/Zimbabwe in the 1970s, to the current Namibia negotiations and the campaign against Libya's Mu'ammar al-Qaddafi in the 1980s—have all been approached as missions that were expected to have a definite beginning and end. One reason we have not yet developed a clear set of guidelines on U.S. interests and diplomatic objectives in Africa is that the U.S. government lacks either a policy planning or intelligence component focused on broad historical goals, realities, and options.

Intelligence Is Not a Dirty Word

For many Africanists in American universities and other non-governmental institutions, intelligence is synonymous with "dirty tricks." The two most convincingly documented covert operations of the Central Intelligence Agency (CIA) reinforcing this stereotype with regard to Africa have been the anti-MPLA operation in Angola, halted by the Congress in January 1976, and the role played by the CIA in 1960-1961 in the coincidental rise to power in the recently de-colonized Belgian Congo (Zaire) of a young colonel named Mobutu and the death, under mysterious circumstances, of the country's first prime minister, Patrice Lumumba.[2] But there is another facet of intelligence—research and analysis—that could be of pivotal importance in gradually developing a working consensus on U.S. interests in Africa.

In a political system such as ours, where changes in senior and even upper middle level policymaking positions are kaleidoscopic and, as noted earlier, the amount of substantive consultation that takes place with each new episode of musical chairs is often governed by such factors as personal style or partisan political considerations, the institutional memory of regional careerists is (or should be) a critical bridge.

As Sherman Kent, a Yale historian who played a major role in the Office of Strategic Services in World War II and subsequently returned to serve for 20 years as director of the CIA's Office of National Estimates, observed in a 1949 study of the relationship between strategic intelligence and U.S. foreign policy, the task of collecting and analyzing the many pieces of information that interact to define or affect U.S. interests throughout the world is "a specialty of the very highest order," quite different from line duty in either the diplomatic or military service. Intelligence, as defined by Kent, is "the kind of knowledge our state must possess regarding other states in order to assure itself that its cause will not suffer nor its undertakings fail because its statesmen and soldiers plan and act in ignorance." Although some of this knowledge may be acquired through clandestine means, "the bulk of it must be had through unromantic open-and-above-board observation and research."[3]

Ray S. Cline, former deputy director of CIA for intelligence, views Kent's book as a seminal work that "provided a generation of intelligence officers with a rational model for their profession of collecting and analyzing information," but cautions that some language suggesting that the author was describing an existing organization is misleading. What Kent outlined was "an idealistic concept" that drew heavily on the role of the Research and Analysis (R&A) branch of the wartime OSS.[4]

To find a unit resembling Kent's "idealistic concept" in the post-war period, one must go back to the 1950s, when the R&A branch of the dismantled OSS had been spun off to the Department of State as a new Office of Intelligence Research (subsequently retitled the Bureau of Intelligence and Research—INR). The INR of that time left "current intelligence" and "morning briefings" to the operating bureaus and the executive secretariat. Its mandate, to which the unit's early leadership and staff of analysts clung with something approaching religiosity, was to lay out trends, to ascertain and describe basic forces and movements, and to define the possible long-term outcomes of alternative policy courses available to *all* those involved in a given situation. The INR of that era had (and wanted) no more than a token presence at the Secretary of State's morning staff meetings and considered it a major tactical victory when senior decision makers were occasionally shaken by career analysts' then-heretical counsel (such as, "Islam is not necessarily a barrier to communism," "neutralism is the wave of the future," "the French cannot win in Algeria," "the Baghdad pact is a loser," or "you may be able to put the shah back on the throne in Iran, but there will be another Mossadeq, or worse.")

The integrity of the contribution of such a service—wherever in the bureaucracy it is located—depends on a blend of respect for scholarship and nonpartisan Washington savvy in its leadership, relative isolation from the overheated atmosphere that surrounds the process of dealing with day-to-day policy questions, and staffing by men and women who expect to spend their lives, in or out of government, honing their understanding of a particular society or region. Although a good case can be made for the dangers of overidentification with one's area of responsibility in the implementation of policy, the policymaking process is well served by some kibitzers with long memories and a commitment to understanding rather than judging human behavior.[5]

An unsettling reminder of conclusions that can be reached concerning U.S. interests in Africa when contextual analysis is missing came across my desk recently in an unclassified African overview of Pentagon origin. "Morocco," the author stated flatly, "is our only friend in Northwest Africa." Aside from the matter of Tunisia, which, conceivably, was excluded as being in north-central rather than northwest Africa, where was the author of this declaration when Algeria's foreign minister played the key role in securing the release of the U.S. hostages held in Iran? And what do we do with the fact that the United States is Algeria's major trading partner, importing more of that nation's oil than any other customer?

As veteran analyst William H. Lewis reported in March 1982: "What dismayed Algerian policymakers [about U.S. policy toward their country during Secretary of State Alexander Haig's tenure] was the disregard for the intricacies and historic roots of North African political relationships and stresses, the rigidly East-West interpretation placed on the Saharan war, and the slighting of Algeria's posture and sensitivities demonstrated by the singlemindedness with which Washington has pressed for stepped-up military collaboration with Rabat."[6]

Any serious analysis of the complex of regional and superpower forces at play in northern Africa must reach the conclusion that the interests of the United States (and, coincidentally, the Soviet Union as well) are best served by a balance of power in the region—that is, a relationship among Morocco, Algeria, and Libya in which none of the three becomes predominant. If the U.S. military had to make a choice, wouldn't it accord greater importance to keeping the Mediterranean coastline free of Soviet bases than to the useful but not absolutely critical logistical support for the nascent RDF that Morocco's King Hassan II is providing in exchange for arms needed to continue military operations in the Western Sahara?[7]

To ask these questions is not to suggest that the United States should downgrade its long-standing friendship with Morocco; rather, it is to emphasize that U.S. interests in Africa are best served if the United States does not conclude that friendship with Morocco precludes amicable economic and political relations with its neighbors.

Policy Planning for Tomorrow as Well as Today

Although the Department of State's Policy Planning Staff has brought some creative minds to the higher echelons of government over the past 35 years and has added an important dimension to the policymaking process under some administrations, the co-option of this unit into day-to-day operations is the rule rather than the exception. We have to go back to the early postwar years to find a time when a secretary of state (George C. Marshall) and his director of policy planning (George Kennan) have been committed in both word and deed to the principle that the policy planning role should be future-oriented, nonoperational, and accorded critical importance.

Ideally, the director of policy planning should be a respected and seasoned authority on international affairs whose writings have been relatively nonpartisan (or at least nonpolemical). This is no job, however, for an academician of ivory tower bent. The effectiveness of the operation would be heavily dependent on the administrative and networking wizardry of both the director and his area officers in seeking out and drawing on the lodes of expertise regarding various geographical and functional areas that are tucked away in corners of the government bureaucracy, in academic institutions here and abroad, in other governments, and among the political risk analysts of corporations.

Such a policy planning staff would be a major customer, of course, for the institutional memory bank discussed earlier as a crucial need in the intelligence community. Unlike the envisaged intelligence unit, however, the policy planning unit proposed here would have to be sensitive to the complex interplay of the legislative and executive branches of the government, various power centers within these branches, personalities, interest groups, and domestic political issues in shaping U.S. foreign policy in the short and long run on any given issue. It would also have to accept as a fact of life the educational function implicit in Dean Acheson's reflection that "it is our sad destiny to put people in the presidency with no experience in foreign affairs."

Ironically, Africa will only take on an identity of its own in the making of U.S. policy when or if an institutionalized advisory group comes into being that has as its sole mandate the determination of how or whether the jumble of perceived U.S. interests and priorities around the globe will fit together a decade or two decades hence. Without such a conceptual framework, Africa policymaking will remain, as it has since World War II, primarily an adjunct of U.S. security interests in Europe, the Middle East, and Asia.

Lessons from the Past

If the intelligence and policy planning capabilities envisaged here were in place, the predictable guidance for decision makers would be to avoid setting up rigid demarcations between "proven friends" and "anti-Western" non-friends. The problem with boxing and labeling African states as good guys and bad guys, as both the United States and the Soviet Union should have learned from their respective experiences in the relatively short time they have been involved in the political affairs of the continent, is that the kinds of boxes and labels devised in either Washington or Moscow tend to disintegrate in the African sun. The French and the British rarely make this mistake, which is a major reason why they so seldom find themselves out on a limb when a given African scene shifts suddenly.

Three perspectives on the risks run in stereotyping African leaders are instructive:

1. In 1969, a young army colonel named Jafar al-Numeri came to power by military coup in Sudan and formed a coalition government in

close alliance with the Sudanese Communist Party. By 1970, the U.S. diplomatic presence had been reduced to an "interest section" level, and the educational system inherited from the British was being drastically restructured by ideologues of the Left. In 1971, the Communist component of the regime organized another coup aimed at displacing Numeri and transforming Sudan into a state organized along unambiguously Marxist lines. Although some 30 officers loyal to Numeri were liquidated, the takeover foundered. Much of the credit goes to Mu'ammar al-Qaddafi's Libya, which forced down the BOAC plane carrying the newly proclaimed head of state and his aide to Khartoum from London. Libyan authorities promptly handed the captives over to Numeri, who had in the meantime regained power as the result of a second uprising that brought the new Communist regime to an end three days after it had taken power. In 1982, for a complex of political and economic reasons that are essentially domestic, Numeri followed the U.S. lead in denouncing Qaddafi as Sudan's major external enemy, and Sudan was second only to Egypt in the hierarchy of recipients of U.S. military and economic assistance in Africa.

The Moral: Just as it was premature to box and label Sudan as "lost to the West" in 1970, so we should be wary of making the assumption that the present close association with the United States is etched in stone. As Colin Legum, dean of Britain's Africanist journalists, has often said:

Those who characterize African governments or movements as being pro-Western or pro-Soviet almost always do so out of a failure to understand why certain African leaders, governments, or movements find it useful to choose a particular foreign ally at a particular point in time. These relationships are largely transient, both because most African governments are short-lived and because the central thrust of continental politics (despite some aberrations) is still toward nonalignment. . . .[8]

2. In the case of President Anwar al-Sadat of Egypt, it is now argued that he focused so much of his attention on developing his image as a "proven friend" of the United States that he lost touch with his own people. Mohamed Heykal, the outspoken former editor of the Cairo daily *al-Ahram*, said in an interview with a U.S. correspondent in February 1982: "I don't mean to be rude, but you [Americans] killed him. . . . He was addressing himself to you, the Barbara Walters of this world, the Walter Cronkites of this world. . . . The friendship with the United States became a target in itself, not a means to achieve something."[9] The inclination "to count too heavily on an individual rather than on across-the-board relations with a nation's people" is viewed by Heykal as a "fatal flaw of American foreign policy."

3. Conversely, there is considerable evidence that the pinpointing by the United States of its own special villains in the Third World may have just the opposite of the intended results. Tanzania's former Minister of Economic Affairs and Development Planning, A. M. Babu, addressed this phenomenon in a recent newspaper column:

President Truman picked North Korea's Kim Il Sung as his arch-villain; . . . President Kennedy's nemesis was Fidel Castro; President Johnson's was Ho Chi Minh; President Nixon settled on Salvador Allende of Chile; and President Carter on Ayatollah Ruhollah Khomeini. Now President Reagan has his Qaddafi. All of these villains in one way or another challenged American policies in their regions, but none of them posed a serious security threat to the United States. Nevertheless, they have been presented consistently to the American public as if their power were deeply dangerous to U.S. survival and to world peace—and their removal essential for the good of humankind. . . .[10]

It is Babu's view that the publicity given to these individuals by U.S. presidents, and thus the world's media, was a significant factor in their becoming folk heroes throughout the Third World. In a similar vein, he notes the irony of the consequences of the 1956 effort led by "the Conservative Anthony Eden of England and Socialist Guy Mollet of France" to oust Egypt's Gamal Abd-al-Nasser over the Suez issue. Nasser emerged as the leading figure in the Middle East and Africa for more than a decade, Babu reminds us, while "both Mr. Eden and Mr. Mollet were thrown out of power in their own countries."

Nicholas O. Berry, writing in the *Christian Science Monitor,* explores at greater length some of the boomerang effects of the attention focused by the United States on Libya's Qaddafi:

By treating Libya and Qaddafi as international menaces, the United States reinforces Libyan bluster and radicalism. The U.S. confirms that the mask is believed, confirms that Libya is considered stronger than it really is. . . .

[A]side from the intervention into Chad, which risked little and served to enhance a radical image, Libyan foreign policy in practice consists largely of words, tokens, asylum giving, monetary grants, guerrilla training, and foreign visits. It is a ceremonial, posturing, ideological, check-writing foreign policy. There is scant physical commitment to reshape the region, much less the world. Qaddafi truly believes in revolution, Arab unity, and national liberation, but the extremes to which he goes are pure theater. . . . The mask of strength had to be created. For to transform a society is itself a weakening process with its untried procedures, misallocated resources, amateur managers, fragile communications, and disgruntled traditionalists.

By threatening Libya with the Sixth Fleet, arms to Egypt and Sudan, and callous musings on the elimination of Qaddafi, the U.S. dumps upon itself huge political and economic costs. . . . The entire Arab press, for instance . . . condemned the U.S. role in the Gulf of Sidra incident.[11]

How Much Diplomatic Manpower Does Africa Warrant?

The demands put upon the U.S. diplomatic establishment by the proliferation of African states in the 1960s prompted Under Secretary of State George Ball to reply to an action alert from Assistant Secretary for African Affairs G. Mennen Williams at the time of the 1964 Zanzibar coup with the observation: "It is my impression that God watches every sparrow that may fall; I do not see why we should compete in that league."[12] The implicit questions in the biblical paraphrase are ones that still hang in the air in the higher reaches of Washington officialdom: How much diplomatic manpower does Africa warrant and aren't there some crises we could leave to the former colonial powers to worry about? The answer, as in the case of any question about Africa, is complicated.

U.S. interests in Africa are indeed served by consultation on a regular basis with European allies whose roles on the continent complement, long antedate, and are often more important than our own. Although such consultation is essential to any serious effort to evolve a more coherent U.S. sense of purpose with regard to Africa, it is not a substitute for direct, informed, and candid relationships with each African state—regardless of size and ideological leanings.

When the United States deals with Africa, not as a superpower drawing the line against the Soviet Union, but through on-the-ground envoys prepared by professional commitment and experience to relate to host governments on the basis of mutual respect and mutual interests, the basis is formed for a policy that can survive and adapt to whatever changes may lie ahead in any given country. The cost of maintaining half a hundred diplomatic missions on the continent and surrounding islands is high (and is higher when consulates are counted), but there are at least two practical reasons for giving serious attention to the style and substance of each bilateral link in Africa.

The first is that Africa accounts for approximately one-third of the total membership of the United Nations. One of the characteristics of small governments is that they tend to place great store in international organizations such as the UN where, for example, a São Tomé or a Djibouti can, at least in the General Assembly, have a vote equal to that of either superpower. Even in the superpower-dominated Security Council there is usually at least one African seat. For all its imperfections, the UN remains a sounding board for the poor and the powerless—which, to a considerable degree, means Africa.

A second reason for maintaining a credible diplomatic presence in each African country is that, as the mini-war over the Falklands demonstrated in 1982, size and intrinsic importance do not necessarily determine where the spotlight will move in the restructured world of the late twentieth century. Nigeria is important to the United States by virtue of its size (an estimated one-third of the population of sub-Saharan Africa), its economic and political influence in the region and in the OAU, its position as the second largest source of U.S. oil imports, and the fact that it is making a second try at democratic civilian government under a constitution largely based on the U.S. model. For defense planners, geographical placement accords special importance to Somalia, Kenya, Morocco, and Sudan. From the point of view of those primarily concerned with the sophisticated and crucial communications facilities that had to be moved from Ethiopia when U.S. relations with that country foundered after the end of Emperor Haile Selassie's rule, the two most important countries in Africa today are Liberia and the tiny cluster of islands known collectively as the Republic of Cape Verde.

Whereas most African governmental changes evoke only yawns above the bureau level, occasionally the falling of a sparrow will send Washington into a state of acute agitation for reasons that border on the inexplicable to those unfamiliar with our folkways. For example, the two magic adjectives that generated an extraordinary mobilization of the U.S. military bureaucracy at the time of an abortive July 1981 coup attempt in the 4,361-square-mile West African republic of Gambia were "Marxist" and "Libyan-assisted." Kwesi Adu's commentary on Ghana radio, like most African analyses, dealt with the coup attempt as something less than a major East-West chessboard move:

One may not be far from right to say that the Gambia is the least likely place for an armed rebellion to take place. With a population of just over a half a million and almost surrounded by Senegal, it has until last week known political stability since independence in 1965. In fact, many refer to the Gambia as the Switzerland of Africa . . . a tiny population, virtually landlocked, and without a standing army. . . .

The Gambia, like most developing countries, has been facing very difficult economic problems. . . . Just as in 1979, agricultural production declined further and slumped to the lowest level in 30 years in the just-ended fiscal year. The severe decline in the country's main export crop, groundnuts, had an extremely adverse effect on the whole economy through a sharp decline in foreign exchange earnings. . . . Such a galaxy of economic problems, compounded by political issues, created a fertile ground for frustration and dissent to germinate.

One of such issues worth considering is the fact that Gambia, since 1965, has known no leader apart from [Alhaji Sir Dawda Kairaba Jawara]. . . . The very prospect of having a new face at Government House, coupled with new ideas . . . gave some sort of support for the rebels, at least at the initial stages of the uprising. This is a major lesson for many African leaders who think without them their countries cannot move. . . .

The least said about the role of Libya and other socialist regimes in the rebellion the better. Although the rebels were clearly of Marxist-Leninist orientation, there is no evidence that outside communists were involved. The earlier African leaders stop blaming every problem on outside interference and put their houses in order, the better. . . .[13]

Professionally staffed U.S. diplomatic missions in all African countries, in touch with all elements of society, are the best insurance available to use against misreading and overreacting to local crises and also against facing a crisis or opportunity with no cards to play.

Closing the Credibility Gap

One subject on which there is a broad consensus among Americans concerned with Africa is that the United States would not fare well in a poll taken to measure the credibility of the external powers playing a significant role in the affairs of the continent. The consensus breaks down, however, when credibility is defined.

Most recently during the Carter presidency (but also under President Kennedy in the early 1960s), the emphasis was on rhetoric and gestures calculated to convey a generalized sense of brotherhood and identification with African aspirations. Problems of credibility arose when rhetoric could not, owing to the complexities of the U.S. policymaking process, be backed up with explicitly or implicitly promised deeds.

For example, the idea of a mini-Marshall Plan for the Sahel that originated during a visit to West Africa by President Carter's mother had a brief lifespan, for the predictable reason that it had no chance of getting off the ground in a Washington where even routine foreign aid legislation moves through the Congress with increasing difficulty. Similarly, the one verifiable result of Vice President Walter Mondale's departure from his briefing book guidance following a meeting with South Africa's Prime Minister John Vorster in Vienna in 1977 (when Mondale replied to a reporter's question by agreeing that there was no real difference between the "full political participation" euphemism put forward in the talks and "one man/one vote") was that Mondale provided Vorster with a "duplicitous Americans" focus for the National Party's campaign in South Africa's November 1977 elections, enabling him to blur issues of genuine substance. Even many of the Americans and Africans who agreed fully with the Mondale statement were concerned that it could create unwarranted or at least premature expectations among South Africa's blacks that the United States would actively support revolution in that country. The analogous example of U.S. rhetoric vs. performance in the case of Hungary in 1956, along with the post-Vietnam syndrome still permeating the United States, were among the reasons for doubting that this was more than a tactical ploy undertaken in response to pressures of the moment.

Reagan administration spokesmen convey a different reading of the term credibility. Many months before he left academia to head the State Department's Africa Bureau in 1981, Dr. Crocker was making the case that "the current U.S. rhetoric aimed at assuring Africans whose side we are on is inappropriate and often counterproductive." Under guidelines of a policy option labeled "Concern for Credibility," he proposed in 1979 that the United States "approach Africa not as a suitor anxious to please, but on a less patronizing basis of shared mutual interest," a stance that would be "hinged openly and directly on a blend of U.S. global and regional interests."[14]

This posture also has its drawbacks, as Vice President George Bush learned in his November 1982 visit to seven African nations during which he sought to explain the logic of linkage between a Cuban departure from Angola and a Namibian settlement. Even President Daniel arap Moi of Kenya, categorized by the Reagan administration as a "proven friend" of the United States and thus the recipient of an increasing share of U.S. sub-Saharan aid, found it necessary for domestic credibility reasons to take strong public issue with the vice president on the grounds that making a Namibia settlement conditional on the Cuban troop issue served no African interests except those of South Africa. U.S. credibility was also strained when the vice president, during his stopover in Zaire, pledged continued support of the "security and stability" of the country, and heaped what some would regard as excessive praise on President Mobutu for his personal courage, his sense of initiative in African affairs, and his resumption of diplomatic relations with Israel.

As noted in Chapter 4, the credibility of Washington's periodic affirmation of support for the "charter and foreign policy principles" of the OAU has been increasingly questioned in both Africa and Europe in the 1980s. Aside from the widely held view that U.S. statements and actions reinforcing Morocco's claim to the Western Sahara helped to scuttle a promising 1981 initiative for a negotiated resolution of the Saharan war, there are also second thoughts about the OAU peacekeeping force sent to Chad in late 1981 with substantial U.S. financial support. For example, A. M. Babu, writing in *Africa Now* of London in May 1982, assailed the United States and France for using "their diplomatic pressure and promises of financial aid to drag the OAU into taking a 'peacekeeping' responsibility which it had neither the means nor the experience to carry out efficiently and effectively [resulting in] a pathetic mess both within the organization and in Chad itself."

Washington provided Babu and like-minded Africans with more ammunition in an address by Assistant Secretary Crocker to the Baltimore Council on Foreign Relations in October 1982 that represented the OAU's Chad operation as a U.S. anti-Libyan success story:

Our cooperative efforts with the OAU have paid off. For example, U.S. policy toward Chad, aimed at countering Libyan military adventurism, has yielded important dividends over the past 12 months. In 1980, 7,000 Libyan troops intervened in the Chadian civil war and quickly became a major source of regional instability, posing a direct threat along Sudan's border and creating great worry among the other states bordering Chad. Seriously concerned by the Libyan presence, we and others encouraged the Chadians to ask for Libya's withdrawal and to seek OAU help in solving internal problems. In late 1981, the then provisional Chadian government, headed by former President Goukouni, called upon Libya to remove its military force. We then worked closely with the OAU to prepare the way for an African peacekeeping force to maintain order in Chad once the Libyans left. . . .

For our part, the United States moved directly to facilitate and support this peacekeeping effort. We allocated $12 million to support the Nigerian and Zairian contingents with nonlethal equipment and to aid transport of supplies to Chad. We also supported OAU efforts to promote reconciliation among various Chadian factions. By June 1982, Goukouni, who refused reconciliation efforts proposed by the OAU, had been forced out of Chad and replaced by his principal rival, Hissene Habré. The OAU concluded that its troops could be withdrawn. For the past four months, Habré has consolidated his control over the entire country and actively pursued the goal of internal political reconciliation. . . . Chad's reconstruction and reconciliation must proceed apace if Libya is to be denied another opportunity for foreign meddling in a sensitive area. Recognizing this, the United States has just signed an agreement to provide $2.8 million in rehabilitation assistance over the coming year. . . .[15]

As the next month's development revealed, the Chad crisis was not behind us. It was a split over seating of the Habré delegation that led to the aborting of the second effort to hold the OAU's nineteenth summit in November 1982.

Will the Real Voice of America Please Stand Up?

The image of U.S. values and interests projected to Africa is shaped not only by government-to-government policies and actions, but also by the content of Voice of America (VOA) broadcasts heard throughout the continent every day by those who own or have access to transistor radios. Controversy over the VOA's mission and content has persisted since its founding in the 1940s—a controversy that centers on whether the Voice should be viewed primarily as a pro-Western/anti-Communist propaganda vehicle, a journalistic venture following professional norms of unbiased world news and commentary, or a window on America, "warts and all."

In 1982, the VOA, which is part of the United States Information Agency (USIA), had a budget of $109 million, some 2,200 employees, and an estimated 104 million regular listeners worldwide for its 981 hours of broadcasts per week in 39 languages. Nobody jams the programs it beams to Africa, and a great many people listen, but extended empirical observation leads to the conclusion that the Voice makes certain flawed assumptions about the reasons Africans turn on their radios, what holds their attention, and what they believe of what they hear. Concerns about the relevance of the Voice fall mainly into three groupings:

· As a source of news and commentary, the Voice cannot compete with the British Broadcasting Corporation (BBC), which is an aspect of the British Empire on which millions of faithful listeners around the world hope the sun will never set. The BBC's reputation for reliability and integrity is so unique that African officials even in the socialist countries are likely to assume that visitors will want to join them in interrupting appointments when the BBC world news is due. The president of Djibouti assailed as "an ugly proposal and a bad governmental decision" a proposed cutback in Somali-language broadcasts in 1981, and the *Washington Star* jumped headlong into the same "penny-wise, pound-foolish" parliamentary debate with an editorial noting that the BBC's external services "give a picture of the world that is universally recognized as about as close to objective truth as human reporting is likely to be."[16]

Although the BBC's external services are an important underpinning of British foreign policy and are nominally and budgetarily under the Foreign Office, the corporation has always looked upon these services "as the flagship of British culture and fairmindedness which produces incidental benefits for the nation."[17] The BBC's political editor, John Cole, notes that the overseas services "are jammed by totalitarian countries of right and left not because they tell lies, but because they tell the truth, and because they are believed."[18] This reputation has been built on a scrupulous dedication to independent and even-handed reporting, even when (as in the Falklands crisis of 1982) this has embarrassed British governments. In further contrast to the VOA, the BBC is wary of periodic efforts by the British government to strengthen transmission hardware when the moving spotlight of world attention shifts to new East-West hot spots (Afghanistan, Poland), on the grounds that any concentration of services on areas under Soviet pressure would provide support for the view that external services are part of a British propaganda machine.

· A significant portion of VOA's programming to Africa now consists of cultural and educational presentations. Books and other works on Africa are reviewed and excerpted at length, and much of the cultural content reflects a conscientious effort to appeal to specifically African or "ethnic" interests, and to educate. These programs are not without interest, but they are subject to credibility problems because they convey a much higher and broader interest level about Africa than in fact exists in the United States. And sufficient account is perhaps not taken of the fact that African radio listeners, like radio listeners in Tennessee or Oregon or New York, have a limited tolerance for uplifting educational fare.

· VOA's return, in the early 1980s, to what USIA Director Charles Wick describes as a more vigorous effort to counteract Soviet disinformation does not arouse the responses in Africa it may in some other parts of the world, because "the Communist menace" does not connect with African realities. It is easy for us to forget that Africans' experience with oppressive externally based masters has been entirely with West European colonial rule; to date, neither the Soviet Union nor Cuba has established a presence in an African country except by invitation and neither has yet declined to depart when asked to do so. In African eyes, moreover, the prospect of an overt or covert intervention by South Africa in an internal power struggle in an African state is perceived as a far greater long-term threat than assistance invited in by one side or the other from Moscow or Havana. South Africa's move into Angola in 1975 and Israel's taking of the Sinai in 1967 and its march to Beirut in 1982 are closer and more real than what has occurred in Poland or Afghanistan.

In a sense, the VOA is a microcosm of the unresolved ambiguities and discontinuities of the entire relationship between the United States and Africa. When Africans listen to BBC programs beamed to Africa, they know precisely what they are hearing—news and commentary calculated to be of interest not only to Africans but to everyone of whatever nationality or occupation who is living, visiting, or interested in Africa. They know that the BBC broadcasts in Britain itself, while the VOA is precluded by law from providing materials to U.S. radio networks and stations. When one turns to the BBC, there is a sense of listening in on the world that an African does not experience when he listens to VOA programs specifically crafted for African audiences. For these reasons, and because the "propaganda" content of VOA varies from administration to administration, Africans have no clear sense of the extent to which the content of what they hear is the official word of the United States.

The answer is that sometimes it is and sometimes it isn't. But who is to figure out for sure unless a given presentation is a verbatim transcript of a presidential or other major policy address? Some long-time students of this problem have suggested that the ambiguity could be resolved if the VOA output were clearly divided into two segments— an official record, on the one hand, of U.S. executive and legislative branch statements, actions, and studies relevant to Africans and those concerned with Africa, and, on the other hand, features drawn exclusively from a noncommercial public broadcasting medium such as National Public Radio. Such a menu, carefully labeled as to official and unofficial components, might be one additional building block to add to those proposed in earlier pages that could, in combination, develop a less episodic U.S. policy toward Africa.

Some Minimal Guidelines

Most European, African, and American analysts take the view that U.S. credibility problems in Africa stem largely from the erratic image created by the tendency of both Democratic and Republican administrations to devise and invoke "principles" to justify ad hoc actions that are often reactive and often dictated or at least shaped by domestic political or anti-Soviet considerations. As the *Wall Street Journal* commented in a 1978 editorial,

[T]he United States has approached Africa in a state of confusion verging on schizophrenia. We waver, hopelessly torn between our legitimate cultural, strategic, and economic affinities and a desire for popularity and moral rectitude. . . . In the end, we achieve neither rectitude nor popularity, or self-interest.[19]

Granted that consensus is an elusive foreign policy goal for a nation that displays its pluralism as flagrantly as does the United States, our best hopes of bettering our credibility score and furthering U.S. long-term (as opposed to transitory and localized) interests in Africa lie

· in getting the facts straight;
· in developing an institutional mechanism for determining what

developments and trends involve interests that are vital or even important to the United States over the longer run;

- in consistently supporting African efforts to prevent or resolve regional conflicts that could escalate into direct or surrogate conflicts between East and West;
- in seeking to maintain access to resources and trading partners and dialogue with African leaders, whatever the shifting ideological commitments of the governments involved;
- in furthering, by keeping open lines of communication and influence with all people by whom the future of South Africa will be shaped, nonapocalyptic change toward a just society in that country;
- in adhering, in such matters as IMF loans and other forms of conditional multilateral assistance where the U.S. vote carries potentially decisive weight, to a firm set of universally applicable behavioral principles;
- in encouraging, with both practical and moral support, the development of the regional economic building blocks envisaged in the Lagos Plan of Action drawn up at the first OAU economic summit in 1980;
- in being wary of making rhetorical commitments or threats whose implementation neither U.S. public opinion nor the U.S. Congress can be counted on to support;
- in operating throughout Africa as a positive force confident of our own values and worth rather than reactively to a Soviet presence that is an inevitable phenomenon of the post-colonial era.

NOTES

1. T. Obinkaram Echewa, "A Nigerian Looks at America," *Newsweek,* July 5, 1982, p. 13.
2. On the role of the CIA in Angola in the 1970s, see John A. Marcum, *The Angolan Revolution,* vol. 2 (Cambridge: MIT Press, 1978), pp. 257, 271, 273, and John Stockwell, *In Search of Enemies: A CIA Story* (New York: W. W. Norton & Company, 1978). The latter book, written by a former CIA operative, also contains the author's account of the circumstances surrounding Lumumba's death (pp. 10, 105, 236-237).
3. Sherman Kent, *Strategic Intelligence For American World Policy* (Princeton: Princeton University Press, 1949).
4. Ray S. Cline, *The CIA Under Reagan, Bush & Casey* (Washington, D.C.: Acropolis Books, Ltd., 1981), pp. 100-101.
5. This discussion of the role of INR in the 1950s originated in an address by the author at a conference at the Naval Postgraduate School in Monterey, California, in 1979 and was subsequently developed into Guidepost 6 in "Eighteen African Guideposts."

6. William H. Lewis, "Why Algeria Matters," *African Index,* vol. 5, no. 2 (March 1, 1982):5.

7. For further discussion of these options, see I. William Zartman's presentation on "Scenarios for Morocco" in the proceedings of the September 1982 CSIS conference on "Strategic Response to Conflict in the 1980s," to be published in 1983.

8. Colin Legum, "African Outlooks Toward the USSR," *Communism in Africa,* ed. David E. Albright (Bloomington: Indiana University Press, 1980), p. 15.

9. From an interview with David Ottaway published in the *Washington Post* on February 20, 1982.

10. Babu, who now teaches at Amherst College in the United States, made these observations in a contribution to the *Sun* (Baltimore, Maryland), January 10, 1982. His column appears regularly in *Africa Now* (London).

11. Nicholas O. Berry, "The High Cost of Threatening Qaddafi," *Christian Science Monitor,* September 30, 1981.

12. George W. Ball, *Diplomacy for a Crowded World: An American Foreign Policy* (Boston: Little, Brown and Company, 1976), p. 223.

13. Ghana radio, August 6, 1981.

14. See Option 5, "Concern for Credibility" in "Options for U.S. Policy Toward Africa," ed. Helen Kitchen, *AEI Foreign Policy and Defense Review,* vol. 1, no. 1 (1979):50.

15. Chester A. Crocker, "Challenge to Regional Security in Africa: The U.S. Response," an address to the Baltimore Council on Foreign Relations (Baltimore, Maryland), October 28, 1982.

16. "Pennies, Pounds and the BBC," *Washington Star,* July 23, 1981.

17. "BBC and the Foreign Office," editorial in the *Financial Times* (London), June 29, 1981.

18. John Cole, "The BBC's War Over Words," *Washington Post,* May 19, 1982.

19. From an editorial in the *Wall Street Journal,* August 23, 1978.

The Gulf: Implications of British Withdrawal

Bernard Lewis et al.

Policy Findings

A decision to withdraw the British military presence and to terminate the treaty and engagements existing between Britain and the littoral states of the Persian Gulf was announced by the Prime Minister in January of 1968. This decision has already produced a changed situation in the Gulf and may well give rise to further developments in and around the region that could affect the political, economic and strategic interests of the noncommunist world in this area. The principal dangers in the Gulf would appear to be:

1. Disturbances within the states themselves. Some of the states of the Gulf region have experienced a dramatic increase in the literate and semi-literate, professional and artisan elements as the result of both an increase in educational opportunities for citizens of the Gulf, and the influx of educated men from other areas of the Arab world. This growth in the size of a politically conscious group that could help to extend unrest in the region threatens the continued existence of some of the states in their present territorial and political forms. Recent events in Nigeria have shown us that oil supplies may be cut off not because some internal or external enemy wishes to do so, but because without a minimum of order, the oil industry cannot function. The same situation could arise in some of the Persian Gulf states.

2. Conflicts between the states themselves. Conflicting territorial claims and other traditional rivalries inhibit the current attempt to set up a federation of Gulf sheikhdoms. The political order in the Gulf during the last century has been maintained by British interest and control. In the very delicate balance of Gulf politics there are many claims that have been in abeyance for a long time without actually being resolved. Under British colonial rule in Cyprus the Greek and Turkish governments accepted the continuance of colonial rule because both sides clearly understood that their claims were, so to speak, on ice. Once British rule ended, or rather once it was made clear that British rule was going to end, both sides were obliged by the political forces within their own communities to put forward their claims, and to do so to the point of virtual war. The principal territorial claims in the Persian Gulf are those of Iran to Bahrain and certain other islands, Iraq to Kuwait and Saudi Arabia to the Buraimi Oasis which is partly in Abu Dhabi and partly in Muscat and Oman. Disputes have not been pursued because the parties concerned recognized that, while the British were present, temporary silence over a claim did not imply its forfeiture. British withdrawal could lead to a renewal of old interstate conflicts and/or the development of new disputes arising from changed economic circumstances.

3. The growth of influence of other powers in the Gulf. In anticipation of British withdrawal and while the Gulf states struggle to reach a new political equilibrium, powers that have previously had little or no influence in the area may be tempted to become involved there. In this situation, attention must be given primarily to Soviet intentions, as a growth in Russian influence in the Gulf could have important and dangerous consequences for the noncommunist world. The British withdrawal does not, of course, imply an open invitation to Moscow, but in the light of experience in Korea it may be seen that a declaration of disinterest by the West could well be read by the Soviet government as equivalent to the granting of a carte blanche to them, and would almost certainly encourage that party within the Soviet leadership which desires a more active and a more forward policy.

It would, moreover, be dangerously facile to assume that Russian policy is formulated within parameters similar to those adopted by the West. The recent invasion of Czechoslovakia serves as a warning that Soviet policy makers are prepared to act in a more determined way than is sometimes assumed. Thus the local opposition, which helped to convince the British government that military bases are not a viable proposition, need not necessarily be a factor of the same influence in Soviet planning.

Definition of Interests: Interest of the Noncommunist World in the Gulf Region

1. Oil: More than half of western Europe's oil supply comes from the Gulf. The Gulf area is also an important supplier to Australia, New Zealand, South Africa, Japan and South Asia. Its oil is of minor importance to the domestic United States, but Persian Gulf oil is used by the United States in Southeast Asia and it fuels the U.S. and NATO allied forces in western Europe.

2. Balance of Payments: The fact that Persian Gulf oil is normally cheaper in western Europe than oil from other regions, and that the money used to purchase it returns to buy goods or to be deposited in the sterling area, means that the consumption of Persian Gulf oil by western Europe helps to prevent a dislocation in the balance of payments. Any disruption of these arrangements could present a serious balance of payments problem to the oil-importing countries.

It follows from these considerations that the strategic interests of the noncommunist world would be in grave jeopardy if freedom of movement in and out of the Gulf were curtailed or denied.

Russian Interest in the Gulf Region

Russian interest in the Gulf is conditioned by several factors.

1. Changes within Russia: As Russia approaches military parity with the United States, Soviet leaders seems to be becoming more adventurous. They no longer see their choice as simply between inaction and full confrontation, but are exploring a range of possibilities between the two. At the same time the role of the military in the formation of Soviet policy, although not yet dominant, is certainly growing.

2. Western attitudes toward the Gulf: The Middle East ranks very high on the Soviet list of priorities and the present Russian government appears to believe that it ranks much lower in American political and strategic thinking.

3. The inherent instability of the Gulf Region: The defensive/offensive dichotomy has little relevance in the discussion of Soviet policy. Their policy could better be described as imperialism in the conventional, traditional sense of the word, though sometimes in the guise of social revolution. There are two essential components to the growth of empire—appetite and a sense of mission. The Soviet Union has both. The defense of the imperial frontier requires a cordon sanitaire, which in turn requires a further cordon sanitaire. This process is capable of indefinite extension. Provinces must be protected from attack, however improbable; people, from ideological contamination. The safeguarding of the Slavs within the frontier requires the control of Slavs beyond the frontier; the same is true of Muslims. The principle of the cordon sanitaire is particularly important in an area of instability and change, which the Soviets might regard as constituting a danger to their security. The defense of Moscow led them to Czechoslovakia. The defense of Baku might well lead them to the Gulf. In view of these considerations British withdrawal from the Gulf makes it a prime target for Soviet penetration.

In this area, as in others, the Soviets may be assumed to have a minimum and a maximum aim. Their minimum aim would presumably be to terminate the western monopoly in the area by establishing a Russian political and naval presence in the Gulf. Their maximum aim could be the complete domination of the Gulf and its closure to western interests as well as a Soviet penetration into the adjacent countries of Asia and Africa.

Until recently, Russian policy was concerned with the promotion of instability in the area; an attitude largely determined by the existence of local British military forces and political influence. As the British withdrawal proceeds, however, Russian policy may be reversed and may seek to create, or impose, a degree of stability as a condition favorable to the exercise of greater Soviet control. If this were to happen, the Soviet government could well find itself confronted with problems and difficulties similar to those that faced Britain as the dominant power in the area. It should be repeated, however, that the Russian response to such a situation would probably differ from that of the British government.

The choice of policies open to Russia is therefore likely to be determined by: conditions prevailing within the states of the area; the diplomacy of the West to protect its interests there; the outcome of struggles within the Soviet leadership; and the effects of current dissensions within eastern Europe. The latter factors will, of course, be affected by the first two.

Recommendations

The change of British policy from one of flexible withdrawal in the 1970s to a public declaration of withdrawal and termination of responsibilities in 1971 has increased the danger of instability in the Gulf region, while at the same time creating new conditions within the area. Although Britain's Conservative Party has indicated an intention, if returned to power, of continuing a British presence in the Gulf, the panel believes that, in the absence of a modification of the present policy in the very near future, such an intention would not be realizable by 1970. It has been assumed that the likelihood of a Conservative government coming to power before 1970 is sufficiently remote to be ignored for present purposes.

Some modification of the present policy of withdrawal in 1971, in response to the sudden and recent changes in both the international and the Middle Eastern regional situations, might be desirable, but politically difficult. Such a change in the present policy would have to be made soon to be effective and would have to allow for the fact that the announcement of withdrawal has already created new conditions in the Gulf. The announcement has in fact set in train a series of political processes that makes it impossible to maintain an exclusive British position based on the existing protection treaties. One of these processes is a move toward full independence for the Gulf states, either through a federation, or individually, and any attempt by the rulers, particularly the ruler of Bahrain, to halt this move could increase the dangers to the stability of their regimes. Independence would lead to membership in the Arab League and this in turn would almost certainly preclude the continued presence of British ground forces; to ignore Arab opinion on this subject would be to invite the involvement of British forces in an Aden-type situation, with all its disastrous consequences. A modification of the present policy would therefore mean the negotiation of new defense arrangements, including possibly a British amphibious force, with ground facilities maintained where necessary by the federation or local governments.

If federation fails and Baharain becomes an independent state, a situation of extreme instability may arise in the southern Gulf where the individual sheikhdoms are too small in population to become members of the United Nations. In such circumstances and for lack of any alternative, British forces might be invited to remain in Sharjah. A withdrawal from Bahrain onto Sharjah would be neither easy militarily nor inexpensive since Bahrain is the nodal point of the British military presence, but the contribution to peace and stability resulting from a continued British presence for a further period would outweigh these considerations. In this event, an extension, by agreement with the Sultan of Muscat, of the very limited military facilities in Masirah would be useful.

Whether the present policy of withdrawal be completed as planned in 1971 or in some way modified, western interests in the area remain of the greatest importance and will need protection. The possibility of simultaneous closure of all Persian Gulf sources of oil is considered remote. Nevertheless, the dependence of oil consumers on this region renders them vulnerable to interruptions in supply. To lessen the dependence, larger stocks should be held in the consuming countries and new sources of supply developed.

A further requirement is to maintain sufficient influence to ensure air communication through the area and in particular U.K. staging rights in Bahrain. To this end and with the aim of forestalling Russian military aid, it is most important that all possible assistance should be given by Britain in the equipment and training of local military forces.

The possible Soviet interpretation of British withdrawal as equivalent to British disinterest has already been mentioned and it is felt that Russian naval visits to the Gulf are bound to increase whether the Suez Canal remains closed or not. To counter this increasing Soviet presence, before it becomes well established, the existing policy of British and American naval visits to Gulf ports should certainly be continued. Visits to the Gulf by naval units from other Western powers should also be encouraged; these visiting units could be of mixed nationality.

The creation of a Soviet Indian Ocean Fleet is a possibility to be taken into account. This would add to the threat of direct Russian political and military action within the Gulf itself, the danger of interference with the seaborne carriage of oil through the Indian Ocean, and is further reason for continuing a matching western naval capability in this area. An American naval presence in the form of an Indian

Ocean task force could serve in a deterrent role. Such an increased American naval presence would be more feasible after a settlement in Vietnam.

It should be emphasized that the purpose of any such military arrangements is to allow additional time for agreements toward intra-regional cooperation to take place. The long-term solution to the region's security problem can be based only on indigenous cooperation within an agreed framework.

Foreign Policy Agenda

Richard G. Lugar

At grass roots town meetings, constituents often ask if we have a foreign policy. They have heard that we have sacrificed the steadiness and consensus of the past for the unpredictability of one crisis after another of the present. Much is made of the disruptions and new beginnings of a succession of presidencies, as well as strong Congressional intervention in foreign policy. Indeed, perhaps too much is made of this.

Nevertheless it does seem clear that the United States has not yet fully recovered from the Vietnam War. Nor has the United States fully adjusted to the role which its values, its economic strength, its geography, and its interests define for it in the world today.

Before Vietnam, some widely shared assumptions were held about the national interest and potential threats to it. Some consensus was apparent on appropriate remedies to our problems. One of the costs of Vietnam was the breakup of this consensus. The United States has been and continues to be uncertain about the use of force in the conduct of U.S. foreign policy. A broader popular involvement in foreign policy questions has deepened the historical reluctance of Americans to employ force to achieve our national purposes.

We continue to employ a strategy which is still best described by the word "containment." But in recent years there is evidence that this has become a very special kind of containment policy: it is containment at minimum cost. In poll after poll, Americans express their concern about hostile governments which imperil our interests in Latin America and elsewhere. But in these same polls, Americans display an equal and overwhelming opposition to any course of action that might actually frustrate governments which are harmful to us.

It is important to restore a greater degree of consensus about our interests and commitments around the world and about our willingness to defend them. Do we really have vital interests all around the globe? Do we have the economic and military capabilities and the political will to support these interests with a safe margin of risk? Do we have a long-term, substantial, and correct view of the Soviet Union? Do we have an appropriate understanding of the economic, political, and spiritual forces that move nations?

There are grounds for optimism. The great majority of the American people agrees upon several basic truths about U.S. foreign policy: a sense of realism about the Soviet Union; an appreciation of the need for a strong defense; solidarity with allies and friends; openness to discussions and negotiations with adversaries; and a strong commitment to justice, human dignity, and economic well-being for all people.

We have just inaugurated President Ronald Reagan for a second four-year term. President Reagan is open to the idea of consensus in foreign policy around the aforementioned themes. The outcome of the recent election should indicate as well to people of diverse political persuasions the importance of foreign policy consensus around the themes which are so fully supported by the great majority of the American people. Questions about commitments and the proper use of force must be resolved in the coming years and strengthen the heart of U.S. foreign policy.

The foreign policy discussion agenda is substantial. The issues include the health of our alliances, the readiness of our forces, regional instabilities, indigenous revolutions, human rights violations, nuclear proliferation, resolution of famine and hunger crises, and the evolution of new economic and technological realities. There are two areas, however, that are surely at the core of our foreign policy: first, East-West relations and arms control; and second, the state of the international economy.

What is to be our relationship with the Soviet Union and with countries that are held within its orbit? This has been an issue for U.S. foreign policy since the end of World War II. Where we have deviated temporarily from the strategy of containment and have settled for less than containment, the result has not been satisfactory.

Much has been said and written about the meaning of detente. As I understand it, its American originators intended it to contain two elements. Coupled with a relaxation in our direct bilateral relationship with the Soviet Union, there was to be an understanding of the continued need for U.S. political will and resoluteness in defending ourselves and those at the margin of the East-West dispute. Two things went wrong. First, it is apparent that the Soviet Union either did not play by the rules of the understanding or that it shared no such understanding in the first place. The Soviet Union continued on a course of unparalleled arms expansion and strenuous activity in Africa, Asia, Latin America, and elsewhere to undermine governments friendly to the West. Second, of course, was Vietnam, which shattered our will to employ force anywhere in the world.

We have been down that road and a substantial majority of Americans in both political parties now maintain a high degree of realism about the Soviet Union. At the same time, most Americans continue to hope that a common interest on the part of the United States and the Soviet Union might result in a reduction of nuclear arms which are poised on both sides.

A key question in analyzing the state of the Soviet-U.S. relationship concerns the place of the arms control process and any arms control agreements in the broad context of that bilateral relationship. Arms control negotiations and possible or actual agreements must be viewed as part of a broad range of policies and actions designed to protect and promote U.S. interests in a world where Soviet power has been steadily increasing and Soviet ambitions are actively asserted. The U.S. purpose must be to see to it that at any given moment and also over time, Soviet leaders recognize that the risks of assertive and aggressive uses of power outweigh the benefits. This is essential for a positive evolution of U.S. relations with the Soviet Union.

The broad purpose of the United States in conducting its policies toward the Soviet Union must be defined in terms of U.S. interests. These interests clearly include the prevention of war and may, in that respect, overlap to a degree with the interest of the Soviet Union. But they cannot ignore, and must centrally incorporate, the protection of U.S. security and well-being in the face of challenges posed to the United States and other nations by the emergence of the Soviet Union as a major military power. There are few signs that the impulses and ambitions which have carried the Soviet Union to the position and status it has reached to date are subsiding. On the contrary, they remain a central ingredient in Soviet conduct. Soviet interests in arms control remain subordinated to these adventurous ambitions. Of course, the Soviet Union wants to see potential enemies constrained, particularly the United States with its impressive economic and technological resources. And Soviet leaders probably wish to have greater certainty in their economic planning. But they are unlikely to want to see their one shining achievement and the principal source of their international influence—military power—significantly curtailed.

The expanded Soviet role and influence in the world, undergirded by growing military power, leads inevitably to the conclusion that we cannot in the foreseeable future expect to avoid maintaining strong and diversified military forces of our own. Arms control arrangements can affect the pace and character of some military programs, but they cannot alone contribute substantially to the balance we require for our security.

This brings us to the present stage of arms control negotiations and the results from the meeting in January between Secretary Shultz and Soviet Foreign Minister Gromyko. The Reagan administration approach to Geneva reflects the need for major changes in the framework of our thinking about arms control policy. Without the introduction of the new strategic defense initiative (SDI), we would have little reason to hope for any substantial or positive development in arms control negotiations. The fact is that the realities of offensive weapons and modernization programs on both sides would have led to little positive incentive for alteration of the stalemate which has existed for over a decade.

The strategic defense initiative offers something which is new and helpful. We do not know the form or the completeness which a strategic defense system might take. But we do know that for the first time there are incentives for both sides to look to something other than the development of newer, more powerful, more precise offensive weapons of mass destruction. The full scope of the changes that will flow from these developments has not yet been sufficiently appreciated. SDI has already made its first contribution to arms control. The Soviet Union is back at the negotiating table. We should not expect the SDI to do too much too quickly, but we should be prepared for the fact that this research effort is here to stay and that its consequences will be great.

The technological capabilities which make it possible to conceive a strategic defense lead to a second set of foreign policy issues, the economic and technological realities underlying many of the political and military decisions which we confront.

Many experts in Washington debate the arcana of arms control negotiating positions, conventional force postures, and a host of other topics well-known to those in the political-military world. These are important in their own right, but the decisions must be grounded more fully in the economic realities which make an adequate defense possible at all.

Defense is costly, as we all know. Defense spending must compete with many other important and worthy programs, not only in this country but also among our allies and among countries in the developing world. We simply must learn to confront the dangers and dilemmas, as well as to maximize the opportunities, inherent in a world economy. Too often, debate about budgets and deficits takes place wholly apart from debates about defense. There are deep connections between our own budget decisions and the defense decisions which we expect from others. Would a freeze in U.S. defense spending have no consequence on our demands for greater burden-sharing on the part of our allies?

We must directly confront the imperative of economic growth. If, for example, the nations of West Europe do not grow at a rate comparable to that of the United States or the countries of the Pacific Basin, will Europe be able to retain, much less expand, its own role in the defense of the West? Europe is challenged by the need for strong leadership to invigorate its economies and, in some cases, to break out of constraining economic rigidities.

In the same vein, we must address complex relationships between the economies of major trading nations. Rapid currency changes have placed intense political pressures on nations to protect their own industries. The dollar has soared against major currencies by some 41 percent since 1980. The strong dollar is the major contributing factor to the record trade deficit in 1984, a deficit calculated to be some $130 billion and growing to some $140 billion in 1985. Imports to the United States in 1984 were up some 27 percent over the 1983 figures, while U.S. exports increased in 1984 by some 8 percent, as the strong dollar that accompanied economic recovery in the United States made American products sold abroad much more expensive. The strong dollar-high interest rate impact of the budget deficit on the U.S. economy has been mixed, with the antiinflationary trends reinforced by low-priced imports more than counterbalanced by increased prices on U.S. exported goods and the resulting impact on U.S. manufacturers.

The accelerating trade deficit is a major cause for concern in efforts to sustain the U.S. economic recovery, for it undermines those key industries that find it increasingly more difficult to sell their products overseas while simultaneously enhancing the pressures for greater protectionism. If the dollar stays high and the trade deficit worsens, demands for action by the U.S. business community are likely to grow more strident. Protectionist sentiment, including even extreme measures such as import surcharges, may find a greater resonance in the Congress as the 1986 elections draw nearer. While the idea of import surcharges may enjoy little support at the moment, that could change if the trade deficit continues to grow and the White House and the Congress prove unable to agree on means for cutting the budget deficit. And, or course, any attempts to restrict imports by quotas or tariffs would likely generate severe trade conflicts between the United States and its trading allies.

Like the future course of the dollar, the direction of U.S. trade will have an important bearing on the overall prospects for the world economy. Increasingly we have come to appreciate the close relationship of trade and development finance issues, especially for Third World debtor countries. World trade volume after exploding by nearly 11 percent in 1984, is likely to grow by only 5 percent in 1985 and 4 percent in 1986. That will hurt Third World debtor nations who can service their debts only by increasing their exports. However, such an expansion of Third World exports will come up against pressures for new barriers to world trade. This means that the Third World debt problem is still a major factor for international instability and must be a constant priority consideration.

As the Senate Foreign Relations Committee seeks to chart its course for the new Congress and inquires into the present and future course of U.S. foreign policy, we will have to grapple with the issues of U.S. commitments and power. We need to better understand how many missions our country has undertaken. We need a better idea of the military forces required to meet our obligations and the economic resources essential to sustain those commitments.

The Committee can probably agree on containment of Soviet adventurism, the value of nuclear reduction negotiations, the importance of worldwide economic growth, of fewer trade barriers, greater building of democratic constitutions and human rights guarantees. We will probably make progress on famine relief and necessary long-term agricultural assistance. We will have a better idea of the strength and the future requirements of international institutions and our proper role in them.

But as the Congress pursues its work in the new session, it should be clear that the fulfillment of the U.S. foreign policy agenda must start at home, that a new foreign policy consensus requires a coming together of the American people at the grass roots, and not simply the efforts of dedicated members of Congress.

Reducing Japanese-U.S. Friction   *Saburo Okita*

Conflicts in Japan-U.S. trade relations have been intensifying in recent years. In discussing the background of this economic friction, it is necessary to differentiate between long-term, structural problems and

short-term, cyclical ones. We must also avoid factual misunderstandings and inaccurate perceptions, and should not allow specific phenomena to make us lose sight of the overall picture.

According to U.S. statistics (FAS base), in its trade with Japan the
United States recorded a deficit of $10.4 billion in 1980 and $15.8 bil-
lion in 1981. This appears to be largely responsible for stirring up
American public opinion and subsequent criticism of Japan.

Often overlooked in this argument is the fact that international
trade requires multilateral dealings, and so should not be judged on a
purely bilateral basis. Concentrating attention on a particular bilateral
relationship tends to invite misunderstanding of the real situation. In
1980, for instance, the United States had a deficit of $10.4 billion in its
trade with Japan but ran up a surplus of $17 billion with the European
Community. In the same year Japan had a trade deficit of $30 billion
with the Middle East and a deficit of $6 billion with Canada and Aus-
tralia combined.

Another important point is that while the visible trade balance is
highly emphasized, balance in service trade, another important factor,
is being ignored. In 1981, the United States sustained a deficit of $27.9
billion in its visible trade with the entire world but had a surplus of
$39.0 billion in service trade, and, with other items added and de-
ducted, recorded a net surplus in its current account of $4.5 billion. By
contrast, in the same year Japan had a $20 billion surplus in visible
trade but a $13.6 billion deficit in service trade, closing its current ac-
count with a surplus of $4.7 billion. In the same way, the United States
had a current account surplus of $3.7 billion in 1980, while Japan ran
up a deficit of $10.7 billion. Thus, in terms of the current account,
which signifies the overall balance of a country's external dealings, the
United States was in better shape than Japan. In these circumstances,
many Japanese find it difficult to understand why Japan alone must be
on the receiving end of criticism.

Exchange Rates and Trade Balance

Judging from the relationship between visible and invisible trade
and the structure of the world's multilateral trade, the United States'
trade deficit of $10 billion with Japan is nothing out of the ordinary.
The most important reason this deficit climbed to $15.8 billion in 1981
was the fluctuation of foreign exchange rates in favor of the dollar and
against the yen. At the beginning of 1981 the dollar was worth only
200 yen. The yen began to weaken later, and in early November 1982

Comparison of Balance of Payments for Japan and the United States ($ billions)

	1977	1978	1979	1980	1981
JAPAN					
Current Balance	+ 10.9	+ 16.5	− 8.7	− 10.7	+ 4.8
Trade (goods) balance	+ 17.3	+ 24.6	+ 1.8	+ 2.1	+ 20.0
Service	− 6.0	− 7.4	− 9.5	− 11.3	− 13.6
UNITED STATES					
Current Balance	− 14.1	− 14.8	− 0.5	+ 1.5	+ 4.5
Trade (goods) balance	− 30.9	− 33.8	− 27.3	− 25.3	− 27.9
Service	+ 21.4	+ 24.0	+ 32.4	+ 33.6	+ 39.0
US-JAPAN TRADE (GOODS) BALANCE (FAS BASE)					
U.S. deficit (−)	− 8.0	− 11.6	− 8.6	− 10.4	− 15.8

it took 278 yen to buy a dollar, but subsequently the yen was sharply appreciated to 235 yen per dollar at the end of the year.

Some American economists say that the drastic jump in 1981 in the United States' trade deficit with Japan would not have occurred if the value of the dollar had been kept at around 200 yen. On the basis of the international competitiveness of products, the yen should have been quoted at higher levels because inflation is lower and the rate of productivity rise is higher in Japan than in the United States. But the high level of U.S. interest rates increased the gap between Japanese and American interest rates, with the result that dollars began flowing out of Japan into the United States, leading to the weakening of the yen against the dollar. The cheaper yen helped Japanese exports while discouraging imports. The Japan-U.S. trade imbalance grew as a result. Thus foreign exchange rates led to a dichotomy between the competitiveness of products and the movement of capital.

Meanwhile, some are of the view that the yen is weak because Japan has not sufficiently liberalized capital transactions, thus refusing to make the yen an international currency. This charge may be justified from a long-term viewpoint. In the short term, however, it is undeniable that the measures taken by the Japanese government in the spring of 1982 to liberalize capital transactions combined with the rising interest rate in the United States encouraged the outflow of yen, which led to the weakening of the Japanese currency. We fully understand that America's high interest rates are the result of the United States' money policy to combat inflation. But we cannot understand why the rate has to remain high when inflation has been forced down to a relatively mild 5 percent. The high U.S. interest rates are a major factor for America's, and for that matter the world's, recession. In this context, we welcome the recent fall in the U.S. interest rates.

The Closed Market

Particularly in recent years, there has been growing criticism of the closed nature of the Japanese market. More and more arguments are being heard that the closed nature of the Japanese market is a major cause of the trade surplus Japan has built up with its trading partners. Despite historical and cultural factors, which stand in the way of opening its market to foreign goods, Japan has continued its efforts to open its market to foreign imports. The progress made in this direction is apparent when the situation today is compared with that of 10 or 20 years ago. In May 1982 Japan decided to move up by two years the across-the-board tariff reductions agreed to in the Tokyo Round of multilateral trade negotiations, remove or lower 67 nontariff barriers, set up the Office of Trade Ombudsman to deal with foreign suppliers' complaints, and take other measures to open its market. These steps are being implemented one by one.

Japan is a parliamentary democracy. In my view, it deserves praise for taking these steps despite the host of complaints politicians are receiving from constituents whose interests are adversely affected by the moves. The Japanese government intends to continue negotiations with the United States concerning the relaxation of residual import restrictions and the expansion of import quotas and to enforce what is agreed on. In the United States it is often said that Japan should take dramatic steps to open its market. Social tradition and custom, however, dictate that Japan make decisions by consensus. For this reason it is difficult to make any dramatic decision. But I believe that Japan's continued efforts to open its market and its policy of persisting in such efforts in the future deserve favorable evaluation by foreign countries. For example, imports of beef from the United States more than doubled and those of citrus fruits increased by 50 percent between 1978 and 1982. In 1981 Japan bought 60 percent of U.S. beef exports and 40 percent of citrus fruits exports.

At his 1983 New Year's press conference Prime Minister Yasuhiro Nakasone stressed his determination to take comprehensive and dramatic measures to remove the remaining import barriers. He also stated that by these and other measures he expected that Japan would not be criticized anymore as "unfair" in its trade policy.

There is also criticism of the fact that the ratio of manufactured products in Japan's total imports is around 24 percent, which is low compared with the United States and European countries. The ratio temporarily dipped in the wake of drastic oil price increases. But with the economy's absorption of the effects of the higher oil prices, the ratio has returned to the trend of increasing yearly. The very structure of its economy requires Japan to import massive amounts of food, energy resources, and raw materials. Even if Japan doubled the ratio of manufactured products in its total imports, it would not be able to reduce its imports of food and raw materials. The increased imports of manufactured products and undiminished imports of food and raw materials would require Japan to step up its exports by some $30 billion to pay for the increased imports. Such an export drive by Japan would exacerbate trade friction.

These circumstances notwithstanding, opening its market is in Japan's own interest, and accordingly, Japan should cooperate in strengthening the free trade system based on the General Agreement on Tariffs and Trade (GATT). If the present rules of free trade are lost, requiring countries to negotiate ad hoc on individual cases of trading and transactions, every country stands to lose. It is necessary to increase the resilience of GATT management, and in compliance with changes in competitive advantage among countries, both importing and exporting countries will be required to share the pains of adjustment. Countries needing time to adjust should be allowed a reasonable period in which to do so. We in Japan have been watching with concern the development in the U.S. Congress of so-called reciprocity bills. The testimony by U.S. Trade Representative William Brock in March 1982 explaining the position of the administration by pointing out the necessity of abiding by existing multilateral agreements was most encouraging.

We are fully aware of the criticism that Japan's recent economic growth, which has been heavily dependent on exports, is undesirable from the viewpoint of promoting the harmonious development of the world economy. It is true that both in 1980 and 1981 Japan's growth in gross national product (GNP) was heavily based on an increase in external demand. Reducing interest rates to encourage private sector investment, however, involves the risk of intensifying trade friction because it will widen the interest gap between Japan and the United States and weaken the yen on the world's foreign exchange markets. Looking at the domestic aspects, to stimulate the economy by pumping in treasury money would be difficult and ill-timed now, for several reasons. Government finance has been in deficit for some years, and the government's outstanding public debt has reached 40 percent of

GNP. In fiscal year 1982, 30 percent of the budget expenditure constituted deficit spending, and the government publicly pledged to rid itself of this bulging deficit as soon as possible. Due to the worldwide recession and Japan's voluntary export restraints—in auto exports to the United States and auto, TV, and machine tool exports to Europe—Japan's export performance has recently shown a definite slump, and the figure for the first half of 1982 was 10 percent below that of the prior year. As a result of sluggish exports and the government's measures to expand domestic demand, 1982 has seen a domestic demand-oriented growth.

Linking Trade and Defense

One of the causes of friction in Japan-U.S. relations is the feeling in the United States that Japan should assume a larger share of its own defense, commensurate with its increased economic power. Some Americans argue that Japan, by spending only about 1 percent of its GNP for defense compared with the 7 percent spent by the United States, is investing the funds saved on defense in private industries so that Japanese exports will be more competitive on the world market. But the main reason for the relatively high level of private investment in Japan is not so much the difference in defense spending between Japan and the United States as the Japanese people's high propensity to save—20 percent compared with 6 percent for the American people.

After World War II, Japan declared in its new constitution that it would not use force as a means of settling international disputes. The country subsequently adopted the basic policy of improving its self-defense only within the framework of an exclusively defensive and nonnuclear capability. For Japan to participate in a collective security arrangement would require a constitutional amendment, which requires passage by a two-thirds majority in the national legislature followed by a national referendum. I do not see such a likelihood in the near future. We understand that U.S. government authorities have agreed to Japan's basic policy of improving its defense capability. From their past experience, the majority of Japanese people fervently hope that nuclear weapons will never again be used. We hope that the United States and the Soviet Union will successfully negotiate a large-scale reduction of nuclear weapons that will lead to worldwide disarmament.

Although Japan will never have the capability to attack other countries, it will continue its efforts, with the use of high technology, to guarantee its capability to defend itself effectively, with the help of the Japan-U.S. Security Treaty, if attacked by a foreign country. The United States may not be satisfied with the speed with which Japan undertakes to improve its defense. But this is an issue that must be judged in light of the world situation, and one that requires a national consensus. Sudden and sharp increases in defense expenditures may destabilize domestic politics and invite suspicions of neighboring Asian countries.

In parallel with its effort to strengthen self-defense capability, Japan should direct its vast economic power to world development, especially through assistance to developing countries in such fields as increasing the production of food and energy and developing such infrastructures as transportation and communication. Japan has more than fulfilled former Prime Minister Takeo Fukuda's pledge to double Official Development Assistance (ODA) in the three years ending in 1980. Former Prime Minister Zenko Suzuki has publicly declared a plan that would increase the ODA total for the five years ending with 1985 to more than double the total for the preceding five years. I personally think it is desirable that Japan accelerate this plan and become, in the not too distant future, the world's largest aid donor. Moreover, Japanese companies, instead of just exporting their products, should enter as often as possible into business connections with foreign companies to create job opportunities abroad by building factories in host countries and to share profits with foreign business partners. In fact, there are more than 200 factories with Japanese participation in the United States and they are creating employment for 65,000 persons directly. Further expansion in this area is expected.

In November 1982, a new cabinet was formed with Yasuhiro Nakasone as prime minister. Both domestic and international problems are likely to burden the new cabinet but there are expectations that the new prime minister will take a more articulate policy stance than his predecessors. He announced that the improvement of Japan-U.S. relations is the highest priority issue for his cabinet. It is hoped that broader understanding on the part of both parties will produce a better relationship in the years to come.

Japan and the United States are bound together not only by common economic interests but also by common political values, such as free elections, freedom of speech, and respect for human rights. Japanese prime ministers have repeatedly stated that Japan-U.S. relations are the backbone of Japanese diplomacy. U.S. presidents have consistently declared that relations with Japan form the basis of America's Asian policy and have stressed Japan's importance as a democratic partner. It would be most unfortunate if the relations between these two countries were to suffer due to economic friction and mutual mis-understandings. Both nations must strive to maintain and develop their friendly relations by deepening mutual understandings from a long-range and comprehensive viewpoint. I hope that the Japan-U.S. rela-tionship will develop into a truly productive partnership.

NOTE

This article is an adapted and updated version of a speech Saburo Okita gave last year to members of the National Press Club in Washington, and was originally published by the Institute for Domestic and International Policy Studies.

U.S. National Security and the Third World

Brent Scowcroft et al.

This panel on U.S. National Security and Third World Policy was con-vened in the hope that a group of private citizens representing a variety of disciplines could define a more comprehensive and coherent national approach to the countries of the developing world. There was total consensus within the panel on the importance of the task and on the urgency of the need to improve the way in which the Third World is incorporated into U.S. national policy considerations. The perfor-mance of the panel, however, inevitably fell short of the aspiration of its members for a variety of reasons, not the least of which was the difficulty, if not the impossibility, of accomplishing such an ambitious task. The discussions of the group, as reflected in this report, were articulate in defining the growing importance of the Third World to important U.S. interests, and in revealing the artificiality of the term "Third World" in describing so disparate a group of political entities. The difficulty of clearly defining a Third World relationship to U.S. needs and purposes became increasingly apparent. The discussion did not, therefore, result in a clear consensus on recommendations for a course of action to cope with the issues involved.

The panel's deliberations have only scratched the surface of a complex subject of major importance for the United States. A number of significant and specific issues within this subject area need further analysis and recommendation. Even as the importance of the Third World grows, aid from the United States dwindles, and its purposes seem to become increasingly vague or unconvincing. Does the United States provide aid primarily to acquire or sustain friends, to alleviate hunger, to promote human rights or other political or social goals, or to assist in economic development? If the latter is our goal, is it development for its own sake? Is aid a way to increase the appetite for U.S. imports on the assumption that economic growth promotes stability, if not democracy? Or is aid given for other reasons?

What should be the balance between governmental assistance and reliance on private enterprise? If the emphasis is to be on private enterprise—because private capital flows will go to areas where the environment is most attractive, not necessarily where the economic or political need is greatest—to what extent and how should the government intervene to try to influence the flow of investment? What should be the balance between bilateral and multilateral aid and to what extent does it matter? How can Third World debt be managed in a way that neither forces default nor imposes an austerity that threatens political stability?

It is entirely possible that this subject cannot be managed adequately at the Third World level of aggregation. And the deliberations of the panel were not extensive enough to resolve that question. What is apparent is that the United States has not yet clearly identified its various objectives in this important group of countries, carefully analyzed the available tools to assist in the attainment of those goals (such as aid, technology transfer, trade, etc.), or devised a comprehensive approach for dealing with the subject.

The panel did not have sufficient time to deal with these and other important issues relating to U.S. policy toward the developing world in a comprehensive manner. If this report, however rudimentary in terms of the dimensions of the task, serves at least to outline the nature and significance of the issues involved and identifies some of the elements requiring resolution, the efforts of the panel will have been well worthwhile.

Background

The panel was convened in the conviction that a broad and realistic view of basic U.S. national interests urgently requires a fresh approach to the developing nations of the Third World. Fundamental changes over the course of past decades have irreversibly transformed the relationship between the United States and the remainder of the

globe. In particular, these changes have served to highlight and intensify a steadily growing interdependence among U.S. security interests,
domestic political and economic factors, and the totality of this nation's international relationships. It is the panel's view that the Third
World has emerged as a significant, yet generally under-appreciated,
component of this matrix.

That the United States no longer stands apart from, or comfortably superior to, the other members of the international system is now
clear. Such pressing national tasks as revitalization of our national
economy and a substantial upgrading of our defense capabilities are
not only intimately related to one another, they are also inextricably
linked to such matters as the European Economic Community (EEC)
tariff structure, exports for the newly industrializing countries, petroleum production levels in the Persian Gulf, NATO military spending, the political stability of Egypt, and socioeconomic conditions in
Central America.

As a result, the United States finds itself approaching a new level
in its international relationships. No longer playing from a position of
unrivaled strength or relative isolation, it must devote far greater conscious attention to the intelligent application of its still vast resources.
It must formulate a coherent and sustainable national strategy that
grasps the complex interrelationships among various national objectives. And it must more effectively mobilize its resources so that they
are applied to appropriate tasks in an integrated manner.

Although the necessary debate over America's future course is
imperfectly joined and far from concluded, there seems to be a growing appreciation of the linkages among national security, the domestic
economy, and U.S. relationships with other major powers of the industrialized world. But it is the distinct impression of this Panel that
there exists a serious danger that the developing nations—which com-
prise the vast majority of mankind—will be left out of our considerations.

In considerable measure, the difficulty in factoring the Third
World into our considerations stems from the prevalence of obsolete
and ineffective attitudes toward this highly disparate group of nations.
During past decades, mainstream foreign policy thinkers have substantially discounted the importance of the Third World countries to the
central purposes of this nation. Our day-to-day relations with these
states have thus been left in the hands of a "development community,"
whose perspectives and policies, however supportive of U.S. interests
in their broadest context, have not contributed to an operational sense
of the importance of these areas to U.S. foreign policy interests. The
lack of policy-oriented interest and of tangible returns has given rise to

the widespread impression that the Third World is to a large extent irrelevant to basic American interests and is essentially a "charity" burden that the United States has chosen to bear.

At the present time these obsolescent and erroneous attitudes constitute a serious and potentially dangerous impediment to the design and implementation of a national strategy equal to the challenges of forthcoming decades. The importance to the United States of many areas in the increasingly heterogeneous Third World, both intrinsically and in the context of other problems and relationships, has increased enormously and will continue to do so in the foreseeable future. Far from being irrelevant and burdensome to the United States, many of our Third World relationships are critically important, and an effective approach to them is an integral component of any viable national strategy. In fact, if based upon proper understanding and implemented with sufficient discernment and skill, U.S. policy toward Third World nations can provide significant assistance in the pursuit of the wider political, economic, and security objectives of this nation.

It is toward the exploration of this key void in U.S. policy that the panel has addressed its concern. The intention has not been to provide detailed and binding answers, rather, it has been to sketch briefly a compelling rationale for markedly heightened U.S. attention to the diverse pattern of our Third World relations, to diagnose why the United States has had difficulty in coming to grips with this broad area of concern, and to offer some general prescriptions on how to make that attention more effective.

The Third World and U.S. Interests

Precisely defining what constitutes the Third World is particularly difficult today. The enormous and growing diversity of this grouping—in culture, interests, and levels of development—has fostered a welter of new classification schemes and profound questioning as to whether the term, Third World, retains any conceptual validity. While appreciating these considerations, the Panel has found the term a convenience in describing a host of diverse nations that have begun serious participation in the modern international system only during recent decades. This grouping is characterized principally by a lack of organic attachment either to the Western industrial community or the Soviet Union and its affiliated group of states and by a relatively low level of socioeconomic development.

However conceived, the Third World was never a very homogeneous grouping. But during the 1960s and early 1970s, Third World opinion did appear more unified on the need for a joint pursuit of policies that could extricate them from great power dominance and contention and that could promote their collective development by means of a general reform of the international political and economic systems.

Despite some enduring similarities, over time, important changes within the developing nations and in the nature of the international system have highlighted existing differences and spurred a process of increasing diversification among the Third World states. There now exist clear and growing differences within this grouping with respect to levels of and prospects for development; values, ideology, and political preferences; national interests; and personal, ethnic, religious, and national allegiances and animosities.

Certain Third World states—notably the petroleum exporters and the Newly Industrializing Countries (NICs)—have exerted powerful economic influence on the world scene. Some nations have managed to fulfill the basic needs of their peoples, while still others seem condemned to long-term, and perhaps worsening, misery. In some cases there is progress and growing self-confidence—in others, stagnation, violence, and even disintegration. A number of Third World states have opted to continue a group approach to international affairs, while others now prefer a more nationally autonomous course of action. Some have sought closer association with one or the other of the two big power blocs. Nevertheless, the Third World states still generally share common concerns and perspectives on a whole range of international issues and often speak and act as if they were a more truly homogenous group. Thus, the United States is faced with the need to recognize the vast and growing differences among Third World nations and to allocate limited resources and attention to those most important to U.S. national interests, while still taking their communality—and aspirations toward communality—into policy calculations.

The possibility of large-scale conflict, involving a nuclear exchange between the major powers of the globe, still constitutes the most dramatic threat to the basic interests of the United States. But large-scale conflict is not the only danger. Vulnerable sources of supply and communication, terrorism, insurgencies, local wars, increasingly severe economic and technological competition, and, over the longer run, problems of population, food, energy, and the environment, raise a specter that may be even more real. And the resulting possibilities of economic decline, military impotence, political isolation, and psychological demoralization may prove virtually as dangerous to basic U.S. and general Western interests.

Guarding against such contingencies requires an active and effective American policy toward a substantial number of Third World countries. Economically, some are major sources of the raw materials indispensable to the continued functioning of the American economy. Approximately one-third of our imports come from these nations. A number of Third World states are also important customers and loci of investment opportunity. Containing a rapidly growing segment of the world's population, they also represent a significant component of the world economic growth potential. Exports to these nations now account for well over one-third of the U.S. total, while more than one-quarter of all U.S. investment abroad is to be found within their borders.

The cumulative indebtedness of these nations, now amounting to well over $600 billion, has become a key, but increasingly fragile, element in the maintenance of international financial stability, as the current world debt crisis amply demonstrates. In addition, it should be noted that a number of Third World countries—Saudi Arabia, Brazil, South Korea, Taiwan, and Mexico, for example—are becoming individually significant economic performers whose policies and problems can have a definite impact. And, overall, growing worldwide interdependence, particularly in economic and financial terms, has reached the stage where the international system as a whole cannot function effectively without the truly broad-based participation of its component parts. It is now quite clear that it must include a substantial number of the key nations-actors of the Third World.

Militarily, many of these states represent—or about—sensitive strategic assets either in geography or in lines of transport and communication. Conflict in the Middle East, Central America, Southern Africa, or South Asia can have direct consequences for U.S. security as well as a possible impact upon our position vis-a-vis the Soviet Union. In addition, a steady worldwide proliferation of conventional military and nuclear technologies carries with it the implication that individual Third World states may be capable of assuaging, aggravating, or generating serious U.S. security concerns.

Another matter affecting U.S. security interests in the Third World is the growing tide of population movement in the direction of the United States. Difficult economic conditions, political instability, and outright conflict in certain Third World areas will serve to augment these flows—perhaps massively. If U.S. policy cannot deal effectively with the root causes, this flow will inevitably lead to expanding foreign communities within our borders that will prove difficult to assimilate or to the adoption of harsh immigration control measures. Such measures could create difficulties at home and prejudice our relationship to the rest of the globe.

On the political level, the policies Third World states adopt can contribute to the resolution of world problems and the achievement of our interests or can complicate our position enormously. Certain issues—such as immigration, population, and pollution control, and the role that U.S. interests can play in the effective development of world resources—will often be determined directly between the United States and various Third World states or in forums, such as the United Nations, where Third World opinion is crucial. Questions affecting the relationships among the United States, the other industrial democracies, and the Soviet Union can also be decisively affected by Third World conditions, views, and capabilities.

Finally, the Third World presents an interesting psychological dimension. It is possible to contend that events that may not directly touch material U.S. interests are of no concern to this country. But, psychologically, an important country that has no vision of its constructive relevance to such a large segment of the remainder of the international system must function at a decided disadvantage in comparison with nations that do possess such a unifying and energizing view.

It is idle to question whether the nations of the Third World are significant in and of themselves or only in the context of other major powers. The world must now be seen as a strategic whole. A substantial number of Third World states are important to us both directly and in the context of our global power relationships—the linkage being inextricable. To a growing extent, our U.S. national interests are directly tied to our relations with many of these nations across a broad economic, political, military, and psychological spectrum. In turn, our relationships with these states often significantly affect our position vis-a-vis more powerful nations, as well as our ability to achieve other national goals.

Toward an Integrated Third World Strategy

The United States, as a nation, has singular difficulty in articulating and implementing a comprehensive strategy toward the rest of the world. This country's traditions, the pluralistic nature of its society, and the division of power within its government all militate against the generation of such a conceptual overarching framework. Nevertheless, current circumstances, both at home and abroad, require that the United States take significant steps toward a comprehensive strategy. U.S. policy toward the Third World suffers acutely in this regard. The Panel has come to the conclusion that important changes in U.S. attitudes and practices are urgently needed to insure the integrations of Third World countries into an American world view that is sufficiently comprehensive to deal with problems on a long-term, global basis, yet sufficiently flexible to accommodate the widely differing circumstances to be found in our heterogeneous international system.

Awareness

As we have mentioned, the bifurcated manner in which Americans tend to view security and major foreign policy questions, on the one hand, and the Third World on the other, is one of the most fundamental problems. National security matters and the "larger" issues on the American foreign policy agenda have generally been contemplated in isolation from Third World questions—and even by different segments of our foreign policy establishment. The term "national security" immediately calls to mind nuclear weapons; modern, large-scale conventional forces; the Soviet Union; and a number of constantly changing hot spots. Those who are principally concerned with such matters constitute a national security community that is, all too often, oblivious to the relationship of Third World countries to these pressing security concerns. Conversely, Third World affairs are commonly—if incorrectly—seen to involve such technical and uninspiring issues as investment, trade, aid, and humanitarian questions that are often subsidiary to, or absent from deliberations on national security questions. These matters are ordinarily the purview of a development community that focuses on issues such as economic growth, social development, basic human needs, and relief activities rather than balance of power and national security considerations.

Thus, in normal times, American policy toward the Third World has tended to proceed substantially on a "developmentalist" basis, to pursue policies more or less in isolation from the more central concerns of domestic and foreign security policy. Consequently, U.S. Third World policy is too often perceived by Americans as a somewhat naive exercise in charity which, even in the best of times, can muster only tenuous political support. The increasing difficulties that traditional foreign assistance programs have encountered in Congress during recent years reflect this clearly. The United States now finds itself near the bottom of the list of OECD nations in percentage GNP devoted to overseas assistance. In times of crisis, however, the opposite may occur, and particular Third World countries may be overwhelmed by attention from economic, political, and security policy specialists who have virtually no grounding in the affairs of these nations nor an appreciation of their internal problems and political dynamics. Thus,

U.S. policy toward the Third World has a strong tendency to oscillate between lack of generalized attention and belated overreaction that employs means of tenuous relevance to local conditions.

The prevailing image of developing nations as simple charity cases unrelated to basic U.S. security concerns must change. The first step in this regard should be a broad-based effort to raise the awareness of the American policy community and the public at large of the enhanced importance of effective interaction with a number of Third World countries—and the particular nature of their problems—in terms of basic U.S. foreign and security interests.

If properly conceived and executed, U.S. Third World policy can be an effective and, in some instances, indispensable tool in the pursuit of this nation's security interests. An efficacious Third World policy can contribute to American security policy in ways that an arms policy alone is simply incapable of doing. At this juncture in international affairs, the economic health and security interests of this nation clearly require a favorable relationship with a substantial number of Third World nations. The forging of an appropriate policy framework requires a perceptive, long-term perspective capable of taking initiatives that match U.S. strengths and interests with the diverse needs of Third World nations.

While not discounting our liabilities in dealing with Third World problems, we should also be aware that our advantages are substantial. In addition to the attractiveness of our political system, which has survived decades of anti-American rhetoric, we have enormous resources in such fields as agriculture; business administration; nutrition; communications; data-processing; health and population planning; a whole range of scientific and technological capabilities; energy and resources planning; manpower development; and soil, water, and forest management. Furthermore, our resources and skills apart, access to U.S. markets and capital is critical to the prospects of developing nations.

The Soviet Union, by contrast, cannot compete in most of these areas. Because of its own economic weakness and unwillingness to commit resources, except where it can obtain an immediate and tangible quid pro quo, the Soviet Union has contributed little to economic development in the Third World. Even in comparison with other industrialized states, the United States remains in a highly competitive position when it does not unduly restrict itself.

Politically, there appears to be an increasing awareness among Third World states that the Soviet Union and not the United States represents the basic threat to their independence. The United States is a power that can live with diversity in the international community. It is the Soviet Union that has few international associates, except for those highly constrained subordinates it attempts to use in support of its ambitious designs. At base, the United States has a far greater ability—in its own enlightened self-interest—to contribute to the political autonomy and economic development that are the basic objectives of most Third World nations. Our comparative advantage is obviously greatest in nonmilitary areas, and we should seek to emphasize economics, communication, education, science and technology, and democratic institution-building, while not neglecting the relevance of our military capabilities to irreducible Third World security needs.

Realism

In addition, a greater degree of realism, both with respect to ourselves and the nature of the Third World, must undergird our policy toward these nations. When disinterested, American policy has traditionally seemed to operate on the premise that expending a bit of philanthropic effort should be sufficient to keep developments in the Third World more or less in line with U.S. interests. On the other hand, when American concern has been aroused, there has emerged the apparent expectation that Third World realities can be rapidly transformed to conform with our values and objectives. American policy has also frequently shown itself to be unrealistic in terms of its expectations of its own citizens. The course of events over recent decades clearly demonstrates that this country simply cannot be expected to support, on a long-term basis, policies that are substantially inconsistent with the nature of our institutions, that are insufficiently well-grounded in concrete American interests, and that are neither understood nor broadly supported by our political leadership and attentive public opinion.

Current circumstances require that a balanced, well-focused sense of our own national interests be the ultimate arbiter of our foreign policy. Without abandoning our values or our concern for the ideal of general development, we must ensure that the limited resources available to our Third World policy be better marshalled and more effectively controlled and allocated in terms of the most important interests of this country.

In this regard, realism requires that we do not base our policies on purely idealistic or ideological lines, but rather that we make careful distinctions among the diverse nations of the Third World on a substantially practical basis. Some countries are simply more important to us than others, but each country is possessed of its own unique characteristics. There may be some Third World states with which, for political or economic reasons, we cannot work in specific areas at particular times. This number should be kept as small as possible, however, and our objections to their conduct purely practical. A frank recognition and admission that we are acting on the basis of our national interests as we conceive them is essential.

We should not believe that American ideals can be realized universally at any time in the foreseeable future. While we must remain faithful to such ideals, our practical objective should be considerably more modest. In the short run, we must strive to show that cooperation with the United States brings positive results and that hostility to its purposes entails disadvantages. And, in the longer term, we must remain confident that our political and economic systems will show themselves superior and worthy of a certain emulation. Our goal, in this respect, is the emergence of viable societies able to stand on their own and capable of making a contribution to stable political evolution and world economic progress. No single and simplistic approach should be expected to encompass the exceedingly complex reality of the Third World. Neither rhetoric nor force will have the enduring impact of example and the careful tending of well thought-out, integrated programs directed to our own needs—programs that, to be effective, must attend to the real needs of Third World nations.

But while undertaking effective programs we must calmly accept the reality that the United States is a uniquely powerful state with a classically liberal, democratic political system, with a conservative foreign policy and a largely capitalistic economic structure. As a purely practical matter, we can be enormously more helpful to states that share our values and our institutional preferences, or that are at least willing to accommodate our needs. Any strategy of meaningful economic assistance to Third World nations must place primary emphasis on American participation in the creation of new wealth rather than utopian schemes based upon charity or redistribution. Any extra assistance should come in the form of support for well-defined political purposes or, in exceptional circumstances, for clearly humanitarian ends.

Consistency and Coordination

Another important deficiency in America's approach to the Third World has been an absence of policy consistency and coordination. Various groups, each with differing interests, manifest concern with and influence upon U.S. foreign policy at different points in time. Radical changes in policy emphasis in successive administrations have been particularly unfortunate with respect to Third World states, especially because they are developing nations. Their developing nature implies that only clearly enunciated and carefully coordinated policies consistently pursued over the long haul offer substantial prospects of assisting these nations and the United States, respectively, to move toward their objectives.

Even when one political point of view is nominally in control of U.S. foreign policy, our various capabilities frequently function with a notable lack of coordination. Organized fundamentally on a domestic basis, the branches of the U.S. government and a welter of federal and even local agencies often contend and duplicate efforts, with inadequate attention to the coherent, efficient implementation of policies that the political leadership may have determined. Moreover, the private sector and various other private institutions frequently, albeit understandably, pursue programs that are not always consistent with national policy, and in fact, are often at odds with it. This is particularly unfortunate in the case of Third World relations because the affairs of these states are treated by a diverse number of governmental agencies—and because, in many cases, private American institutions could be more effective in dealing with them than any combination of government agencies. Although no U.S. government could or should rigidly dictate the activities or relationships of private institutions overseas, consultations and coordination should be encouraged.

Domestically, we must strive for consensus on a Third World policy based on our interests rather than fancy or faction. In the context of efforts to accomplish this on a global basis, we must ensure that our overall policies have an important Third World dimension—a dimension that clearly contributes to overall national security policy and that can and will be carried out in a coherent and consistent manner over the long term. Coherence requires great care and wide consultation in order to design an approach that is effective and that can command widespread, long-term support among critical domestic constituencies and the public at large. Concurrently, a strong effort must be made to harness and coordinate the enormous range of U.S. capabilities toward realization of the objectives of our Third World policy. Foreign policy, generally, and foreign assistance in particular, must be more centrally coordinated and effectively managed. In addition, a much greater effort must be made to engage and support the enormous capabilities of the private sector overseas for identifying commercial opportunities, for promoting foreign interest in American investment, products, and services, and for harnessing these activities in support of wider U.S. interests. Also, the value of the private voluntary organizations (PVOs), international associations, universities, and research institutes are frequently underestimated. While attempting to mobilize our capabilities more effectively across the board, we should recognize that the basic pluralism of our society is itself an advantage in dealing with complex and often contradictory Third World realities.

Conclusions

The basic conclusion of the panel's deliberations is that there is a clear and increasingly urgent need for U.S. policy to view and address a substantial number of issues—heretofore considered "Third World questions"—in terms of this nation's basic foreign and security interests. Such matters as the trade and debt aspects of development, the cultivation of bilateral relations with a number of emerging powers, and the provision of long-term support for lesser nations situated in critical geostrategic areas must be elevated to the major agenda of U.S. foreign and security policy concerns. They should be treated on a realistic, integrated basis with the other pressing issues to be found there.

This effort can be justified by the direct relationship between these questions and basic U.S. interests. A major obstacle, however, is that the perceptions of American elites have lagged badly behind the rapid pace of change in the international system. A substantial effort, therefore, will be required to raise the awareness of the American foreign policy process to these new realities—and to design and implement fresh approaches appropriate to the needs of the present and the future.

Bold leadership by the executive and within the Congress and a broad-based campaign aimed at clearly demonstrating the growing interrelationship between basic U.S. interests and objectives on the one hand and various Third World relationships on the other is probably the only manner in which the necessary changes in perception could be achieved and sustained. Presidential addresses on this theme and the establishment of a high-level group of concerned citizens charged with documenting the case, mobilizing public opinion, and distilling concrete policy recommendations would represent highly positive steps in this regard. Any new approach should also be accompanied by considerable thought and planning involving:

1. placing in explicit priority America's Third World concerns;

2. conducting a detailed inventory of available policy instruments and a careful matching of means to ends;

3. devoting careful and intelligent attention to reforming old institutions and practices (and the possible creation of new ones) to see that capabilities are fully mobilized and coordinated and that future

initiatives are followed through and sustained. This effort would, of necessity, have to involve both a sharpened focus and improved coordination within the U.S. government and a more effective employment of potential resources outside our government.

On the governmental side, primary attention should be given to focusing the responsibility for Third World affairs and assuring that these matters are fully integrated into the process by which U.S. foreign and security policy are made. At the most general level, an effort should be made to design mechanisms that would at once enhance the discretion of the executive and improve the efficacy of consultation with the Congress. Within the executive branch, strong consideration should be given to specific definition of responsibility for the conduct of relations with Third World nations. This might include eliminating the distinction between developmental assistance and support funds, increasing their integration with military assistance, and concentrating all foreign assistance matters in a single office. In budgetary matters, some manner should be found of melding Third World policy into broader foreign security policy deliberation, while assuring that all foreign and security needs are given more systematic, integrated, and effective consideration in the process of resource allocation.

Some institutionalized form of foreign and security guidance for the Office of Management and Budget (OMB) or even a move to establish a unified budget for foreign and security affairs (in which important Third World questions would be included) could be considered in this regard. Only when the real needs of American policy in the Third World are adequately addressed can the necessary support be generated to sustain and improve the effectiveness of such critical programs as the United States Information Agency, trade promotion, military assistance groups, and various other efforts to promote stability and development and enhance scientific, technological, educational, and political interchange with key Third World areas. Government policymakers must also be encouraged to employ more effectively the enormous and diverse strengths of the private sector that give the United States such an enormous comparative advantage.

To coordinate an improved U.S. policy toward the Third World with institutions outside the U.S. government, a great number of initiatives can be constructively undertaken. A better understanding of the international financial institutions' relationship to U.S. interests should be a prime objective. Such an integrated relationship can work toward long-term infrastructural development efforts and large scale emergency loans for which these institutions are particularly suited. The more immediate day-to-day economic objective should place increased emphasis on involving the U.S. private sector whenever possible. The basic purpose in this regard is to identify governmental policies that might more effectively promote U.S. business activity abroad, while at the same time improve consultation between policymakers and the private sector—all with a view toward harnessing U.S. economic capabilities to the service of this nation's foreign and security policy around the globe.

Serious attention should also be accorded to improved and enhanced governmental efforts to multiply policy efficacy by working with and through private cultural, scientific, and educational institutions. Political parties and labor unions should be encouraged to work with their counterparts to promote the establishment and strengthening of Third World institutions and infrastructures. These steps, together with PVOs, which have programs in fields ranging from general promotion of international understanding to concrete charity and relief activities, would immensely supplement U.S. government policy initiatives aimed at establishing a more substantial, constructive U.S. presence in critical Third World areas.

Nationalism, Nations, and Western Policies

Hugh Seton-Watson

Nationalism is one of the two great plagues of late twentieth-century man, being equalled only—if at all—by communism, not only as a source of worry to politicians but as a direct threat to the personal security or even existence of most members of the human race. Yet, the nature of the phenomenon is widely misunderstood in Western countries, whether one thinks of government officials, ministers, intellectuals, or the general public. The misunderstanding is itself a consequence of the inflation of words, pursued by the mass media with a reckless enthusiasm, in no way inferior to that with which our banks of issue inflate our currencies, and with no less deadly effect.

"Nationalism" in common parlance has come to mean little more than selfishness. A "nationalist" policy is one pursued by a foreign government (not, of course, by one's own) which ignores or overrides the interests of other governments or peoples. A "nation" may be any sort of political, legal, or even geographic unit (as in the frequently used American phrase "across the nation," meaning simply the geographical area of the United States). Yet selfish rulers and policies have existed since the dawn of history, as has the habit of calling one's neighbors selfish when they obstruct one's aims. A nation may overlap with, but is not the same thing as, a state, or a clan, or a religious group, or a language group, or the population of a territory.

After many years of study, both in books and in real life, I have been forced to conclude that there can be no precise scientific definition of either nationalism or nation; but at least the approximate boundaries of these phenomena can be drawn, and the margin of error and confusion reduced. The word "nationalism" should be confined to two main meanings: a doctrine about the interests and aims of a nation, and a movement to achieve these alleged aims (which usually amount to the creation of an independent state, or the union of several territories in one state, or the diffusion among the inhabitants of a state of a sense of forming a nation). As for the word "nation," it is easier to say what it is not than what it is. It is not a state. It is true that there are some outstanding historical examples of how the process of formation of a state and of a sense of belonging to a nation developed simultaneously and interdependently: England and France will serve. But this was not the typical experience, whether in Europe or anywhere else. The process misnamed by so many historians "the rise of the *nation*-state"—which dominates European history from the late-fifteenth to the mid-nineteenth centuries—was in fact "the rise of the *sovereign* state." The inhabitants of many of the early sovereign states did *not* feel themselves to be nations; and many communities which *did* feel themselves to be nations were obliged to break the fetters of existing sovereign states in order to achieve their national aims. This was strikingly true in Central Europe a hundred years ago, and is equally true today in tropical Africa, the Middle East, the Soviet empire, and parts of North America and Western Europe.

A nation is a community of persons living within a state, bound together by a national consciousness. Essentially this is based on a common culture—in which usually religion, language, economics, historical traditions or myths, and love for a specific territory play their parts. However, not all these factors need always be present, and there is a great range of possible admixtures. What is the difference between national consciousness and tribal or clan loyalty? This difficult and important question has no fully satisfying answer. The difference between "nation" and "tribe" is essentially the difference between levels of culture and degrees of intensity with which cultural loyalty is felt. Sometimes the difference can be clearly seen: for example, between the Scottish nation and clan Campbell (not that this distinction has not been blurred in the past, with fatal consequences for thousands of men and women!). In others, it is not at all clear: are the Yorubas of Nigeria a "tribe" or a "nation"? The truth is that all attempts to allocate the one label or the other to a particular community must be subjective: neither from within the community nor from outside it are judges likely to be objective. The type of argument: "my group is a nation; yours is a tribe," or "I am a patriot; you are a nationalist" (or "chauvinist") is all too familiar, and gets us nowhere.

It is indeed arguable that nationalism is a curse for modern man. The crimes committed in its name are legion, though it is also true that it has been a source of great cultural achievements, especially in literature and to some extent in music. However, to rail against fate is not much use to any of us. It is wiser to distinguish between "nationalism" and "national consciousness." Nationalism becomes dangerous and a potential cause of wars when the national consciousness of a significant number of people within one or more states conflicts with the existing frontiers of one or more sovereign states and with the interests of the dominant political class within that state or those states. It is perfectly legitimate for democrats and for reasonable civilized persons in general to object to nationalist fanaticism, but it is foolish to refuse to admit that national consciousness is a powerful force in men's and women's minds, neither good nor bad in itself but potentially constructive or destructive.

It might be convenient for politicians, social scientists, journalists, and the common run of humanity if national consciousness were a minor by-product of the struggle for material prosperity (as the plutocratic-hedonist ethos of the capitalist West would imply) or of the class struggle (as the Marxist-Leninists would have it). But neither view is supported by the historical record or by an unprejudiced look at the world around us today. Certainly the leaders and members of nationalist movements pursue material prosperity, and certainly in many—probably most—nationalist movements class struggle and struggle for national independence have been and are closely interwoven. But this does not mean that national consciousness can be explained away by economic or social doctrines, or that nationalism can be cured (even though its intensity can be temporarily mitigated) by economic growth, peaceful redistribution of incomes, or social revolution. Of this, the history of postwar Canada and of the Soviet Union since 1917 are two outstanding pieces of evidence.

The issue is also often confused by the argument as to whether, in the world of interdependent economies and intercontinental missiles, "the nation state" is an anachronism. There is a strong case against the sovereign state as the basic unit in world politics (but also a strong case in its favor). But whether or not wise statesmanship ought to replace a large number of small sovereign states by a few large regional combinations, the problem of national consciousness and national culture remains. In order to reduce the importance of state frontiers, or even to absorb sovereign states in larger units, it is not necessary to do violence to national consciousnesses, to crush developing or reviving national cultures, or to cause existing nations to believe that their long-established national cultures are being suppressed.

The cliché that nationalism is a cause of wars should perhaps be reformulated to the effect that when deeply felt widespread national consciousness comes into conflict with the boundaries of existing sovereign states and the dogmas of those who rule them, tensions arise which may lead to a danger of war between states.

Situations of this kind frequently recur, and will certainly recur in the future. They deserve more thorough consideration than they receive from Western intellectuals, either in the media or in the academic world. The phenomena of national consciousnesses, and of the fierce reactions produced by attempts to suppress them, should have a larger place in the common fund of practical political wisdom on which Western statesmen draw. Unfortunately, the peculiar traditions and climate of political thinking in those Western countries which have produced the greatest quantity of Western political doctrine, both theoretical and practical, are rather unfavorable to such consideration.

France, England, and America

France is one of the two oldest nations. The main instrument in the creation of French national consciousness was the monarchy, which, despite periodic reverses, succeeded over several centuries in extending its authority to all the "natural frontiers" except the middle and lower Rhine. This process required the brutal destruction of potentially no less brilliant national cultures, especially in the South, where, nevertheless, Occitanian aspirations survived and have made themselves felt in recent years. The monarchy identified itself with relentless centralization, which went still further under the successive republics. It has been forcefully argued that it was not until around 1914 that the conscious French nation became more or less coextensive with the population of France, rural as well as urban (see Eugen Weber,

Peasants into Frenchmen: The Modernization of Rural France 1870-1914 [Stanford University Press, 1976], and even today there are discordant noises at four of the six angles of the hexagon.

The French rulers resigned themselves to the loss of Quebec, the only colony of French settlement, in 1763 and again in 1782. In the new colonies of the nineteenth century, the blessings of French national culture were offered to those natives who could acquire them (though acquisition was impeded by *pieds noirs* and various *petits blancs*); but no other national consciousnesses were respected—until, at the eleventh hour, De Gaulle in a magnanimous gesture renounced France's black Africa. The French political mind still finds it difficult to conceive of national identity as distinct from citizenship in a state— though of course individual French minds have grasped the distinction with penetrating wisdom. The centuries-old obsession of rulers and officials with centralizing uniformity, the anarchic rejection which it provokes from the other France (Left and Right elements being found on both sides of this barricade), and the harmful effects of both for Frenchmen have often been discussed by Frenchmen, never perhaps so brilliantly as in recent years. It is argued again, with great insight and considerable originality, in Alain Peyrefitte, *Le mal français* (Paris: Librairie Plon, 1976).

Yet whatever the gaps in French culture and the fallacies in French political thinking, one great advantage the French still possess: they know that they are Frenchmen and that the French nation stands above all others. Nothing has ever shaken this conviction, not even in 1870 or 1940, nor can one see when or how anything could.

This can hardly be claimed with equal confidence for the other oldest nation, England. In the formation of English national consciousness, like the French, the monarchy and the state apparatus played a leading part, but another decisive influence was the language. The kings of France made great use of the French language in their centralizing policies: Richelieu founded the *Académie Française;* and in the last stages of the process studied by Eugen Weber, the diffusion of the language through the conscript army and the school was most important. But the role of the English language was relatively greater, even though kings and bureaucrats paid much less attention to it, or to the literature which emerged from it, than did their French equivalents. The English language came into being by the flowing together of Anglo-Saxon and French streams. This new river was in spate by the end of the fourteenth century, from which time, not earlier, the English nation dates. Little over a hundred years later, the English Bible, English Protestant thinking and pamphleteering, English secular poetry, and English piracy on the high seas formed different aspects of the upsurge of English national consciousness, whose militancy under-standably dismayed civilized Europeans. In the seventeenth century the piracy continued, but much of the furious energy of the English was turned upon one another in their various civil wars, wherein they were imitated, with no less talent, by their northern neighbors, the Scots. In the eighteenth century, as we can see now but could not, even as recently as my schooldays, a great change came. The union with Scotland in 1707 created Great Britain, and the annexation of vast lands overseas created the British Empire. The same period saw the development of new forms of government and of political liberty, whose pace accelerated with the great reforms of the nineteenth cen-tury. The unexpected and fateful result was that by the mid-twentieth century politically conscious persons in England had ceased to think of themselves as Englishmen: their loyalties were to the British Empire, to British Democracy, or even at times to the British Army, not to mention the Royal Navy and the Royal Air Force. At a lower level there was Manchester United football club or the Transport and Gen-eral Workers' Union; but to look for an object of loyalty in 1978 pre-ceded by the adjective "English" is a vain search. But this process did not affect the geographical periphery: Scots, Welsh, and Irish re-mained Scots, Welsh, and Irish.

The Irish were victims for centuries of English oppression, and Ireland was then torn by religious dissension: since the Reformation never won the Irish peasants, the division continued, and even after the English made their rule milder and then cleared out altogether, the religious hatreds remained. Indeed, the departure of the English made inter-Irish hatreds worse: to blame the English after they had gone was a useful way of relieving feelings, but solved no problems.

The Scots, or at least most Scots, can hardly be called victims in the last two centuries: they did well under the British Crown and in the British Empire and the British economy. It was when the British Em-pire withered away and the British economy succumbed to stagflation that the Scots began to think again. In the mid-twentieth century, when things go wrong, modern man blames government, because gov-ernment is assumed to work miracles. Government was in West-minster, so Scots blamed London and the English for their woes. Though the English had stopped feeling English, the Scots remained Scots. Much the same would seem to apply to the Welsh periphery as well. It is a mistake to regard the revival of Scottish and Welsh na-tionalisms as economic phenomena: they reflect national identities, a compound in which admittedly there are very large economic ingre-dients.

All   this,   however,   remains   incomprehensible   to   English bureaucrats (including those Scots and Welsh whose continued loyalty to Britain leads them unconsciously but inextricably to identify Britain with England). They have not the least desire to oppress the Scots. Imperialism is not their motive. They are only too pleased to discuss reforms and liberties, couched in bureaucratic jargon. But when Scots talk of a Scottish nation, these enlightened and high-minded gentlemen simply do not know what they are talking about.

From my piecemeal knowledge of American history, it seems doubtful to me whether the Americans who fought for independence 200 years ago felt themselves to be a nation, or wished to become one. They wanted the liberties of Englishmen; some of them wanted the more far-reaching liberties of which the thinkers of the European Enlightenment talked and wrote; and all of them wanted to be rid of the interference of ignorant busybodies, with supercilious manners and arrogant pretensions who lived 3,000 miles away. Geography, economics, and political radicalism were the motives. But when the war was won and the new republic founded, the process of nation-building had to begin. For the first time a synthetic nation was to be created on the basis of moral and political principles. In this at least, the young United States and the young Soviet Union resemble each other (whatever reservations one may have about some of George Kennan's arguments on the affinities of Americans and Russians). The new republic came into existence, firmly resting on its new Constitution, negro slavery, and the expropriation of the indigenous Amerindians. The founders could not have seen what was coming: half a million dead in a war fought to prevent a third of the population from breaking away to form its own state; millions of Teutons, Slavs, and Latins of Catholic, Jewish, or Baptist faith pouring in year by year; the pullulation of vast new cities and industries; and the emergence of the world's first superpower. But it worked. Success followed on success. The Constitution accommodated fantastic social changes. An American nation was created. From it all, certain sacred dogmas emerged. Equality was good, elites bad—though America's success was due as much to an enlightened, relatively open, self-renewing, but predominantly WASP elite as to anything else. Ethnic groups were bound to be absorbed into the American melting pot, and this was a desirable fate for all ethnic groups—though the distinction was not made between the chances of absorption of uprooted immigrants seeking a new home thousands of miles from their native lands and those of peoples living in compact communities within a hundred miles or so of the metropolis (Francophone Canadians and Montreal, let alone Slovaks and Budapest, Tatars and Kazan, or Azeri Turks and Baku). Most important of all, self-determination was good, but secession was bad: George Washington, Thomas Masaryk, and Ahmed Sukarno were angels of light, but Jefferson Davis, Emeka Ojukwu, and Moise Tshombe were children of darkness.

The French identification of nationality with the uniform, centralized state, the English illusion that national identity is an outworn superstition that will simply fade away, and the American preference for virtuous synthetic patterns make the "progressive" intellectuals of these three leading western countries, and their pupils among the professional politicians, uniquely unfitted for dealing with the national conflicts (as distinct from conflicts between states) which bulk so large in world politics today.

Regional Nationalism

Conflicts between national consciousness and the sovereign state exist today in most parts of the world. They may, or actually do, seriously affect the relations between governments and between the superpowers, thus becoming a danger to world peace, or they may have no such effects. It makes sense to distinguish three regions in which conflicts of this kind have arisen: sub-Saharan Africa, the Soviet bloc, and the western advanced industrial countries. Other regions (the Arab lands, South Asia, Latin America) are also affected, but I shall confine myself here to some examples from the three regions just named, seeking not to sum up each problem, but to note points relevant to my earlier general argument.

The national conflicts of the advanced countries are less obviously dangerous to peace than those of the other two regions, but it would be foolish to ignore them. Ability or failure of the governments concerned to come to terms with the discontented nationalists will affect European and Atlantic security. It will depend largely, though not of course wholly, on the ability or failure of rulers to enter into the minds of nationalists.

From this point of view, it looks, in the autumn of 1978, as if the most promising outlook is in Spain: the Western country which has had for 40 years the most tragic experience of civil war and dictatorship. The government in Madrid and the nationalists in Catalonia seem equally determined to reach agreement. Both appear to understand that the task is to reconcile Catalan national culture with the unity of the Spanish state. Castilians and Catalans have known and quarrelled with each other for centuries. The Catalans have long memories and have not forgotten how their search for foreign protection against

Madrid brought disaster when their patrons abandoned them (1641-1652 and 1705-1714). Both remember the Barcelona revolt of 1934 and the even greater horrors of 1936-1939. Both sides seem to be making great efforts in a conciliatory spirit. This is less true of the Basque situation, in which separatist terrorists are strong enough to keep up a wrecking action. Certainly it is too soon to assume that extremism in either nation or rigid centralist dogma in the Spanish armed forces have been overcome. But difficulties are at least not due to misconceptions.

In Britain, nationalism is less acute than in Spain, but arguably more intractable. The Irish horrors at least are not due to misunderstanding. Everyone knows very well that there is an insuperable conflict between two passionately held beliefs—that there is only one Irish nation, which is being frustrated by a minority of about one-quarter of the population, and, alternatively, that the people of Ulster do not belong to that nation and form a two-thirds majority in their own country. Nothing will persuade the Irish Republican Army, and political inhibitions prevent the British army from using methods ruthless enough to destroy it. The governments in Dublin and London both know that the IRA's main objective is not Ulster but total power in all Ireland, and that if that were achieved, the foreign patrons of the IRA would have struck a deadly blow at naval security in the Atlantic; yet their dependence on the mythology of their voters prevents them from cooperating. Whether the government in Washington understands any of these things is far from obvious.

The problem of Scotland, by contrast, is not at present deadly, yet in the long term it may prove no less painful if no greater wisdom can be found. Scotland is not a region, but a country and a culture. The Scots are not just a people with awkward local economic problems and a desire to grab profits from North Sea oil (though they are that): they are a nation. This the English, especially their bureaucrats, seem incapable of understanding. The reason is not that—as some tartan demagogues will argue—they are imperialists seeking to exploit the Scots; it is that, having lost their own national consciousness as Englishmen or Englishwomen, they are unable to understand how any people of English speech can have a national consciousness of their own. To be a Scot, aware of one's Scottish national identity, need not mean to desire a separate Scottish state. Scottish and English nations lived together rather happily in Great Britain: they should be able to live together in medium-sized (and not necessarily mediocre) Britain. There are probably more Scotsmen living in England than in Scotland, and probably most of these still feel themselves to be Scots. But at Westminster and in Whitehall these things appear to be ignored.

Whitehall produces pages of bureaucratic jargon and plays with soulless words like "devolution." As for Westminster, the first priority for the Labour Party is to maintain the existing system of parliamentary gerrymandering which gives certain Scottish districts with safe Labour majorities a disproportionate representation in the Westminster House of Commons. Provided that the Scottish nationalists are willing to leave Labour its rotten boroughs in Westminster, to enable it to force through its policies of wrecking the hospital and school system of England against the wishes of a majority of the English, then Labour will make concessions—though doubtless it will try hard to stultify their effects at a later stage.

The Quebec problem has some similarity to the Scottish. Here too we have a people with a strong national consciousness facing one which has very little. The difference between Britain and Canada is that the English (as I have argued earlier) once had a strong national consciousness and have lost it, whereas the Anglophone Canadians never had one at all. The Quebec problem is simpler than the Scottish in this sense: that the difference in culture is self-evident, whereas the borderline between the English and Scottish cultures is blurred as a result of the common language. However, the inability of most Anglophones to think themselves into the minds of Quebecois, and of many Quebecois to think themselves into the concept of a common Canadian homeland stretching from ocean to ocean, remain facts. The Canadian example can also be instructive for other North Americans: it is the clearest historical proof of the falsity of the comfortable belief that the example of the United States as an industrial melting pot points the way for the natural and desirable merging of nationalisms in a larger whole. The different ethnic groups which immigrated into the United States after independence consisted of persons who had decided to leave their homelands and live in a new country. In Canada, a large compact population of French-derived culture in Quebec lived next to large compact populations of English-derived culture in Ontario and the Maritimes. In the first case the immigrants wished to be absorbed into a new nation, and industry and school were the instruments by which absorption was achieved (though how fully it has been achieved even in 1978 is still arguable). In the second case, a solid compact community went on living in its homeland and grew into a new nation: industry and school served only to intensify its national consciousness. The urbanized, educated, secularized Quebecois of 1978 are not less but more nationally conscious than the rural semiliterate priest-ridden Quebecois of 1928. This is a historical and social phenomenon which Americans would do well to ponder in order to better understand the problems of more distant lands, and perhaps even of their own.

The possibility of an independent Quebec is also of potential importance for North Atlantic strategy. Such fantasies as a northern Cuba bolstering Soviet Arctic power or an association of four small peace-loving northern democracies (Quebec, Iceland, Scotland, and Norway) miraculously maintaining a disarmed neutrality across the oceans need not be taken very seriously; but there is plenty for politically adult Americans to think about.

Africa

In sub-Saharan Africa one may distinguish between two types of conflict between national consciousness and the sovereign state.

The first type is anti-European or antiwhite. It is directed partly against the former imperial metropolitan nations, feeding on resentment for past actions; partly against the remaining white rulers in the continent—in Rhodesia and South Africa, neither of which is a colony or belongs to an overseas empire; and partly against the United States, as the protector of the former metropolitan countries and as the strongest state of predominantly white population in the world. From this hostility the Soviet Russian whites have escaped insofar as they never held African territories, though there is some evidence that where Soviet advisers of various kinds have been present in considerable numbers, they have provoked a similar resentment among Africans.

The nature and causes of this antiwhite nationalism are fairly clear to everyone, but there is less understanding of the mentalities which resist it. In particular, Westerners tend to forget, or not even to know, that the white South Africans, and in particular the Afrikaner majority of them, are an African nation, with a deep-rooted national consciousness older than that of most black African nations.

The second type of national conflict in Africa is interblack African. Here we get at once into semantic difficulties. Americans and West Europeans tend, in the African context, to reserve the use of the word "nation" for the whole population of each African state, and to describe communities which live side by side with other quite distinct communities within one state, or which sprawl across state boundaries, as "ethnic groups" or "tribes." It is undoubtedly true that there is a qualitative difference between primitive communities of elementary culture, which we may call "tribes," and communities of well-developed culture which are best described as "nations." Yet, as I have argued earlier, it is impossible to draw a scientifically precise dividing line between them. Conflicts between African nations cannot simply be explained away as childish quarrels between backward tribes, artificial hatreds worked up by demagogues, or creations of imperialists resolved to divide and rule. It is easy to understand that the governments of the Organization of African Unity (OAU) should wish to prevent territorial disputes (of which they rather naively believed that the Balkan states of Europe had presented shocking and warning examples) by insisting on the sanctity of existing state frontiers. Unfortunately, wishing, like patriotism, is not enough. King Canute's courtiers no doubt sincerely wished the tidal waters to obey their orders not to advance over the monarch's feet; but as Canute himself had warned them, the sea was stronger than their wishes.

Ethiopia is one of the oldest states in the world (though its boundaries have shifted to and fro during 2,000 years), and it is an unshakable belief of politically conscious Ethiopians that Ethiopian territory includes not only Eritrea but also the eastern provinces of Somali population (which Menelik conquered a century ago, and Ethiopia has thus held for about half as long as the British held India). But imperial dogma is no more defense against political realities than Canute's feet against the tide. The Hungarian rulers at the beginning of this century rightly pointed out that Transylvania had been ruled by Hungarians for over 1,000 years; yet this did not prevent the Rumanian majority in that province from uniting with their kinsmen in the neighbor state Rumania. Attempts to coerce and re-educate Slovaks into becoming Hungarians also failed.

Of course nothing is inevitable in politics until it happens. The Rumanians were not *bound* to win, nor are the Somalis. But so many African states have so many ethnic groups—that is, potential nations—within their borders that we can be quite certain that repetition of ritual incantations about the sanctity of frontiers is not going to solve their problems. Of course, these are *their* problems, not ours. Obviously it cannot be the task of Western governments to solve them. Nevertheless, American policymakers, and those who influence American public opinion through the media, would do well to think seriously about them, and there is not much sign that they are doing so. African governments cannot escape the task of trying to satisfy the divergent cultural needs of their component ethnic groups before these turn into irreconcilable nations demanding separation. Those who ignore this task can expect a rather more drastic treatment than kind King Canute meted out to his courtiers.

Those who most seriously addressed themselves to this problem in the past were the Austrian socialists Renner and Bauer, 70 years ago.

Their warnings and proposals were ignored, and Austria collapsed. Africa in 1978 is obviously different from Austria in 1908, but the hard thinking which is needed for Africa might well be stimulated by a glance at their works. The complacent assumption that new African governments will succeed in "nation-building" by a magic mixture of urbanization, industrialization, and mass mobilization through schools and one-party systems, the whole process to be conducted in most cases in the language of the former colonial rulers, will not get us very far.

The Soviet Empire

The most eloquent refutation of the doctrine that nationalism is a by-product of the class struggle, and will disappear with the destruction of "the bourgeoisie" and the establishment of "socialism," is provided by the history of the Soviet Union itself. The multinational Russian empire of 1917 has become the multinational empire of 1978, buttressed on its western border by an area of multinational Soviet neocolonialism embracing a population about one-half that of the empire itself. The people of this whole vast region, numbering some four hundred million, are officially stated to consist of "socialist nations." This phrase makes sense insofar as the old upper and middle classes have been destroyed or transformed, and those who make or influence policy are predominantly and increasingly children of persons who at least began their working lives as manual workers or peasants.

However, the "socialist nations" have no less powerful national consciousnesses, and no less bitter objections to being dominated by Russians, than did their predecessors, the "feudal nations" or "bourgeois nations." For their part, the Soviet rulers are no less determined to maintain their rule by force and fraud than were their predecessors. With that admirable capacity, which they possess and which Western commentators seem so often to have lost, to see the naked emperor through his fictitious clothes, the Chinese have rightly dubbed them "the new Tsars."

To be sure, Soviet policy differs somewhat from that of the last Tsars. It is not its overriding aim to Russify the non-Russian peoples: rather, the intention is to impose on Russians and others alike the same synthetic totalitarian culture, in essence an amalgam of residual Marxism-Leninism and an imperialist chauvinism which is not explicitly Russian. However, the instruments of the policy are mostly Russian bureaucrats impregnated with that parochial intolerance of any deviation from uniformity, and that absolute lack of generosity toward other outlooks, which has been the mark of their species for the last 500 years. It is also true, and an important truth, that the Russian nation is a victim, not a beneficiary, of this policy, which is a denial of the true tradition of Russian culture as expressed in Orthodox saintliness and in nineteenth century literature. This point, which has been made by Solzhenitsyn with a genius to which a pedestrian historian cannot aspire, needs no elaboration here.

The discontents which the quasi-Russification policies of the Moscow rulers create within the Soviet empire and the Soviet semicolonies constitute one of the main dangers to world peace. There is a direct causal connection between the Soviet "nationality question" and the personal security of every American, French, British, German, or other West European citizen. This connection is worth brief exploration.

Ever since 1945 the Soviet government has not been content with a traditional type of "Great Power sphere of influence" in Eastern Europe, giving Moscow control over the foreign policy of these countries but leaving the management of internal affairs to their peoples. Finland is the one exception to this statement. Elsewhere the Soviet rulers insisted on imposing, by force and fraud, blueprints of their own political institutions and copies, not only of their economic policies, but of their own particular type of bureaucratic planning structure. But this was not enough. National cultures too (including the writing of history and the publication of works of literature, classical as well as contemporary) had to be distorted and crippled in the interests not only of Marxism-Leninism but also of a Great Russian chauvinist view of the world. (Polish, Czech, and Rumanian history and Polish and Rumanian literature have suffered especially). All this added up to a policy of deliberate national humiliation, which was bitterly resented not only by professors of history and literature but also by working men and women in factory and field, to whom the national historical-literary mythology (part truth, part fiction) with which they have grown up at home and at school has been the breath of life for a century and more past. It is this combination of social oppression and national humiliation which has kept Eastern Europe for 30 years in a condition of simmering resentment, boiling up from time to time into violence. Soviet policy has had its plain failures—it has lost Yugoslavia and Albania (whether the recent quarrel between the Albanian leadership, apparently linked with the Gang of Four, and the Chinese leadership of Chairman Hua will lead to a reconciliation between Albania and the Soviet Union is one of the more interesting open questions in this region)—and it has made concessions—to Poland in the treatment of the Catholic Church and the peasants, to Hungary in economic

management, and to Rumania in the presentation of national culture—
but these are only partial, and may well be revoked. The result is that
Eastern Europe, the area of Soviet neocolonialism, remains one of the
most explosive regions in the world; and the fact that the crises of
1953, 1956, 1968, 1971, and 1976 did not spill over into East-West
confrontation is no guarantee that the inevitable future conflicts will
not do so.

Why does the Soviet government persist in these odious, provocative, and dangerous policies when it could get all that it needs for its
security if it were to treat the East European nations as mildly as it
treats Finland? This question cannot be answered with complete certainty, but almost certainly the explanation lies in the multinational
nature of the Soviet empire. If Moscow were to allow Poles to live as
Poles, Hungarians as Hungarians, and so forth, without interference in
their social and economic policies or their national cultures, then the
Ukrainians, Estonians, Tatars, Uzbeks, and dozens of other nations of
the empire would ask for similar treatment. "Well, why not?" an
American may ask. "Why shouldn't the nominally federal Soviet state
be made into a real federation?" At this point attempts at rational
argument with Russians break down. Immediately nightmare visions of
separatism, foreign intervention, and breakup of the Soviet Union
flood the Russian imagination. The non-Russians, the *inorodtsy
(persons of other stock),* must be kept under the Russian yoke, if need
be with the *knut*—this traditional reflex is as automatic and as powerful under Brezhnev as under Nicholas I.

So Eastern Europe has to remain in its explosive condition. For
most Americans and West Europeans, accustomed to the pursuit of the
joys of consumer society and interrupted every few years by a few
minutes of warm sentimental tears for the poor Hungarians and
Czechs, this state of affairs in Eastern Europe is acceptable. But is it
acceptable for the Soviet leaders? In particular, is it acceptable for
those now rising to key posts just below the top in civil government,
the communist party, and the armed forces who do not remember the
horrors of 1941-1945? As they see it, the ferment in Eastern Europe is
caused not by their own policies (which are "scientifically" Marxist-
Leninist), but by constant incitement from the "capitalist" West. Thus
the very existence of the "capitalist" West, by the yearnings which it
maintains in Eastern Europe, appears as the main cause of the vast
drain on Soviet resources for military purposes, which retards material
progress for Soviet citizens, and of which no end is in sight. Yet the
societies of these European capitalist states, and of their protector
across the Atlantic, are demonstrably decadent, the rulers of all of

them are weak and cowardly, and their armed forces are arguably inferior to those of the Soviet Union. However, there is increasing talk in the capitalist world of the need to rearm, and the possibility must be taken seriously that, granted the basic technological inferiority of the Soviet Union, the West may within some years recover a definite military superiority.

The present mood of the Soviet political class, insofar as it may be judged by public statements, alarmingly recalls that of William II's Germany. There is the same fist-thumping bullying boastfulness: "We will be a *Weltmacht*, we will be present in every ocean." There is the same predicament: armed strength is at its peak, yet it may fall behind the rival in the coming decades (this was what the German General Staff dreaded in 1914 with regard to the rapidly recovering army of Imperial Russia). There is only one logical conclusion from these reflections: Brezhnev may not draw it, but what of the *obkom* secretaries and General Staff colonels now in their mid-forties who will be at the top in a few years' time?

The purpose of this article was not to discuss these military issues, which are beyond its author's knowledge, but to show the connection between the multinational nature of the Soviet empire and the Soviet Union's expansionist foreign policy; and in a wider perspective, to insist on the importance, for world peace and Western security, of the conflicts between national consciousness and state sovereignty which are too often blurred by the use of the ambiguous word "nationalism." Complacent views about melting pots as natural solutions—derived from simplistic comparisons with United States experience—and facile assumptions that the Soviet empire (despite its admitted faults) is in principle a sound organization and should be preserved in its present boundaries because, like the United States, it is big, is composed of numerous "ethnic groups," and is based on a proclamation of ideological principles can only obfuscate the judgment of statesmen. May a non-American be forgiven for arguing that, no less than his own compatriots and fellow Europeans, Americans in government, in universities, and in still wider realms of public life need to think much more often and much harder about these things?

6

THE POLICY PROCESS

The Three Requirements for a Bipartisan Foreign Policy

Zbigniew Brzezinski

Since America's massive entry into the world in the wake of World War II we can discern two very distinctive patterns in the democratic process of shaping our foreign policy. From roughly the postwar era—from 1945 on—until somewhere around the mid-1960s, our foreign policy was made on the basis of genuine bipartisan consensus.

Since then, and certainly throughout much of the 1970s, and, alas, still currently, our foreign policy has been made largely through a process of partisan contestation. These two patterns—of consensus and of contestation—have produced significantly different processes of decision making, different relations between the executive and the legislative branches, and different styles of our national discourse on the subject of foreign policy.

You will remember without a doubt that the era of bipartisan consensus was ushered in, perhaps symbolically, through Senator Vandenberg's willingness to support America's engagement in the postwar era in the new institution to be called the United Nations. And that willingness of his put behind us the danger that many feared at the time that the United States might again then repeat the painful experience of the immediate post-World War I era when Senator Lodge led successfully the opposition to America's active participation and membership in the League of Nations.

Vandenberg's willingness to put his prestige on the line to obtain the support of his colleagues for an act of enduring American commitment to international participation made possible in turn one of the most creative phases in American foreign policy. It produced a series of strategic initiatives, many of them expressed institutionally, which designed a creative and constructive American relationship with the world. The Marshall Plan, the OECD, NATO—all created an institutional framework which was effectively sustained in the course of the next two decades through bipartisan support throughout the country.

There was thus a pattern of relative continuity in American foreign policy, and I emphasize the importance of the word continuity. Though at times there were strains in the relationship between the two parties, most notably during the Korean war, personally expressed through antipathy and conflict between President Truman and General MacArthur, the continuity nonetheless endured and it was a major American asset in our relations with the world. America was viewed as reliable, as constant.

It was also an era of close executive-legislative cooperation. There was genuine consultation between the executive branch and the legislative branch. Just recall the personal relationship between President Truman and Senator Vandenberg or between President Eisenhower and Senator Connally. This made real bipartisanship possible. It was reinforced also by the practice—an accepted practice, not an exceptional practice—of appointing to leading policy-making positions members of the opposite party. Let me just evoke the names of Lovett or Harriman or Hoffman.

All of that in turn made possible effective executive leadership in the area of foreign policy and the acceptance of such executive leadership as legitimate. Our national discourse on the subject of foreign policy, particularly in the press, reflected the general confidence in the broad global purposes of the United States, a general trust in the word and deed of the U.S. government, an inclination to give the United States the benefit of the doubt as America tried to refine its commitment to world affairs.

It was, to be sure, not an idyllic situation, and I do not mean to idealize it retroactively; but it was truly a workable relationship in a creative and pluralistic democracy which thereby demonstrated that it had the capacity to translate its pluralism, its mosaic of interests, into common and purposeful international action.

That condition came to naught sometime in the course of the 1960s. The catalysts for the rupture were the Vietnam war and the political and personal tragedy of Watergate. But I suspect it came to naught even more so because such a sustained and enduring commitment of America to the world bred an escapist reaction from the enduring realities of complexity and infinity.

Complexity in the sense that increasingly it became more and more difficult to reduce the problems of the world to the simple dichotomies of black and white, good and evil, to which we had become so accustomed in the course of World War II. Mass democracies, such as ours, inherently tend to simplify problems, and the dichotomy of good and evil is the simplest way in which to comprehend the world. Yet the world became increasingly complicated with the entrance of the Third World into the picture, with divergences in the communist world, with the Sino-Soviet split, with the emergence of national communism. Unfortunately, often the easiest way to deal with complexity is to turn one's back on it.

Second, infinity became an increasingly perplexing reality since our cultural style is to resolve problems; indeed, if necessary, it is to overwhelm enemies. But the essence of international politics is that there is no permanent resolution of issues, that it is an infinite process in which the resolution of one set of issues almost inevitably generates a new set of challenges and problems. And that is fatiguing and difficult to comprehend. There is no such thing as enduring peace, or a complete peace. The reality of world affairs is a shading of a variety of colors from black to white, but mostly different pastels of grey. And a mass democracy finds it difficult to sustain a prolonged engagement with no seeming end. There is thus an inherent tendency to move toward grand oversimplifications.

In that context, our foreign policy became increasingly the object of contestation, of sharp cleavage, and even of some reversal of traditional political commitments. The Democratic Party, the party of internationalism, became increasingly prone to the appeal of neo-isolationism. And the Republican Party, the party of isolationalism, became increasingly prone to the appeal of militant interventionism. And both parties increasingly found their center of gravity shifting to the extreme, thereby further polarizing our public opinion.

This has produced a situation in which it is difficult now to speak of continuity in American foreign policy. Even our own use of words reflects this condition. We less and less often speak of American foreign policy. We more and more often speak of Nixon's foreign policy, of Ford's foreign policy, or Carter's foreign policy, or Reagan's foreign policy; and who knows whose foreign policy tomorrow. Foreign policy is now a disjointed, discontinuous reality in contrast to what it has been for a long time.

In that setting, the close executive-legislative cooperation of the past and the acceptance of executive leadership (and I emphasize that executive leadership was accepted in the context of close executive-legislative cooperation) has given way to conflict, to trials of strength, and to deliberate limits on executive power. We have witnessed in the last few years a massive intrusion of the legislative branch into the executive prerogative of shaping foreign policy. Congressmen and senators now find themselves entitled, and feel entitled, to legislate not only on our defense budget, which is their constitutional right and duty, but also on the nature and characteristics of particular weapons systems, on the precise characteristics of such systems. They find themselves free to legislate how such weapons ought to be deployed or how they should not be deployed. They find themselves passing, sometimes with a stunning lack of discretion, on the appropriateness of particular covert activities. They find themselves even trying to legislate the location of our embassies abroad.

All of that is destructive to the ability of the United States to manage foreign policy. Five hundred thirty-five legislators see themselves as putative secretaries of state or secretaries of defense, and each one of them is assisted by full-time paid experts whose job it is to make every congressman or senator into a would-be secretary of state or secretary of defense.

Our national discourse has become dominated by distrust, by investigative reporting in the area of foreign policy assuming a largely adversary relationship with the government, with little concern for genuine national interest. My first experience when in office in that regard was to try to deal with the intention of *The Washington Post* to reveal a very legitimate intelligence activity of the United States conducted in cooperation with Jordan, fully in keeping with existing laws, not in violation of any legislative or executive regulations. *The Washington Post* simply chose to reveal this operation, thereby destroying it, on the grounds that it was its sacred right to do so, without the least concern whether the national interest would thereby be damaged. And that incident was by no means the only one in recent years.

This condition of national division and debate has also affected the nature of our political competition. Lately, it has produced such spectacles as presidential candidates groveling before special interest groups, with little regard for whether their advocacy is or is not damaging to the national interest. It involves making promises which are not intended to be kept and which the candidates know they made only for electoral gain, thereby degrading the quality of our political discourse.

It has even had the disturbing effect of politicizing our top military echelons. The commander in chief of that most sensitive branch of our armed forces, the Strategic Air Command, considered it appropriate while on active duty to send secret messages to the opposition candidate for president, while serving his Commander in Chief, seeking a private meeting so that he could undermine his Commander in Chief. And our Supreme Allied Commander Europe (SACEUR) who had been most desirous of reappointment to that post by his Commander in Chief, thought it appropriate to travel secretly to the United States to hold political consultations, while on active duty, with a presidential candidate. It is not a healthy condition for it undermines the apolitical integrity of the uniform.

Look also at the terms in which foreign policy issues are currently discussed. When it comes to East-West relations it is considered appropriate by many to paint the President of the United States as a mindless cold warrior, who is gravely endangering the stability of the peace and who should therefore make preemptive concessions to the Soviets so that they are willing to negotiate with him. I have been struck by the number of Americans who go on visits to the Soviet Union and come back breathlessly reporting that the Soviets' feelings have been hurt by presidential rhetoric and that they will not negotiate with us unless we make concessions. The Soviets are said to have confided that they may even engage in some conflict with us unless we change our course. Usually, after pressing, we discover that the allegedly senior Soviet officials engaging in these startling confidences turn out to be propagandists like Arbatov, Zamyatin, and Zagladin. This is part and parcel of the Soviet negotiating process: the stonewalling of the willingness to negotiate is itself an integral part of negotiating. Yet it is quite commonplace today to blame primarily the President of the United States for a dangerous stalemate in American-Soviet relations.

That extreme is echoed on the other side. I have just read the memoirs of a very recent secretary of state who described President Carter as engaging in "an exercise of obsequiousness" vis-a-vis the Soviet Union—a president whom, incidentally, he was then serving as SACEUR and who was in the process of increasing for the first time in peacetime the U.S. defense budget.

On arms control we are treated to such spectacles as the freeze proposal which anyone knows is fundamentally a hoax designed to placate certain segments of the population and not a workable solution for effective arms control. And, of course, we are also treated to unrealistic prospects of foolproof defense systems becoming attainable in the near future.

It is not surprising that in that context our policy on the Middle East today is so paralyzed or that our policy on Central America today is so polarized.

Can all this be corrected? Can we move towards bipartisanship? We certainly should. We certainly could do much better than we are doing, but we should have no illusion that it will be easy to do so, for the splits in our society have become deeply rooted as the ideologization of our politics has become more intense. But an effort has to be made and an effort has to be made above all else by the one person in whom this nation reposits its entire trust—that is, the president. He is the only official whom we all elect, and it is the president, the next president, who in my judgment has a special obligation to try to move this country again towards bipartisanship.

President Carter did it on Panama by working with Senator Baker. And it is to the credit of both men that this effort was made and it was successful. But I would be the first to concede that the administration with which I was associated did not do enough to promote bipartisanship.

President Reagan could have done so for he was elected with a very large mandate. And to be specific about it, he should have coopted into his cabinet Senator Jackson, who would have immediately brought to that cabinet a measure of truly significant bipartisanship. Reagan did not do it, and I believe he missed an important opportunity.

I hope the next president, whoever he is—whether it is Mr. Reagan or one of the Democratic candidates—will try. But trying means more than talking about it. And it is not enough to appeal for bipartisanship when all it means is that the opposition should blindly support the administration.

Genuine bipartisanship means a very deliberate, self-disciplined effort on three levels: on the level of rhetoric, on the level of policy, and on the level of people.

Insofar as rhetoric is concerned, it means deliberately stressing the genuine continuity in American foreign policy and not highlighting in a self-serving fashion the alleged contrasts between one's own administration and its predecessor. In the final analysis, there is a great deal of continuity in our foreign policy—be it vis-á-vis Europe, or the Soviet Union, or the Far East, as well as on other issues, including international-functional cooperation.

But our presidents in recent years have chosen to stress their own new contributions, highlighting the alleged contrast between their own creative innovation and the ineptness of their predecessors. This is pernicious to bipartisanship, and it behooves the next president to put deliberate emphasis on the element of continuity in the discussion of American foreign policy. I would wish presidential candidates—including the incumbent—would do that as well, for they would thereby serve their country better.

On policy, it means a deliberate effort to try to articulate policies in terms more susceptible to winning bipartisan support. It means deliberately moderating one's own most extreme aspirations. It means making concessions on substance to the views of the opposite party.

On defense, it means commitment to a steady and progressive increase in defense spending, somewhere, to be more precise, around 5 percent per annum rather than dramatic oscillations from year to year. And it means also a serious commitment to arms control. For example, in the short run I do not believe it is possible to achieve the Eureka proposals that President Reagan has put forward, but I do think that a limited interim agreement based on the very simple formula of 1,800 launchers and 7,000 warheads is possible. Movement in that direction would, I believe, generate a measure of significant domestic support regarding an issue on which indeed our public opinion is sharply divided.

On the Middle East, it means negotiations in keeping with both the Reagan Plan and Camp David. That requires assertive American leadership, for peace in the Middle East is in America's interest, while paralysis on this subject leads to domestically divisive competition in promises, with destructive consequences for the ability of the United States to manage a serious foreign policy in a vital region.

On Central America, it means accommodation between the two dimensions of the problem which tend to be so politically emphasized. The issue is not only the immediacy of the Soviet-Cuban strategic danger to us, though it exists; nor is it only the need for long-term socio-economic reforms, though they are needed. It clearly is both, but one happens to be more immediate than the other, and therefore military assistance is now necessary, for without military assistance the issue would be foreclosed and there will be no opportunity for an enduring American commitment to social reform. But in that context such little words as "human rights" and "morality" perhaps ought to be used more often with substantive seriousness by those who now shape our policy and who are being criticized for overly militarizing our response.

But beyond all that, bipartisanship means also dealing with the problem of who makes policy—and that means people. That compels me to talk frankly about individuals even at the risk of becoming more unpopular than I am already. One has to be explicit when talking about people if one wishes to drive home the point that to make policy on a bipartisan basis you have to have people who have the capacity to make bipartisanship work and who themselves symbolize such bipartisanship. Presidents have to choose individuals to make policy who can work with other people of different political persuasions. It is not only a question of choosing the best and the ablest and the most congenial. It is also a question of choosing those who have the capacity to draw others outside of the victorious party's spectrum into the process of making foreign policy.

To be specific, I consider Secretary Weinberger to be a remarkably gifted and talented individual who has rendered this country historical service by revitalizing our defense. But I wonder whether he would be well positioned to fashion a bipartisan foreign policy if he were to be secretary of state, given the kind of opposition that he would immediately generate from Democrats and from some interest groups which he has alienated and which are fearful of his foreign policy views. An appointment like this could be certainly controversial.

Henry Kissinger is one of our great living statesmen whose views on international affairs are based on an extraordinary grasp of history and geopolitics. And yet there is little doubt that if he were to be the secretary of state again the Democrats would have a field day with their attacks on him, and segments of the Republican Party's right wing would undermine the effectiveness of his tenure in office.

A Democratic president would be well advised not to choose as a secretary of state an individual who makes a fetish out of arms control or who is strongly on record as opposing our national defense, for such a person would find it extremely difficult to fashion a bipartisan coalition on behalf of our broader national security concerns.

But what if a Republican president were to choose, for example, Senator Nunn or Congressman Hamilton or Ambassador Linowitz as his secretary of state? It certainly would be in keeping with the precedents of the 1940s and the 1950s, for such individuals have demonstrated capacity to work across the political spectrum and to represent the creative middle which has to be resuscitated.

And what if a Democratic president were to choose Senator Mathias or Ambassador Anne Armstrong or Elliot Richardson, all of whom have demonstrated capacity in the area of foreign policy and the respect needed to work with members of the opposite party? And last but not least, what about individuals who could serve a president of either political stripe well and who could fashion the needed relationships with members of the other party? I have in mind someone like Senator Howard Baker, who would make an extraordinarily effective secretary of state either for a Republican or for a Democratic president. Or Jim Schlesinger, who has served both Republican and Democratic presidents.

A change in our rhetoric, a deliberate emphasis on a centrist policy, the selection of policymakers from the opposition party would all help to give this country again the kind of a foreign policy which is based on continuity, on constancy, and on historical courage.

Managing National Security

Robert Hunter

Introduction

Why does the U.S. national security policy either succeed or fail? In most commentaries, management and bureaucratic organization are usually poor stepchildren to factors like presidential leadership, the quality of senior officials, the nature of issues and challenges to the United States, and the vagaries of domestic politics. Yet any president who does not pay close attention to, and exercise firm control over, the *how* as well as the *what* of U.S. national security policy will likely find both himself or herself and the nation in deep trouble. In fact, it may be argued that the most immediate, and among the most consequential, tasks in national security policy facing the president elected this November—whether Ronald Reagan or Walter Mondale—will be to review, revise, and if need be reform the existing structure for making and carrying out policy.

Of course, their tasks would be different. After four years in office, a reelected president has accumulated both practical experience and a legacy of behavior that condition what he can and will want to do in setting a course for his second administration. By contrast, a new president has to staff the senior levels of his administration and may want to restructure its organization; he also can never anticipate all the problems of management and organization that he will confront after Inauguration Day. While pointing out differences, however, it is also important to understand similarities: what are almost iron laws of making and implementing U.S. national security policy, as well as lessons for either Reagan or Mondale as president.

For any president, there are limits to what can be done in practice. All U.S. national security policy is conducted in the name of the National Security Act of 1947, which created the National Security Council, denoted its statutory members, and set forth broad powers in the realm of foreign and defense policy. Trying to change that basic structure goes beyond what any president would want or need to do in order to be in full command. The Act itself, however, is notably lacking in detail, and each president since Harry Truman has adapted both structure and management to suit the needs of the times and his own predilections.

Indeed, there is no perfect system that can or should be adopted. Each president's own style of leadership and governing is critical—for example, whether he wishes to be deeply involved in the details of national security policy (as did Carter) or prefers to set broad guidelines and to leave most policy management to others (as does Reagan). Nor is there anything inherently wrong, within limits, with either choice or with something in between—provided it works for that particular president and the people he assembles in key foreign policy and related posts. Leadership is the primary quality; structure and management must be adapted to allow leadership to be expressed effectively.

Nevertheless, whoever is elected president in November must face some important institutional choices and challenges in at least six key areas—whether to ensure greater national security policy success in a second Reagan term or to lay the basis for success under Mondale; again, choices and challenges that must be faced by any future president.

The Power of Appointments

First, whom should a president appoint to senior office? Clearly, a new president faces more difficult appointment problems than one reconfirmed in office. For the latter, four years of experience should provide a reasonable basis for judging the talents of those individuals who have already undertaken demanding government responsibilities. But for the former, the task is of greater proportions and thus merits some extended comment.

Critics often argue that the 11-week period between the presidential election and Inauguration Day is too long and that we should amend the Constitution to shorten the lame-duck period along the lines followed in most other Western democracies. In Britain, for example, a new prime minister assumes power within hours of the election results.

The system in the United States, however, is unique. Unlike many parliamentary democracies, the U.S. opposition party does not develop a shadow cabinet, whose members gain experience in working together politically as a team and are therefore ready to assume office on fairly short notice. Moreover, even if a new president has decided before his election whom to appoint to cabinet offices, these individuals cannot be expected to have in mind the people they wish to appoint to all subsidiary positions. These political appointments extend to a level farther down in the ranks of the bureaucracy than is true in almost all other countries. Throughout the British government, for example, perhaps 150 offices change hands following a general election in which power is transferred; in the United States the comparable figure is close to 6,000. The recruiting, nominating, processing, confirming, and acclimatizing of new appointees takes time to achieve.

Similarly, a new U.S. president—or one seeking to bring in new blood—is handicapped in appointing a national security team because he cannot, in advance, judge accurately how newcomers to the administration will actually work together. Unlike a major corporation or even the U.S. military and foreign services—where officers move as cohorts up through the ranks—senior political appointees in a new administration are unlikely to have extensive experience in working together, certainly not in the precise relations ordained by their appointments. Trial and error are inevitable—as witnessed, for example, by changes Ronald Reagan made early in his presidency in the positions of secretary of state and national security adviser and that he may make in these or other positions if reelected.

In judging the future performance of his national security team, however, a new or reelected president can follow several general rules. In the first place, a broad understanding of foreign or defense affairs is only one factor essential in senior advisers: A particular set of talents is needed to develop and articulate goals for the United States abroad; a second to create a general strategy for achieving those goals; and yet a third to devise specific tactics against a background of fast-changing events and the stress of crisis. Few individuals possess all these talents; yet a president must have ready access to all three.

At another level, a new or reelected president needs to recognize that his senior officials must perform four separate and distinct functions, above all else: devising a coherent set of foreign policy ideas, conducting diplomacy, managing the bureaucracy and the national security process, and integrating policy within U.S. domestic politics. Again, few candidates for appointment are likely to be adept at all four. But any president—with either a wholly new team or just a handful of change—must ensure that all these talents are present somewhere in his administration; indeed, that they are present in each of the three major national security policy agencies: the State and Defense Departments and the staff operating under the national security adviser (a staff often referred to by the misnomer National Security Council or NSC).

For success, a rule of complementarity must apply, the neglect of which has plagued several recent administrations. If the secretary of state is a superb craftsman of issues but is weak on management, his deputy should make up for what he lacks. If the secretary's strength is economics, a key deputy must understand national security issues, or vice versa. If no top official has much experience in, or vocation for, U.S. domestic politics, someone with the necessary skills should be appointed at a senior level of each department. In any event, the lines of authority in national security policy need to include the White House political and congressional relations staffs, because they reflect interests particularly important to the president. The directors of these staffs should be informal members of the National Security Council and its subsidiary bodies. The idea that policy can be made without politics or the setting of legislative priorities is a myth; institutionalizing a domestic political viewpoint within the process is only realistic.

In addition, a president must balance two separate and often conflicting requirements in terms of the general foreign and defense policy orientation of his senior appointees: compatibility with his view of the world and of the U.S. role in it, on the one hand, and guaranteed access for dissenting views on the other. Straying too far in the former direction can blind an administration to realities abroad; straying too far toward the latter can severely inhibit a president in developing coherence in national security policy, particularly in its execution.

A president must also grapple with an age-old problem: the role of the foreign service. Interests are competitive: Presidents want to maximize the chance to promote their own viewpoints and initiatives by bringing in outsiders at the expense of foreign service officers in senior State Department and other posts; and they want to appoint some ambassadors for either policy or partisan political reasons. In contrast, the foreign service wants to see the members of its career service promoted to the highest levels possible and also to have as many ambassadorships abroad as possible. This struggle is not likely to be resolved. But there can be a viable compromise: fill most policy-making positions with the president's men and women—bearing in mind the demands of experience and diplomatic craft; and fill all but a few ambassadorial positions with career officers—bearing in mind that some foreign countries virtually require that the U.S. ambassador be politically or personally close to the president.

In considering personnel issues, a special caveat is important: There is a need for someone, somewhere at the senior levels of an administration, to set a style of intellectual coherence for U.S. national security policy. This is more than the development of general themes to be articulated by a president. It is recognition that, more than ever before, different aspects of national security policy must be clearly and carefully related to one another and managed together. This need is partly a function of the world's greater complexity, partly a function of the relative decline of U.S. economic and military power—the result less of any American failure than of efforts by other countries. More than ever before, the United States faces a necessity for choice and correlation—a necessity understood in European countries for generations. A crisis in the Persian Gulf, for example, could require sophisticated, simultaneous management of questions, among others, relating to the Soviet Union, Western Europe and Japan, the Arab-Israeli conflict, the Islamic world, energy markets, the strength of Western economies, the role of the dollar, the structure of U.S. military forces, and gasoline rationing at home.

The conduct of U.S. national security policy thus needs far more conceptual depth and strength than was true in the days when U.S. power and position let us rely more on what was termed pragmatism. In brief, the task of integrating different aspects of national security policy with one another within some realistic, nonideological, and more-or-less coherent view of the world must be accorded increasing importance, and a president must ensure that this quality of thought is available to him at senior levels of his administration—most likely with either the secretary of state or national security adviser being preeminent. This attitude toward policy does not happen naturally; it must be nurtured and developed.

Key Relationships

The record of recent administrations indicates that the key personnel decision to be made, at the outset or on later reflection, is the role the president wishes his national security adviser to play. This decision cannot be left until experience with a new appointee provides the president with guidance, because both the nature of the individual selected and the bureaucratic powers he or she is given will largely define the role.

This position, not formally recognized by the National Security Act, has gained significant power and influence during the past three decades and has become the recurrent center of controversy both within the bureaucracy and in analyses of presidential management of national security policy. The increased role is not surprising, as the nature of national security problems has progressively engaged more and more departments and agencies. Distinctions have become blurred between foreign and domestic concerns, on the one hand, and between economic issues and those considered diplomatic or security-related on the other. Nor is the reaction to this increased role surprising, as more authority has gravitated from the cabinet departments, with their keenly-felt interests, toward the White House.

Reagan was not the first president to come to the White House determined to restore cabinet government; nor was he the first—at least in national security affairs—to learn that effective management and presidential leadership require a large measure of centralized authority within the presidential household. The issue, both for him and for his successors, is not whether the national security adviser will be important—that point should long-since have been settled—but precisely what the adviser's role should be relative to that of other key officials, especially the secretaries of state and defense.

The temperament of, and personal relations among, these key individuals and others, like the director of central intelligence, are clearly important; but they can be overemphasized as central to success. No president can afford to assemble a team of yes-men and women. Nor should any president expect senior appointees to put aside the strong personal ambition that more often than not brings them to the top and helps make them effective when there. The president must manage that ambition; if inevitable competition gets out of hand, it is his responsibility. In the process, he has two key decisions to make and, if need be, to remake: where he chooses to center basic foreign policy thinking—either at the State Department or the NSC (or rarely, but conceivably, at the Defense Department)—and how he will structure the organization to strike a workable balance among contending bureaucratic interests.

Much of the former decision should depend on the president's own predilections in national security policy: whether the depth of his own interests leads him to want his key interlocutor close at hand in the White House, or whether he is prepared to entrust the basic shaping of U.S. policy, with his guidance, to his secretary of state. Presidents Nixon and Carter were examples of the former style, Ford the latter, while Reagan has evinced a combination of the two. Either of these choices is plausible, provided a president is comfortable with it and truly understands his own strengths and weaknesses; but it is essential that he choose and if the choice does not work, choose again.

In terms of organization, however, U.S. presidents—whether newly in office or seeking to improve national security policy performance in a second term—have far less choice. They may decide to limit the conduct of diplomacy to the Department of State and, in its own domain, the Department of Defense. But because of the increasing complexity of national security issues and the bureaucratic factors cited above, one function—that of chief coordinator of the process of making policy—must henceforth be entrusted to the national security adviser. At its simplest, coordination means deciding what departments need to be involved in any decision, at what level a decision should properly be taken, whether a formal meeting is required to prepare matters for the president's attention and, if so, who should chair it: tasks that sound mundane but are vital. A cabinet officer could have the breadth of view to formulate policy across the range of U.S. interests; none can have the bureaucratic purview either to provide the needed insight into the way other departments work or to exercise coordinating authority without severe challenge from his cabinet and agency colleagues. Indeed, the only time that this came close to being achieved—when Henry Kissinger was at the State Department and had relinquished his role as national security adviser—it entailed a virtual duplication of the NSC staff and exclusion of large elements of the State Department bureaucracy from key decisions; even then, the national security adviser still played a significant coordinating role.

At the same time, it would be unwise for a president to seek to make his national security adviser the bureaucratic czar of national security policy—formally recognized as such by making his appointment subject to Senate confirmation. Bureaucratic strains would be inevitable—especially with the secretary of state; the NSC staff would likely have to be expanded severalfold; and the president could lose a source of independent advice—not subject to review by the Congress—that is indispensable.

A new or reelected president can, however, choose to blend temperament, talent, and organization, by judicious selection of his two key officers: a national security adviser skilled in management and flexible in his approach to issues—who can foster a respected role as neutral arbiter in bureaucratic struggles; and a secretary of state with a strong conceptual bent, backed by talent in depth. This does not argue for a weak national security adviser or NSC staff—whenever that has been tried it has failed. Both must be thoroughly competent to be respected as valid coordinators and also to provide the president with intelligent insight unencumbered by viewpoints naturally conditioned in the bureaucracy. (Such an arrangement argues for a two-tiered NSC staff: a small senior level to give overall policy advice, a larger junior level to handle routine coordinating tasks). White House "second guessing" may be anathema to the departments and agencies; for a president seeking to maintain control over national security policy, "second guessing" is indispensable.

Structuring the Process

A new president must also decide on the basic system whereby issues for decision flow upward in the bureaucracy to the Oval Office and then back down again for implementation; a reelected one would be wise to correct errors detected in his first term. In the former case, this system also takes time to develop between election and inauguration, as a new president shifts his sights from the rigors of campaigning to the demands of governing: quite different requirements. In the latter case, reviewing the system at periodic intervals—especially on a president's being reconfirmed in office—is essential and requires overcoming bureaucratic rigidities developed during his first four years.

Few presidents have chosen to rely heavily on plenary meetings of the National Security Council—the exceptions being Dwight Eisenhower and Reagan, as befitting their own personal styles of governing. All presidents in between found this approach either too constricting or too time-consuming and progressively used the Council less as a primary instrument for making decisions. Most presidents have increasingly relied on a system of organization that places emphasis on what happens either below or in place of the National Security Council.

This basic system perforce consists of two elements: the means whereby papers are prepared within the bureaucracy that culminate in decisions and the formal relations devised to force different cabinet departments and the NSC to reconcile their divergent views—without at the same time depriving the president of a range of choice or unduly limiting his flexibility.

As national security adviser in 1969, Kissinger first made his mark with the large number of questions he posed to the bureaucracy soon after Inauguration Day—the so-called 76 trombones. The object was only in part to question a wide range of established policies to permit presidential initiative; it was also intended to set a pattern for bureaucratic behavior and White House mastery of the process—thus increasing the authority of the president. Not surprisingly, as their terms have progressed, recent administrations have made less use of the peremptory demand from the White House for major studies of national security issues: once patterns of behavior and expectations are set within the bureaucracy, less formal procedures become possible. Any new president would also be well advised to employ this technique. It would also be a valuable technique for a reelected president, if only to permit some renewal of the power of initiative usually available to him only in his first few months in office.

The processing of papers for decision making is also not just a concession to a bureaucratic mind-set. In a government where, for example, the exchange of messages with its embassies abroad numbers upward of a million yearly, some orderly procedures are indispensable. The National Security Study Memoranda (Nixon-Ford), Policy Review Memoranda (Carter), and National Security Study Directives (Reagan) have been similar instruments with different names; but—along with less structured means of reducing issues to paper—they have been critical in placing policy in a management mold whereby all elements of the bureaucracy can relate to the same framework and approach. This has also been true of one form in which the results of presidential decision have been expressed: This form has been called in respective administrations National Security Decision Memoranda, Presidential Directives, and National Security Decision Directives. They have not only set forth major policies but have also provided both approaches and methodological benchmarks against which the bureaucracy has measured its subsidiary actions. In addition, they have provided a basic structure that then has permitted deviation, for example, in ad hoc decisions that relate to a larger bureaucratic process without crippling it.

Neither the request from the White House for major policy studies nor formal presidential directives need to be pursued by a second Reagan or first Mondale administration in the forms of the past. But any president must have some such basic organization of paperwork—and must periodically review its effectiveness—if the system as a whole is to have any predictability or if the president and his senior officers are to be able to exercise effective control.

Policy-making Committees

Similarly, since the early days of the National Security Council, an elaborate system of committees has been gradually created to do the bulk of the day-to-day work of shaping issues for presidential decision—indeed, also of deciding what matters should not be referred either to the full National Security Council or separately to the president. The obverse of "the buck stops here" is that no president's time and energies should be burdened with issues not of presidential quality.

The modern NSC system was developed at the beginning of the Nixon administration and was followed, with some variation, through that of Carter. Of key importance was a set of cabinet-level committees operating under the aegis of the National Security Council but without the participation of the president. Under Carter, these were most streamlined: a Policy Review Committee, usually chaired by the secretary of state, and a Special Coordination Committee chaired by the national security adviser. Both generally included the same participants at the table, both met in the White House, and both relied upon subcommittees and working groups drawn from different government agencies to do key preparatory work before engaging cabinet level officers. The former committee dealt with issues that fell primarily within the compass of a single cabinet department—State, for example; the latter with issues that cut across bureaucratic lines where a broader purview was required and where no one department could claim primacy without being challenged by others—namely, arms control negotiating strategy, covert action, and crisis management.

The Reagan administration, by contrast, has experimented with a more decentralized means of management, by reviving and upgrading a dormant set of Senior Interdepartmental Groups—one each for foreign policy, defense policy, intelligence, and international economics, each chaired by senior officials of the respective departments and agencies and each with membership below cabinet rank, except for the chairmanship of the international economics panel by the treasury secretary. This system differs in two key respects from that of the three preceding administrations: no formal set of meetings regularly requires cabinet-level officers to meet to prepare decisions for the president or, if possible, to render his involvement unnecessary; and at first no committee was chaired by the national security adviser or met in the White House (except for the group on international economics). The latter choices were presumably an effort to avoid past friction between the national security adviser and, in particular, the secretary of state by upgrading the role of the cabinet departments at the adviser's expense. Notably, however, the national security adviser now chairs less formal but still highly-structured committees on arms control, space, and public diplomacy—similar to past practice and in part reflecting similar considerations of bureaucratic competition.

The differences between these two approaches to management are not trivial. Indeed, any president must steer between Scylla and Charybdis: to avoid becoming overly mired in the details of national security policy and, at the same time, to avoid the risk of providing inadequate direction to his senior officials on the vast array of issues facing the U.S. government. For this to happen, the basic organizational lessons of the Nixon through Carter period—whether honored during those years in the breach or the observance—need to be relearned: cabinet officers in national security policy must be required to meet regularly, with formal agendas, in the absence of the president; the White House is the best venue for purposes of maintaining bureaucratic comity; and someone must be able to act as a more-or-less neutral arbiter on issues deeply affecting the interests of different departments and agencies. Organizational details—how many committees and how formally structured—are of less consequence.

Here, too, basic patterns of behavior and expectation are important. Indeed, it is by creating these patterns in national security policymaking—provided they prove effective—that any administration can then ignore the formal structure when rapid decisions are required, as in some crises, or when invoking the full system would be too cumbersome to settle isolated matters that are in deep contention among cabinet departments or that require personal discussion with the president. Then it becomes possible at times to utilize informal instruments. These include the presidential breakfasts and the lunches involving the national security adviser and the secretaries of state and defense that existed during the Carter administration and that, in different form, are used by the Reagan administration. A system that works well under normal circumstances can be short-circuited under extraordinary conditions; by contrast, regularly trying to make national security policy on an ad hoc basis through informal instruments is destined at some point to lead to confusion and major error, beginning with the precious quality of accurate communication up and down the ranks of the bureaucracy.

Managing Crises

Whatever means a president chooses for managing national security policy during times of relative quiet, special requirements are imposed during times of crisis. Regular, effective patterns of bureaucratic behavior can help but the management of crises imposes its own demands. Indeed, a central problem for the United States during the past several administrations has been that the emergence of crises abroad is no respecter of our bureaucratic limitations—like sorrows, crises tend to "come not single spies, but in battalions."

The Nixon-Ford-Carter and Reagan administrations adopted different formal approaches to crisis management: the first three administrations established what under Carter was called the Special Coordination Committee, chaired by the national security adviser: the Reagan administration created the Special Situation Group under the leadership of the vice president. The latter method does have the advantage that the chairmanship is in the hands of someone who is not viewed—either factually or inherently—as a bureaucratic competitor. But it has a potential weakness in that a crisis may come so quickly and require such intimate knowledge of everyday detail that no one without regular line responsibilities for dealing with noncrisis issues can expect to be sufficiently cognizant of the flow of events, policies, and bureaucratic action to be entirely on top of fast-breaking developments. However much the vice presidency has been elevated under the last two administrations, it does not include line responsibility. There is a clear trade-off; but a system of crisis management is most likely to be effective if its guidance is in the hands of a senior official who is also regularly engaged in the policy process—a further argument for developing the role of the national security adviser along the lines suggested above.

Such bureaucratic decisions, however, do not dispose of the need to anticipate crises, to manage more than one at a time, or to attend to other pressing national security matters while the crisis is underway. It may be argued, for example, that problems facing the Carter administration over Iran were intensified in late 1978 because of unavoidable preoccupation with the Camp David Summit and its aftermath. The Reagan administration's Crisis Pre-Planning Group, chaired by the deputy national security adviser, is a useful innovation. But more systematic effort is still needed.

Defining a crisis is part of the matter: when should special methods come into operation? There can be no hard and fast rule, and repeated testing is required. Indeed, in an ideal world, no new president would face a major foreign policy crisis in the early months of his administration while his national security team is learning to work together; but he would have a crisis about the end of the first year that would test the effectiveness of the system. Unless there is a relatively smooth development of bureaucratic relations among the departments and with the NSC such as that outlined above, declaring a crisis can also become a form of bureaucratic gamesmanship, a means of shifting authority for chairing meetings and managing issues, say, from a secretary of state (noncrisis periods) to the national security adviser (crisis periods). There would be value in creating a team of designated uppermiddle level officials, drawn from different agencies, who would do nothing else but help to manage crises—experts, at least, in the types of questions to be asked and the types of communications channels to be kept ready. But any crisis worthy of the name will entail issues and bureaucratic responsibilities sufficient to require engagement of the president's top advisers and probably his own: no "utility infielders" can substitute.

In the final analysis, the effective management of national security crises depends on two factors: the way in which relationships have developed over time among the key participants in the process—where the strong hand and will of the president will most likely be needed— and the sensitizing of senior officials to potential crises. Regarding the latter point, the special handicap of time intrudes most forcefully. There are just so many hours in the day, and major themes of U.S. foreign policy also have to be advanced if action is not always to be overshadowed by the need for reaction—the Gresham's Law of national security policy. Each department needs its own particular means of keeping senior officials abreast of what could go wrong or what might challenge U.S. interests. Cabinet officers need to develop special staffs precisely for this purpose, where these do not now exist, and commit themselves to pay attention on a regular basis.

The canvassing of possible crises needs to include extensive communication among the various departments and agencies. Ideally, this function should be centered in the NSC. In addition, a president must ensure that both he and his top officials receive a wide variety of foreign intelligence from different agencies. Homogenized products from the intelligence community often lack value. Crisis-alert procedures that now exist often lead either to unevaluated lists of potential trouble spots or to bureaucratic suppression of ambiguous data as the by-product of deliberation-by-committee. Competitive intelligence is essential; but it will only be of value if top officials require themselves to pay heed. Again, system is important, especially as the burden of information management rapidly escalates. Viewed in retrospect, the U.S. government rarely has gained no information in advance on impending developments that could seriously affect U.S. interests.

Planning U.S. Policy

Any president now must also grapple with a problem analogous to anticipating crises: that of planning U.S. national security policy. All presidents come to office with some view of the major themes they wish to pursue and a rough agenda for action—sometimes general, as with Reagan, sometimes highly specific, as with Nixon and Carter. Each must also rapidly develop a set of priorities, both for U.S. action abroad and for efforts that require public education or participation of the Congress. But a systematic means is also needed for planning beyond the initial list of objectives with which an administration begins, especially as events in the outside world dictate changes of course or open up new opportunities to advance U.S. interests. This is as true of an administration in its second term as in its first, especially after the agenda of initial goals has been exhausted. Planning has indeed long been the bête noire of U.S. foreign policy—always recognized as valuable, always attempted, never particularly successful beyond the articulation of general goals in documents like National Security Decision Directives. Over the years, planning has proved particularly difficult, for a variety of reasons, in a central area of U.S. foreign policy: namely, U.S.-Soviet relations.

For observers outside of government, the recurrent failure of efforts at planning in national security policy-making—both long-range goals and specific strategies for reaching them—may seem quixotic and inexplicable, even allowing for the world's complexity, the pace of events, or the fact that the United States does not act in a vacuum: other countries also have active foreign policies designed, in some cases, to confound our own. Much of the explanation lies in the tendency of planning to succumb to a bureaucratic trap. Officials who wish to be actively involved in making decisions and executing policy either do not have the time to engage in systematic planning or find that this discipline weakens their ability to concentrate on immediate concerns; by contrast, officials engaged only in planning must generally sacrifice their involvement in day-to-day bureaucratic national security activities, without which their plans risk becoming sterile "wish lists" rather than the outgrowth of established patterns of policy—that is, what it is possible for a particular administration to do. In the latter case, a shorthand rule has applied: no action portfolio, no real involvement in the process. Furthermore, mid-level planners rarely are given preference for advancement within the bureaucracy; line responsibility carries more career opportunity as well as potential for short-term satisfaction.

The requirement for more systematic planning that now faces any president is deeply connected with a step argued for earlier: the recruitment by an administration—from the career services or from outside—of people who are able to think about the world as a whole and to relate disparate aspects of policy to one another. Unless an administration has one or more individuals of extraordinary gifts and energy—and, over the life of an administration, even then—system is again important. Each key national security department and agency now has its planning staff. The Reagan administration has also experimented with a small team on the NSC staff and has set up a National Security Planning Group that is, in fact, the National Security Council with restricted attendance. If systematic planning across a broad range of subjects is to have value, however, it must be conducted at a level that does not depend on presidential participation, and it must work in parallel with the regular bureaucratic system—ultimately coordinated in the same manner, preferably within the NSC.

Thus whoever becomes president next year would benefit from

creating a Senior Planning Council—including a special group of advisers on Soviet affairs with access to both government and academic communities. This council should be formally composed of officials at the deputy secretary rank and be housed in the White House. In addition, it should be designed to have lasting value in helping to develop policies that can be sustained beyond the life of a single administration—that is, in laying a basis in long-range planning for greater bipartisanship. Thus it needs to be managed day-to-day by a high-quality staff that includes individuals who are treated as part of a senior career service, not subject to termination or automatic reassignment with change of administrations. This last injunction may be difficult for any new president to countenance. Institutional memory, however, is a critical part of looking at the future and should not be discarded lightly; nor do formal papers passed from one administration to another suffice because so much of the craft and experience of U.S. foreign policy is never written down. New presidents will replace most senior officials; the one elected in November should do his successor and the nation a service by establishing a principle of continuity for most of the proposed Senior Planning Council staff. Indeed, he should also apply this advice to much of the NSC staff, especially where career foreign service, military, and intelligence community officers can provide critical institutional memory that is more natural—but even there not assured—to cabinet departments with their continuing bureaucracies.

Beyond organizational steps, the issue for effective planning is leadership and self-discipline at the top of each department and on the part of the president. The planning function can become important if these leaders will make it so—not as an afterthought but as an integral part of the system and their own appointment schedules. The craft of longer-range planning has to be respected, the individuals involved must have bureaucratic niches where they can command attention, they must be rewarded for their efforts through career advancement, and the president and his cabinet-level officials must visibly demonstrate that they are taking the process seriously.

Integrating Economics

Finally, in recent years U.S. presidents have discovered that the most difficult national security issues, at least in terms of process, tend to involve matters of economics—in particular, integrating international economic issues with those involving traditional diplomacy and security and relating all to key choices in domestic economics. Nor is this just a matter of budgets, although resources committed to defense, for example, have a sizeable impact on macroeconomic policy. In addition, problems of integrating policy include the interaction of domestic economic choice and management with our diplomatic and security activities abroad—for example, trade in agriculture and high-technology, embargoes, the securing and financing of energy imports, and the politics of key alliances as affected by U.S. domestic economic decisions. Unlike our European allies with their longer history of vulnerability to international economic forces, the intensity of economic issues in foreign policy and the blurring of foreign and domestic distinctions are relatively new to us, as growth of global and domestic economic constraints has combined with our deeper relative involvement in the world economy. The complexities are clearly vast, especially when they affect so many facets of government action. In the past decade, for example, U.S. energy policy has engaged more parts of the government bureaucracy, more parts of the Congress, and more aspects of American life than any other matter in our history except for the conduct of major wars.

This complexity manifests itself in bureaucratic action. Not only do international economic issues deeply involve the regular membership of the National Security Council, but they also affect virtually all departments and agencies, plus the Congress, to a degree beyond anything in more traditional diplomatic and security areas. It should not be surprising, therefore, that no administration has thus far been able to develop a process for managing these economic questions that approximates the relatively simple and straightforward tools for other national security issues. For example, even if the national security adviser were accepted as a neutral arbiter for coordinating other matters, he is unlikely either to have the competence in domestic economic issues or to be able, bureaucratically, to be *primus inter pares* in coordinating the broader agenda.

Different solutions have been tried, with mixed results. The Carter administration developed an Economic Policy Group involving key economic officials. The Reagan administration has relied heavily on the Senior Interdepartmental Group for international economic policy, chaired by the treasury secretary, and at times on a Cabinet Council on Economic Affairs. On paper at least, the most successful approach so far has been that tried by the Nixon administration, which created a Council on International Economic Policy, with a status roughly equal to that of the National Security Council.

As a high priority in management, the president elected this November should create an International Economics Council, involving cabinet level officers and representatives of key White House institutions—namely, the NSC, Domestic Council, Office of Management and Budget, Council of Economic Advisers, the Office of the Special Trade Representative, and both political and congressional relations staffs. The actions of the Council should parallel those of the National Security Council structure, with much overlapping of membership; it should hold its meetings in the White House; it should be staffed by individuals more adept at coordinating the policy process than at trying to impose their own views; and its mandate should place special emphasis on integrating domestic and foreign economic issues. Given the complexities inherent in such a wide purview, plus the fact that economic issues have domestic constituencies far stronger than those found—except for defense—in national security policy, this Economics Council needs to be less bureaucratic and more flexible in its organization and management than is the National Security Council structure. Its formal leadership could be in vested in the treasury secretary but with an executive director responsible to the Council as a whole—although experimentation would be needed, especially regarding competition among departments and agencies, before a final judgment could be made. Indeed, this process could be an outgrowth of today's Senior Interdepartmental Group for international economic policy.

Creating this International Economics Council would involve increased demands on the time of senior officials and can never be a watertight system; but at least there must be recognition that the process of making policy in this area requires special arrangements ensuring that contending interests—foreign and domestic—are brought together at a level just below the president.

Conclusions

No doubt, the president elected or reelected this November will want to consider other matters of organization and management in national security policy—especially regarding Congress, as lines are progressively blurred between domestic and foreign affairs. The six principal issues discussed here, however, are most in need of careful review, both now and in the future. At the same time, developing and operating the right structure and procedures are no guarantees of success in the area of national security policy. Content of policy is still likely to be controlling in most circumstances; the setting of priorities can sometimes make or break an administration's efforts; the wisdom and effectiveness of presidential leadership can be decisive. But there is also little doubt that any president who does not confront the issues raised here—either at the outset of his administration or as he gains experience—will find success in national security policy far more elusive. And if there are major failures of either structure or management, a president has only himself to blame.

The Pleasures of
Self-Deception   *Roberta Wohlstetter*

Quite a few years ago, I looked into why we were surprised at Pearl Harbor. I examined the signals available to us that pointed to an attack on Pearl Harbor and the background of ambiguities in which they were embedded. I looked at what we wanted to believe the Japanese were up to, as well as what it turned out they were actually up to.

In this connection it was useful to borrow a distinction originating in information theory between signals and noise—signals pointing to Pearl Harbor that might have actually changed our expectations of the likelihood of an imminent attack (what the theorists grandly call a change in the a priori probabilities, or even more mysterious, the negative logarithm of the probability) and the noise or huge clutter of signs pointing in other directions, for example, to an attack on the Soviet Union or to no attack at all. While the distinction derives from information theory, it has obvious common-sense meaning. It is clear that one has to distinguish between deliberately created or amplified noise and the noisy background generated by random events, by "line noise," by the operation of one's own equipment and procedures, or by "normal" traffic. Of course the deliberate and the undeliberated are related. An adversary, for example, must design his attack so as not to be heard against the normal or random background. Even the suppression of his signals, like going into radio silence, must not arouse suspicion. As an alternative to skirting a warning system, as the Japanese did in coming at Pearl Harbor from the north, an adversary may deliberately conceal radar returns from his low-flying aircraft in the normal ground clutter. Or he may accept radar detection of his aircraft as he penetrates, but time it in a way that fits the normal traffic patterns of unknowns and therefore does not alter the prior probabilities. Or the adversary may *create* a normal pattern by a sequence of exercises or penetrations of the warning system before the attack. He may, in short, *condition* his opponent.

But all such conditioning or other forms of deception have to be based on a shrewd appreciation of the normal background, or what the victim thinks of as normal, and how far that background can be altered. It will come as no surprise that most surprise attacks involve deception by an adversary. They are generally done with malice aforethought.

What has interested me from the beginning but more so in recent times is the role the victim often plays in deceiving himself. This seems especially important in cases that occur between wars, where the critical time to recognize what an adversary is up to may take years, and where perceptions may be shaped by extended negotiations, past, present, and future, on the assumed common interests of the opposing sides. These are the slow Pearl Harbors, so to speak. Let me mention a few examples:

1. The reluctant recognition by the British in the 1930s that Hitler was really less interested in avoiding an "unlimited arms race,"[1] as he put it, than he was in speeding his own rearmament and slowing down the British. That is to say, he was interested in winning the arms race.

2. The even slower and more reluctant recognition by American intelligence that the Russians were not merely interested in having a minimum deterrent force of 200 ICBMs, nor even satisfied with the same numbers as our own, but thought it would be rather nice to have 50% more; in short, they were not simply being dragged along reluctantly by the mad momentum of an arms race we were running with ourselves, but were continuing to run along quite smartly long after we had stopped.

Russian intentions on these matters clearly have some significance for various SALT treaties. SALT I and II, and especially hopes for future SALTs, tend to affect our willingness or reluctance to recognize the signals of what the Russians have in mind.

3. The refusal of our government to recognize India's military nuclear preparations. The Indians, in a succession of regimes (Nehru, Shastri, Mme. Gandhi, and Desai), have been able to use as a cover for their military program the peaceful atom and the desires of the Americans and the Canadians to propagate civilian nuclear electricity—and to sell reactors—and more recently to conclude a comprehensive test ban treaty. The noise of these civilian arrangements confused otherwise plain signals of their accumulation of separated missile material directly usable in weapons, their capacity to separate more, the manufacture and detonation of a nuclear explosive, and current bland statements that they may make more nuclear explosives, if these should seem to be economic for mining or other purposes. The

Indians have managed to maintain this position while being offered as a prime example of the utility of a comprehensive test ban in slowing the spread of nuclear explosives.

In all of these errors persisting over a long period of time in the face of increasing and sometimes rather bald contrary evidence, cherished beliefs and comforting assumptions about the good faith and common interest of a potential adversary play a very large role. The victims in such cases may be the principal deceivers. An adversary may only have to help the victim along a bit. The victim will explain what might otherwise look like a rather menacing move. So the British who had other priorities after World War I which entailed keeping their defense budget down, started in 1919 to assume that no major war was likely to occur in the following 10 years and continued to base their planning on this increasingly less tenable assumption well into the decade before the outbreak of World War II. This "prediction" always had a component of wish and fiat in it, and it came to be called appropriately "The Ten Year *Rule*."[2] British estimates beginning in 1933, as to the number of firstline aircraft the Germans would be able to field, seem to have been much lower than the reality in good part because making them higher would have dictated a course of action that would have been extremely difficult politically to undertake. One can also use the example of the Anglo-German Naval Agreement of 1935: British officials resisted recognizing Germany's intention to develop a fleet that might be used against them and delayed in acknowledging strong evidence that the Germans were violating the agreement. This had something to do with the discomfort of recognizing the truth. It was difficult to do anything first of all about the violations of the Versailles Treaty which the Anglo-German Naval Agreement legitimized and later to do anything about the violations of the 1935 agreement itself. Not to be deceived was uncomfortable. Self-deception, if not actually pleasurable, at least can avoid such discomforts.

The Germans had agreed in the Anglo-German Naval Treaty of June 1935 to limit battleships to 35,000 tons displacement. But Admiral Raeder ordered the *Bismarck* and *Tirpitz* built to displace 45,000. The particulars of the *Bismarck's* design, confided by the German Embassy to the British Foreign Office, revealed a beam 15 feet wider than Britain's *King George V* (which did have a displacement of 35,000 tons), and other dimensions which were apparently incompatible with the 35,000-ton limitation. The British director of naval construction suggested that the large beam went with the shallow draft which was necessary for navigating the Kiel Canal and the Baltic; and the Plans

Division in London, which had been involved in the limitation agreement and therefore had a stake in believing it would be faithfully observed, seized on this anomaly and the shallow draft explanation to provide an even cheerier evaluation: the Germans were looking towards the Baltic, rather than towards the British—they were aiming at the Russians.

In Donald McLachlan's excellent account[3] there is no indication that the Germans offered the explanation that they were aiming at the Russians or that they expected the British to elaborate that cover story for them. Admiral Raeder simply lied to the British naval attache in Berlin about the displacement of the *Bismarck* and the head of the British Plans Division worked out an explanation for some of the troubling inconsistencies. As McLachlan says, the Plans Division in London had been "closely involved in—and therefore believed in—the various treaties limiting naval armaments."[4] The director of plans had "allowed himself to write, 'Our principal safeguard against such an infraction of treaty obligations lies in the good faith of the signatories.'" Yet he was by nature "a skeptical and aggressive man."[5]

In fact, the *Bismarck*'s draft differed little from that of British capital ships. Statements about the shallow draft were a cover by the Germans, gratefully accepted by the British, to save their belief in the fidelity of their German opposite numbers, and to save their belief in the safety of the agreement. The director of naval construction in England, according to Donald McLachlan, didn't push the questions about the *Bismarck*'s specifications even though he was building battleships to oppose the *Bismarck* because he was "hard pressed with the new programme and deeper probing of the German design would almost certainly not have led . . . to a change in our own designs which would mean breaking treaty limitations."[6] As a further nice twist, it appears that the Plans Division in Germany, which knew that the *Bismarck*'s true displacement was over one-fifth greater than allowed and than that announced by the British, argued against revealing the violation on the delicate ground that "we shall be accused of starting an armament race."[7]

It appears, then, that the cheater in an arms agreement and the side cheated may both have a stake in allowing the error to persist. They both need to preserve the illusion that the agreement has not been violated. The British fear of an arms race, so skillfully manipulated by Hitler, led to a naval agreement, in which the British without consulting the French or the Italians tacitly revised the Versailles Treaty. And British fear of an arms race prevented them from recognizing violations of the new agreement.

The second example is the American error in underestimating the number of ICBMs, SLBMs, and bombers that the Russians would have in their strategic force. This error persisted for about a decade—a very much longer time than the British underestimates of Hitler's aircraft program. Moreover, it persisted in the face of precise evidence gathered year after year with all the marvels of high-altitude reconnaissance using satellites, high-resolution cameras, and other optical and nonoptical sensors which told us exactly what silos and submarines the Russians had completed, what they had under construction, and what bombers were still part of their operational force.

My colleagues at Pan Heuristics have made a series of careful studies of forecasts of the Soviet strategic force made by each of the services, of predictions by the intelligence community in consensus, and of those consensus forecasts which the various secretaries of defense used in their annual defense reports as the basis for their budget requests.[8] I will cite only one example of their results.

American long-term projections of Soviet ICBM silos were not only systematically under the mark from 1962 through the end of the 1960s, but in the face of gathering evidence that the forecasts were under the mark, they drifted even further under the mark. In 1962 we predicted that the increase in the Soviet force would be about 85% of what actually materialized. In 1969 we predicted an increase that turned out to be less than 20% of what the Soviets actually fielded. And the ratio of our predicted increases to the actual increases worsened at the rate of about 8 percentage points a year. For all our improved means of collecting information compared to those primitive devices available to the British in the 1930s, we did even worse than they in anticipating this military buildup. Like the British, our interpretation of the data was strongly affected by our strategic doctrines and political predispositions. Moreover, while qualitative forecasts are harder to confirm or disconfirm, it would be quite wrong to suppose that our forecasts of Soviet improvements in unit performance erred on the other side, or even were much better in avoiding underestimation than the predictions on numbers of vehicles in the strategic force. Nor is it clear that we are doing any better now on these qualitative forecasts. I observe each year that our secretaries of defense, like children with their familiar Christmas stocking, express a kind of surprise that is familiar. It seems the Russians once again have improved their CEPs (circular error probables) more than we had expected in the preceding year.

The third example is the Indian nuclear program. The Americans in their negotiations with the Indians in the field of nuclear energy have been amazingly cooperative in going along with some of the Indian fictions. This is partly explained, of course, by the fact that U.S. nuclear officials had entertained some of the same fictions, most notably the belief in the early coming of the plutonium breeder and in the Plowshare program (the peaceful use of nuclear explosions in mining or digging canals). The Plowshare program came to an end in the late 1960s. The plutonium breeder, however, is still on the scene and provides the ultimate justification in most non-weapon states for accumulating stockpiles of weapons material.

I don't want to go into the pros and cons of the breeder. My purpose here is to explore the effects on the intelligence process of a continuing negotiation on what is or is not contained in our agreement with India for nuclear cooperation, and which country is or is not in violation of that agreement.

The Indian military nuclear program has been underway—in a state described by Norman Gibbs in another context as one of "open secrecy"—since the early 1970s. It actually had its beginnings much earlier, in the mid-sixties, when relations with the People's Republic of China became openly hostile, after the Sino-Indian War of 1962 and the first Chinese nuclear tests of 1964. Nevertheless, the Indians continue to protest that they do not have a military nuclear program.

The Indians used heavy water of U.S. origin in a research reactor of Canadian origin, to produce plutonium that they separated in a plant of U.S. design, and made it into a nuclear explosive which they detonated. We and the Canadians have both since the mid-sixties made explicit many times that a nuclear explosive, even if it were said to be contemplated for eventual use in engineering, in digging a canal, had a more obvious and patent military use. That canal could always be dug suddenly in the middle of an adversary's city. We made clear that the use of equipment, material, or services of American or Canadian origin for the manufacture of a nuclear explosive, however labeled, would violate the obvious common-sense meaning of our agreements with the Indians that they would limit their use of what we had provided to "peaceful," that is, civilian purposes *only*.

When the Indians detonated their nuclear explosive, the Canadians cut off further aid. The United States on the other hand went through a series of contortions, first ignoring the whole thing, but reiterating our belief in general that spreading nuclear explosives to more countries would be unfortunate. Then, in defiance of what we had been saying for many years, we allowed that if the Indians said their nuclear explosive was peaceful, we could hardly doubt them. And, in any case, it was a problem for the Canadians, since it was their reactor, and we had nothing directly to do with it. But when nasty questions were raised about our heavy water, we replied that the Indians had said that all the materials, equipment, and personnel were 100% Indian, and we believed them. Then, when it was clear that our heavy water had been used in the CIRUS reactor, we maintained that by the time of the manufacture of the bomb our heavy water must have been replaced by 100% Indian heavy water. When it appeared that the last statement defied some well-established laws of physics and arithmetic, we said yes, there was some heavy water. On the other hand, the Indians were telling the truth—there was none.

This might appear to be troubling on some of the familiar standards of Western logic—that the CIRUS should have been both empty and non-empty of our heavy water. However, by that time some of our officials through long dealings with the Indians appear to have gone native. In some Indian writings, for example, those of the Madhyamika School of Buddhist philosophy, founded by Nagarjuna, a rather more relaxed view is taken of such matters. There are other possibilities than simply being empty or non-empty. For as Nagarjuna says, "If something non-empty existed, then there might be something termed empty; there is no something non-empty, and so nowhere does there exist an empty something."[9] In some cases, one can say that something or someone is "not to be called empty, nor non-empty, nor both, nor both-not." "Everything is either true or not true, or both true and not true, or neither true nor not true; that is the Buddha's teaching."[10] That may explain why the Buddha was smiling on the occasion of the Indian nuclear explosion.

Whatever suspicions Westerners might harbor about the validity of the logic involved, one can hardly doubt that an attitude of mind that can contemplate with equanimity a statement being simultaneously true and false has its diplomatic uses. In fact, it seems to have penetrated our own officialdom.

The story of how our preferences and predispositions affected the writing of the various agreements and our estimates of what the Indians were doing up to May 1974, the date of their nuclear explosion, would take a good deal of time to state adequately here. However, the developments of American policy and the estimates of Indian nuclear activity since that time are related to the negotiations on the Comprehensive Test Ban Treaty (CTBT), and form an interesting parallel to the other cases discussed here: England in the thirties and the U.S. strategic force predictions. The American position on CTBT is based in part on the argument that what is driving countries like India to the acquisition of nuclear weapons is the fact that to make a distinction between nuclear have and have-not states is inequitable. Any step, therefore, by the two superpowers to restrict themselves is a step towards greater equity.

But the Indians developed their nuclear explosive program with an eye to the People's Republic of China. They have little active interest in the armament of the two superpowers. The original motivation for the nonproliferation treaty as expressed by the Irish resolution was based on the interests of the nonweapon states in seeing to it that potentially hostile neighbors did *not* get nuclear weapons. In the treaty, there is naturally a good deal else about encouraging peaceful nuclear developments, and steps toward general nuclear disarmament and in fact general and comprehensive disarmament. But these are rhetorical flourishes that have little to do with actual concerns. They can, however, as in the case of the Treaty of Versailles, serve as a justification for the acquisition of arms, in this case nuclear arms.

In fact, the Indians have produced a welter of statements about the circumstances in which they would explicitly give up nuclear explosives. Our foreign service officers and the State Department have selected those that sound rather hopeful in that they suggest that if only the United States and Soviet Union take this long stride towards nuclear disarmament, the Indians will follow suit. But an examination of the full range of signals and noise emerging from the official declarations and policies, press statements, and debates in the Lok Sabha make quite clear that this selection is as wishful as our prior perceptions of Indian policy. In thinking of this as a stride it is useful to see what the prime minister has in mind as just the first step.

In his address to the UN General Assembly on June 9, 1978, Mr. Desai made clear that among other things there was no point in considering a total ban on testing that extended to some countries and not all. It would have to include the entire globe. "It is idle," he said, "to talk of regional nuclear free zones . . . the whole world should be declared a nuclear free zone." In short, Mr. Desai makes clear in this context that no CTBT that is less than universal, that fails to include China and France among its signatories, will fulfill the conditions that he is stipulating for Indian cooperation.

Mr. Desai went on to say that we should take decisive steps towards the general acceptance of the philosophy and practice of non-violence and Satyagraha. However, conceding that this will take time, he calls only for "one step": That step, however, involves quite a leap. The "first step" he outlines includes (1) a declaration outlawing the use of or research on nuclear technology for military purposes; (2) "qualitative and quantitative limitations on nuclear armament and immediate freezing of present stockpiles under international inspection"; (3) the reduction of stocks of nuclear weapons and their total elimination in no more than 10 years; (4) the comprehensive test ban treaty "with provision for safeguards to prevent breach of the treaty, which in my view can only be through independent inspection"; the ban must be "universal and nondiscriminatory"; (5) a program of drastic reductions in conventional arms should be initiated before the end of the decade. "In fact, we should visualize a time when the use of armed forces would not be necessary even for internal security."

In the past, members of the Ministry of External Affairs in India who advocated the acquisition and testing of nuclear bombs have referred to nuclear and conventional disarmament as an "adorable dream." As a dream we should all cherish it. But we should be clear that stipulating it as a condition for nonproliferation is simply a justification for the spread of nuclear weapons.

One of the points to be made in reviewing this history is that when Hitler talked about his sincere desire to avoid an unlimited arms race, he referred to the outbreak of World War I as the result of such an arms race. In this way, he was drawing on a body of beliefs about the causes of World War I which were very much in the center of British pacifist writings of the interwar period. Lord Grey, who had been foreign secretary at the outbreak of WWI, and Lewis Fry Richardson, the Quaker physicist and meteorologist, are outstanding exponents of this cluster of beliefs. The revival of an interest in Richardson at the beginning of the 1960s has accompanied the growth up to the present time of some current beliefs that the process of negotiation with the Russians is the only way to stave off an unlimited arms race and the certain nuclear holocaust that would follow. And as in the thirties, the facts about what was happening to the armaments of both sides have had to be stretched and pushed entirely out of shape to preserve the doctrine. Revisionist history of the Cold War today, and the related notion that the United States has been forcing the reluctant Russians to spend money on arms which they would rather spend otherwise—all of this resembles the British belief that it was the Allied failure to disarm after Versailles that compelled the Germans reluctantly to rearm. Hitler many times reiterated that he would much prefer to forego armament altogether, if only the Allies would disarm completely.

Other beliefs that have been popular since the early sixties have it that just as our unilateral acts of arming forced the arms race, so a unilateral act of self-restraint will induce reciprocation. Among other things, this view is likely to make us rather relaxed about the bargains we strike. If they seem a little one-sided against us, our objection may be regarded as either a quibble or a useful example of our restraint. And the belief in reciprocity is likely to make us relaxed about the precise interpretation of the bargain, and about intelligence that seems to suggest our adversary may be violating the agreement or at any rate interpreting it very differently from what we had said it meant.

One of the disabilities of the current mind set and the optimistic forecasts about adversary behavior which it encourages is that the adversary may be tempted to exploit our trust. This sort of optimistic forecast has a way of undermining itself.

For those who want—against an abundance of evidence—to believe that the world is really not a very dangerous place, the sociologists' category of self-confirming beliefs offers some reassurance. On this view, the adversary who becomes a threat because we distrust him and arm to meet his threat in a threatening way can once again become no threat at all, if only we trust him. The proposition "He is trustworthy" is as potent in making itself come true as the proposition "He is not to be trusted." So the theory goes.

But, alas, in the hard world not everyone can be trusted to act peacefully, even when not themselves threatened. They may make war because they believe it's easy pickings. "I am in no danger whatsoever" is an example of a self-annihilating proposition. According to the sociologist Robert Merton,

This mechanism, picturesquely termed the "suicidal prophecy" by the nineteenth century logician John Venn, involves beliefs which prevent fulfillment of the very circumstance which would otherwise come to pass. Examples of this are plentiful and familiar. Confident that they will win a game or a war or a cherished prize, groups become complacent, their complacency leads to lethargy, and lethargy to eventual defeat.[11]

The British Ten-Year Rule predicting that, "There will be no war in the next 10 years," when uttered in the early 1930s, justified a lack of preparation for defense and vain hopes of disarmament negotiations. And these in turn encouraged the Germans to believe they could rearm without calling forth sanctions or rival rearmament until it was too late. In this way, the prediction that there would be no war in 1942 helped to lead to war three years earlier and so to its own disconfirmation. Such self-destroying prophecies then can be suicidal in two senses. They endanger both the prophecy and the prophet.

In the between-war period—as in the sixties and seventies—the main perverse kinds of fashionable prophecy were those which converted innocent men deserving of trust into something untrustworthy. The bank run started by false rumors of insolvency was a favorite example in the thirties, as was the minister of defense or prime minister of "Any country" or "Jedesland" who wanted only to defend his country but was misinterpreted as being interested in aggression and so frightened his neighbor, and was himself frightened into an arms build-up leading to war. That was Richardson's concern.

In fact, in the 1930s Hitler was busy talking like the minister of Jedesland in Richardson's theory, making exactly the noises that the British wanted to hear, while his behavior was signalling the opposite—that the governments of *some* countries at any rate had something in mind other than self-defense. While the fashionable political and sociological theories concentrated on *self-fulfilling* prophecies, the actual practice (reinforced perhaps by the sociological theories) illustrated the use of what John Venn called suicidal prophecies. Hitler, when trusted, did not become trustworthy. He took advantage of British trust and complacency and guilt.

Similarly, recent history suggests that the unilateral restraints embodied in our informal practices in advance of an agreement and in our lax agreements themselves in SALT, and in our lax interpretation of these agreements, encourage the Russians to believe that they can gain an advantage through the continued expansion of their defense effort.

A basic underlying characteristic of these prophecies which are perverse or have perverse effects is that there are genuine ambiguities in the evidence supporting them. The unanticipated consequences upset the initial assumption. But policy predispositions, desires, and prejudices may lengthen the time it takes to recognize that the prophecies are false or have perverse effects.

It is, of course, by no means certain that we will persist in our beliefs in self-destroying prophecies. The instinct for self-preservation is after all a strong one. Our political birdwatchers often misidentify an ostrich as a dove. But the habit of sticking one's head in the sand is not a survival trait. We have so far survived. The British finally pulled their heads out of the sand. So, I hope, can we.

NOTES

1. Sir Charles Webster and Noble Frankland, *History of the Second World War, The Strategic Air Offensive Against Germany: 1939-1945*, Volume I: "Preparation," London: Her Majesty's Stationery Office, 1961, p. 158.
2. Ibid. p. 57.
3. Donald McLachlan, *Room 39, Naval Intelligence in Action, 1939-45*, London: Weidenfeld & Nicholson, 1968, pp. 135-42.
4. Ibid., p. 136.
5. Ibid., p. 137.
6. Ibid., p. 137.
7. Ibid., p. 139.

8. Albert Wohlstetter, "Racing Forward? Or Ambling Back?," *Defending America,* New York: Basic Books, Inc., 1977.

9. Ibid., p. 302.

10. Richard H. Robinson, "Some Logical Aspects of Nagarjuna's System," *Philosophy East and West,* vol VI, no. 4, January 1957, p. 297.

11. Robert K. Merton, *Social Theory and Social Structure,* Glencoe, Illinois: The Free Press, 1949, p. 121.

12. There is, of course, a more attractive class of self-destroying predictions. For example, the prediction that "The enemy is mobilizing for an attack on you" can lead to your mobilization, and cancellation of the attack.

Intelligence for Policymaking

Richard K. Betts

Intelligence is more important to the United States than ever before because we can afford ignorance or misjudgment less. The rise of Soviet military power and decline of American economic hegemony have shrunk the margin for error. With the last shreds of detente going up in smoke, the United States could be entering a period where tension is as great as it was in the 1950s and 1960s, but the old cushion of American material predominance is gone. Important as it always was, it is now even more vital that American leaders understand the nature of challenges in the international arena and know the full implications of their own policy initiatives and reactions. Such understanding requires first-class intelligence.

Yet the increased importance of intelligence has not been matched by adequate understanding of its true nature and its proper use to improve government decisions. By and large, intelligence is properly appreciated where it is most successful and least controversial: the collection of raw information. Confusion is greatest where the problems are trickier, impossible to fix by changes in resource allocation or organizational procedure, and infected by controversy: analytic interpretation and projections of foreign military and political developments.

Expectations, Types, and Timing of Intelligence

Policymakers often complain about failures of the intelligence community to give them information that is timely or relevant to the nature of their responsibilities, but they rarely realize that they themselves are a big part of the problem. Henry Kissinger reportedly said, "I don't know what kind of intelligence I want, but I know it when I get it." And when authorities *are* more communicative about their needs, intelligence professionals frequently feel they ask the wrong questions. Officials also often prefer to get "hard facts," rather than extensive analytical interpretations, feeling they are better equipped to make their own assessments.

In some ways, and at some times, they *are* better equipped: they usually have more political experience than professional analysts do, and they know more about high-level activity and day-to-day developments in negotiations both external (with foreign governments) and internal (between various U.S. agencies and committees). As generalists, competent policymakers can make better sense of the relationships between pieces of data in widely different subject areas. But precisely because they are generalists, they also are less sensitive to the particularities, intricacies, and ambiguities of specific problems. Raw data mean nothing out of context, and whereas leaders may understand the context of the big picture, they are less likely to grasp the context of the little picture. Hard facts without interpretation by specialists thus may lead high-level decision makers astray; highly general interpretations by specialized analysts about issues that cut across subject boundaries may strike decision makers as either obvious or naive.

The kind of intelligence that is most frequently likely to be useful, therefore, lies in the middle range: analyses of specific problems that marshal recent information acquired through multiple channels, link it with relevant data from the past, outline the range of possible implications, and estimate probabilities without attempting to state definitive or sweeping conclusions. When isolated facts are so clear that they speak for themselves, there is no real job for intelligence, aside from the transmission of those facts. When the data are highly uncertain, they are virtually meaningless, and the intelligence job is impossible. To be useful, intelligence analyses must truly inform decision makers.

Simple logic suggests that intelligence should precede the decision process: estimators should turn out their products and only then should officials read and use them. In the real world of international politics, though, apart from long-range analyses of problems that have not yet become critical, the division of labor can rarely be so logically neat and discrete. In crises or on rapidly developing issues, the formal process of producing National Intelligence Estimates (NIEs) is too slow, and useful contributions from intelligence may have to come in the form of quick memos. Complicated and pressing issues are in flux, not frozen in time. The information available, its significance or meaning, the process of policy choice, change, implementation, and adaptation are all constantly changing—feeding into, and altering, each other. Estimates themselves can be self-fulfilling or self-negating prophesies, by prompting leaders to take actions that change the situation and change the facts behind the prediction. Intelligence pushes decision makers' ideas in one direction, and their decisions affect the environment, thus changing the intelligence picture again. In short, there is a political Heisenberg effect: measuring the phenomenon changes it. Intelligence assessment and the policy process become one big ball of wax.

When intelligence products are successfully kept out of this maelstrom, remaining untainted by the hurly-burly of policy debate, they may preserve purity at the price of irrelevance. Almost two weeks before the U.S. incursion into Cambodia in 1970, for example, the Office of National Estimates drafted a memorandum entitled "Stocktaking in Indochina: Longer Term Prospects," which noted that denial of North Vietnamese base areas in Cambodia would hurt, but not eliminate, the Communist military effort. Director of Central Intelligence (DCI) Richard Helms did not forward the draft to the White House immediately. He had been told of the impending operation on the condition that he not inform his analysts, and he considered it unwise to forward a memo drafted in ignorance of this plan.[1] Helms' caution was reasonable, given the political realities of the situation. The draft did not contain blockbuster conclusions that forcefully invalidated the president's reasons for deciding to invade, and the decision was so far advanced that last-minute reconsiderations were almost impossible. The memo would probably just have provoked the president's wrath, especially since Nixon already had a strong visceral antipathy toward "Ivy League" CIA analysts.[2] Nevertheless, both the White House secrecy and Helms' need for prudent reticence were unfortunate. As a matter of principle, analysts should never be inhibited from foisting their views on policymakers, even at the last minute and even if their views send the president through the roof. Policymakers also have to trust intelligence professionals enough to tell them about decisions that bear on their analyses. Otherwise, exercises in estimation like "Stocktaking in Indochina" are an utter waste of time and taxes. In dispensing with professional intelligence appreciations, even if they are general in nature and arrive at an inconvenient time, decision makers increase their own risks of acting in ignorance of things they ought to know.

Of course, the melding or confusion of analysis and decision can be overstated. In most instances the functions of intelligence estimation and policy judgment are quite clearly and easily separable in time and space. This is more often the case, though, for the comparatively clear, easy, and temporary or remote problems than for the murky, difficult, and continuing or pressing ones. For these latter cases it may be a misdirected effort to ask "at what stage" intelligence should fit into the policy process, because it fits in at almost all stages: defining a problem, listing the constraints that bound the range of choices, assessing foreign reactions to those choices, and reassessing the variables as U.S. policy unfolds. Moreover, it is obvious that the best way to avoid or temper the consequences of crises is to think about them and plan well in advance, before they become full-blown. This is hard to do in the real world of policymaking, but it is among the most urgent of tasks of a revitalized intelligence community.

Political Sensitivity, Analytical Risks, and Foresight

The conventional wisdom, which has come under challenge only in recent years, stresses the need to guard the objectivity of analysts by separating them from the decision process. Involvement in policy councils is generally held to offer either an invitation to intellectual corruption (analysts' becoming "yes men") or an opportunity to walk the plank (honest analysts' being marked or passed over for their insistent espousal of unpopular views). But if the careful separation of the analytical and decisional functions is impossible without sacrificing estimators' influence and turning the intelligence community into an ivory tower, how can the analyst's integrity or reputation be protected? Finding a satisfactory solution to this dilemma is not merely a philosophical exercise, for if leaders lose confidence in the objectivity of intelligence, intelligence cannot do its job of informing them.

Unhappily, there are no hard and fast answers. Success depends on maintaining a delicate balance between discrediting analysts as a result of their total absorption into policy debate or isolating them and keeping them pure but unhelpful to decision makers. How well this can be done depends very much on the personalities involved, and especially on the adeptness at bureaucratic politics of the intelligence managers (for example, the deputy to the DCI for National Intelligence or the State Department's director of intelligence and research), who can act as brokers or salesmen for their subordinates' products and as buffers against political pressure. This management of intelligence-policy interaction is more art than science, and cannot succeed unless both policymakers and managers agree on the need for the delicate balance. In short, there must be a consensus that a top-flight analyst must navigate between a destructive political promiscuity and a sterile and impossible political virginity.

If the "consumers"—the policy-level officials who use the intelligence products—do not understand the interdependence of analysis and decision, if they do not encourage close communication between users and producers, or if they just do not think about how the intelligence process can serve them, no amount of artful management or mechanical innovation will help.

If consumers want stimulating inputs to their deliberations from intelligence, they must also allow analysts to be occasionally wrong, and even to be nuisances. Paradoxical as it may sound, analysts should be encouraged to take these risks, as long as the consumers regard intelligence as both something that lays out the range of important possibilities rather than a single best estimate and something that should alert them far enough in advance of a problem that they have time to behave appropriately.

Some of the greatest surprises are discontinuities that would not be predictable in a prudent estimate of single probability. For example, despite the fact that the president's Foreign Intelligence Advisory Board encouraged more attention to the issue in late 1972, American intelligence failed to warn sufficiently of the Organization of Petroleum Exporting Countries (OPEC) oil price rise of 1973-74. Certainly estimates should have warned that a sudden rise was quite possible.[3] But if intelligence had been asked to give a yes-or-no prediction much in advance of the event, an estimate that definitively predicted such a move during that year would have been unwarranted. OPEC had existed since 1960, but had done nothing so drastic (though it did show some muscle in 1971) during its thirteen years. Evolution of oil import patterns should naturally have alerted observers that a big change could occur but did not necessarily indicate that a revolution in Saudi policy (the determining factor) would occur in 1973, 1974, or the immediate future. If an analyst's reputation were to hinge on a single prediction for the year, he would have been reckless to say the event would happen. If he were to be judged, however, by how well he flagged dangerous possibilities rather than by whether he was always "right," a strong warning about a price rise in the near term would have been warranted even several years earlier.

This takes us to the second point. Before the events of 1973, U.S. decision makers at the highest levels simply were not interested in OPEC. They were preoccupied by other insistent problems, such as the war in Vietnam, peace negotiations in Paris, Strategic Arms Limitation Talks (SALT), the Conference on Security and Cooperation in Europe (CSCE), rapprochement with China, war in the Indian subcontinent, currency exchange rates, and tension between Israel and non-oil-producing Arab states. With never enough time to think or read about all the aspects of even these problems, they were not about to launch into excursions about the kind of oil crisis that only "could" happen sometime in the future and that at any rate had never happened before. Of course, they should have worried about it then, and professional intelligence specialists who knew the potential seriousness of the problem should have had a license to nag them. It should be possible and penalty-free for analysts to lobby with top managers to have such subjects discussed at a National Security Council meeting. And when there is such a meeting, the analysts with expertise, rather than just their superiors at the level of assistant secretary, should attend. If the problem fails to become real, policymakers should not feel peeved that the intelligence bureaucracy has "wasted" their time.

There are four obvious obstacles to these prescriptions. First, some consumers do not want to be warned; they do not want to be bothered about hypothetical or potential dangers that may, after all, never develop. To take time out to worry about hypothetical is to take time from other present, real, and demanding questions. Second, if nuisance mongering is encouraged, too many energetic analysts will be trying to foist their pet concerns on higher authorities, and the opportunity for policymakers to be warned early about major problems may drown in a sea of special pleaders. A third barrier comes from protocol and hierarchy. Attendance at highest-level meetings must be kept small to be manageable, and it is hard to justify inviting relatively low-level analysts when much higher-ranking officials are excluded. Finally, my proposals violate the traditional norm of keeping intelligence professionals out of policy debates. In many respects this is a good norm, but it is often impractical; and even when practical it may still be undesirable. Most of the time, increased interchange between analysts and policymakers would improve the work of both.

Fuzzy Lines Between Facts and Judgment

Intelligence assessments and policy goals are inevitably linked, for the significance of information depends on our national interests, and those interests are politically defined. Thus, the focus of cogent estimates should be on the facts that affect the available policy choices. As Steve Chan has written, "An intelligence system totally divorced from the thinking of the political leadership is neither practical nor desirable. . . . In the absence of a referent system provided by those commitments, efforts to collect and analyze information will 'drift' aimlessly."[4] So at least at a general level estimators need to frame their evaluations in these political terms, but they also should be encouraged to challenge the empirical basis of underlying assumptions. Smart policymakers should recognize that despite the inconvenience this poses for the decision-making process, such challenges are valuable because they may alert them to incipient problems resulting from mistaken challenges. If policymakers are not so astutely sensitive, though, intelligence officers criticizing the assumptions behind policy may be ignored or slapped down for overstepping their responsibilities.

The political context of intelligence assessment presents the fewest problems in those aspects of intelligence that are least controversial or are purely descriptive, such as lists of different types of Soviet military hardware. But these are no longer the most demanding challenges in strategic intelligence. Simply discovering how many and which kinds of missiles, aircraft, and tanks existed in the U.S.S.R. was a huge and important task in the 1950s because intelligence collection resources were very limited. With comprehensive and high-quality reconnaissance systems now in place, however, counting and listing things is only the starting point for good intelligence. Our descriptive knowledge about what forces the Russians have is now far from perfect, but still quite good. Today the bigger problems still lie where intelligence has fallen down before: figuring out (1) what capabilities the Soviets will have five or 10 years in the future, and (2) what they think those forces can do for them.

Both of these questions involve a complex and politically charged blend of judgments about technical capabilities, elite perceptions, and government intentions. Even at the easier end, good intelligence cannot stop with lists and descriptions. The wartime capabilities of weapon systems cannot automatically be deduced from their technical characteristics, but depend on the operational concepts, strategy, and tactics that would direct their use. For example, British intelligence had estimates of the German order of battle in May 1940 that were not wildly inaccurate, and the allies and the Wehrmacht were about evenly matched in hardware and manpower (if either side had an edge, it was certainly the French and British). Yet the Germans were able to overrun France in a stunning rush, because those estimates had no grasp of the nature and implications of the revolutionary blitzkrieg strategy, which massed and maneuvered the limited German armored forces and coordinated them with air support in a novel and devastating way.

American intelligence on Soviet capabilities today is certainly much better than allied intelligence in 1940. But the stakes are higher, too. And there is still much we do not know and, I would guess, much that some U.S. leaders do not know that we do not know. Strategic debate takes place in a deceptive atmosphere of precise knowledge about the capabilities of nuclear forces—an atmosphere that is fed by the great quantity of data available from sophisticated intelligence-collection mechanisms and highly refined computer calculations. With no experience in large-scale nuclear operations, however, or even large-scale coordinated testing of forces, we really know very little about how an attempted attack would unfold. We have only educated guesses about the timing, targets, and success of a Soviet first strike, guesses that rest on assumptions about Soviet planners' views of their opportunities, constraints, and alternatives.

Calculations prevalent among experts involved in strategic analysis usually assume that the Soviets would do what *we* think would maximize their capabilities: put multiple independently targeted reentry vehicles (MIRVs) on as many of their heavy intercontinental ballistic missiles (ICBMs) (especially SS-18s) as possible, and replace old heavy missiles like the SS-11 with newer ones like the SS-17 or 19 as quickly as possible. But the Russians have done neither as rapidly as they could. This apparent anomaly may not be crucial, and there are indeed logical hypotheses floating around the intelligence community to explain it. The only point I am making is that even to judge capabilities, good analysis has to take account of the adversary's intentions and strategy and the possibility that his view of the appropriate military use of technological innovation may depart from what we see as logical. This takes intelligence into much more controversial areas, with crucial implications for U.S. policy choices, and makes it progressively harder to separate factual assessment and political judgement.

Interdependence of Policy and Assessment

Much has been made of the intelligence community's persistent underestimates throughout the 1960s of the number of ICBMs the Soviet Union would deploy.[5] The exposure of this failure was a healthy warning, but its significance really depends on the policy preferences of the beholder. Hawks have correctly pointed out the effect of unsubstantiated assumptions about Soviet aims—that the U.S.S.R. was striving in the 1960s only for minimal deterrence, or for parity—in skewing projections. It is not clear, though, that the failure to project numbers deployed was in itself quite as dangerous or egregious as some hawks maintain.

First, projecting numbers of a weapon that will be deployed can never be more than an informed guess, especially if the projections go years into the future, to a point where the adversary himself may not even have decided the number yet. The guess in this case should have been better, since ample clues were available (though their salience or determinacy is "obvious" only in hindsight), but it still would have been a guess. Second, other estimates in this period, such as those concerning qualitative improvements in weaponry, were not all comparably far off the mark. (On the controversial issue of whether or not the Soviet SS-9 missile had a MIRV capability, for example, the CIA analysts took a bureaucratic beating for a while in 1969 but turned out to be right.) Third, just because the failure to predict the number of Soviet ICBMs concerned a crucial area of policy does not mean that the failure itself had severe consequences. The crucial estimates in this period were those about Russian antiballistic missile (ABM) developments, and these did not err on the side of optimism.[6] It is not obvious that less-mistaken projections of ICBM totals would necessarily have prompted substantially different American policy choices. The quantitative scale of our own ICBM investments had already been set in the early 1960s, before the full accumulation of misestimates, and there is no evidence that the ABM decision, SALT positions, or modernization programs would have been altered in a major way by more accurate projections. (The cancellation of the B-1 and slowdown of MX development, for example, were decisions made long after recognition of the mistaken estimates.)

None of this excuses the failure, but it does make its significance contingent on other judgments, such as those concerning Soviet intentions and strategic doctrine, and those related to our own conception of deterrence and military adequacy. The significance of ICBM misestimates depends on the competing logic of strategies of mutual assured destruction (MAD), damage limitation, and limited nuclear war. And these considerations lie in the world of theological polemics. There is no evidence whether any of these strategies are correct, because they have never been tested. Policymakers have to settle their own theological beliefs. On this issue, a quest for intelligence objectivity is doomed, except insofar as objectivity is defined by rigor of argument.

The import of intelligence success or failure, in short, depends on U.S. policy just as the wisdom of policy also depends on intelligence. This has been the crux of the strategic debate since the mid-1970s. If asymmetrical counterforce capabilities and numerical Soviet advantage in the ballistic missile elements of our triad are not in themselves a threat, the mistaken estimates of the 1960s were an embarrassing but inconsequential failure. If, on the other hand, an American posture based generally on the theory of MAD is inadequate or dangerous— and the consensus in the defense community has indeed swung back in this direction in recent years—then the intelligence and policy failures discussed by Albert Wohlstetter and others, failures that reinforced each other, are important. How then might they have been avoided?

One way would have been to facilitate the articulation of dissent from low levels in the analytical bureaucracy. The goal of producing a single coordinated National Intelligence Estimate does not prevent this, but it does inhibit it. As long as the NIE is supposed to be produced separately from, and prior to, discussions in a policy forum, and negotiated among various agencies, indulging dissent poses costs— first, for timeliness; second, for cogency.

If justice is to be done to all viewpoints within a trim document, it will take longer to produce. And the production process for NIEs is already quite constipated, to the point that they may not be useful for fast-breaking problems.[7] For the strategic NIEs, timeliness may not be so crucial—unless we get into a latter-day Cuban missile crisis—but here we run into the second problem. The 1976 Team B critique jolted the production process of the NIE 11/8 (the central strategic estimate) into less certainty and more attention to alternative explanations of Soviet programs. The 11/8s of the past few years reportedly have grown even longer than they used to be—already too long and flabby for many high-level officials to take time to read.

Recognizing and Using Biases

The simple norm of tolerating or encouraging dissent is not especially helpful. It has become so widely accepted in principle that it is now a cliché before which almost all observers ritually genuflect. A related solution to avoiding the self-reinforcing ideological consensus that some critics saw as the source of error is a more radical one: to institutionalize contending biases within the analytical bureaucracy. To some extent this is already done in effect by the dispersion of analytic assets across intelligence units in different departments—such as CIA, the State Department's Bureau of Intelligence and Research (INR), the Defense Intelligence Agency (DIA), and the service intelligence agencies—where professional subcultures and predispositions tend to differ somewhat from each other. But this is an unconscious and un-systematic institutionalization of bias, and, as many observers have begun to notice, pluralism in itself does not guarantee fewer mistakes. I have in mind a more conscious and admittedly politicized standard for personnel selection within units, such as the CIA's Office of Strategic Research. Managers would purposely install several analysts with different fundamental views about the Soviet Union and the nature of arms competition, so that in arguing with each other consistently they make it harder to write and build on unsubstantiated generalizations than it would be if they were comfortably surrounded by likeminded colleagues. This scheme would not guarantee better decisions (it is similar to the concept of "multiple advocacy,"[8] which has a number of drawbacks)[9] but it would guarantee better analyses. At the least it would inhibit the unrecognized drift toward ideological homogeneity that was attacked by the Team B critics of strategic NIEs.

This kind of personnel strategy would, to say the least, be controversial and tricky to organize. If it is not done purposely, however, bias will still be institutionalized unsystematically and by default. Some degree of bias is inevitable. Except in its primitive and rigid form, bias does not mean fanaticism or closed-mindedness. It simply means the general view of international reality, the set of assumptions that any analyst has about how the world works, the notions that form the complex of intellectual shortcuts that help analysts make sense out of information. Good analysts will question their own biases and revise them in the face of contrary evidence, but they cannot get along without some set of working assumptions. Nor should they. Zealots are dangerous, but an analyst who has no predispositions at all has probably not learned or thought very much. And the most challenging issues for intelligence are those that are controversial, concerning basic uncertainties (such as Soviet aims) where biases differ. If political-intellectual biases are inevitable, they should be organized intelligently, not suppressed, ignored, and left to pop up in unrecognized ways in the estimating process. Moreover, highlighting the contention between varying biases within the estimate should make it harder for policymakers to glide over such differences of opinion in their own deliberations.

This recommendation may be as unrealistic and impractical as the orthodox separation of intelligence and policy that I am criticizing. Even if officials agreed with the idea in principle—which is doubtful—there would probably be endless disagreements about how to implement it and debilitating recriminations and results. But the notion is worth exploring at least as much as solution via bureaucratic reorganization (the more usual—and in the last several years, absolutely chronic—response to dissatisfaction with the intelligence system). Although the recent managers of the intelligence community evidently disagree, it is probable that we have reached the point of diminishing returns in finding new organizational and politically neutral fixes for what in many ways are old and politically charged intellectual problems.

To an extent that is not fully appreciated outside the executive branch, the decision-making system has already adapted to, and promoted the integration of, intelligence and policy judgments; but the implications of this development have not been matched by explicit changes in priorities in the intelligence process. Especially since the beginning of the Nixon administration, the traditional principal products of the analytical bureaucracy—the NIEs—have become less important to consumers at the highest levels. In some respects they have been supplanted by an elision of analysis and policy alternatives in the interagency studies known as National Security Study Memorandums (NSSMs) under Presidents Nixon and Ford, and Presidential Review Memorandums (PRMs) under President Carter. These studies are produced by committees with participants from both the intelligence community and the policy bureaus of the State, Defense, Commerce, Treasury, and Energy Departments, and the Arms Control and Disarmament Agency and the National Security Council (NSC) staff. Intelligence assessments and policy options are considered together in the same document, which is then discussed by principals at the NSC level. There is a place in the system both for such high-level studies and for the NIEs, which retain the traditional divorce between estimation and policy options. But the higher de facto profile of PRMs suggests that, at least implicitly, presidents and their top lieutenants find it more useful to see the two elements addressed together.

Acceptance, Rejection, and Blame

When an unpleasant surprise hits a policymaker in the face, it is natural for that policymaker to feel that intelligence has let him down. Sometimes (though not often) intelligence does fail abjectly. Sometimes it fails because success was impossible, and sometimes the intelligence is good while the decision is bad. Half the battle in improving the contribution of intelligence to policy choice and implementation is to recognize the limits of analysis. If high officials think good intelligence will offer "the answer" and make their decisions easy, they will not only fail to live up to their own responsibilities but will also fail to make the best use of the analysis.

On the most challenging issues—such as Soviet strategy or political developments in important but volatile Third World countries—

success in terms of precise prediction is usually impossible. Analysts cannot be expected to divine foreign leaders' decisions when those leaders themselves do not even yet know what they will do, or whether they will hinge their decisions on what the United States government does (which is, again, something the American analysts or officials do not know themselves). What can be expected from the analyst is a clarification of the variables in play, a highlighting of details that generalists are not aware of, a narrowing of the range of probabilities, and a series of tentative propositions about alternative developments. Even when the trends or the probable eventual occurrences seem clear, analyses can rarely tell a president what would be most helpful to him: exactly *when* the generally predictable development will happen.

The revolution in Iran offers some clues. Much of the failure to anticipate the seriousness of the challenge to the Shah was avoidable. With hindsight it is clear that signs abounded of the underlying conditions for the revolution: an autocratic regime that substituted repression for political institutionalization and channeled and controlled social mobilization and co-optation; rapid and uneven economic development and modernization, with its attendant dislocations and frustrations; a population and urbanization explosion; and other explosive social and political developments.[10] The trouble is that this picture also characterizes a number of other societies, too. Should estimates now be saying that these regimes will fall within a year or two—or ten? There are other cases in which the grounds for predicting the imminent demise of a ruler were even better, yet the ruler survived. As General Shlomo Gazit, former chief of Israeli military intelligence, has noted, it seemed utterly obvious to experts twenty years ago that King Hussein of Jordan could not last, but he is still around. In these situations, a good estimate can only note the probability of disaster, not pinpoint it.

But because such analyses are equivocal, there are situations in which intelligence estimates are reasonably accurate about the odds and offer good warnings; yet policymakers nevertheless feel compelled to take actions inconsistent with the warnings. They may accept the pessimism but take a plunge anyway, because of (1) what they perceive as the alternative consequences, which strike them as even worse, and (2) their willingness to take risks, to gamble that the worst possibilities will not come to pass. In these circumstances, disaster is a policy failure, not an intelligence failure.

One example is Vietnam policy. The record of NIEs in the 1950s and 1960s looks quite good today, in that they warned cogently and consistently of the odds against success from increased American involvement and military escalation. Yet Presidents Kennedy and Johnson persevered, despite the odds, because until the late 1960s the consequences of losing appeared so bad and unacceptable that there was no alternative to pushing on and hoping for the best. Perhaps another example might be the recent hostage crisis, although at this writing only speculation and fragmentary press stories are available for making guesses about what led to the president's decision to admit the Shah to the United States. Reportedly there were ample warnings that violence would follow in Teheran, and the president himself considered the possibility of an attack on the embassy. Maybe the risk was judged necessary for the sake of preserving credibility with allies (perhaps the reasoning was that the spectacle of American insouciance while the Shah wasted away and died might make someone like King Khalid worry about whether the United States would stand by him in adversity). Moreover, while destructive invasion of the embassy was predictable (and, reportedly, predicted), the events that followed—government tolerance and support for prolonged occupation of the embassy and the official kidnapping of U.S. personnel—are thoroughly unprecedented in recent history and were therefore not predictable.

To sum up: officials cannot expect intelligence warnings to be precise or unequivocal, except in the area of last-minute tactical warning. Analyses that are to be pointedly useful in policy deliberations may also sometimes be those that tread across the line into the political debate. The intelligence and policy processes can be clearly segmented only in the comparatively easy instances when there is plenty of time for leisurely policymaking and in the rare cases in which appraisals of foreign capabilities and decisions do not depend on U.S. policy initiatives and the reactions they provoke in foreign capitals. For the messy, tough issues in which foreign developments are quick and their consequences immediate and in which foreign decisions may be in response to the U.S. stance on the matter, trenchant estimates may have to suggest that U.S. policies are creating problems. Formally, this is usually *verboten*. Practically, decision makers may find it in their best interests to let professional intelligence analysts needle them.

NOTES

1. U.S. Congress, Senate, Select Committee to Study Governmental Operations with Respect to Intelligence Activities, *Final Report,* Book I: *Foreign and Military Intelligence,* 94th Cong., 2d sess., 1976, pp. 80-1.
2. Henry Kissinger, *White House Years* (Boston: Little, Brown, 1979), pp. 11, 36.
3. U.S. Congress, Senate, Select Committee on Intelligence, *Staff Report, U.S. Intelligence and the Oil Issue,* 1973-1974, 95th Cong., 1st sess., 1977.

4. Steve Chan, "The Intelligence of Stupidity: Understanding Failures in Strategic Warning," *American Political Science Review* 73, no. 1 (March 1979), p. 178.
5. Albert Wohlstetter, "Racing Forward or Ambling Back?" in James Schlesinger et al., *Defending America* (New York: Basic Books, 1977).
6. Lawrence Freedman, *U.S. Intelligence and the Soviet Strategic Threat* (Boulder: Westview Press, 1977), pp. 108, 137-44.
7. U.S., Congress, House Permanent Select Committee on Intelligence, *Staff Report, Iran: Evaluation of U.S. Intelligence Performance Prior to November 1978,* Committee Print, January 1979.
8. Alexander George, "The Case for Multiple Advocacy in Making Foreign Policy," *American Political Science Review 66,* no. 3 (September 1972).
9. Richard K. Betts, "Analysis, War, and Decision: Why Intelligence Failures Are Inevitable," *World Politics* 31, no 1 (October 1978), pp. 76-8.
10. An example of this argument is Abul Kasim Mansur (pseud.), "The Crisis in Iran: Why the U.S. Ignored a Quarter Century of Warning," *Armed Forces Journal International* 116, no. 5 (January 1979), pp. 26-8.

Congress and Intelligence Oversight   *Barry Goldwater*

During the early 1970s, it appeared Congress was going to hamstring the U.S. intelligence services with its public investigations of the alleged abuses within the intelligence community. Today, six and a half years after formation of the Senate Select Committee on Intelligence and its counterpart on the House side, I believe it is possible to say that the intelligence community is recovering very well.

The reason for this promising outlook is that congressional oversight of our intelligence agencies is working.

The committee that held the public investigation was given one cumbersome title, the Senate Select Committee to Study Governmental Operations with Respect to Intelligence Activities. Chaired by former Senator Frank Church of Idaho, the committees performance was a sorry demonstration of the way Congress deals with its problems. We spent nearly $3 million and over 15 months investigating the intelligence community with a peak staff of over 130 professionals, consultants, and clerical personnel. I wish we could try to do to the Soviet KGB what we tried to do to ourselves.

Clark Clifford, that wise adviser to many presidents over the years, lamented the committee's efforts at the time and I agreed.

That committee was formed to determine the extent of abuses mentioned in the Rockefeller Commission Report, made upon the request of President Ford. I endorsed the Senate's decision because I felt it was necessary to investigate any possible abuses of the privacy of American citizens. After endorsing it, however, I refused to sign the two final reports put out by the committee as I felt both were inaccurate and played too much to the sensational publicity.

In my comments at that time, I said that the free-wheeling, self-righteous, and frequently moralizing thrust of the report assured recommendations which were premised on wish and speculation rather than fact and testimony. It presented a strong dose of 20/20 hindsight that raised more questions than answers. It also blackened the reputation of agencies and persons that have served the country well. The Senate resolution that set up this committee had promised a calm and deliberative investigation. That promise was not fulfilled. The committee is out of business now and has been replaced by the current permanent committee.

The formation of this new committee is the only positive aspect to emerge from this investigation. It has consolidated for the first time all the government's intelligence activities under the jurisdiction of one committee in the Senate. It has focused on the problems raised by the previous method of accountability rather than on abuses.

The Senate majority picked a wise man, Senator Daniel K. Inouye (D-Hawaii), to be the first chairman. Through his good judgment, common sense and order was restored and this in turn led to trust and respect between the intelligence community and Congress. Now, the intelligence community must account for its activities, including covert action, and request allocations for every dollar it wants to spend. It's the best form of accountability known in a free society and is similar to that which other committees of Congress have regarding the agencies under their jurisdiction. The intelligence community welcomed this greater accountability to Congress, the Congress was ready for it, and the American people are better off as a result.

In the mid-1970s, I emphasized the importance of having an effective system for collecting information and assessing the events that bear on U.S. strategic interests, particularly at a time when turmoil and anti-American sentiment seemed to be increasingly widespread. In reviewing our intelligence capabilities at the time, I commented that we had been through an extended period in which intelligence agencies of our government had been pictured more as enemies of the American people than as contributors and necessary adjuncts to our national security.

The media have never shown any marked sympathy for the collection and use of intelligence information, especially if such activity required the use of secret or clandestine methods. Nor have they shown any sympathy for the men and women of the American intelligence community who suffer great hardship and sacrifice in performing their day-to-day tasks. There seems to be built-in abhorrence on their part for anything of a confidential nature, even in the interests of protecting American people and interests.

In 1975, I was asked to serve on the so-called "Church Committee" of the U.S. Senate to investigate alleged improper intelligence activity. In my humble opinion, the Church Committee went out of its way to do as much as it possibly could to disrupt the activities of the Central Intelligence Agency and other elements of our intelligence family. Not once did that committee keep in mind, nor did the newspapers that reported on its activities keep in mind the fact that everything they criticized about intelligence activity was done by those agencies on direct orders from the various presidents of the United States. The operations that the media have depicted as reprehensible in the intelligence business occurred in the past two decades, and all of it was approved by the president—these activities were undertaken because the man elected to the highest office in the land decided that they were in the best interest of the American people.

Throughout this entire period of attacking, criticizing, and undermining our intelligence agencies, the question of ultimate responsibility was conveniently ignored. The effect of all this public breastbeating was to reduce the government's capability to gather needed intelligence and to assess it properly.

Since the mid-1970s, world events have begun to persuade the American people and many members of Congress of the vital need for a healthy intelligence community. Even some members of the media are beginning to understand that abuse cannot be heaped upon the agencies and individuals whose job it is to serve this country's intelligence interests without eventually doing them grave damage.

The U.S. intelligence system is the most public intelligence system in the world. Through proper congressional oversight, we may be able to maintain this openness and still come up with the intelligence we need to safeguard our freedom. But it is not easy.

Recovery

The Senate Select Committee on Intelligence has been in business since May 19, 1976. There were two compelling reasons why it was formed. First, to consolidate all national and foreign intelligence activities under the jurisdiction of our committee in both Houses, and second, to develop charters that would put the agencies under the rule of law. Both tasks were intended to make intelligence more accountable to the Congress.

Senate Resolution 400, which describes the committee's functions, duties, and organization, established the permanent committee on intelligence. Previously, jurisdiction for intelligence matters was shared by at least four committees.

The attempt to put together charters was a cumbersome one. There was a great deal of criticism because we were unable to agree on a 150-page intelligence charter that was a dubious undertaking from the start. The committee tried unsuccessfully to revise the original draft, and neither effort was approved. The first time around the proposals were too long and too restrictive. The second version which emerged two years later, was shorter, but still too restrictive. We finally set aside both charters and agreed on a shorter version, which we use today.

That version, known as the Intelligence Oversight Act of 1980, repealed the congressional reporting requirement of the unworkable Hughes-Ryan amendment and required that significant, anticipated intelligence activities be reported to the two intelligence committees of the House and Senate instead of all eight congressional committees. This new law strengthened the system of congressional oversight of intelligence activities of the United States by requiring the agencies to keep the two committees fully and currently informed, provide full access to information, and give prior notice of significant intelligence activities.

By agreeing on this legislation, along with the already established budget authorization procedure, we overcame the biggest obstacle, which was ourselves.

The budget authorization process is standard procedure now, though no other nation in the world has such a process. This method ensures that our constitutional responsibilities are fulfilled, while at the same time maintaining the confidentiality necessary for an effective intelligence system. We examine in detail the budget of the Central Intelligence Agency, the National Security Agency, and the intelligence activities of the Departments of Defense, State and Treasury, and of the Federal Bureau of Investigation and the Drug Enforcement Administration. This process allows us to determine if intelligence is being well managed and responsive to the country's needs. It gives us a chance to focus on a wide range of national security issues, such as international trade and monetary policy, nuclear proliferation, energy and other scarce natural resources, political developments in Third World countries, and international terrorism and narcotics.

In arriving at the shorter version of the charter, two important items were deferred. One was relief for the intelligence community from the Freedom of Information Act (FOIA) and the other was intelligence identities protection legislation to preserve the anonymity of our intelligence operatives around the world.

In June of 1982, the Senate finally took steps to protect our covert agents by passing the Intelligence Identities Protection Act. The act helps to protect our intelligence employees abroad from other American citizens who would expose them by the unauthorized disclosure of their names. These unauthorized disclosures have not been infrequent: most have been made by former CIA employees. At least 1,200 names had been made public in magazines or newspapers, and another 700 names appeared in one book. A bi-monthly bulletin exposed alleged CIA, FBI and military intelligence personnel and assignments, and a worldwide network called "CIA Watch" operated for the purpose of eliminating the CIA. Until passage of this legislation, we had no legal means to stop such disclosures.

The bill had broad support but had been delayed over a misunderstanding that it might interfere with the First Amendment rights of the news media. These were considered and the resulting law will protect those rights while allowing for prosecution of those who unlawfully disclose names of foreign intelligence operatives.

The act sends out a clear signal that U.S. intelligence officers will no longer be fair game for those members of their own society who wish to take issue with the existence of CIA or find other motives for making these unauthorized disclosures.

FOIA Needs Adjustment

There's very little doubt anywhere that the intelligence community needs relief from the FOIA, yet this will likely be just as hard to get as was the identities law.

The Senate Intelligence Committee hearing on charter legislation demonstrated considerable opposition to exemptions to FOIA for the intelligence community but, in my view, we must sooner or later come to grips with the fact that openness in government must be tempered by consideration of how much openness our national security can afford.

The Freedom of Information Act of 1966 was designed to recognize the individual's right of access to the government's records that concerned him. Unfortunately, the act has had an unintended side effect on the intelligence community, because of its dealings with classified intelligence from sources in foreign countries. President Johnson warned us of this when he signed the law in 1966, saying that "the welfare of the nation or the rights of individuals may require that some documents not be made available." In 1974, President Ford refused to sign stronger FOIA amendments because of his concern "that our military or intelligence secrets and diplomatic relations could be adversely affected."

These warnings have now come home to roost. Even the Russians can make requests to the intelligence agencies and, under this law, their requests must be answered. Since the act was passed in 1966 and amended in 1974, the intelligence community has been denied intelligence that it normally could have expected from foreign agents, friendly foreign services, and Americans traveling abroad because these sources no longer believe that the U.S. government can protect them from public disclosure. At present, many sources have stopped sharing information with the United States altogether, while others share only what they think will not harm them if disclosed. The FOIA has also created a problem with the CIA's record-keeping system by necessitating distribution of and access to information that goes beyond what is considered consistent with good security practices. Testifying before the committee recently, Frank Carlucci, former deputy director of Central Intelligence, noted that "If we believe we need intelligence, then we have to accept some secrecy. FOIA has called into question around the world our ability to keep a secret. Its application in its current form is inappropriate, unnecessary in light of current oversight by the Senate and House Intelligence Committees, and harmful."

In closed testimony before my committee, we were told of a request that involved 150 reports and 600 documents from a foreign resident in Europe. The documents involved in this and many similar cases are filled with names, dates, places, and details of operations which, if released, would predictably lead to the deaths or incarceration of numerous people who had assisted the U.S. government in our intelligence collection mission.

The last question of that testimony poses this question: "Would you cooperate with the United States intelligence if you knew that the information which you delivered, often at risk of death, was subject to review for disclosure under American law?" That's a sobering question.

In addition to the serious situation this law has created, it costs the taxpayers $16 million or more per year to process FOIA requests just for the intelligence agencies. In effect, this is like an expensive government subsidy to those who make the request and I'm not sure that this is fair to the other taxpayers.

Human Side of Intelligence

Four years ago, in commenting on press publicity on intelligence collection, I suggested in a *Congressional Record* statement that a disturbing trend has become evident regarding the future course of our intelligence efforts. Whether this trend is the result of fascinations with "gee-whiz" technology or whether it represented the selling of SALT II does not matter. What does matter, however, is that our intelligence effort is based on a triad concept not unlike that of our regular armed forces. The three legs of the triad are communications intelligence (COMMINT), imagery intelligence (IMINT), and human intelligence (HUMINT). If we are not careful, we may end up crippling the HUMINT leg of the triad.

In this regard, a recent newspaper article sought to downplay the valuable role that the HUMINT plays in our intelligence process. Its conclusion was that since we have superior technology, HUMINT is an outdated relic of the past—a conclusion with which I fundamentally disagree.

Our satellites can give us little or no information on the intentions of hostile agents, their plans and targets. In these areas, it requires humans to be in the right places at the right time, which is often a long, tedious, and dangerous process. A satellite cannot be expected to tell us where, when, and how the next terrorism bomb will explode.

For all their sophistication, satellites can only tell us information of a quantitative nature—how many missiles or how many submarines the enemy has. Knowing what the enemy may do with his armament is completely beyond the satellites' capabilities, and this constitutes the basic reason for having a strong human intelligence effort. In an age of nuclear uncertainty, having a sense of the intentions of our enemies becomes more and more critical if we are to preserve our freedom. Too much reliance on our technical systems could ultimately exclude a third alternative in world affairs, namely, covert and/or paramilitary operations. By limiting ourselves to diplomatic responses or all-out military intervention, we would deprive this country of an important tool to influence events that require more than words and less than direct military intervention.

And let us not forget that however useful our satellites may be, they are still susceptible to technical countermeasures and deception.

Just as in modern warfare, we have a variety of new technical systems, yet it ultimately comes down to the human eyes and ears as well as the human mind to make the judgmental decisions which thousands of computers can never make. If we are to maintain a successful intelligence service, we must keep a proper balance between technology and man.

Perhaps because of the American love of technology or the desire to avoid getting our hands dirty, there has been a tendency to ascribe an excessive value and promise to the space systems. The advent of the space reconnaissance programs has been the single most important contribution to intelligence since the radio receiver. But the fact is that technical and human collection resources are both essential in assessing what is going on in foreign countries. Our experience in recent years has reinforced this, and has resulted in a rebuilding of the more traditional capabilities.

The sanctuary of space, however, is clearly in jeopardy. Although we believe that peacetime operations are not presently at risk, the capability to incapacitate space vehicles exists today. Soviet initiatives in this area have forced us to respond in kind, but more important is the challenge these developments present to the collection of intelligence.

U.S. initiatives in space, and especially in the intelligence field, have always been at the forefront of technology. There is no reason to believe that we have exhausted our technical know-how or that we have reached a plateau in our capabilities. On the contrary, opportunities abound for enhancing sensing technology, propulsion technology, and data processing technology. While technology is unquestionably a vital ingredient in our use of the high ground of space, we must not lose sight of an even more important factor. At the core of all our progress and potential are the dreamers and the builders and the operators of these magnificent devises. The intelligence space program has profited from the application of the best minds in this country, and the best of the best will be needed in the future to carry on in the fine tradition of the early space pioneers. But where will they come from? Will there be enough to go around? Will they have that extra capacity and vision so essential to tackle the challenges of the future? The education and encouragement of the next generation of space scientists and engineers may well be the most critical challenge we face.

Conclusion

Because the intelligence community went through a difficult period during the 1970s, the quality of collection was bound to suffer. Unfortunately, we seem to have reached a point where cynicism and distrust have replaced goodwill and trust. Too often we are ready to enact laws, pass regulations, and use the other coercive forces of government against all sorts of seeming ills. If we continue this trend, mediocrity and do-nothingism could become the watchword of the governors and governed alike. The Senate Intelligence Committee, by the very nature of the subject it is dealing with, cannot operate in the open and is therefore taken to task as being excessively secretive or being a captive of the intelligence agencies. If we are to be successful in obtaining good intelligence information for the protection of our freedom, we must also understand how to safeguard it. As chairman of the Senate Intelligence Committee, I am very concerned with our tremendous responsibility in this regard. Because committee members need access to classified information in order to perform our legislative and oversight responsibilities, we cannot afford to risk poor security and "leaks."

Recently, however, we have begun to restore the trust and confidence between the intelligence community and Congress. We share the goal of getting the best intelligence information possible to serve our national security and protect our freedom.

Recent years have witnessed a growing public awareness of the importance of intelligence that is timely, relevant, and of the highest quality.

We have enjoyed freedom for 200 years. We worked hard for it, many have fought for it, and some have died for it. It is up to us to decide whether we can make it last another 200 years. I think we can if we realize that freedom and intelligence go hand in hand.

Foreign Policy and the English Language   *Walter Laqueur*

Psittacism is the habit of using words without thought. The habit has spread in recent years as far as the coverage, the comment, and the analysis of foreign affairs in our media are concerned, and the same is also true in quasi-scholarly publications. Terms such as "conservative" and "liberal," "fascist" and "Marxist," left and right, "revolutionary" and "reactionary," "detente" and "cold war," "corrupt" and "progressive," let alone "socialist" and "democratic" are frequently used without reference to their real meaning. But is it always a case of psittacism, of thoughtlessness and confusion? On one hand, we know far too little about the psychology of parrots and parakeets (psittaci) after whom the habit is named, and on the other, it is just possible that the mistakes are sometimes quite deliberate.

Let us analyze some typical cases of apparent psittacism. It is perfectly nonsensical to call the inhabitants of a poor Lebanese mountain village "right wing" because they are Christian, and their neighbors from the next village "leftist"—just because they are Muslim. Yet the habit is by now almost universal. One suspects that those who were originally responsible for the use of these labels knew better and that there was a political intention behind it. (In the Third World, left wing has a positive connotation; right wing, on the other hand, is bad.) But subsequently these terms were adopted by others with no particular knowledge of the Middle Eastern scene.

Another interesting case of psittacism is the indiscriminate use of the term "guerrilla." The *London Times* would never report about a major bomb outrage or assassination or kidnapping by "Irish guerrillas" in London, just as *Le Monde* would never refer to Corsican guerrilla fighters in Paris, or the *New York Times* would never use the term guerrillas when reporting the activities of some Puerto Rican extremists in New York. But the same newspapers will not hesitate to report about guerrillas—though they quite obviously mean terrorists—if these happen to operate in other countries. There is a very considerable substantive, not just a semantic, difference between terrorist and guerrilla; furthermore, guerrilla has, on the whole, a positive public relations image, which terrorist has not.

As our examples have shown, reporters and subeditors are quite sensitive to this difference, at least as far as their own countries are concerned. Their word blindness is not total, only partial.

The misuse of the term "moderate" is another frequent case of psittacism. According to the dictionaries it means avoiding extremes, to be temperate in conduct and expression, not to be strongly partisan, one who holds moderate opinions, in politics, religions, etc., such as the Girondists in the French Revolution. But in contemporary usage, moderate sometimes means the very opposite. Thus, the *Christian Science Monitor,* quoting the Washington-based Center for Defense Information (CDI), introduces it as a moderate institution. The Center for Defense Information stands for a clear political line: in its frequent publications it strongly argues that the United States and its allies spend far too much on defense, that the United States is much stronger than the Soviet Union, which has far more severe security problems than the United States. It also believes that Soviet intentions are basically peaceful; it is not equally certain about U.S. intentions. It is not the purpose of this essay to comment on issues of substance; for all one knows, CDI may be right in its predictions, the Warsaw Pact may suddenly collapse out of sheer weakness, or the Soviet leaders may announce their conversion to a Gandhian-style pacifism. All this is possible, if somewhat unlikely. It is impossible to define a political approach of this kind as moderate, temperate, and nonpartisan. And the question then arises whether to describe an extreme point of view as moderate (or centrist) is a genuine mistake or a deliberate action.

The corruption of political language has been going on for a long time. It certainly did not end with the downfall of fascism, which made a notable contribution to the brutalization of language by leaving little to the imagination. But equally often the fascist political language was used as a means of deception: When the Japanese proclaimed a "Co-prosperity Sphere" in Asia they were not, of course, concerned with the prosperity of other countries such as Burma or Indochina. When Hitler talked about the German "New Order" in Europe, he did not make it clear that this "order" was to be based on German occupation, or at the very least on German hegemony and the extermination of all opponents. He frequently referred to his desire for peace but was discreet about the specific character of this peace; the murder of the Jews was called the "final solution" (which could mean a great many things). Even such circumlocution was too strong for a sensitive man like Himmler who preferred "transport to the East." The official name of Hitler's party was "National Socialist Workers' Party"; it was, as Goebbels said, the only true socialism. Stalin's constitution of 1936, on the other hand, was officially known as the "most democratic" in human history. A well-known Soviet song of the period ("Shiroka strana moya rodnaya") announced that there was "no other land in the world in which people were breathing equally freely." It is by now generally accepted that when Soviet spokesmen refer to "peace" and "progress," "freedom" or "democracy," they do not mean quite the same thing as noncommunists would mean. Since "imperialism" or "aggression" in the Soviet vocabulary apply a priori only to capitalist countries (and to those misguided communist countries that have rejected Soviet leadership), it is vain to look for a West-East consensus on the definition of aggression.

Tactical considerations are of great importance for the choice or rejection of political terminology. Thus Soviet leaders have noted that as a result of "hostile propaganda," the term "communism" has assumed a broad negative connotation to a much greater degree than socialism. It is, of course, impossible to change at this late date the name of old established communist parties like those of Italy and France. But on the other hand, the Warsaw bloc countries are always referred to as the socialist, not the communist, countries. This habit has been accepted by those in the West who usually follow the Soviet lead; by others, on the opposite end of the political spectrum who cannot be bothered with what they regard as minor differences between communism and democratic socialism; and lastly by those suffering from advanced psittacism. The noncommunist left in Europe will hardly make this verbal concession, for if it were conceded that Russia or, say, Albania were indeed socialist societies there would be no justification for the existence of social democratic parties in Western Europe.

Use has just been made of the term "left," which, as its opposite, goes back to the French Revolution when it referred to the sitting order in Parliament. The habit of seating slowly spread to other countries; in the British Parliament it was adopted only in the 1930s. By that time, serious doubts began to prevail with regard to the use of the terms: Was fascism, for instance, a movement of the left or the right? The question continues to preoccupy experts to this day; in many ways it is a futile question because fascism combined certain elements of both, while belonging neither to the left nor to the right. It gradually appeared that nineteenth-century terminology belonging to the era of parliamentary democracy could not be transposed to the movements of different inspiration without causing much confusion. Furthermore, there were great differences between countries, and between one fascism and another. No one in his right mind would have regarded the Franco dictatorship as a movement of the left, but likewise no one familiar with the situation in Romania would have claimed that the native brand of fascism was right wing. In short, the use of terms such as "left" and "right" did not help to clarify the character of fascism but, on the contrary, obfuscated it.

It did not help in other respects either. Was there such a thing as a "left-" or "right-wing" foreign policy in the 1930s, and if so, what did it mean? "Left," it was widely believed, was a synonym for international reconciliation, whereas "right" stood for patriotism and an aggressive foreign policy. But in France, the left had been the party of patriotism (Jacobinism) and even expansionism, whereas many of the right preferred Hitler to Leon Blum. The great issue in Britain in the 1930s was whether the dictators should be appeased and this cut across existing party lines. Some labor leaders were in favor of pacifism, others advocated rearmament. Winston Churchill was an extreme right-wing Tory, an unabashed imperialist who had opposed the majority of his party because it gave more freedom to India. But on the decisive issue of appeasement, Churchill and his friends took a line dimetrically opposed to that of Neville Chamberlain and his circle, who constituted the moderate wing of the Conservative party. Had Churchill suddenly become a man of the left? Hardly, Churchill had not changed, simply the great foreign political issues could no longer be defined using the nomenclature of an earlier age. The situation in the United States was similar; there was isolationism of the left and of the right, from the eve of the First World War to the aftermath of the Second.

In our time, Ed Clark's Libertarian party offers an interesting illustration. In domestic politics, it is right-wing conservative: it stands for greatly reduced taxation, for strict monetarism, for heavy cuts in government spending, for decontrol and deregulation all along the line, for the abolition of a minimum wage and so on. In foreign affairs, on the other hand, its mouthpiece, *Inquiry,* advocates the dissolution of NATO, wishes to reduce the defense budget to a fraction of the present level, and would like to abolish the CIA. While demanding absolute freedom of the press in the United States, it warns that more of such freedoms in communist countries (which it chooses to call socialist countries) such as Poland would have disastrous consequences. Generally speaking, it draws its inspiration from writers such as Professor Noam Chomsky. All of which has led at least one commentator to marvel how far leftward the right wing of American politics stands.

It is a curious argument, for if the far right has moved to the left, as far as foreign policy is concerned, why use the terms in the first place? The phenomenon is by no means altogether novel; some of the founding fathers of American fascism propagated a left-wing foreign policy after the Second World War without reneging on their erstwhile fascist convictions.

The only political party that for a long time was not internally divided on foreign policy was the Communist party; its aim was the defense and the strengthening of the Soviet Union. However, the correct party line was subject to radical and abrupt change: in 1933 the Communists said the Social Democrats were the greatest danger, not Hitler; in 1935 Nazism became the greatest threat; in 1939 Hitler made his peace with the Soviet Union and the attitude towards him changed accordingly; in 1941, the Nazis again became the enemies of mankind. Thus, the correct "left" position in July 1941 was the opposite of what it had been the year before; always on the assumption that support for the Soviet Union was the decisive test for every communist and that "left-wing" and communist were synonymous. After 1945, the situation became far more complicated from the communist point of view: Were men and women of left-wing and progressive views to support Russia or China, Yugoslavia or Albania, Indochina or Cambodia? Surely the attitude towards capitalism was no longer the decisive yardstick, private ownership of the means of production having been abolished in all these countries. Communist leaders still accuse each other of sundry "left-" or "right-wing" deviations but they do it less frequently than in years past and, in any case, the exercise is perfectly meaningless. Only reluctantly has the use of the terms "left" and "right" been dropped by the Western media with regard to the conflict between communist countries.

But in other respects it is now used with a vengeance: not a day passes without some reference in the columns of the newspapers to "liberal" or "conservative" (and "ultra-liberal" and "ultra-conservative") views and approaches to foreign policy. "Liberal" in this context refers to sympathy for "progressive" Third World countries, belief in detente, opposition to defense spending, opposition to American "interventionism," etc. "Conservative" on the other hand stands, broadly speaking, for the opposite. This practice is based on the assumption, correct in part, that in domestic politics there are great differences between "left" and "right," between "conservative" and "liberal"; if so, why not use the same classification with regard to foreign policy as well? Even in domestic affairs the scheme can be used only with reservations for the differences are much less clear now than they were 30 or 40 years ago, as new problems and challenges have arisen that transcend the traditional pattern. The international scene has very little in common with American (or West European) domestic affairs; signposts and demarcation lines that make sense in the United States are only misleading when applied to other political regimes. The American political compass does not function south of the Rio Grande, let alone in other continents. Likewise, standards are not the same with regard to the orientation among foreign political systems, societies, and the definition of our attitudes towards them. Thus, a Khomeini or a Qaddafi becomes a conservative or a liberal or a revolutionary conservative (or vice versa) or a radical populist or a radical democrat or an Islamic revolutionary—there is no limit to human ingenuity (and folly) as far as attaching labels are concerned.

Those who use these labels may believe that they serve some useful purpose, but what could the purpose be? One can perhaps understand the psychological motivation of those in the West who believe that a revolution is a priori a good thing, deserving our sympathy and support, even if it may be a little extreme, confused, and committing occasional errors. Seen in this light, people in foreign lands who use revolutionary, or at the very least populist, verbiage cannot be all bad. This solidarity syndrome is well known: it always ends in disappointment (the case of Khomeini was only the most recent incident), yet hope springs eternal. Every discussion in the Third World (yet another misnomer) requires these slogans. The "popular masses" are always invoked in the speeches; "liberation" and "revolution" are always welcomed even though this can mean nowadays about anything from Pol Pot to the bomb in the Bologna railway station, placed by the neofascist "revolutionary nuclei." There is the tendency to welcome any populist demagogue, any self-styled revolutionary, and to extend credit to him, frequently for a long time, until it is reluctantly realized that there has been no liberation, that a great many people have been killed and imprisoned, and that the condition of the masses has not changed. But this explains only the behavior of a small minority.

The corruption of the political language manifests itself in many ways—in fact, one of them is the use of the term "corruption." Hardly a month passes without reports to the effect that the regime in a certain country is about to fall or has been overthrown because of its "corrupt" and "oppressive" (or "repressive") character. Oppressive (or repressive) according to the dictionaries is to be subject to unjust hardship, cruelty, tyranny. That there is a great deal of tyranny in the world is not open to doubt and it would be a comforting thought if we knew for certain that tyrants cannot escape their fate, and that the greater the tyranny the greater the punishment. But this is not what historical experience shows; the truly tyrannical regimes are hardly ever overthrown unless they are incautious enough to engage in war and be defeated. It is only those who practice repression halfheartedly, or even try to improve their wicked ways who are defeated. About the crimes of truly effective tyrannical regimes one hears relatively little because they are careful to keep out the Western media, or at the very least limit the media's movements and impose stringent controls. As a result of censorship or self-censorship there is not much information, and certainly not much that is offensive to the regime. Western newspaper readers were exposed to a rich diet on the inequities of the rule of the late shah, or of South Korea, or of Egypt. They will seldom if ever hear such stories about North Korea, Iraq, Libya, Syria, Ethiopia, or contemporary Iran, not because there has been, or is, less oppression but because the Western media have no access or are threatened or cajoled into silence.

While the flow of news can be impeded or even stopped, it is almost impossible to mislead the outside world about the true character of a regime for any length of time unless there is a willingness to be deceived. Such willingness is by no means infrequent and it has linguistic consequences to be discussed presently. According to the more primitive argument, things are not what they appear to be—tyrannies are havens of freedom, whereas the so-called democracies practice fascism and slavery. On a slightly more sophisticated level it is maintained that there are in the world only various degrees of unfreedom; consequently, there is not much to choose between the regimes. Somewhere in between these two schools of thought is Professor Richard Falk of Princeton. He has established a model to differentiate between various kinds of dictatorships (or potential dictatorships), which provides our next exhibit. Professor Falk has discovered nine categories:

- Brazilian (including Egypt, Mexico, Saudi Arabia, Nigeria, and South Africa).
- Left Praetorian (including Amin's Uganda).
- Right Praetorian (Costa Rica, Burma, Lebanon).
- Leninist (including Benin, Ethiopia, Cambodia).
- Trilateral (the "capitalists" from Austria to Lichtenstein).
- Stalinist (the obvious).
- Left pre-authoritarian (Finland).
- Centrist pre-authoritarian (Mauritania, Mauritius, and Portugal).
- Right pre-authoritarian (including Israel, Malta, and Nauru).

This fascinating list can provide entertainment for many a long winter evening. In the present context a random question will have to suffice: Why is North Korea regarded as a Leninized state? The term, according to the author, points to a "larger degree of freedom" in contrast to the "pathological expression of state socialism" that reached its peak in the Soviet Union and lives on there in diluted form: North Korea is a much freer country because "the socialist advantage arising from its promises about, and achievements of equality, solidarity, and liberation." The promises are certainly not in doubt, but if one moves from the level of promises to the level of realities, one will find little that is "Leninist" about North Korea, let alone freedom and liberation. It is a nationalist dictatorship. It is not a capitalist country, nor was Egypt under the Pharaohs or China under the T'ang dynasty. In fact, a comparison with ancient Egypt or with Europe in the age of absolute monarchy could be more helpful than references to Leninism, solidarity, and liberation. As for the "larger degree of freedom" there is reason to believe that in comparison with North Korea, the Soviet Union, not to mention Hungary and Poland, are wildly permissive, almost anarchical societies. But why single out North Korea? With even greater justification it could be asked why poor Costa Rica, which does not even have an army, should be termed a "praetorian" state—and a right-wing one at that? Why focus on Professor Falk? Yet another legitimate question: One is not dealing with individual eccentrics but with psittacism on a massive scale, almost an epidemic.

"Corruption" is the other favorite term of the theorists of the law of decline and fall in the modern world. The term has several meanings—lack of integrity and honesty, it also implies the acceptance of money for dishonest ends. But people can be corrupted not only by money but also, sometimes far more effectively, by flattery, and, of course, by power.

To what extent do repression and corruption—in the narrow specific sense—go hand in hand? The theoreticians use them frequently as synonyms but this is quite misleading. The truly savage dictators—a Hitler, Stalin, even a Mussolini—were not financially corrupt; they did not accept bribes, not even on a grand scale (Goering did, but in his case, too, this was a minor blemish—the lust for power was always dominant.). It could even be argued that corruption implies a certain degree of freedom, for the stronger the controls in a dictatorship the less room for corruption: some will exist under any circumstances. It has been said about certain countries that a certain measure of corruption mitigates what would otherwise be an intolerable situation. Nor is it true that widespread corruption necessarily undermines a political regime; on the contrary, the wider the corruption, the stronger the vested interest in maintaining the status quo, the less opposition to it. There are societies and whole political cultures that would hardly function without a certain measure of corruption: the regime may be overthrown from time to time but the prime motive underlying the circulation of the elites is the desire to get part of the spoils. The history of Latin America—but by no means only of Latin America over the last 150 years—offers a great many examples. To say that a political regime is corrupt is one thing, but to infer from this that it is weak and therefore likely to be overthrown is a non sequitur. Some elites are far more adept than others in hiding corruption and for this reason it may not be easy to prepare comparative statistics about the incidence of corruption in the Middle East and Africa. But the final result is a foregone conclusion: there is in these parts no correlation between the prevalence of corruption and the stability of the regime.

It is easy to point to the misuse of language in the foreign policy field, but it is far more difficult to say with any degree of certainty whether this is done deliberately or whether it is the result of neglect or sloppiness. Sometimes one can think of mitigating circumstances: the case of Lebanon has been noted. As Neville Chamberlain used to say in such circumstances, this is a faraway country about which we know little, hence the confusion about "left-wing" Muslim and "right-wing" Christian mountain villagers. Equally, Qaddafi seems to be somewhat unstable, so why blame the media if he is sometimes described as a man of the left, and at other times a right-winger? In short, one can find excuses for lack of precision (and worse) for those who do not specialize in the study of and comment on foreign affairs.

But what if the misuse is perpetrated by seasoned reporters and commentators, by experts who surely must know better? Even they may be subject to inexplicable lapses. But if there is consistency in their behavior, this charitable explanation no longer applies and there is room for suspicion. They know that the use of terms such as "liberal" or "conservative," of "left" and "rightist" in foreign policy does not add to our understanding. They know that one can be for or against detente quite irrespective of one's feelings about the control of the money supply or the introduction of a national health service. They know that Khomeini and Qaddafi are neither liberals nor conservatives, that Benin (Dahomey) is not Marxist, that the Lebanese mountaineers are not really right or left wing, and that one does not have to be a Friedmanite to accept the fact that the Soviet Union is spending a great deal of money on its military forces. Thus, one is bound to reach the conclusion that while laziness and ignorance may be the reason for use of ill-fitting clichés in some cases, this is not so in others. Could it be perhaps the desire to save newsprint by using "abbreviations"? It is so much cheaper to refer to "Marxist regimes" in Benin or in Congo-Brazzaville, rather than trying to describe the true character of these governments; the number of experts on Benin is small, there will not be many protests against the use of abbreviations, and it can always be argued in defense that Benin usually votes with the Soviets in the United Nations and that it must therefore be "Marxist." And does not the same refer, *mutatis mutandis,* to the "left" and "right," the "liberal" and the "conservative" labels in writing on foreign policy in general? But the abbreviation theory is not very convincing either, for even more newsprint could be saved if the adjectives were dropped altogether.

Do we have to suspect fraudulence? Words are symbols and this is true a fortiori in political language. Such symbols can be manipulated, they are a means to influence public opinion by creating confusion and disinformation. In the 1930s and 1940s the Axis powers tried to appropriate for themselves with varying success the term "peace"; regardless of how often Hitler, Mussolini, and the Japanese engaged in naked aggression, they were always fighting for peace against the plutocratic (and later also the Bolshevik) warmongers. After the Second World War, "peace" became the most frequently used term in the Soviet dictionary. The "Partisans of Peace" engaging in the "defense of peace" against the "imperialist warmongers" were mobilized all over the globe; they had their annual congresses, published a great deal of literature, engaged in mass meetings and demonstrations. The fact that the "peace movement" still exists is not widely known; perhaps the Russians forgot to wind it up, perhaps they are holding it in cold storage, to be revived at some future date. But it has certainly been much downgraded: once it became known that it was just another front organization with the sole purpose to justify Soviet foreign policy, it had outlived its usefulness.

In the 1970s "detente" replaced "peace" as the key word in political warfare. No other term in our political vocabulary has caused so much needless confusion. But one cannot fairly blame Soviet propaganda; on the contrary, detente *(razriadka)* is used much less frequently in the communist countries than in the West. The problem with detente is not that it does not exist, but that it means different things in different places, and that some well-meaning (and perhaps also some not-so-well meaning) people in the West have systematically created the impression that their own conception of detente is shared by everyone else. The following statement should serve as an example: "Detente has to be saved if mankind is going to survive whatever the current misunderstandings between the superpowers." This sentence clearly wishes to convey the impression that detente is a synonym for peace, an antonym for war and cold war; that unless detente is restored, the danger of war will grow; that there is unanimity between West and East as to what detente means; that if sufficient efforts were made by Western statesmen and if the intrigues of Western hawks were thwarted, detente could be saved; and that those who oppose detente endanger the survival of mankind. We are not told that the Soviet leaders never implied that detente means bridge building, not gaining advantages at the cost of the other side; that they never promised that political tensions would lessen; that political warfare would be discontinued; that military action outside Europe and North America would not be undertaken during detente. They never made a secret of their belief that detente (as they understood it) was to create better conditions for a decisive shift in the global balance of power. Seen in this light, the tensions and crises of the last few years are not the breakdown of detente but its result.

*   *   *

All this became fairly obvious several years ago and President Ford was so disenchanted at one stage that he vowed to banish the term from his vocabulary. It took President Ford's successor three years and some major disappointments to reach similar conclusions. The term "detente" makes sense only as a synonym for "Soviet-Western relations," a neutral term, value free, neither good nor bad. But so deeply rooted is the belief that detente has somehow an existence of its own, quite irrespective of how the Soviets view it, that it is still used as a synonym for peace in newspaper columns and even in discussions among experts. There still is a fairly widespread belief that a consistent "detente" line is the only virtuous and sane policy constituting the best chance to safeguard world peace. Those who fail to understand this simple truth are either acting out of dishonorable motives (the military-industrial complex) or out of negative psychological reasons (they fail to understand the enormity of the destruction likely to be caused by a Third World War). The example of "detente" shows the dangers of ambiguity in political language and how difficult it is to eradicate such misuse even after it has become abundantly clear that the indiscriminate use of the term causes confusion. And there is no doubt that at least some of this confusion has been deliberately caused.

Accuracy in the use of language is not a panacea, it does not constitute a guarantee for the correct understanding of political reality. As a wise statesman once noted, world affairs are constructed most unfairly; there is an infinite number of possibilities to misunderstand and misconstrue realities and usually only one to get them right. Spinoza said that one of the most frequent causes of mistakes is to attach the wrong name to a thing, but Spinoza was too trusting a soul, he apparently did not consider that such practices would be used quite deliberately. Even if the term "detente" were used correctly, even if it were clear that it meant different things to different people, there still would be wide scope for misunderstandings. But it is also true that the necessity to clarify one's language is a precondition for the clarification of thought.

In April 1946, George Orwell published his famous essay on "Politics and the English Language." Today, scores of Orwells would be needed to clear up the accumulated rubbish of more than three decades; the United Nations alone could employ a dozen. His basic thesis that there is a vicious circle is still true; the English language has become inaccurate (or deliberately misleading) because it is used to express foolish thoughts—and the slovenliness of the language makes it easier to have foolish thoughts. Partly this is a matter of bad habits, partly of deception, but the decadence of language may still be curable—psittacism is not usually a fatal disease. Silly words and misleading expressions can be made to disappear if exposed to ridicule. A beginning should be made by showing a little less tolerance towards the use of silly, deceptive, and unnecessary words in the debates on foreign policy. At the very least the work of the terrible simplificateurs will become more difficult. When they next invoke "detente" or refer to "liberal" or "conservative" foreign policies, they should be asked, politely but firmly, what, if anything, they mean. They may not like it, and their answers will not be very instructive, but the exercise will still be of considerable educational value.

7

INTERNATIONAL ECONOMICS

Strategic Leverage from Aid and Trade   *James R. Schlesinger*

This paper is based on the twin premises: (a) that American policies regarding aid and trade may legitimately be employed as strategic weapons in the Cold War, and (b) that, in such employment, flexibility is both appropriate and necessary. These postulates will be resisted in various quarters. They involve, first of all, rejection of the idealistic-utopian view that aid should be extended essentially on humanitarian grounds and that considerations of power should be scrupulously avoided in the aid program. By contrast, the position taken here is that the primary intent of both our aid and trade policies should be to serve the interests of the United States and, also, to assist our principal allies, whose long-run interests and cultural traditions are more or less coincident with our own. While it is perfectly proper to recognize that extension of aid or increase of trade serves a humanitarian objective of increasing the aggregate income and possibly the standard of life in many nations unaligned in the Cold War, some of which are close to the margin of starvation, for the present the elimination of poverty cannot be the *paramount* objective of our policies. In the world in which we now find ourselves ideal goals must be subordinated to the more pressing objective of enhancing the security of America and the West.*

A second locus of resistance to the underlying premises of this paper is represented by those who fear that strategic flexibility in the use of these weapons will, for one reason or another, result in the compromising of freedom. Aid and trade policies should reflect the values of freedom. Any compromising on these values, such as would be represented by the conscious adoption of discriminatory trade practices, would weaken the American economy and reduce the moral strength of the society. If we wish to encourage the growth of freedom, aid should either not be extended, or should be extended only with great reluctance, to any nation whose social order departs markedly from our own brand of liberal capitalism. At the outer margin this

---

*Though there is no need to belabor the point, it bears mentioning that there is no necessity to emphasize our security objectives in foreign policy statements directed toward the underdeveloped world. Some window dressing seems advisable. Nevertheless I think that leading figures in the Government should have firmly in mind what the principal objective is.

would, of course, exclude nations which have developed Communist systems and which are to a greater or lesser degree satellites of the Soviet Union. It is contended that any aid to, or even trade with, such nations represents an abetting of the enemy and in some way results in self-contamination.

To accept any of these contentions as guiding principles would be unwise. If we are to be flexible, each situation should be examined on its own merits to assess the net benefits and costs involved. Such an assessment should, of course, take place within the context of a general policy, and policy-makers should be alert to the broader implications of individual decisions. But policies must to some extent be pragmatic and experimental. The public ought not expect perfect consistency between specific decisions and general policies.

Before embarking on a detailed discussion of how the economic weapons of strategy might be used, it seems appropriate to mention a few general considerations that should guide our policy. First, the United States has in the past been accused of lacking a positive policy and of determining its actions negatively and belatedly in response to Soviet actions. There is some justice in such criticism. It ought not be inferred, however, from such comments that it would be advisable for the United States to formulate some kind of positive program and adhere to it in the face of changing developments. If the United States is to employ its power effectively, it must be flexible enough to adjust its policies to take advantage of unforeseen opportunities or to counter a deterioration in its own position with which the over-all program had not been intended to deal. Part of American grand strategy must be to alter its policies and ambitions with alterations in the international posture. Without such flexibility we may be assured that the Soviets will take notice of the character of an unchanging policy, and will design measures which will counter the main thrust of American effort. Power which is spent in attacks on relatively invulnerable points of the Soviet Cold-War battle array or is repeatedly used against the same vulnerable points with diminishing returns is wasted. Whether wasted power is power at all is a question which we may leave to the philosophers. But to design an ideal and permanent policy which is impervious to changing developments and altered Soviet attitudes and actions is a losing venture. One may hope that national policy will not be altered indiscriminately in response to every changing breeze and that the longer-term guidelines and the cost of their abandonment will be taken into consideration in day-to-day control of policy. Nevertheless, there must be tactical and even strategic flexibility. There would be no need to mention this obvious point regarding what might be called the "economy of power" were it not for the fact that many critics of recent policies seem to assume that it is practicable to designate an array of permanent policy objectives and to follow this program willy-nilly.

There is a second consideration which deals with the objectives and, therefore, at one remove, with the guidelines and allocative mechanisms of the program for international assistance. If aid allotments are graduated in accordance with the degree of support provided by the recipient nation of Western strategic objectives, the aid program is unlikely, save by coincidence, to provide a powerful spur to economic progress in the underdeveloped world. On the other hand, if assistance is extended exclusively or primarily to those nations which can most effectively employ those resources in achieving growth, the program may be a weak (or even treacherous) instrument of policy. Elsewhere I have argued, at least tentatively, the advantages to be gained by distributing aid primarily on the basis of the recipient nations' attitudes toward our foreign policy objectives.[1] There is still something to be said for such a procedure. Through it one is in a position to minimize the mutual jealousies that are created by the assistance program—by creating a relatively objective standard which all potential recipients can understand even if they dislike it. It is relatively riskless in that it seeks to preserve the status quo, but it is riskless in this sense because it lacks daring. It is based on the premise that it is difficult to foretell or significantly to influence long-range changes in the pattern of hostility and alliance among independent states.

Whatever the advantages of a policy of graduating aid in accordance with support of Western objectives, it is plain that the decision in this Administration and in its predecessor has been against it. The primary thrust of the aid program will be, unless a nation is under direct assault, to provide assistance to those that can most profitably employ it to expand aggregate output. Within the context of such a policy, the question is how the aid can be used to serve our own objectives. It may be noted that some of the tensions which exist between an alliance-oriented and a development-oriented aid program have been eliminated by the displacement of SEATO by India as the principal bulwark against Chinese expansionism. These tensions have not been entirely eliminated, as the Pakistani response to American military assistance to India bears witness, yet the sharp conflict between the two patterns of assistance which existed in the late fifties no longer exists.

Deterrence: Carrots and Sticks

In the past decade considerable ingenuity has been invested in studying the type of force structures which will deter the Soviets from outright military assault. In much of the discussion there was a failure to recognize that the concept of deterrence has a broader applicability than to military matters alone. It is, in fact, relevant to the whole range of foreign policy issues. The Austrian peace treaty provides the Soviets with an excellent device to deter the Austrians from abandoning neutrality and joining forces with the West—a step they might well take were they in a freer position. The risk of Soviet intervention is sufficiently great to preclude such action. The Finns are even more effectively deterred—and the Soviet military presence frustrates the hope for *rapprochement* with the West in at least several of the satellite nations.

On our side we wish to deter the underdeveloped nations from taking steps which are frankly hostile to Western interests. In addition, we should like to have some means of encouraging the satellites to resist Soviet pressures. Conceptually at least, the answer is simple: we must consciously strive to develop mechanisms of deterrence. The very existence of such mechanisms will encourage greater circumspection in dealing with Western interests. They would be most useful if they do not have to be employed, but they may be—in the event of a substantial provocation. Mistakenly in the past we have consciously considered deterrence only in our dealings with the Soviets, and have assumed that it was unnecessary for dealing with the underdeveloped nations and irrelevant for dealing with the Satellites. As a result our responses have been belated and ad hoc.

This failure to think through the nature of deterrent measures that might be applied to areas other than those representing a primary threat may be sheer oversight, but the implicit analysis is faulty. Even where relationships are basically those of coordination rather than rivalry, elements of deterrence are always implicit in the situation.[2] In the past we have not hesitated to threaten our allies with "agonizing reappraisals"—and, in practice, we have made such reappraisals with less advertisement, more subtlety, and perhaps with less agony than we thought might be required. Our policy toward those who are neither wholly with the West nor wholly with the Soviets will be far more effective when a system of deterrence has been constructed—a system of rewards and sanctions which is at least vaguely perceived in advance. In our attitude toward the newly emerging nations we have tended to assume—what it is unwise to assume—that we can be "permissive" and that eventually the new nations will learn to be responsible and reasonable according to our lights.

The implicit analogy to American child-rearing methods, now somewhat out of fashion, is quite relevant, for social attitudes tend to form a complex whole. Where public opinion influences policy, views on child-rearing are likely to be related to those on foreign policy. "Young" nations are supposed to go through the same stages of development as humans. This is, of course, not the case, but even with respect to children, permissiveness is unworkable. Even the most permissive of parents have sneaky ways of obtaining the behavior they desire—ways which children understand even if the parents are themselves deceived. We cannot afford to wait for other nations to acquire a feel for the American temperament; we should instead consciously devise a pattern of techniques for influencing the conduct of others— which combines the values of firmness with independence for others.

During much of the twentieth century the American disposition has been to regard employment of the stick in minor international tensions as immoral. We have instead attempted to achieve our objectives through the overwhelming use of the carrot. But this is hardly an effective method in the long run. Any system that has only reward but no sanctions provides a temptation to those affected to run the minor risk of unfriendly words or adjustment of the reward in order to bring their behavior into conformity with their own ambitions or the expectations of those outside the system.

Even if the primary goal of the assistance program is to promote economic development and social change in the assisted nations, it should be implicit in the program that we look upon our own interests with a little tenderness, and that aid or trade may be curtailed if actions are taken which are provoking as well as provocative. In dealing with the Caribbean nations the existence of the sugar-control system automatically supplied us with an effective mechanism for bringing pressure to bear. Ultimately the Cubans provoked us into taking more forceful steps—on a more or less ad hoc basis. Normally, however, there is no established mechanism for bringing pressure to bear. Before we can expect other nations to be deterred from taking actions hostile to the West we must not only have a carefully designed system of responses, but we must have made it credible to those whom we hope to deter that we might actually put such retaliatory measures into use.

Much of the disappointment we have felt in recent years regarding the behavior of the neutrals may be attributed to our earlier failure to establish an incentive system which would help elicit the type of behavior we desired. Not only was there little risk of punitive action, but on the part of the neutrals there was an awareness, possibly unconscious, that concessions might be obtained from the West by an unsympathetic posture, while nothing could be gained from the Soviets by a similar response. A posture of moral superiority may be disturbing to Anglo-American public opinion, and by generating self-doubt might bring concessions. The Soviet Union was impervious to this sort of pressure. The upshot was that through the absence of firm policies we help to create a situation ripe for Soviet exploitation in which Soviet accomplishments appear large in relation to either their natural advantages or the resources which they were willing to invest in the underdeveloped lands.

We should move toward a posture in which it is recognized by all parties that, while we regard use of military force as only the last possible resort, we have access to a variety of intermediate responses in the event of provocative action. Section 232 of the Trade Expansion Act (originally passed in 1955 as the so-called national security amendment to the Trade Agreements Act) provides for the specification of *commodities* whose importation (allegedly) threatens national security by eliminating domestic sources of supply and provides for limitation of such imports. There is no reason why the law cannot be changed to specify *nations* from which importation can be limited—and to far better purpose.* Access to the American market is something that no underdeveloped nation can lightly surrender. The threat becomes all the stronger, of course, if joint arrangements can be worked out with the Common Market, and to a lesser degree with Britain, Japan, and other industrialized countries. The dependence of the underdeveloped nations taken together on Western markets is very great. Even for a *single* country, like Cuba, the substitution of Bloc markets for Western markets represents a very poor trade—the terms of which would become harsher if any large number of underdeveloped nations tried to "go East" simultaneously.

Making access to American and other Western markets contingent on avoidance of overtly hostile acts, by providing a sanction, would

---

*If the authority to restrict application of the law to Communist-dominated or controlled nations, conferred on the President by Section 231 of the Trade Expansion Act, is interpreted broadly enough, the President may already possess the necessary powers. Though the wording is quite general, the plain intent of the section is, however, to prevent or to eliminate tariff concessions which have been or might be extended to Communist nations under the most-favored-nation clause, rather than providing the power to impose more general restrictions on trade. A very generous interpretation of Presidential powers and a very dubious interpretation as to what constitutes a "Communist-dominated" area would be necessary before the present section could be used to put pressure on unfriendly nations in the underdeveloped world.

alter the way in which underdeveloped nations perceived the environment. Take a concrete example. Some people have argued that Ghana has been unduly troublesome as the center of anti-Western ferment in sub-Saharan Africa. I do not find the present situation particularly disturbing, but assume, for purposes of discussion, that it were to deteriorate. Suppose Ghana were to make use of its solid foreign-exchange position to encourage anti-Western moves in Nigeria. The standard American response would be to augment assistance to Nigeria, but under such circumstances a far more direct approach to the issue would be to bring measured retaliation against Ghana. In this case the policing problems would be relatively simple, for the trade in cacao is sufficiently limited that discovering the source of supply should not be difficult. As heavy a blow against the Ghanian economic position as desired might be struck. To be sure, the Soviets might take advantage of the opening, but the Soviet tendency has been to be niggardly in aid and incompetent in performance. The long-run therapeutic effect on other states of such action might be substantial. And for such a goal the American and possibly the European consumer may be asked to forego chocolate bars—at least temporarily.

I do not believe that the knowledge that sanctions exist need seriously interfere in the long run with our objective of encouraging growth and reform in the underdeveloped areas. In some ways the prospects might be improved, for in the majority of the underdeveloped countries energies that might have been wasted in tilting against the West (with the by-product of discouraging outside investment) may be more productively employed. Nor do I believe that establishing a mechanism of deterrence in this manner needs to imply more than a slight modification of our policy of moving toward liberalized, multilateral trade. The bulk of our trade will continue to be with the industrialized nations of Western Europe, Canada, Japan, etc. At the very most, no more than five per cent of our trade should be very much affected by these restraints.

When the decision is made to apply pressure to a nation for which there is an aid program, the usual assumption might be that aid should be cut first. Under ordinary conditions this may be the case, but there may be circumstances in which it is appropriate to continue with the aid program. Aid implies commitments, and it may be wisest to bring to a successful conclusion projects which have been inaugurated. The maximum psychological effect may be obtained in this way. Also, it may be unwise to sacrifice the personal and informal relationships which have been established by officials of the aid program. Finally, it may be possible to bring pressure to bear more discreetly via the trade route.

One final consideration—it would be unwise to use potential weapons of this sort for niggling purposes. The balance of payments has been troublesome and is properly an object of concern in Washington, but surely it is not a first-order consideration in our relations with the underdeveloped nations. Suggestions have been bruited about that we should make use of the aid program to force recipients to buy from us in ways that go beyond tied aid. Under the best of circumstances, our bargaining power is limited, and shooting away strategic ammunition for so paltry an economic goal would seem to reflect a poor sense of proportion.

Aid

Within an over-all framework designed to discourage hostile or predatory attitudes toward the West, the aid program may seek to foster the maximum rate of economic and social progress. In the basic policy of AID, the Kennedy Administration has explicitly adopted this goal. As has been indicated there are costs to this decision. Outsiders are not likely to be much liked even under the best of circumstances, which hardly apply to the underdeveloped countries, and their intervention in whatever direction will in the long run excite antagonism based on real or fancied wrongs. Nevertheless, the basic decision has been made. Let us examine in what way we may proceed so that the good effects clearly outweigh the ill effects.

There are two initial postulates: (1) our bargaining power will be limited, and (2) American notions of social reform and of equity are neither necessarily applicable in the underdeveloped lands, nor need we assume that those whose cooperation we must win will find them appealing. These postulates are interrelated. Jointly they imply that we cannot press forward on all fronts to create a society in which a good American democrat will feel at home, but must instead concentrate our energies on those social changes which will spur economic growth even if the immediate results are more consistent with the cultural genius of the peoples involved rather than our own tastes. We ought not expect them to make the same choices as we would, or, if they make the same choices, to achieve in a ten-year period what it took us eighty years to achieve. Finally, in reaching judgments on social processes in other lands, we cannot apply what are our own—or, in reality, higher—standards of purity.

As outsiders, we will be unable to perceive the social function of behavior which is superficially corrupt, and will tend to lump it together with that which is purely parasitical. With respect to our own history, retrospectively we have come to find merit in what once were regarded as the disreputable procedures of an organization like Tammany Hall in that it provided a kind of social security and a welcome for the newly arrived immigrant. We are accustomed to the daily dangling of new post offices, good committee assignments, and bridges over creeks in the outback before wavering Congressmen, and warm approval is given, for its fine sense of political realism, to whatever administration is doing the dangling by those who agree with its goals. Toward similar procedures abroad we are inclined to take a simple muckraking attitude. We look askance at the higgling of the political market—with a naiveté that would do credit both to missionaries and old-style political reformers. If we hope to achieve a fair measure of success, we shall have to sharpen our critical faculties and learn to distinguish between unappetizing social devices which are functional and those which are simple barriers to progress.

The statement of objectives by AID is a very ambitious one. The purposes of the assistance program include stimulation of self-help, encouragement of progressive forces, and achievement of governments based on consent, which recognize the dignity and worth of individuals who are expected to participate in determining the nation's goals. No doubt, a statement of aspirations is in large part window dressing, but the criteria by which self-help is moving toward social and political progress are more specific: a more equitable distribution of income, a more equitable tax system with increased yields, expanded welfare programs, increased political participation and civil liberties, and so on. Several points may be made regarding the objectives: first, there are too many; second, they are to some extent inconsistent; and third, they ignore the real resources available.

There is, in the first place, the long-perceived clash between economic progress, on the one hand, and the combined goals of equitable distribution of income, immediate improvement in living standards, and security on the other. This underlying conflict spills over into a tension between rapid economic progress and the introduction of democratic processes. On this issue there appears to have been a revolution in informed opinion in the United States during the past five years. During the late fifties, it had become almost an axiom that authoritarian, if not totalitarian, governments had innate advantages in guiding economies toward rapid growth. The prevailing view was based, no doubt, on an assessment of the record of the Soviet regime, and an exaggerated notion of how much the Chinese "Great Leap Forward" would accomplish. Perhaps the earlier "pessimism" regarding the relative performance potential of "free" and "controlled" economies was overdone, but have we not gone too far in the now prevailing "optimism" that any clash between economic progress and the democratic institutions which insure the dominance of the *vox populi* is minimal?

The average citizen—particularly when he is ill-housed, ill-clothed, ill-fed, and ill-educated—seems most likely to be interested in the here and now. A government which is responsive to the desires of the public will continually be tempted to mortgage the future for the present. The "abstinence" or "waiting" which classical and neoclassical economics state to be necessary ingredients in economic progress will be hard to require, as will be the incentive schemes (and the accompanying conspicuous consumption) which are likely to strike the average voter as inequitable. We may recall that the Perón regime was (and still may be?) the most popular regime in recent Latin American history. Or we may observe the economic consequences of Brazilian democracy, and have our doubts. The inflow of American resources may be able to make showpieces out of several small, recently-democratized nations like the Dominican Republic, but we ought not assume either that democracy assists in economic development, or that the Dominican example is widely applicable. This is not to say that some judicious prodding in the direction of democracy may not be a wise policy, but it must be *judicious,* and cannot be based on the assumption that democracy necessarily fosters the political stability essential to growth.

One of the criteria by which self-help can be judged as justifying additional aid is an improvement in the savings ratio. Some students of the aid program would put major emphasis on changes in the savings ratio in that it provides a relatively objective standard by which an improvement in economic performance can be judged.* If we apply an objective standard, complaints about the distribution of aid and subjectivity in the judgment of self-help can be minimized. But such a standard points to the conflict inherent in the wider ambitions of AID. To the extent that a rise in the savings ratio is a primary objective of policy, it will be hindered by movement toward a more equal distribution of income. Achievement of relative income equality either directly or through a progressive income tax may interfere with incentives. Just what the appropriate degree of progressivity is for the tax structure is a delicate question upon which judgments can vary widely. No doubt in

---

*Charles Wolf, Jr. of RAND has been attempting to develop an econometric model which will provide an objective measure of the performance of aid recipients in terms of self-help. The criterion is the savings ratio. In the model the attempt is made to eliminate the influence of other variables, such as per capita income, income distribution, and degree of urbanization, which account for a good deal of the observed variation in the savings ratio as between nations and between different periods of time.

most underdeveloped nations there is considerable scope for increasing progressivity without affecting incentives—and without affecting significantly the funds available for investment outlays (even though the savings ratio may be reduced). But this is not universally true, and, even where it is true, there is a danger that enthusiasts will push progressivity too far. The upshot is that for the time being only elimination of the grosser forms of inequality seems to be a reasonable goal. If the goal is to foster growth, we shall very much desire to retain skewness of the income distribution as long as it is related to economic function. American experience is relevant here. Since the Kennedy Administration is now talking about reducing the progressivity of the American income tax and the need for unshackling "initiative," it may be hoped that the urging of greater progressivity abroad and lessened progressivity at home will not be taken as inconsistent. It seems likely, however, that the wrong inferences will be drawn—and the net effect will be to reduce the persuasiveness of the Administration's position.

The emphasis which we have placed upon the paraphernalia of democracy, on income equality, on welfare programs seems to me to be misleading. What we are fundamentally interested in is stable, non-Communist governments which command—and can retain—the support of their peoples. What the aid program should attempt to do is to encourage changes in which currently disillusioned people may perceive a greater degree of legitimacy and effectiveness in their own social systems. Regimes acquire legitimacy in the eyes of their own people, not because of external forms, but because they work. Only ideologues will assume that the average individual can become deeply concerned about forms alone.

The influence of ideology on the ordinary man is quite limited. In the main he will be interested in security and—if he is ambitious—in opportunities for advancement commensurate with his deserts. Ideologies will flourish only where incompetency is dominant and hope disappears. The mission of the aid program should be to enhance acceptance of the legitimacy of society by helping to unblock opportunities. The primary concern should be to provide opportunities for the ambitious, the capable, and the unideological within the existing social framework. If an individual has the capacity and inclination for work, if he can make a contribution, his way to the top should not be blocked by nepotism, incompetency, jobbery, and functionless upper classes. It is the primary goal of the aid program to help remove such barriers—not to reform society as such. We are interested in the redistribution of income, for example, so that it is functional, so that it encourages work, so that it is regarded as justifiable and legitimate—not to arrive at some preconceived distribution. The acquisition of legitimacy by governments in the underdeveloped areas is consistent with a very great variety of social forms—almost all of which should be acceptable to us.

Discussion of the assistance program in the context of enhancing the legitimacy of the social order in the eyes of the people concerned casts some light on the vexing question of "socially disruptive" reforms. Those who are hostile to the assistance program, particularly in its new orientation, have objected to the making of "reforms," which are "socially disruptive," a condition of assistance. Reforms, however, are by definition disruptive. There are short-term costs—and most of those whose interests are adversely affected may be counted on to oppose the changes. The real question is whether the long-term social and economic benefits are sufficiently great to outweigh the costs of short-term disruption. In some societies reform is necessary to preserve social health, to eliminate mechanisms which frustrate progress, even to prevent social disintegration. Under such conditions, it is meaningless to say that reforms are disruptive simply because of the short-term costs. It all depends on the nature of the specific reforms suggested. They may be well-conceived in light of the given circumstances, or they may represent simply the attempt to write American values into other cultures. In the latter case, the reforms may both reduce the hope for social cohesion and the likelihood of a foreign policy orientation not hostile to the West.

Too early insistence on the introduction of the forms of democracy where the spirit of democracy does not exist may provide opportunities, not for the ordinarily ambitious and capable men who are willing to advance by making a productive contribution within a reformed system, but to those who would bring systematic change—to those who would bring revolution. It would be unwise deliberately to bring changes that will probably bring to the top those who, from our point of view, would subvert the society. One of the most successful examples of both economic growth and social change, which we have influenced, has been in Taiwan. At the moment Chiang's regime would probably have popular support if an election were held. Yet, if we had listened to those Americans who urged the introduction of democratic procedures in the early or mid-fifties, the regime would undoubtedly have been swept away—and with it, in all probability, the chances for the substantial social improvements that have taken place. There is a time for the introduction of democratic procedures, and there is a time to avoid such introduction.

I have emphasized this point at some length because I believe a misdirection of our effort is potentially very dangerous. By providing opportunities for the ideologies, we may succeed only in making the existing social order in the underdeveloped areas wholly unworkable, and make probable substantial Soviet gains. Strong leadership is still essential in the underdeveloped world if steady though unspectacular improvement is to be achieved. This implies that we may have to acquiesce in techniques for maintaining the strength of leadership of which we would disapprove under other conditions.

Trade

Aside from the economic advantages which trade conveys, the expansion of trade under present conditions is useful in that by creating interdependence it provides a medium for non-military deterrence. Some of these possibilities have been suggested in the section on "deterrence," but some amplification is appropriate. Nations which are dependent on trade are reluctant to see the disappearance of substantial markets or cheap sources of supply of essential commodities. Moderate pressures can be brought to bear by great trading entities against their smaller trading partners by threatening to terminate what had been hoped to be permanent trade relationships. The threat to restrict trade has a clear limitation as a strategic weapon in that, like a missile, when it is employed it is gone. When one uses the weapon, one forfeits the threat. Therefore one must consider the costs of employing the weapon. For the United States the economic costs are likely to be slight, but the cost in terms of reduced future influence may be heavy. The cost of using the weapon, however, does not imply that it is inadvisable to build up trade and let it be known that trade may be curtailed under given conditions. In itself, the creation of such a mechanism will give smaller nations pause.

In order to be able to employ the trade weapon, one must be in a position to bargain effectively. Under some circumstances this may imply that a nation should be able to "bilateralize" trade with those it seeks to influence—to ensure that the volume of purchases can be made dependent on political negotiations. The amount of pressure may be too much reduced if sales of foreign producers remain dependent on impersonal multilateral markets. Any movement toward the bilateralization of trade would, of course, require a change in the American perspective on commercial policy. However, one can foresee the continued existence of multilateral trade in our dealings with most nations, especially the principal industrial producers in the Free World. Nevertheless, for the small proportion of total trade carried on with our principal rivals or with smaller nations that might become hostile, the establishment of instrumentalities which can negotiate directly on the terms of volume of trade seems advisable. In the kind of world in which we live, and in which we are reluctant to make use of direct military pressure, it might be unwise to forego use of the trade weapon.

An important step forward would be taken if both the United States and the EEC were to establish trading organizations which had the power to bargain directly with their Soviet counterparts over commercial transactions with the West—and which could exclude from this line of activity firms in these two great economic units. This does not imply that a reduction in trade is desirable. On the contrary, expansion of trade might convey certain advantages. An increase of this type of contract with the Soviet Union would probably be beneficial. The damage that we can do by *refraining* from such trade is slight. We must keep a sense of proportion about these matters. The Battle Act kind of notion that by cutting off trade with the Soviets, we could beat them to their knees in six months is so outlandish it does not deserve comment. When one recalls that the Soviet economy is growing at a rate of six to seven per cent each year, it is clear that the benefits that the Soviets would extract from trade under the best of circumstances are marginal—only a drop in the bucket. However, if trade is built up, the damage that we could do by *curtailing* trade, even though it is slight, might well be the deciding factor between taking some provocative step and avoiding it.

The objections to expanding trade with the Soviets seem unconvincing. Many people would argue that on principle we should not trade with our foes, but why forego the establishment of these connections, if they carry strategic advantages for us?* We must get over this belief that whoever comes into contact with the Soviets is irretrievably lost. The notion that either the United States or the EEC might become strategically dependent on Soviet sources of supply strikes me as ludicrous—although Western producers have been energetically spreading it.† A more interesting argument is that the Soviets would extract undue advantage from such trade because of the difference be-

---

*The current drive by several right-wing organizations to persuade stores not to stock goods produced in Communist countries is probably something of a strategic boomerang. If we refuse to buy Polish hams (the principal target) or other Polish goods, our influence in Poland will certainly not be strengthened. A potential weapon is being wasted in a petty emotional display. The triviality to which the campaign descends may be illustrated by the exhortation of a Freeport, New York housewife: "I've been told that Russian peat moss is being sold in many nurseries on Long Island. Remember to ask where your peat moss comes from." The whole episode makes an interesting study in frustration.

†One of the three purposes stated for the Trade Expansion Act is "to prevent Communist economic penetration." Whatever relevance the term may have for Iceland or Afghanistan, its relevance for the United States or the EEC is approximately zero. The provisions in the Act have the sole function of protecting American producers; its strategic impact, for the reasons mentioned, is probably negative from our standpoint.

tween their low marginal costs and world prices. Oil is a case in point. Of course, it makes commercial as well as strategic sense to attempt to limit Soviet gains, but this calls for an attempt to bargain prices down toward marginal costs. Presumably two Western trading organizations would possess considerable bargaining power in such matters, and we might well be able to obtain Soviet commodities not only below Western production costs (with the inherent saving of our own resources), but possibly below the full cost of production to the Soviets.

With some modification, the same kind of perspective might govern our trade with the Satellites. In this case the costs of refusing to trade or drastically limiting trade are more impressive. The net effect will be to ease the Soviet strategic problem by forcing the Satellites to integrate their economies more thoroughly into the Bloc than they might otherwise do. The West should hardly cooperate in smoothing the path toward the achievement of Soviet objectives. Moreover, by refraining from trade we forfeit an instrument which potentially could influence the Satellites either to resist Soviet pressures or to avoid provocations against the West. Since one of the assumptions of our foreign policy has been that the Satellites reluctantly accept Soviet dominance because they have no alternative, it would appear desirable that this awareness of various shades of gray existing in the Bloc be reflected in our trade policies—rather than accepting the uncritical notion that trade with Communists is reprehensible under any circumstances, etc.

In controlling trade with the Satellites, it is not necessary, and it might prove to be a disadvantage, for trade to be put on a bilateral basis. The same is true with respect to the underdeveloped countries, although, if the circumstances arise, it may be advisable to be in a position to shift to bilateral negotiations through a national organization in order to bring maximum pressure to bear. In general, it should be remembered that in this era the "supply effect" has shrunk in importance relative to the "influence effect" in using trade strategically. In order to gain influence, one must put other nations in a position in which they have something to lose, if they are uncooperative. With respect to the supply effect, in light of technological advance and the easy availability of substitutes, no technically sophisticated nation can be significantly hurt by the interdiction of some so-called strategic material. The main exception to this rule is in dealing with underdeveloped countries, where curtailment of deliveries or technical services by the normal suppliers of capital equipment may impose a very sharp increase in costs on the affected nations, because of the difficulty of finding alternative sources of parts, replacements, and advice on maintenance. Investment in capital equipment at any time means the provision of something of a hostage to fortune. It is desirable that the West retain control of this hostage, and consequently, it would seem advantageous to maintain the current dominance of the United States and its major allies in the supply—and the servicing—of capital equipment in the underdeveloped world. Such dependence implies a source of leverage.

The kind of procedures, which have been suggested to exploit the strategic potential implicit in aid and trade, would require the adoption of an attitude toward nations with which we are not at war tougher than has existed in the past. It would require some extension of controls and further departure from the goal of nondiscriminatory trading practices. However, I can see no fundamental objection to having trade with the Soviet Union and China, as well as the Satellites and some of the "neutralists" if necessary, centrally controlled. I do not find the "wedge" argument convincing—i.e., the controls which exist on the five per cent of our trade carried on with hostile nations must inevitably spread to the bulk of our trade which is carried on with friendly nations, thus destroying multilateral trade. If the case for the market or for decentralization in general rests on such a weak basis that it will collapse on account of an occasional deviation from "principle," then it is too weak to survive in any event. My own reading of the situation is different: the area of influence of ideology on economic organization has been very much narrowed since the 1940's, and the argument for decentralization is accepted by most of those who in the earlier period might have been regarded as favoring *dirigisme* in principle. Thus, I would have few hesitations. Without significantly weakening pursuit of its other objectives, I think that the United States can move ahead in designing techniques which will result in greater exploitation of the strategic potential embodied in our aid and trade policies.

NOTES

1. James R. Schlesinger, *The Political Economy of National Security* (New York: 1960), pp. 227-32.
2. It seems almost sententious to cite the seminal work on the subject, Thomas C. Schelling, *The Strategy of Conflict* (Cambridge, Mass: Harvard University Press, 1960), Part I.

A Bipartisan Trade Strategy

Robert S. Strauss

My subject today is our nation's trade policy, a topic which for too long has had a low priority on our national agenda. The economy of the United States is at a crossroads. The decisions we make in the next few years will in large measure determine the economic strength of our country and its future role in the world. Trade is second only to strategic arms limitation and national security in its importance to our country. In many ways international trade will have the most immediate and direct impact on our economy and on the well-being of the American people.

This afternoon I would like briefly to review our domestic trade situation, the international economic situation, and then propose a broad framework, with some specific suggestions for a national policy. The time has come for bold political leadership and international economic diplomacy if we are to manage current difficulties and ensure an international economic system which will facilitate growth and accommodate change.

As a youngster growing up in West Texas fifty years ago, it seemed to me that the only thing that really affected our economic welfare was whether it rained in the spring and summer. If the rains came, the cotton grew, the farmers had cash to spend on a new tractor, clothes for the family, payments to the bank and possibly a good used car. Economic conditions were good if rain fell within a five-mile radius of the town square. Our very lives seemed to depend upon the rain that fell or didn't fall. That's all that seemed to matter.

Now, life around the square in Stamford is affected far more dramatically, within seconds, by decisions made daily in Riyadh, Brussels, London and Tokyo, to name a few.

I tell this story because, to me, it illustrates how the world economy has changed during the postwar period and how this change has brought benefits to America but also harsh disruptions and economic stress to many regions of our country and sectors of our economy.

The experience of recent years, in particular the overvaluation of the dollar and the massive merchandise trade imbalance, has accelerated even more the pace of change and telescoped the period of adjustment that our basic industries are undergoing. When change comes too fast, political pressures build to preserve the status quo and to insulate key industrial sectors from the impact of that change. This process challenges political leaders and economic diplomacy becomes exceedingly difficult.

It's a setting in which political choice for national leaders is easy and predictable: apply the brakes to imports, look more to protectionism, and ignore the fundamental causes of the erosion of national competitiveness. The political expedient is to blame foreigners for whatever is going wrong. This phenomenon is not exclusively ours— it's the same in virtually every country in the world. Foreigners don't vote; they are easiest to blame. The situation becomes exacerbated when that blame is well founded.

This process of resisting adjustment to change, and blaming trade problems on foreigners, is at work in every capital in the world. Today every government in the world is trying to limit imports and boost exports in order to husband domestic employment and insulate key economic sectors and regions. One does not have to be an economist to recognize that if every government in the world is attempting to manage trade artificially to enhance domestic conditions, the result will be a world marketplace that will no longer grow to the benefit of all. Trade becomes a zero sum game. From the U.S. perspective, let's look at a few givens:

1. We are now the world's leading debtor nation. As recently as five years ago we were the world's largest creditor nation. For the first time since 1914 we owe the rest of the world more than it owes us. Developing countries are now shifting capital to the U.S.

2. Record shattering trade deficits, if improving at all, are doing so only marginally, and it appears obvious that we face future years of merchandise trade deficits "as far as the eye can see."

3. Massive federal budget deficits continue to soak up scarce capital, inhibiting productive investment in the United States as well as abroad.

4. Our national debt has doubled since 1980.

5. U.S. productivity gains continue to fall behind those of our trading partners. In the 1960s, our productivity grew at a rate that doubled our standard of living every 23 years. At today's rate of growth, it will require 70 years. Meanwhile the productivity gains of our principal trading partners continue to exceed ours by a growing margin.

6. Leaders in both government and business have failed to appreciate the rapid internationalization of markets and the consequences of this for national policy and private business decisions.

7. Expenditures in research and development and investment in new plants and equipment have been lagging.

8. The international trading system is weak and ineffective. The GATT is premised on a notion of free market forces which no longer exist, if indeed they ever did. In many sectors there is no such thing as free trade. It doesn't exist in agriculture or airplanes, steel or services, telecommunications or ships or autos or computers.

9. The Uruguay Round is a positive step and should be aggressively pursued, but its completion under the best of circumstances is years away.

Into this setting, add the lack of international economic coordination, the Third World debt crisis, exchange rate volatility and distortion. It is easy to become pessimistic about the future, especially when there is so little international leadership to address these problems.

Secretary Baker has achieved some very significant success during the past year, most recently and notably the U.S.–Japan accord on international economic coordination. However, other countries, especially West Germany, have been recalcitrant.

In general the Administration's exchange rate initiative has been successful primarily against only two currencies, and our efforts to date have dramatized and underscored the tremendous volatility in exchange rates which we now face. This volatility is driven by the surge in the volume of global capital flows and has produced fundamental and profound changes in the way exchange rates move. Responding to enhanced capital mobility, exchange rates now are having a more pronounced impact on trade and increase disruption. Although the Group of Seven is now considering the problem, a real return to broad exchange rate stability is not on the horizon.

Furthermore, global disequalibrium has put additional strain on the established international economic institutions. This change of pace has exceeded the political capacity of the institutions of governments, such as the World Bank, the IMF, the GATT, and others to adjust. They also suffer from limited mandates and even greater limitations on political clout.

When I became trade negotiator for the United States, I worried about my lack of knowledge of international trade. But I soon realized that trade policies were the manifestations of political responses to the forces of change that were working relentlessly throughout the world. It became clear that the toughest trade barriers being maintained were those that survived attacks by trade negotiators over the years because they were put in place by powerful political forces working in each country.

Obviously the only way to begin dislodging these hardened national political positions was to obtain agreement at the highest political level that changes were imperative and have it flow down to the

bureaucracy. This political mandate could not be achieved at the min-
isterial level. A broad bargain was needed that left every government
with something positive to show. The details could and should be left
to ministers—but the political outlines and timetables for change had
to be set by heads of government acting courageously if we had any
hope of cutting across the jurisdictions of bureaucratic agencies and
across the conflicting political interests of each nation. The London
and Bonn Summits, with Carter, Schmidt, and Fukuda leading the
effort, made possible the success of the Tokyo Round in the face of
considerable economic and political adversity. It wasn't done by ministers like me nibbling around the edges of the most difficult issues.

If America hopes to regain control of its economic destiny, it must
reassert its role as a leader in the Western alliance in this economically
interdependent world. Today far too much depends upon what happens outside our borders and beyond our control. We must demand
that those who enter our domestic markets permit us equal access to
theirs. We must further insist that they enter our markets fairly, free of
dumping and other predatory practices. On this we must be stronger
and clearer and more aggressive than ever before. But if we are to
avoid the self-destructive process of ever-growing protectionism and
economic nationalism, we must also devise strategies to ensure our
domestic growth and international economic competitiveness so that
market access becomes genuine opportunity. And we must build the
domestic political consensus that will support our efforts to achieve
those goals.

Nearly two years ago, the Young Commission Report offered several necessary proposals and prescriptions to improve the country's
competitiveness. The Commission's recommendations include long-
term productivity-boosting measures designed to spur high technology,
provide incentives for research and development, revitalize the drive
to improve our education system, encourage worker training and increase the supply of productive capital in key sectors of our economy.
None of these are short-term measures and none are sufficient, but all
are essential if market access is also to mean opportunity.

My purpose here today is not to dwell on these problems or to
elaborate on their details. It is rather to begin to lay the outlines for a
broad, long-term strategy because our nation stands at a crossroads in
our economic history.

Interestingly, with all of their differences, Western nations are
governed by leaders who share many common views; certainly share
enough common values and concerns to enable them to work together
to bring about real breakthroughs if they combine forces. In the next
two years we should seize this opportunity to forge an international

consensus to strive for continued growth of the world economy in this century and the next.

The next economic summit should be a very special one. The Administration should take the lead in seeing that this summit meeting is entirely new and different from those of the past. Instead of meeting to tinker with the great problems we face, intense planning by the participants should begin immediately so that the leaders, with their ministers, can agree upon and enter into a substantive package of recommendations, actions and agreements. They must face up to the impending world economic chaos that present policies, or lack thereof, are creating. They must truly enter into a new global bargain or compact. They must reach for joint, mutually beneficial, long-term commitments that are politically impossible for any one of them to make alone but viable if taken in concert. They must strike a comprehensive global bargain with each putting enough on the table to make it viable for the others to return home with enough in their hands to secure the political support necessary to go forward.

The United States, for example, must among other things commit to immediately act with credibility, using real, not make-believe, measures to begin to reduce its federal budget deficits. It must agree to take action to stop the siphoning of world capital to finance our budget deficits.

Japan, for its part, must put its procurement and internal spending policies on the bargaining table and must accelerate the long cultural changes that would have the effect of genuinely opening its markets to foreign producers. It must move its economy away from export lead growth to domestic demand. It must accelerate its assumption of the global responsibilities of a great nation.

The European Community, among other things, must take the political steps that are necessary to begin to harness and eventually, over a period of time, to deal constructively with the common agricultural policy. Europeans know better than anyone else that they cannot continue to function effectively with an agricultural policy that requires an ever-growing share of the budget of the European Communities. Let me emphasize here that we have no more difficult problem than our agriculture mess, and I assure you we will never solve our domestic agricultural problems unless we do so in an international context. For another example of European commitment, West Germany must adopt policies aimed at achieving growth and shouldering a greater responsibility for the expansion of the world economy, not through pump-priming, but through structural reforms and reduced subsidies.

A global compact should deal with a more equitable sharing of responsibilities among nations. A classic example of an unbalanced burden can be quickly seen in the fact that between 1982 and 1985, the U.S. absorbed 55 percent of the increase in non-OPEC LDC exports while Japan took only 10 percent and Europe about 20 percent. We cannot let this continue.

Another element of this comprehensive global compact should be the institutionalization of the Group of Seven. The Group of Seven has political symmetry with the summit leaders, and a summit mandate for a more structured group to deal with broader issues would give it the political muscle that is imperative for it to assume those designated responsibilities outside the existing international institutions. No doubt there are those who worry about such a mechanism outside established institutions. The Group of Seven of course should not replace or duplicate any of these existing institutions, but should serve a role of high-level political and economic coordination as an ongoing process. It should also involve those non-members of the Group who account for about one-half of our trade deficit.

Any sound strategy must also focus on the interconnected debt and growth issues, as well as the current lack of international economic coordination. Secretary Baker and Minister Miyazawa have made an important contribution, but more is needed.

Domestically, we must take steps to be certain that comprehensive sensible trade legislation is enacted in 1987 on a bipartisan basis. Reading the press these past few days would lead one to believe that the Congress intends to be confrontational and irresponsible on this issue. I don't believe that must or will be the case. The new Chairman of the Finance Committee, Senator Bentsen, is an astute and intelligent legislator and a wise observer of the international economic scene. He will provide fresh, strong and responsible leadership that will be forward-looking and growth-oriented with emphasis on protecting our national interest. While it certainly is time to get tougher, a toughened trade posture does not have to be synonymous with protectionism. And it is time to get tough, not only with our trading partners but also on ourselves. I predict he will develop bipartisan support in the Senate and that the House will also act with bipartisan leadership.

Why do we need new trade legislation? There are several answers. First and most importantly the President will need an extension of his authority to bring home trade agreements in the Uruguay Round and to submit them to the Congress for an up or down vote. This authority is essential if the President's negotiators are to have credibility. In addition, we need legislation to improve Section 301 of the Trade Act of 1974 to deal with foreign unfair trade practices. We need to strengthen the protection of intellectual property and to assist in the fight against counterfeiting. We need new authorities to compel the opening of foreign markets in high technology, especially telecommunications, where state-owned and -influenced monopolies make market penetration almost impossible. We need new trade laws designed to deal with the problems faced by our growing service sector.

In addition, in trade legislation we need to restructure our own governmental trade organization. Although many have opposed a new governmental structure to deal with our trade issues, I have reluctantly come to the conclusion that part of any comprehensive bipartisan trade legislation should be the creation of a new Department of Trade. Not a Department of Protectionism, not a Department of Free Trade, but a new department that would be the centerpiece of a sensible, aggressive U.S. trade policy based on national self-interest and also committed to global responsibility. The idea of the Department of Trade is not new. It now needs to be reviewed and reconsidered in a new light, not as an old idea that has been discredited by bureaucratic infighting over who will control policy making. We must find the most sensible way to organize the U.S. Government to deal effectively with trade and foreign economic policy. Democrats and Republicans must join in this effort with Administration leadership or at least support. Representatives of business, labor, and agriculture should join in carefully reviewing a variety of possibilities, eventually structuring one that makes functional sense and can muster sufficient political support to put it in place. There are many more modest and significant steps that can be immediately taken. For example, although international monetary coordination is of the highest priority, we no longer have an Undersecretary at the Treasury whose sole responsibility is to coordinate international monetary issues with domestic financial issues. That position should be reestablished. Further, the agricultural export position established two years ago by the Congress to give us a stepped-up export thrust should be filled immediately.

Finally, in my judgment there is nothing President Reagan could do to demonstrate more dramatically to the world that we understand the extent of the global economic crisis than to negotiate with Chairman Volcker of the Fed, surely one of the most respected and reassuring people on the world economic scene, to encourage him to accept another term. This would relieve a great deal of uncertainty in the financial markets at home and abroad and assure stability and judgment in that special institution.

Finally, as I conclude, I would respectfully urge President Reagan to make trade and economic policy one of the centerpieces of his last two years in office. The leadership belongs in the Oval Office and, as indicated, I'm convinced he would find the Congress ready to join.

We can, and I'm confident we will, work out our problems. It will take time, it will take steadfastness and intelligence, it will take ideas and judgment. But we have these qualities. Now we should try to put things in focus, discuss them with America and then do our damnedest to build and sustain a political consensus for achieving our goals.

And there is so much more involved than dollars. As long ago as 1844, Ralph Waldo Emerson wrote a few lines about trade and America that I sometimes quote that are probably more pertinent today than when written. He said, and I quote:

The philosopher and lover of man have much harm to say of trade but historians will see that trade was the principle of liberty, that trade planted America and destroyed feudalism, that it makes peace and keeps peace, and it will abolish slavery.

Technological Challenges to National Economic Policies of the West   *Harald B. Malmgren*

Throughout the industrialized nations of the West there seems to be a growing sense of urgency about the need for new policies to strengthen national economies and improve competitiveness. Even in the United States there is an increasing preoccupation with flagging national competitiveness and a rapidly widening controversy about means to restore world economic leadership.

In policy debate, the role of technology has become a focal point virtually everywhere. Countless proposals are being made for boosting national technological advances to help industries meet intensified global competition.

Yet, in spite of a near-universal interest in the role of technology, there is in public policy discussion very little analysis of the actual impact of technological change on the world economy. There is a widen-

Harald B. Malmgren was deputy U.S. trade representative in the mid-1970s, and is now an international management and economic consultant with offices in Washington and London. This article is adapted from a chapter in *The U.S. and the World Economy*, edited by John Yochelson, to be published in 1987.

ing sense of need for faster structural change to adapt to the new realities of economic competition. But there is little recognition of the revolutionary character of emerging technologies and their potentially overpowering effects on governments and their national economic policies.

The Rise of Protectionism and Economic Nationalism

New policies are being devised, but their orientation tends to be inward-looking and based on past experience. Thus, there is a growing tendency toward economic nationalism, based on traditional conceptions of how to use trade policy to improve competitiveness: boosting exports, limiting imports, and artificially enhancing home-based production and jobs. The consequence is that mutually conflicting policies are being generated among the Western nations that threaten to fragment their economic and political interests. Multilateral economic cooperation is being undermined as nations attempt to find their own separate ways to harness and restrain the forces of change.

In relying on trade policies to improve competitiveness, governments are essentially attacking the symptoms of rapid change without addressing the causes. One need not resort to sophisticated economic analysis to reach the obvious conclusion that if every nation acts to limit imports and boost exports, the ultimate result will be global economic contraction.

A major example of these tendencies can be found in the United States, where the national debate on economic policy is becoming permeated with references to the need to improve competitiveness and to deal more effectively with the technological challenges of Japan and other nations. There is a degree of recognition that exchange rates and profligate domestic economic policies have hurt U.S. competitiveness. But much of the policy discussion is formulated in terms of criticizing the practices of other nations, placing blame for deterioration of U.S. competitiveness on the allegedly unfair policies and practices of foreign governments.

One response has been a political push for import restrictions and import-retarding remedial actions in key industrial sectors. There have been demands for trade-restrictive counter-measures against alleged industrial-targeting policies of foreign governments. There are growing demands for greater protection of U.S. technology through much tougher actions against imports that allegedly infringe upon U.S. patents, copyrights, trademarks, and licensing arrangements. Some officials and politicians are advocating a drive to build up the so-called defense industrial base within a framework of national security objectives, excluding foreign enterprises or discriminating against them in key industries.

Furthermore, there was in the early 1980s an extensive national debate in the United States concerning the possible need for industrial policies aimed at enhancing competitiveness in key sectors. There was considerable public attention to the suggestion that government should play a more active role in stimulating, assisting, and guiding industrial innovation and adaptation. Given the constraints on government spending imposed by the federal budget deficit, and a long-standing public skepticism about government effectiveness in guiding the economy, these industrial policy suggestions soon evolved into arguments for greater protection against imports.

These discriminatory and trade-limiting responses have not, of course, been the only proposals made. Reforms of antitrust policy to allow more cooperation among enterprises in research and development (R&D), tax policies to favor innovation, changes in patent policy for government-funded R&D, and other positive proposals have also been widely discussed, and in the 1980s some policy changes along these lines have already been made.

This perceived need to improve national competitiveness in the face of global economic challenges is evident throughout the West. For example, among the member nations of the European Communities (EC) there is a growing apprehension about what is perceived as a Japanese-American technological challenge to Europe's future competitiveness and economic well-being. There is a widespread feeling that Europe is falling behind and becoming vulnerable to economic domination by external interests. A prevailing sentiment is that technological rejuvenation of European industry is urgently needed, and for this to happen a way must be found to generate sufficient economies of scale and size of market to guarantee adequate returns on R&D for European companies. The solution most often presented is that the EC must really become a single, integrated marketplace as quickly as possible, and cooperation among EC companies across national boundaries must be vigorously encouraged. Governments, it is also argued, must join hands in supporting European-scale technological projects—projects that will enhance Europe's relative global trading position in advanced technologies.

But this West European obsession with economies of scale and size of home market overlooks completely the international technological successes of many business enterprises based in comparatively small European economies such as Sweden, Finland, and Switzerland. In spite of the smallness of their home market bases, a significant number of companies in each of these countries has emerged as world-class industrial competitors alongside the giant Japanese and U.S. multinationals.

Moreover, the widespread apprehension about the Japanese and U.S. competitive challenges seems to have caused a European blindness to the rapid emergence of the comparatively small newly industrialized countries (NICs) as significant world competitors in many advanced technology sectors. South Korean industrial enterprises, for example, are rapidly becoming internationally competitive in advanced consumer electronics, semiconductors, and small computers, and South Korean technology in the production of steel and in shipbuilding is second to none. The scale of domestic markets in the NICs can hardly be said to be the foundation of their rapid advances in technological capabilities and world competitiveness.

In Japan, there has long been a feeling of vulnerability to external forces. Technological progress for many years has been perceived as the principal avenue to growth, world competitiveness, and diminished dependence on the vicissitudes of global political and economic developments. The economic shocks of the 1970s—oil prices, exchange rate volatility, inflation, the emergence of Third World competitors—gave increased impetus to the development and the application of emerging technologies in Japan. Government policymakers devoted much attention to the encouragement of technological advances, in part through direct assistance to industry but mainly through facilitation of, and sometimes even forcing of, R&D cooperation and sharing of knowledge among independent commercial enterprises. The government in turn would periodically articulate its national "visions" of the direction and character of technological change, and the implications for the structure of the Japanese economy and its global competitiveness. These visions provided a framework for business planning and financial commitments.

In more recent years, Japanese commercial enterprises have gradually pulled away from government guidance of their R&D. Public policy has become more focused on the promotion of what are called next-generation or emerging technologies. Acquisition of existing technologies from other nations is less of a concern now than autonomous generation of new technologies. The focus of competition among Japanese enterprises is shifting from cost competitiveness in producing and selling off-the-shelf goods to competitiveness in the generation of entirely new products and new methods of production. On the one hand, this shift is being spurred by a growing desire to catch up with the United States. On the other hand, there is a growing fear of the progress being made by the NICs in closing the competitive gap and challenging Japanese enterprises in world markets in both traditional and technologically advanced manufactures. Increasingly, there seems to be a feeling in Japan that world technological competition is becoming a race, with victory going to the swiftest, rather than the most efficient.

Even the NICs seem increasingly preoccupied with enhancing their technological potential, and their industrial and trade policies have in recent years been adapted to this preoccupation. The intense economic nationalism and protectionism which characterize Brazil's informatics policy is one of the most visible examples.

One important conclusion that can already be reached is that many of the measures being considered or being taken in the West to shield national markets from external pressures are aggravating the difficulties of structural adjustment to changing international competitiveness. Since technology is increasingly transferable across borders, restrictions on the exports of certain countries simply encourage expansion of production in other countries, particularly the NICs. The rapid emergence of new entrants increases world productive capacity and artificially stimulates even more intense competition.

Major exporters increasingly respond to perceived protectionism by stepping up their foreign direct investment, jumping national borders, and building new production facilities in the major importing countries. At first glance this seems to help create new jobs, but its longer-term effect may often be to create additional domestic competitive pressures and even excess capacity. Ironically, the new foreign-owned plants are relatively more able to withstand intensified competition because of their state-of-the-art production technologies. (For example, there can be little doubt that the U.S. automotive industry will suffer from excess domestic production capacity in the next few years. This problem will be greatly aggravated by the large capacity of Japanese-owned automotive plants already in place or now being built inside the United States, mainly in response to fears of protectionism and U.S. pressures for job creation.)

Such industrial responses to accelerate movement up the ladder of technological progress and to employ new technologies in plants built in foreign markets cannot readily be stemmed by protectionism or a revival of economic nationalism. Put simply, government efforts to shield key sectors and guide structural adjustment are being overrun by the force and pace of technological change.

Technological Thrusts and Structural Change

Thus, it is no longer possible to devise effective economic policies without taking into account the underlying technological thrusts and their implications for the structure of national economies and the pattern of world trade, investment, and delivery of services.

There are a number of major technological forces now at work that will require fundamental structural adjustments on the part of national economies. Among them:

The development of new, man-made materials which will increasingly compete with, and substitute for, traditional materials generated from natural resources. There has been a fundamental reversal in the direction of technological change in materials science. Traditionally, technology has been used to process materials found in the ground or growing from it. Recent advances in materials science and engineering are making it possible "to start with a need and then develop a material to meet it, atom by atom."[1] These advances are widely characterized as constituting a "materials revolution."

These "new materials" now being developed in Japan, Western Europe, and the United States will have a profound effect on the economic value of natural resources. The new man-made materials will be generated by new industrial processes and even new industries.

In the 1980s there have been many public expressions of concern about a potential deindustrialization of U.S. industry, as a result of a perceptible decline of traditional basic industries like steel and copper. Little public attention has been given to the potentially expansive role of emerging new industries that produce super-polymers, composites, fiber optics, fine ceramics, etc.

Even by itself, the materials revolution should force a refocusing of public policy away from the prospects for traditional industries and toward the emergence of entirely new industries and processes. For example, our policymakers should be asking whether the relative economic importance of key natural resources will diminish, leaving some countries such as the resource-dependent LDCs much worse off and the United States better off. They should reexamine the supposed criticality to national security of domestic resources (and selected imported raw materials) in the new context in which the Defense Department gives its highest R&D priorities to the generation of substitute new materials (because of their greater capabilities in military applications).

Accelerating advances in the technology of computers, telecommunications, and information-processing which provide enormous economies of scale in supplying services and transferring technology.

The changes taking place in the area of information management are so far-reaching that they have been characterized as the "information revolution." Many scientists believe that this revolution is generating historic changes on a scale comparable to, or even greater than, the changes that took place during the Industrial Revolution. This revolution is not simply a matter of faster, more powerful memories and rapidly declining costs of processing information. Advances in telecommunications represent only a part of the revolution taking place.

Applied research is becoming faster, as past knowledge becomes more readily available to researchers and experimentation is assisted by simulation and the bare beginnings of artificial intelligence (AI). Product life cycles are shortening. Process and product technologies are becoming instantly transferable through global computer-telecommunication links, widening dramatically the potential suppliers of goods and services in the world marketplace. Goods suppliers increasingly are able to provide accompanying engineering services, enabling much closer and more interactive producer-consumer relationships, thereby changing the nature of competition from selling previously designed machinery, equipment, and components to provision of design services, process technology, tailored equipment and components, redesign, and continuous engineering support. These developments sharply reduce the significance of geographic distance and dramatically shorten the response time needed to meet changing consumer demand.

The reorientation of industrial processes within the framework of computer-integrated manufacturing (CIM) and flexible manufacturing systems (FMS). The emerging reorientation of industrial processes is based upon multipurpose, reprogrammable equipment and systems combined with entirely new materials processing techniques. The changing character of production processes will provide opportunity for much greater flexibility, small lot production, minimal inventories, rapid market response, and product adaptation, while maintaining and even enhancing economies of scale in use of plant and equipment.

The greater reliance on CIM, and the improvements in production systems that are possible with CIM (such as robotics, automated transfer, industrial lasers, and new techniques for precision forming and shaping) will tend to reduce the importance of labor costs in competitiveness. There may be a substantial labor-displacing effect, and this could have significant implications for competitiveness of enterprises in countries which rely on low labor costs for export competitiveness. (For example, the automation of sewing could greatly alter the world pattern of apparel production and trade, leaving massive job displacement in its wake in some of the LDCs as well as in the United States).

CIM will inevitably result in shorter product life cycles, as continuous adaptation and tailoring or products become easier. Competitiveness will increasingly depend upon speed of response and character of product-related services.

Improvements in transportation, especially in the technology of aircraft, bringing production centers and markets much closer in terms of time and relative cost. Lighter but stronger airframes and lighter, higher-performance aircraft engines will mean greater weight capacity, greater distance feasibility, and shorter landing and takeoff requirements, thereby intensifying competitiveness of air transport relative to other modes of transportation, and giving even greater emphasis to speed of response to consumer requirements.

Rapid advances in life sciences that are likely to alter demographic profiles, and enhance human capabilities across all age brackets. The human resource development of nations will become increasingly important to the dynamics of growth and competitiveness. The share of services in total national employment is likely to continue to grow in virtually every nation, placing growing importance on the quality of the human resource base in maintaining and improving competitiveness. This growing dependence on the overall strength of the human resource base will give greater emphasis to reforms of education and the quality and distribution of services (health maintenance, life-sustaining services, and quality-of-life services).

Thus, it must be anticipated that competitiveness will depend upon more rapid and more tailored responses of suppliers to rapidly evolving and increasingly individualized demand.

Biotechnology developments which may open the way for major advances in the production (and location of production) of food and improvements in such diverse areas as industrial processes, management of wastes, memory technology, and even in animal and human characteristics. The unknowns of biotechnology—the dangers as well as the potential benefits—are central to any assessment of future thrusts. Developments currently under way only reveal a glimmer of what these future thrusts might be. It can nonetheless already be said that developments in this field are likely to change greatly the nature of world food production and distribution, with major effects on agricultural and agribusiness technologies and competitiveness.

The Accelerating Pace of Change

Throughout history technological change has brought about changes in the pattern of world economic activity. What is new is the acceleration of the pace of change, combined with the emerging capability of changing the character of nature's building blocks to open entirely new avenues of production—and even, potentially, new avenues of evolution.

In essence, an entirely new paradigm is unfolding. In this perspective, scientists who characterize the current changes as an information revolution or a materials revolution may be somewhat understating the profound significance of the wide array of technological advances now cumulatively coming to bear upon national economies. This technological revolution is, in other words, likely to generate historical discontinuities—with past experience sometimes a poor guide for future policy decisions and commitments of human and financial resources.

The acceleration of change brings about a compression of time, from the point of view of decision makers. The economic behavior patterns which presently characterize the world economy, and which are embodied in institutional and political processes of decision making, are very time-sensitive. Time is taken to evaluate new ideas and assess their commercial potential. Producers seek, and plan on, adequate time to ensure that expected returns can be achieved from plant and equipment investments that implement new technologies. Competitive countermeasures take time to put in motion. Petitions for government assistance or action against foreign interests take time to consider. Legislative policy changes take a long time to develop. Government-to-government negotiations on salient problems take years.

Rapid economic change invariably means disruption to sectors and geographic regions—bringing about political pressures to alleviate the pains of adjustment or retard its pace. There are congenital tendencies in our economic institutions and political processes to slow things down, to seek breathing time, and to retard the pace of structural change through measures that shield disrupted enterprises or industrial sectors from global forces of change.

Against these built-in institutional tendencies to stretch out the time taken for change, the emerging technology thrusts are accelerating the pace of change. Information technology is shortening the time required to produce a new service or a new good embodying an idea; it is shortening the time necessary for managers to respond to changing demand and supply characteristics of their markets; and it is shortening the time lag in international diffusion of technology.

One of the consequences of a shortened economic time span is faster product obsolescence in world competition. As the market life cycle of many products shortens, there is a growing need for faster responses and faster adaptation of production systems, without time-consuming investment in new plant and equipment. The time factor in competition—responding quickly and staying ahead through rapid innovation—is itself altering the way in which products and services are generated, forcing producers and suppliers to devise flexible, adaptable, reprogrammable production and delivery systems, and increasing both the incentive and the need to provide supporting services in conjunction with the sale of goods.

In such a competitive environment, R&D cannot be attributed to particular products; R&D becomes an ongoing process necessary to remain a viable, competitive entity. Measurement of performance, accounting standards, tax treatment—all such traditional concepts become obsolete. Only contemporaneous measurement of the performance of R&D makes sense. This means treating R&D as current nonattributable overhead costs, or, in public policy terms, treating the level of R&D spending as an underlying measure of the strength of a corporation, much like capital asset value.

Structural Implications

What are the structural implications of these fundamental technology thrusts, and the compression of time allowed to deal with them?

First, it is likely that there will be significant shifts in relative competitiveness among industrial sectors, and shifts in relative economic power among nations. These shifts may not always move continuously in a single direction. Building plants in other nations and securing components from foreign suppliers ("outsourcing") may prevail for some periods, while domestic consolidation and centralization may prevail in other periods. (For example, the U.S. automotive industry may for a time move toward global sourcing, but there are strong economies to be gained from consolidation when CIM and the novel characteristics of new materials become more widely relevant to automotive production.)

Emergence of new materials will not only have an effect on traditional resource-processing industries and countries; there will also be significant effects on production methods (obsolescence of machine tools and emergence of precision-forming, laser treatment, and other entirely different processes of cutting, bending, shaping, and refinishing based on CIM) and on the global management of remote production facilities (on-line programming by engineers in remote locations).

In assessing relative economic and political power of nations in coming years, it is apparent that countries which adapt quickly will tend to be stronger, and those which have difficulty adapting will tend to fall behind. The resilience and flexibility of an economy will therefore be vital determinants of relative power as technological change works through national economies.

In this regard, relatively rigid, centrally managed economies like that of the Soviet Union will have great difficulty keeping pace. Indeed, even if the decentralization efforts of Chairman Gorbachev were to be widely implemented, it is difficult to foresee any circumstances in which the economy of the Soviet Union could adapt to the pace of change likely in the West. The United States, Japan, Canada, Western Europe, and the NICs will probably stretch their technological lead over all the centrally planned economies. Among the Western countries, some of the European nations could lag unless there is further loosening of the constraints on independent enterprises imposed by regulations and social policies.

This leaves a question mark over the future of such economies as those of South Asia and China. Perhaps more historically significant is the very poor outlook for many of the developing countries, which are heavily dependent on natural resources and are already in difficult circumstances.

Second, major transformation of national and global systems for delivery of services is under way, particularly through advances in information technology. Vast economies of scale globally are achievable through consolidation of a variety of services and delivery through computer-telecommunications networks (witness the emergence of so-called financial supermarkets). On the other hand, small, innovative entities can provide services globally through the same kinds of mechanisms, in such varying fields as engineering, software support, medical diagnostics, and management information services. Once supporting services such as software development can be routinized, it will be possible to assign such services activities to remote locations (e.g., assignment of technical support activities to underemployed technicians in South Asia).

Third, growing world competition from new entrants at home and abroad can be expected to be generated by the accelerated international diffusion of technology. Countries that remain "plugged in" to globally available services and technology information can keep pace with world markets, but countries that try to develop indigenous technologies through protectionist measures and exclusion of foreign technologies and communication will eventually find themselves falling back, "plugged out" from world competition. (The nationalistic, restrictive informatics policy of the Brazilian government poses this long-term danger for Brazil's economy.)

Fourth, the acceleration of change will tend to undermine or counteract government policy measures taken to limit or impede imports of particular products. The consequence of import-restraining measures may often be to accelerate the introduction of new, substitutable products and the establishment of new foreign and domestic sources of production, greatly intensifying competitive pressures. Thus, ironically, protectionist actions will tend to increase, rather than moderate, the very competitive pressures which initially gave rise to pleas for protection from firms and workers.

Fifth, there is likely to be change in the global pattern of demand for labor, but in uncertain ways. Transformation of manufacturing processes, such as through automation of sewing and bonding in production of apparel, will tend to change fundamentally the industrial development path for many LDCs. Labor demand in some regions may fall, while rising in other regions characterized by new technologies of production in new facilities. Skill requirements may vary continuously throughout the life of individual workers, and their versatility may become more important than specific skills and experience in specific tasks.

Industrial and agricultural jobs will continue to shrink as a share of total employment, even if present levels of production are maintained in key sectors. The orientation of education will have to be altered, but the appropriate direction of change is still very unclear (for example, will there be a need for lifetime reeducation?).

Sixth, private enterprises will have to become far more knowledgeable about worldwide developments among both present and potential competitors. To limit risks from competitive surprises and to enhance the ability to synthesize a variety of technologies, enterprises may increasingly seek to devise cooperation arrangements among two or more industrial partners in various parts of the world. Engineers operating at different geographic points will increasingly work interactively through global telecommunications networks to develop new technologies cooperatively. These tendencies will increasingly obscure the national origins of particular technologies.

It is also likely that there will be a decreasing emphasis in some manufacturing enterprises on making things to sell, and on direct investment in foreign production facilities, and growing emphasis on global provision of services (R&D, design, engineering, procurement, trading, finance, customer support, etc.).

Competitiveness of private enterprises will tend to depend upon the basic strategies of those enterprises. Planning for change, and adapting quickly to it, may become the most vital element in maintaining and enhancing competitiveness. This will often require increased emphasis on diversification and risk management, through diversification of markets (geographically and among demand segments), products, production location, production methods, financial arrangements, and R&D.

Policy Responses

The pace of technological change and of the responses by private enterprises is overrunning the ability of governments to guide or manage structural adjustments. Existing regulatory regimes are rapidly being made obsolete, and traditional concepts of competition based on national markets are being made irrelevant by growing transborder competition spurred by the accelerated diffusion of technology on a global basis. As already noted, national measures to shield domestic industries from global competition will often tend to be counterproductive and aggravate the underlying problems of structural adjustment.

Government-to-government negotiations on specific product issues, particularly those negotiations aimed at official management of trade flows, will be made increasingly irrelevant by the accelerating pace of change. There will instead be a growing need for governments to set aside short-term microeconomic concerns and turn to cooperation aimed at improving the macroeconomic environment for fostering and facilitating change. Thus, governments will need to think about devising international guidelines or consultative arrangements aimed at insuring mutual compatibility of their respective industrial and economic policies.

Overt, explicit economic nationalism will be more difficult for governments to practice. Unilateralist policies on the part of the major economic powers will tend to be rejected by some governments, and the ability of any single nation to control technology transfer will inevitably diminish over time. In essence, a degree of sovereignty and assertion of national power may have to be yielded, even by the United States, in order to obtain greater multilateral cooperation.

This is particularly relevant to the handling of controls on the East-West transfer of technology, and on the parallel West-West controls that supplement and support them. Washington has been pushing to widen the scope of export controls to encompass many currently available, commercially developed technologies, and to include many potential technologies which are expected to emerge in the next few years. This drive to expand controls over international technology transfer is increasingly threatening commercial activities of non-U.S. enterprises, and it is opening new rifts in Western economic relations.

The U.S. effort to widen the control system is based on the rapidly expanding scope of the so-called Militarily Critical Technologies List (MCTL) developed by the Defense Department. This list is being broadened to include technologies which might benefit the "defense industrial base," broadly defined, of the Soviet Union and other potentially hostile nations. Thus, it is being expanded to include many of the new materials and new technologies of industrial production that are emerging.

Moreover, the growing importance of computer architecture, new materials, sensors, lasers, advanced energy devices, and other commercially developed technologies in defense planning and procurement inevitably will lead to a growing overlap of defense and nondefense technologies. There is considerable evidence that many new technologies now being sought in the military-security sphere are initially being generated in the commercial sphere. The conceptual framework of the MCTL increasingly reflects this shift in the origins or technologies which have, or could have, defense or security applications.

The concept of "dual use" technologies used by defense experts to justify controls on many specific technologies and products will lose meaning as most technologies become dual use. The legitimacy of export controls will thereby be undermined, because of a singular failure to take into account the profound effects of the technological thrusts that are now under way. Similar admonitions apply to recent Defense Department efforts to broaden controls on international technology transfers through parallel systems of government classification of defense-related technology development; of government control over scientific communication and access to information; of government control over foreign investment in, or ownership of, domestic facilities that provide products or services to the Defense Department and the military services; and unilateral controls over applications of R&D involved in projects like the Strategic Defense Initiative (even when some of that R&D may have originated in a commercial context prior to participation in a DoD-sponsored project).

This rapid extension of Defense Department concepts and controls into areas of commercial R&D in Europe and Japan will not be sustainable, and Western cooperation will sooner or later fragment under the evolving pressures of global technological change.

The convergence of defense and nondefense technology development also suggests the need for a reexamination of national technology policy. It has long been argued, for example, that defense and space

R&D were of limited commercial significance. Thus, although about half of U.S. R&D is funded by the government—and well over half of that government support is for defense R&D—it is often said that there is little benefit to economic competitiveness. Other governments, it is sometimes argued, focus some of their R&D funding on achieving improvements in commercial competitiveness. This line of reasoning has given rise to considerable support in the United States for counter-measures against foreign government targeting policies.

These arguments, however, have decreasing relevance to European and Japanese technology policies, but they probably could be applied in reverse, with increasing relevance, to U.S. technology development. Defense Department and NASA R&D programs overlap more and more with major commercial R&D thrusts, and are increasingly supportive of those thrusts. This means that there is an urgent need for fundamental reexamination of the dual-purpose consequences of government supported R&D, especially in the areas of defense and space.

Conclusion

The sheer force of technological changes now under way will cause fundamental structural adjustments, whatever governments try to do about them. Controlling these forces of change through policies of protection and economic nationalism will tend to be counterproductive.

Unilateralism in technology transfer policies will accelerate the fragmentation of Western cooperation and will intensify the search for technology autonomy in many countries, aggravating the very problems that controls are designed to resolve. A greater degree of international cooperation among governments, and of transnational cooperation among private enterprises and research establishments, seems to provide the only sensible path.

Government and industry therefore need to rethink the costs and benefits of cross-border cooperation in devising technology policies, in assisting basic research, in the encouragement and exploration of emerging technologies, and in generating policy responses to the structural adjustments being forced upon the world economy.

Vague thinking along such lines was initiated at the 1982 Western Economic Summit, but little came of it. The OECD Committee on Science and Technology is exploring some dimensions of these issues, but with little policy impact on capitals. The EC is moving in its own way, with emphasis on European projects and internal market-opening measures to provide larger-scale market opportunities for European technologies. Japan and the United States spend much time in policy combat, and little in the exploration of long-term mutual interests.

Thus, acting together, governments can hope to avoid mutually conflicting policies. But there are two important roles that each of the governments could play independently.

First, governments could try to improve their macroeconomic policies to encourage faster innovation, investment, and growth. They could try to improve the tax treatment and other incentives for innovation, with particular attention to stepping up the speed of innovation and the pace of competitive responses to foreign challenges. Governments could create an environment that favors creation of new businesses and institutional change. But policies that rely on assisting existing large enterprises, and on concentrating new technology development in them, as seems to be the tendency in the EC, will tend to aggravate the difficulties of structural adjustment.

Second, governments could educate their publics, including their business enterprises, about the nature of the forces now at work and the fundamental structural changes that will be necessary to meet them. When political pressures build for intervention in specific sectors, governments should illuminate for the public at large the underlying structural problems and the complexity of adjustment to changing global circumstances. Perhaps, in this connection, the United States and Western Europe could learn a lesson from the Japanese government by generating their own consensus visions of the nature and direction of industrial change.[2]

In educating their citizenry, governments should avoid publicly blaming other governments whenever there is an underlying problem of structural adjustment. The politics of blame may play well in the short term; but in the long run, shifting blame simply diverts public attention from the need for change, while encouraging counterproductive foreign responses.

There is no hope to be found in policies that try to halt or to slow the historic forces now at work throughout the world. The way forward to enhanced economic well-being and quality of life must lie through policies which encourage more rapid structural change in our economies, and more rapid adaptation of our education and lifestyles. Technology is opening up revolutionary opportunities for us all, if we go with the flow, rather than fight it.

Notes

1. J.P. Clark & M.C. Fleming, "Advanced Materials and the Economy," *Scientific American,* October 1986, p. 41.
2. In the United States, a substantial effort to develop perspectives on the implications of technological changes has already been set in motion by the National Research Council, in conjunction with the National Academy of Sciences and the national Academy of Engineering. See, in particular, Manufacturing Studies Board, National Research Council, *Toward a New Era in U.S. Manufacturing: The Need for a National Vision* (Washington, D.C.: National Academy Press, 1986).